Fundamentals of
FINANCIAL
ACCOUNTING

THE
WILLARD J. GRAHAM SERIES
IN ACCOUNTING

CONSULTING EDITOR

ROBERT N. ANTHONY   *Harvard University*

Fundamentals of
FINANCIAL
ACCOUNTING

GLENN A. WELSCH
College of Business Administration
University of Texas at Austin

and

ROBERT N. ANTHONY
Graduate School of Business Administration
Harvard University

 1974

RICHARD D. IRWIN, INC. *Homewood, Illinois* 60430
Irwin-Dorsey International, London, England WC2H 9NJ
Irwin-Dorsey Limited, Georgetown, Ontario L7G 4B3

First Printing, April 1974
Second Printing, August 1974
Third Printing, June 1975

ISBN 0-256-01544-9
Library of Congress Catalog Card No. 73–91787
Printed in the United States of America

To our wives,
Irma and Katherine

Preface

Many accounting instructors believe that it is sound pedagogy to divide the first course in accounting into two parts, the first semester or quarter focusing on financial accounting and the second on management accounting. Most texts, however, are not arranged so that such an approach is feasible with a single text. Consequently, instructors tend to select one text for financial accounting and a different text for management accounting, which causes a certain amount of confusion because of differences in terminology, point of view, and coverage. Moreover, the second text usually contains considerable review material on financial accounting because its author could not assume that students would have a common body of knowledge.

This volume and its companion, *Fundamentals of Management Accounting,* are designed to overcome these problems. They provide material for a fully coordinated first course. As their titles indicate, this volume deals with the fundamentals of financial accounting, and its companion with the fundamentals of management accounting. Each volume can be used either for a one-semester or a one-quarter course. Both are designed to provide maximum flexibility for the instructor in the selection and order of materials for the classroom. They emphasize those aspects of accounting we believe essential for interpretation and use of accounting information. Mechanical and procedural details are minimized, while the conceptual, measurement, and communication aspects are emphasized.

This book is an introduction to financial accounting, which has as its primary subject the communication of relevant financial information to external parties. We strongly believe that a certain level of knowledge of the accounting model, the measurement processes involved, the data classifications, and terminology, is essential to the interpretation and effective use of financial statements and we have provided the necessary information in this volume. The key to sound use of financial statements is to understand what they do and do not say, the measurement approaches used, and the standards observed in their development. This is the case both for students who will continue their study of accounting and for those who will not. The materials are arranged to meet the requirements of a wide range of academic institutions and curricula. This volume is designed to support subject matter presented in *Fundamentals of Management Accounting.*

This volume represents a significant departure from the traditional financial accounting textbook. A number of topics not traditionally covered in an elementary book have been included. In our judgment, much of the traditional material is essential; however, the recent thrusts and changes in financial accounting make it imperative that certain significant topics be accorded comprehensive treatment. This volume is unique because it focuses on these new directions with special emphasis on concepts, rationale, measurement, and reporting. Certain traditional procedural topics, are presented in appendixes should coverage of them be desired.

The primary features of the book and the instructional materials that accompany it are as follows:

- – At the outset the characteristics of the environment in which the accounting process operates are emphasized.
- – Accounting is viewed as an information processing model designed to enhance communication between the entity and the users of its financial reports.
- – The discussions emphasize concepts, standards, and generally accepted accounting principles as the rationale for the way certain things are done in accounting.
- – Throughout the chapters, the measurement approaches used in accounting and in reporting to decision-makers are emphasized.
- – At the outset, the student is presented with a comprehensive description of the end products of the financial accounting process —the financial statements. Thus, the student learns what the goals are before being introduced to the ways in which those reporting goals are attained.
- – Throughout, the focus is on the corporation rather than on the sole proprietorship or the partnership. Actual case examples are utilized. As a consequence, income taxes, dividends, earnings per share, capital stock, and the APB Opinions are encountered throughout.
- – Relevant topics, not ordinarily treated in a first course, are discussed. These include cash flow, present value, consolidated

statements, purchase versus pooling, statement of changes in financial position (both working capital and cash bases), compensating balances, and price-level effects.

– – Some chapters are divided into *Parts* to provide flexibility in the selection of materials, and in making daily assignments that cover separable parts of the chapter.

– – One or more *Appendixes* follow some of the chapters. These appendixes focus on the clerical and mechanical aspects of the accounting process such as special journals, subsidiary ledgers, payrolls, and petty cash. Separation in appendixes facilitates their exclusion, or order of selection, without affecting the continuity of the course.

These features are of particular importance to nonaccounting majors since the first semester will be their only exposure to the fundamentals of financial accounting. For example, most of the external financial statements coming to the attention of the nonaccounting majors, both in school and in real life, will be consolidated statements. Similarly, an understanding of the effects of inflation on financial information is essential in these times to the interpretation of reported results.

The subject matter of the sixteen chapters and nine appendixes that comprise this volume has been arranged in what we believe to be a pedagogically sound sequence; nevertheless, considerable rearrangements can be made if the instructor so desires. Each chapter has a summary and almost all have a demonstration case, with a suggested solution. The purpose of the demonstration cases is to tie together the various subtopics discussed in the chapter. Following each chapter are study materials classified as (*a*) discussion questions, (*b*) short exercises (suitable for homework, class illustrations, and examinations), and (*c*) comprehensive problems. Each of these groups of study materials is arranged to follow the topical sequence of the chapter.

In addition to the text itself, a wide selection of supplementary materials are available for students and for the instructor.

Answers to questions such as how much time should be spent on each chapter, how much homework should be required, and what materials should be omitted, depend on the objectives of the particular course, the time constraints, and the backgrounds of the students. This volume presents more material than can ordinarily be covered in a one-semester undergraduate course. Therefore, some choices usually must be made by the instructor. We have arranged the topical materials to permit maximum flexibility in selecting among various options and in giving varying topical emphasis to fit practically all situations. Appendixes, parts of chapters, and even entire chapters may be omitted without adversely affecting the continuity of the course. The Instructor's Manual includes comments and suggestions that are particularly helpful in selecting among a number of possible options.

The list of students and faculty members to whom the authors feel a sense of gratitude for ideas and suggestions is too long to enumerate here. With respect to this volume, we are particularly grateful to the following individuals who devoted considerable time in discussions, reviewing manuscript, and testing materials:

Professors Gale E. Newell, Western Michigan University; Michael J. Barrett, University of Minnesota; Richmond O. Bennett, Lamar University; Henry A. Genery, Colby College; Yvonne R. Knight, Colby College; Vern Odmark, San Diego State College; and Jack Helmkamp, Purdue University; and to graduate students Gary Cunningham; Beverley Spikes; Beverly Hicks; Morley Lemon; Bill Bailey; Karen Lowe; Charles Raimond; and Mary Ann Welsch.

Our thanks to the American Institute of Certified Public Accountants, American Accounting Association, and the authors identified by citations, for permission to quote from their publications and to J. C. Penney Company and Clark Equipment Company for materials from their annual reports.

And finally, sincere appreciation to I. L. Grimes, Jack Young, and the editors and staff at the Irwin company who worked so diligently in putting the manuscript together. And perhaps the most important debt of gratitude is owed to Dick Irwin for suggesting and encouraging us to collaborate in developing these two volumes.

Suggestions and comments on the text and the related materials are solicited.

March 1974   GLENN A. WELSCH
                                                    ROBERT N. ANTHONY

Contents

Purpose of the chapter. Categories of operational assets. Principles underlying accounting for operational assets. Measuring and recording acquisition cost. Matching the cost of an operational asset with future revenues. Fixed assets subject to depreciation. Repairs and maintenance. Disposals of fixed assets. Trading in used assets. Natural resources. Intangible assets. Amortization of intangibles. Deferred charges.

Purpose of the chapter. **Part one: Accounting for liabilities.** Measurement of liabilities. Current liabilities: *Accounts payable. Accrued liabilities. Payroll liabilities. Deferred revenues.* Long-term liabilities. Notes payable. Deferred income taxes. Lease liabilities. Contingent liabilities. Controlling expenditures: *The voucher system.* **Part two: Concepts of future value and present value.** Basic concepts: *Future amount of $1. Present value of $1. Future amount of an annuity of $1. Present value of annuity of $1.* Some measurement and accounting applications. Appendix A: *Payroll accounting.* Appendix B: *The voucher system.*

Purpose of the chapter. **Part one: Fundamentals of bonds payable.** Nature of bonds payable. Classification of bonds. Advantages of issuing bonds. Measuring bonds payable and bond interest expense: *Bonds sold at par. Bonds sold at a discount.* **Part two: Some complexities in accounting for bonds payable.** Accounting for bonds sold between interest dates. Adjusting entry for accrued bond interest. Bond sinking fund. Effective interest amortization on bonds payable.

Purpose of the chapter. **Part one: Shareholders' equity.** Characteristics of a corporation. Types of capital stock: *Common stock. Preferred stock.* Accounting and reporting capital stock: *Sale of capital stock.* Treasury stock. Accounting for dividends. Nature of a cash dividend. Dividends on preferred stock: *Current dividend preference. Cumulative dividend preference. Participating dividend preference.* Stock dividends. Dividend dates. Stockholder records. Reporting retained earnings. **Part two: Owners' equity for sole proprietorship and partnership.** Owner's equity for a sole proprietorship. Owners' equity for a partnership.

Purpose of the chapter. **Part one: Long-term investments in equity securities.** Nature of long-term investments in the capital stock of other corporations. Measuring long-term investments in common stock. No significant influence or control (cost method). Significant influence exists (equity method). **Part two: Long-term investments in bonds.** Nature of a bond investment. Measuring and reporting bond investments. Bonds purchased at par. Bonds purchased at a discount. Bonds purchased at a premium. Bond investment purchased between interest dates. Sale of a bond investment. Effective-interest amortization on bond investments.

1 Perspectives — the environment of accounting

Purpose
of the
chapter   The objective of this book and its companion volume *Fundamentals of Management Accounting** is to develop your knowledge of, and your ability to use, accounting information. This volume, on financial accounting, focuses on the role of accounting information in the decision-making processes of external parties; that is, owners, investors, potential investors, creditors, and the public at large. The second volume, on management accounting, focuses on the role of accounting information in the decision-making processes of managers who have responsibilities inside the organization. Whether you ultimately become an owner, a manager, an investor, or a creditor, or even if your interest in an organization is only that of a concerned citizen, an understanding of accounting will significantly enhance your abilities as a decision maker. As you study these two volumes you will develop an understanding of how accounting information influences resource–allocation decisions in all types of organizations: profit-making enterprises, nonprofit endeavors, governmental entities, and social programs. In practically all organizations, success depends in large part on the quality of the resource–allocation decisions that are made for them. Accounting information, in the broad sense, is used to aid in the decision-making process and to measure the results after the decisions are made and implemented.

The purpose of this chapter is to present a broad perspective of accounting and the environment (i.e., the surroundings) in which it operates. We will focus on those features of the environment that bear

---

* Robert N. Anthony and Glenn A. Welsch, *Fundamentals of Management Accounting* (Homewood, Ill.: Richard D. Irwin, Inc., 1974).

directly on, and strongly influence, accounting. We also will seek to explain the basic role of accounting in the decision-making process and in the measurement of the financial results, irrespective of the particular type of endeavor.

A complex
environment

In many, perhaps most, aspects of life, we are associated with social, political, and economic organizations, such as businesses, churches, fraternal organizations, political parties, states, counties, schools, environmental groups (both public and private), chambers of commerce, and professional associations. Many of these organizations are complex and pose critical problems on which decisions must be made. The future quality of our society depends in large measure upon the collective decisions of the managers of organizations. These organizations are essential to the workings of a society; indeed, they constitute much of what we call "society." Although they should be characterized by service to the "public interest," it must be recognized that they are subject to manipulation by self-interests and, perhaps more importantly, that some of them constitute a drag on the society because they are inefficient, lack high purpose, and take inappropriate actions.

Fundamental to a dynamic and successful society is the ability of each organization to measure and report its organizational accomplishments, to undergo critical self-analysis, and, by means of sound decisions, to renew and grow so that the individual organization and societal objectives are served adequately. Essentially, society, and the various organizations that comprise it, thrives in direct proportion to the efficiency with which it allocates scarce resources: human talent, materials, services, and capital. To accomplish these broad goals, organizations and persons interested in specific organizations need information about the resources that the organization controls and how those resources are used. Accounting information is designed to meet these needs.

A monetary system provides one way for the measurement and communication of the flow of resources in and out of an organization. In a monetary system, the unit of exchange (dollars in our case) is the common denominator of measurement, the medium of exchange, and a store of value. Thus, it provides a basis for expressing, in large measure, the available resources and the resource flows of both the society as a whole and of the various organizations that comprise it. Accounting is directly concerned with measuring and reporting available resources and their flow. It provides monetary measurement of inputs (resources received) and outputs (goods produced and services rendered), and, as a consequence, it measures the efficiency of organizational performance. It also measures the available resources held and the claims against those resources.

Accounting measures the resources and resource flows of organizations within a society in terms of the monetary unit of that society. Thus, accounting utilizes the monetary system of each country within which it operates. This is one of the critical problems in accounting—the conversion of financial amounts from one monetary system to another monetary system in measuring resources and resource flows for multinational businesses. Since accounting measures and reports financial resources in terms of the society's monetary unit, it is based on what is called the **unit-of-measure assumption.** The common denominator or yardstick used for accounting measurements in the United States is the dollar; the assumption is that the dollar is a stable measuring unit.[1]

**Accounting
defined**   Accounting focuses on the **measurement** and **reporting,** in monetary terms, of the flows of resources into (inflows) and out of (outflows) an organization, of the resources controlled by the organization, and of the claims against those resources. In doing this, accounting collects, processes, evaluates, and reports certain information. In addition, accounting involves broad judgmental and interpretative roles in the reporting and use of financial results. Accounting also measures, in monetary terms, the efficiency with which an organization uses the scarce resources available to it for carrying out its objectives.

Accounting communicates primarily monetary information to internal parties (i.e., managers and others within the organization) and external parties (i.e., owners, investors, creditors, governmental agencies, and the public at large). This volume focuses on communication to owners, investors, and the public.

Accounting serves those that use the information it provides in three separate, but related, ways:

1. Accounting provides information that is helpful in making decisions. Most important decisions, irrespective of the type of endeavor involved, are based, in part, upon complex financial or monetary considerations. **Accounting provides an important information base and a particular analytical orientation that help the decision maker assess the potential financial implications and potentials of various alternatives that are being considered.** The primary role of accounting, then, is to aid decision making.

2. Accounting reports what happened after a decision was made. Once decisions are made and implemented, critical and often subtle financial effects generally start happening. These financial effects often are critical to the success of the endeavor. Thus, they must be continuously measured and reported so that the decision maker can be

---

[1] The exchange unit (dollars) changes in purchasing power due to the effects of inflation and deflation; simply, the dollar does not always command the same amount of *real* goods. Since the dollar is the common denominator (the yardstick) in the accounting process, as we shall see later, a special and complex problem is posed by inflation and deflation.

appropriately informed of continuing and new problems and of successes, over time. **Accounting provides a continuing measurement of the financial effects of a series of decisions already made, the results of which are communicated to the decision maker by means of periodic financial statements.**

3. **Accounting keeps track of a wide range of items to meet the scorekeeping and safeguarding responsibilities imposed on all organizations.** These include how much cash is available for use; how much customers owe the company; what debts are owed by the organization; items owned, such as machinery and office equipment; and inventory levels.

We have said that accounting measures the resources and resource flows of an organization. Each such organization is called an **entity** for accounting purposes. In order to measure resources and resource flows a careful identification of the entity must be made.

One of the essentials of any measurement process is a precise definition of specifically what is to be measured. Examples of specific things to be measured are the population of California, the rainfall in Michigan, the voter registrations in New York, or the bank deposits in Texas (each for a stipulated time). Similarly, in the measurement of resources and resource flows, accounting requires precise definition of the **specific entity** for which monetary or financial data are to be collected, measured, and reported. When a specific entity is carefully defined, such as the Adams Company, it is often referred to as an **accounting entity.** The whole nation is a specific entity, so is each business unit, and so are individual persons. In any measurement scheme, the definition of that which is to be measured often involves difficult problems. For example, in measuring the population of California, should the amount include servicemen? college students? jail inmates? long-term visitors? hotel guests? Similarly, in defining an accounting entity, there are important problems to be resolved. For example, if we are to account for, say, the Adams Company, it is defined as a separate and specific accounting entity. The accounting entity has a specialized definition that is known as the **separate-entity assumption.**[2] The separate-entity assumption holds that, for accounting measurement purposes, the particular entity being accounted for is carefully distinguished from all other similar and related entities and persons. Under this assumption, an accounting entity is held to be separate and distinct from its owner(s). A business is viewed as *owning the resources* (i.e., *assets*) used by it and as *owing the claims* (or *debts*) against those assets. The assets, debts, and activities of the business are kept completely separate, for measurement purposes, from those of the owners and other entities. For example, in the case of the Adams

---

[2] A list of the fundamental assumptions and principles underlying accounting is given on page 29.

Company, the personal activities of the owners are not included in the accounting measurements of the business itself.

Types of business entities

This book will focus primarily on accounting for business entities. There are three main types of business entities. Since they will be referred to often throughout this volume, their primary characteristics are explained below.

Sole proprietorship—a business owned by one person. This type of business entity is common in the fields of services, retailing, and farming. Generally, the owner is also the manager. Legally, the business and the owner are not separate entities—they are one and the same—however, accounting views the business as a separate entity to be distinguished from its owner.

Partnership—a business owned by two or more persons known as partners. The agreements between the owners are set forth in a partnership contract. The contract specifies such matters as division of profits each period and distribution of resources when the business is terminated. As in the case of a sole proprietorship, a partnership is not legally separate from its owners; legally, each partner is responsible for the debts of the business (i.e., each partner usually has what is called unlimited liability); however, accounting views the partners' personal activities as separate from the activities of the partnership.

Corporation—a business incorporated under the laws of a particular state whereby the owners are known as shareholders or stockholders. Ownership is represented by shares of capital stock that can be freely bought and sold. The state issues a charter, which gives the corporation the right to operate legally as an entity, separate and apart from its owners. The owners enjoy what is called "limited liability"; that is, they are liable for the debts of the corporation only to the extent of their investment. Most states require a minimum of two or three shareholders and a minimum amount of resources to be contributed at the time of organization. The shareholders elect a board of directors, which in turn employs managers and exercises general supervision of the corporation.[3] Accounting focuses on the corporation, not on the directors and managers as individuals.

In respect to economic importance, the corporation is the dominant form of business organization in the United States. The advantages of the corporate form include limited liability for the stockholders, continuity of life, ease in transferring ownership (stock), and opportunities to raise large amounts of money by selling shares to a large number of people. As a result of these advantages, most large and medium-sized businesses (and many small ones) are organized as corporations. We

---

[3] There are a number of specialized types of entities that we do not discuss, such as joint ventures, mutual funds, cooperatives, investment trusts, and syndicates. Consideration of these is outside the scope of this book.

shall emphasize, therefore, this form of business. Nevertheless, the accounting concepts, standards, and measurement procedures apply generally to the other types of business.

Accounting
and
economics in
combination

Economics has been defined as the study of how men and society end up choosing, with or without the use of money, to employ scarce productive resources that could have alternative uses to produce various commodities and distribute them for consumption, now or in the future, among various people and groups in society.[4] This definition suggests a relationship to the definition of accounting. Like economics, accounting has a conceptual foundation. It focuses on the collection, measurement, and communication of the flows of scarce resources and the resources held by specific entities. Accounting generally is viewed as also encompassing the **financial planning process** (discussed in *Fundamentals of Management Accounting*), which focuses on the planning and projection of **future** flows of scarce resources. Thus, accounting collects data and measures, interprets, and reports on those human activities that are the focus of economics. Economics basically attempts to *explain* economic relationships primarily on the theoretical level, whereas accounting attempts to *measure* the economic relationships primarily on a practical level. However, accounting measurements must be made as consistent as is feasible with economic concepts. Accounting must deal with the complex problems of measuring, in a practical way, the monetary effect of exchange transactions (i.e., resources inflows and outflows), the resources held, and the claims against those resources for each entity. Throughout these two volumes many of the theoretical and practical issues that arise in the measurement process will be discussed from the accounting viewpoint.

The use of
accounting
information
in the
decision-
making
process

We have said that your role as a future decision maker is significant, whether you become a manager, investor, professional man, owner of a business, or simply an interested citizen. Decision makers use various approaches for selecting one alternative from among a set of alternative solutions to a given problem. Selection of the preferred alternative constitutes the basic decision. In the process of reaching decisions, the decision maker is concerned about the future since a decision cannot change the past; however, the effective decision maker does not neglect the past. Knowledge and interpretation of what has happened in the past aid in making decisions since history may shed considerable light on what the future is likely to hold. Thus, one of the fundamental inputs to decision making is dependable and relevant historical data. A large portion of historical data that are relevant to business decisions

---

[4] Paul A. Samuelson, *Economics,* 8th ed. (New York: McGraw-Hill Book Co., 1970), p. 4.

are expressed in monetary terms. They include costs (i.e., resources expended), revenues (i.e., resources earned), assets (i.e., things owned), liabilities (i.e., amounts owed), and capital. Thus, accounting provides an important information base for decision making. The information provided by accounting must be understandable to the decision maker in order to preclude unwarranted interpretations in the decision-making process. This is a primary reason why measurements in accounting must adhere to certain standards and concepts.

On page 3, three separate, but interrelated, ways in which accounting can aid in the decision-making process were outlined briefly. At this point we will re-emphasize that the measurement and information reporting encompassed in the accounting process is essential to effective control, and sound decision making, by those individuals directly concerned with, and interested in, the endeavor, irrespective of its character.

Most entities, such as a business, a hospital, or a program to educate the disadvantaged, carry on their activities over an extended period of time, during which resources are committed and used with the expectation that desirable outputs will result in the form of goods and services. During the period of continuing activity, those involved in the organization, be they owners or managers, must have information about the continuing amounts of resources committed, resources used, resources on hand, and the outputs (goods and services), and this information must be periodically reported, interpreted, and evaluated. The accounting process is designed to provide a continuing flow of such information to all interested parties. The financial statements constitute the primary means of communicating the relevant information on a continuing basis.

The management, sponsors, and owners of each organization need a constant and periodic flow of accounting information in their decision-making activities. In order to meet this need on a continuing basis, there must be a cycle of information flow and uses in the organization. This cycle is diagramed in Exhibit 1–1.

Now, let's see how the flow of accounting information may aid decision makers in three different kinds of entities. We will consider a business, a hospital, and a community educational program for a disadvantaged group.

A business. First, the objectives of the business are formulated by the organizers. Initially, the owners provide the funds, which often are supplemented by funds provided by creditors. These funds then are used to acquire machinery, inventory, services, and other resources. As the business operates, additional resources are generated from the sale of goods and services. Many other things happen, most of which involve either the inflow or outflow of resources. The manager of the business needs information, on a continuing basis, that tells him about the status of the resources. He wants to know such things as sources and amounts of funds, revenues (sales and services sold), expenses, how

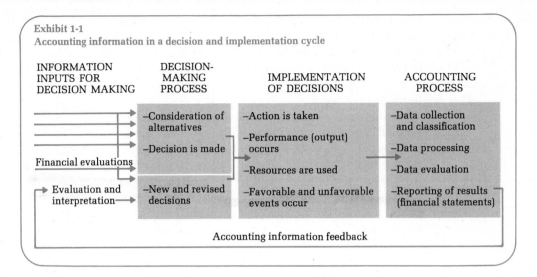

Exhibit 1-1
Accounting information in a decision and implementation cycle

INFORMATION INPUTS FOR DECISION MAKING	DECISION-MAKING PROCESS	IMPLEMENTATION OF DECISIONS	ACCOUNTING PROCESS
	–Consideration of alternatives	–Action is taken	–Data collection and classification
		–Performance (output) occurs	
	–Decision is made		–Data processing
Financial evaluations		–Resources are used	–Data evaluation
Evaluation and interpretation	–New and revised decisions	–Favorable and unfavorable events occur	–Reporting of results (financial statements)

Accounting information feedback

much is invested in inventory, what is the cash situation, how much is being spent for research and development, and how much money is being spent in the sales efforts.

The interested parties need answers to questions such as these for two fundamental reasons. First, accounting information in response to these and similar questions may aid importantly in making decisions about the entity to improve its effectiveness and efficiency. Second, accounting information tells the interested parties what the score was during the immediate past periods. This scorekeeping is important to the control and evaluation of performance. In Exhibit 1–1, financial evaluations are shown as one of the information inputs to the decision-making process. The exhibit also depicts the accounting process. Throughout this process, data such as that cited above are collected, measured, and reported. Through the reporting phase, the accounting information is communicated as an aid in making new decisions and in revising prior decisions.

Now, consider a shareholder (an owner) who has a substantial amount of funds invested in it but has little opportunity to directly influence the management. Such an owner must decide whether to (1) retain his ownership interest, (2) expand or contract it, or (3) dispose of it completely. He also is interested in decisions that will lead to expansion of the business and raise its level of efficiency. As a consequence of these concerns, he would want to know such things as the trend of sales, the level of expenses, the amount invested in various assets (such as inventory and machinery), the debts of the business, and the cash balances. In other words, he would be very interested in knowing how the management is allocating the scarce resources provided them by the owners and the creditors. This information would be basic to his taking one of the three actions listed above, or to guide the management. The financial reports provided on a continuing basis by the accounting process have as their primary objective the furnishing of information bearing on these questions. The accounting information thus provided should flow into the decision-making process of the owners in the ways depicted in Exhibit 1–1.

A hospital. Assume you are on the Board of Governors of a local hospital and, as a consequence, share the responsibility for the basic decisions and guidelines for its continued operation at an efficient level. Similar to the owner of a business, you have a wide variety of questions concerning its revenues, expenses, funds tied up in buildings and equipment, cost of charity services, etc., that are in the scorekeeping category. You also are concerned with whether enough resources are being allocated to such activities as emergency care, sanitation, and nursing services. Before any sound decisions in these areas can be made for the future, you must have information about the past and current allocation of resources to them and what the output (quality and quantity of benefits) was. Thus, as a sponsor, you have many information needs that are important to your decisions for the future.

Now, consider the manager of the hospital. He needs accounting information about the operations of the hospital similar to that discussed above for the manager of a business, and for the same reasons. Typically, he will need more *detailed* accounting information than the sponsor. In any event, whether a sponsor or a manager of the hospital, financial measurement and the reporting results should be continuing inputs to the decision-making processes.

An educational program for a disadvantaged group. As with the business and the hospital, there are both sponsors and managers of the program. They are vitally concerned with its resource needs and uses, the level of operational efficiency, and the extent to which the entity is attaining the goals set out for it. In addition to the all-important dedication and efforts of those carrying out the day-to-day activities, the financial problems and related decisions command the major attention of both the sponsors and the management—how resources are being committed, how they are being allocated, are they being allocated to the most critical phases of the program, are they being used efficiently, what additional resources are needed? These are indicative of the wide range of accounting information that is needed to make sound decisions and to direct the effort in a responsible way. The accounting process, if adequately designed for the situation, can provide, through the medium of continuing financial statements, information responses to many of these questions. The sponsors and the management, if they have a reasonable understanding of the financial considerations, can utilize the financial statements as important inputs to their decision-making process.

In summary, irrespective of the type of endeavor or the position of the decision maker, the need for a continuous flow of accounting information is useful to the decision maker. The flow of accounting information in the decision-making/implementation cycle, as depicted in Exhibit 1–1, is needed in all types of endeavors.

Historical
perspectives

Accounting is as old as the transaction processes (whether barter or monetary) that gradually developed with civilization. The earliest written records, including the Scriptures, contain references to what is now called accounting. Accounting records have provided some of the most detailed insights into the history of civilization.[5]

Accounting has evolved in response to the economic needs of society. Prior to the 15th century it apparently followed no well-defined pattern except that it developed in answer to specific governing and trading needs of the era. The first known treatment of the subject of accounting was written in 1494, two years after the discovery of America by Christopher Columbus. An Italian monk and mathematician, Fr. Luca Paciolo, described an approach that had been developed by the Italian merchants of the time to account for their activities as owner–managers of business ventures. Paciolo laid down the foundations of the "accounting model" that is used to this day. As economic activity moved from the feudal system to agriculture and then to the Industrial Revolution, accounting adapted to the evolving needs. As business units became more complex and broader in scope, accounting evolved in response to the increased planning and control responsibilities of management. As governments increased in size and became more centralized, accounting was developed to meet the increased responsibilities.

In the 17th and 18th centuries, in England the Industrial Revolution provided the impetus for the development of new approaches in accounting. The impetus was particularly in the direction of management accounting and the accumulation of data concerning the cost of manufacturing each product. In the latter half of the 18th century, English accountants, small in numbers but large in competence, appeared on the American scene. By 1900, the lead in accounting developments, provided earlier by the English, began to shift to America. Since the turn of the century, spearheaded by the accounting profession in the United States, accounting has experienced dynamic, and sometimes controversial, growth.

At the present time, four important groups in the United States predominate in the development of financial accounting concepts and practice. A general knowledge of their respective historical and continuing roles is important to your understanding of accounting. The

---

[5] For example, the financial records personally prepared by Thomas Jefferson (which have been carefully preserved) provided much of the detailed and interesting history still being written about this outstanding man. See *Journal of Accountancy* (April 1972), pp. 33–47.

groups are: the American Institute of Certified Public Accountants; the Financial Accounting Standards Board; the U.S. Securities and Exchange Commission; and the American Accounting Association. The past and present roles of each group will be briefly reviewed.

American Institute of Certified Public Accountants (*AICPA*). This institute was organized a few years prior to the turn of the century by a group of accountants engaged in public and industrial accounting. Membership is limited to certified public accountants (see pages 13 and 14). In terms of direct impact on financial accounting practice, the AICPA, by far, has been the strongest force in accounting in recent decades. It carries on a wide-ranging program encompassing professional development, publications (including the magazine *Journal of Accountancy*), and the development and communication of accounting standards and procedures. During the approximate period 1930 to 1950, the AICPA's Committee on Accounting Procedure issued a number of Accounting Research Bulletins (ARB's) that enunciated certain *recommended* financial accounting principles and procedures. These recommendations were followed by much, but by no means all, of the accounting profession. In the realization of a developing need for increased effort and more adherence to prescribed accounting guidelines, in 1959 the AICPA organized the Accounting Principles Board (APB) to replace the former committee. The APB issued 31 numbered *Opinions* during its existence from 1959 through 1973. Basically, accountants are required to follow the provisions of the *Opinions*. The *Opinions* dealt with many of the tough issues of financial accounting and, as a consequence, many of them were highly controversial. Throughout this volume you will encounter a few references to the ARB's and numerous references to APB *Opinions*.

Financial Accounting Standards Board (*FASB*). Usually referred to as the FASB, this organization began operating June 1, 1973. It is appropriate to review its background. Accounting is a complex and frequently controversial professional activity. The intensity of the controversies in recent years is indicated by the fact that a wide range of interested individuals and groups (frequently representing special interests) have committed significant amounts of resources and time in attempting to influence the setting of accounting concepts and standards. The controversy on occasion entered the political arena, which is generally viewed as an inappropriate area in which to establish sound accounting concepts and standards. Accounting issues increasingly have been important in litigation in the courts.

As you study accounting you will realize that the economic results reported by financial accounting, such as asset valuations, net income, and earnings per share, may have impacts on the economy, on the capital markets (including the stock market), and on many major decisions of individuals, groups, and entities. You also may appreciate how the selection of a particular financial accounting approach frequently has a significant impact on the financial results reported through the accounting process (such as net income and earnings per share). In the light of these issues, the AICPA in 1972 decided to reassess the approaches to establishing financial accounting concepts and standards. As a consequence of this reassessment, the APB was discontinued and in its place the Financial Accounting Standards Board was established. The seven FASB members are appointed by an independent Board of Trustees and serve on a full-time basis. The trustees are appointed by the AICPA. The FASB was organized to be independent. It has as its sole function the establishment and improvement of accounting concepts and standards. At present, an assessment of it cannot be made; however, the direction of accounting under its guidance will be both interesting and significant. The accounting profession, through the FASB, intends to keep the standards-setting function in the private sector rather than by laws and governmental agencies.

U.S. Securities and Exchange Commission (SEC). This government regulatory agency was established by the Securities Acts of 1933 and 1934. The acts gave the SEC authority to prescribe accounting guidelines for the financial reports required to be submitted by corporations that sell their securities in interstate commerce (i.e., registered companies). This includes all sizable corporations. The SEC requires these corporations to submit periodic reports, which are maintained in the files of the commission as a matter of public record. From the beginning, the SEC, as a matter of policy, generally followed the accounting concepts, standards, and procedures established by the AICPA committees. The SEC publishes "Regulation SX," which prescribes the special guidelines to be followed by registered companies in preparing the financial reports submitted in conformance with the Securities Acts. Throughout its existence the SEC has exerted a significant impact on accounting. Its staff has worked closely with the accounting profession on the evolution and improvement of accounting standards.

American Accounting Association (AAA). This association was organized during the World War I period by a group of college accounting professors. The association sponsors and encourages the improvement of accounting teaching and accounting research (primarily on a theoretical plane), and publishes a magazine, *The Accounting Review.* Its committees issue reports that, coupled with the research activities of individual academicians, continue to exert a pervasive influence on the development of accounting theory and standards.

Judgment in
accounting

Financial accounting concepts and standards have been developed and articulated to increase the reliability and relevance of accounting measurements and reporting. Since accounting is man-made and, as explained above, must evolve to meet changing needs, it has a limited number of "provable" approaches. As you study accounting you will appreciate that it requires much professional judgment in application on the part of the accountant in order to capture the economic essence of transactions. Thus, accounting is intellectually stimulating since it is not a cut-and-dried subject, but, rather, it is one that calls upon your intelligence, analytical ability, creativity, and judgment. Since accounting is a communication process involving an audience (users) of a wide diversity of knowledge, interest, and capabilities, it will call upon your ability as a communicator. The language encompasses concisely written phrases and symbols used to convey information about the resource flows measured for specific organizations.

The accounting profession

In the period since 1900, accountancy has attained the stature of a profession similar to law, medicine, engineering, and architecture. As with all recognized professions, it is subject to licensing, observes a code of professional ethics, requires a high level of professional competence, is dedicated to service to the public, requires a high level of academic study, and rests on a "common body of knowledge." The accountant, in addition to meeting specified academic requirements, may be licensed by his state to be a **certified public accountant,** or **CPA.** This designation was first established in 1894. The primary objective was the attainment of high standards of professional competence. It is granted under the law only upon completion of requirements specified by statute. Although the CPA requirements vary somewhat between states, generally they include a college degree with a major in accounting; high moral character; from one to five years specified experience; and successful completion of a three-day examination. The CPA examination, scheduled in each state simultaneously on a semiannual basis, is prepared by the American Institute of Certified Public Accountants and covers accounting theory, auditing, business law, and accounting practice.

As is common with physicians, engineers, lawyers, and architects, accountants (including CPAs) commonly are engaged in professional practice or are employed by businesses, government entities, nonprofit organizations, etc.

PRACTICE OF PUBLIC ACCOUNTING

A CPA, practicing public accounting, is one who offers his professional services to the public for a fee, as does the lawyer and physician. In this posture he is appropriately known as an **independent CPA,** because certain of his responsibilities also extend to the general public (third parties) rather than being limited to the specific business or other entity that pays for his services. The independent CPA is not an employee of his clients. This concept of independence from the client is an aspect of the accounting profession that is unique. The consequences of this aspect are not so widely understood as perhaps they should be. For example, the lawyer and the physician, in case of malpractice or incompetence, generally are subject to potential liability (lawsuits) that may extend only to the client or patient involved. In contrast, the independent CPA, in case of malpractice or negligence in the audit function, is subject to potential liability that may extend to all parties (whether known to him or not) that suffered loss through reliance on financial statements "approved" by him.

While a single individual may practice public accounting, usually two or more individuals organize an accounting firm in the form of a partnership. These firms vary in size from a one-man office, to regional firms, to the "big-eight" firms, which have hundreds of offices located around the world. Nearly all accounting firms render three types of services: auditing, management advisory services, and tax services.

Auditing. An important function performed by the CPA in public practice is the **audit** or **attest function.** Its purpose is to lend credibility to the financial reports; that is, to insure that they are dependable. Primarily this function involves an examination of the financial reports prepared by the management in order to insure that they are in conformance with generally accepted accounting concepts and standards. In carrying out this function the independent CPA examines the underlying transactions, including the collection, classification, and assembly of the financial data incorporated in the financial reports. In performing these professional tasks he must conform to professional standards that have been established and assure that the information reported conforms to "generally accepted accounting principles" appropriate for the entity involved. Additionally, he is responsible for verifying that the financial reports "fairly present" the resource inflows and outflows and the financial position of the entity. The magnitude of these responsibilities may be appreciated when it is realized that the number of transactions involved in a major enterprise such as General Motors runs into the billions each year. The CPA, of course, does not examine each one of these transactions; rather, he utilizes professional approaches to ascertain that they were properly measured and reported.

Occasionally, the auditor may encounter attempts, for example, to increase reported profit by omitting certain expenses or to overstate financial position by omitting certain debts. There are many intentional and unintentional potentialities for preparing misleading financial reports. The audit function performed by an independent CPA is the best protection available to the public in this respect. Many investors have learned the hazards of making investments in enterprises that do not have their financial reports examined by an independent CPA.

Management advisory services. Many independent CPA firms also offer advisory or consulting services. These services generally are accounting based and encompass such activities as the design and installation of accounting, data-processing, profit-planning, and control (i.e., budget) systems; financial advice; forecasting; inventory controls; cost-effectiveness studies; and operational analyses. This facet of public practice is experiencing a rapid growth.

Tax services. The CPA in public practice usually is involved in rendering tax services to his clients. This includes tax planning as a part of the decision-making process and determination of the tax liability (by means of the annual tax return). The increasing complexity of state and federal tax laws, particularly income tax laws, demands a high level of competence.

The CPA's involvement in **tax planning** often is quite significant. Virtually every major business decision carries with it significant tax impacts; so much so, in fact, that tax-planning considerations frequently govern the decision. To illustrate the significance of tax effects in a simple way, assume two taxpayers, each of whom desires to borrow $100,000, and a going (i.e., actual) interest rate of 8% per year. Assume that taxpayer A has an average tax rate of 30%, whereas taxpayer B has a 50% rate. Let's evaluate the annual **net or effective interest cost** of each. The effective interest cost is the net cost of borrowing. It is the **actual interest, less the reduction in income taxes** resulting from including the interest cost on the income tax return as a deduction. To continue the illustration:

	Taxpayer A	Taxpayer B
Actual annual interest to be paid ($100,000 × 8%)........	$8,000	$8,000
Less: Tax saving:		
A ($8,000 × 30%).....................................	2,400	
B ($8,000 × 50%).....................................		4,000
Net or effective after-tax interest cost...............	$5,600	$4,000
Net or effective after-tax rate:		
A ($5,600 ÷ $100,000).........................	5.6%	
B ($4,000 ÷ $100,000).........................		4.0%

The **tax saving** is due to the fact that the $8,000 interest paid is a deductible expense on the income tax return of each party. Since this would reduce taxable income by $8,000, it would serve to reduce the amount of income taxes to be paid, the amount of which would depend upon the tax rate of the person or entity. The key amount in the decision model of each party in determining whether to borrow or not is the net or effective after-tax interest rate, rather than the actual interest rate. The cost of borrowing, net of tax, may turn out to be materially less than the cost of funds provided by owners. Significantly, tax planning must occur during the decision-making process rather than at the end of the year when the tax return is prepared.

EMPLOYMENT BY ORGANIZATIONS

Many accountants, including CPA's, are employed by profit-making and nonprofit organizations. A company or other organization, depending upon its size and complexity, may employ from one up to hundreds of accountants. In the business enterprise, the chief financial officer, usually a vice president or controller, is a member of the management team. This responsibility generally entails a wide range of management, financial, and accounting duties. Exhibit 1–2 shows a typical organizational arrangement of the financial function in a business enterprise. In the business entity, accountants typically are engaged in a wide variety of activities, such as general management, general accounting, cost accounting, profit planning and control (i.e., budgeting), internal auditing, and electronic data processing. A common pattern in recent years has been the selection of a "financial expert" as the chief executive or president of the company. One primary function of the accountants in organizations is to provide data that are useful for managerial decision making and for controlling operations. In addition, the functions of external reporting, tax planning, control of assets, and a host of related responsibilities normally are performed by accountants in industry. The role of accountants within organizations is emphasized in *Fundamentals of Management Accounting* of this series.

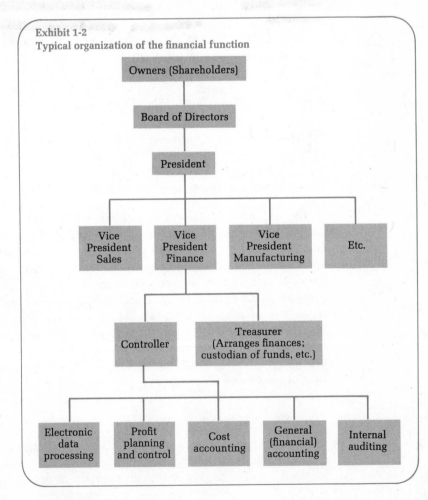

Exhibit 1-2
Typical organization of the financial function

EMPLOYMENT IN THE PUBLIC SECTOR

The vast and complex operations of governmental units, from the local to the international level, create a great need for accountants. Accountants employed in the public sector perform similar functions to those performed by their counterparts in private organizations. Additionally, the General Accounting Office (GAO) and the regulatory agencies, such as the Securities and Exchange Commission, Interstate Commerce Commission (ICC), Federal Power Commission (FPC), and Federal Communications Commission (FCC), utilize the services of accountants in carrying out their regulatory duties.

Finally, accountants are involved in varying capacities in the evolving programs of pollution control, health care, minority enterprises, and other socially oriented programs, whether sponsored by private industry or by government.

Social and economic significance of accounting

The broad areas of public-policy formulation and the ranking of national priorities are important issues to many citizens. Even casual knowledge tells us that the financial complexities of public-policy formulation are a compelling, if not overriding, consideration. Accounting information assists policy makers to bring the financial complexities into focus for study, evaluation, and selection of the more favorable alternatives. First and foremost, the financial information that underlies policy formulation must have credibility; that is, the financial information must be dependable. The independent audit function provided by the accounting profession, coupled with the expertise of the accountant in sorting out relevant financial analyses and relationships, helps to meet this need. Similarly, the credibility of financial reports on business units is indispensable in the conduct of the business, the administration of the taxation process, and the protection of the broad public interest. Inefficiencies, errors, and selfish interests would cause the whole system to break down if these reports were not reliable. In the Federal government, the General Accounting Office was established to audit and report to the Congress on the administration of public funds. Regulatory bodies such as the SEC and the ICC were established by law to protect the public interest. These and similar agencies, in good measure, rely upon audited financial reports in carrying out their statutory missions.

The growth of business organizations in size, particularly publicly held corporations, has brought pressure from stockholders, potential investors, creditors, governmental agencies, and the public at large, for increased financial disclosure. The public's right to know more about organizations that directly and indirectly affect them (whether or not they are shareholders) is being increasingly recognized as essential. An open society is one that has a high degree of freedom at the individual level and typically evidences an effective commitment to raising its quality of life. These characteristics make it essential that the members of that society be provided adequate, understandable, and dependable financial information from the major institutions that comprise it. Voters are asked to decide upon taxation proposals, allocations of resources to many sources, and other questions. All of these decisions should be based upon adequate financial knowledge. Labor negotiations, environmental programs, economic opportunity programs, foreign aid, and education programs are but a few of the difficult problem areas important to all citizens that, for enlightened decision making, require extensive use of accounting information.

Some naive misconceptions

Some people naively confuse a bookkeeper with an accountant and bookkeeping with accounting. In effect they confuse one of the minor parts with the whole of accounting. It is tantamount to comparing the simple administration of first aid with the complex practice of medicine by the physician. Bookkeeping is the routine and clerical side of accounting and requires only minimal knowledge of the accounting model. A bookkeeper records the repetitive and uncomplicated transactions in most businesses and may maintain the simple records of a very small business. In contrast, the accountant is a professional who is competent in systems design, analysis of complex economic events, interpretative and analytical processes, financial advising, and managerial endeavors.

Another prevalent misconception is that all of the financial affairs of an entity are subject to precise and accurate measurement and that the results of accounting, as reflected in the financial statements, are absolute facts. For example, that the profit figure is influenced by estimates in many respects will be illustrated in subsequent chapters. Many people believe that accounting should measure and report what a business is "worth," but accounting does not attempt to do this. In order to understand financial statements and to interpret them wisely for use in decision making, the user must be aware of their limitations as well as their usefulness. He should understand what they do and do not attempt to accomplish.

As a student of accounting, you must be wary of these and other similar misconceptions. To adequately understand financial statements and to be able to interpret the "figures" wisely, one must have a certain level of knowledge of the concepts and standards and the measurement procedures used in the accounting process. He must learn what accounting "is really like" and appreciate the reasons why certain things are done the way they are. This level of knowledge cannot be gained simply by reading a list of the "principles" and a list of the misconceptions. Neither can a generalized discussion of the subject matter suffice. A certain amount of involvement, primarily problem solving as used in mathematics courses, is essential in any study of accounting focused on the needs of the user. Therefore, we provide problems aimed at the desirable knowledge level for the user of financial statements.

The chapters in this volume have been divided into parts primarily to provide reasonable study units; however, this also provides your instructor with flexibility in priority selection of materials consistent with the time available. Most of the procedural aspects of accounting are presented in appendixes to the chapters to further provide flexibility to your instructor in attaining the knowledge level desired consistent with time constraints and course objectives.

Demonstration case for self-study

This introductory case is presented to start you thinking, in monetary terms, of some of the resource inflows and outflows of a business. It deals with measuring and reporting certain accounting information for an individual involved in a simple business situation. The discussions in the chapter will not help you much with the monetary amounts or the format of the report. See what you can do with the case before studying the recommended solution that follows the case.

JOHN'S BREAD COMPANY

John Rath entered college in September 1967 with $600 he had saved during high school by working as a "bag boy" in a local grocery, plus $400 obtained on a loan from a local businessman "payable at no interest until after you graduate and get a job." Unfortunately, John could expect no parental help. He realized that before the end of the year he would have to get a job sufficient to pay the full cost of his college education above the $1,000 cash on hand. The college was in a relatively small town and employment opportunities for students were limited. At the end of the first semester John had not located a job. Eventually he did come up with an idea that he thought might be profitable. While working back home in the grocery, he had observed that "day-old" bread always sold out at a reduced price. He surveyed the grocery stores in the college town and found that they were serviced by a chain bakery from a distant town and that none of them sold day-old bread. He purchased an old sedan for $150 cash (including the registration fees), drove to another town (75 miles away), and located a local bakery that would provide him day-old bread at a reasonable price. Thereupon, he loaded the trunk and back seat with bread at a cost of $30 and returned. The first two stores he contacted took the entire load at a price of $50 and indicated a desire to obtain the same amount each Tuesday and Friday. John took one-half of his remaining cash of $300 and set it aside in a separate bank account for the bread business. Within the month John was making one round trip every Monday and Thursday to supply the four grocery stores he had lined up. Not counting his time and the cost of operating his car, John earned $20 on the bread for each trip. His car averaged 15 miles per gallon of gasoline (regular at $.30 per gallon). Each of the 28 trips made during the spring semester required 1 quart of oil

($.50 per quart). During the semester he spent $42 for repairs, license, and insurance. All transactions were cash. At the end of the spring semester John ended up as follows: grade point average, 3.1; tires and motor worn-out; an increase in his bank balance; income taxes owed equal to 20% of his profit; and the belief that he could expand his business to include more grocery stores. A fellow student offered him $500 for the business—"lock, stock, and barrel." Instead of selling, John decided to expand during the summer. The first step was to analyze the potential demand and the resources that would be needed. He immediately decided that he should acquire a used pickup truck (he located one he liked, priced at $1,250, less a $50 trade-in on his old car) since it would enable him to triple the amount of bread he could handle. He estimated that this amount would saturate the market. He estimated 12 miles per gallon of gas for the pickup; service, license, repairs, and insurance for one year of $150; and a value for the pickup after one year of $800. He then approached a local banker for a $900 loan to purchase the pickup, the loan to be payable at the end of 12 months (interest rate 7%). The banker was agreeable on the condition that John would develop for him a "profit report that would show for the spring semester just ended his sales, expenses, and profit for the bread operation." John was enthusiastic and, although he had never studied accounting, proceeded to prepare the report for the banker the next day. Required: Prepare the report for the banker. Include any comments that you consider relevant.

Solution:

JOHN'S BREAD COMPANY
Financial Report for the Banker
Spring Semester, 1968

Sales, Expenses, and Profit:

Sales (bread) 2 trips × 14 weeks × $50)......................		$1,400
Less cost of the bread (2 trips × 14 weeks × $30)..............		840
Gross...		560
Less expenses:		
Gasoline (2 trips × 150 miles × 14 weeks = 4,200 miles		
4,200 miles/15 = 280 gallons @ $.30)......................	$ 84	
Oil (28 quarts @ $.50)......................................	14	
Repairs, license and insurance..............................	42	
Automobile*		
Cost at start.......................................	$150	
Trade-in value at end...............................	50	
Cost of using the automobile........................		100
Total expenses (excluding taxes).....................		240
Profit subject to income taxes..................................		320
Income taxes ($320 × 20%)...................................		64
Profit for the semester (excluding John's time)....................		$ 256

* This is the cost of using the automobile itself for the semester. This cost was occasioned by "wear-and-tear" through use for the semester. The $100 expense for use is frequently called *depreciation*. A later chapter will explain more precisely the nature of depreciation as a cost of using equipment and similar items that have a limited life.

Epilogue: At the end of five years, John left college with a degree (including much more knowledge of accounting) and, having sold the business, with $11,000 cash in his pocket.

Summary   Accounting interfaces with practically all aspects of the environment: social, economic, and political. Any open society is a complex one that is characterized by organizations—businesses, political parties, governmental entities, churches, social institutions, and private groups and associations. Each organization, whether local or international in scope, is an accounting entity. The essence of accounting is the measurement and reporting of financial information for an accounting entity. The measurement and reporting of the inflows and outflows of scarce resources and the financial position of each accounting entity is essential to (*a*) effective management of each such organization and (*b*) the understanding and evaluation of it by interested outside parties. Measurement of the financial characteristics of each such organization is essential because each of us is an important decision maker, both in respect to our individual interests and as a concerned citizen in the broader sense. Our decision-making potential is enhanced if we understand the financial impacts of alternative solutions to particular problems.

Important   **Accounting**   **Independent CPA**
terms   **Unit-of-measure assumption**   **Auditing**
            Separate-entity assumption   **Management advisory services**
            Accounting entity   **Tax services**
            Sole proprietorship   **Net or effective interest cost**
            Partnership   **Bookkeeping**
            Corporation

Questions   1. Any open society is characterized by social, political, and economic
for   organizations. Why is it essential that their accomplishments (or lack
discussion   of accomplishments) be measured and reported?

2. Each entity, such as a church, welfare organization, or business, in a progressive society is involved in the allocation of scarce resources. These frequently are expressed (measured) in terms of the monetary unit. How is accounting information used in the allocation of resources in such entities?

3. In general, how does an interpretative knowledge of the resources held and the resource flows of an organization aid in decision making for the organization?

4. What is meant by an accounting entity?

5. Briefly distinguish between a sole proprietorship, a partnership, and a corporation.

6. In general, why is a knowledge of the financial implications of public-policy questions important to a concerned citizen? Where would you expect to find data concerning these implications?

7. What is the primary focus of accounting, irrespective of the type of entity?

8. Explain your general concept of the decision-making process. Refer to Exhibit 1–1.

9. Explain what is meant by the designation CPA.

10. Distinguish, in general terms, between the practice of public accounting and employment as an accountant in private organizations and in the public sector.

11. The independent CPA firm normally renders three services: auditing, management advisory, and tax. Briefly explain each.

12. In general, what are the duties of a controller in a business?

13. Distinguish between accounting and bookkeeping.

14. Explain the unit-of-measure assumption as applied in accounting.

15. Explain the separate-entity assumption as applied in accounting.

Exercises   E1–1.   In the practice of public accounting one offers professional services as an independent CPA for a fee. Explain the meaning of the word "independent."

E1–2.   Reo Retailers, Incorporated, owns and operates eight department stores located in five different cities. The corporate charter, granted by the state, authorized 100,000 shares of common stock (par value $20 per share). The bylaws provide for the annual election of a board of directors numbering ten individuals, three of whom must be "outside directors." In addition to the president, the officers will include three vice presidents: finance, merchandising, and promotion. In the finance function there will be a controller and a treasurer. You are asked to prepare an organization chart for Reo and to include thereon a recommended subdivision of responsibilities under the controller.
(Hint: Use your present knowledge of a department store and your imagination.)

E1–3.   Assume you are the owner of a small store that sells clothes for men (specializing in the college crowd). Because of your excellent management and financial control, you are in the "40% tax bracket." You are considering adding a department that will entail an outlay of $20,000 cash, 75% of which will have to be borrowed (for one year) at 7½% interest per year. What would be your net or effective interest cost (*a*) in dollars and (*b*) as an effective after-tax rate of interest? Show computations.

E1–4.   Assume you are the owner of "The College Shop," which specializes in items of interest to college students. At the end of January 1975 you find that (for January only):

Sales, per the cash register tapes, totaled $31,000, plus one sale on credit (a special case) of $200.

With the help of a friend (who had majored in accounting) you determined that the goods sold during January had cost you $16,000 when they were purchased.

During the month, according to the checkbook, you spent $11,000 for salaries, utilities, supplies, advertising, and other expenses; however, you have not yet paid the $300 monthly rent on the store (including the fixtures).

On the basis of the data given, how much was the profit for January (disregard income taxes)? Show computations.
(Hint: A convenient form to use would have the following major side captions:

Revenue from sales:
Expenses:
Difference–profit before income taxes:)

E1–5. Arrow Company, a small service organization, prepared the following report for the month of January:

Sales, Expenses, and Profit

Sales:		
Cash sales (per cash register)..............	$ 5,000	
Credit sales (per charge tickets;		
not collected)........................	15,000	$20,000
Expenses:		
Salaries and wages (paid by check).........	11,000	
Supplies (taken from stock)................	2,000	
Estimated cost of wear-and-tear on used		
delivery truck for the month		
(depreciation).........................	100	
Other expenses (paid by check).............	2,900	16,000
Difference – pretax profit...............		4,000
Estimated income taxes thereon		
(to be paid next quarter).................		1,000
Profit for January........................		$ 3,000

You have been asked by the owner (who knows very little about the financial side of business) to compute the "amount of cash that was generated in January by the above operations."

You decided to prepare a report for the owner with the following major side captions:

Cash Inflows (collections):
Cash Outflows (payments):
Difference–net increase (or decrease) in cash:
(Hint: There was a cash decrease; that is, a negative cash flow.)

Problems P1–1. Upon graduation from high school, Jack Kane immediately accepted a job as a plumber's helper for a large local plumbing company. After three years of hard work, Jack received a plumber's license, whereupon he decided to go into business for himself. He had saved $3,000, which he decided to invest in the business. His first step was to transfer this amount from his savings account to a business bank account for "Kane Plumbing Company." He then purchased, for cash, a used panel truck for $1,000 and $800 worth of tools; rented limited space in a small building; inserted an ad in the local paper; and opened the doors on October 1, 1974. Immediately, Jack found himself very busy and, after one month, employed a helper. Although he knew practically nothing about the financial side of the business, he realized from his prior experience that a number of reports were required and that costs and collections had to be controlled carefully. Accordingly, at the end of the year, prompted in part by concern about his income tax situation (previously he only had to report his salary), he recognized the need for financial statements. At his urging, his wife undertook "to develop some financial statements for the business." With the advice of a friend, on December 31, 1974, she gathered the following data for the three months just ended: deposits in the bank account of collections for plumbing services, $9,540; checks written: plumber's helper $600, payroll taxes paid $30, supplies purchased and used on jobs $5,000, oil, gas, and mainte- nance on truck $650, insurance $150, rent $200, utilities and tele- phone $120, and miscellaneous expenses $400. In addition, there were uncollected bills to customers for plumbing services amounting to $800, and the rent for December amounting to $100 had not been paid. Jack's income tax rate may be assumed to be 20%. Also as- sume that the "wear-and-tear on the truck and tools due to use dur- ing the three months" amounted to $90.

Required:
Prepare a financial report for Kane Plumbing for the three months. Use the following main captions:
   Revenues from services:
   Expenses:
   Difference–profit subject to income taxes:
   Income taxes:
   Profit:
(Hint: Expenses totaled $7,340.)

P1–2.   During the summer, between his junior and senior years, Randy Walker was faced with the need to earn sufficient funds for the com- ing academic year. Unable to obtain a job with reasonable remunera- tion, he decided to try the lawn-care business for three months. After a survey of the potential, Randy acquired an old pickup truck on June 1 for $300. On each door he painted "Randy's Lawn Service, Ph. XX." Additionally, he spent $150 for mowers, trimmers, etc. To acquire these items he borrowed $500 cash on a note (endorsed by a friend) at 8% interest per annum, payable at the end of the three months (ending August 31).

At the end of the summer Randy realized that he had "done a lot of work and his bank account looked good," which prompted him to become concerned about how much profit his business had earned.

A review of his check stubs showed the following: deposits in the bank of collections from customers, $4,200; checks written: gas, oil, and lubrication $360, pickup repairs $85, repair of mowers $40, miscellaneous supplies used $70, helpers $1,200, payroll taxes $68, payment for assistance in preparing payroll tax forms $50, insurance $120, telephone $30, and $510 to pay off the note plus interest (on August 31). A notebook kept in the pickup, plus some unpaid bills, etc., reflected that customers still owed him $450 for lawn services rendered and that he owed $47 for gas and oil (credit card charges) and income taxes (estimated tax rate 20%). He estimated that the "wear-and-tear" for use of the truck and the other equipment for three months amounted to $100.

Required:

Prepare a financial report for Randy's Lawn Service covering the three months June, July, and August. Use the following main captions:

Revenues from services:

Expenses:

Difference—profit subject to income taxes:

Income taxes:

Profit:

(Hint: Profit before deducting income taxes amounted to $2,470.)

2 Communication of accounting information

Purpose of the chapter

In this chapter we will consider the fundamentals of financial statements, which are the primary end products of the financial accounting process. Knowledge of what the financial statements are intended to communicate will enable you to understand better the concepts and measurement procedures that underlie the accounting process that generates them. Accounting is an information system and the financial statements constitute an important communication medium.

The focus of the chapter will be on the communication of financial information about profit-making business entities to owners, potential investors, creditors, and other interested parties. Some of the problems encountered in the measurement and classification of resources will be introduced. Finally, we will be interested in what financial statements say and will begin to learn some accounting terminology.

It is important to keep in mind as you study this chapter that we will focus on the purposes and nature of financial statements—not on how the amounts were derived. Since financial statements are a means of communication, we will consider briefly this broad area first.

Communication of accounting information

Communication consists of a flow of information from one party to one or more other parties. For communication to be effective, the parties must have a common understanding of the information. In the process of communication there are obviously great problems in understanding precisely the words, symbols, and sounds used. Accounting comprises an information system that is designed to convey relevant financial information. First, accounting seeks to communicate with the users of

26

the financial information—owners, potential investors, creditors, and other decision makers. Second, accounting seeks to identify the primary types of decisions that require financial information. Finally, accounting, on the basis of these two determinations, attempts to report the kinds of financial information needed in the decision-making process. Fundamentally, managers, owners, potential investors, creditors, and other decision makers, as a basis for assessing the present and future potentials of a business, want answers to three important questions: (1) What has been the performance of the business? (For example, how much profit has it earned?) (2) How does the business stand financially at the present time? (For example, what are its resources and how much does it owe?) (3) What are its future potentials? The financial statements discussed in this chapter are primary means of communication, developed by the accountant, that respond in part to questions (1) and (2). Although they are not directly responsive to the third question, they provide an important starting point in assessing the future.

Before looking at the financial statements, we should consider communication in general. As we make decisions of varying sorts, we must rely upon certain information that often is unique to each type of decision. Often, we must make decisions without adequate information. Either the needed information is not available to us or the cost and time entailed in developing it is prohibitive when compared to its potential benefits.[1] The nature and form in which information reaches us often affects our decision. For example, some individuals are more influenced by graphic than by quantitative presentations; others find narrative preferable to tabular expression; some prefer summaries rather than details; and still others object to technical presentations of any sort. The way in which accounting information is communicated determines its usefulness to, and impact upon, decision makers.

Financial information and the means of communicating it frequently have strong and pervasive **behavioral impacts**[2] upon decision makers. The behavioral impacts of accounting extend to both positive and negative motivations of people. The frequency, form, and quality of one's communications with others are often important to motivations.

The terminology and symbols of accounting were devised over a long

---

[1] This suggests the concept of *cost-benefit analysis;* that is, a comparison of the cost of a particular course of action, compared with the economic benefits or advantages derived from that course of action.

[2] A behavioral impact is an individual response to external forces. An individual may be motivated toward or away from certain courses of action by information or observations that come to his attention. For example, one may be motivated to purchase a large automobile rather than a small one for reasons of prestige. However, a financial report showing the relative costs of operating the two automobiles may motivate the individual to purchase the small automobile. Thus, the report exerted a significant behavorial impact on the decision maker.

period of time in the search for ways to communicate financial information effectively. As is common with other professions, such as law and medicine, the terminology and symbols of accounting are somewhat technical. Accounting has developed in direct response to the needs of people. As a consequence, it is continuously evolving new concepts, terminology, procedures, and means of communication. In these two volumes, one of our considerations will be the terminology of accounting.

Accounting:
an informa-
tion system

Accounting records the detailed financial history of the business entity and, from that information, derives the financial statements. Thus, the **accounting process** involves the accumulation, analysis, measurement, interpretation, classification, and summarization of the results of each of the many business transactions that affect the business during the year. After all of this processing, accounting then transmits or projects the message to the decision makers. The message is in the form of financial statements and the decision makers are the users. Accounting does not generate the basic information (raw financial data); rather, the raw financial data are derived from the day-to-day transactions initiated, participated in, and completed by the employees of the enterprise. As an *information system,* the accounting process is designed to record these data and capture the **economic essence** of each transaction.[3]

The accounting system must be designed to classify the financial information on a basis suitable for decision-making purposes and to process the tremendous quantities of data efficiently and accurately. The information system must be designed to report the results periodically, in a realistic and concise format that is comprehensible to users who generally have only a limited technical knowledge of accounting. The information system also must be designed to accommodate the special and complex needs of the internal management of the entity on a continuing basis. These internal needs extend primarily to the planning and control responsibilities of the managers of the enterprise; they are discussed in *Fundamentals of Management Accounting.*

The accountant has the primary responsibility for developing the accounting information system that is essential for most entities, whether operating on a profit or nonprofit basis. In designing an information system, the accountant must consider the factors of (a) cost, (b) benefit, (c) timeliness (i.e., reports must be rendered early), and (d) requirements of various outside influences, such as governmental regulatory agencies (examples are the Securities and Exchange Commission and the Internal Revenue Service).

Now, we are ready to consider the fundamentals of **external financial**

---

[3] The accounting information system should be viewed as a part of the overall information system that necessarily operates in all entities.

statements prepared for owners, potential investors, creditors, and other interested parties.

<table>
<tr><td>Fundamen-
tals under-
lying
accounting</td><td>In Chapter 1 we briefly discussed the roles of the American Institute of Certified Public Accountants (AICPA), the Securities and Exchange Commission (SEC), and the American Accounting Association (AAA) during the last fifty years. Although the efforts of these and other organizations were significant, much of the evolution in accounting was initiated by industry and by firms of practicing accountants. As a result of all these forces, certain assumptions, concepts, principles, and standards evolved that today constitute the **fundamentals underlying accounting.** These fundamentals are man-made. They are continually being changed to meet the evolving needs of society and to keep financial measurement and reporting relevant to current trends and problems. They change primarily because of the research efforts of accountants and the activities of the above-named organizations.</td></tr>
</table>

Exhibit 2–1
Fundamentals underlying accounting

	Text Reference	
Basic Assumptions, Principles, and Procedures*	*Chapter*	*Page*
1. *Underlying Assumptions:*		
a. Separate-entity assumption	1	4
b. Continuity assumption	2	35
c. Unit-of-measure assumption	1	3
d. Time-period assumption	5	126
2. *Underlying Principles:*		
a. Cost principle	2	35
b. Revenue principle	2	32
c. Matching principle	5	128
d. Objectivity principle	2	35
e. Consistency principle	7	238
f. Full-disclosure principle	3	68
g. Exception principle	8	270
(1) Materiality		
(2) Conservatism		
(3) Industry peculiarities		
3. *Practices and Procedures:*		
a. Those related to income and asset measurement		
b. Those related to the reporting of accounting results		Illustrated and discussed throughout the chapters to follow
c. Those not related to asset or income measurement or to the reporting of accounting results		

* A similar tabulation including a brief explanation is presented in Exhibit 16–1.

The accounting profession has not agreed upon a single listing of the fundamentals underlying accounting; therefore, throughout the literature of accounting you will find variation in terminology and definition. For purposes of this book we will use the list given in Exhibit 2–1. At this point, we will simply list these fundamentals for your convenience in future reference. We have also listed the chapter and page numbers where each fundamental is *first* introduced. Throughout the discussions we will return to these fundamentals in order to explain the rationale for a particular accounting approach.

External financial statements

A primary objective of the accounting process is the development of financial statements that communicate relevant information to decision makers. An understanding of financial statements at the outset places you in an excellent position to interpret them and to understand how the accounting process operates. The three primary financial statements for a profit-making entity for external reporting to owners, potential investors, creditors, and other decision makers are the:

1. Income Statement (more descriptively, statement of revenues, expenses, and profit)
2. Balance Sheet (more descriptively, statement of assets, liabilities, and owners' equity)
3. Statement of Changes in Financial Position (more descriptively, statement of working capital, or cash inflows and outflows)

These three statements summarize the financial activities of the business entity for each specific period of time. They can be produced at any time (such as end of the year, quarter, or month) and can apply to any time span (such as ten years, one year, one quarter, or one month). The heading of each statement contains a very specific statement of the time dimensions of the report. Although these three reports relate to each other, for convenience, at this point in your study, they will be considered separately. We will first illustrate them for a simple business situation; the next chapter discusses and illustrates a more complex situation.

THE INCOME STATEMENT

The income statement is designed to report the profit performance of a business entity for a specific period of time, such as a year, quarter, or month. Profit, or net income, represents the difference between revenues and expenses for the specified period. In other words, an income statement presents the results of operations; that is, it reports, for a specific period of time, the items that comprise the total revenue and the total expense and the resulting net income.

Exhibit 2–2 presents the income statement for the first year of operations of Business Aids, Incorporated, an enterprise that renders professional secretarial, reproduction, and mailing services for a fee. Busi-

Exhibit 2–2

BUSINESS AIDS, INCORPORATED	←Name of entity
Income Statement	←Title of report }HEADING
For the Year Ended December 31, 1974	←Time

Revenue:

Stenographic revenue...........................	$30,000	
Printing revenue..............................	20,000	
Mailing revenue...............................	13,000	
Total revenue............................		$63,000
Expenses:		
Salaries expense...............................	30,750	
Payroll tax expense............................	1,100	
Rent expense on office space....................	2,400	
Rental payments for copier......................	6,600	
Utilities expense...............................	400	
Advertising expense............................	960	
Supplies used expense..........................	120	
Interest expense...............................	70	
Depreciation expense on office equipment..........	600	
Total expenses...........................		43,000
Pretax income.................................		20,000
Income tax expense ($20,000 × 22%)........		4,400
Net Income....................................		$15,600
Earnings per share ($15,600 ÷ 3,000 shares)........		$ 5.20

ness Aids was organized by three individuals as a corporation. Each owner (who is called a shareholder or stockholder) received 1,000 shares of capital stock as evidence of his ownership. The heading of the statement specifically identifies the name of the entity, the title of the report, and the period of time over which the reported net income was earned. Note that the date encompasses a period of time—in this case, one year. There are three major captions: *Revenue, Expenses,* and *Net income.* The detail presented under each caption is intended to be sufficient to meet the needs of decision makers interested in Business Aids, Incorporated. This latter point is significant because the composition and the detail of a financial statement vary, depending on the characteristics of the business entity and the needs of the users.

    Revenue. Revenues are inflows of cash and other items of value received for goods sold or services rendered. Although some of the revenue inflows are cash, others may include rights, such as receivables that ensue from extending credit to customers, or property received from a customer who is paying for a service with merchandise from his own shelves. Typical sources of revenue, in addition to those illustrated for Business Aids, are sales of goods, commissions earned, rent revenue, dividends received on stock, and interest revenue.[4] Revenue is expressed in dollars as the bargained price agreed on by the two

---

    [4] Revenue sometimes is called "income," such as rent income, interest income, and royalty income, but this practice leads to confusion. *Income should always refer to the difference between revenue and expense.*

parties to the transaction. One of the fundamentals listed in Exhibit 2–1 is called the **revenue principle**; it is also called the *realization principle*. This principle governs the accounting for revenue. The revenue principle (a) incorporates a definition of revenue, as above; (b) states that revenue should be recognized[5] in the period when the sale is made or when the services are rendered rather than when the related cash is collected; and (c) specifies that revenues should be measured as the cash received plus the cash equivalent (i.e., the fair-market value) of any other items received. The revenue principle is discussed in Chapter 5 also.

Expenses. Expenses represent outflows of resources, or the incurring of a debt, for goods and services by an entity to earn revenues. Expenses may require the immediate payment of cash or, in the case of credit, the payment of cash some time after the expense is incurred. In some cases cash is paid *before* the expense is incurred, as in the case of the payment of office rent in *advance of occupancy*. For accounting purposes, an expense is recognized in the period in which it is incurred rather than in the period in which the cash is paid. Incurred means the period in which the goods are used or the services are received.

An expense may represent the cost of using equipment or buildings that were acquired and are being held for use in operating the business rather than for sale. Such items often have a high initial cost at the date of acquisition and, through use, are worn-out over an extended period of time known as their useful life. As they are used in operating the business, a portion of their initial cost becomes an expense. This kind of expense is known as depreciation. For example, on January 1, 1974, Business Aids purchased office equipment for its own use at a cost of $6,000. It was estimated that the office equipment would have a useful life of ten years. Therefore, the depreciation expense each year for using the equipment is measured as $6,000 ÷ 10 years = $600. The income statement for 1974 (Exhibit 2–2) reports this amount as an expense.[6]

Since a corporation must pay a 22% tax rate on the first $25,000 of profits earned each year (and a 48% rate for profits above that amount), Business Aids incurred an income tax expense of $4,400.[7] Income tax expense may be listed along with the other expenses; however, Business Aids prefers to report it separately as illustrated, so that both pretax and after-tax income is shown.

---

[5] Recognized, as used in this context, means that the amount involved should be accounted for (i.e., recorded in the accounting system) at the specified time.

[6] Accounting for depreciation is discussed in detail in Chapter 9. In respect to expense recognition, see the Matching Principle, Chapter 5, for a detailed discussion.

[7] Corporations, except those that qualify under Subchapter S of the Internal Revenue Code, are required to pay income taxes. Sole proprietorships and partnerships, as business entities, and Subchapter S corporations are not subject to income taxes.

Net income. Net income is the excess of total revenues over total expenses. If the total expenses exceed the total revenues, a net loss is reported. When revenues and expenses are equal for the period, the business is said to have operated at breakeven.

Earnings per share. The amount of earnings per share (EPS) is reported immediately below net income if the business is organized as a corporation. EPS is derived by dividing net income by the number of shares of stock outstanding. Since Business Aids had 3,000 shares of stock outstanding (i.e., 1,000 shares were owned by each of the three shareholders) and a net income of $15,600, EPS was computed as: $15,600 ÷ 3,000 shares = $5.20 per share for the year. Especially in recent years, EPS has been accorded an extensive amount of attention by security analysts and others. As a consequence, the accounting profession has come to accept it as an important information input for investors. Specific accounting guidelines were developed by the APB for computing and reporting EPS in complex situations.

It is frequently said that the income statement is the most important of the three financial reports. It is designed to communicate to the user the results of operations of the business for a specific period of time. The accounting model for the income statement is:

$$\text{Revenues} - \text{Expenses} = \text{Net Income} \quad (\text{i.e., } R - E = NI)$$

The amount of net income obviously represents a net increase in resources that flowed into the business entity during the period.

THE BALANCE SHEET

The purpose of the balance sheet is to report the financial position of a business at a particular point in time. This is in contrast to the income statement, which covers a period of time. Financial position refers to the amount of resources (i.e., assets) and liabilities of the business on a specific date. As a consequence, this statement is frequently called the statement of financial position. A more descriptive title would be the statement of assets, liabilities, and owners' equity, since these are the three major captions on the statement.[8]

Exhibit 2–3 presents the balance sheet at the end of the first year of operations for Business Aids, Incorporated. Observe that the heading specifically identifies the name of the entity, the title of the report, and the specific date of the statement. Note that a specific point in time—in this case, December 31, 1974—is stated on a balance sheet. This contrasts with the dating on the income statement, which indicates a period

---

[8] The designation "balance sheet" is unfortunate since it is not descriptive in any sense. It implies that the central fact is that it balances arithmetically, although this is actually an incidental feature. Because of the widespread use of the term, however, it will be used in this book.

Exhibit 2–3

BUSINESS AIDS, INCORPORATED
Balance Sheet
At December 31, 1974

Assets			*Liabilities*	
Cash.................		$13,600	Accounts payable..... $ 900	
Accounts receivable....		13,000	Income taxes payable.. 1,500	
Land.................		20,000	Note payable, short-	
Office equipment....... $6,000			term.............. 1,000	
Less accumulated de-			Total Liabilities.	$ 3,400
preciation........	600	5,400		
			Shareholders' Equity	
			Contributed capital:	
			Capital stock (3,000	
			shares, par value	
			$10 per share).... $30,000	
			Contributed capital in	
			excess of par...... 3,000	
			Retained earnings..... 15,600	
			Total Sharehold-	
			ers' Equity ...	48,600
			Total Liabilities and	
Total Assets..........		$52,000	Shareholders' Equity	$52,000

---

of time (such as one year). Below the heading the Assets are listed on the left and the Liabilities and Owners' Equity on the right; the result is that the two sides "balance." Later, we will discuss alternative formats for the balance sheet. The accounting model for the balance sheet is:

Assets = Liabilities + Owners' Equity (i.e., A = L + OE).

As is the case with any equation, its elements may be transposed. For example, the model frequently is expressed to reflect the fact that owners' equity is a residual (i.e., the difference between the assets and liabilities of the entity), viz.:

Assets − Liabilities = Owners' Equity (i.e., A − L = OE).

The accounting model is a basic building block in the total accounting process.[9] We will define and discuss each of the three variables in this model next.

Assets. Fundamentally, assets are resources owned by the business. They may be tangible (physical in character), such as land, buildings, and machinery, or intangible (characterized by legal claims or rights), such as amounts due from customers (a legal claim called accounts re-

---

[9] The model also may be expressed as: Assets = Equities. Equities is used to denote (a) liabilities or creditors' equity, which represent claims of creditors; and (b) owners' equity, which represents claims of the owners.

ceivable) and patents (a protected right). In short, assets are the things of value, whether physical or not, owned by the business entity.[10]

Observe in the balance sheet that each of the assets listed has an assigned dollar amount. The prevailing accounting view is that assets should be *measured* on the basis of the *total cost incurred in their acquisition.* In accounting, this is known as the cost principle (listed in Exhibit 2–1). To illustrate, the balance sheet for Business Aids reports "Land, $20,000"; this is the amount of resources that was paid for the land when it was acquired. It may well be that, because of market changes, the fair-market value of the land at December 31, 1974 (date of the balance sheet), was actually $22,000. Nevertheless, under the cost principle, the report would reflect the land at its original acquisition cost. The conclusion is that a balance sheet does not necessarily show the current fair-market value of the assets listed.

It is appropriate to inquire why accountants do not change the measurement of the assets for each subsequent balance sheet to reflect the then fair-market value or price. This is not done because of the objectivity principle listed in Exhibit 2–1. This principle holds that accounting must be carried out on an objective and factual basis. There are four important reasons why fair-market values are not used.

Because of the objectivity principle:

1. To restate asset measurements at each balance sheet date would require that estimates (usually costly appraisals) be made of the current market value of each asset.

2. Accurate estimates for some assets would be difficult to determine since they would be subject to wide ranges of judgment. Accounting must be objective and factual. At acquisition, a buyer and a seller, each driving for the best bargain for himself, establish a factual valuation of cost. Such "bargained costs" are an objective and factual measure of the value of the asset when acquired.

3. Estimated fair-market values have the potential to be deliberately misstated to make the asset amounts look more favorable than is the case.

Because of the continuity assumption:

4. Many assets are acquired for use and not for resale.

The financial statements of a business are prepared on the assumption that it is a continuing enterprise; that is, a going concern. This is known as the continuity assumption in accounting (see Exhibit 2–1). The underlying assumption is that the business will not be sold or liquidated in the near future but will continue to carry on its operational

---

[10] Assets also include prepaid expenses and deferred charges, since these generally represent valid rights or claims for goods and services paid for in advance. These kinds of assets are considered in later chapters.

objectives indefinitely. Consequently, the current estimated fair-market value or prices of assets such as land, buildings, and machinery that will not be sold is of no particular importance.

The measurement of assets is one of the most complex and controversial issues in accounting; we shall explore it further in subsequent chapters.

You should particularly note how the asset "Office equipment" is reported on the balance sheet. You will recall from page 32 that this equipment cost $6,000 when it was acquired by Business Aids. Also, it was estimated that the equipment would have a ten-year useful life; thus, depreciation was calculated to be $600 per year. On the balance sheet, assets that depreciate, such as this one, are reported at cost in accordance with the cost principle. From the cost of the asset, a deduction is made for the *accumulated* depreciation from the date of acquisition to the balance-sheet date. Thus, the equipment is reported on the balance sheets at December 31, 1974, and December 31, 1975, as follows (explanatory detail added):

	December 31	
	1974	1975
Office equipment (cost at acquisition).............	$6,000	$6,000
Less: Accumulated depreciation (1 year × $600)...	600	
(2 years × $600)..		1,200
Carrying, or book, value (at end of one year)......	$5,400	
(at end of two years).....		$4,800

Liabilities. Liabilities are debts or obligations owed by the entity to the creditors. They arise as a result of the purchase of goods or services from others on credit and through cash borrowings to finance the business. If a business fails to pay its creditors, the law may accord the creditors the right to force the sale of assets sufficient to meet their claims.[11]

Business entities frequently borrow money on a note payable. In this case, a liability known as notes payable is created. A note payable, which may be short-term or long-term, specifies a definite maturity or repayment date and the rate or amount of interest charged by the lender. Also, many businesses purchase goods and services on open account that does not involve a note, thus creating a liability known as accounts payable. Income taxes frequently are paid, at least in part, several months after the end of the year. As a consequence, a liability to the government, income taxes payable, must be reported until the taxes are fully paid. You may observe in Exhibit 2–3 that Business Aids listed three liabilities and the amount of each. In respect to amounts, liabilities present few measurement problems since most liabilities are reported at

---

[11] In case of dissolution or sale of all the assets of a business, legally, the creditors must be paid first and any remainder goes to the owners.

the amount of the debt established by the parties to the transaction.

Owners' equity. The accounting model (page 34) shows owners' equity to be equal to the total assets minus the total liabilities of the business. Thus, the owners' equity is a residual interest or claim of the owners to the assets because creditor claims legally come first. Owners' equity sometimes is called net worth, capital, or proprietorship; however the preferable designations are for a sole proprietorship: owner's equity; for a partnership: partners' equity; and for a corporation: shareholders' or stockholders' equity. Owners' equity in a business derives from two sources: (1) contributed capital, which is the investment of cash or other assets in the business by the owner or owners; and (2) retained earnings, which are the accumulated profits of the business less the losses and withdrawals. When the owners receive cash or other assets from the business through withdrawals (defined later), the total amount of owners' equity is reduced. When the business incurs a loss, owners' equity also is reduced.

In Exhibit 2–3, the shareholders' equity section reports the following:

1. Contributed capital—The three shareholders invested a total of $33,000 in the business and received 3,000 shares of capital stock having a par value of $10 per share (par value will be discussed in Chapter 12). They invested $11 per share, or $1 above par value. The 3,000 shares issued are reported at their par value (3,000 × $10) as "Capital stock" and the remainder, often called a premium (3,000 shares × $1 = $3,000), is reported as "Contributed capital in excess of par value."[12]

2. Retained earnings—The accumulated earnings less all dividends paid since formation of the corporation is reported as "Retained earnings." During the first year the business earned $15,600, as shown on the income statement (Exhibit 2–2). This amount is reported on the balance sheet for Business Aids at this date as Retained earnings since no dividends had been paid to the shareholders.

3. Total shareholders' equity is the sum of the investment ($33,000) plus the retained earnings ($15,600) = $48,600. This amount may be verified: Assets ($52,000) − Liabilities ($3,400) = Shareholders' equity ($48,600)

If, by contrast, a dividend of $6,000 had been paid to the three shareholders, the balance sheet would have reflected cash of $7,600 and retained earnings of $9,600.

The form of organization utilized for Business Aids was a corporation. If the business were a sole proprietorship or a partnership, the "Owners' Equity" classification on the balance sheet would appear somewhat differently. Owners' equity for both a sole proprietorship

---

[12] Par value has a legal meaning that is discussed in Chapter 12.

and a partnership is illustrated below, utilizing the amounts for Business Aids from Exhibit 2–3.

Owners' Equity for a Sole Proprietorship

Owner's Equity:

Raymond Nalle, capital.............................. $48,600

Owners' Equity for a Partnership*

Partners' Equity:

John Doe, capital......................................	$16,200
Richard Moe, capital.................................	16,200
Samuel Roe, capital..................................	16,200
Total Partners' Equity..........................	$48,600

* This assumes that each partner invested $11,000 and that the earnings of $15,600 were divided equally among them.

Corporations may be required by law to maintain a distinction between contributed capital and retained earnings, as reflected in Exhibit 2–3. This is because the amount of dividends normally cannot exceed the amount of retained earnings. In a partnership, the capital of each partner usually is increased by his share of the net income and decreased by his withdrawals of assets from the business. In a sole proprietorship, earnings are added to the proprietor's original invested capital and withdrawals are deducted.

STATEMENT OF CHANGES IN FINANCIAL POSITION

In recent years the **financing activities** of businesses have become increasingly complex. The business entity of today requires substantial funds for operations and expansion. These funds necessarily come from three sources: (1) owner investment, (2) borrowings, and (3) internally by earning net income. In recognition of the need by users of financial statements for information concerning the investing and financing activities of the business, the APB issued *Opinion No. 19* in March 1971. This *Opinion* requires a statement of changes in financial position[13] to accompany the income statement and the balance sheet.

The objective of the statement of changes in financial position is to communicate to the user information about the inflows and outflows of cash (or, alternatively, of working capital, defined later). Exhibit 2–4 presents a statement of changes in financial position for Business Aids. At this point you need not be concerned about the derivation of the amounts. Rather, your attention is called to the two basic classifications: cash generated (inflows of cash) and cash applied (outflows of cash). The difference between them represents the change in cash during the

---

[13] This statement is an outgrowth of a "Statement of Sources and Application of Funds," which was optional.

period. Since investors and creditors often think in terms of present and potential future cash flows, this statement provides an important information input to the decision-making process. The accounting model for this statement is:

Resource Inflows — Resource Outflows = Change in Resources

The statement of changes in financial position is derived from an analysis of the balance sheet and the income statement. For example, total revenue reported on Exhibit 2–2 (the income statement) of $63,000, less $13,000 of the revenue (Mailing) rendered on credit, equals $50,000, reported as the cash inflow from revenue on Exhibit

Exhibit 2–4

BUSINESS AIDS, INCORPORATED
Statement of Changes in Financial Position—Cash Basis
For the Year Ended December 31, 1974

Cash Generated (Inflows):		
From operations:		
From revenue.	$50,000	
Less: Cash used for expenses.	44,400	
Cash generated from operations.		$ 5,600
From other sources:		
Investment by owners (stock issued).	33,000	
Loan—note payable.	1,000	
Cash generated from other sources.		34,000
Total cash generated during the year (inflows).		39,600
Cash Applied (Outflows):		
To purchase office equipment.	6,000	
To purchase land.	20,000	
Total cash applied during the year (outflows).		26,000
Change—increase in cash during the year.		$13,600

2–4. Similarly, Total expenses of $47,400 (including income tax expense), shown on Exhibit 2–2, less the noncash expenses of $600 for depreciation and $2,400 for accounts payable and income taxes payable, equals the $44,400 reported on Exhibit 2–4 as the cash used for expenses. Detailed discussion of the statement of changes in financial position is deferred to Chapter 15 because it requires special procedures that are best understood after your knowledge level of the accounting process is substantial.

Accrual basis accounting   In the definition of revenue on page 31, we stated that revenue is recognized when earned rather than when the resulting cash is collected. Similarly, in defining expenses, we stated that an expense is recognized when *incurred* rather than when the required cash is paid. These definitions reflect the accrual basis of accounting, as contrasted with the cash basis. Frequently, revenue may be *earned* long before the cash is collected. For example, an appliance company may sell a refrigerator for $300 on November 1, 1974, for a $100 down payment and the balance payable later, on May 1, 1975. Under the accrual basis, the $300 sale would be recognized in 1974. In other situations, cash may be collected before the revenue is earned. For example, a publishing company generally receives cash for subscriptions before the magazines or newspapers are delivered. In this situation the revenue from the subscriptions would be recognized as the magazines are delivered rather than when the cash subscription price was collected. Similarly, expenses may be *incurred* before or after the cash payment date. For example, an outsider, such as a plumbing firm, may have completed a service job for the company in December 1974 and cash payment is to be made in February 1975. Under the accrual basis, the expense should be recognized in 1974 rather than in 1975. Or, expenses may be prepaid; that is, the cash is paid *before* the expense is incurred. For example, a company may choose to pay in advance a three-year premium of $300 for insurance on an automobile. The insurance expense would be $100 for each of the three years since the expense is *incurred* as the time covered by the policy passes.

The accrual basis is used in accounting so that revenues and expenses will be recognized in the period in which the activities occurred that caused those revenues and expenses. Cash inflows and outflows reflect financing activities, whereas revenues and expenses recognized on the accrual basis reflect the results of operating activities.

Demonstra- tion case for self-study	## ABC CORPORATION Try to resolve the case before studying the suggested solution that follows it.

The ABC Corporation was organized by three investors on January 1, 1974. On that date, as initial, or start-up, capital, each investor bought 2,000 shares of capital stock (par $10 per share) and paid $12 per share in cash. In addition, the corporation borrowed $40,000 cash from a local bank, giving a three-year note payable. The note was dated January 1, 1974, and called for 8% interest per year. The interest is payable each December 31 and the maturity, or due date, of the note is December 31, 1976. Operations were started immediately.

On December 31, 1974, it was determined that the net income of the ABC Company for the first year was $21,000, after deducting interest expense and income taxes. On that date, each shareholder was paid a cash dividend of $2.00 per share. The income tax rate for the year was 22%.

Required:

1. What were the sources and amounts of cash to start the business?
2. Prepare the shareholders' equity section of the balance sheet for the ABC Corporation at December 31, 1974.

Solution:

ABC CORPORATION

1. Sources and amounts of initial cash:

From owners (6,000 shares of stock at $12 per share).......	$ 72,000
From creditors (note payable, 8% interest, 36 months to maturity)...	40,000
Total	$112,000

2. Balance sheet at December 31, 1974:

Shareholders' Equity

Capital stock (6,000 shares, par $10 per share)..............	$ 60,000
Contributed capital in excess of par value..................	12,000
Total contributed capital..........................	72,000
Retained earnings (see Note *a*)...........................	9,000
Total Shareholders' Equity....................	$ 81,000

Notes:
(*a*) Computation of retained earnings:

Starting balance, January 1, 1974....................................	$ –0–
Add net income for 1974...	21,000
Total...	21,000
Deduct dividends paid during 1974 (6,000 shares × $2)..................	12,000
Ending balance, December 31, 1974...............................	$ 9,000

(*b*) The $40,000 note payable will be reported on the balance sheet under the liability caption. The $3,200 interest paid will be reported on the income statement under the expense caption.

Summary   The focus of this chapter was on the communication of accounting information to external users as a basis for their decision making. Your attention was directed primarily to profit-making entities, or business enterprises. The chapter explained and illustrated the basic features of the three required **external** financial reports—the income statement, the balance sheet, and the statement of changes in financial position.

The income statement, as a statement of operations, reports revenue, expenses, and the net income for a stated **period** of time. Earnings per share (EPS), which expressed the relationship between net income and the number of shares of common stock, was illustrated.

The balance sheet, as a statement of financial position, reports dollar amounts for the assets, liabilities, and owners' equity at a specific **point** in time.

The statement of changes in financial position, as a statement of the inflows and outflows of resources, reports those flows for a specific **period** of time.

The fundamental accounting model **Assets = Liabilities + Owners' Equity** was introduced as the foundation for the balance sheet and the accounting process in general. The distinction between the accrual basis and the cash basis was explained. The financial statements for a small company were illustrated. In the next chapter we will move one step forward and look at a more complex situation and, at the same time, add more concepts to your knowledge about the characteristics of the financial statements for a business entity.

A list of the broad fundamentals underlying accounting was given in Exhibit 2–1. Of those listed, the following have been defined and illustrated up to this point in your study:

Designation	*Underlying Fundamentals*
Unit-of-measure assumption	Measurement in accounting predominately is in terms of the monetary exchange unit. The dollar is the common denominator—the yardstick—for measurement in the accounting process.
Separate-entity assumption	For accounting purposes the entity must be specifically defined; a business is assumed to be separate and apart from its owners and other parties.
Revenue principle	Revenue should be given accounting recognition only when it is earned; that is, when a sale of goods is made or a service is rendered.
Cost principle	Assets acquired should be accounted for at the bargained cost when acquired and are subsequently carried at that cost.
Continuity assumption	Unless there is evidence to the contrary, accounting assumes that the business entity is not being sold or liquidated; that it will continue indefinitely as a "going concern" to carry out its intended operational objectives.
Objectivity principle	Accounting measures and reports the financial effects of transactions on an objective, factual, and verifiable basis. Insofar as possible, only objectively determined measurements are used.

Important terms

Communication	Balance sheet
Information system	Assets
Accounting process	Liabilities
External financial statements	Owners' equity
Income statement	Statement of changes in financial position
Revenue	
Expenses	Unit-of-measure assumption
Depreciation expense	Cost principle
Net income	Separate-entity assumption
Earnings per share (EPS)	Continuity assumption
Accrual basis	Objectivity principle

Questions
for
discussion

1. Financial statements are the end products of the accounting process. Explain.

2. Generally, how would you define communication?

3. The accounting process generates financial reports for both "internal" and "external" audiences. Identify some of the groups in each audience.

4. Explain why accounting may be viewed as an information system.

5. Complete the following on a sheet of paper:

Name of Statement		A More Descriptive Name
a. Income statement	a.	_____
b. Balance sheet	b.	_____
c. Statement of changes in financial position	c.	_____

6. What information should be included in the heading of each financial statement?

7. Explain why the income statement and the statement of changes in financial position are dated "For the Year Ended December 31, 19XX," whereas the balance sheet is dated "At December 31, 19XX."

8. Explain the revenue principle.

9. Briefly define revenue and expenses.

10. Briefly define the following: net income; net loss; breakeven.

11. What are the purposes of: (a) the income statement, (b) the balance sheet, and (c) the statement of changes in financial position?

12. Explain the accounting model for the income statement. What are the three major items reported on the income statement?

13. Explain the accounting model for the balance sheet. Define the three major components reported on the balance sheet.

14. Explain the accounting model for the statement of changes in financial position. Explain the three major components reported on the statement.

15. Why is owners' equity frequently referred to as a residual interest?

16. What are the two primary sources of owners' equity in a business?

17. What are appropriate titles for owners' equity for (a) a sole proprietorship, (b) a partnership, and (c) a corporation?

Exercises E2–1. Decision makers, in utilizing financial reports to assess the future potential of a company, generally want answers to the three important questions listed below. In respect to each of them, you are to complete a format similar to the following:

Question	Name of statement that responds to the question	Briefly, the way in which the statement responds to the question
a. What was the profit performance of the business?		
b. What resources are owned, what debts are owed, and what is the amount of the owners' claim?		
c. What were the sources and uses of cash?		

E2–2. The Oakley and Kane Grocery is a corporation that has been in operation for three years. The 1974 annual financial statements are being prepared for the use of the management and for submission to the bank as support for a line of credit. You have been requested to draft an appropriate heading and list of major captions for each of the three external reports that should be prepared.

E2–3. Jones Realty, Incorporated, has been operating for five years and is owned by three investors. Sam Jones owns 60% of the stock (6,000 shares) and is the managing executive in charge. On December 31, 1974, the following financial items for the year were determined: commissions earned and collected in cash, $100,000, plus $10,000 uncollected; rental service fees collected and earned, $18,000; salaries expense paid, $50,000; commissions expense paid, $40,000; payroll taxes paid, $3,000; rent paid, $1,100 (not including December rent yet to be paid); utilities expense paid, $500; promotion and advertising paid, $5,800; and miscellaneous expenses paid, $200. Jones Realty rents office space for its own use but owns the furniture therein. The furniture cost $3,000 when acquired and has an estimated life of ten years. The corporate income tax rate is 22%. Also, during the year, the company paid the owners "out of profits" cash dividends amounting to $10,000. You have been requested to prepare an income statement for 1974.

(Hint: EPS is $2.106.)

E2–4. Taylor's is a retail store that specializes in men's furnishings. The company owns two small panel trucks utilized for deliveries and general hauling associated with the operation of the store. The two trucks are as follows:

	Cost When Acquired	Date Acquired	Estimated Useful Life
No. 1	$2,400	Jan. 1, 1972	4 years
No. 2	3,600	Jan. 1, 1974	5 years

You are requested to compute the depreciation expense on each truck for the year ended December 31, 1974. Show your computations.

E2–5. The University Bookstore was organized as a partnership by James Nash and Roy Opel; each contributed $15,000 cash to start the business. The store completed its first year of operations on December 31, 1974. On that date the following financial items were determined: cash on hand and in the bank, $22,000; due from customers from sales of books, $1,000; store and office equipment, purchased January 1, 1974, for $30,000 (estimated useful life ten years); amounts owed to publishers for books purchased, $4,000; and a note payable to a local bank for $2,000. The partners divided the annual profit of $14,000 equally, although none of it was withdrawn since they "needed it for growth of the store." You have been requested to prepare a balance sheet for the bookstore at December 31, 1974.

(Hint: Total liabilities and partners' equity is $50,000.)

E2–6. The Macon Corporation is in the process of preparing a balance sheet at the end of 1974. The following amounts have been determined: retained earnings amount at the start of 1974 was $37,000; cash dividends paid to stockholders at the end of 1974 amounted to $20,000; and net income (after income taxes) for 1974 amounted to $24,000. You have been requested to determine the amount of retained earnings at the end of 1974.

E2–7. Ace Trucking Line, Incorporated, is in the process of completing the financial report for shareholders. For the first time a statement of changes in financial position—cash basis is being prepared. You have been asked to help design the report. The following data on cash flows have been developed for the year ended December 31, 1974: cash inflow from operating revenues, $190,000, less cash expended for operating expenses, $160,000; cash dividends paid to shareholders during the year, $10,000; and payments on long-term notes payable, $25,000. During the year, three used moving vans were sold for $14,000 cash, and $15,000 cash was expended for two new vans of a different type.

Required:

Prepare a statement of changes in financial position—cash basis for 1974. Follow the format illustrated in the chapter.

(Hint: Cash decreased $6,000 during the year.)

E2–8. On June 1, 1974, the Rand Corporation prepared a balance sheet just prior to going out of business. The balance sheet totals reflected the following:

Assets (no cash)	$100,000
Liabilities	60,000
Stockholders' equity	40,000

Shortly thereafter, all of the assets were sold for $75,000 cash.

Required:
(a) How would the balance sheet appear immediately after the sale of the assets?
(b) How should the cash be distributed? Explain.

Problems P2–1. The Aztec Rental Company was organized as a corporation in January 1974 by five investors. Each investor paid in $11,000 cash and received 200 shares of $50 par value stock. Immediately thereafter, the company obtained a $15,000 loan from a local bank. Rental equipment costing $52,000 was purchased for cash, and operations began. Careful records were maintained during the year. As a consequence, the following accurate amounts were available at the end of December 1974:

Rental fees collected	$65,000	Cash on hand and in bank	$23,000
Rental fees uncollected	3,000	Rental equipment (cost)	52,000
Repair fees collected	10,000	Land for future building site	14,000
Salaries and wages paid	30,000	Other assets	3,000
Payroll taxes paid	600	Rent payable (December)	200
Repair parts purchased and used	700	Income taxes payable	1,400
Rent paid (11 months)	2,200	Notes payable, long-term	15,000
December rent not yet paid	200	Capital stock	50,000
Utilities paid	400	Cash dividends paid	10,000
Advertising expenditures paid	2,100	Accounts receivable	3,000
Insurance premiums paid		Accumulated depreciation	10,000
for 1974	100	Contributed capital in	
Miscellaneous expenses paid	1,500	excess of par	5,000
Depreciation for the year on			
rental equipment	10,000		
Maintenance costs paid	200		
Income tax rate (flat rate)	22%		

Required:
You have been requested to utilize the above data to prepare an income statement and a balance sheet.

(Hint: EPS was $23.40 and the balance sheet total is $85,000.)

P2–2. At December 31, 1974, the Big J Corporation had been in operation for one year. At the date of organization, each of the ten investors paid in $10,000 cash and each received 100 shares of capital stock. Due to a need for more capital, on January 1, 1974, the corporation also borrowed $100,000, at 7% interest per year, on a note from a local bank. Interest on the note was payable each December 31 and the loan matures December 31, 1977. On December 31, 1974, the income statement and the balance sheet (summarized) were as follows:

Income Statement
For the Year Ended December 31, 1974

Total revenue....................................	$70,000
Total expenses.....................................	44,360
Pretax income....................................	25,640
Income tax expense ($25,640 × 22%)................	5,640
Net Income......................................	$20,000

Balance Sheet
At December 31, 1974

Assets		*Liabilities*	
Cash.......................	$ 30,000	Income taxes payable........	$ 5,640
Remaining assets............	195,640	Notes payable, long-term......	100,000
		Owners' Equity	
		Capital stock (1,000 shares)....	100,000
		Retained earnings............	20,000
		Total Liabilities and Owners'	
Total Assets................	$225,640	Equity.................	$225,640

An independent CPA has audited the above amounts. He found that the bookkeeper had neglected to include two transactions that occurred on December 31, 1974:

(1) Payment of a cash dividend of $8.00 per share to each shareholder.

(2) Cash payment of interest on the long-term note payable to the bank.

Required:

Other than for these two transactions, the figures were correct. You have been asked to recast the income statement and the balance sheet to include the effects of these two transactions. Assume a 22% tax rate.

(Hint: Revised net income is $14,539 and the balance sheet total is $210,640.)

P2–3. The ABC Furniture Store was organized at the start of 1974 with an investment of $60,000. At the end of the year, it was determined that net income after income taxes amounted to $15,000. During the year, the owners had not withdrawn any cash. You have been requested to develop the owners' equity section of the December 31, 1974, balance sheet under each of three different cases as follows:

Case A—Assume a sole proprietorship (owner Sam Bass).

Case B—Assume a three-way partnership (Kane, Myron, and Null) whereby each partner invested the same amount of cash at the start and net income is divided ⅓ to each.

Case C—Assume a corporation whereby 2,000 shares were issued to each of three shareholders at $10 par value per share.

P2–4. The Oakland Realty Company was organized early in 1969 as a corporation by four investors, each of whom invested $2,500 cash. The company has been moderately successful, despite the fact that financial controls are inadequate. Although financial reports have been prepared each year (primarily in response to income tax requirements), sound accounting practice has not been followed. As a consequence, the financial performance of the company was only vaguely known by the four shareholders. Recently, one of the shareholders, with the agreement of the others, sold his shares to a local CPA (not in public practice). The new shareholder was amazed when handed the report below, which was prepared by a secretary for the last meeting of the Board of Directors. He could tell at a glance that the reported profit was wrong. He quickly observed that there was no interest expense shown for a $9,000, 8% note payable that had been outstanding throughout the year. Also, no recognition had been given to office equipment that was purchased on January 1, 1974, at a cost of $10,000 and having an estimated five-year useful life.

OAKLAND REALTY
Profit Statement
December 31, 1974

Commissions earned (all collected).....................	$120,800
Property management revenue (exclusive of $1,200 not collected).......................................	7,000
Total.....................................	127,800
Salaries paid.......................................	30,000
Commissions paid..................................	37,480
Payroll taxes paid..................................	2,100
Office supplies expense.............................	110
Rent paid..	1,800
Utilities paid......................................	390
Advertising (excluding the December bill for advertising of $4,000 not yet paid)............................	26,000
Miscellaneous expenses.............................	400
Total.....................................	98,280
Profit for the year................................	$ 28,080

EPS: $28,080 ÷ 1,000 shares = $28.08

Required:

You have been asked to redraft the income statement, including corrections. Assume a 22% income tax rate.

(Hint: The correct EPS is $18.72.)

P2–5. In January 1974, Boston Stores, Incorporated, purchased a building at a cost of $200,000 and immediately put it to use as an expansion of the main store. It was determined that $50,000 of the purchase price applied to the land on which the building was located and the remainder applied to the building. At the end of the year, the management felt that the fair-market value of the property had increased "by about 10%." A local real estate agent, thinking he might line up a good deal, indicated that he would "ask and perhaps get $240,000 for the property." Although the company had no intention of selling the property, there were discussions to the effect that the property should be "listed on the balance sheet at $240,000, and certainly no less than $220,000." You have been asked for a definite statement, with reasoning, as to the proper accounting measurement to be shown, separately for the building and the land on the balance sheets at December 31, 1974 and 1975. Assume a 20-year estimated useful life for the building. In your response show the following:

Assets:	1974	1975
Building...........................		
Less: Accumulated depreciation.....		
Land..............................		

Explain the basis for the amounts you show for each item.

(Hint: Land is not subject to depreciation since it is not "used up" over time.)

P2–6. Minor's Men Store owns the following items of equipment and fixtures utilized in operating the business:

Item	Date Acquired	Cost When Acquired	Estimated Useful Life
Store fixtures...........	Jan. 1, 1971	$32,000	10 years
Delivery auto (panel)....	Jan. 1, 1972	4,000	4 years
Office equipment........	Jan. 1, 1973	3,000	10 years
Land.................	Jan. 1, 1974	15,000	Indefinite—not subject to depreciation

You have been asked to compute depreciation expense for 1974 for each of the above assets (show your computations). Can you think of any factors that might be missing that would affect the computation of depreciation? Explain.

3 Content of financial statements

Purpose
of the
chapter
The preceding chapter introduced the concepts underlying the income statement, balance sheet, and statement of changes in financial position. In this chapter we turn our attention to appropriate *subclassifications* of the information presented in these statements. Classification is employed to enhance the usefulness of the information presented. In addition, we will introduce ratio analysis, which often is helpful in the interpretation of financial statements. In the course of the discussions in this chapter, we will illustrate, first, the financial statements for a medium-sized enterprise. We will then discuss a more complicated set of financial statements for a large business.

In this chapter you should concentrate on understanding the nature of the classifications and the presentation of accounting information in the financial statements rather than on how the amounts shown are accumulated. At this time in your study of accounting, we do not anticipate that you will absorb all aspects of the financial statements that are presented; however, you should comprehend the primary features of each statement. You also should appreciate the importance of the end product of the accounting process—the financial statements—and be able to maintain perspective in the chapters to follow when studying the details of information processing, measurement, and reporting in terms of the accounting model. As you study the subsequent chapters, you should return frequently to this one for reference points and further study. Also, the exhibits will be helpful as a guide in solving some of the assigned problems in subsequent chapters.

Classification
of items
on the
financial
statements

In order to assist the user of financial statements, some standardization of classifications has evolved. As a basis for discussion of these classifications, this section presents the financial statements for Diamond's, Incorporated, a large department store that has been in business for over 40 years. When these classifications are included on the statements, they are sometimes referred to as **classified financial statements.** Classified financial statements vary in terminology and arrangement from those for Business Aids, given in Chapter 2. These differences reflect the fact that financial statements are tailored to the **needs of users,** depending on the type of company and the nature of the industry.

THE INCOME STATEMENT

Exhibit 3–1 presents an income statement for Diamond's.[1] It follows the basic concept that: **Revenue — Expenses = Net Income.** Therefore, Exhibit 3–1, stripped of the detailed items, shows the following subclassifications:

> *Revenue:*
>   Sales
>
> *Expenses*
>   Cost of goods sold
>   Selling expenses
>   General and administrative expenses
>   Financial expenses
>   Income tax expense
>
> *Difference*—income before extraordinary items
>   Extraordinary gains and losses (a special category of items)
>
> *Difference*—net income

We will discuss the meaning of each of these classifications.

Revenue. The total revenue of a business that sells physical products or merchandise is called **sales.** Merchandise sold and later returned by the customer represents **returned sales** and is not a revenue. Similarly, allowances granted to customers, say for a defect in the goods purchased from the store, reduces revenue. Therefore, **gross sales** for the period must be reduced by these amounts in order to derive the correct net revenue amount, or **net sales,** for the period.

Expenses. An income statement may be designed to reflect several classifications of expenses. These classifications tend to vary, depending upon the type of business. For a merchandising business, which is one

---

[1] The income statement discussed and illustrated in this section sometimes is referred to as a *multiple-step* income statement since it shows several groupings of data and after each group (or step) shows a difference. Each such difference is appropriately labeled, such as gross margin on sales. In contrast, a single-step income statement would be similar to that illustrated in Chapter 2 since only two major categories were shown and there were no "step" differences. Many published income statements follow the single-step format. The classifications illustrated for Diamond's are used frequently; however, they are not mandatory.

Exhibit 3–1

DIAMOND'S, INCORPORATED
Income Statement
For the Year Ended December 31, 1974

Gross sales revenue............................		$3,620,000	
Less sales returns and allowances............		5,000	
Net sales revenue............................			$3,615,000
Less cost of goods sold......................			2,416,000
Gross margin on sales.......................			1,199,000
Operating expenses:			
Selling expenses:			
Sales salaries...........................	$409,000		
Advertising and promotion...............	200,000		
Depreciation of store equipment..........	15,000		
Insurance...............................	18,000		
Taxes (excluding income tax expense)......	3,200		
Warranty expense.......................	3,000		
Amortization of trademarks..............	2,000		
Miscellaneous...........................	9,800		
Total selling expenses..............		660,000	
General and administrative expenses:			
Administrative salaries...................	179,000		
Office supplies used......................	8,100		
Estimated losses on doubtful accounts.....	3,600		
Depreciation on office equipment..........	1,000		
Insurance...............................	2,000		
Taxes (excluding income tax expense)......	400		
Miscellaneous...........................	1,900		
Total general and administrative expenses.		196,000	
Total operating expenses.............			856,000
Income from operations......................			343,000
Financial expenses and revenues:			
Interest expense.........................		56,000	
Revenue from funds and investments......		13,000	
Net financial expense..................			43,000
Pretax Income.............................			300,000
Income tax on operations.................			138,000
Income before extraordinary items............			162,000
Extraordinary items:			
Gain on sale of land held for appreciation..		51,000	
Less Income tax on the gain		13,000	38,000
Net Income................................			$ 200,000
Earnings per share of common stock:			
Income before extraordinary items........			$ 9.13
Extraordinary items.....................			2.54
Net Income.............................			$11.67

---

that sells goods manufactured by others, the usual classifications of expenses are:

1. *Cost of goods sold.* This expense reflects the amount that was incurred for the merchandise (or goods) that was sold during the period. For example, Diamond's sold goods during the period, at selling price, amounting to $3,615,000. This merchandise, when purchased by Dia-

mond's, cost $2,416,000. The difference between these two amounts is
known as the gross margin on sales. For Diamond's, the gross margin
was $1,199,000. The gross margin indicates the markup on the goods
sold. To illustrate, the average markup *on cost* for Diamond's was
$1,199,000 ÷ $2,416,000 = 49.6%, and *on selling price,* it was
$1,199,000 ÷ $3,615,000 = 33.2%.

2. *Operating expenses.* These are the usual expenses that were
incurred in operating the business during the period. Often they are
subclassified further, as reflected in Exhibit 3–1, between selling expenses and general and administrative expenses. *Selling expenses* comprise all amounts incurred during the period in performing the sales
activities. *General and administrative expenses* include the overall business expenses, such as the president's salary and the expenses of operating the accounting department.

3. *Financial expenses.* These are the expenses incurred as a result
of borrowing money or for credit extended to the company. The cost
of money usually is referred to as interest expense. Since interest on
debt is a financing expense rather than an operating expense, it is set
out in a separate category from cost of goods sold and operating expenses. Some businesses also collect interest for credit they have extended to others and receive revenue from investments (discussed in a
later chapter). Rather than include these inflows under the revenue
category, they are often offset against interest expense as shown on
Exhibit 3–1.

4. *Extraordinary items.* This classification is used to report non-
operating losses and gains. Since these items are unusual in nature and
occur infrequently, they are set out separately to aid the user in evaluating the profit performance of the business. To include them in the usual,
regularly recurring revenue or expense categories would lead the user
to believe they are normal and will occur again in the future. Observe
in Exhibit 3–1 that, when there are extraordinary items to report, there
will be income amounts shown immediately before and immediately
after the extraordinary items.[2]

Income tax expense. This is the amount of income taxes incurred
for the period, based upon taxable operating income, before the extraordinary items. The amount of income subject to tax is defined by
the Internal Revenue Code and often does not agree with the "accounting" income amount shown on the income statement. Detailed consideration of income taxes is beyond the scope of this book. However,
we will utilize simplified tax rates and computations of income taxes to
demonstrate appropriate reporting of the income tax expense and income taxes payable.

---

[2] APB *Opinion No. 30* requires that the following format be used at the
bottom of the income statement when there are extraordinary items:
    Income before extraordinary items.
    Extraordinary items (net of income tax).
    Net income.

In Exhibit 3–1, observe that total income tax expense is $138,000 + $13,000 = $151,000. When there are extraordinary items, income tax expense must be reported in two parts:

1. Income taxes based on normal operations is reported above the caption "Income before extraordinary items" ($138,000 in Exhibit 3–1).
2. Income taxes based on the extraordinary items is reported with those items ($13,000 in Exhibit 3–1).

Net income. Net income is always the last item in the body of the income statement; as a result it is often called the "bottom-line figure." It is after extraordinary items and has no qualifications—it is the difference between total revenues and total expenses.

Earnings per share. A corporation is required to show earnings-per-share amounts on the income statement for income before extraordinary items and for net income.[3] In Chapter 2, the computation of earnings per share was discussed and illustrated. In that chapter, Business Aids, Incorporated, reported only one EPS amount since there was no extraordinary items. In contrast, Diamond's reported three EPS amounts since there was an extraordinary item.[4]

THE BALANCE SHEET

In order to assist users, the assets, liabilities, and owners' equity are classified on the balance sheet into useful categories of similar items. The following classifications commonly are used.

Balance Sheet

Assets	*Liabilities*
Current assets	Current liabilities
Funds and long-term investments	Long-term liabilities
Fixed (or operational) assets	
Intangible assets	*Owners' Equity*
Deferred charges	Contributed capital
Other assets	Retained earnings

---

[3] APB *Opinion No. 15* requires that the two EPS amounts listed above be reported. Many companies also report EPS for the extraordinary category as shown on Exhibit 3–1.

[4] Earnings-per-share amounts are computed only for common stock outstanding. At this point in your study you need not be concerned about the computation of EPS amounts when both common and preferred stock are outstanding. This will be discussed later. However, for those interested, the computations for on Exhibit 3–1 are:

Income before extraordinary items:
($162,000 − $25,000, the dividend
claim of the preferred) ÷ 15,000 shares = $ 9.13
Extraordinary gain:
$38,000 ÷ 15,000 shares =   2.54
Net income:
($200,000 − $25,000) ÷ 15,000 shares = $11.67

Exhibit 3–2 presents a balance sheet for Diamond's, Incorporated. This reports items under each of the *three major* categories—assets, liabilities, and owners' equity. These major categories were defined in Chapter 2. Exhibit 2–3 (Business Aids) presented a balance sheet in account form; that is, with assets on the left and liabilities and owners' equity on the right. In contrast, Exhibit 3–2 (Diamond's) presents a balance sheet in statement form, which reports the major captions in a vertical relationship. Both formats are widely used.

Current assets. Under this classification are listed cash and other resources that are expected to be realized in cash or sold or consumed either within one year from the date of the balance sheet or during the normal operating cycle of the business, whichever is the longer. The normal operating cycle tends to vary for each business because it is the average time required to go from cash to cash. For a merchandising company it may be graphically presented as shown in Exhibit 3–3.

Current assets generally are listed on the balance sheet in order of decreasing liquidity. Liquidity is the average period of time required to convert a noncash resource to cash. In addition to cash, current assets include temporary or short-term investments, accounts receivable, inventories, and prepaid expenses. Prepaid expenses are expenses paid in advance, such as a two-year insurance premium and office supplies purchased some time before their actual use. Thus, they are goods and services paid for in advance that will be utilized in the near future (not over one year) in operating the business. When used, they will become expenses. In the meantime, since resources were expended to attain them prior to their actual usage and they will be used in the near future, they are classified on the balance sheet as current assets until utilized. To illustrate, assume a two-year insurance premium of $600 was paid on January 1, 1974. At the end of 1974, one-half of the insurance period would have expired. Therefore, *insurance expense* for 1974 would be $300 and the remaining $300 would be reported on the balance sheet as a current asset because the company still has insurance coverage due for one year. Similarly, in 1975, insurance expense would be $300 and there would be no prepaid insurance at December 31, 1975.

Creditors that have loaned money to the company on a short-term basis look primarily to current assets for payment when the amounts are due. Thus, a banker making a decision to grant short-term credit to a business is very much interested in the amounts of accounts receivable, inventory, and other current assets.

Short-term investments in the marketable securities of another company are shown under current assets because they are being held only temporarily and will be converted to cash for use in the business through sale within the next year or next operating cycle. Otherwise, investments must be reported under the caption "Funds and Long-term Investments."

Funds and long-term investments. The second classification of

Exhibit 3–2

DIAMOND'S, INCORPORATED
Balance Sheet
At December 31, 1974

Assets

Current Assets:		
Cash............................		$ 150,000
Temporary investments....................		40,000
Accounts receivable......................	$425,000	
Less allowance for doubtful accounts......	15,000	410,000
Notes receivable........................		20,000
Merchandise inventory....................		1,510,000
Office supplies inventory..................		1,000
Prepaid insurance.......................		4,000
Total current assets....................		$2,135,000
Funds and Long-term Investments:		
Stock of X Corporation...................		10,000
Sinking fund to pay bonds................		200,000
Total funds and long-term investments...		210,000
Fixed Assets:		
Store equipment.........................	150,000	
Less accumulated depreciation...........	50,000	100,000
Office equipment........................	16,000	
Less accumulated depreciation...........	4,000	12,000
Total fixed assets....................		112,000
Intangible Assets:		
Trademarks.............................		50,000
Other Assets:		
Land acquired for future store site..........		18,000
Total Assets.........................		$2,525,000

Liabilities

Current Liabilities:		
Accounts payable.......................	$ 180,000	
Notes payable..........................	100,000	
Wages payable..........................	16,000	
Income taxes payable....................	30,000	
Estimated warranty obligations............	24,000	
Total current liabilities................		$ 350,000
Long-term Liabilities:		
Bank notes payable (maturity 1976).........	100,000	
Bonds payable (7%, maturity 1984).........	500,000	
Total long-term liabilities..............		600,000
Total Liabilities.....................		$ 950,000

Stockholders' Equity

Contributed Capital:		
Preferred stock, 5%, cumulative,		
5,000 shares outstanding, par $100........	500,000	
Common stock, 15,000 shares outstanding,		
no-par...............................	750,000	
Contributed capital in excess of par, preferred		
stock................................	50,000	
Total contributed capital.............	1,300,000	
Retained Earnings (see Statement of Retained		
Earnings below).........................	275,000	
Total stockholders' equity.............		1,575,000
Total Liabilities and Stockholders'		
Equity...........................		$2,525,000

Exhibit 3–2 (continued)

DIAMOND'S, INCORPORATED
Statement of Retained Earnings
For the Year Ended December 31, 1974

Beginning balance, retained earnings, January 1, 1974	$220,000
Add net income for 1974	200,000
Total	420,000
Less dividends paid during 1974	145,000
Ending balance, retained earnings, December 31, 1974	$275,000

assets reports the investments the company intends to hold for the long run (more than one year). Long-term or permanent investments include such items as the stocks and bonds of other companies that have been purchased as investments. This classification also includes cash set aside in special funds (such as a savings account) for use in the future for a specified purpose. The sinking fund to pay bonds reported in Exhibit 3–2 represents cash set aside for a special purpose. Eventually this fund will be expended to retire the bonds payable reported under Long-term Liabilities.[5] While the fund is in existence, it will earn interest that will be reflected on the income statement as revenue from investments and funds (see Exhibit 3–1).

Fixed Assets. This subcategory frequently is called "Operating Assets" or "Property, Plant, and Equipment." It includes those assets having physical substance (i.e., they are tangible) that were acquired for use in operating the business rather than for resale as regular goods

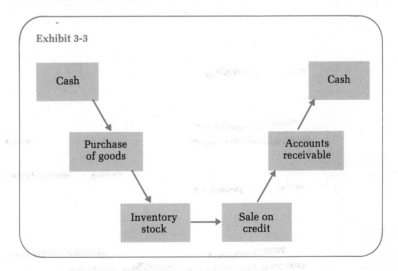

Exhibit 3-3

[5] The term "sinking fund," although widely used in accounting, is not descriptive. It simply refers to a cash fund set aside to pay a long-term debt at the maturity or due date.

or as an investment. Typically, they include buildings owned; land on which the buildings reside; and equipment, tools, and furniture and fixtures used in operating the business. They are long-lived and are used in the production and/or sale of other assets or services. Fixed assets, with the exception of land, are depreciated over time as they are used. Since their productive usefulness decreases as they are used, their initial cost is apportioned to expense over their estimated useful life. This apportionment of cost over their useful life is known as deprecia-tion. Land is not depreciated because it does not wear out as do ma-chinery, buildings, etc. The amount of depreciation computed for each period is reported on the income statement as an expense, and the cumulative amount of depreciation expense for all past periods since acquisition is deducted on the balance sheet from the cost of the asset. To illustrate, for Diamond's, the depreciation for office equipment was determined and reported as follows:

(1) Income Statement (Exhibit 3–1)—Depreciation expense for 1974, $1,000. This was computed as follows:

$$\frac{\text{Cost of the equipment}}{\text{Estimated useful life}} = \frac{\$16,000}{16 \text{ years}} = \$1,000 \text{ depreciation expense (each year)}$$

(2) Balance Sheet (Exhibit 3–2)—The amounts shown for office equipment represent the following:

Office equipment, cost when acquired on January 1, 1971	$16,000
Accumulated depreciation expense from January 1, 1971, to December 31, 1974 ($1,000 × 4 years)	4,000
Difference—amount of equipment cost not yet allocated to depreciation expense	$12,000

The difference, $12,000, generally is referred to as the book value, or carrying value, of the store equipment. At the end of the 16th year, the book value of the office equipment will be zero. Depreciation is discussed in detail in Chapter 9.

Intangible assets. This classification includes those assets having no physical existence (i.e., they are intangible) and having a long life. Their value is derived from the rights and privileges that are incident upon ownership. Examples are patents, trademarks, copyrights, fran-chises, and goodwill. Intangible assets generally are not acquired for resale, but, rather they are used by the business as a part of operations. Thus, in this respect, they are akin to fixed assets. Intangible assets are discussed in detail in Chapter 9.

Deferred charges. This is a classification for long-term prepay-ments for goods and services that are expected to contribute to the generation of revenue in the future. They are the same as prepaid expenses (defined above), except that the prepayment is for more than

one year. For example, the prepayment of a five-year insurance premium would be classified as a deferred charge rather than as a current
asset.

Other assets. Some businesses own assets that do not reasonably
fit into one of the preceding classifications. Thus, a miscellaneous category called other assets may be needed. For example, fixed assets re-
tired from service and being held for disposal would be reported under
this category.

Current liabilities. The first category of liabilities reports the
short-term debts. It encompasses those debts that will be paid out of
the current assets. Thus, current liabilities are expected to be paid
within the coming year or within the normal operating cycle of the
business, whichever is longer. The normal operating cycle was defined
on page 55. Examples of current liabilities are short-term notes payable,
amounts payable to creditors (called accounts payable), wages payable,
income taxes payable, payroll taxes payable, interest payable, and unearned revenue (discussed in a later chapter).

At this point we can conveniently define a widely used concept—
that of working capital—which is *the difference between total current
assets and total current liabilities.* Thus, Diamond's working capital at
December 31, 1974, was: $2,135,000 − $350,000 = $1,785,000. The
significance of this amount will be discussed in later chapters.

Long-term liabilities. The long-term debts; that is, those not classified as current liabilities.

Owners' equity. Owners' equity represents the residual claim of the
owners. This claim is the sum of the shareholders' investments plus the
accumulated earnings of the company less the dividends paid. Exhibit
3–2 reports these two categories of stockholders' equity. These two
categories are intended to report the sources of owners' equity. Each
class of capital stock is reported separately. Diamond's balance sheet
shows two classes of capital stock:[6] (1) Preferred stock, 5,000 shares
outstanding; (2) Common stock, 15,000 shares outstanding.

The amount labeled "Contributed capital in excess of par, preferred
stock" means that the preferred stock initially was sold at an average of
$10 per share above the par value of $100 per share since the "excess"
was $10 × 5,000 shares = $50,000. The par value is reported as one

---

[6] Preferred stock is so designated because it has certain specified preferences
over the common stock. In this particular case the preferred stock is reported
as having two preferences; (1) a dividend preference of 5%—this means that
dividends on the preferred stock must be paid each year equivalent to 5% of the
par value per share of the preferred before any dividends can be paid on the
common stock; (2) a cumulative preference—this means that, should dividends
equivalent to 5% not be paid on the preferred stock for any year, the amount
not paid will cumulate and must be paid in subsequent years before any
dividends can be paid on the common stock. Capital stock is discussed in detail
in Chapter 12.

amount and the excess is reported separately. The sum of the two amounts represents the amount contributed by the stockholders when the stock was sold initially. The amount of owners' equity does not represent what the residual claim is worth; it is the "book value" of the claim.

STATEMENT OF RETAINED EARNINGS

Below the balance sheet for Diamond's (Exhibit 3–2), a supplementary statement is presented with the title "Statement of Retained Earnings." This statement, although optional, generally is presented; it explains the increases and decreases in retained earnings during the period. The statement starts with the balance in retained earnings at the beginning of the period. To that balance, net income for the year is added and dividends paid during the year are deducted. The result is the balance of retained earnings at the end of the period. Retained earnings is one of the primary sources of stockholders' equity in most corporations. The statement of retained earnings is the connecting link between the income statement and the balance sheet. In accounting for a sole proprietorship or partnership, this statement is not used.

STATEMENT OF CHANGES IN FINANCIAL POSITION

The purpose of this statement was discussed in Chapter 2. Basically, it reports the inflows and outflows of resources during the period. Exhibit 3–4 presents a statement of changes in financial position for Diamond's. Since much of the terminology on financial statements is optional to the preparer, you will observe some differences between the illustrations in Chapter 2 and in this chapter. Subclassification of the sources of cash (cash generated) as between Operations, Extraordinary items, and Other sources was prescribed in APB *Opinion No. 20* in order to enhance the usefulness of the statement.

Observe that Diamond's statement is typical in that most of the cash generated during the year came from operations. Of the $271,700 cash generated, most of it, $228,700 or 84%, came from this one source.[7]

For instructional purposes, the statements of changes in financial position illustrated in Chapter 2 and in this chapter were based on cash flow. Many accountants prefer to base it on working capital. Either approach is permitted by APB *Opinion No. 19*. The choice between one that emphasizes working capital flows and one that emphasizes cash depends on the circumstances in the particular company. The statement of changes in financial position is discussed further in Chapter 15.

---

[7] To avoid misunderstanding—the land was sold for $56,000 cash, as shown in Exhibit 3–4; it cost $5,000; the resulting pretax extraordinary gain of $51,000 was reported on the income statement, Exhibit 3–1.

Exhibit 3–4

DIAMOND'S, INCORPORATED
Statement of Changes in Financial Position—Cash Basis
For the Year Ended December 31, 1974

Sources of Cash:

From operations:

Sales revenue..............................		$3,615,000
Income from investments..................		13,000
		3,628,000
Adjustments for noncash revenue (deduction).		5,000*ᵃ
Cash inflow from sales and investments.....		3,623,000
Expenses and cost of goods sold............	$3,466,000*ᵇ	
Adjustments for noncash expenses deduction.........................	(71,700)*ᶜ	
Cash outflow for expenses.............		3,394,300
Net cash inflow from operations and investments......................		228,700
From extraordinary items (net of income taxes): Disposal of land ($56,000–$13,000)..........		43,000
Total cash generated.............		271,700

Uses of Cash:

To pay dividends:

On preferred stock.......................	25,000	
On common stock.......................	120,000	
To purchase land for future store site.........	18,000	
Total cash applied...............		163,000
Increase in cash during the year...............		**$108,700**

* At this point in your study, there is no need to be concerned with the derivation of these amounts; however, they may be reconciled with Exhibit 3–1 as follows:
a. The adjustment of $5,000 to revenue was due to an increase in accounts receivable of that amount during the period.
b. $2,416,000 + $856,000 + $56,000 + $138,000 = $3,466,000.
c. $15,000 + $2,000 + $3,600 + $1,000 + $50,100 (the net change in accruals, deferrals, and accounts payable) = $71,700.

A more
complicated
set of
financial
statements

Up to this point you have studied two simplified sets of financial statements, stripped of much of the surrounding features. To complete this overview of financial statements for a business, we present a set of **published** financial statements for a well-known company, J. C. Penney Company, Inc. Corporations such as this one are said to "publish" their annual report because it is printed and distributed to each shareholder and to others upon request. Companies selling their stock on the exchanges (and some others) distribute such annual reports. The published annual report typically includes a number of features in addition to the financial statements, such as the president's letter to the shareholders, a list of the principal officers of the company, information on the company's products (including pictures), and other materials deemed to be of interest.

The following components from the 1972 annual report of J. C. Penney Company, Inc., are included in Exhibit 3–5 for your study:[8]

---

[8] The statements are labeled "J. C. Penney Company, Inc., and Consolidated Subsidiaries." The latter two words indicate that J. C. Penney, as the parent

1. Statement of income.
2. Statement of reinvested earnings (i.e., retained earnings).
3. Balance sheet.
4. Statement of changes in financial position (working-capital basis).
5. Accountant's report.
6. Summary of accounting policies.
7. Selected notes to the financial statements.

As recommended by the APB, comparative amounts are presented. That is, amounts for each item are reported for the current year and the preceding year.

There are a number of items reported on these statements you will not understand at this point in your study. A good number of them will be discussed in subsequent chapters.

Income statement. The statement of income is dated "52 weeks ended January 27, 1973." This means that the company uses a fiscal year rather than the calendar year. The fiscal year for a business also is referred to as the natural business year since it ends when the business normally is at its lowest level of activity. For a retail business such as Penney's, this naturally comes as soon as the January clearance sales end. Accountants strongly recommend that a business use its natural fiscal year rather than the calendar year. The period selected by the business for its usual operating purposes also is used for accounting. It often is referred to as the accounting period as well as the fiscal year.

Accountant's report or opinion. The independent CPA, as the outside auditor, is required to express an opinion on the financial statements or to state that an opinion cannot be expressed. The accountant's report on the statements of J. C. Penney Company, Inc., in the first paragraph, states the scope of the examination performed. In the second paragraph, the independent CPA has stated that, in his opinion, the statements "fairly present" the results of operations (i.e., the income statement), the financial position (i.e., the balance sheet), and the changes in financial position (i.e., the statement of changes in financial position). The key words are "fairly present." If the statements do not meet this standard, the independent CPA must explain why an opinion cannot be expressed. Since the accountant's opinion relates to the "fairness" of the financial statement in its entirety, it is generally viewed as a particularly important feature.

Summary of accounting policies. Because of its importance this section is required by APB *Opinion No. 22.* Its purpose is to explain the

---

company, owns over 50% of the outstanding stock of some other corporations. This ownership gives the parent company a controlling interest, and the other companies are designated as subsidiaries. To prepare the statements on a *consolidated basis,* the financial statement of the subsidiaries are added on a line-by-line basis to those of the parent company. This subject is discussed further in Chapter 14.

Exhibit 3–5

Statement of Income
Statement of Reinvested Earnings

J. C. Penney Company, Inc.
and Consolidated Subsidiaries

Statement of Income	52 weeks ended January 27, 1973	52 weeks ended January 29, 1972
Sales	$5,529,621,697	$4,812,238,548
Costs and expenses		
Cost of goods sold, occupancy, buying, and warehousing costs	3,947,282,521	3,432,060,221
Selling, general, and administrative expenses	1,211,380,650	1,061,140,073
Interest, after deduction of income of J. C. Penney Financial Corporation		
before income taxes	59,763,739	53,467,845
Total costs and expenses	5,218,426,910	4,546,668,139
Income before income taxes and other unconsolidated subsidiaries	311,194,787	265,570,409
Income taxes	155,320,000	134,300,000
Net income before other unconsolidated subsidiaries	155,874,787	131,270,409
Net income of other unconsolidated subsidiaries	6,758,007	4,445,349
Net income	$ 162,632,794	$ 135,715,758
Per share of common stock		
Primary	$2.86	$2.46
Fully diluted	2.86	2.43

Statement of Reinvested Earnings		
Reinvested earnings—beginning of year	$ 761,100,305	$ 680,698,275
Net income for the year	162,632,794	135,715,758
Dividends	(59,456,022)	(55,313,728)
Reinvested earnings—end of year	$ 864,277,077	$ 761,100,305

See 1972 Review of Operations and Financial Information on pages 19 to 26, and 31.

Exhibit 3–5 (continued)

Balance Sheet

J. C. Penney Company, Inc.
and Consolidated Subsidiaries

Assets	January 27, 1973	January 29, 1972
Current assets		
Cash	$ 45,016,423	$ 55,302,033
Receivables, net	146,956,183	110,201,186
Merchandise inventories	1,047,064,287	879,381,432
Properties to be sold under sale and leaseback agreements	39,318,060	30,903,716
Prepaid expenses	38,925,098	35,100,024
Total current assets	1,317,280,051	1,110,888,391
Investment in unconsolidated subsidiaries	221,298,447	184,951,730
Properties, net	603,983,174	614,295,248
Other assets	11,118,073	13,734,759
	$2,153,679,745	$1,923,870,128

Liabilities and Stockholders' Equity		
Current liabilities		
Accounts payable and accrued liabilities	$ 547,144,900	$ 490,367,101
Dividend payable	15,343,706	14,602,202
Due to unconsolidated subsidiaries	—	980,000
Income taxes	22,107,225	50,244,679
Deferred credits, principally tax effects applicable to installment sales	175,000,000	138,200,000
Total current liabilities	759,595,831	694,393,982
Long term debt	216,856,393	210,146,889
Deferred credits, principally tax effects applicable to depreciation	39,200,000	29,700,000
Stockholders' equity		
Preferred stock without par value: Authorized, 5,000,000 shares—issued, none		
Common stock, par value 50¢: Authorized, 75,000,000 shares—		
issued, 57,091,093	273,750,444	228,528,952
Reinvested earnings	864,277,077	761,100,305
Total stockholders' equity	1,138,027,521	989,629,257
	$2,153,679,745	$1,923,870,128

Exhibit 3–5 (continued)

Statement of Changes in Financial Position

J. C. Penney Company, Inc.
and Consolidated Subsidiaries

(In millions)	52 weeks ended January 27, 1973	52 weeks ended January 29, 1972
Funds were generated from:		
Operations		
Net income	$162.6	$135.7
Undistributed net income of unconsolidated subsidiaries	(18.1)	(14.8)
Depreciation	52.5	45.5
Deferred credits, principally tax effects applicable to depreciation	9.5	7.3
Stock issued to retirement plans	16.2	14.1
Stock issued under stock bonus plan	9.5	5.1
Total	232.2	192.9
External sources		
Properties sold and leased back	125.6	96.0
Other disposals of properties including future sale and leaseback agreements	17.6	40.7
Increase in long term debt, excluding convertible debentures retired	21.9	18.7
Stock options exercised	4.4	4.4
Stock issued principally upon conversion of debentures	15.2	132.3
Total	184.7	292.1
Total funds generated	416.9	485.0
Funds were used for:		
Dividends	59.5	55.3
Capital expenditures (fixed assets)	185.5	237.2
Retirement of convertible debentures	15.1	135.3
Investment in subsidiaries	18.2	.7
Change in other assets	(2.6)	1.0
Total funds used	275.7	429.5
Increase in working capital	141.2	55.5
Increase in other deferred credits, principally tax effects applicable to installment sales	36.8	7.2
Increase in working funds	$178.0	$ 62.7

(The Changes in Working Capital Accounts section
is shown in the Notes to the Financial Statements.)

Accountants' Report

To the Stockholders and Board of Directors of J. C. Penney Company, Inc.

We have examined the balance sheet of J. C. Penney Company, Inc. and consolidated subsidiaries as of January 27, 1973 and January 29, 1972, and the related statements of income, reinvested earnings and changes in financial position for the 52 week periods then ended. Our examination was made in accordance with generally accepted auditing standards, and accordingly included such tests of the accounting records and such other auditing procedures as we considered necessary in the circumstances.

In our opinion, the accompanying financial statements present fairly the financial position of J. C. Penney Company, Inc. and consolidated subsidiaries at January 27, 1973 and January 29, 1972, and the results of their operations and changes in financial position for the 52 week periods then ended, in conformity with generally accepted accounting principles applied on a consistent basis. Also, in our opinion, the accompanying statistical data on pages 33 to 35 present fairly the information shown therein.

345 Park Avenue
New York, N.Y.
March 20, 1973

Peat, Marwick, Mitchell & Co.

Exhibit 3–5 (continued)

Summary of Accounting Policies

The accounting policies employed by the Penney Company are consistent with generally accepted accounting principles. In those instances in which more than one generally accepted accounting principle can be applied, the Company has adopted the accounting principle that it believes most accurately and fairly reflects the situation, as described in the following paragraphs.

Definition of Fiscal Year. The Company's fiscal year ends on the last Saturday in January. Fiscal year 1972 ended January 27, 1973; fiscal year 1971 ended January 29, 1972. Each year comprised 52 weeks.

The accounts of several subsidiaries, including the insurance companies, are on the calendar year basis.

Basis of Consolidation. The financial statements present on a consolidated basis the results of all domestic and European merchandising operations. Not consolidated are J. C. Penney Financial Corporation, three insurance companies, JCP Realty, Inc., and several small nonretail subsidiaries.

The income before income taxes of J. C. Penney Financial Corporation is included in the statement of income as a reduction of interest expense. The combined income of all other unconsolidated subsidiaries is included as a single item in the statement of income.

The financial statements of insurance subsidiaries are presented in accordance with generally accepted accounting principles. The accounts of insurance subsidiaries are maintained in accordance with accounting practices prescribed or permitted by insurance regulatory authorities, which differ in certain respects from generally accepted accounting principles. Realized investment gains and losses are included in net income.

Sales. Sales include merchandise, services, and licensed departments, net of returns, and exclude value added and sales taxes. Layaway sales are recorded upon receipt of the initial deposit.

Sales are attributed to the operating division that makes the sale to the customer.

Accounts Receivable. Service charge income arising from customer accounts receivable is treated as a reduction of selling, general, and administrative expenses in the statement of income.

The allowance for doubtful accounts represents 2 per cent of customer accounts receivable at year end.

Inventories. Merchandise inventories in stores are stated at the lower of cost or market, determined by the retail method. Other inventories in warehouses or with manufacturers are stated at the lower of cost (first-in, first-out) or replacement market.

Properties. The cost of properties includes interest and certain other carrying costs on construction in progress and land held for future use. Maintenance and repairs are charged to current operations as incurred, and improvements are capitalized.

Depreciation. The cost of buildings and equipment is depreciated on a straight line basis over the estimated useful lives of the assets. The principal annual rates used in computing depreciation are 3 per cent for store buildings, 2½ per cent to 4 per cent for warehouse buildings, and 10 per cent for furniture and fixtures. Improvements to leased premises are amortized on a straight line basis over the life of the lease or the useful life of the improvement, whichever is shorter.

Income Taxes. The Company uses the "flow through" method whereby income taxes are reduced currently for the amounts of investment credits.

Foreign Exchange Transactions. All foreign currency accounts are translated into U.S. dollars at exchange rates in effect at each year end for current assets and liabilities, at historical exchange rates for depreciation and noncurrent assets and liabilities, and at average exchange rates during the year for income and expense. Gains and losses are charged or credited to operations as incurred.

Deferred Charges. Expenses associated with the opening of new stores are written off in the year of store opening, except for those of stores opened in January, which are written off in the following fiscal year. Catalog printing costs are written off over the estimated productive lives of the catalogs, not exceeding six months. Research and other development costs are charged to operations as incurred.

Pension Cost. The cost of pension benefits has been determined by the entry age normal method. The plan in effect in 1971 used the attained age normal method. Past service liabilities are amortized over 30 years.

Exhibit 3–5 (concluded)

Notes to the Financial Statements

J. C. Penney Company, Inc.
and Consolidated Subsidiaries

Sales in 1972 were $5.5 billion, an increase of 14.9 per cent over the $4.8 billion in 1971. Operating divisions contributed to sales as follows:

(In millions)	1972	1971	Per cent increase All units	Per cent increase Comparative units
Penney stores				
Full line	$2,566.8	$1,993.9	28.7	13.1
Soft line	2,084.9	2,079.0	.3	3.1
Total	4,651.7	4,072.9	14.2	7.9
The Treasury stores	284.5	242.3	17.4	1.7
Thrift Drug stores	132.5	112.2	18.0	10.8
Supermarkets	100.2	96.6	3.8	2.1
Mail order	89.0	76.9	15.9	—
European operations	271.7	211.3	28.6	4.4
Total sales	$5,529.6	$4,812.2	14.9	7.7

Catalog merchandise sold through Penney stores is included in the sales of Penney stores. Thrift Drug and food supermarket sales through Penney and Treasury stores are included in the sales of the latter divisions. Food sales by European operations are included in that division's sales. Licensed department sales represent less than 1 per cent of total Company sales, and are included in the sales of Penney and Treasury stores. Comparative units are those in operation throughout both 1972 and 1971. For further analyses of sales, see the discussion below of each division's operations and the Operations Summary on page 35.

In the eight years ended January 27, 1973, sales have grown at a compound annual rate of 12.5 per cent.

Properties at year end were as follows:

(In millions)	January 27 1973	January 29 1972
Land	$ 35.8	$ 34.0
Buildings	163.9	152.2
Fixtures and equipment	548.1	497.4
Leasehold improvements	87.5	64.3
Construction in progress and land held for future use	60.4	134.5
	895.7	882.4
Less accumulated depreciation and amortization	291.7	268.1
Properties, net	$604.0	$614.3

Net income was $162.6 million in 1972, an increase of 19.8 per cent from the $135.7 million earned in 1971.

Income before income taxes and other unconsolidated subsidiaries was $311.2 million in 1972, which is 17.2 per cent higher than the $265.6 million in 1971.

Net income per share increased in 1972 as shown in the following table, which also lists the unaudited amounts for each quarter:

	1972	1971	Increase
Primary			
First quarter	$ .35	$ .31	$ .04
Second quarter	.51	.46	.05
Third quarter	.78	.68	.10
Fourth quarter	1.22	1.01	.21
Year	$2.86	$2.46	$ .40
Fully diluted—year	$2.86	$2.43	$ .43

In the eight years ended January 27, 1973, primary net income per share has increased at a compound annual rate of 9.8 per cent.

Fully diluted net income per share in 1971 assumed conversion of the Company's 4¼ per cent convertible debentures during the period outstanding prior to their redemption date of August 12, 1971.

Working funds increased $178.0 million during 1972, compared with an increase of $62.7 million in 1971. Working funds consist of current assets less current liabilities, excluding deferred credits, principally tax effects applicable to installment sales. Following is an analysis of changes in working capital and working funds:

(In millions)	1972	1971
Cash	$ (10.3)	$(10.4)
Receivables, net	36.8	26.8
Merchandise inventories	167.7	89.9
Properties to be sold under sale and leaseback agreements	8.4	30.9
Prepaid expenses	3.8	2.9
Accounts payable and accrued liabilities	(56.8)	(93.6)
Dividend payable	(.7)	(1.3)
Due to unconsolidated subsidiaries	1.0	31.3
Income taxes and deferred credits	(8.7)	(21.0)
Increase in working capital	141.2	55.5
Deferred credits, principally tax effects applicable to installment sales	36.8	7.2
Increase in working funds	$178.0	$ 62.7

accounting policies being followed by the company. This information significantly aids the user in interpreting the amounts reported. Observe that this company explained its accounting policies in respect to 11 different items.

Full disclosure. One of the broad fundamentals underlying accounting, listed in Exhibit 2–1, is the principle of full disclosure. This relates directly to the financial statements. It specifies that there should be complete and understandable reporting on the financial statements of all **significant information** relating to the economic affairs of the entity. To meet the requirements of this principle, the quantitative expressions in the financial statements frequently require narrative and detailed elaboration. As a consequence, practically all published financial statements will include a section called "Notes to the Financial Statements." The notes are considered to be an integral part of the financial statements and are important to understanding and interpretation of the amounts reported. To illustrate typical notes, four were selected from the J. C. Penney statements (see page 67).

Interpretative or proportional relationships

When using financial statements the decision maker often may gain further interpretative insight into the amounts if one or more **proportional relationships** are computed. A proportional relationship is based on *two* selected amounts from the financial statements that are related in a meaningful way. One, known as the **base amount,** is divided into the other to express the proportional relationship between the two. The result may be expressed as a ratio, a percent, or, sometimes, as a dollar amount. To illustrate, assume we are interpreting the income statement of hypothetical Company X. On the statement we observe two amounts of particular significance to our problem at hand. They are: (1) net sales, $300,000 and (2) net income, $45,000. Clearly, these two amounts are related. To analyze one aspect of their relationship, we can apply the concept of proportional analysis. We will use net sales as the base amount. Therefore, the computation would be:

$$\frac{\text{Net income}}{\text{Net sales}} = \frac{\$45,000}{\$300,000} = .15$$

The computed result can be expressed in any of the following ways: (*a*) as a ratio—net income was .15 of net sales; (*b*) as a percent—net income was 15% of net sales; or (*c*) as a dollar amount—for each $1.00 of net sales there was $.15 net income. The relationship just computed is known as the **profit margin** since it is the relationship between **sales** and **profit** for the period.[9]

-----

[9] In computing the profit margin when there are extraordinary items, income before extraordinary items rather than net income generally should be used to avoid the distortion caused by the unusual and infrequently recurring items.

The concept of **earnings per share (EPS),** already illustrated, is another widely used relationship. EPS reflects the relationship between income and the number of shares of common stock outstanding.

The concept of **return on investment (ROI)** is still another relationship especially useful to decision makers. It is particularly significant since it expresses the relationship between profit and investment. The income statement provides the income amount and the balance sheet provides the figure for the investment.

The concept of return on investment is frequently applied by almost everyone in one way or another. To illustrate, suppose you invested $1,000 on January 1, 1974, and at the end of the year you got back $1,200. Disregarding income taxes, you may say that you earned $200 during the year on your investment. Based on these amounts what would be your ROI (i.e., your return on investment)? You may assert that your return for the year was $200 ÷ $1,000 = 20% on the investment. Similarly, the return on investment for a business for a specific period of time may be computed as follows:

$$\frac{\text{Net income}}{\text{Investment (owners' equity)}} = \text{Return on investment}$$

The return on investment earned by Diamond's for 1974 would be computed as follows:[10]

$$\frac{\$162,000 \text{ (from Exhibit 3–1)}}{\$1,575,000 \text{ (from Exhibit 3–2)}} = 10.29\%$$

These three examples are sufficient at this point to introduce the concept of proportional analysis as applied to the interpretation of financial statements. In the chapters to follow, several more particularly useful relationships will be introduced and illustrated. Finally, in Chapter 16 the concept will be revisited and discussed in more detail.

Although a proportional relationship may be expressed as a ratio, a percent, or a dollar amount, the concept often is loosely referred to as **ratio analysis.**

Financial statements related to the decision process

Throughout the preceding pages, we have emphasized the point of view of the decision maker; that is, the user of the financial reports. In making decisions of various kinds, he must assess future prospects and probable future outcomes. Decision making deals with the future rather than with the past; therefore, the decision maker must make projections. Recent past events and trends generally provide the background for most projections if they are to be realistic. The financial statements

---

[10] Depending upon the nature of the problem and the preference of the decision maker, the income amount may be either (a) income before extraordinary items or (b) net income. Similarly, investment may be either (a) owners' equity or (b) total equities (i.e., liabilities plus owners' equity).

provide valuable information concerning past transactions and their economic effects on the business. In making many decisions relating to a business entity, the decision maker must carefully interpret and evaluate the various financial factors. In addition, he must bring to bear his knowledge of such factors as technological constraints, environmental influences, and competitive forces in making certain decisions relating to the business. The following case is presented to demonstrate how accounting information may be important in decision making.

John Smith, Individual. It was five years after John Smith received his B.A. in history at State University. During that time, John worked for a local business, first in sales and now as the general office manager. Since John did not take any business courses at State, his increasing responsibilities made it desirable that he enroll in several business courses in night school for the last three years. During the five years since his graduation, John saved approximately 10% of his salary, which he deposited in a savings account. The potential impact of inflation on this type of investment concerned him. A co-worker gave him a tip: "Purchase some of the stock of the X Corporation, which recently went public. The price is down now and I was told confidentially that it would double in the next two to three years based on their expected EPS trend." Since the X Corporation was in a distant state, John was unable to get much information about the management of the company. As to products, he was told that "the company is in the automotive parts manufacturing business." John was about ready to invest his savings of $4,000 in the stock when a friend suggested that he should "analyze the financial statements of the company for several years running before taking the big jump." Accordingly, John wrote to the company and received the annual financial reports for the past three years. In discussing these statements with a friend, who was an accountant, they discovered several disconcerting facts. Among them were the following:

1. The cash position, if one eliminated borrowings, had steadily deteriorated.
2. The money tied up in inventory had increased at a greater rate than sales, suggesting the possibility of inadequate controls on the part of management.
3. The plant and equipment was largely depreciated, indicating it to be old and probably inefficient. Large outlays might be required in the near future for replacement.
4. The working-capital ratio was very low, compared with the industry average (as reported by Dun & Bradstreet, a New York-based firm that publishes such averages).
5. There appeared to be excessive debt in relation to owners' equity.
6. The EPS amounts were as follows:

	Last Year	1st Year Prior	2d Year Prior
On income before extraordinary items.............	$1.60	$1.80	$1.80
On net income...............................	4.50	3.00	2.00

Examination of the income statement indicated that the dramatic increase in EPS on net income was due to sales of several pieces of land the company had owned for many years. The land had been acquired at a very low price and, when sold, brought premium prices. John realized that these unusual gains would not be repeated.

7. The footnotes revealed that the company had been sued for a large sum of money for negligence related to a serious accident in the plant. The case was still pending.

On the basis of the above and some other information inputs to his decision process, John decided against making the investment. Subsequently, John learned that the business had encountered severe financial difficulties.

Summary

In this chapter, you encountered the commonly used subclassifications of financial information on the income statement, balance sheet, and statement of changes in financial position. You learned some of the interpretative and evaluative approaches that should be utilized by the decision maker when relying on financial reports. You also learned to expect variations in the terminology and format of financial reports.

Financial reports of an existing company were presented to reinforce your conceptions and for reference as you study the accounting process in the chapters to follow. The knowledge of financial statements, gained in Chapter 2 and in this chapter, should assure that, in studying the details and complexities of accounting, you will maintain a broad view of accounting and keep in mind the nature of the end product—the financial statements. We re-emphasize this point because, not infrequently, students soon become immersed in details and lose the broad perspective that is desirable.

We looked at a case where financial information exerted a significant impact on the decision maker. We will continue to focus on decision making because the overriding objective of accounting, as we have said, is to contribute to sound and realistic decisions.

In this chapter, we defined another of the broad fundamentals underlying accounting as listed in Exhibit 2–1, viz:

Full-disclosure principle—There must be complete and understandable reporting on the financial statements of all significant economic information relating to the entity that may influence decisions. Notes to the financial statements generally are necessary to meet the full-disclosure principle, especially in respect to unusual transactions and circumstances.

In the next chapter your attention will be turned to the accounting process that collects and reports the financial data of an entity.

Important
terms

Cost of goods sold
Gross margin on sales
Operating expenses
Financial expenses
Extraordinary items
Income tax expense
Current assets
Normal operating cycle
Prepaid expenses
Funds and long-term investments
Fixed assets
Book value

Intangible assets
Deferred charges
Other assets
Current liabilities
Long-term liabilities
Statement of retained earnings
Fiscal year
Accountant's opinion
Full disclosure
Return on investment (ROI)
Profit margin

Questions
for
discussion

1. What is the primary purpose of subclassification of the information presented on financial statements?

2. What is gross margin? Why is it that the income statement for a service business does not include this specific item?

3. What are the two primary subclassifications of operating expenses reported on the income statement of a retail store?

4. Explain the subclassification "Financial expenses and revenues" on the income statement.

5. What are extraordinary items? Why should they be reported separately on the income statement?

6. Explain EPS. What EPS amounts should be reported on the income statement?

7. Briefly explain how income tax expense is reported on the income statement when there are extraordinary items.

8. Briefly define (a) current assets, (b) current liabilities, and (c) working capital.

9. What is a prepaid expense?

10. On a balance sheet, investments may be reported under either (a) current assets or (b) funds and long-term investments. Explain.

11. In respect to fixed assets, as reported on the balance sheet, briefly explain (a) cost, (b) accumulated depreciation, and (c) book value.

12. Briefly explain the two major subclassifications of owners' equity for a corporation.

13. What is meant by a comparative statement? Why is it desirable?

14. Briefly, what does the independent auditor's report encompass?

15. What is proportional analysis? Why is it often useful in interpreting financial statements?

16. Explain the full-disclosure principle.

Exercises   E3–1.   The Lewis Tire Company, a local tire store, is developing the annual financial statements for 1974. The following amounts have been determined to be correct: sales, $240,000; selling expenses, $33,000; interest expense, $1,000; administrative expenses, $19,000; extraordinary item—loss due to hurricane damage—$4,400; sales returns and allowances, $4,000; cost of goods sold, $136,000; and income tax on operations expense, $14,100; $1,100 taxes were saved because of the extraordinary item.

You have been requested to prepare a classified income statement for 1974. Assume 10,000 shares of common stock outstanding during the year.

(Hint: EPS is $2.96 per share.)

E3–2.   Brownlee Jewelers is developing the annual financial statements for 1974. The following amounts have been determined to be correct at December 31, 1974: cash, $18,500; accounts receivable, $6,000; merchandise inventory, $160,000; investment in stock of the Z Corporation (long-term), $10,000; store equipment, $32,000; used store equipment held for disposal, $13,500; allowance for doubtful accounts, $400; accumulated depreciation on store equipment, $9,600; accounts payable, $26,400; long-term notes payable, $40,000; income taxes payable, $5,100; retained earnings, $53,500; and common stock, 10,000 shares outstanding, par $10.00 per share (originally sold at $10.50 per share).

You have been requested to prepare a classified balance sheet at December 31, 1974.

(Hint: The balance sheet total is $230,000.)

E3–3.   Royal Bakery is developing the annual financial statements for 1974. The following cash-flow data have been determined to be correct for the year: sales revenue (including $12,000 not collected), $260,000; expenses, $239,000 (including $21,000 of noncash items); cash received for extraordinary item, $900; cash borrowed on a five-year note payable, $10,000; cash disbursement for dividends, $12,000; and cash expenditure to purchase two new delivery trucks, $9,900. You have been requested to prepare a statement of changes in financial position on the cash basis for 1974.

(Hint: Cash increased $19,000.)

E3–4.   The Samson Department Store averages a 20% markup on net sales. During 1974, gross sales amounted to $228,000 and return sales were $6,000. You are requested to prepare the annual income statement from sales through gross margin on net sales. Show your computations.

E3–5.   The Weber Corporation has just completed the 1974 income statement (there were no extraordinary items), except for the EPS computations. Net income has been determined to be $125,000. Common stock outstanding during the year was 40,000 shares and preferred stock (5%, $10 par value) outstanding was 10,000 shares. You are requested to compute the EPS amount for the income statement.

(Hint: First subtract the preferred dividends of $100,000 × 5% = $5,000.)

E3–6.   The Maxey Corporation (common stock, 2,000 shares outstanding) is preparing the income statement for 1974. The pretax operating income has been determined to be $50,000 and there was a $22,000 pretax loss on storm damages to one of the plants (i.e., an extraordinary item). Total income tax expense has been correctly determined to be $11,200 on the basis of a 40% tax rate on operations and on the storm loss. You have been requested to complete the income statement starting with pretax income.

(Hint: EPS on income before extraordinary items was $15.00.)

E3–7.   The following is a list of major classifications and subclassifications on the balance sheet. You are to indicate, by numbering them on a sheet of paper, the order in which they normally would be on a balance sheet.

_8_	Current liabilities	_4_	Fixed assets
_7_	Liabilities	_2_	Current assets
_10_	Owners' equity	_13_	Retained earnings
_9_	Long-term liabilities	_11_	Contributed capital
_3_	Funds and long-term investments	_1_	Assets
		_6_	Other assets
_5_	Intangible assets		

E3–8.   Berger, Incorporated, was organized in 1965 by ten investors. Each investor paid in $5,200 cash and received 500 shares of $10 par-value common stock. In 1970, to raise more capital, Berger, Incorporated, issued 3,000 shares of 5% preferred, nonparticipating, cumulative stock, par $20 per share, and received $68,000 in cash for it. On December 31, 1974, retained earnings amounted to $80,000. You have been requested to prepare the stockholders' equity section of the balance sheet at December 31, 1974.

E3–9.   The Barber Manufacturing Company is preparing the annual financial statements at December 31, 1974. The company has acquired two investments:

(a)   Common stock of M Corporation, purchased for $75,000, during 1970. M Corporation is a supplier of parts to Barber; therefore, the latter "intends to hold the stock indefinitely." The shares acquired represented 2% of the total shares outstanding.

(b)   Municipal bonds of the city of Macon, purchased at a cost of $10,000, during 1974. Barber made this investment to "temporarily use some idle cash that probably will be needed next year."

You have been requested to illustrate and explain the basis for the reporting of each investment on the 1974 balance sheet of Barber.

E3–10.   The Fisher Company is preparing the balance sheet at December 31, 1974. The following assets are to be entered thereon:

(1)   Building, purchased 15 years ago (counting 1974); original cost, $80,000; estimated useful life 20 years from date of purchase.

(2)   Land, purchased 12 years ago (counting 1974); original cost, $6,000.

You are requested to show how these items should be included on the balance sheet being prepared. Also indicate the amount of depreciation expense that should be reported on the 1974 income statement.

E3–11.   River City Retailers, on January 1, 1974, paid $3,600 cash for a two-year insurance premium. The premium was for an insurance policy covering all of the assets owned. Two-years' premium in advance was paid to take advantage of a 20% discount. It is now December 31, 1974, and you are asked to respond to the following questions (show your computations):

(a)   On the 1974 annual income statement, how much should be reported for *insurance premium expense?*

(b)   At the end of 1974, what was the amount of *prepaid insurance premium?*

(c)   How should the amount determined in (b) be reported on the balance sheet?

E3–12.   This exercise is designed to aid in your understanding of the contents of published financial statements and to observe differences in form and terminology. You are to refer to the financial statements of J. C. Penney Company, Inc., presented in this chapter and respond to the following (note: 1972 refers to the year ended January 29, 1972 and 1973 refers to the year ended January 27, 1973):

(a)   Income Statement:
  1.   What title is used?
  2.   Is it a comparative statement? Explain.
  3.   Are there any extraordinary items?
  4.   Compute the profit margins.
  5.   Did EPS increase?

(b)   Statement of Retained Earnings:
  6.   What title was used?
  7.   What was the amount carried from the income statement?
  8.   What was the amount of dividends each year?

(c)   Balance Sheet:
  9.   What was the amount of working capital at the end of each year?
  10.   Was accumulated depreciation reported on the balance sheet?
  11.   What was the amount carried from the statement of retained earnings?

(d) Statement of Changes in Financial Position

    12. Was this statement prepared on a working-capital basis or on a cash basis?

    13. What was the largest source of working capital?

    14. What was the largest use of working capital?

(e) Accountant's Report:

    15. Did the independent CPA believe that the statements "present fairly" the results of operations and financial position? Were there any exceptions on this point?

(f) Summary of Accounting Policies:

    16. How many accounting policies were explained?

    17. When are "layaway sales" recorded as revenue?

(g) Notes to the Financial Statements:

    18. How many different categories of sales are reported? Which one contributed the largest amount of sales in 1972?

    19. What amounts in the first note agree with a single line on the income statement?

    20. What was the amount of accumulated depreciation each year?

Problems **P3–1.** Bill's Auto Supply Store is developing the annual financial statements for 1974. The bookkeeper has been able to develop the information given below and you can assume it has been verified as correct. Assume there are 10,000 shares of common stock outstanding. You will note that, in some instances, only totals are provided in order to shorten the solution.

Financial Information, 1974

Income Statement			Balance Sheet	
Sales.............		$243,000	Cash.......................	$ 25,700
Selling expenses......		42,000	Accounts receivable..........	15,000
Interest expense......		1,000	Allowance for doubtful accounts	500
Administrative ex-			Accounts payable............	32,000
pense............		23,400	Retained earnings............	103,600
Return sales.........		3,000	Merchandise inventory........	155,000
Cost of goods sold....		134,000	Investment in stock of K Corp.	
Extraordinary loss on			(long-term)................	4,000
hurricane damage..		1,500	Income taxes payable..........	5,000
Income tax expense on			Accumulated depreciation......	16,600
operations (40%)...	$16,000		Store equipment.............	70,000
Tax savings on extraor-			Used equipment held for dis-	
dinary item (40%)	600	15,400	posal....................	16,000
Revenue from divi-			Common stock, par $10	
dends on stock in-			per share.................	100,000
vestment.........		400	Long-term notes payable.......	10,000
			Contributed capital in excess of	
			par......................	18,000

Required:

On the basis of the listed data, you have been asked to prepare a classified income statement and a balance sheet for the year ended

December 31, 1974. Also compute the return on investment, on shareholders' equity, at the bottom of the balance sheet.

(Hint: EPS on net income is $2.31.)

P3–2. Although Baker's Retail Store has been operating for only four years, the sales volume increase each year has been outstanding; apparently it was occasioned by the excellent location, a friendly atmosphere in the store, and a large stock for customer selection. Despite this appearance of success, the company has continually experienced a severe cash shortage, and a recent analysis by a consultant revealed significant inventory overstocking in numerous lines. Baker's Retail Store was organized as a corporation by Samuel Baker (now president) and four additional investors. Each owner invested $41,000 cash and received 400 shares of common stock (par value $100 per share). Although Sam Baker is recognized as an "excellent retailer," he exhibits very little interest in the financial reports. At a recent meeting of the Board of Directors, the "inadequacy of the financial reports" was raised. The board voted to engage an independent CPA "to examine the accounting system, submit audited financial statements, analyze the financial situation, and make appropriate recommendations to the Board." The independent CPA has just been handed the following reports prepared for the last board meeting by the "store bookkeeper" (to simplify this case, assume that all of the figures are correct; also, only representative amounts have been included):

BAKER'S RETAIL STORE
December 31, 1974
Profit Statement

Revenues:		
Sales for the year	$572,000	
Interest collected on charge accounts	1,000	
Dividends received on stock of Y Corporation	200	$573,200
Costs and expenses:		
Salaries—sales	66,500	
Salaries—administrative	36,000	
Depreciation—office equipment	1,200	
Depreciation—store equipment	6,000	
Store rent	18,000	
Office supplies used	800	
Store supplies used	1,900	
Cost of goods sold for the year	340,000	
Bad debt losses (estimated)	300	
Promotion costs	60,000	
Interest on debts	5,000	
Loss on fire damage	1,200	
Insurance and taxes (⅔ selling and ⅓ administrative)	6,000	
Miscellaneous expenses—sales	2,000	
Miscellaneous expenses—administrative	700	
Sales returns	8,000	
Income taxes on operations $8,000, less tax saving on fire loss $400; net taxes	7,600	561,200
Profit		$ 12,000

Balance Sheet

Assets:		Liabilities:	
Cash......................	$ 11,500	Accounts payable.............	$ 20,000
Accounts receivable (offset for		Notes payable, short-term......	10,000
allowance for bad debts $500).	23,500	Notes payable, long-term......	80,000
Merchandise inventory (at cost).	269,200	Rent due (1 month)..........	1,500
Office supplies inventory.......	300	Income taxes payable.........	4,600
Store supplies inventory.......	1,600	*Capital:*	
Prepaid insurance............	1,200		
Stock investment in Y Cor-		Stock, par $100, 2,000 shares...	200,000
poration..................	5,000	Excess paid over par..........	5,000
Store equipment (offset for accu-		Retained earnings............	34,000
mulated depreciation $25,600)	36,800		$355,100
Office equipment (offset for accu-			
mulated depreciation $6,000).	6,000		
	$355,100		

Required:

Prepare an income statement and a balance sheet classified as illustrated in the chapter.

(Hint: EPS on income before extraordinary items is $6.40.)

P3–3. The Weber Company, a successful local automobile repair shop, is preparing the 1974 financial statements. On January 1, 1974, the company acquired a substantial quantity of new shop equipment (and related tools) for use in its testing and repair operations. The equipment involved a cash expenditure of $8,000. On the basis of past experience, John Weber, the owner, estimated the useful life of the new equipment to be five years, at which time he would sell it for approximately 20% of the original cost.

He has requested your advice on two questions: (a) How much should be reported on the 1974 income statement for depreciation expense? (b) How should the new equipment be reported on the 1974 balance sheet? Show your computations and explanations.

(Hint: Residual value is represented by the 20% and should not be depreciated since it will be recovered at the time of disposal.)

P3–4. You are considering making a $20,000 investment in the common stock of either X Corporation or Y Corporation. The companies operate in different industries, and their managements have followed different financing policies. In reviewing the latest financial statements you observe the following data:

	X Corporation		*Y Corporation*	
From the balance sheets:				
Total assets........................		$240,000		$240,000
Total liabilities.....................		100,000		10,000
From the income statements:				
Revenues...........................		$ 93,800		$ 93,800
Expenses:				
Interest expense (rate 8%)...........	$ 8,000		$ 800	
Income tax expense (rate 40%)........	24,000		24,000	
Remaining expenses.................	25,800	57,800	33,000	57,800
Net income.........................		$ 36,000		$ 36,000

From these amounts you observe that the two companies have (1) the same total amount of assets ($240,000), (2) the same amount of revenues ($93,800), and (3) the same net income ($36,000). However, as part of your analysis, you decide to compute their return on investment.

Required:
(a) Compute the return on investment for each company based on owners' equity. Which one appears to be more favorable?
(b) Compute the after-tax, or effective, interest cost to each company.
(Hint: Refer to Chapter 2).

P3–5. We are considering investing $50,000 in either A Corporation or B Corporation. Both companies have been operating in the same industry for a number of years. Our decision process calls for an evaluation and interpretation of the financial statements for the last five years; however, we have obtained the statements for last year only. Those statements provided the following data:

	A Corporation	B Corporation
Sales...	$500,000	$700,000
Gross margin on sales............................	210,000	301,000
Income before extraordinary items..................	50,000	49,000
Net income......................................	20,000	63,000
Total assets.....................................	300,000	400,000
Total liabilities (average interest rate 8%)...........	100,000	100,000
Owners' equity (total)............................	200,000	300,000
Shares outstanding...............................	10,000	30,000
Income tax rate (average).........................	40%	40%

Based upon the above data (aside from other factors), what analytical steps would you suggest? Provide computations and comments in support of the analytical steps suggested. On the basis of your analytical steps only, which company appears preferable as the investment choice?

P3–6. The financial statements at the end of the fiscal year for Mason Corporation are summarized below at June 30, 1974:

Income Statement		*Balance Sheet*	
Sales........................	$800,000	Current assets................	$ 70,000
Cost of goods sold............	450,000	Investments...................	90,000
Gross margin on sales.........	350,000	Fixed assets..................	330,000
Operating expenses and		Other assets..................	10,000
income taxes..............	270,000	Total assets...............	$500,000
Income before extraordinary			
items.....................	80,000	Current liabilities............	$ 60,000
Extraordinary loss (net of		Long-term liabilities..........	40,000
income taxes)..............	60,000	Total liabilities............	100,000
Net income..................	$ 20,000		
		Capital stock, 5,000 shares.....	350,000
		Contributed capital in excess	
		of par....................	3,000
		Retained earnings............	47,000
		Total stockholders' equity....	400,000
		Total liabilities and stock-	
		holders' equity............	$500,000

Required:

Several important investment decisions are under consideration by a large shareholder. Among the analytical data needed are certain financial ratios. Accordingly, assume you have decided to compute the following ratios for him:

Profit margin:
    (a)   Profit margin based on net income
    (b)   Profit margin based on income before extraordinary items
Return on investment:
    (c)   Return on investment based on net income and total stockholders' equity
    (d)   Return on investment based on income before extraordinary items and total stockholders' equity
Earnings per share:
    (e)   Earnings per share based on income before extraordinary items
    (f)   Earnings per share based on net income

For each of the three categories select those that you would deem most important and explain the basis for your choice.

P3–7.   This problem is designed to aid you in understanding the content of published financial statements and to observe differences in form and terminology.

You are to refer to the financial statements of J. C. Penney Company, Inc., presented in this chapter and respond to the following (Note: 1972 refers to the year ended January 29, 1972 and 1973 refers to the year ended January 27, 1973):

(a)   Income Statement:
    1. Is this a comparative statement? Explain.
    2. Is this a consolidated statement? Explain.
    3. Are there any extraordinary items?
    4. What is the percent of income tax expense to pretax income?
    5. What were the profit margins?
    6. How many EPS amounts were reported?

(b)   Statement of Retained Earnings:
    7. What title was used?
    8. Did the balance in retained earnings increase or decrease during 1973? What items caused the change?

(c)   Balance Sheet:
    9. What was the working capital at the end of 1973?
   10. How can one determine the amount of accumulated depreciation for each period?
   11. Did "other assets" change from 1972 to 1973?
   12. Were there any unpaid income taxes at the end of 1973? How does this compare with income tax expense for 1973?
   13. What amount was carried to the balance sheet, for 1973, from the statement of retained earnings?

14. How many classes of capital stock have been issued? Did the stock sell at par?

15. At the end of 1973, what percent of stockholders' equity was represented by prior earnings retained in the business?

(d) Statement of Changes in Financial Position:

16. Can you tell from the heading whether it is based on working capital or on a cash basis?

17. Do you like the caption "External Sources"? Explain.

18. In which year did working capital increase by the greater amount?

19. In 1973, what item generated the largest amount of working capital? What item used the largest amount of working capital?

20. In which year did the company invest the greater amount in subsidiaries?

(e) Accountant's Report:

21. Who were the independent CPA's?

22. May this particular "accountant's report" presumably increase the reliability of the financial statements? Explain why.

(f) Summary of Accounting Policies:

23. How many accounting policies are explained?

24. Are all of the subsidiaries on the fiscal-year basis ending January 29, 1972?

25. When are lay-away sales recorded as revenue?

26. What depreciation rate is used for furniture and fixtures?

(g) Notes to the financial statements:

27. What was the percentage increase of 1973 sales over 1972 sales for European operations (all-units basis)?

28. Which fixed asset showed the largest amount of investment at the end of 1973?

29. In 1973, which quarter generated the largest amount per share of net income?

30. What was the increase in working capital in 1972 and in 1973? What were the increases in cash balances for the same periods? Do these amounts suggest the need for more information? Explain.

4 Transaction analysis and information processing

Purpose
of the
chapter
We have considered the objectives of financial accounting and studied the end product—the financial statements. We now turn our attention to the accounting process; the way in which the ongoing transactions are recorded, analyzed, and classified in a form suitable for generating the periodic financial statements. In this chapter we will learn the fundamentals of the accounting model and the analysis of transactions to determine and capture quantitatively their economic impacts on that model. We will focus on **transaction analysis** and **information processing.**

PART ONE: TRANSACTION ANALYSIS AND THE ACCOUNTING MODEL

Nature of
transactions
Accounting focuses on certain events that have an economic impact on the entity. Those particular events are recorded in the accounting process and are generally referred to as **transactions.** This is a broad view of transactions and includes (1) those events that involve an exchange of resources (assets) and/or obligations (liabilities) between the business (i.e., the accounting entity) and one or more parties other than the entity; and (2) certain events (or economic occurrences) that are not between the entity and one or more parties but yet have a direct and measurable effect on the accounting entity.[1] Examples of the first

---

[1] A narrow definition of a transaction limits it to the first category; that is, events between the entity and one or more parties other than the entity. This narrow definition is useful in certain circumstances but is not suitable for accounting purposes.

82

category of transactions include the purchase of a machine, the sale of merchandise, the borrowing of cash, and the investment in the business by the owners. Examples of the second category of transactions include a casualty loss (such as a flood loss), depreciation of a fixed asset (as a result of use), and the "using up" of prepaid insurance. Throughout this book the word "transaction" will be used in the broad sense to include both types of events.

Most transactions are evidenced by an original business document of some sort; in the case of a sale on credit, a charge ticket is prepared and, in the case of a purchase of goods, an invoice is received. In certain other transactions, such as a cash sale, there may be no document, other than the cash register tape. The documents that underlie, or support, business transactions are usually called source documents. The important requirement, from the accounting point of view, is that there must be some procedure that will capture the raw economic data of each transaction as it occurs. Once this has been done, the data-processing characteristics of the accounting model move the economic impact of each transaction on to its final place—the periodic financial statements.

The fundamental feature of a transaction is that the business entity both gives up something and receives something in return. For example, in the case of a sale of merchandise for cash, the entity gives up resources (the goods sold) and receives in return another resource (cash). In the case of a credit sale of merchandise, the resource received at the time of sale is an account receivable (an asset). Later, another transaction occurs when the account receivable is collected; here, the resource relinquished is the receivable and the resource received is cash. As another example, in the purchase of an asset (either merchandise for resale or a truck purchased for use in the business), the entity acquires the asset and gives up cash, or, in the case of a credit purchase, incurs a liability. In the case of a credit purchase, another transaction occurs later when the debt is paid. At that time, the entity gives up a resource (cash) and "receives" satisfaction of the debt. The sale or purchase of services can be analyzed in the same way. Thus, every transaction has a dual economic effect on the accounting entity. We will return to this dual effect when we consider the accounting model in the next section of this chapter.

| The fundamental accounting model | The fundamental accounting model expresses in algebraic format the status of the resources, debts, and owners' claims of an accounting entity at any specific point in time. In Chapter 2 you learned the fundamental accounting model when you studied the balance sheet (the position statement), viz: |

$$Assets = Liabilities + Owners' Equity$$

You also learned that owners' equity is (*a*) increased by investments (i.e., contributions) by the owners; (*b*) decreased by withdrawals by owners (such as dividends); (*c*) increased by revenues; and (*d*) decreased by expenses.[2] Thus, we can expand the fundamental accounting model as follows:

Assets = Liabilities + Owners' Equity

Increased by:	Decreased by:
Investments	Withdrawals
Revenues	Expenses

This model, since it is a broad economic description of an accounting entity, accommodates the *recording* of each transaction and that directly affects the enterprise. The dual economic effect of each transaction is recorded in terms of this expanded accounting model. The dual effect is captured by the accounting process, whether the processing system is handwritten, mechanized, or computerized.

To illustrate how specific transactions are analyzed and the dual effect is recorded in terms of the fundamental accounting model, let's take a simple but realistic situation. Throughout the example you should particularly note that (a) each transaction is recorded separately; (b) in each recording the integrity of the accounting model is maintained (that is, assets will always equal liabilities plus owners' equity); and (c) the dual effect, as discussed in the preceding section, will be recorded for each separate transaction.

Assume that Bill Bass and three friends started a dry cleaning business, on January 1, 1974, by investing $10,000 cash from their personal savings accounts. Each investor was issued 100 shares of capital stock. Remember that the accounting entity, Bass Cleaners, Incorporated, is to be distinguished from the four investors. Exhibit 4–1 lists a series of transactions for the year 1974 and illustrates the dual effect of each transaction on the accounting model for the business. It also provides the information for developing the income statement and balance sheet shown in Exhibit 4–2. On the balance sheet, since this is a corporation, owners' equity is represented by the two sources: contributed capital and retained earnings. Retained earnings represents the accumulated earnings of the corporation to date, less all dividends paid to date. This aspect of the balance sheet was explained and illustrated in Chapter 2 (pages 34–37) and in Chapter 3 (pages 55–59).[3] From this simple situation you can view the broad perspective of the accounting process. Transactions occur that create raw economic data. Each is subjected to

---

[2] Owners' equity frequently is referred to as equity capital and, sometimes, net worth. The latter term is not recommended because it implies that owners' equity on the balance sheet states what it is actually worth, which is not the case.

[3] If Bass Cleaners were a sole proprietorship or a partnership instead of a corporation, owners' equity would be shown as "Capital, owners' name" for each owner (see page 38).

Exhibit 4–1

BASS CLEANERS, INCORPORATED
Transaction Analysis

Transaction:	Assets	=	Liabilities	+	Stockholders' Equity
(a) Bass Cleaners received $10,000 cash invested by owners; 400 shares of stock issued.	Cash + $10,000				Capital stock (400 shares) + $10,000
(b) Borrowed $5,000 cash on 8% note payable.	Cash + 5,000		Note payable + $5,000		
(c) Purchased delivery truck for cash at cost of $3,000. . . .	Cash − 3,000 Delivery truck + 3,000				
(d) Cleaning revenue collected in cash, $30,000.	Cash + 30,000				Cleaning revenue + 30,000
(e) Cleaning revenue earned but the bill is not yet collected, $4,000.	Accounts receivable + 4,000				Cleaning revenue + 4,000
(f) Operating expenses paid in cash, $20,000.	Cash − 20,000				Operating expenses − 20,000
(g) Operating expenses incurred but not yet paid, $2,000.			Accounts payable + 2,000		Operating expenses − 2,000
(h) Paid 8% interest on the $5,000 note payable, (b) above, with cash ($5,000 × 8% = $400).	Cash − 400				Interest expense − 400
(i) Depreciation expenses for one year on truck ($3,000 ÷ 5 years = $600).	Truck − 600				Operating expenses depreciation − 600
(j) Cash dividend of $1,500 paid to shareholders.	Cash − 1,500				Dividends paid − 1,500
(k) Collected $1,000 cash on accounts receivable in (e).	Cash + 1,000 Accounts receivable − 1,000				
(l) Paid $500 cash on accounts payable in (g).	Cash − 500		Accounts payable − 500		
Totals (end of accounting period).	Total Assets $26,000	=	Total Liabilities $6,500	+	Total Stockholders' Equity $19,500

Exhibit 4–2

BASS CLEANERS, INCORPORATED
Income Statement
For the Year Ended December 31, 1974

Cleaning revenue......................................		$34,000
Operating expenses...............................	$22,600	
Interest expense...................................	400	23,000
Net income.....................................		$11,000

Note: To simplify the illustration, income taxes are disregarded.

BASS CLEANERS, INCORPORATED
Balance Sheet
At December 31, 1974

Assets:		
Cash..		$20,600
Accounts receivable..............................		3,000
Delivery truck..................................	$ 3,000	
Less accumulated depreciation....................	600	2,400
Total Assets		$26,000
Liabilities:		
Notes payable...................................	$ 5,000	
Accounts payable...............................	1,500	
Total Liabilities...............................		$ 6,500
Stockholders' equity:		
Contributed capital:		
Capital stock (400 shares).......................	10,000	
Retained earnings (net income, $11,000 minus dividends		
paid, $1,500).................................	9,500	
Total Stockholders' Equity......................		19,500
Total Liabilities		
and Stockholders' Equity.........................		$26,000

---

transaction analysis and then is recorded in terms of its dual effect on the fundamental accounting model. Finally, the financial statements at the end of the period are constructed from data provided by the accounting model.

This example, as reflected in Exhibits 4–1 and 4–2, indicates that we have two primary data-processing problems. First, we need an efficient method for keeping track of the amounts of: each kind of asset (cash, accounts receivable, equipment, inventory, etc.); each kind of liability (notes payable, accounts payable, bonds payable, etc.); and each category of owners' equity (capital stock, dividends paid, revenues, and expenses). Second, we need a systematic method for recording the increases and decreases in assets, liabilities, and owners' equity.

The account. These two data-processing problems led the early accountants to the use of a series of accounts. A separate account is used for each kind of asset, liability, and owners' equity. An account is simply a standardized arrangement for recording data by categories. Thus, in most accounting systems, you will find separate accounts, individually labeled, for each item such as cash, inventory, accounts receivable, equipment, land, accounts payable, notes payable, taxes payable, capital stock, sales revenue, service revenue, and various kinds of expenses. It is very useful to think of an account as having two sides: the left or debit side and the right or credit side. The increases are recorded on one side and the decreases on the other side.[4] For example, the Cash account for Bass Cleaners may appear as in Exhibit 4–3.

Exhibit 4–3

Ledger account (T-account form)

Cash

Left or Debit Side		Right or Credit Side #101	
(Increases)		(Decreases)	
Investment by owners	10,000	To purchase truck	3,000
Loan from bank	5,000	Operating expenses	20,000
Cleaning revenue	30,000	Interest expense	400
Collections on ac-		Dividends paid	1,500
counts receivable	1,000	Payment on accounts	
		payable	500

Since the left or debit side of the Cash account (Exhibit 4–3) sums to $46,000 and the right or credit side sums to $25,400, the balance of cash is the difference: $46,000 − $25,400 = $20,600. This is the amount of cash on hand at the end of the period, and this amount is the source of the balance-sheet amount for cash reported in Exhibit 4–2. To facilitate the processing of accounting data, whether handwritten, mechanized, or by computer, each account generally is assigned an identification number for ready reference. For example, the Cash account may be assigned an identification code number such as 101. Although the above T-account is used for instructional convenience, a standard account form often used in manually maintained systems is shown in Exhibit 4–4.[5] Although rearranged, in effect it still has the debit side and credit side feature.

---

[4] Historically, and continuing to the present, accountants always refer to the left side as the debit side and to the right side as the credit side. For accounting purposes, the terms debit and credit have no other meanings. The words "to debit" and "to credit" should not be confused with "increase" or "decrease" as will become clear in the next few paragraphs. Contrary to what some people think, there is no implication of "goodness" attached to credits or "badness" attached to debits (or vice versa).

[5] Handwritten or manually maintained accounts in the formats shown here generally are used only in small businesses. Highly mechanized and computerized systems retain the concept of the account but not this format. T-accounts are very useful for instructional purposes.

Exhibit 4–4
Ledger account (account form)

| Account Title | *Cash* | | | Account Number | *101* |

Date	Explanation	F	Debit	Credit	Balance
Jan. 1	*Investments*	*1*	*10,000*		*10,000*
etc.	*Borrowing*	*etc*	*5,000*		*15,000*
	Truck purchased			*3,000*	*12,000*
	Cleaning revenue		*30,000*		*42,000*
	Operating expenses			*20,000*	*22,000*
	Interest expense			*400*	*21,600*
	Payments to owners			*1,500*	*20,100*
	Collections on receivables		*1,000*		*21,100*
	Payments on accounts payable			*500*	*20,600*

Recording increases and decreases in the accounts. In respect to the second data-processing problem cited above, a systematic and algebraically consistent accounting for each increase and decrease in assets, liabilities, and owners' equity is provided by the fundamental accounting model. This is a unique and significant characteristic of the accounting model. You may recall from Chapter 1 that a mathematician (Paciolo) in 1494 first described the fundamental accounting model used today. Perceiving the problem at hand, and after designing the T-account (as illustrated above for cash), Paciolo applied an algebraic concept that has proven to be of great significance in increasing the accuracy in the accounting process. The fundamental accounting model, Assets = Liabilities + Owners' Equity, itself is an algebraic model that balances and can be rearranged mathematically. Paciolo added another algebraic balance feature to it to accommodate the recording of increases and decreases in each account. Let's see how it was done.

Paciolo perceived that, having designed the T-account with two sides in order to reflect increases and decreases, he could add still another algebraic balancing feature by simply *reversing* the position in the account of the "increases" and "decreases" on the *opposite sides* of the equal sign. To illustrate the point, he could have designed the system as follows:

Assets		=	Liabilities		+	Owners' Equity	
Debit	Credit		Debit	Credit		Debit	Credit
+	−		+	−		+	−

Instead, in order to introduce a second algebraic balance feature, he designed the system with the "+" and "−" in reverse order on the opposite sides of the equal sign as follows:

Assets		=	Liabilities		+	Owners' Equity	
Debit	Credit		Debit	Credit		Debit	Credit
+	−		−	+		−	+

The addition of this algebraic concept resulted in the second "balancing" feature; that is, debits always equal credits. Thus, the system for recording increases and decreases in the accounts may be conveniently tabulated as follows:

	Increases	Decreases
Assets........................	Debit	Credit
Liabilities.....................	Credit	Debit
Owners' equity................	Credit	Debit

Another way to view the debits = credits feature is in terms of the algebraic relationship: "The signs reverse on opposite sides of the equal sign."

It follows that for each transaction, and for all transactions, the debit amounts will always equal the credit amounts. To summarize, the two balancing features of the fundamental accounting model are:

(1)   Assets = Liabilities + Owners' Equity
(2)   Debits = Credits

Debit and credit for revenue and expenses.   Owners' equity is increased by credits and decreased by debits. Revenues are increases in owners' equity, so they are also increased by credits. Expenses are decreases in owners' equity, so they are increased by debits. In other words, the debit/credit relationship for owners' equity accounts is applied to revenues and expenses as follows:[6]

Revenues are recorded as credits.
Expenses are recorded as debits.

---

[6] To "charge an account" is a frequently used expression meaning to *debit* an account. Thus, the word "debit" is used as both a verb and a noun.

Transaction analysis is a term frequently used to describe the process of studying each transaction to determine its dual effect on the entity in terms of the accounting model. In transaction analysis a distinction is made between the cash basis and the accrual basis viewpoints. In Chapter 2, pages 39 and 40, the distinction between *cash basis accounting* and *accrual basis accounting* was discussed. The concept of **accrual accounting** requires that revenues and expenses be measured and reported in the accounting period in which they occur rather than when the related cash is received or paid. To illustrate, assume a sale of merchandise for $1,000 in 1974. In the case of a cash sale, there is one transaction to be recognized. In 1974, cash is increased by $1,000 and sales revenue of $1,000 has been earned. In this situation, sales revenue is measured at the same time that the cash is collected since they occur at the same time. Now, assume instead that it was a credit sale in 1974 and that the cash will be collected in 1975. In this situation, there would be two separate transactions to be given accounting recognition: (1) In 1974 the sales revenue and a receivable from the customer is recognized when the sale is consummated; (2) Later, in 1975 when the cash is collected on the receivable, a transaction must be recognized that would increase cash and decrease the receivable.

Now, let's see how each transaction is subjected to transaction analysis to determine (1) the dual economic effect and (2) how that dual effect is recorded in the accounts (i.e., in the fundamental accounting model). For each transaction recorded, the **two separate balances** must be maintained, viz: (1) Assets = Liabilities + Owners' Equity, and (2) Debits = Credits. Bass Cleaners, Incorporated, will be used to demonstrate, on the next few pages, the transaction analysis and the recording process. You should analyze each transaction (listed on page 85) and trace the manner in which the dual effect is recorded in the T-accounts. The transactions are keyed with letters for ready reference.

(*a*) Received $10,000 cash invested by the four owners and issued 400 shares of capital stock (par value $25 per share).

Cash (asset)

Debit	Credit
(a) 10,000	

Capital Stock (owners' equity)

Debit	Credit
	(a) 10,000

Transaction analysis—The transaction increased the company's cash by $10,000, which was recorded in the Cash account as a debit (increase); liabilities were unaffected; owners' equity was increased by $10,000, which was recorded in the Capital Stock account as a credit (increase). Thus, the entry meets the test of both equations: assets equal liabilities plus owners' equity and debits equal credits.

(*b*) Borrowed $5,000 cash from the bank on an 8% note payable.

Cash (asset)

Debit	Credit
(a) 10,000	
(b) [5,000]	

Transaction analysis—The transaction increased the cash by $5,000, which was recorded in the Cash account as a debit (increase); liabilities were increased by $5,000, which is recorded in Notes Payable as a credit (increase); and owners' equity was unchanged. The entry meets the test of both equations.

Notes Payable (liability)

Debit	Credit
	(b) [5,000]

(*c*) Purchased a delivery truck for cash at a cost of $3,000.

Cash (asset)

Debit	Credit
(a) 10,000	(c) [3,000]
(b) 5,000	

Transaction analysis—The transaction increased the asset, delivery truck, by $3,000, which was recorded in that account as a debit (increase); the cash decreased by $3,000, which was recorded in the Cash account as a credit (decrease). Liabilities and owners' equity were not affected. The entry meets the test of both equations.

Delivery Truck (asset)

Debit	Credit
(c) [3,000]	

(*d*) Cleaning revenue collected in cash, $30,000.

Cash (asset)

Debit	Credit
(a) 10,000	(c) 3,000
(b) 5,000	
(d) [30,000]	

Transaction analysis—The transaction increased cash by $30,000, which was recorded in the asset account Cash as a debit (increase); liabilities were unaffected; owners' equity was increased by $30,000 as a result of the earning of revenue. Owners' equity was credited (increased) by $30,000. A separate account, "Cleaning Revenue," is used to keep track of this revenue. The entry meets the test of both equations.

Cleaning Revenue (owners' equity)

Debit	Credit
	(d) [30,000]

(*e*) Cleaning revenue earned but the bill is not yet collected, $4,000.

Accounts Receivable
(asset)

Debit	Credit
(e) 4,000	

Transaction analysis—The transaction increased the company's asset, Accounts Receivable, by $4,000, which was recorded as a debit (increase) to that account; liabilities were unaffected; and owner's equity was increased by $4,000 as a result of earning revenue. Owners' equity was credited (increased) by $4,000. A separate account, "Cleaning Revenue," is used to keep track of this revenue. The entry meets the test of both equations.

Cleaning Revenue, (owners' equity)

Debit	Credit
	(d) 30,000
	(e) 4,000

(*f*) Expenses paid in cash, $20,000.

Cash (asset)

Debit	Credit
(a) 10,000	(c) 3,000
(b) 5,000	(f) 20,000
(d) 30,000	

Transaction analysis—The transaction decreased the cash by $20,000, which was recorded in the Cash account as a credit (decrease); liabilities were unaffected; owners' equity was decreased by $20,000 as a result of paying expenses. Owners' equity was debited (decreased) for $20,000. A separate account, "Operating Expenses," is used to keep track of this expense. The entry meets the test of both equations.

Operating Expenses (owners' equity)

Debit	Credit
(f) 20,000	

(*g*) Expenses incurred but not yet paid, $2,000.

Accounts Payable (liability)

Debit	Credit
	(g) 2,000

Transaction analysis—This transaction increased the company's liabilities by $2,000, which was recorded as a credit (increase) to Accounts Payable; assets were unaffected; owners' equity was decreased by $2,000. A separate account, "Operating Expenses," is used to keep track of this expense. The entry meets the test of both equations.

Operating Expenses (owners' equity)

Debit	Credit
(f) 20,000	
(g) 2,000	

(h) Paid cash for interest on note payable in (b) ($5,000 × 8% = $400).

Cash (asset)

Debit		Credit	
(a)	10,000	(c)	3,000
(b)	5,000	(f)	20,000
(d)	30,000	(h)	400

Transaction analysis—This transaction decreased the cash by $400, which was recorded as a credit (decrease) in the Cash account; the amount of the liability ($5,000) was unchanged; however, owners' equity was decreased by the amount of the interest ($400) since the payment of interest (but not principal of the note) represents an expense. Owners' equity was debited (decreased) for $400. A separate account, "Interest Expense," is used to keep track of this type of expense. This entry meets the test of both equations.

Interest Expense (owners' equity)

Debit		Credit
(h)	400	

(i) Depreciation expense for one year on the delivery truck computed ($3,000 ÷ 5 years = $600).

Operating Expenses (owners' equity)

Debit		Credit
(f)	20,000	
(g)	2,000	
(i)	600	

Transaction analysis—This transaction is caused by the internal utilization of an asset owned for operating purposes. The use gives rise to depreciation expense. Owners' equity was debited (decreased) to record the fact that an expense was incurred, the debit was recorded in a separate account, "Operating Expenses," established to keep track of this type of expense. Asset (delivery truck) was decreased due to the fact that a "part of the cost of the asset was used up in operations." Instead of crediting the asset account "Delivery Truck" directly, a related **negative asset** account, "Accumulated Depreciation on Delivery Truck," is credited so that the depreciated amounts can be kept separately. This will be explained in detail in Chapter 9. This entry meets the test of both equations.

Delivery Truck (asset)

Debit		Credit
(c)	3,000	

Accumulated Depreciation on Delivery Truck (negative asset)

Debit	Credit	
	(i)	600

(j) Paid $1,500 cash dividend to the stockholders.

Cash (asset)

Debit		Credit	
(a)	10,000	(c)	3,000
(b)	5,000	(f)	20,000
(d)	30,000	(h)	400
		(j)	1,500

Transaction analysis—This transaction decreased the company's cash by $1,500, which was recorded in the Cash account as a credit (decrease); liabilities were unaffected; owners' equity was decreased by $1,500 as a result of the resources (cash) paid out of the business to the stockholders. Owners' equity was debited (decreased) by $1,500. A separate account, "Dividends Paid," is used to keep track of this decrease in owners' equity. This entry meets the test of both equations.

Dividends Paid (owners' equity)

Debit		Credit
(j)	1,500	

(*k*) Collected $1,000 cash on accounts receivable in (*e*).

Cash (asset)

Debit		Credit	
(a)	10,000	(c)	3,000
(b)	5,000	(f)	20,000
(d)	30,000	(h)	400
(k)	1,000	(j)	1,500

Transaction analysis—This transaction increased the cash by $1,000, which was recorded as a debit (increase) in the Cash account; an asset (Accounts Receivable) was credited (decreased) by the same amount; liabilities and owners' equity were unaffected since there was simply a change in two assets but no change in total assets. This entry meets the test of both equations.

Accounts Receivable (asset)

Debit		Credit	
(e)	4,000	(k)	1,000

(*l*) Paid $500 cash on accounts payable in (*g*).

Cash (asset)

Debit		Credit	
(a)	10,000	(e)	3,000
(b)	5,000	(f)	20,000
(d)	30,000	(h)	400
(k)	1,000	(j)	1,500
		(l)	500

Transaction analysis—This transaction decreased the cash by $500, which was recorded as a credit (decrease) in the Cash account; liabilities (Accounts Payable) were decreased (debited) for $500; owners' equity was unaffected since there were no revenue or expense involved in this transaction, merely the payment of a debt. This entry meets the test of both equations.

Accounts Payable (liability)

Debit		Credit	
(l)	500	(g)	2,000

Now we may summarize the fundamental accounting model and the mechanics of the debt–credit concept in T-account format as follows, where + means increase and − means decrease:

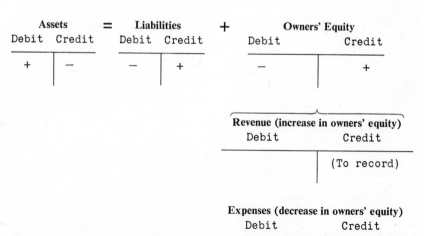

Assets		=	Liabilities		+	Owners' Equity	
Debit	Credit		Debit	Credit		Debit	Credit
+	−		−	+		−	+

Revenue (increase in owners' equity)

Debit	Credit
	(To record)

Expenses (decrease in owners' equity)

Debit	Credit
(To record)	

Note particularly that an increase in **revenue** (a credit) represents an **increase** in owners' equity and an increase in **expense** (a debit) represents a **decrease** in owners' equity. When a revenue is earned, the resources of the business are increased and, because of the dual effect, owners' equity is increased by the same amount. In contrast, when an expense is incurred, the resources of the business are decreased and, because of the dual effect, the owners' equity is decreased by the same amount.

PART TWO: THE FUNDAMENTALS OF INFORMATION PROCESSING

The ledger   In the preceding illustration a separate account was maintained for each kind of asset, liability, and owners' equity. From this you can

Exhibit 4–5

BASS CLEANERS, INCORPORATED
LEDGER

| ASSETS | = | LIABILITIES | + | OWNERS' EQUITY |

Cash | **Notes Payable** | **Capital Stock**

(a) 10,000 (c) 3,000	(b) 5,000	(a) 10,000
(b) 5,000 (f) 20,000		
(d) 30,000 (h) 400		
(k) 1,000 (j) 1,500		**Dividends Paid†**
(l) 500		(j) 1,500

Accounts Receivable | **Accounts Payable** | **Cleaning Revenue**

(e) 4,000 (k) 1,000	(l) 500 (g) 2,000	(d) 30,000
		(e) 4,000

Delivery Truck | **Operating Expenses**

(c) 3,000	(f) 20,000
	(g) 2,000
	(i) 600

Accumulated Depreciation on Delivery Truck* | **Interest Expense**

(i) 600	(h) 400

| Totals | 26,000 | = | 6,500 | + | 19,500 |

* Accumulated depreciation is a negative, or contra, asset account. For further explanation see Chapter 9.

† Dividends Paid represents a decrease in owners' equity since it shows the amount of cash that was paid out as dividends to the stockholders. For further explanation see Chapters 5 and 12.

see that an accounting system will contain a large number of accounts. Collectively, the accounts are known as the **ledger.** The ledger may be organized in numerous ways. Handwritten accounting systems may use a loose-leaf ledger—one page for each account. In the case of "machine accounting," a card ledger generally is used and there is a separate machine card for each account. In the case of a computerized accounting system, the ledger is maintained on magnetic tape or similar electronic storage devices, but there are still separate accounts as in the other systems.

Exhibit 4–5 shows the ledger for Bass Cleaners in T-account form. The accounting model, Assets = Liabilities + Owners' Equity, as given at the top of this exhibit, and the totals at the bottom are shown only for your convenience in study; they would not appear in an actual ledger.

**The trial
balance**

At the end of the accounting period, as a matter of convenience, a **trial balance** is prepared from the ledger. A trial balance is simply a listing, in ledger-account order, of the accounts and their respective debit or credit balances. Exhibit 4–6 shows the trial balance for Bass

Exhibit 4–6

BASS CLEANERS, INCORPORATED
Trial Balance, December 31, 1974

	Account balances	
Ledger accounts	*Debit*	*Credit*
Cash...............................	$20,600	
Accounts receivable..................	3,000	
Delivery truck......................	3,000	
Accumulated depreciation on delivery truck......................		$ 600
Notes payable......................		5,000
Accounts payable...................		1,500
Capital stock (400 shares)		10,000
Dividends paid......................	1,500	
Cleaning revenues...................		34,000
Operating expenses..................	22,600	
Interest expense.....................	400	
Totals.......................	$51,100	$51,100

Cleaners at December 31, 1974. Basically, there are two convenience factors: (1) the equality of debits and credits is easily checked; and (2) it provides data in a convenient form for construction of the income statement, balance sheet, and statement of changes in financial position.

The journal   In a very simple situation one could record the transactions of a business entity directly into the ledger accounts as was done for Bass Cleaners. However, in more complex situations, it is essential, as each transaction is analyzed, that its dual economic effect on the accounting model (i.e., the resultant entry) be recorded in one place in chronological order (i.e., in order of date). The accounting record designed for this particular purpose is known as the journal. The dual effects are later transferred, or posted, to the appropriate accounts in the ledger. The journal contains a chronological listing of the entries for each of the transactions. The format of the entry in the journal for each transaction is designed so that the dual effects on the accounting model and the debit and credit features are physically linked. For example, transaction (a) for Bass Cleaners would appear in the journal in the following format:

```
(Date)  Cash.............................. 10,000
             Capital Stock.................        10,000
        To record investment of cash by
        owners.
```

This feature is in contrast to the ledger, where each entry is physically separated between two or more accounts. For example, you will recall that the above entry for Bass Cleaners would appear in the ledger as follows:

Cash		Capital Stock	
(Date) 10,000			(Date) 10,000

If for some reason one desires to trace an entry subsequently, knowledge of the approximate date of the entry would not be helpful in locating it in the ledger. Similarly, one would have to examine two or more ledger accounts (cards, sheets, etc.) to review the complete effects of a particular transaction. To facilitate your understanding, let's see how the journal might appear in a manually maintained system. The first five transactions for Bass Cleaners have been entered in a typical journal as shown in Exhibit 4–7. Recording the transactions in this manner is known as journalizing the transactions and events. In respect to the journal entries, you should observe in particular that (a) each transaction and event is first recorded in the journal with a separate entry, (b) each entry is dated and entries are in chronological order, (c) the debits (accounts and amounts) are entered first; the credits follow and are indented, and (d) as a consequence, the effects on the accounting model and the debits and credits are linked in one entry. These features, since they provide an "audit or tracing trail,"

Exhibit 4–7

Journal				Page ___1___
Date	Account Titles and Explanation	Folio	Debit	Credit
Jan 1	Cash	101	10,000	
	Capital stock	301		10,000
	Investment of cash by owners			
etc.	Cash	101	5,000	
	Note payable	202		5,000
	Borrowed cash on 8% note			
etc.	Delivery Truck	111	3,000	
	Cash	101		3,000
	Purchased delivery			
	truck for use in			
	the business.			

facilitate subsequent examination of past transactions, the location of errors, and simplify subsequent accounting (as will be demonstrated later). Because it is the place of first recording of each transaction, the journal is referred to as a **book of original entry.** In contrast, the ledger is referred to as a **book of final entry.**

Posting to the ledger   In the preceding section we stated that the data for each entry recorded in the journal are transferred, or *posted,* to the appropriate accounts in the ledger. In a business using a manual system, one may expect the entity to record the transactions in the journal each day and the posting (to the ledger) to occur less frequently, say every few days. Of course, the timing of these **information-processing activities** varies with the particular situation.

In posting, the debits and credits, as stated in the journal entries, are transferred directly as debits and credits to the indicated accounts in the ledger. In both the journal (Exhibit 4–7) and ledger (as in the

Cash account, Exhibit 4–4), you can observe that there is a **"folio"** column, which is included to provide a numerical cross-reference between the journal and the ledger (to provide the audit trail). For example, the journal shown in Exhibit 4–7 shows a folio number of 101 for Cash, which indicates the account to which that amount was posted. You will recall that this is the account number we assigned to cash in Exhibit 4–4. Similarly, if you look at the ledger account for Cash, as shown in Exhibit 4–4, you will see on the first line of the account a folio number of 1, indicating that the particular amount posted came from page 1 of the journal. Entry of the folio numbers also indicates to what point the posting has been carried.

LA PALOMA APARTMENTS, INCORPORATED

Demonstra-tion case for self-study

(Try to resolve the case before studying the suggested solution that follows.)

In 1971 Mark Hall and Paul Garza formed a corporation to build and operate an apartment complex to be called La Paloma. At the start, each invested $40,000 cash and received 3,000 shares of $10 par-value stock. Therefore, at that date the following entry was recorded in the accounts:

```
Cash....................................... 80,000
   Capital Stock, par $10 (6,000 shares)....      60,000
   Contributed Capital in Excess
      of Par.................................      20,000
```

Shortly thereafter, land was acquired for $30,000 and a construction contract was signed with a builder. The first apartments were rented on July 1, 1972. The owners decided to use a *fiscal year* for business purposes—July 1 through June 30. It is now June 30, 1974, and the occupancy rate during the year has been over 96% due to the quality of the apartments and the excellent management by Hall and Garza.

We have selected this case of a small business to demonstrate the complete accounting *information-processing cycle* from the capture of the raw economic data to the financial statements developed at the end of the period. Only representative and summary transactions have been selected in order to keep the length of the case within reason. You should study each step in the solution carefully since it reviews the concepts, principles, and procedures introduced in the chapters to this point.

Since this is the second year of operations, certain accounts in the ledger will have balances carried over from June 30, 1973. Below you will find a complete list of the ledger accounts that will be needed for this case, with the balances carried over from the previous fiscal year. Ledger account (folio) numbers are provided at the left.

LA PALOMA APARTMENTS
Ledger Balances,
July 1, 1973

Account Number	Account Title	Debit	Credit
101	Cash...	$ 5,000	
103	Accounts receivable (or rent receivable)............		
105	Supplies inventory..............................	2,000	
A 112	Prepaid insurance..............................		
121	Land (apartment site).........................	30,000	
122	La Paloma apartment building....................	200,000	
123	Accumulated depreciation on apartment building....		$ 10,000
125	Furniture and fixtures...........................	60,000	
126	Accumulated depreciation on furniture and fixtures...		12,000
131	Land for future apartment site....................		
151	Accounts payable...............................		6,000
152	Property taxes payable...........................		
153	Income taxes payable............................		
161	Mortgage payable (on apartment building).........		179,000
162	Note payable, long-term.........................		
201	Capital stock (par $10, 6,000 shares)..............		60,000
202	Contributed capital in excess of par...............		20,000
203	Retained earnings (accumulated earnings to June 30, 1973)...............................		10,000
211	Rent revenue...................................		
221	Utilities and telephone expense...................		
222	Apartment maintenance expense...................		
223	Salary and wage expense........................		
224	Insurance expense..............................		
225	Property tax expense............................		
226	Depreciation expense...........................		
227	Miscellaneous expenses..........................		
231	Interest expense................................		
232	Income tax expense.............................		
	Totals..................................	$297,000	$297,000

Representative transactions (most of them summarized) for the 12-month fiscal period—July 1, 1973, through June 30, 1974—are listed below. To facilitate tracing, instead of a date, we will use the letter notation to the left of each transaction.

(a) Paid $3,000 cash for a three-year insurance premium covering the building and contents and liability.

(b) Rental revenue earned: collected in cash, $90,000; uncollected, $1,800.

(c) Paid accounts payable (amounts owed from last year for expenses), $6,000.

(d) Purchased a tract of land, at a cost of $35,000, as a planned site for another apartment complex to be constructed in "about three years." Cash amounting to $5,000 was paid and a long-term note payable (8% interest per annum, interest payable each six months) was signed for the balance.

(e)   Operating expenses incurred and paid in cash were:

      Utilities and telephone expense $26,000

      Apartment maintenance expense   1,200

      Salary and wage expense   3,000

(f)   At the end of the fiscal year (June 30, 1974) the following bills for expenses incurred had not been recorded or paid: June telephone bill, $40, and miscellaneous expenses, $1,100.

(g)   Paid interest for six months on the long-term note at 8% per annum. (Refer to item (d).)

(h)   An inventory count at the end of the fiscal period, June 30, 1974, showed supplies on hand amounting to $400. Supplies used are considered a miscellaneous expense.

(i)   By the end of the fiscal period, June 30, 1974, one-third of the prepaid insurance premium of $3,000 paid in transaction (a) had expired.

(j)   Depreciation expense for the year was based on an estimated useful life of 20 years for the apartment and 5 years for the furniture and fixtures.

(k)   The property taxes for the year ending June 30, 1974, in the amount of $1,700 have not yet been recorded or paid.

(l)   Cash payment on the mortgage on the apartment was:

On principal	$ 8,000
Interest	10,700
Total paid	$18,700

(m)   Income tax expense for the year ending June 30, 1974, was computed to be $4,900. This obligation will be paid in the next period.

Required:

(1) Set up a ledger in T-account form that includes all of the accounts listed above; include the account numbers as given. Enter the July 1, 1973, balances in each account in this manner:

Cash	101
Balance 5,000	

(2) Set up a journal and journalize each of the transactions listed above for the period July 1, 1973, through June 30, 1974. Number the journal pages consecutively.

(3) Post all entries from the journal to the ledger; utilize the folio columns.

(4) Prepare a trial balance at June 30, 1974.

(5) Prepare a classified income statement for the fiscal year.

(6) Prepare a classified balance sheet at June 30, 1974.

Suggested Solution:

Requirement   (2):

JOURNAL   Page 1

Date 1973–74	Account Titles and Explanation	F	Debit	Credit
(a)	Prepaid Insurance	112	3,000	
	Cash	101		3,000
	Paid insurance premium for 3 years in advance			
	(Explanatory note—An asset account, Prepaid Insurance, is debited because a future service, insurance coverage, has been paid for in advance of this date.)			
(b)	Cash	101	90,000	
	Accounts Receivable (or Rent Receivable)	103	1,800	
	Rent Revenue	211		91,800
	(Explanatory note—To record rent revenues earned for the year, of which $1,800 has not yet been collected.)			
(c)	Accounts Payable	151	6,000	
	Cash	101		6,000
	Paid obligations carried over from previous year.			
(d)	Land for Future Apartment Site	131	35,000	
	Cash	101		5,000
	Note Payable, Long-term	162		30,000
	Purchased land as a site for future apartment complex. (This is a second tract of land acquired; the present apartment building was constructed on the first tract.)			
(e)	Utilities and Telephone Expense	221	26,000	
	Apartment Maintenance Expense	222	1,200	
	Salary and Wage Expense	223	3,000	
	Cash	101		30,200
	Paid expenses.			
(f)	Utilities and Telephone Expense	221	40	
	Miscellaneous Expenses	227	1,100	
	Accounts Payable	151		1,140
	Expenses incurred but not yet paid.			

JOURNAL

Date 1973–74	Account Titles and Explanation	F	Debit	Credit
(g)	Interest Expense	231	1,200	
	Cash	101		1,200
	Paid six months' interest on long-term note ($30,000 × 8% × 6/12 = $1,200).			
(h)	Miscellaneous Expenses	227	1,600	
	Supplies Inventory	105		1,600
	To record as expense supplies used from inventory during the year. (Explanatory note—Supplies are bought in advance of use, hence, at that time are recorded as an asset, Supplies Inventory. As the supplies are used from inventory, the asset thus used becomes an expense.)			
(i)	Insurance Expense	224	1,000	
	Prepaid Insurance	112		1,000
	To record as an expense the cost of the insurance that expired ($3,000 × 1/3 = $1,000).			
(j)	Depreciation Expense	226	22,000	
	Accumulated Depreciation on Apartment Building	123		10,000
	Accumulated Depreciation on Furniture and Fixtures	126		12,000
	Depreciation expense for one year. Computation: Apartment: $200,000 ÷ 20 years = $10,000 Furniture and Fixtures: $60,000 ÷ 5 years = $12,000			
(k)	Property Tax Expense	225	1,700	
	Property Taxes Payable	152		1,700
	Property taxes for the year not yet paid.			
(l)	Mortgage Payable	161	8,000	
	Interest Expense	231	10,700	
	Cash	101		18,700
	Payments on principal of mortgage payable plus interest expense.			
(m)	Income Tax Expense	232	4,900	
	Income Taxes Payable	153		4,900

Requirements   (1)and(3):

LEDGER

Cash   101

Date	F	Amount	Date	F	Amount
Balance		5,000	(a)	1	3,000
(b)	1	90,000	(c)	1	6,000
			(d)	1	5,000
			(e)	1	30,200
			(g)	2	1,200
			(1)	2	18,700

Furniture and Fixtures   125

Date	F	Amount	Date	F	Amount
Balance		60,000			

Accumulated Depreciation on Furniture and Fixtures   126

			Balance		12,000
			(j)	2	12,000

Accounts Receivable   103

(b)	1	1,800

Supplies Inventory   105

Balance		2,000	(h)	2	1,600

Land for Future Apartment Site   131

(d)	1	35,000

Prepaid Insurance   112

(a)	1	3,000	(i)	2	1,000

Accounts Payable   151

(c)	1	6,000	Balance		6,000
			(f)	1	1,140

Land (Apartment Site)   121

Balance		30,000

Property Taxes Payable   152

			(k)	2	1,700

La Paloma Apartment Building   122

Balance		200,000

Income Taxes Payable   153

			(m)	2	4,900

Accumulated Depreciation on Apartment Building   123

			Balance		10,000
			(j)	2	10,000

Mortgage Payable (On Apartment Building)   161

(1)	2	8,000	Balance		179,000

Note Payable, Long-term						162
Date	F	Amount	Date	F	Amount	
			(d)	1	30,000	

Insurance Expense						224
Date	F	Amount	Date	F	Amount	
(i)	2	1,000				

Capital Stock		201
Balance		60,000

Property Tax Expense		225
(k)	2	1,700

Contributed Capital in Excess of Par		202
Balance		20,000

DF 6

Depreciation Expense		226
(j)	2	22,000

Retained Earnings		203
Balance		10,000

Miscellaneous Expenses		227
(f)	1	1,100
(h)	2	1,600

Rent Revenue		211
(b)	1	91,800

Interest Expense		231
(g)	2	1,200
(l)	2	10,700

Utilities and Telephone Expense		221
(e)	1	26,000
(f)	1	40

Income Tax Expense		232
(m)	2	4,900

Apartment Maintenance Expense		222
(e)	1	1,200

Salary and Wage Expense		223
(e)	1	3,000

Requirement   (4):   **LA PALOMA APARTMENTS**
Trial Balance, June 30, 1974

Account Number	Account Title	Debit	Credit
		Balance	
101	Cash..	$ 30,900	
103	Accounts receivable............................	1,800	
105	Supplies inventory.............................	400	
112	Prepaid insurance.............................	2,000	
121	Land (apartment site)..........................	30,000	
122	La Paloma apartment building..................	200,000	
123	Accumulated depreciation on apartment building....		$ 20,000
125	Furniture and fixtures...........................	60,000	
126	Accumulated depreciation on furniture and fixtures..		24,000
131	Land for future apartment site...................	35,000	
151	Accounts payable.............................		1,140
152	Property taxes payable.........................		1,700
153	Income taxes payable..........................		4,900
161	Mortgage payable (on apartment building).........		171,000
162	Note payable, long-term........................		30,000
201	Capital stock (par $10, 6,000 shares).............		60,000
202	Contributed capital in excess of par..............		20,000
203	Retained earnings (accumulated earnings to June 30, 1973)...............................		10,000
211	Rent revenue..................................		91,800
221	Utilities and telephone expense..................	26,040	
222	Apartment maintenance expense..................	1,200	
223	Salary and wage expense.......................	3,000	
224	Insurance expense.............................	1,000	
225	Property tax expense...........................	1,700	
226	Depreciation expense..........................	22,000	
227	Miscellaneous expenses........................	2,700	
231	Interest expense..............................	11,900	
232	Income tax expense...........................	4,900	
	Totals....................................	$434,540	$434,540

Requirement   (5):   **Income Statement**
For the Year Ended June 30, 1974

Revenue:

Rent revenue........................ $91,800*

Operating expenses:

Utilities and telephone expense.........	$26,040	
Apartment maintenance expense........	1,200	
Salary and wage expense..............	3,000	
Insurance expense....................	1,000	
Property tax expense.................	1,700	
Depreciation expense.................	22,000	
Miscellaneous expense................	2,700	
Total operating expenses.......		57,640

Income from apartment operations........   34,160
Financial expense:

Interest expense........................   11,900

Pretax net income.......................   22,260
Income tax expense.....................   4,900

Net income........................... $17,360

Earnings per share: $17,360 ÷ 6,000 shares = $2.89

* Notes:
(a)   These amounts were taken directly from Requirement (4), the trial balance.
(b)   Since no products are sold by this business, there is no gross margin.

Requirement (6):

LA PALOMA APARTMENTS
Balance Sheet
At June 30, 1974

Assets

Current Assets:
Cash......................................	$ 30,900*	
Accounts receivable..........................	1,800	
Supplies inventory............................	400	
Prepaid insurance...........................	2,000	
Total current assets......................		$ 35,100

Fixed Assets:
Land—apartment site........................		30,000	
La Paloma apartment building.................	$200,000		
Less accumulated depreciation on building.....	20,000	180,000	
Furniture and fixtures.........................	60,000		
Less accumulated depreciation on furniture and fixtures.................................	24,000	36,000	
Total fixed assets........................			246,000

Other Assets:
Land acquired for future apartment site.........	35,000
Total Assets.............................	$316,100

Liabilities

Current Liabilities:
Accounts payable...........................	$ 1,140	
Property taxes payable.......................	1,700	
Income taxes payable........................	4,900	
Total current liabilities....................		$ 7,740

Long-term Liabilities:
Mortgage payable...........................	171,000	
Note payable, long-term......................	30,000	
Total long-term liabilities.................		201,000
Total Liabilities		208,740

Stockholders' Equity

Contributed capital:
Capital stock, par $10 (6,000 shares)...........	60,000	
Contributed capital in excess of par............	20,000	
Total contributed capital...................	80,000	
Retained earnings (beginning balance $10,000 + net income $17,360)........................	27,360	
Total stockholders' equity.................		107,360
Total Liabilities and Stockholders' Equity...		$316,100

* These amounts were taken directly from Requirement (4), the trial balance.

Summary   In this chapter we focused on the fundamental accounting model and the accounting information-processing system; they are outlined for study purposes in Exhibit 4–8. We discussed the nature of transactions that provide the raw economic data for input into the accounting information system. We learned that the fundamental accounting model— Assets = Liabilities + Owners' Equity—provides the basic framework for transaction analysis. The accounting model provides for recording the dual effect of each transaction. It encompasses two balancing features, the conditions of which must be met with respect to each transaction and event recorded, viz: (1) assets equals liabilities plus owners' equity, and (2) debits equal credits. After analysis, the transactions are recorded (journalized) in the journal first; the resultant effects (i.e., the amounts debited and credited) then are posted to the

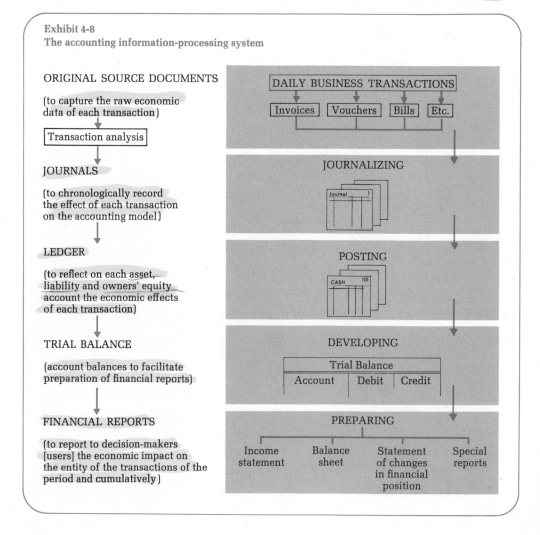

Exhibit 4-8
The accounting information-processing system

ORIGINAL SOURCE DOCUMENTS

(to capture the raw economic
data of each transaction)

Transaction analysis

JOURNALS

(to chronologically record
the effect of each transaction
on the accounting model)

LEDGER

(to reflect on each asset,
liability and owners' equity
account the economic effects
of each transaction)

TRIAL BALANCE

(account balances to facilitate
preparation of financial reports)

FINANCIAL REPORTS

(to report to decision-makers
[users] the economic impact on
the entity of the transactions of the
period and cumulatively)

DAILY BUSINESS TRANSACTIONS

Invoices | Vouchers | Bills | Etc.

JOURNALIZING

Journal   1

POSTING

CASH   101

DEVELOPING

Trial Balance

Account | Debit | Credit

PREPARING

Income   Balance   Statement   Special
statement   sheet   of changes   reports
                            in financial
                             position

ledger. The ledger reflects a separate account for each kind of asset and liability and for owners' equity. Normally, asset accounts will have debit balances, whereas liability and owners' equity accounts usually will have credit balances. The information-processing system, as a consequence, generates the data needed to develop the periodic financial statements: the income statement, balance sheet, and statement of changes in financial position.

The discussions in this chapter establish the basis for the accounting information-processing cycle for a business entity. It represents a cycle because it repeats itself each accounting period (usually one year). The steps in the information-processing cycle may be outlined as follows:

Step 1. Raw data collection—Economic data are collected for each transaction at the time of occurrence. Sales invoices, charge tickets, freight bills, notes, signed receipts, etc., are source documents used in this step.

Step 2. Transaction analysis—Each transaction undergoes transaction analysis to determine how it affects the fundamental accounting model: Assets = Liabilities + Owners' Equity.

Step 3. Journalizing—Each transaction is recorded *chronologically* in the journal, which indicates the date; accounts to be debited and credited; amounts; and, frequently, an explanation.

Step 4. Posting—Each amount entered in the journal is transferred, or posted, to the appropriate account in the ledger.

Step 5. Trial balance—At the end of the accounting period the balance in each account in the ledger is determined. The balance of each ledger account then is listed on a trial balance. The equality of debits and credits is checked.

Step 6. Financial statements—The information on the trial balance is utilized to develop the periodic financial statements composed of the income statement, balance sheet, and statement of changes in financial position.

As we progress in our study, additions to and elaborations of this information processing cycle will be introduced.

Important terms		
Transactions	Journal	
Account	Journalizing	
Debit	Posting	
Credit	Ledger	
Transaction analysis	Trial balance	
Fundamental accounting model		

	Questions for discussion	
Questions for discussion	1.	Define a business transaction. Why does accounting focus on the individual business transaction?
	2.	Accounting focuses on certain events. Define what is meant by a business transaction.
	3.	Give the fundamental accounting model and briefly explain each variable included in it, including revenues, expenses, and investments and withdrawals by owners.
	4.	Explain why revenues increase and expenses decrease owners' equity.
	5.	What is the meaning of "to debit" and "to credit"?
	6.	Complete the following matrix by entering either debit or credit in each cell.

Item	Increases	Decreases
Assets	DEBIT	CREDIT
Liabilities	CREDIT	DEBIT
Owners' equity	CREDIT	DEBIT
Revenues	DEBIT	CREDIT
Expenses	CREDIT	DEBIT

7. Complete the following matrix by entering either increase or decrease in each cell.

Item	Debit	Credit
Assets	I	D
Liabilities	D	I
Owners' equity	D	I
Revenues	I	D
Expenses	D	I

8. Define the ledger. What purpose does it serve?
9. Define the journal. What purpose does it serve?
10. What is a trial balance? What purpose does it serve?
11. Distinguish between a book of original entry and a book of final entry.
12. Distinguish between journalizing and posting.
13. Outline the information-processing cycle for a business entity.
14. What does the term "audit trail" imply?
15. Define a fiscal period as used in accounting.

Exercises E4–1. The PT Service Company has just been organized by Paul Tate, the sole owner. The following transactions have been completed:
(a) Tate invested $20,000 cash in the business.

(b) Equipment for use in the business was purchased at a cost of $2,000; one-half was paid in cash and the balance is due in six months.

(c) Service fees were earned amounting to $30,000, of which $5,000 was on credit.

(d) Operating expenses incurred amounted to $20,000, of which $3,000 was on credit.

(e) Cash was collected for $2,500 of the service fees performed on credit in (c) above.

(f) Paid cash, $1,500, on the operating expenses that were on credit in (d) above.

Required:

You are requested to set up a format similar to the following and enter thereon each of the above transactions. Transaction (*a*) is entered as an example.

Transactions	*Assets*	=	*Liabilities*	+ *Owner's Equity*
(*a*) Investment of cash in the business	Cash + $20,000			Capital, P. Tate + $20,000

Also determine the total amounts for assets, liabilities, and owner's equity after entry (*f*).

E4–2.   The Cox Service Company completed the following transactions during the current accounting period:

Transaction (a)   Fees earned for services amounted to $20,000, of which $18,000 was collected in cash.

Transaction (b)   Operating expenses incurred amounted to $14,000, of which $13,000 was paid in cash.

Transaction (c)   Acquired two machines for operating purposes at the start of the year at a cost of $600 each; paid cash.

Transaction (d)   One of the machines was destroyed by fire one week after purchase; it was uninsured. The event to be considered is the fire. (Hint: Set up a fire loss account.)

Transaction (e)   The other machine has an estimated useful life to Cox of three years. The event to be considered is the depreciation of the equipment since it was used for one year in rendering services.

Required:

Set up T-accounts and enter in them the dual effects on the accounting model of each of the above transactions. Key the amounts to the letters (a) through (e). Number the accounts starting with 101 for Cash.

E4–3.   The following T-accounts for Blye Service Company, owned by T. Blye, reflect five different transactions (entries). You are requested to write a description of each transaction; also indicate the debits and credits by account.

	Cash				Accounts Payable				Capital, T. Blye	
(a)	10,000	(c)	7,000	(e)	1,000	(c)	2,000		(a)	10,000
(b)	13,000	(e)	1,000							
(d)	2,000									

Service Revenue Earned

	Accounts Receivable						(b)	16,000
(b)	3,000	(d)	2,000					

Operating Expenses Incurred

(c)	9,000

E4–4. On January 1, 1974, Roy Roe and Sam Sly organized the R&S Service Company as a partnership. The transactions of the company for the first 45 days are stated below. You are requested to analyze each transaction and enter it in a journal similar to the one illustrated in Exhibit 4–7.

Jan. 1   Cash invested by the partners was: Roe $10,000, Sly $5,000.

Jan. 3   Paid monthly rent, $200.

Jan. 15   Purchased equipment for use in the business costing $15,000; paid ⅓ down and signed a 6% note payable for the balance. Monthly payments comprised of part principal and part interest are to be paid on the note.

Jan. 30   Paid cash for operating expenses amounting to $8,000; in addition, operating expenses of $2,000 were incurred on credit.

Jan. 30   Service fees earned amounted to $17,000, of which $14,000 was collected and the balance was on credit.

Feb. 10   Collected $1,000 on account for service fees previously performed on credit.

Feb. 15   Paid $250 on the equipment note, including $50 interest expense.

E4–5. Brown's Air Conditioning Service Company, Incorporated, has been operating for three years. Tim Brown, the majority shareholder, has built it up from a one-man to a ten-man operation. Very few records have been maintained; however, Mr. Brown is beginning to realize the need for a complete accounting system. The size and complexity of the business is partially indicated by the following selected transactions for 1974.

Jan. 15   Purchased two new service trucks at $3,600 each; paid ½ down and signed a one-year note for the balance. Monthly payments, including interest, are to be made on the note.

Jan. 31   Service revenue earned in January amounted to $23,000, including $3,000 on credit (due in 90 days).

Feb. 5   Dividends amounting to $1,000 were paid in cash. (Hint: This decreases owners' equity.)

Feb. 6 Operating expenses incurred in January amounted to $16,000, including $2,000 on credit (payable in 60 days).

Feb. 15 Paid $350 on the truck note, which included $36 interest.

Apr. 15 Paid 1973 taxes on business property, $100; this amount was recorded in 1973 as a liability.

May 1 Collected $2,500 of the services extended on credit in January.

Required:

(a) Journalize the above transactions in a form similar to that illustrated in Exhibit 4–7. Number the journal pages consecutively, starting with 51.

(b) Post to T-accounts in the ledger; utilize the folio columns and enter dates. Number the ledger accounts consecutively, starting with 101 for the Cash account. As you post, keep in mind that there would be prior amounts carried over from 1973 in most of the ledger accounts.

E4–6. The Stacey Service Company is in a situation where a considerable amount of credit is typical. When it was first organized by Oral Stacey, the only records maintained were for cash receipts and cash payments. Stacey reported that "I watched my cash balance to see how I was doing; if cash went up I assumed a profit, and, to the contrary if cash went down I assumed a loss." As Stacey Company grew and became more involved in credit, Oral realized that "I must look at the revenue earned and the expenses incurred on an accrual basis, as well as just the cash situation." Illustrative of the situation is the following information for Stacey Company for the month of January 1974:

Service revenues:	
Cash collected for services performed in January 1974	$30,000
Services performed in January 1974 on credit	2,000
Operating expenses:	
Cash paid for expenses incurred in January 1974	15,000
Expenses incurred in January 1974 on credit	18,000

Required:

(a) Prepare a special statement on a cash basis to reflect cash inflows, cash outflows, and the change in cash occasioned by the above summarized transactions.

(b) Prepare an income statement (accrual basis) to show computation of revenues earned, expenses incurred, and the differences (i.e., net income or loss).

(c) Basically, what does this suggest as to the inappropriateness of cash amounts in reflecting profit performance for January?

E4–7. The bookkeeper of Tacy Company, a sole proprietorship, prepared the following trial balance at December 31, 1974:

Accounts	Debit	Credit
Accounts receivable.................	$ 4,000	
Accounts payable.................	800	
Land...........................	16,000	
Capital, Tacy.....................		$20,000
Cash...........................	7,000	
Notes payable, long-term............		5,000
Operating expenses.................	19,000	
Interest expense...................		800
Other assets.....................	9,583	
Service revenues...................		30,583
Total.....................	$56,383	$56,383

The independent CPA (auditor) casually inspected the trial balance and concluded there were two errors on it. You have been requested to draft a correct trial balance.

(Hint: All of the amounts are correct.)

Problems P4–1.   Listed below are the ledger accounts of the AAA Rental Company, Incorporated. Indicate whether the balance in each account usually would be a debit or a credit.

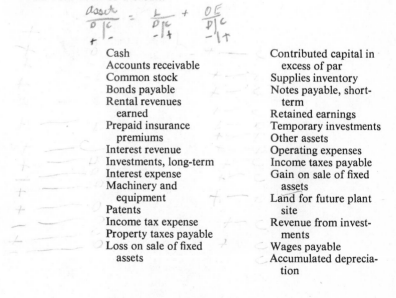

Cash	Contributed capital in
Accounts receivable	excess of par
Common stock	Supplies inventory
Bonds payable	Notes payable, short-
Rental revenues	term
earned	Retained earnings
Prepaid insurance	Temporary investments
premiums	Other assets
Interest revenue	Operating expenses
Investments, long-term	Income taxes payable
Interest expense	Gain on sale of fixed
Machinery and	assets
equipment	Land for future plant
Patents	site
Income tax expense	Revenue from invest-
Property taxes payable	ments
Loss on sale of fixed	Wages payable
assets	Accumulated deprecia-
	tion

P4–2.   Listed below are a series of accounts for Quality Service Company, Incorporated. The accounts are numbered for identification. Below the accounts are a series of transactions. Using the format in the example, list the transaction letters, write the appropriate account identification number(s) beside them, and indicate whether the accounts should be debited or credited.

1. Cash	9. Notes payable
2. Accounts receivable	10. Wages payable
3. Supplies inventory	11. Income taxes payable
4. Prepaid insurance premiums	12. Capital stock
5. Equipment	13. Contributed capital in excess of par
6. Allowance for depreciation of equipment	14. Service revenues earned
7. Patents	15. Operating expenses
8. Accounts payable	16. Income tax expense
	17. Interest expense

Transaction	Debit	Credit
a. Investment by shareholders to start the business (example).	1	12,13
b. Purchased equipment for use in business; paid ½ cash and gave note payable for balance.		
c. Paid cash for salaries and wages.		
d. Collected cash for services performed this period.		
e. Collected cash for services performed last period.		
f. Performed services this period on credit.		
g. Paid operating expenses incurred this period.		
h. Paid cash for operating expenses incurred last period.		
i. Incurred operating expenses this period, to be paid next period.		
j. Purchased supplies for inventory; paid cash.		
k. Used some of the supplies from inventory for operations.		
l. Purchased a patent; paid cash.		
m. Made a payment on the equipment note (b) above; the payment was in part on principal and in part interest thereon.		
n. Collected cash on accounts receivable for services previously performed.		
o. Paid cash on accounts payable for expenses previously incurred.		
p. Paid ¾ of the income tax expense for the year; the balance to be paid next period.		
q. On last day of current period, paid in cash an insurance premium covering the next three years.		

P4–3. Bowles Home Repair Service was started two years ago by Henry Bowles as sole owner. By the end of the second year, three "crews" were operating and Harry felt that the business was a success. Although his prices were high, his customers appeared pleased in view of the quality of the work done and the efficiency with which repairs were completed. The following account balances were reflected by the ledger on January 1, 1974:

Accounts	Debit	Credit
Cash...	$ 8,500	
Accounts receivable............................	3,400	
Building supplies inventory		
(for use on repair jobs)........................	1,000	
Trucks..	12,000	
Accumulated depreciation on trucks................		$ 4,800
Accounts payable..............................		4,000
Note payable, short-term........................		5,000
Wages payable................................		100
Note payable, long-term.........................		10,000
Capital, Harry Bowles...........................		1,000
Totals................................	$24,900	$24,900

During 1974 the following transactions occurred:

(a) Paid the $100 wages payable carried over from 1973.

(b) Purchased, for cash, additional building supplies for future use, $1,200 (debit the Building Supplies Inventory account).

(c) Purchased an additional truck "as a backup" for $4,200 cash.

(d) Collected $2,400 cash on the accounts receivable.

(e) Paid off the $5,000 short-term note, plus six months' interest at 8% per annum.

(f) Bowles invested an additional $3,000 cash in the business.

(g) Repair fees earned in 1974, $67,000 including $5,000 earned in 1974 but uncollected.

(h) Paid operating expenses of $44,000 cash. Additional operating expenses of $3,000 were incurred; the cash will be paid for these in 1975.

(i) According to an inventory count of the building supplies at December 31, 1974, unused supplies amounted to $800.
(Hint: Supplies used should be debited to operating expenses: supplies used = amount on hand at start + additional purchased − ending inventory.)

(j) Depreciation on the three trucks was computed on the basis of an estimated useful life of five years. The new truck will not be depreciated in 1974 since it was acquired near the end of the year.

(k) Paid $5,000 on the long-term note, plus 7% interest on the $10,000 for one year.

(l) Paid $6,000 on accounts payable.

Required:

(1) Set up the ledger accounts listed above and enter the beginning balances; label these as "Balance."

(2) Analyze each transaction, then enter it directly in the ledger accounts (you will have to add a few additional accounts). Key your entries with the letter designation (in place of a date).

(3) Prepare a trial balance at December 31, 1974.

(4) Show computation of net income.
(Hint: Net income is $15,300.)

P4–4.   Braley's Stenographic and Mailing Service, Incorporated, was organized by three individuals during January 1974. Each investor paid in
$2,500 cash and received 200 shares of $10 par-value stock. During
1974 the transactions listed below occurred. The letters at the left of
each item will serve as the date notation.

a.   Received the investment by the organizers.
b.   Purchased office equipment costing $4,000; paid cash.
c.   Paid $300 cash for a three-year insurance premium on the office
equipment.
d.   Purchased a panel delivery truck at a cost of $3,400; paid $2,000
down and charged the balance.
e.   Purchased office supplies for cash to be used in the stenographic
and mailing operations, $2,000. The supplies are for future use;
therefore, debit Office Supplies Inventory.
f.   Revenues earned during the year were:

	Cash	On Credit
Stenographic fees.	$38,000	$4,000
Mailing fees.	7,000	1,000

g.   Operating expenses incurred during the year were:

Cash.	$16,000
On credit.	14,000

h.   On October 1, 1974, borrowed $5,000 from the bank on a 90-
day, 8% per annum note. The interest is payable at maturity
date of the note.
i.   Purchased land for a future building for operations at a cost of
$19,000; paid cash.
j.   Depreciation on the truck for 1974 was computed on the basis
of a five-year useful life; on the office equipment, useful life of
ten years was assumed (compute a full year depreciation on
each).
k.   By December 31, 1974, insurance for one year had expired.
Prepaid Insurance should be decreased and an expense recorded.
l.   An inventory of the office supplies reflected $200 on hand at
December 31, 1974. Supplies Inventory should be reduced and
an expense recognized.
m.   Paid the $5,000 note to the bank on December 31, 1974, plus
interest for 90 days.

Required:

(1)   You have been asked to analyze and prepare a journal entry
for each item listed. Use a form similar to Exhibit 4–7 and
include an explanation for each transaction.
(2)   After the above transactions are completed, compute the following amounts at the end of 1974:

Cash balance
Operating expenses
Interest expense

P4–5. The AB Delivery Service was organized as a corporation on June 1, 1973. The management decided that the fiscal year for the company would be June 1 to May 31. The following transactions were selected from the first year for case purposes; for convenience the letter identification has been used as the date.

a. Cash invested was $10,000 and 1,000 shares of $10 par-value capital stock was issued.

b. Three new delivery vehicles were purchased at a total cost of $10,000. One-half was paid in cash and an 8% note payable was signed for the balance.

c. Operating supplies costing $300 were purchased for cash. These supplies are to go into Operating Supplies Inventory and will be used gradually.

d. Delivery revenues earned amounted to $60,000, of which $10,000 was yet uncollected.

e. Operating expenses incurred amounted to $40,000, of which $7,000 was not yet paid in cash.

f. Paid cash for a three-year insurance premium in advance to insure the delivery equipment, $600.

g. Collected $6,000 on the credit extended for delivery services (item (d) above).

h. Paid $4,000 on the obligations for operating expenses (item (e) above).

i. An inventory count showed that ⅔ of the operating supplies purchased ((c) above) had been used by May 31, 1974.

j. Paid $1,000 on the note given on the delivery vehicles ((b) above), plus 12 months' interest (on $5,000).

k. Computed depreciation on the delivery vehicles for one year (up to May 31, 1974), assuming a five-year useful life.

l. On May 31, 1974, insurance for one year had expired.

Required:

(1) Set up a journal similar to Exhibit 4–7, then journalize each item.

(2) Post the journal entries to ledger accounts; number the ledger accounts starting with 101 for Cash.

(3) Prepare a trial balance at May 31, 1974.
    (Hint: The trial balance totals are $79,000.)

P4–6. The ledger accounts for Black Real Estate Agency, a corporation (organized three years previously) owned by Roy and Bill Black, provided the annual trial balance shown below at March 31, 1974 (the end of the fiscal year).

Trial Balance at March 31, 1974

Account Title	Debit	Credit
Cash..	$ 33,000	
Accounts receivable...........................	48,900	
Office supplies inventory.......................	200	
Automobiles (company cars).....................	6,000	
Accumulated depreciation on automobiles...........		$ 4,000
Office equipment..............................	2,000	
Accumulated depreciation on office equipment........		1,000
Accounts payable..............................		2,000
Salaries and commissions payable..................		1,000
Notes payable, long-term........................		20,000
Capital stock (3,000 shares)......................		30,000
Contributed capital in excess of par...............		3,000
Retained earnings (on April 1, 1973)...............		5,000
Dividends paid during the year....................	10,000	
Sales commissions earned........................		70,000
Management fees earned.........................		6,000
Operating expenses (detail omitted to conserve time)..	40,000	
Depreciation expense (on autos and office		
equipment)..................................	500	
Interest expense...............................	1,400	
Totals................................	$142,000	$142,000

Required:

(a) Prepare a classified income statement for the year ending March 31, 1974. To simplify, disregard income taxes.
(Hint: EPS $11.37.)

(b) Prepare a classified balance sheet at March 31, 1974.
(Hint: Refer to Chapter 3 for examples of classified statements.)

P4–7. Able, Baker, and Cain organized ABC Realty as a corporation to conduct a real estate and rental management business. Each contributed $12,000 cash and received 100 shares of stock (par value $100 per share). They commenced business on January 1, 1974. The transactions listed below are representative of those during the year. We have selected only a few of the actual transactions for case purposes. Also assume that these transactions comprise all of the transactions for the year. This case demonstrates the information processing cycle from the capture of raw economic data to the final output —the financial statements. Use the numbers at the left as the date notation.

1. Receipt of $36,000 cash invested by shareholders and issuance of 300 shares of stock.
2. Purchase of office equipment costing $3,000; paid ⅓ cash and charged the balance (⅓ due in 6 months, remainder due in 15 months). Credit Accounts Payable for the amount not paid in cash.
3. Purchased land for future office site at a cost of $20,000; paid cash.
4. Paid office rent in cash, 11 months at $100 per month. Be-

ginning with this transaction, set up separate accounts for each type of expense.

5. Sold nine properties and collected commissions of $37,000. Set up an account "Realty Commissions."
6. Paid salaries and commissions amounting to $27,800 and miscellaneous expenses amounting to $1,000.
7. Collected rental management fees, $8,000. Set up an account "Rental Management Fees."
8. Paid utilities, $900.
9. Paid auto rental fees (auto rented for use in business), $1,800.
10. Paid for advertising, $5,000.
11. At year end, the December rent had not been paid.
12. The estimated life of the office equipment was ten years; assume use for the full year in 1974.
13. At year end, commissions earned during 1974 on sale of real estate amounting to $13,000 were uncollected and had not been recorded.
14. Paid the installment on the office equipment (see (2) above).
15. Assume a corporate income tax rate of 22%; the tax expense will be paid in 1975.

Required:

(a) Analyze, then journalize, each of the above entries; number your journal pages consecutively, starting with 1.
(b) Post each transaction from the journal to the ledger; use T-accounts and number your ledger accounts consecutively, starting with 101 for Cash. Use folio cross-references.
(c) Take a trial balance from the ledger; check the equality of debits and credits.
   (Hint: Trial balance total is $99,800.)
(d) Use the data on the trial balance to prepare a classified income statement and balance sheet. Refer to Chapter 3 for examples of classified statements. Because of its complexity, we will defer preparing a statement of changes in financial position until a later chapter.
   (Hint: EPS $52.)

P4–8. The Ace Moving and Storage Company was organized four years ago as a partnership by Oscar Snow and Ray Dean; they share profits equally. Each contributed $20,000 cash initially and, since that time, a good portion of the profits have been left in the business for growth. Ace owns a large warehouse and 11 hauling vans. At the beginning, very few financial records were maintained; however, they now have one person who devotes all of his time to records and reports. Some disagreements with the Internal Revenue Service and tentative discussions of the possibility of changing to a corporation prompted Snow and Dean to approach an independent CPA for advice. As a consequence, the first audit was performed for 1973. For purposes of this case, we will utilize only representative accounts and transactions in order to minimize the time requirements. Assume that the accounts for Ace showed the following balance on January 1, 1974 (the fiscal and calendar years agree):

Account No.	Account	Debit	Credit
101	Cash.....................................	$ 20,000	
103	Accounts receivable........................	12,000	
110	Supplies inventory........................	3,000	
112	Prepaid insurance..........................		
131	Land (on which warehouse is located)........	10,000	
133	Warehouse................................	60,000	
134	Accumulated depreciation, warehouse........		$ 12,000
135	Moving vans..............................	75,000	
136	Accumulated depreciation, moving vans.......		30,000
151	Land for future office building...............		
201	Accounts payable..........................		9,000
210	Notes payable, long-term (7%)..............		30,000
301	Capital, Oscar Snow.......................		48,000
302	Withdrawals during the year, Oscar Snow......		
305	Capital, Ray Dean.........................		51,000
306	Withdrawals during the year, Ray Dean.......		
401	Trucking revenues.........................		
402	Storage revenues..........................		
501	Operating expenses........................		
502	Depreciation expense.......................		
505	Interest expense...........................		
	Totals.................................	$180,000	$180,000

Representative transactions for 1974 follow (use the letter notation at the left for dating purposes):

(a) Purchased land for future office building at a cost of $15,000; paid cash.

(b) Revenues earned:

	Cash	Credit
Trucking...............	$180,000	$30,000
Storage................	20,000	1,000

(c) Paid $1,500 cash for a three-year insurance premium covering trucks, warehouse, etc. (assume this payment was made on January 1, 1974).

(d) Purchased additional supplies for use in operations for cash, $1,300; these supplies are to be used as needed. Debit account 110.

(e) At end of 1974 paid $10,000 on the long-term note payable, plus 7% interest on the $30,000 for 12 months.

(f) Operating expenses incurred:

Cash..................	$150,000
On credit.............	17,000

(g) Collections on accounts receivable (for trucking and storage services on credit), $35,000 (see (b) above).

(h) Payments on accounts payable (expenses and services previously incurred on credit), $18,000 cash.

(i) Withdrawals of cash by partners for personal use: Snow, $12,-000; Dean, $11,000. Debit accounts 302 and 306.

(j) Depreciation expense for 1974 was computed on the basis of a useful life of: warehouse, 20 years; moving vans, 5 years.

(k) On December 31, 1974, an inventory showed supplies on hand (unused) amounting to $1,000. Reduce Supplies Inventory and recognize an expense.

(l) On December 31, 1974, insurance for one year had expired (see item (c) above).

Required:

(1) Set up T-accounts for each account listed above (this list includes all of the accounts needed) and enter therein the balances given in the following manner:

Cash	101
Balance 20,000	

(2) Set up a journal similar to Exhibit 4–7 and enter each of the transactions. Use the letter designation for dating and include short explanations. Number the journal pages consecutively.

(3) Post each transaction entered in the journal to the ledger; use the folio columns in both the journal and ledger.

(4) Prepare a trial balance from the ledger accounts at December 31, 1974.

(Hint: the trial balance total is $418,000.)

(5) Prepare a classified income statement and balance sheet. See Chapter 3 for examples of classified statements. Show the following detail on the balance sheet for the owner's equity of each partner:

```
Capital, name, January 1, 1974.................. $xx
Add: Share of net income for 1974..............  xx
     Total.....................................  xx
Less: Withdrawals during 1974..................  xx
Capital, name, December 31, 1974..............       $xx
```
(Hint: Net income is $40,100.)

P4–9. (Note: This is a special case to test your analytical skills.) Simon Lavoie, a local attorney, decided to sell his practice and retire. He has had discussions with an attorney from another state who desires to relocate. The discussions have entered the complex stage of agreeing on a price. Among the important factors have been the financial statements on Mr. Lavoie's practice. Mr. Lavoie's secretary, under his direction, maintained the records. Each year they developed a "Statement of Profits" on a cash basis from the incomplete records maintained, and no balance sheet was prepared. Upon request, Mr. Lavoie provided the other attorney with the following statement of profits for 1974 prepared by his secretary:

S. LAVOIE
Statement of Profits, 1974

Legal fees collected............................		$62,000
Expenses paid:		
Rent for office space.........................	$ 3,900	
Utilities....................................	360	
Telephone.................................	2,900	
Office salaries..............................	19,000	
Office supplies.............................	900	
Miscellaneous expenses......................	1,600	
Total expenses.....................		28,660
Profit for the year............................		$33,340

Upon agreement of the parties, you have been asked to "look into the financial figures for 1974." The other attorney appeared to question the figures, especially since they are on a "100% cash basis." Your investigations have revealed the following additional data at December 31, 1974:

a. Of the legal fees collected in 1974, $18,000 was for services performed prior to 1974.

b. At the end of 1974, legal fees of $7,000 that were performed during the year were uncollected.

c. Office equipment owned and used by Lavoie cost $3,000 and had an estimated useful life of ten years.

d. An inventory of office supplies reflected $200 worth of items purchased during the year that were still on hand.

e. At the end of 1974 a secretary, whose salary is $7,200 per year, had not been paid for December since she had taken a trip that extended to January 15 of 1975.

f. The phone bill for December, 1974, amounting to $300, was not paid until January 11, 1975.

g. The office rent paid of $3,900 was for 13 months (it included the rent for January 1975).

Required:

On the basis of the above information, prepare an income statement for 1974 on an accrual basis. Show your computations for any amounts changed from those in the statement prepared by Lavoie's secretary.

5 Periodic matching of expenses with revenue and information processing

Purpose
of the
chapter

Net income is one of the more significant single amounts developed through the accounting process. In this chapter we will focus on several critical issues involved in the measurement of net income and the processing of revenue and expense data. In Part One we will examine some of the complications posed when the life span of a business is divided into selected time periods, such as one year. We will consider the problem of realistically identifying revenues within the selected time period and then identifying the expenses that were incurred in order to generate the revenue for that period. In Part Two the information-processing cycle, introduced in Chapter 4 (pages 95 and 99), will be expanded to include certain procedures used in matching expenses with revenue for the period.

PART ONE: MATCHING EXPENSES WITH REVENUE EACH PERIOD

Relation-
ships among
financial
statements

In the preceding chapters the three periodic financial statements required for external reporting were discussed; however, the relationships among them were considered only indirectly. In Chapter 3 we stated that the three statements, plus the accompanying notes and the auditor's opinion, should be viewed as a single reporting package. In order to understand the overall financial aspects of a business, and for many decisions, the entire reporting package generally is needed. Exhibit 5–1 presents the basic relationships among the three financial statements for a fiscal year—January 1 through December 31, 1974. In this exhibit you can visualize the starting point as the financial position or

124

balance sheet at the beginning of the year and the ending point as the financial position or balance sheet at the end of the year. The changes in financial position between the starting and ending points are communicated to the users by two different change statements; they are:

1. Income statement—The income statement reports changes during the period as a result of operations. Net income increases owners' equity and this is graphically shown in Exhibit 5–1, Part (1). The detailed amounts that caused this change in owners' equity (or financial position) during the period appear on the income state-

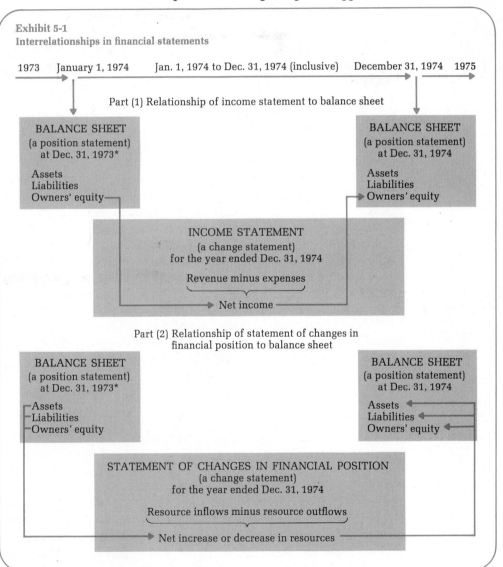

Exhibit 5-1
Interrelationships in financial statements

1973   January 1, 1974   Jan. 1, 1974 to Dec. 31, 1974 (inclusive)   December 31, 1974   1975

Part (1) Relationship of income statement to balance sheet

BALANCE SHEET
(a position statement)
at Dec. 31, 1973*

Assets
Liabilities
Owners' equity

BALANCE SHEET
(a position statement)
at Dec. 31, 1974

Assets
Liabilities
Owners' equity

INCOME STATEMENT
(a change statement)
for the year ended Dec. 31, 1974

Revenue minus expenses

Net income

Part (2) Relationship of statement of changes in
financial position to balance sheet

BALANCE SHEET
(a position statement)
at Dec. 31, 1973*

Assets
Liabilities
Owners' equity

BALANCE SHEET
(a position statement)
at Dec. 31, 1974

Assets
Liabilities
Owners' equity

STATEMENT OF CHANGES IN FINANCIAL POSITION
(a change statement)
for the year ended Dec. 31, 1974

Resource inflows minus resource outflows

Net increase or decrease in resources

* This also is the balance sheet at the beginning of 1974.

ment. Therefore, the income statement also reports detailed information to explain one of the changes in financial position during the period.

2. Statement of changes in financial position—This statement has been designed to report, or explain, the causes of the changes in assets, liabilities, and contributed capital during the period. Thus, this statement reports the inflows and outflows of resources during the period. It explains how resources were generated and used.

The
time-period
assumption
in
accounting

Each financial statement should include in the heading a specific statement as to the time dimension of the report (see Chapter 2, page 31). Exhibit 5–1 re-emphasizes the point that the balance sheet is at a specific date, and the two "change" statements cover a specified period of time.

The life span of most business entities is indefinite. Society in general "lives by the calendar." This fact requires that the life span of an entity be divided into short time periods, such as one year, for many measurement purposes, including financial reporting. The business community assumes that the activities of a business can be divided into time periods. Thus, the time-period assumption (see Exhibit 2–1) is fundamental to the accounting process and financial reporting. Under this assumption, the business activities of the entity are divided into a specific time period, such as one year, for accounting measurements. As a consequence, we focus on the annual financial statements.

Because annual periods tend to be dominant throughout our society, the accounting period generally is viewed as being 12 consecutive months. Many firms utilize a fiscal year that corresponds to the natural cycle of the business rather than to the calendar year. In addition to the annual financial statements, many businesses also prepare and publish quarterly reports for external parties. These usually are called interim reports. Monthly financial statements frequently are prepared; however, they are exclusively for internal management purposes. In the paragraphs to follow you will see that dividing the life span of a business into short periods of time often poses complex measurement and reporting problems.

Matching
expenses
with
revenue

Dividing the life span of a business into short time periods, such as a year, for measurement purposes often poses complex accounting problems because some transactions start in one accounting period and are concluded in a subsequent period. For example, the prepayment of a three-year insurance premium occurs in one accounting period, yet each of the three periods covered by the insurance must be assigned a fair share of the expense. As another example, assume a machine is purchased this year that has an estimated useful life of ten years.

During each of those ten years a fair share of the cost of the machine must be apportioned as the annual depreciation expense. Similarly, revenue may start in one accounting period and conclude in a subsequent period. For example, the collection by a magazine publisher of a three-year subscription price in one accounting period requires that a fair share of the total be assigned to each of the three periods as the revenue is earned.

Earning revenues through sales and services and the incurring of expenses necessary to generate those revenues is a continuous process. Some transactions cover an extended period of time between their initiation and final completion; yet, financial reports must be made for a specific time period, such as a month, quarter, or year. Thus, there must be a cutoff between periods so that the revenues and expenses for each period can be accurately measured.

Frequently, it is difficult to identify each specific revenue and expense with a particular accounting period. In response to this problem, the revenue principle and the matching principle have evolved as two of the broad fundamentals underlying accounting (see Exhibit 2–1). These two principles focus on the measurement of net income for each period. *The revenue principle takes precedence in the measurement process.* First, the revenue earned for the period from the sales of goods and services is measured; next, the matching principle is applied to measure the expenses incurred in generating that revenue. For accounting measurement purposes, the revenue and matching principles require a careful cutoff of revenues and expenses at the end of each accounting period.

The revenue principle. The revenue principle was defined in Chapter 2 (page 32). This principle holds that revenue should be measured in the period in which it is earned, or realized. In identifying revenues with a specific period for measurement purposes, one must look to *when* the various transactions occurred rather than to the period in which the cash inflows occurred. The income statement for each particular period must report all of the revenue earned, or realized, in the period but must not report any revenue earned in a prior or following period.

The general guideline is that revenue is earned when a sales transaction is made (consummated) or when services are rendered. In the case of sales or services for cash, this guideline is easy to apply; however, in the case of credit sales or services, problems often arise. Sales or services made on the "normal" short-term credit basis follow the general rule, irrespective of whether there is a down payment. In contrast, sales and services made on a long-term credit basis, and with little or no down payment, pose the question of the risk that complete payment will not be made ultimately. The accounting profession has developed guidelines for such situations. For example, in the case of land development companies, it is the practice to sell undeveloped land for a down payment of around 5% with a 10- to 30-year payout period. For this particular industry, the guideline is that sales revenue cannot be recognized until the period in which the down payment reaches 10%. (There are some related accounting complexities in this industry that are beyond the scope of this book.)

Many companies sell large items of merchandise (such as a television set) on the **installment plan.** The usual provisions of an installment plan are: (a) a relatively small down payment is required; (b) the payment period is long and calls for monthly payments on principal plus interest; and (c) the seller retains conditional title to the goods. These provisions, in combination, mean that there is a relatively high risk of reclaims of the merchandise because of nonpayment. The installment method of accounting has been developed to meet this type of situation. Under this method the revenue is recognized as the **cash is collected.** As a consequence, this method is very close to cash-basis accounting.

Another difficult problem arises in respect to long-term construction contracts. For example, assume a building contractor signs a contract to build a large building at a cost of $3,500,000, and the construction period is three years, starting January 1, 19A. Now, assume further that the cost of the building to the contractor is estimated to be approximately $3,200,000; that is, a net income of approximately $300,000. The question is: Should the $300,000 income be reported as earned in 19C or allocated on a fair basis to each of the three years? One method, called the **completed-contract method,** is a conservative one in that no revenue is recognized until net income (the $300,000) can be measured with certainty; that is, in 19C, the period of final completion. In contrast, the **allocation method** permits the recognition of revenue on the basis of estimates covering the three-year period. Thus, a portion of the $300,000 would be recognized as revenue each year. The allocation method generally is called the **percentage-of-completion method.** At the present time the contractor is permitted to select either method. Many accountants believe that this choice between two alternatives for the same set of facts is not sound. Many believe that the $300,000 income should be allocated to each of the three periods based upon percentage-of-completion of the building by years (generally estimated by the architects). Of course, other accountants prefer the completed-contract method. Lack of agreement as to the best measurement approach primarily is the reason for the permission of alternatives. There are a number of other areas of accounting where measurement alternatives are permitted for the same set of facts. The profession is striving to eliminate this type of alternative.

The matching principle. Expenses were defined in Chapter 2 (page 32). The matching principle focuses on the measurement of expenses and the matching of them with the periodic revenues generated as a result of the resources used. *Directly, the matching principle holds that all of the expenses incurred in generating revenue should be identified, or matched, with the revenue generated, period by period.*

In measuring and matching expenses with revenue, one must look to the **purpose** for which the expenses were incurred. If it was to generate revenue, as is the usual purpose, those expenses should be identified with the period in which the revenues were recognized as earned. In this way the expenses are matched with the revenue of each period so that net income for each period is correctly measured. Expenses incurred in generating the revenue earned for the period must be reported in that period. Resources expended in one period to generate revenues in other periods must be apportioned to those other periods.

Application of the matching principle often requires that special accounting entries be made at the end of the accounting period so that a cutoff of revenues and expenses is attained for measurement purposes as between periods. These special entries generally are called **adjusting entries** because they result in the adjustment of some account balances at the end of the accounting period. There are four types of transactions that often cause adjusting entries:

Expenses:

1. *Recorded costs* that must be apportioned between two or more accounting periods. Three examples are:
    (a) The cost of a three-year insurance premium paid in advance and recorded as a prepaid expense. The prepaid cost must be apportioned, as insurance expense, over each of the following accounting periods.
    (b) The cost of a machine having a five-year useful life and recorded as an asset. The cost must be apportioned to each of the five years as depreciation expense.
    (c) The cost of items purchased in advance of use, such as supplies, and recorded as an asset (Supplies Inventory). The cost must be apportioned as an expense to the periods in which the supplies are actually used.
2. *Unrecorded expenses* that nevertheless must be identified with the current period. Three examples are:
    (a) Wages earned by employees in the current period but not paid until the next period. They must be recorded as an expense in the current period because that is when the services were received. Unpaid wages are often called *accrued* wages.
    (b) Taxes incurred in the current period but not paid until the next period.
    (c) Interest cost on money borrowed during the current period with payment of the interest in the next period.

Revenue:

3. *Recorded revenue* that must be apportioned between two or more accounting periods: Example: rent revenue collected in advance

of the period in which occupancy occurs. The revenue must be *deferred* and identified with the period of occupancy.

4. *Unrecorded revenues* that were earned in the current period but are to be collected in a subsequent period. Example: rent revenue earned due to occupancy during the current period but uncollected at the end of the current period.

At the end of each accounting period, after the regular entries are completed, the accountant must make a careful check of the records and supporting documents to determine whether or not there are any situations such as those listed above for which **adjusting entries** should be made. One or more such entries invariably will be required at the end of each accounting period. If these adjusting entries are overlooked, revenue may be measured incorrectly and expenses may not be matched with revenues for the period. In either instance, the result would be incorrect measurement of amounts on both the income statement and the balance sheet.

Adjusting entries are not unusual. They require no additional competence, only a knowledge of the actual facts in respect to each item. In Chapters 3 and 4, the illustrations, exercises, and problems include several adjusting entries (depreciation expense, prepaid insurance, supplies used, and accrued or unpaid wages) routinely made without special identification or concern.

The two terms "accrued" (or to accrue) and "deferred" (or to defer) frequently are used in accounting. A straightforward and practical definitional statement for our purposes is: Accrued means unpaid (in the case of expenses) and uncollected (in the case of revenues); deferred means prepaid (in the case of expenses) and precollected (in the case of revenues). Thus:

KNOW

Item	Brief Definition	Balance Sheet Classification
1. Deferred expense	An expense paid, but not yet incurred	Asset
2. Accrued expense	An expense incurred, but not yet paid	Liability
3. Deferred revenue	A revenue collected, but not yet earned	Liability
4. Accrued revenue	A revenue earned, but not yet collected	Asset

Adjusting entries illustrated

Several examples of each of the four general types of adjusting entries were cited above. In this section we will examine each of the examples, the analysis of them, and the **adjusting entry** that should be made at the end of the period. This examination will serve to increase your understanding of the application of the accounting model and the measurement of revenues and expenses. Throughout the examples to follow, we will refer to High-Rise Apartments, and will assume that the current annual fiscal period ends December 31, 1974.

RECORDED COSTS APPORTIONED BETWEEN ACCOUNTING PERIODS

A company frequently must make an expenditure or incur a liability for assets or services that will benefit one or more future accounting periods. When such a transaction occurs, an asset is increased (debited). As the future periods pass, the asset cost is apportioned to *expense* so that there is a matching of expense with revenue for each of the periods affected. For High-Rise Apartments we will analyze three such transactions that occurred in 1974. (Note: Each entry is letter coded for reference in the illustrations to follow.)

Prepaid insurance. On January 1, 1974, High-Rise paid in advance a three-year insurance premium of $3,600 on an apartment building. The sequence of entries for this prepaid expense would be:

Entry on date of payment, January 1, 1974:

```
Prepaid Insurance........................... 3,600
    Cash....................................       3,600
    To record payment of premium.
```

(a) Adjusting entry at end of current period, December 31, 1974:

```
Insurance Expense........................... 1,200
    Prepaid Insurance.......................       1,200
    To record insurance expense for 12 months
    ($3,600 × 12/36).
```

The latter entry would be repeated at the end of 1975 and 1976. The adjusting entry serves two measurement purposes: (1) it apportions insurance expense to the current period for matching purposes, and (2) it adjusts (reduces) the Prepaid Insurance account to the correct asset amount for the unexpired insurance at the end of 1974. That is, at the end of 1974 the company was still entitled to two years of insurance protection and hence had an asset amounting to $2,400.

Depreciation. On January 1, 1973, a contractor completed an apartment building for High-Rise. The contract price of $360,000 was paid in cash. The building has an estimated useful life of 30 years and an estimated $60,000 *residual value* at the end of that time. The sequence of entries would be:

Entry on date of purchase, January 1, 1973:

```
Apartment Building...................... 360,000
    Cash................................       360,000
```

(b) Adjusting entry at end of current period, December 31, 1974:

DEC EXP
DEC ASSET

```
Depreciation Expense...................... 10,000
     Accumulated Depreciation, Building.....              10,000
     To record depreciation expense for one
     year.
```

The adjusting entry would be repeated at the end of each year over the life of the building. The **estimated** amount expected to be recovered when the asset is finally sold or disposed of is known as the **residual value** (sometimes it is called scrap value). For computing depreciation, the cost of the asset must be reduced by the residual value. The difference—$360,000 − $60,000 = $300,000—is the amount to be depreciated over the estimated useful life. Thus, the annual depreciation expense on the apartment building would be ($360,000 − $60,000) ÷ 30 years = $10,000.[1] The residual value of $60,000 is deducted since it is expected to be recovered at the end of the useful life. Again, the adjusting entry serves two measurement purposes: (1) it apportions a part of the cost of the building to expense for the current period for matching purposes, and (2) it adjusts (reduces) the amount of the asset to the amount of the unexpired cost of the asset. The credit to "Accumulated Depreciation, Building" could have been made directly to the building account with the same effect; however, it is desirable, for reporting purposes, to keep the balance of the asset account "Apartment Building" at original cost. This is accomplished by setting up a **contra,** or **offset,** account entitled "Accumulated Depreciation, Building." You will recall from Chapters 3 and 4 that on the balance sheet the building is shown on one line at cost with a deduction on the next line for accumulated depreciation (see Exhibit 3–2).

Supplies inventory. On March 1, 1974, maintenance supplies were purchased at a cost of $600. At the date of purchase they were placed in the supply room to be used as needed on a day-to-day basis. At the end of 1974, an inventory of the supply room was taken which indicated that $200 of supplies were still on hand; therefore, $400 must have been used in 1974. The sequence of entries would be:

Date of purchase, March 1, 1974:

INC   ASSET
DEC   ASSET

```
Inventory of Maintenance Supplies............... 600
     Cash.........................................          600
     To record purchase of supplies inventory.
```

(c)   Adjusting entry at end of current period, December 31, 1974:

---

[1] This example assumes straight-line depreciation; that is, an equal amount of depreciation expense is apportioned to each period. Other methods of depreciation will be discussed in Chapter 9.

> Maintenance Expense............................. 400
>   Inventory of Maintenance Supplies............   400
>   To record the amount of supplies used from
>   inventory ($600 − $200).

The adjusting entry serves two measurement purposes: (1) to apportion expense to 1974 for matching purposes, and (2) to adjust (reduce) the asset account Inventory to the cost of the supplies on hand carried over at the end of the period.

UNRECORDED EXPENSES

Most expenses are incurred and paid for during the same period; however, at the end of the period there usually are some expenses that have been **incurred** (i.e., the benefit realized) but not recorded since payment has not been made. These unpaid and unrecorded expenses frequently are referred to as accrued expenses. We will analyze three different situations encountered by High-Rise Apartments that started in 1974 and carried over to affect one or more future accounting periods.

Salary expense. On December 31, 1974, the manager of High-Rise was on a trip and due to return January 10, 1975. As a consequence, his December salary of $600 was not yet paid. The sequence of entries for the accrued salary expense would be (disregard payroll taxes at this time):

(d)   Adjusting entry at end of current period, December 31, 1974:

> Salary Expense.................................. 600
>   Salaries Payable (or Accrued Salaries
>   Payable)...................................   600
>   To record salary expense and the liability for
>   December salary not yet paid.

At date of payment, next period, January 10, 1975:

> Salaries Payable................................ 600
>   Cash.......................................   600
>   To record payment of a December 1974 salary.

The adjusting entry serves two measurement purposes: (a) to record an expense incurred in 1974 for matching purposes, and (b) to record the liability for the salary owed at the end of 1974.

Property tax expense. On December 30, 1974, a tax bill amounting to $4,700 was received from the city for 1974 property taxes. The taxes are due on February 15, 1975, hence they were unpaid at the end of 1974. The sequence of entries would be:

(e)   Adjusting entry at end of current period, December 31, 1974:[2]

DEC EXP
INC LIAB

```
Property Tax Expense........................ 4,700
    Property Taxes Payable..................        4,700
To record 1974 property taxes incurred
and the related liability.
```

The adjusting entry serves the same two measurement purposes enumerated above for salaries. When the taxes are paid, Cash will be credited and Property Taxes Payable debited for $4,700.

Interest expense. On November 1, 1974, the business borrowed $30,000 cash from a local bank on a 90-day note with an annual interest rate of 8%. The principal plus the interest is due in three months. The sequence of entries is:

At date of loan, November 1, 1974:

INC ASSET
INC LIAB

```
Cash........................................ 30,000
    Note Payable, Short-term..............        30,000
To record a three-month, 8% loan from
the bank.
```

(f)   Adjusting entry at end of current period, December 31, 1974:

DEBIT EXP
CRY LIAB

```
Interest Expense............................. 400
    Interest Payable (or Accrued Interest
    Payable)..................................        400
To record accrued interest expense for two
months on note payable ($30,000 × 8% × 2/12 =
$400).
```

At date of payment of loan principal and interest, January 31, 1975:

DEC LIAB
DEC LIAB
DEBIT EXP
DEC ASSET

```
Note Payable, Short-term.................. 30,000
Interest Payable (per adjusting entry).....    400
Interest Expense (1975—$30,000 × 8% × 1/12)    200
    Cash....................................        30,600
To record payment of note and interest at
maturity date.
```

At the end of 1974 the note payable is a liability of the business. Since the note has been outstanding for two months up to December 31,

---

[2] This is an example of a situation where there may or may not be an adjusting entry. For example, assume the tax bill was received on December 5, 1974. At that date a *current entry* may be made identical to the adjusting entry given above. Obviously, under these circumstances, an adjusting entry at December 31, 1974, would not be needed.

1974, there also is a liability for **accrued interest** for two months. This is because interest legally accrues with the **passage of time,** notwithstanding the fact that the interest is payable in cash at the maturity date of the note. The adjusting entry accomplishes two measurement purposes: (1) to record interest expense incurred in 1974 for matching purposes, and (2) to record a liability for the interest accrued at the end of 1974. The December 31, 1974, balance sheet will report two liabilities in respect to this note: one for the principal amount ($30,000) and one for the interest liability ($400).

RECORDED REVENUE APPORTIONED BETWEEN ACCOUNTING PERIODS

Some businesses collect revenue in advance of rendering the service or the sale of goods. In such situations the revenue must be apportioned to the period in which the services are rendered or the sale is consummated in accordance with the revenue principle (see page 127). Such a situation requires an adjusting entry at the end of the period. We will analyze one such situation for High-Rise Apartments that occurs because a few tenants pay their rent on the 15th of each month.

Rent revenue collected in advance. On December 15, 1974, two tenants paid rent for the period December 15, 1974, to January 15, 1975, in the amount of $1,200. The sequence of entries would be:

Entry at date of collection of rent, December 15, 1974:

```
Cash........................................1,200
      Rent Collected in Advance................      1,200
      To record one month rent for the period De-
      cember 15, 1974, to January 15, 1975.
```

Observe that the $1,200 cash collected included rent revenue for one-half month in 1974 and rent collected in advance for one-half month for 1975. As a consequence, at December 31, 1974, the rent collected in advance was only $600. This amount is a liability for High-Rise Apartments because there is a future obligation to provide occupancy for one-half month in 1975.

(g)   Adjusting entry at end of 1974:

```
Rent Collected in Advance...................... 600
      Rent Revenue................................      600
      To record fulfillment of occupancy obligation
      for one-half month rent.
```

The adjusting entry serves two measurement purposes: (a) to apportion rent revenue for one-half month to 1974 for matching pur-

poses, and (b) to adjust (reduce) the obligation to furnish future occupancy to one-half month.

UNRECORDED REVENUE

On occasion, at the end of the period, there may be revenue that has
been **earned** (in accordance with the revenue principle) but not yet
recorded. Unrecorded revenue must be given accounting recognition in
the period in which it was earned. We will analyze a typical situation
for High-Rise Apartments.

Rent revenue. On December 31, 1974, the manager of High-
Rise Apartments, upon checking the rental records, found that two
tenants had not paid their December rent amounting to $400. The
sequence of entries would be:

(h)   Adjusting entry at December 31, 1974:

```
Rent Revenue Receivable......................... 400
    Rent Revenue.................................        400
    To record rent revenue earned in 1974 but not
    collected by year end.
```

Entry at date of collection in January 1975:

```
Cash...............................................400
    Rent Revenue Receivable......................        400
    To record collection of receivable for 1974
    rent revenue.
```

The adjusting entry at the end of 1974 served two measurement
purposes: (a) to record rent revenue earned for matching purposes,
and (b) to record "Rent Revenue Receivable" as an asset for occupancy provided in 1974. Rent Revenue Receivable would be reported
on the December 31, 1974, balance sheet as a current asset.

The above examples demonstrate that adjusting entries involve application of the fundamental accounting model in the same manner as
all other transactions. The only reasons they are singled out for special
consideration in the measurement process is that they usually require
an analysis of each situation through examination of the records and
related sources since, by their nature, specific documents (such as
invoices, bills, etc.) may not flow into the system to generate an entry;
and they are **end-of-the-period entries** that usually are made immediately after all of the regular transactions are recorded. In some instances, it is difficult to draw a distinct line between regular and
adjusting entries. There are no reasons, other than the two listed
immediately above, for making such a distinction. The important point
is that adjusting entries (as well as most other entries) are necessary

to appropriately measure revenue and match expenses with revenue for the period.

PART TWO: INFORMATION PROCESSING

Manual, mechanical, and electronic data processing

In Chapter 4, page 109, the information-processing cycle in accounting was outlined briefly. At that point we stated that the cycle is repeated each period. In this part we expand that outline and illustrate the expanded cycle.

Information processing means the order and ways in which the work is accomplished in collecting the source documents, recording their effects in terms of the accounting model, classifying the data, and, finally, in preparing the periodic financial statements. In most firms a large amount of data must be handled. Although information processing can be time-consuming and costly to the enterprise, a well-designed system can provide a smooth, uninterrupted, and efficient flow of data from the point of occurrence of the transaction to the various financial reports. The processing of accounting data may be performed in one of three ways, or, as is the usual case, by a combination of them. The three approaches may be briefly described as follows:

(1) Manual data processing. When this approach is used, all of the work is performed manually; that is, by hand. In the discussion and illustrations up to this point, manual processing has been employed. The manual approach is used extensively in small businesses. Also, in large and medium-sized businesses, certain elements of data processing continue to be performed manually. The manual approach is quite useful for illustrating the application of accounting principles measurement procedures. It also is convenient for explaining and illustrating the accounting process because the learner can readily see what is being done. One cannot see what is going on inside a computer.

(2) Mechanical data processing. Mechanical data processing is used for repetitive transactions that occur in large numbers. Mechanical processing employs accounting machines that vary widely in type and application. They encompass mechanical devices, some of which display a combination typewriter–adding machine keyboard. They encompass not only the strictly mechanical devices, such as a posting machine, but also punched-card equipment. The latter consists of (1) key-punch machines, on which cards are punched to record the transactions; (2) sorting machines, which sort the cards in any pre-determined order; and (3) tabulating machines, which print the output, such as a listing of the expenses for the period. Although mechanical data processing is widely used today, it is rapidly being superseded by electronic data processing.

(3) Electronic data processing. Electronic data processing is based upon use of electronic computers. The manual and mechanical

activities in data processing are reduced to a minimum. Because of their large capabilities to store data and the speed with which such data can be manipulated and recalled, electronic data processing has become widely used in accounting. This process involves the use of "hardware" and "software." The computer and other machines related to it (usually called peripheral equipment) constitute the hardware. The software includes the programs that must be designed as instructions to the computer and all other items related to the operation of the system. Other items include materials used in operating the system, training materials, and studies of various sorts. Electronic data processing is widely applied to such accounting problems as payrolls, billings for goods and services, accounts receivable, accounts payable, and inventories.[3]

Expanding the information-processing cycle

In this part of the chapter we will expand the information-processing cycle that was outlined in Chapter 4, page 109, to illustrate the additional **phases** of the processing of accounting data. The cycle is expanded to encompass the following phases. (Phases added to those previously discussed and illustrated are indicated with an asterisk.)

1. Collection of raw economic data generated by transactions
2. Analysis of the regularly occurring transactions to determine the economic effects on the business in terms of the accounting model
3. Journalizing the results of this analysis of the transactions. This encompasses recording the entries in chronological order in the journal
4. Posting the entries from the journal to the ledger
5. Preparation of a trial balance from the ledger
*6. Preparation of an accounting worksheet
   a. Collection of data for adjusting entries and analysis of the data in the context of the accounting model
   b. Segregation of data for the income statement and balance sheet
7. Preparation of financial statements
   a. Income statement
   b. Balance sheet
   c. Statement of changes in financial position (discussed in Chapter 15)
*8. Adjusting entries
   a. Entered in the journal
   b. Posted to the ledger
*9. Closing the accounts
*10. Post-closing trial balance

---

[3] This subject is discussed in more depth in *Fundamentals of Management Accounting*, Chapter 16.

The four phases added (6, 8, 9, and 10) are strictly information-processing phases and involve no new accounting concepts and principles beyond those that you have already learned in the first four chapters. These four phases are designed to provide an orderly flow of the data processing work and, although not absolutely necessary, generally are desirable in order to complete the financial statements with minimum effort. They also tend to decrease the potential for errors and omissions. Each of these added phases will be discussed and illustrated in order. In the illustrations we will employ a manual system for instructional purposes.[4]

The
worksheet
(Phase 6)

After the regular transactions for the period are journalized and posted to the ledger, and before the adjusting entries are determined, a trial balance is taken from the ledger (Phase 5 above). Next, it is generally desirable, although optional with the accountant, to prepare what is known as a worksheet. The worksheet is an efficient tool that has as its only purpose essential data-manipulation steps and the grouping of amounts for the income statement and the balance sheet. It brings together in one place, in an orderly way, the trial balance, adjusting entries, financial statements, and closing entries (explained later). The worksheet normally is prepared in pencil (for ease in making changes) since it is not presented to management or to other parties. After the worksheet is completed and determined to be correct, it then becomes the guide for the subsequent phases in the information-processing cycle (Phases 7, 8, and 9 above).

Preparing the worksheet. A typical worksheet, shown in Exhibit 5–2 is for High-Rise Apartments for the year ended December 31, 1974. Note that the ledger accounts are listed vertically in the first column and there are debit and credit columns for Trial Balance, Adjustments, Adjusted Trial Balance, Income Statement, and Balance Sheet. The steps involved in developing this worksheet are:

Step 1—After the regular transactions and events for the year were entered in the journal and posted to the ledger, a trial balance was developed. This trial balance is entered directly in the first two money columns on the worksheet. The equality of debits and credits was verified at this point (totals $481,460).

Step 2—The second pair of money columns, headed "Adjustments," are completed by entering the *adjusting entries* directly onto the worksheet. The adjusting entries for High-Rise Apartments to be placed on the worksheet were determined as explained earlier in this chapter. To facilitate examination (for potential errors), future reference, and

---

[4] The discussions from this point to the Summary may be omitted without affecting the continuity of the materials. However, this relatively concise discussion of data processing often is found to be useful for instructional purposes in subsequent areas.

Exhibit 5–2

HIGH-RISE APARTMENTS
Worksheet
For the Year Ended December 31, 1974

Account Titles	Trial Balance Debit	Trial Balance Credit	Adjustments Debit	Adjustments Credit	Adjusted Trial Balance Debit	Adjusted Trial Balance Credit	Income Statement Debit	Income Statement Credit	Balance Sheet Debit	Balance Sheet Credit
Cash	1,097				1,097				1,097	
Prepaid insurance	3,600			(a) 1200	2,400				2,400	
Inventory maintenance supplies	600			(c) 400	200				200	
Land	25,000				25,000				25,000	
Apartment building	360,000				360,000				360,000	
Accumulated depreciation, building		10,000		(b) 10,000		20,000				20,000
Notes payable		30,000				30,000				30,000
Rent collected in advance		1,200	(g) 600			600				600
Mortgage payable		238,037				238,037				238,037
Capital stock, 500 shares		50,000				50,000				50,000
Retained earnings		23,760				23,760				23,760
Dividends paid	12,000				12,000				12,000	
Rent revenue		128,463		(g) 600 / (h) 400		129,463		129,463		
	481,460	481,460								
Advertising expense	500				500		500			
Maintenance expense	3,000		(c) 400		3,400		3,400			
Salary expense	17,400		(d) 600		18,000		18,000			
Interest expense	19,563		(f) 400		19,963		19,963			
Utilities expense	34,500				34,500		34,500			
Miscellaneous expenses	4,200				4,200		4,200			
Insurance expense			(a) 1,200		1,200		1,200			
Depreciation expense			(b) 10,000		10,000		10,000			
Salaries payable				(d) 600		600				600
Property tax expense			(e) 4,700		4,700		4,700			
Property taxes payable				(e) 4,700		4,700				4,700
Interest payable				(f) 400		400				400
Rent revenue receivable			(h) 400		400				400	
			18,300	18,300	497,560	497,560	96,463	129,463	401,097	368,097
Net Income*							33,000			33,000
							129,463	129,463	401,097	401,097

* This was a Subchapter S Corporation, therefore, no income taxes were owed.

study, the adjusting entries usually are coded on the worksheet as illustrated in Exhibit 5–2. Some of the adjusting entries require the addition of one or more account titles below the original trial balance listing. After the adjusting entries are completed on the worksheet, the equality of debits and credits for those entries is checked (totals $18,300).

Step 3—Next, the columns headed "Adjusted Trial Balance" are completed. Although not essential, they are used for insuring accuracy. They simply represent, line by line, the combined amounts of the trial balance, plus or minus the amounts entered in the adjustment columns. For example, the Rent Revenue account reflects a $128,463 credit balance under Trial Balance. To this amount is *added* the credit amounts under Adjustments—$600 and $400 (debit amounts would be subtracted)—giving a combined amount of $129,463, which is entered as a *credit* under Adjusted Trial Balance. For those accounts that were unaffected by the adjusting entries, the Trial Balance amount is simply carried across to the Adjusted Trial Balance column. After each line has been completed in this manner, the equality of the debits and credits under Adjusted Trial Balance is checked (total $497,560).

Step 4—The amount on each line, under Adjusted Trial Balance, is extended horizontally across the worksheet and entered (a) as a debit, if it was a debit under Adjusted Trial Balance, or as a credit, if it was a credit under Adjusted Trial Balance; and (b) under the financial statement heading (income statement or balance sheet) on which it must appear. You can see that each amount extended across (1) was entered under *only one* of the four remaining columns, and (2) that debits remain debits and credits remain credits in the extending process.

After the amounts on each line are extended to the last four columns of the worksheet, the four columns are totaled. At this point you can observe a very interesting and useful feature of the worksheet: the difference between the debit and credit columns under Income Statement is the *net income* or *net loss*. Likewise, the difference between the debit and credit columns under Balance Sheet is the net income or net loss. If this result does not occur, there is an error in the extending process.

Step 5—This step completes the worksheet. Observe on Exhibit 5–2 that the last item listed in the left column (Account Titles) is Net income and that the amount of income (the difference explained above) is entered under *both* the Income Statement and the Balance Sheet in debit and credit format. The amount of net income is entered in the *debit* column under Income Statement in order to make the two columns balance, and as a *credit* under Balance Sheet for the same reason. The credit under Balance Sheet for Net income (or, alternatively, debit if a loss) also indicates that this amount must be added to the balance sheet accounts representing owners' equity.

Despite the several balancing features of the worksheet, errors may exist; that is, the balance features are not absolute proofs of accuracy. For example, in extending the amounts to the four remaining columns, one could enter an expense (a debit) under Balance Sheet instead of under the Income Statement (where it should be), and the worksheet would still balance; however, Net income would be incorrect. Clearly, special care should be exercised in the extending process.

Preparing statements from the worksheet (Phase 7)   The completed worksheet provides all of the amounts needed, in convenient form, to prepare the income statement, balance sheet, and statement of retained earnings. The statement of retained earnings, although not listed as a required statement, generally is prepared by corporations (see pages 57 and 63). It ties together the income statement and the stockholders' equity section of the balance sheet. For example, the statement for High-Rise Apartments would be as follows:

HIGH-RISE APARTMENTS, INC.
Statement of Retained Earnings
For the Year Ended December 31, 1974

Retained earnings balance Jan. 1, 1974	$23,760
Add net income for 1974	33,000
Total	56,760
Less dividends paid in 1974	12,000
Retained earnings balance, Dec. 31, 1974	$44,760

The task of preparing the income statement and balance sheet is simply one of classifying the data provided by the worksheet for the two statements. Since we illustrated such statements in Chapter 4, they will not be repeated here.

The worksheet described above does not provide data for the statement of changes in financial position. This statement requires special analytical procedures; as a consequence, a special worksheet must be used to develop it. The special worksheet will be discussed and illustrated in Chapter 15.

Recording adjusting entries in the accounting records (Phase 8)   Next, the adjusting entries entered on the worksheet (in the Adjustments column) are entered in the journal and then posted to the ledger. This is a clerical task since they are merely copied from the worksheet. The adjusting entries for High-Rise Apartments, showing a folio notation for posting completed, is illustrated in Exhibit 5–3. The ledger, with the adjusting entries posted, is shown (in blue to facilitate your identification) in Exhibit 5–5.

Closing the accounts (Phase 9)   In our study of the fundamental accounting model, we have emphasized that the revenue and expense accounts are subdivisions of owners' equity. The revenue and expense accounts may be viewed as the "income-statement accounts," whereas the remainder of the accounts can be viewed as "balance-sheet accounts." The revenue and expense

Exhibit 5–3
Adjusting entries

JOURNAL				Page 6
Date 1974	Account Titles and Explanation	Folio	Debit	Credit
Dec. 31	Insurance Expense......................	96	1,200	
	Prepaid Insurance...................	45		1,200
31	Depreciation Expense..................	97	10,000	
	Accumulated Depreciation, Building....	53		10,000
31	Maintenance Expenses..................	91	400	
	Inventory of Maintenance Supplies.....	47		400
31	Salary Expense.........................	92	600	
	Salaries Payable....................	63		600
31	Property Tax Expense..................	98	4,700	
	Property Taxes Payable..............	64		4,700
31	Interest Expense......................	93	400	
	Interest Payable....................	65		400
31	Rent Collected in Advance...............	62	600	
	Rent Revenue.......................	81		600
31	Rent Revenue Receivable................	42	400	
	Rent Revenue.......................	81		400

accounts are often called temporary accounts in the sense that data are collected in them for current accounting periods only. At the end of the period their balances (and the Dividends Paid account) are transferred, or closed, to the Retained Earnings account. This clearing out, or closing, serves two purposes: (1) it transfers net income (or loss) to retained earnings and (2) it establishes a zero balance in the revenue and expense accounts to start the new accounting period. In contrast, the balance-sheet accounts (assets, liabilities, and owners' equity) are not closed; therefore, they are often called permanent accounts. The balance at the end of the period in each balance-sheet account is carried forward as the beginning balance for the next period. As a consequence of these differences, the balance-sheet accounts frequently are called real accounts and the income-statement accounts are called nominal accounts.

The clearing out, or closing, at the end of the accounting period of the revenue and expense accounts is simply a mechanical phase. The closing entries are entered in the journal in the normal format and are immediately posted to the ledger. The mechanics of the closing procedure may be illustrated by assuming one revenue and one expense account. A special clearing account called "Income Summary" often is used to facilitate the procedure. Before continuing with High-Rise, we will use a highly simplified set of data to illustrate the closing procedure. Assume the following summarized data from the accounts of XYZ Corporation at December 31, 1974:

Stockholders' Equity Accounts

Capital stock, 500 shares..............................	$ 50,000
Retained earnings (beginning balance Jan. 1, 1974)........	15,000
Dividends paid during 1974..........................	10,000
Revenue earned (during 1974).......................	100,000
Expenses incurred (during 1974).....................	80,000

The closing mechanics for this corporation may be diagrammed as follows:

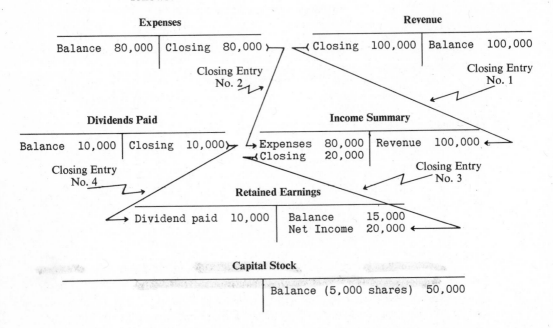

The four closing entries would appear in the journal and dated December 31, 1974, as follows:

```
1  Revenue.......................... 100,000
      Income Summary...............           100,000
      To close the Revenue account and
      transfer its balance to Income
      Summary.
2  Income Summary...................  80,000
      Expenses....................            80,000
      To close the Expense account and
      transfer its balance to Income
      Summary.
3  Income Summary...................  20,000
      Retained Earnings............            20,000
      To close the Income Summary ac-
      count and transfer net income to
      Retained Earnings.
4  Retained Earnings................  10,000
      Dividends Paid..............             10,000
      To close Dividends Paid account
      and to reduce Retained Earnings.
```

Now, let's return to High-Rise Apartments and apply the same closing mechanics. The closing entries are shown in Exhibit 5–4 as they would be entered in the journal; the posting to the ledger is indicated also. The ledger accounts with (a) the trial balance totals, (b) the adjusting entries posted (in blue), and (c) the closing entries posted (in black box) are shown in Exhibit 5–5 in T-account format. The colors and boxes are utilized to facilitate your study of the mechanics of

Exhibit 5–4
Closing entries

JOURNAL Page 7

Date 1974		Folio	Debit	Credit
Dec. 31	Rent Revenue............................	81	129,463	
	Income Summary......................	73		129,463
	To transfer revenues to Income Summary.			
31	Income Summary...........................	73	96,463	
	Advertising Expense	90		500
	Maintenance Expense..................	91		3,400
	Salary Expense........................	92		18,000
	Interest Expense.......................	93		19,963
	Utilities Expense......................	94		34,500
	Miscellaneous Expenses...............	95		4,200
	Insurance Expense.....................	96		1,200
	Depreciation Expense..................	97		10,000
	Property Tax Expense..................	98		4,700
	To transfer expense accounts to Income Summary.			
31	Income Summary...........................	73	33,000	
	Retained Earnings.....................	71		33,000
	To transfer net income to Retained Earnings.			
31	Retained Earnings........................	71	12,000	
	Dividends Paid........................	72		12,000
	To transfer Dividends Paid to Retained Earnings.			

each step. You should observe that all of these amounts are verifiable directly on the completed worksheet (Exhibit 5–2).

There are two points that should be commented on. First, the closing entry for expenses is in one **combined entry,** which saves time and space (of course, a separate entry could be made for each expense). Notice that the **total debit** to Income Summary in that entry is taken directly from the worksheet. Second, since the **Dividends Paid** account also is a temporary account, it should be closed to Retained Earnings.

After the closing is completed, you can observe that all of the nominal (i.e., the revenue and expense) accounts are closed and are ready for reuse during the next accounting period. The Retained Earn-

Exhibit 5–5

LEDGER

Cash 41		Property Taxes Payable 64		Salary Expense 92	
1,097			(6) 4,700	17,400	[(7) 18,000]
				(6) 600	

Rent Revenue Receivable 42		Interest Payable 65		Interest Expense 93	
(6) 400			(6) 400	19,563	[(7) 19,963]
				(6) 400	

Prepaid Insurance 45		Mortgage Payable 66		Utilities Expense 94	
3,600	(6)1,200		238,037	34,500	[(7) 34,500]

Inventory Maintenance Supplies 47		Capital Stock 70		Miscellaneous Expenses 95	
600	(6)400		50,000	4,200	[(7) 4,200]

Land 51		Retained Earnings 71		Insurance Expense 96	
25,000		[(7) 12,000]	23,760	(6)1,200	[(7) 1,200]
			[(7) 33,000]		

Apartment Building 52		Dividends Paid 72		Depreciation Expense 97	
360,000		12,000	[(7) 12,000]	(6)10,000	[(7) 10,000]

Accumulated Depreciation 53		Income Summary 73		Property Tax Expense 98	
	10,000	[(7) 96,463]	[(7) 129,463]	(6)4,700	[(7) 4,700]
	(6)10,000	[(7) 33,000]			

Notes Payable 61		Rent Revenue 81	
	30,000	[(7) 129,463]	128,463
			(6) 600
			(6) 400

Rent Collected in Advance 62		Advertising Expense 90	
(6) 600	1,200	500	[(7) 500]

Salaries Payable 63		Maintenance Expense 91	
	(6) 600	3,000	[(7) 3,400]
		(6) 400	

Balances are in black.
Adjusting entries are in blue.
Closing entries are enclosed in boxes.

ings account now has an ending balance of $44,760, which will be reported on the balance sheet under stockholders' equity.[5]

Post-closing trial balance (Phase 10)

Despite the guidance provided by the worksheet, occasional errors are made in the adjusting and closing mechanics. After the completion of these two phases, it is desirable to retest the equality of the ledger account balances. This is normally accomplished by simply running an adding machine tape on the ledger—the debits are entered as plus and the credits as minus and the resultant total should be zero. Some individuals prefer to prepare another formal trial balance, called a **post-closing trial balance,** before starting the new period. In any case the accounts after adjustment and closing should have the identical balances as reflected in the last two columns of the worksheet, with the exception of the Retained Earnings account, which must be calculated as the net of the beginning balance plus net income minus dividends paid.

We cannot emphasize too strongly that the worksheet, the closing entries, and the post-closing trial balance steps are **only mechanical data-processing procedures** and do not involve any new accounting principles or measurement approaches.

Reversing entries

Some accountants add one more phase to the accounting cycle, which is known as "reversing entries." This phase is dated on the first day of the following period and is used for the sole purpose of simplifying certain subsequent entries in the accounts. Reversing entries relate only to certain adjusting entries already made in the accounts. When appropriate, certain adjusting entries are reversed on the first day of the next period. Reversing entries are strictly optional and involve only bookkeeping mechanics rather than accounting principles and procedures. Appendix A discusses and illustrates reversing entries for those who desire to become familiar with this facilitating procedure.

Summary

This chapter, in Part One, focused on the revenue and matching principles. Matching expenses with revenue for the period is critical

---

[5] A common bookkeeping approach to "ruling a T-account" with a carry-forward balance is as follows:

Retained Earnings

Dividends (1974)	12,000	Jan. 1, 1974, balance	23,760
Balance carried forward	44,760	Net income (1974)	33,000
	56,760		56,760
		Jan. 1, 1975, balance	44,760

because the life span of an enterprise, although indefinite in length, must be divided into short time periods (usually one year) for periodic performance measurements. Primary among those measurements are the economic effects as reported in periodic financial reports.

In the measurement of net income, the revenue principle holds that revenues earned in the period through sale of goods or performance of services must be identified, measured, and reported for that period. The matching principle holds that costs and expenses incurred in generating those revenues must be identified, measured, and matched with revenues of the period to determine periodic net income. To implement the matching principle, certain transactions and events that extend over two or more accounting periods must be analyzed at the end of each accounting period to apportion their effects to the proper periods. The apportionment of many such transactions requires the use of adjusting entries. Adjusting entries follow the same concepts and procedures as entries for the usual transactions. At the end of the accounting period they are entered in the journal and posted to the ledger in the same manner as all other entries.

In Part Two the end-of-the-period phases of the information cycle were discussed and illustrated. These are mechanical data-processing procedures that do not involve any new accounting principles or measurement approaches.

Important terms		
Interim reports	Mechanical data processing	
Revenue principle	Electronic data processing	
Matching principle	Real accounts	
Adjusting entries	Nominal accounts	
Accrued expenses	Closing entries	
Manual data processing	Reversing entries	

Appendix   REVERSING ENTRIES

After completion of Phase 10 of the information-processing cycle (i.e., the post-closing trial balance), an optional phase may be added as Phase 11 (see page 138). This final phase is known as "reversing entries." Reversing entries are dated at the beginning of the next period. Unlike most of the phases in the information-processing cycle already discussed, reversing entries are not required by accounting principles or practice. They are made solely to simplify or facilitate subsequent entries in the accounts. The reversing-entry phase is presented here because (1) it introduces a very common data-processing mechanism used in most companies, whether the system is manual, mechanical, or computerized; and (2) a knowledge of the circumstances under which it is used to advantage gives some additional insight into certain relationships in the efficient processing of accounting information.

Reversing entries are given this name because they reverse, at the start of the next accounting period, the effects of *certain adjusting entries* made previously. Reversing entries are *always* the opposite of the related adjusting entry. In some situations it may be desirable to "reverse" certain adjusting entries and the other adjusting entries should not be reversed. To illustrate reversing entries and the type of situation where a reversing entry will simplify the subsequent entry, assume that Day Company is in the process of completing the information-processing cycle at the end of its accounting period, December 31, 1974. In order to place the adjusting entry in context, we have presented in Exhibit 5–6 a tabulation of entries that shows (1) an adjusting entry on December 31, 1974; (2) the reversing entry that could be made on January 1, 1974; and (3) the subsequent entry on

Exhibit 5–6
Reversing entries illustrated

DAY COMPANY

a) The payroll was paid on Dec. 28, 1974; the next payroll will be on Jan. 13, 1975. At Dec. 31, 1974, there were wages earned of $3,000 for the last three days of the year that had not been paid or recorded.

With Reversing Entry: *Without Reversing Entry:*

Dec. 31, 1974, adjusting entry to record the unpaid wages:

Wage Expense................... 3,000		Wage Expense................... 3,000	
Wages Payable (a liability)...	3,000	Wages Payable (a liability)....	3,000

b) The revenue and expense accounts are closed to Income Summary after the adjusting entries are completed and posted to the ledger.

Dec. 31, 1974, closing entry:

Income Summary.............. 3,000		Income Summary.............. 3,000	
Wage Expense............	3,000	Wage Expense............	3,000

c) The information-processing cycle in 1974 is complete. All closing entries have been posted and the post-closing trial balance has been verified. At this point in time, Jan. 1, 1975, the accountant decides whether it is desirable to make any reversing entries to simplify the subsequent entries. Question: Would a reversing entry on Jan. 1, 1975, simplify the entry on Jan. 13, 1975 when the wages are paid?

Jan. 1, 1975, reversing entry:

Wages Payable (a liability) 3,000		No reversing entry to be made.
Wage Expense............	3,000	

d) The payroll of $25,000 was completed and paid on Jan. 13, 1975. This payment entry is to be recorded. Question: Did the reversing entry simplify this entry?

Jan. 13, 1975, payroll entry:

Wage Expense.............. 25,000		Wages Payable	3,000	
Cash	25,000	Wage Expense..............	22,000	
		Cash		25,000

Observe that with the reversing entry having been made, this last entry required only one debit, contrasted with two debits when no reversing entry was made. This difference was due to the fact that the reversing entry served to (1) clear out the liability account "Wages Payable," and (2) set up a temporary *credit* in the Wage Expense account. After the last entry, to record the payment of the payroll, both accounts affected—Wage Expense and Wages Payable—are identical in balance under both approaches. If the reversing entry is not made, the company must go to the trouble of identifying how much of the $25,000 paid on Jan. 13, 1975, was expense and how much of it was to pay the liability set up in the prior adjusting entry.

January 15, 1975, that was simplified. Also, to demonstrate the effect of a reversing entry, we have presented in the tabulation the same sequence without the reversing entry. You should study carefully the sequence of entries and the explanatory comments in Exhibit 5–6.

In the above discussion it was indicated that certain adjusting entries could be reversed to simplify subsequent entries and that certain adjusting entries would not be reversed. How does one decide the entries that may be reversed with advantage? There is no inflexible rule that can be provided. The accountant must analyze each situation and make a rational choice. He then identifies those situations where reversal is useful and issues instructions to that effect or programs the computer to make the reversals in each period.

In this part of the discussion we will refer to the illustrations in this chapter for High-Rise Apartments. Adjusting entries (d) (page 133), (f) (page 134), and (h) (page 136), if reversed, would simplify the subsequent entries related to them. The remaining entries for High-Rise normally would not be reversed.

To explain further the type of entry that may be reversed, we will analyze in a somewhat different manner than in the preceding tabulation entry (d) (page 133) for High-Rise. First, let's look at the adjusting entry that was made on December 31, 1974:

```
Salary Expense............................................. 600
    Salaries Payable.......................................        600
    To record the salary expense and the liability for December
    salary not yet paid.
```

On the date of payment, January 11, 1975, it would be correct to record payment of the salary as follows:

```
Salaries Payable........................................... 600
    Cash...................................................        600
```

Let us assume, however, the books for High-Rise are maintained on a computer (a common situation) and that the computer is programmed to make the following entry *every time* a salary payment is made:

```
Salary Expense............................................. XXX
    Cash...................................................        XXX
```

Such a program is completely logical for all of the salary payments for the year; yet, the first payment entry as given above does not debit Salary Expense. It may make little economic sense to write a special program for the January payment entry and separate programs for the remaining months of the year, or to manually interrupt some of the January computer runs to make an occasional "special" payment entry. This undesirable effect can be avoided by utilizing a reversing entry. A reversing-entry computer routine could be included in the end-of-the-period information-processing cycle. The reversing procedure could be included in the same group of computer runs as those to record the closing entries with no additional cost. The computer would be programmed to effect the following reversing entry at the end:

Salaries Payable... 600
    Salary Expense.......................................   600

As demonstrated in Exhibit 5–6, the ledger accounts then would reflect appropriate balances for the continuation of the routine entry programmed to debit Salary Expense for all salary payments. Thus, adjusting entries should be reversed only in those situations where *an analysis* of the *subsequent entry* shows that the subsequent recording would be simplified and the clerical or computer costs reduced.

In contrast, let's examine a situation where reversals are not made. Examine entry (e) (page 134) for Property Tax Expense for High-Rise Apartments; it was as follows:

Property Tax Expense.................................... 4,700
    Property Taxes Payable...............................   4,700

When the payment is made on January 15, 1975, the payment entry would be:

Property Taxes Payable.................................. 4,700
    Cash...   4,700

As property tax payments are made only *once each year* in most communities, the computer input would be written to debit Property Taxes Payable for the payment. Thus, future bookkeeping would not be simplified (nor the cost reduced) by using a reversing entry.

The adjusting entry to record depreciation and entries of this type should never be reversed. In these situations the adjusting entry is not followed by a subsequent "payment" entry; therefore, it would be not only pointless to reverse it but also would introduce an error into the accounts. Thus, most adjusting entries are not candidates for reversal, and those that are candidates are easily identified if one considers the nature of the subsequent related entry.[1]

Perhaps the most compelling reason for reversing entries is to reduce the likelihood that the effects of certain adjusting entries will be overlooked when recording the next related transaction in the following period.

In summary, reversing entries are optional and are made for the sole purpose of simplifying subsequent related entries. When appropriate, they are the reverse of the related adjusting entry and are dated the first day of the following period. They represent a data-processing mechanism and do not involve accounting principles or practice.

---

[1] In general it may be said that accruals, but not deferrals, are candidates for reversal.

1. Identify the two *change* statements and briefly explain why they are so designated.

2. Explain the time-period assumption.

3. What is the "natural business year"? How does it relate to accounting?

4. Explain the revenue principle and the matching principle.

5. What are adjusting entries? Why are they necessary?

6. Briefly define each of the following: accrued expense, accrued revenue, deferred expense, deferred revenue.

7. What two purposes generally are served by an adjusting entry for expenses?

8. What two purposes generally are served by an adjusting entry for revenues?

9. Distinguish between manual, mechanical, and electronic data processing.

10. Give in sequence the ten phases of the information-processing cycle.

11. What is the purpose of the worksheet?

12. Why are adjusting entries entered in the journal and posted to the ledger?

13. What is meant by closing entries? Why are they necessary?

14. Distinguish between real and nominal accounts.

15. What is a post-closing trial balance? Is it a necessary part of the information-processing cycle?

16. What are reversing entries? When are they useful? Give an example of an adjusting that (1) should be reversed, and (2) that should not be reversed. Refer to the Appendix.

Exercises E5–1. This exercise focuses on the definition and classification of accrued and deferred revenues and expenses. You are to complete the following requirements:

(a) Complete the following:

Term	Brief Explanation	Balance Sheet Classification
1. Deferred expense		
2. Accrued expense		
3. Deferred revenue		
4. Accrued revenue		

(b) Assume there is a deferred expense of $100; an accrued expense of $200; a deferred revenue of $300; and an accrued revenue of $400. Give a typical example of each and provide the entry that would normally be made to recognize each.

E5-2. Gold's Department Store is in the process of completing the accounting process for the year just ended, December 31, 1974. The worksheet has been started and the following data in respect to adjusting entries are available:

a. Office supplies purchased and debited to Office Supplies Inventory during the year amounted to $360. The year-end inventory showed $80 worth of supplies on hand.

b. Wages earned but unpaid and unrecorded at December 31, 1974, amounted to $1,100.

c. Three-fourths of the basement of the store is rented to another merchant, John Smith, who sells compatible, but not competitive, merchandise. On November 1, 1974, the store collected six months' rent in advance, amounting to $3,600, which was credited to Rent Income.

d. The rest of the basement is rented to Spears Specialty; rent of $250 per month is payable monthly. On December 31, 1974, the rent for November and December 1974 had not yet been collected.

Required:

Give the adjusting entry for each situation that should be entered on the worksheet and in the records at December 31, 1974.

E5-3. The information-processing cycle for the fiscal year ended December 31, 1974, has been completed up to the adjusting entries by Fox Retailers, a men's store. Information from the records and related documents revealed the following:

a. Delivery equipment costing $12,000 was being used by the store. Estimates in respect to the equipment were: (1) useful life five years, and (2) residual value at the end of five years' use, $2,000. Assume depreciation for a full year.

b. On July 1, 1974, a three-year insurance premium amounting to $1,800 was paid in cash; the debit was to Prepaid Insurance.

c. Fox rents one-half of the building occupied by the store to another merchant, Brand Ladies Shop. The rent of $400 per month is payable six months in advance, each September 1 and March 1. The last rent collection credited to Rent Income was on September 1, 1974.

d. Fox operates an alteration shop to meet its own needs. In addition, the shop does alterations for Brand. At the end of December 31, 1974, Brand had not paid for alterations completed amounting to $320; this amount had not been recorded as Alteration Shop Revenue.

Required:

Give the adjusting entry for each situation that should be entered on the worksheet and in the records at December 31, 1974.

E5-4. Matson Company, on August 1, 1974, in order to meet a cash shortage, obtained a $6,000, 8% loan from a local bank. The principal, plus interest, was payable at the end of 12 months. The annual fiscal period for Matson ends on December 31, 1974.

Required:

a.   Give the journal entry on date of the loan, August 1, 1974.
b.   Give the adjusting entry required on December 31, 1974.
c.   Give the journal entry on date of payment, July 31, 1975.

E5–5.   On April 1, 1974, the Mark-Hale Corporation received a $9,000, 8% note from a customer in settlement of an open account receivable. According to the terms, the principal of the note, plus the interest, was payable at the end of 12 months. The annual fiscal period for Mark-Hale ends on December 31, 1974.

Required:

a.   Give the journal entry for receipt of the note on April 1, 1974.
b.   Give the adjusting entry required on December 31, 1974.
c.   Give the journal entry on date of collection, March 30, 1975.

E5–6.   The Baker Company is in the process of making adjusting entries for the year ended December 31, 1974. In developing information for the adjusting entries, we learned that on September 1, 1974, a three-year insurance premium of $1,800 was paid.

Required:

a.   What amount should be reported on the 1974 income statement for insurance expense?
b.   What amount should be reported on the December 31, 1974, balance sheet for prepaid insurance?
c.   Give the adjusting entry at December 31, 1974, under each of two cases:

   Case 1.   Assume that when the premium was paid on September 1, 1974, the bookkeeper debited Prepaid Insurance.

   Case 2.   Assume that when the premium was paid on September 1, 1974, the bookkeeper incorrectly debited Insurance Expense.

   (Hint: In Case 2 be sure you end up with the same amount in the Prepaid Insurance account as in Case 1.)

E5–7.   The Ball Manufacturing Company uses a large amount of shipping supplies, which are purchased in large volume, stored, and used as needed. At December 31, 1974, in collecting information as a basis for making the adjusting entries, the following data relating to shipping supplies were obtained from the records and supporting documents:

Shipping supplies on hand, January 1, 1974. . . . . None
Purchases of shipping supplies during 1974. . . . . $11,000
Shipping supplies on hand, per inventory, December 31,
   1974.   4,000

Required:

a.   What amount should be reported on the 1974 income statement for shipping supplies expense?

b. What amount should be reported on the December 31, 1974, balance sheet for shipping supplies inventory?

c. Give the adjusting entry at December 31, 1974, assuming the purchases of shipping supplies were debited to Shipping Supplies Inventory.

d. What adjusting entry would you make, assuming the bookkeeper debited Shipping Supplies Expense when the $11,000 supplies were purchased?

(Hint: In solving c. and d., be sure that each solution ends up with the same amount remaining in the Shipping Supplies Inventory account.)

E5–8. Assume that the worksheet at December 31, 1974, for Blue Realty Corporation has been completed through "Adjusted Trial Balance" and we are ready to extend each amount to the several columns to the right. These columns are listed below with code letters:

Code No.	Columns
a	Income statement, debit
b	Income statement, credit
c	Statement of retained earnings, debit
d	Statement of retained earnings, credit
e	Balance sheet, debit
f	Balance sheet, credit

Below are listed representative accounts to be extended on the worksheet of Blue Realty Corporation. You are to give a code letter for each account indicating the proper worksheet column to the right of "Adjusted Trial Balance" to which the amount in each account is to be extended.

KNOW

DO

Accounts	Code No.
Cash	
Inventory of office supplies	
Interest payable	
Capital stock	
Commissions earned	
Rent collected in advance	
Salary expense	
Return sales	
Retained earnings, beginning credit balance	
Building	
Mortgage payable	
Income taxes payable	
Cash dividends paid during year	
Sales commissions receivable	
Accumulated depreciation on building	
Contributed capital in excess of par	
Unearned sales commissions	
Income tax expense	
Net income:	
Code number for the debit	
Code number for the credit	
Net loss:	
Code number for the debit	
Code number for the credit	

B/S

A = L + OE

I S

R − E = NI

E5–9.   This exercise has three cases that relate to the closing procedure. Case A deals with a sole proprietorship; Case B, with a partnership; and Case C, with a corporation. In each case you are to (1) enter the owners' equity balances in T-accounts and (2) enter therein the appropriate closing entries.

Case A: Smith Cleaners (sole proprietorship) accounts reflected the following on December 31, 1974, end of the fiscal year: Capital, $15,000; Withdrawals, $8,000; Revenues, $40,000; Expenses, $29,000.

Case B: Bob and Ray (partnership) accounts reflected the following on December 31, 1974, end of the fiscal year: Capital, Bob, $14,000; Capital, Ray, $15,000; Withdrawals, Bob, $9,-000; Withdrawals, Ray, $10,000; Revenues, $68,000; Expenses, $50,000. Profits are divided equally.

Case C: Stein Corporation accounts reflected the following on December 31, 1974, end of the fiscal year: Capital Stock $100,000; Contributed Capital in Excess of Par, $10,000; Retained Earnings, Jan. 1, 1974, $43,000; Cash Dividends Paid (during 1974), $25,000; Revenues, $160,000; Expenses, $130,000 (income taxes already deducted).

In developing the solution, complete the following two steps:

Step 1.   Enter the above amounts in the following accounts for each case.

Sole Proprietorship	Partnership	Corporation
Capital, Smith	Capital, Bob	Capital Stock
Withdrawals, Smith	Withdrawals, Bob	Contributed Capital in
Income Summary	Capital, Ray	Excess of Par
Revenues	Withdrawals, Ray	Retained Earnings
Expenses	Income Summary	Dividends Paid
	Revenues	Income Summary
	Expenses	Revenues
		Expenses

Step 2.   Enter in the accounts the closing entries for each case. Key the closing entries with letters such as (a), (b), etc.

E5–10.   (Based on the Appendix.) The Dikins Corporation is completing information-processing cycle at December 31, 1974. The adjusting entries have been made and posted to the ledger. Following that phase, the closing entries also were entered in the journal and posted to the ledger. The post-closing trial balance has been verified as being correct.

This exercise focuses on two of the adjusting entries that were made at December 31, 1974. They were:

(a)   Rent revenue amounting to $10,000 was collected on December 15, 1974. These collections were for the period December 15, 1974, to January 14, 1975. At the date of collection they were processed through the computer, which was programmed to make the following entry for rent collections:

Cash.................................... 10,000
    Rent Revenue Earned.................   10,000

     (b)   Depreciation expense of office equipment for the year was $8,000.

Required:

(1)   Give the adjusting entry for each of the above items on December 31, 1974.

(2)   Give the closing entry for each item.

(3)   Give the reversing entry that could be made on January 1, 1975, to simplify the subsequent entry. If no reversing entry is advantageous, explain why not.

(4)   Give the next entry (a) for the collection of rent again from these tenants on January 15, 1975, amounting to $10,000; and (b) the next adjusting entry for $8,000 depreciation at the end of 1975.

Problems   **P5–1.**   The Ace Transportation Company (a corporation) is now in the process of completing the information-processing cycle for the year ended December 31, 1974. The trial balance has been entered in the first two columns of the worksheet and has been determined to be correct. The adjusting entries are now to be entered on the worksheet. The following data that must be considered have been developed from the records and related documents:

(1)   On September 1, 1974, a three-year insurance premium on certain equipment was paid amounting to $720, which was debited to Prepaid Insurance.

(2)   During the year, office supplies amounting to $1,200 were purchased for cash and debited to Supplies Inventory; at the end of 1974 an inventory of supplies showed $300. There was no inventory of supplies on hand at January 1, 1974.

(3)   On December 31, 1974, the B & R Garage completed repairs on a truck at a cost of $450; the amount was payable by January 30, 1975.

(4)   In December 1974, the tax bill on equipment for 1974 amounting to $600 was received from the city; the taxes are due February 15, 1975.

(5)   On December 31, 1974, Ace completed a hauling contract for an out-of-state company. The bill was for $2,700, payable within 30 days. No entry has been made.

(6)   On July 1, 1974, Ace purchased a new hauling van at a cash cost of $7,100. The estimated useful life of the van to Ace was five years, with an estimated residual value at that time of $1,100. Compute depreciation for six months.

(7)   On October 1, 1974, Ace borrowed $6,000 from the local bank on a one-year, 8% note payable. The principal and interest is payable at the end of 12 months.

Required:

Give in journal-entry form the adjusting entry for each of the above transactions that would be entered on the worksheet for 1974. Give a brief explanation with each entry.

P5–2.   The following information was provided by the records and related documents of El Patio Apartments (a corporation) at the end of the annual fiscal period, December 31, 1974:

Revenue:

1. Rental revenue collected in cash during 1974 for occupancy in 1974. . . . .$90,000
2. Rental revenue earned for occupancy in December 1974 but not to be collected until 1975.   5,000
3. In December 1974, collected rent revenue in advance for January 1975; that is, rent collected in advance.   3,000

Salary expenses:

4. Cash payment made in January 1974 for salaries incurred (earned) in December 1973.   2,000
5. Salaries incurred and paid during 1974. 16,000
6. Salaries earned by employees during December 1974 but not to be paid until January 1975.   1,000
7. Cash advanced to employees in December 1974 for salaries to be earned in January 1975.   3,000

Supplies used:

8. Supplies purchased for cash during 1974 and debited to Supplies Inventory.   5,000
9. Supplies on hand (Supplies Inventory) on December 31, 1974 (there were no supplies on hand January 1, 1974).   2,000

Required:

(a)   What amount should be shown on the 1974 income statement for: (1) rent revenue; (2) salary expense; and (3) supplies expense?

(b)   Give the 1974 journal entry, including date and explanation, for each of the above events and transactions.

P5–3.   This case, taken from the experiences of May's Department Store (a corporation), has been selected to give you an opportunity to test your analytical ability in transaction analysis and in developing the adjusting entries where there are both notes receivable and notes payable. The annual fiscal period ends on December 31, 1974. Each of the two situations otherwise are independent.

Situation A—May's has arranged a line of credit whereby a local bank will provide them cash for short-term working capital needs. Repayment will vary from 60 to 90 days. Occasionally, the company borrows a substantial amount on longer terms. On August 1, 1974, the corporation borrowed $30,000 on a one-year, 8% note. Both principal and interest are payable at the end of 12 months.

Situation B—May's sells approximately 42% of their goods on credit; terms are 2/10; n/30 (i.e., 2% discount is granted if the customer pays in 10 days and, if not, the amount is due in 30 days from date of the sale). From time to time, special efforts must be made to collect an account. John Doe was such a case; he owed the store $1,800 on an account that they had been unable to collect. Finally, on November 1, 1974, he gave them an 8% note for the $1,800, coupled with a mortgage on his two automobiles. The note was for two years. At the end of the first full year he agreed to pay one-half of the principal ($900), plus interest on the principal outstanding, during the year; final payment of principal and interest was due at the end of the second year.

Required:

(a) What amount should be shown on the income statement for 1974 for: (1) interest expense; (2) interest revenue?

(b) What amount(s) should be shown on the balance sheet at December 31, 1974, for: (1) the note payable and the related accrued interest expense; (2) the note receivable and related interest revenue earned?

(c) Give the adjusting journal entry for each situation at December 31, 1974. Show your computations.

P5–4. The All-Purpose Service Company is in the process of completing the information-processing cycle at the end of the annual fiscal year, December 31, 1974. The worksheet and financial statements have been prepared and the next step is journalization of the adjusting entries. The two trial balances given below were taken directly from the completed worksheet.

		December 31, 1974			
		Trial Balance		Adjusted Trial Balance	
		Debit	Credit	Debit	Credit
(a)	Cash..........................	$ 8,000		$ 8,000	
(b)	Service revenue receivable.........			400	
(c)	Prepaid insurance................	300		200	
(d)	Fixed assets.....................	120,200		120,200	
(e)	Accumulated depreciation, equipment........................		$ 21,500		$ 25,000
(f)	Income taxes payable.............				5,500
(g)	Capital stock....................		50,000		50,000
(h)	Retained earnings, Jan. 1, 1974......		14,000		14,000
(i)	Service revenues earned...........		60,000		60,400
(j)	Salary expense...................	17,000		17,000	
(k)	Depreciation expense..............			3,500	
(l)	Insurance expenses...............			100	
(m)	Income tax expense...............			5,500	
		$145,500	$145,500	$154,900	$154,900

Required:

By examining the amounts in each trial balance, reconstruct the four adjusting entries that were made between the trial balance and the adjusted trial balance.

P5–5. You are in the process of developing the adjusting entries for Box Service Company at December 31, 1974. Three items are of special concern. Data at hand concerning the three items are:

Cash inflows and outflows:
Prepaid Insurance—cash spent during 1974......... $ 600
Interest Expense—cash spent during 1974........... 700
Service Revenue—cash collected during 1974........ 6,700

Balance sheet amounts:

	Dec. 31, 1973	Dec. 31, 1974
Prepaid Insurance (asset–debit).....	$100	$400
Interest Payable (liability–credit)....	300	200
Unearned Service Revenue (liability–credit)...............	300	500

Required:

How much should be reported on the 1974 income statement for (show computations):
(1)   Insurance expense? *300.⁰⁰*
(2)   Interest expense? *600.⁰⁰*
(3)   Service revenue earned? *6500.⁰⁰*

P5–6. Morris Transportation Company, a corporation, has been in operation since January 1, 1974. It is now December 31, 1974, the end of the annual fiscal period. The company has not done well financially during the first year, although hauling revenue has been fairly good. The two stockholders manage the company, and they have not bothered with record keeping. In view of a serious cash shortage, they asked the local bank for a loan. The bank requested a "financial statement." The statements were presented in the format given below:

MORRIS TRANSPORTATION COMPANY
December 31, 1974

Income Statement		*Balance Sheet*	
Hauling revenue.........	$90,000	Assets:	
Expenses:		Cash..................	$ 1,000
Salaries..............	20,000	Receivables...........	4,000
Maintenance.........	15,000	Inventory maintenance	
Other expenses........	–25,000	supplies.............	5,000
Total Expenses.	60,000	Equipment............	30,000
Net Income..............	$30,000	Other assets...........	37,000
		Total assets.....	$77,000
		Liabilities:	
		Accounts payable.....	$ 7,000
		Capital:	
		Capital stock........	40,000
		Retained earnings.....	30,000
			$77,000

After reviewing the statements and "looking into the situation," the bank requested that the statements be redone (with some expert help) to "incorporate depreciation, accruals, inventory counts, corporate income taxes, etc." As a consequence of a review of the records and supporting documents, the following additional information was developed:

(a)   The inventory of maintenance supplies should be $2,000, instead of the $5,000 shown on December 31, 1974.
(Hint: Increase Maintenance Expense.)

(b)   Prepaid insurance at December 31, 1974, amounted to $1,000. All of the insurance premium had been debited to Miscellaneous Expenses.

(c)   The equipment cost $30,000 and has an estimated useful life of five years.

(d)   Unpaid salaries at December 31, 1974, amounted to $1,000.

(e)   Unearned hauling revenue at December 31, 1974, amounted to $2,000. This had been credited to Hauling Revenue.

(f)   The corporate income tax rate is 22%.

Required:

(1)   Give the six adjusting entries required by the above additional information for December 31, 1974, in journal form with explanations.

(2)   Correct the above statements after taking into account the additional data. You do not need to use subclassifications on the statements.
Suggested form:

Items	Amounts Reported	Changes Plus	Minus	Corrected Amount
(List here each item from the two statements)				

(Hint: Correct net income is $14,820; correct balance sheet total is $69,000.)

P5–7.   (Note: This is a longer problem designed to review Chapters 3, 4, and 5.)

R&S Service Company was organized as a corporation three years ago by two individuals. During the first two years, practically no records were kept. In June 1974 they employed on a part-time basis a college student who was majoring in accounting "to get an accounting system going." With the advice of one of his instructors, the student has been able to establish a simple, yet efficient, system that will generate monthly financial statements for internal purposes and financial statements at the end of the year. The shortened list of accounts (and amounts) used in this case are representative of operations for 1974. The first set of financial statements are to be prepared for the year ended December 31, 1974. The student has worked very diligently to gather all the raw data for the year and to record it in the information-processing system that he designed. This case starts with the worksheet, which has been completed through the columns headed "Adjusted Trial Balance, December 31, 1974." You are to pick up from there and complete the requirements listed below. The Adjusted Trial Balance on the worksheet follows:

Debit		Credit	
Cash...................	$ 18,200	Accumulated depreciation.	$ 4,500
Accounts receivable......	4,000	Accounts payable.......	1,900
Supplies inventory.......	200	Property taxes payable....	300
Prepaid insurance.......	600	Unearned service fees.....	100
Land (future building site).	13,000	Interest payable.........	200
Equipment.............	15,000	Note payable, long-term...	10,000
Dividends paid..........	16,000	Capital stock............	30,000
Salary expense..........	23,000	Retained earnings........	–0–
Rent expense...........	4,800	Service fees earned.......	53,000
Insurance and tax expense.	500		
Advertising expense......	1,400		
Utilities expense.........	900		
Depreciation expense.....	1,500		
Interest expense.........	800		
Miscellaneous expenses ...	100		
	$100,000		$100,000

Note: Since this is a Subchapter S corporation, there will be no corporate income taxes

Required:

(a) Set up a worksheet starting with "Adjusted Trial Balance" as given and complete the worksheet in every respect.
(Hint: Net income is $20,000.)

(b) Based upon the worksheet, prepare the closing entries in journal form. Date and provide a brief explanation for each entry.

(c) Prepare an unclassified income statement, statement of retained earnings, and balance sheet.
(Hint: The balance sheet total is $46,500.)

(d) Prepare a post-closing trial balance.

P5–8. (Note: This is a mini-practice set designed to review Chapters 3, 4, and 5.)

W&P Moving and Storage Service has been in operation for several years as a corporation. Revenues have gradually increased from both the moving and storage services. The *annual* financial statement is inadequate for management needs. Therefore, during 1974, the current year, the president decided to have the accounting system improved so that it will provide *monthly* income, balance-sheet, and cash-flow information for internal purposes. The first step was to employ a full-time bookkeeper and they called upon a local CPA firm for assistance. It is now December 31, 1974, the end of the current fiscal year. The bookkeeper has developed a trial balance. A member of the staff of the CPA firm will advise and assist the bookkeeper in completing the information-processing cycle for the first year. The trial balance at December 31, 1974, follows:

Debit		Credit	
Cash..................	$ 25,010	Accumulated depreciation.	$ 15,000
Accounts receivable......	2,030	Accounts payable........	6,000
Office supplies inventory..	150	Property taxes payable....	
Prepaid insurance........	1,440	Interest payable.........	
Land for future building		Unearned storage fees....	
site.................	6,000	Notes payable..........	30,000
Equipment.............	58,000	Capital stock, 200 shares..	20,000
Dividends paid..........	24,000	Retained earnings, Jan. 1,	
Salary expense...........	74,000	1974................	8,600
Advertising expense......	1,000	Hauling fees earned.......	106,400
Utilities expense.........	1,300	Storage fees earned.......	14,000
Maintenance and fuel			
expense..............	6,500		
Miscellaneous expenses....	570		
Insurance and tax expense.			
Depreciation expense.....			
Interest expense.........			
	$200,000		$200,000

Note: This is a Subchapter S corporation; hence, there will be no income taxes.

Examination of the records and related documents provided the following additional information that should be considered for adjusting entries:

(a) Office Supplies Inventory at December 31, 1974, reflected $100 on hand. Office supplies used are considered to be a miscellaneous expense. No office supplies were purchased during the year.

(b) On January 1, 1974, a three-year insurance premium was paid amounting to $1,440. Set up an account for "Insurance and Tax Expense."

(c) The equipment cost $58,000 when acquired. It is estimated to have a ten-year useful life to the company and an $8,000 residual value on the used market at that time.

(d) Information obtained at the County Courthouse indicated that the 1974 tax bill on property will be $200. It is payable by March 1, 1975.

(e) The $30,000 note payable was signed on October 1, 1974, for an 8% bank loan, principal and interest due at the end of 12 months from that date.

(f) Storage fees collected and recorded as earned before December 31, 1974, included $400 collected in advance from one customer for storage time in 1975.
(Hint: This $400 should be regarded as Unearned Storage Fees.)

(g) Gasoline, oil, and fuel purchased for the vehicles and used during the last two weeks of December 1974 amounting to $300 have not been paid for or recorded.

Required:

(1) Enter the trial balance on a worksheet, then, based on the above data, enter the adjusting entries. Complete the worksheet.

(Hint: Net income is $30,000.)

(2) Using the worksheet, prepare a classified income statement, statement of retained earnings, and balance sheet.

(Hint: The balance-sheet total is $72,100.)

(3) Using the worksheet, enter the adjusting entries in the journal.

(4) Using the worksheet, prepare closing entries in journal form.

(5) Prepare a post-closing trial balance.

P5–9. (Note: This is a mini-practice set designed to review Chapters 3, 4, and 5.)

Charter Air Service, Incorporated, was organized on January 1, 1970, to operate a charter service in a city of approximately 300,000 population. The eight organizers were issued 7,500 shares of $10 par-value stock for a total of $75,000 cash. The company rents hangar and office space at the airport for a flat monthly rental. The business has prospered because of the excellent service and the high level of maintenance on the planes. It is now December 31, 1974, end of the annual fiscal period, and the information-processing cycle is in the final phases. Following are representative accounts and amounts selected from the ledger at December 31, 1974, for problem purposes:

Debit		*Credit*	
Cash	$ 14,600	Accumulated depreciation,	
Prepaid insurance	6,000	aircraft	$ 60,000
Maintenance parts inven-		Notes payable, long-term	90,000
tory	18,000	Capital stock, par $10	75,000
Aircraft	260,000	Retained earnings, Jan. 1,	
Cash dividends paid in		1974	20,600
1974	15,000	Charter revenue earned	262,400
Salary expense	90,000		
Maintenance expense	24,000		
Fuel expense	63,000		
Advertising expense	2,000		
Utilities expense	1,400		
Rent expense	14,000		
	$508,000		$508,000

For the adjusting entries, the following additional data were developed from the records and supporting documents:

(a) On January 1, 1974, the company paid a three-year insurance premium amounting to $6,000.

(b) The aircraft, when purchased, cost $260,000 and it is estimated that the useful life to the company is approximately ten years. At that time the equipment will have an estimated residual value on the used market of $60,000.

(c) On March 1, 1974, the company borrowed $90,000 from the bank on a five-year, 8% loan. Interest is payable annually starting on March 1, 1975.

(d) Charter revenue, on occasion, is collected in advance. On December 31, 1974, collections in advance amounted to $1,000; this amount has been recorded as earned.

(e) Rent amounting to $14,000 on hangar and office space was paid. This included rent paid in advance amounting to $2,000 for January and February 1975. The total amount was recorded as rent expense in 1974.

(f) The inventory of maintenance parts on December 31, 1974, showed $7,000. All parts purchased are debited to Maintenance Parts Inventory when purchased.

(g) For case purposes, assume the corporate income tax rates to be: first $25,000 net income, 22%; above $25,000, 48%.

Required:

(1) Enter the above accounts and balances from the ledger on a worksheet. (The following accounts should be added to the worksheet since they will be needed for the adjusting entries: Insurance Expense, Depreciation Expense, Interest Expense, Interest Payable, Unearned Charter Revenue, Prepaid Rent Expense, Income Tax Expense, and Income Taxes Payable.)

(2) Based on the additional data given above, enter adjusting entries on the worksheet.

(3) Complete the worksheet.
(Hint: Income tax expense is $7,900 and net income is $22,100.)

(4) Based on the worksheet, prepare an income statement, a statement of retained earnings, and a classified balance sheet.
(Hint: The balance sheet total is $207,600.)

(5) Journalize the adjusting entries.

(6) Prepare the closing entries.

P5–10. (Based on the Appendix.) The Brookshire Manufacturing Company operates two separate plants that manufacture specialty tools sold through hardware outlet channels. Their line of tools appeals to mechanics, machinists, and general repair specialists. One of their most popular small tools has been their "nut cracker," a tool designed to cut the nuts off of corroded bolts without damaging other parts when disassembling machinery. The company has a large number of individuals on hourly pay and, as a consequence, a payroll is prepared each week for payment on Friday. At the end of each accounting period, there is a significant amount of wages earned but not yet paid. This is due to the fact that the accounting period ends on the last day of the period, which is seldom on Friday. Accordingly, an adjusting entry must be made at the end of each period for the wages earned (accrued) but not yet paid. The adjusting entry at the end of the last period was:

December 31, 1974:

Wage Expense	29,000	
Wages Payable		29,000
To record wages earned in 1974 but not yet paid.		

The next Friday, in this particular case, was on January 3, 1974; accordingly, the following "regular payroll" entry was made for January 3, 1975:

Wages Payable................................. 29,000
Wage Expense (1975)........................... 47,000
    Cash......................................   76,000
    To record weekly payroll, including unpaid
    wages carried over from 1974 (Monday and
    Tuesday).

The bookkeeper has presented you with a problem in respect to these two entries. "When I go to make the payroll entry, there is a tremendous amount of time spent and inconvenience in keeping up with the amount of the cash disbursement that must be matched with the debit to Wages Payable ($29,000 in this instance). Is there some way that we can simplify the procedure to make it less inconvenient?" Your immediate response is: "Sure, it's very simple; just back out the adjusting entry. Here is how it is done!"

Required:

Illustrate and explain "how it is done." (Note: Remember that Wage Expense account is closed to Income Summary at each December 31.)

6 Accounting for sales revenue and measurement of revenue deductions

Purpose
of the
chapterThe dominant features of many business entities are the purchasing and selling functions, whether the business is retail, wholesale, or manufacturing. Decision makers that use financial reports often focus considerable attention on the marketing successes and failures of a business.

A merchandising business, whether retail or wholesale, devotes most of its energies to the buying and selling of goods, either raw or finished. Practically all manufacturing businesses also devote significant efforts and resources to purchasing and selling activities. Generally, a manufacturing business purchases raw materials for conversion into finished products, which then are sold. It is not uncommon for a service business also to sell some merchandise. For example, a retail appliance store frequently includes a combined sales-and-service-type operation. These activities of a business have a major impact on net income.

Although the discussions and illustrations in the preceding chapters relating to the measurement of resources, liabilities, and net income are as appropriate for merchandising and manufacturing enterprises as for service businesses, for instructional reasons they were limited primarily to service businesses. This chapter will focus on the measurement and reporting problems for selling and purchasing activities in all types of businesses. It will not consider manufacturing activities. That topic is discussed in *Fundamentals of Management Accounting*.

PART ONE: ACCOUNTING FOR SALES REVENUE

This part focuses on the accounting for sales revenue. Marketing has two sides the accountant must consider in measuring net income.

167

One side is revenue and the other is expenses directly related to revenue generation. The revenue side requires careful measurement of economic effects of each sale of goods and services. On the expense side, under the matching principle when sales revenues are earned during a particular period, the cost of the merchandise sold, and the selling and administrative expenses incurred in making those sales must be measured and reported. The cost of the merchandise sold is usually called cost of goods sold on the income statement and it is reported

Exhibit 6–1

CAMPUS CORNER, INCORPORATED
Income Statement
For the Year Ended December 31, 1974

Gross sales......................................		$808,000
Less: Sales returns.............................	$ 6,000	
Sales allowances...........................	2,000	8,000
Net sales.......................................		800,000
Cost of goods sold:*		
Beginning inventory of merchandise, January 1, 1974.	40,000	
Purchase of merchandise during 1974†..............	515,000	
Goods available for sale.....................	555,000	
Less: Ending inventory of merchandise,		
December 31, 1974..........................	35,000	
Cost of goods sold..........................		520,000
Gross margin on sales.............................		280,000
Operating expenses:		
Selling expenses................................	110,000	
Administrative expenses........................	90,000	
Income tax expense‡..........................	31,900	231,900
Net Income.....................................		$ 48,100
Earnings per share ($48,100 ÷ 10,000 shares).........		$4.81

* This illustration assumes a periodic inventory system (see page 179).
† In a manufacturing company this may be called "Cost of Goods Manufactured.
‡ Often reported after pretax income; see pages 31 and 52.

---

immediately after the sales revenue amount.[1] Selling or distribution expenses are reported on the income statement as a subclassification of operating expenses.[2] Exhibit 6–1 is presented to emphasize the purchasing and selling activities of a typical small business. Observe the detail in respect to sales revenue and cost of goods sold. Compare this income statement with one for a service type of business such as Exhibit 2–2. There are two primary differences: (1) revenue is represented by an amount for sales rather than by service fees, and (2) inclusion of an additional expense captioned "Cost of Goods Sold." This feature makes it feasible to utilize a "step," or difference, called "Gross Margin on

[1] Some accountants prefer the designation "cost of sales."

[2] In this chapter, to simplify the illustrations, we shall not ordinarily show the detailed operating expenses.

Sales" (or simply gross margin).[3] This amount is the difference between net sales and cost of goods sold. It shows the average markup above cost realized on the goods sold during the period. The relationship between gross margin and net sales is called the gross margin ratio or percent. To illustrate, for Campus Corner, Inc., the gross margin ratio is: $280,000 ÷ $800,000 = .35. From this it can be said that for each $1.00 of net sales the gross margin is $.35.

On published financial statements the net sales amount, without the revenue details shown on Exhibit 6–1, normally is reported. However, there is a trend to reporting sales revenue by product lines, as was illustrated for J. C. Penney Company, Inc. (page 67), because this is considered particularly useful information for external decision makers.

Reporting and accounting for revenues from sales

Exhibit 6–1 reports gross sales revenue less (1) sales returns and (2) sales allowances. In accordance with the revenue principle, a sale generally is considered to be realized and, therefore, recorded in the accounts when title to the goods passes from the seller to the buyer, regardless of when the cash is collected. In Chapter 5, page 127, the revenue principle was discussed; it will not be repeated here. In these discussions we will assume the usual sales transaction and that sales revenue is to be recognized when the sales transaction is made. Thus, under the revenue principle, sales would be recorded as follows:

a. Cash sales for the day per cash register totals:

```
Jan. 15  Cash........................... 12,760
                Sales (or Sales Revenue)......      12,760
```

b. Credit sales for the day per charge tickets:

```
Jan. 15  Accounts Receivable..............  4,120
                Sales (or Sales Revenue)......       4,120
```

Alternatively, if it is desired to maintain a separate sales account in the ledger for the sales by each department, entry a, for example, could be as follows:[4]

```
a.  Jan. 15  Cash......................... 12,760
                  Sales, Dept. 1............        4,120
                  Sales, Dept. 2............        7,890
                  Sales, Dept. 3............          750
```

---

[3] Occasionally the obsolete designation "Gross Profit on Sales" is used.

[4] See Appendix A to this chapter for an applicable data-processing procedure.

Sales returns and allowances.   Many businesses permit a customer to return unsatisfactory or damaged merchandise and receive cash or credit upon the return. In some cases, rather than taking back such merchandise, a cash or credit allowance may be given to the customer. To appropriately measure sales revenue, such transactions must be recorded, whether or not the goods are returned. Although the Sales account could be debited (i.e., reduced) in recording these reductions in sales, for management control purposes (that is, so that management will be informed of the volume of returns and allowances), a separate account entitled "Sales Returns and Allowances" generally is used. This account is always viewed as a deduction from gross sales. To illustrate, assume a customer returned unsatisfactory merchandise for which he had paid $25; the entry would be:[5]

```
Jan. 18   Sales Returns and Allowances.............. 25
              Cash (or Accounts Receivable, if
                applied to his account)............       25
          See later section for perpetual inventory system.
```

Sales discounts.   A substantial portion of the sales made by some businesses are on credit. When merchandise is sold on credit, the terms of payment should be definite so there will be no misunderstanding as to the amounts and due dates. In fact, credit terms usually are printed on each credit document. Frequently, credit terms are "n/10, EOM," which means the net amount (i.e., the sales amount less any sales returns) with no discount is due not later than 10 days after the end of the month (EOM) in which the sale was made. In other cases the terms may be "n/30," which means that the net amount is due 30 days after the date of the invoice (i.e., after date of sale). In still other cases, **sales discounts** (often called cash discounts) are granted to the purchaser for early payment. For example, the credit terms may be "2/10, n/30," which means that, if payment is made within 10 days from the date of sale, the customer (debtor) may deduct 2% from the invoice, or sales price; if he does not pay within the 10-day discount period, then the full sales price (less any returns) is due in 30 days from date of sale.

A customer is motivated to pay within the discount period in order to reduce the cost of his purchase. As a consequence, the usual case is to take advantage of the sales discount. In accounting for sales discounts, the normal situation should govern the accounting procedure. The revenue principle holds that sales revenue is measured by the cash or cash equivalent received for the sale of goods. Since the sales

---

[5] If the goods were returned in the year following the year of sale, the matching principle would be violated; however, no special accounting is undertaken since the amount generally is not material.

discount will almost always be taken, to properly measure revenue the Sales Revenue account should be credited (i.e., increased) for the cash to be received rather than for the gross amount. To illustrate, assume a sale is made for $1,000 with terms 2/10, n/30. The sequence of entries would be as follows:[6]

    (a)   Jan. 18, date of sale on credit:

```
Accounts Receivable............................ 980
    Sales Revenue...............................     980
    Terms: 2/10, n/30 ($1,000 × .98 = $980)
```

    (b)   Jan. 27, date of collection (within the discount period):

```
Cash.......................................... 980
    Accounts Receivable.........................     980
```

If the payment were received after the discount period, the entry would be:

Jan. 31, date of collection (after the discount period):

```
Cash.......................................... 1,000
    Interest Revenue*...........................      20
    Accounts Receivable.........................     980
    * Or Sales Discount Revenue.
```

Cash discounts should not be confused with **trade discounts.** A cash discount is a price concession given to encourage early payment of an account. A trade discount is a device used by the vendor for quoting sales prices; the amount *after* the trade discount is the sales price. For example, an item may be quoted at $10 per unit subject to a 20% trade discount on orders of 100 units or more; thus, the price for the large order would be $8 per unit.

In recent years there has been a trend toward more credit sales, particularly at the retail level. The extension of credit may entail a significant increase in record keeping for the business. Unless the business has its credit sales handled by a credit card company, which charges a fee for this service, detailed records must be maintained for each credit customer. Appendix A discusses the nature of these detailed records.

Measuring bad debt losses. When goods and services are sold on credit, despite careful credit investigation, there will always be a few

---

[6] Some people prefer to record sales revenue at date of sales as $1,000. If the payment date is *within* the discount period, a debit of $20 to a "Sales Discount" account would be recorded at that time. Sales discount is then deducted from sales on the income statement. This approach is conceptually deficient since it overstates both the sales and accounts receivable amounts.

customers who do not pay their obligations. If an account receivable proves uncollectible, the business incurs a **bad debt loss.** Businesses that extend substantial amounts of credit do so with the expectation of a certain **average rate** of bad debt losses on credit sales. As a matter of fact, an unusually low rate of losses due to uncollectible accounts may give evidence of too tight a credit policy. If the credit policy is too restrictive, many customers who will pay their bills may be turned away. In the measurement of net income for the period, the bad debt losses of that period must be measured.

In bad debt losses, the matching principle requires that the bad debt losses be matched with the period's sales that gave rise to those losses. This requirement is difficult to implement because a bad debt loss may not materialize until one or more years after the particular sale was made. To illustrate, assume credit sales in 1972 amounted to $100,000. All of these accounts were collected except one from John Doe for $100, which was not determined to be uncollectible until the end of 1974. One approach in accounting for this sequence of events would be as follows:

```
1972: Accounts Receivable................. 100,000
            Sales Revenue...................          100,000
1972-1974: Cash........................... 99,900
            Accounts Receivable........           99,900
End of 1974: Bad Debt Expense............    100
            Accounts Receivable
            (John Doe)..............                  100
```

The above approach is known as the **charge-off method.** Note that the effects are reported over a three-year period. Therefore, it is clearly deficient because it violates the **matching principle** since the sales revenue was recognized in 1972 and a directly related expense was not recognized until 1974. The charge-off method, then, normally should not be used.

To satisfy the matching principle in such situations, the **allowance, or estimating, method** has been developed to measure bad debt losses. It recognizes that bad debt losses really are incurred in the year in which the sales were made that generated those losses. Since there is no way of telling in advance which individual accounts will ultimately prove worthless, the method is based upon the concept of **estimating** in each accounting period what the probable amount of bad debt losses due to uncollectible accounts will be. The estimate is made on an aggregate basis, because the individual accounts that will be bad will not be known in the period of sale. The question is: What percent of the aggregate credit sales for the period probably will be bad debts?

Estimating the probable amount of losses due to uncollectible accounts generally is not complex nor fraught with major uncertainties.

For a company that has been operating for some years, past experience provides a sound basis for projecting probable future bad debt losses related to credit sales. For example, an analysis of accounting data on aggregate **credit** sales and aggregate uncollectible accounts for the past five years may indicate an average bad debt loss of 1.2% of aggregate credit sales (that is, losses divided by credit sales equals 1.2%). This bad debt loss rate could simply be used for the coming year, or alternatively, assuming more care will be exercised in credit granting and more efficient collection efforts, the rate may be estimated at 1%.

Now, let's see how the allowance method would be applied to the above example. Assuming net **credit** sales in 1972 of $100,000, we would record bad debt expense of $100,000 × 1% = $1,000 **in 1972.** This would require the following adjusting entry be made on December 31, 1972 (end of the accounting period):

```
Bad Debt Expense.............................. 1,000
    Allowance for Doubtful Accounts..........         1,000
    To record the estimated bad debt loss for
    the period based on credit sales and an
    average expected loss rate of 1%
    ($100,000 × 1% = $1,000).
```

Bad debt expense would be reported on the 1972 income statement as an expense and thus would be matched with the sales revenue of the year in which the credit was granted (1972 in this case). The Bad Debt Expense account would be closed at the end of each accounting period along with the other expense accounts.

In the above entry, rather than crediting the Accounts Receivable account, the credit was made to an **offset,** *or* **contra, account** descriptively titled "Allowance for Doubtful Accounts." Other acceptable titles are "Allowance for Bad Debts" and "Allowance for Uncollectible Accounts." The Allowance for Doubtful Accounts is **always** considered to be an offset or deduction to the Accounts Receivable account. Thus, the two accounts would be reported on the balance sheet, under current assets, as follows:

```
Current assets:
  Cash......................................      $ 34,000
  Accounts Receivable........................  $148,600
    Less: Allowance for Doubtful
          Accounts..........................     2,400    146,200
```

The Allowance for Doubtful Accounts carries a cumulative **credit** balance and, since it is a balance-sheet account, it is not closed. It is sometimes described as a contra account, an asset reduction account, an offset account, or a negative asset account, but more frequently as a **valuation account.** These titles, particularly the last one, derive from the fact that it carries a cumulative credit balance that is always deducted from the Accounts Receivable account and thus serves to measure the fair (or true) value of accounts receivable. In the above example, the difference between the two accounts—$146,200—represents the expected **net realizable value** of the accounts receivable (sometimes called book value).

The above illustration based the bad debt estimate on credit sales. Occasionally, one observes a company that bases the loss rate on total sales (i.e., cash plus credit sales). This approach seems illogical since (a) cash sales obviously do not cause credit losses, and (b) a shift in the relative proportion between cash and credit sales would render such a rate meaningless. Since the total amount of credit sales for each period can be determined (because they are also recorded in Accounts Receivable as debits), there is no reason for not using credit sales as the base. Another method of estimating bad debt losses is known as "aging accounts receivable"; this method is explained and illustrated in Appendix B to this chapter.

Recording an uncollectible account. Whenever a particular receivable from a customer ultimately is determined to be uncollectible, the amount should be removed from Accounts Receivable. At this time no bad debt loss should be recorded in respect to this particular account since the loss was estimated and recorded earlier in the period of sale. The Allowance for Doubtful Accounts was established to absorb this loss. Accordingly, the entry to record an uncollectible account in the period in which uncollectibility is determined would be:

```
Dec. 30  Allowance for Doubtful Accounts......... 100
            Accounts Receivable................         100
         To write off a receivable from John
         Doe determined to be uncollectible.
```

Observe that this entry does not affect the income statement since no expense is recorded at this time. Also, the entry does not change the realizable value (i.e., the book value) of the accounts receivable. The difference between accounts receivable and the allowance account remains the same as before the entry, viz:

	Before Write-off	After Write-off
Accounts Receivable......................	$148,600	$148,500
Less: Allowance for Doubtful Accounts...	2,400	2,300
Difference—estimated realizable value.......	$146,200	$146,200

Actual write-offs compared with estimate. The actual uncollectible accounts written off seldom will agree exactly in amount with the estimates previously recorded. If the accounts actually written off are less than the allowance provided, the Allowance for Doubtful Account normally will have a credit balance.[7]

The caption "Accounts Receivable" often appears on the balance sheet under current assets without additional descriptive terms; however, a more descriptive designation such as "Receivables from Trade Customers" is preferable. Receivables from other than the regular trade customers, such as loans to officers or employees, should not be included in the accounts receivable category. Rather, as a special kind of receivable, they should be reported as separate items.

PART TWO: MEASUREMENT OF REVENUE DEDUCTIONS

In the measurement of net income for a period, in addition to carefully measuring all aspects of the revenue generated, the revenue deductions must be measured and reported. The revenue deductions, related to sales activities, are comprised of two categories of expense: cost of goods sold and selling expenses. This section focuses on the measurement of cost of goods sold. It is often the largest single item of expense to be measured and reported for the period.

Measuring inventory and cost of goods sold

In the cost-of-goods-sold section of the income statement, shown in Exhibit 6–1, the component amounts making up cost of goods sold (inventories and purchases) were reported separately. The components represent important concepts in the measurement of net income. Cost of goods sold, as an expense, is a relatively simple concept. It is the cost of the merchandise sold during the period and, therefore, excludes all goods still on hand at the end of the period (i.e., the ending or final inventory). Typically, a business will start each period with a supply of merchandise on hand, which generally is called the beginning, or initial, inventory. To that stock will be added the merchandise purchased (or manufactured) during the period.

Clearly the beginning inventory plus the purchases (or goods manufactured) during a period represent the merchandise available for sale during that period. If all the merchandise available for sale were sold in the period, there would be no ending inventory. In a typical situation, however, a quantity of the goods remains unsold at the end of each period. Thus, we must subtract the ending inventory from the goods available for sale to determine the cost of goods sold for the period.

To compute cost of goods sold, three amounts must be known: (1)

---

[7] On the other hand, occasionally the amount written off may be more than the allowance balance. In such instances there will be a temporary debit balance in the allowance account. This situation will be resolved when the next "allowance entry" is made. It may be that the estimated loss rate being used is too low.

beginning inventory, (2) purchases during the period, and (3) ending inventory. The ending inventory of one accounting period is the beginning inventory of the next period. Therefore, the beginning inventory amount will be available from the prior period. The amount of purchases for the period can be accumulated in the accounting system. Determining the amount of the final inventory presents a special problem.

There are two distinctly different systems that are used in measuring inventories. They are:

(1) Perpetual inventory system—This approach involves the maintenance of detailed inventory records in the accounting system. For each type of goods stocked, a detailed record is maintained that shows (a) units and cost of each purchase, (b) units and cost of the goods for each sale, and (c) the units and amount on hand. This continuous record is maintained on a transaction-to-transaction basis throughout the period. Thus, the inventory record provides the amount of ending inventory and the cost of goods sold for the period.

(2) Periodic inventory system—This approach involves an actual physical count of the goods on hand at the end of each period. The number of units of each type of goods on hand is multiplied by their purchase cost per unit to compute the dollar amount of the inventory. Thus, the balance of goods on hand is not known until the last day of the period.

Perpetual
inventory
system

A perpetual inventory system may involve a considerable amount of clerical effort; however, it is very effective in measuring inventory and cost of goods sold. The maintenance of a separate inventory record for each type of goods stocked on a transaction-to-transaction basis can be time-consuming and costly. In businesses stocking very few items, a manual system may be feasible; however, most perpetual inventory systems are computerized. Whether manual, mechanical, or computerized, the data to be recorded and reported are the same. For instructional purposes let's look at a manual approach. For example, Modern Equipment Company sells heavy construction equipment. It maintains a separate perpetual inventory record for each type of machine stocked. The inventory record for a mower, code 330, is shown in Exhibit 6–2.[8]

The perpetual inventory record shown in Exhibit 6–2 reflects an ending inventory balance of 21 units and a total inventory cost of $6,300. A similar inventory record for each type of equipment sold would provide the total inventory for the company. The computer does exactly what was done manually in Exhibit 6–2; however, a comput-

---

[8] Measuring inventories and cost of goods sold when there are different *unit* purchase costs is deferred to Chapter 7.

Exhibit 6–2

PERPETUAL INVENTORY RECORD

| Item | Mower (heavy) | Code | # 330 | Minimum stock | 10 |
| Location | Storage# 4 | Valuation basis | Cost | Maximum stock | 40 |

| | | Purchases | | | Sales | | | Balance on Hand | | |
Date	Explanation	Units	Unit Cost	Total Cost	Units	Unit Cost	Total Cost	Units	Unit Cost	Total Cost
Jan. 1	Beginning inventory							10	300	3,000
14	Purchase	30	300	9,000				40	300	12,000
30	Sale				20	300	6,000	20	300	6,000
31	Return sale				(1)	300	(300)	21	300	6,300

erized system does it with tremendous speed and has wide ranges of capacity to handle voluminous data. The perpetual inventory approach is widely used because it can be programmed for computer-based systems and measures very effectively.

A perpetual inventory system may be described as follows:

(1) During the period, the purchase cost of each type of goods bought is entered in the Inventory account as an increase and in a detailed perpetual inventory record (Exhibit 6–2). Thus, a cash or credit purchase of goods for resale would be recorded as follows (refer to Exhibit 6–2):

```
Jan. 14, 1974:
Inventory* (Mower # 330)..................... 9,000
        Accounts Payable (or Cash)..............        9,000
    * Also entered in the perpetual inventory record.
```

(2) During the period, each sale is recorded by means of **two companion entries.** One entry is to record the **sales revenue at sales price,** and the other entry is to record the **cost of goods sold at purchase cost.** The sales revenue is accumulated in the Sales Revenue account and the cost of goods sold is accumulated in the Cost of Goods Sold account. Thus, a credit or cash sale would be recorded as follows (refer to Exhibit 6–2):

```
Jan. 30, 1974:
(1)  To record the sales revenue at the sales
     price of $400 per unit:
        Accounts Receivable (or Cash)......... 8,000
           Sales Revenue (20 units × $400)...        8,000
(2)  To record the cost of goods sold (at
     cost per the perpetual inventory record-
     Exhibit 6-2):
        Cost of Goods Sold................... 6,000
           Inventory (Mower # 330)*..........        6,000
```
* Also entered in the perpetual inventory record.

(3) During the period, purchase returns and sales returns are recorded in the Inventory account and on the perpetual inventory card at cost. For example, the return by a customer of one mower on January 31 would be recorded as follows:

```
Jan. 31, 1974:
To record the return of one mower:
   Sales Returns and Allowances.................. 400
      Accounts Receivable (or Cash).............        400

   Inventory (Mower # 330)*...................... 300
      Cost of Goods Sold........................        300
```
* This amount was provided by the perpetual inventory record; also restored to the perpetual inventory record.

(4) At the end of the period, the balance in the Cost of Goods Sold account would measure the total amount of that expense to be reported on the income statement. There would be no computations to be made of cost of goods sold like those shown on page 180 in situations where the periodic inventory system is used. Similarly, the Inventory account would measure the ending inventory amount that would be reported on the balance sheet. The sum of all the inventory balances on the various perpetual inventory records would be the same as the balance in the Inventory account in the ledger at all times.

This simple illustration demonstrates that, when a perpetual inventory system is used, it is not necessary to take a physical inventory count of the merchandise on hand at the end of the year in order to find the ending inventory amount and to measure cost of goods sold. However, since clerical errors are apt to occur, a physical inventory should be taken from time to time to check upon the accuracy of the perpetual inventory records. When an error is found, the inventory records must be adjusted to agree with the physical count.

For various reasons some companies do not use a perpetual inventory system. One of the primary reasons is the nature of the business. For example, a variety store or a grocery store could experience considerable difficulties and cost in implementing such a system because of the large number of low-priced items stocked and the high stock turnover rates. For example, when you purchase groceries for cash, no record is made at the cash register of the specific items purchased. Rather, the dollar amount of sales revenue is recorded on the cash register tape. Clearly, the grocery store in this instance is not accumulating the physical quantity of goods sold that would be needed for each type of item to implement a perpetual inventory system. Businesses that do not use a perpetual inventory system necessarily use a **periodic inventory system.** A periodic inventory system, in many respects, is more difficult to understand and more accounts are required. Also, a periodic inventory system does not provide an important element of **inventory control** that can be attained through a perpetual system.

A periodic inventory system may be described as follows:

(1)   During the period, the purchase cost of all goods bought is accumulated in an account called Purchases (or Merchandise). Thus, a credit or cash purchase would be recorded as follows:

```
Jan. 14, 1974:  Purchases................... 9,000
                     Accounts Payable (or Cash)      9,000
```

(2)   During the period, the sales price received for all goods sold is accumulated in a Sales Revenue account. In contrast to the perpetual inventory approach, no companion entry is made to record the cost of goods sold since the periodic system cannot provide such unit cost data during the period. Thus, a credit or cash sale would be recorded as follows:

```
Jan. 30, 1974:  Accounts Receivable (or Cash) 8,000
                     Sales Revenue...........      8,000
```

(3)   At the end of the period, the **Inventory account** still reflects the inventory amount carried over from the prior period. Thus, to measure the ending inventory for the current period, a physical count must be made of all goods on hand. This count is made at the end of each period. A physical count is necessary since, under the periodic inventory system, a transaction-by-transaction **unit record** is not maintained for purchases, cost of goods sold, and the inventory balance. Inventory taking is discussed later.

(4)   The dollar amount of the ending inventory quantities is
computed by multiplying the number of units found to be
on hand times their unit purchase cost. The dollar amounts
thus determined for all of the types of goods stocked are
summed to measure the total ending inventory for the company.

(5)   After the ending inventory is measured, as in (4), cost of
goods sold for the period can be computed as follows:

Beginning inventory (carried over from the last period in the Inventory account).............................	$ 40,000*
Add purchases for the period (accumulated balance in the Purchases account). :...........................	515,000
Total Goods Available for Sale.................	555,000
Less ending inventory (determined by physical count)...	35,000
Cost of Goods Sold.......................	$520,000

* Based on the data shown in Exhibit 6-1.

To summarize, a comparison of the perpetual and periodic inventory
systems will reveal two basic differences between them:

1.   Inventory:
  a.   Perpetual—During the period, the Inventory account is
       increased for each purchase and decreased (at
       cost) for each sale. Thus, at the end of the
       period, it measures ending inventory.
  b.   Periodic—During the period, the Inventory account is
       not changed, thus, it reflects the beginning in-
       ventory amount. During the period, each pur-
       chase is recorded in the Purchases account. As
       a consequence, the ending inventory each pe-
       riod must be measured by physical count, then
       "costed" at purchase cost.
2.   Cost of goods sold:
  a.   Perpetual—During the period, cost of goods sold is re-
       corded at the time of each sale and the In-
       ventory account is reduced. Thus the system
       measures the cost of goods sold amount for
       the period.
  b.   Periodic—During the period, no entry is made for cost of
       goods sold (in this instance there is no Cost of
       Goods Sold account). At the end of the period,
       after the physical inventory count, cost of goods
       sold is measured as: beginning inventory +
       purchases − ending inventory = cost of goods
       sold.

Some
issues in
measuring
purchases

In accordance with the cost principle, goods purchased for resale are recorded at the date that title passes to the buyer. Normally, title is considered to pass when the goods are received and not when the purchase order is placed. The goods should be recorded at their cash equivalent price in accordance with the cost principle. Cost, as defined, includes the cash equivalent price paid to the vendor plus other amounts paid for freight and handling in order to get the goods to their intended location. Cost does not include any financing expenditures, such as interest paid on funds borrowed to make the purchase. In accounting for purchases, several measurement problems frequently are encountered; they are discussed below.

Purchases returns and allowances. Goods purchased may be returned to the vendor because they are unsatisfactory or damaged. When the goods are returned or when the vendor makes an allowance because of the circumstances, the effect on the cost of purchases must be measured. The purchaser will receive a cash refund or a reduction in his liability to the vendor for the purchase. To illustrate, assume Company A returned to Company B, for credit, unsatisfactory goods that cost $160. The return would be recorded by Company A as follows:

DEC LIAB
DEC ASSET

```
Accounts Payable................................. 160
    Purchase Returns and Allowances*............       160
    * Inventory is credited when perpetual inventory procedures are being used.
```

Purchase returns and allowances are viewed as a deduction to the cost of Purchases.

IMPORTANT

Transportation-in. Under the cost principle, assets acquired should be measured and recorded at their cash equivalent cost. Thus, the purchase cost of goods acquired for resale should include all freight and transportation-in costs incurred by the purchaser. When a perpetual inventory system is used, transportation costs paid on goods purchased should be included in the inventory cost amount entered in the perpetual inventory record. When a periodic inventory system is used, such costs should be entered as a debit (i.e., increase) to the Purchases account. However, for control and reporting purposes, and because of problems of apportioning a freight bill to the several items it may cover, it may be more practical to use a separate ledger account entitled "Transportation-in," or "Freight-in." Thus, the journal entry to record a payment for transportation charges upon delivery of merchandise acquired for resale would be:

```
Jan. 17  Transportation-in......................... 18
             Cash.....................................       18
```

At the end of the period, the balance in the Transportation-in account would be reported as an addition to the cost of Purchases.

Purchase discounts.   Recall the discussion of sales discount on page 170. Essentially, a corresponding situation occurs when merchandise is purchased for resale—except that the discount is received rather than given. When merchandise is purchased on credit, terms such as 2/10, n/30 are common. This means that if payment of the purchase invoice cost is made within 10 days from date of purchase, a 2% discount may be taken. If payment is not made within the discount period, then the gross purchase invoice cost is due 30 days after purchase. To illustrate, assume Company A purchases goods from a number of suppliers. The company always pays cash at date of purchase or within the discount period. On January 17, the company purchased goods from Vendor B that had a $1,000 invoice price with terms 2/10, n/30. Under these terms, Company A, following its own payment policy, will pay $980 for the goods. Therefore, the purchase should be recorded by Company A as follows:[9]

```
Jan. 17--Date of purchase:

Purchases (or Inventory)....................... 980
    Accounts Payable...........................         980

Jan. 26--Date of payment, within the discount period:

Accounts Payable............................... 980
    Cash.......................................         980
```

If for any reason Company A did not pay within the ten-day discount period, the following entry would result:

```
Feb. 1

Accounts Payable............................... 980
Discounts Lost (an expense).................... 20
    Cash.......................................       1,000
```

Taking a physical inventory.   We explained above that, whether a periodic or perpetual inventory system is used, a physical inventory count must be taken from time to time. When a periodic inventory system is used, the inventory must be counted physically at the end of each period because the financial statements cannot be prepared without

---

[9] Some people prefer to record the transaction at the date of purchase at the gross amount, i.e., at $1,000. In this instance, payment within the discount period would result in credit to the account Purchase Discount, $20. The purchase discount credit would then be reported as a revenue, or as a deduction from purchases. This credit is not income and, if deducted in full from purchases on the income statement, would tend to misstate both inventory and purchases. For these reasons it is conceptually deficient.

this amount. When a perpetual inventory system is used, the inventory count may be scheduled at various times to verify the perpetual inventory records. The two steps in taking a physical inventory are:

(1)   Quantity count—The count of merchandise is made after the close of business on the last day of the period. Normally, it would be difficult to accurately count goods during business hours when sales are taking place. A physical count is made of all items of merchandise on hand and entered on an appropriate form. For example, an inventory sheet, such as the one shown in Exhibit 6–3, may be used. The quantity

Exhibit 6–3

Campus Corner PHYSICAL INVENTORY SHEET							
Date of Inventory _12/31/74_ Department _# 4_ Taken by _M. R._							
Location	Identification of Merchandise	Quantity on Hand	Date Purchased	Unit Cost Price	Unit Market Price*	Unit Cost	Inventory Amount
1	Headsets #8-16	20	12/2/74	$19.95	$11.50	$11.50	$230
2	Television Sets #17-961	7	11/5/74	349.50	220.00	220.00	1,540
2	Radios #23-72	4	10/26/74	49.95	34.00	34.00	136
	Total Department Inventory	XXX	XXX	XXX	XXX	XXX	
TOTAL INVENTORY VALUE--ALL DEPARTMENTS 12/31/74							$35,000

* Price that would have to be paid if the item were being purchased on the inventory date (see lower-of-cost-or-market discussion in Chapter 7).

determined to be on hand is recorded in a quantity column as shown in the exhibit. Of particular importance in the quantity count is to be sure that all of the merchandise owned by the business is included, wherever located, and that all items for which the entity does not have legal title are excluded. On occasion a business will have possession of goods it does not own.

(2)   Inventory costing—After the physical count to determine the quantity of goods on hand has been completed, each kind of merchandise must be assigned a unit cost. Each quantity is multiplied by the unit purchase cost to derive the inventory amount for each different kind of goods, as illustrated

in Exhibit 6–3. The sum of the inventory amounts for all merchandise on hand measures the total ending inventory amount for the business. Exhibit 6–3 reflects computation of the ending inventory shown on the income statement for Campus Corners (Exhibit 6–1). In costing inventory quantities, the cost principle is applied; therefore, unit purchase cost, as defined above, must be used. However, there are several ways to identify unit purchase cost for inventory purposes such as the *first-in, first-out (Fifo)*, *last-in, first-out (Lifo)*, or *average cost* approaches. These alternative approaches to costing inventories are discussed in detail in Chapter 7.

Inventories, since they frequently represent large amounts of tied-up resources (cash), often present management with complex planning and control problems. For example, decisions should be made as to the maximum and minimum levels of inventory that should be observed; when to reorder; how much to reorder; and the characteristics of the items to stock, such as size, color, style, and specifications. Some of these issues are discussed in *Fundamentals of Management Accounting*. From the viewpoint of the investor, creditor, and other interested parties, the investment in inventory frequently is important in decision making. Thus, explanatory footnotes are frequently observed that relate to inventories that are included in the financial reports.

Data processing— adjusting and closing entries

In this chapter a number of new accounts related to selling and purchasing activities have been introduced. Further explanation, in terms of the adjusting and closing phases of the information-processing cycle, is needed.

The Sales Revenue, Sales Return and Allowance accounts normally do not involve any adjusting entries (see discussion in Chapter 5). These accounts are closed to the Income Summary account along with the other revenue and expense accounts. Thus, these new accounts do not present new problems for you in the adjusting and closing phases of the information-processing cycle. In contrast to the revenue accounts, however, the Inventory and Cost of Goods Sold accounts do present new procedures in the adjusting and closing phases. The adjusting and closing phases for these two items are affected by the inventory system used.

ADJUSTING AND CLOSING PHASES FOR A PERPETUAL INVENTORY SYSTEM

When a perpetual inventory system is used, no additional adjusting entries are required. The only new closing entry is to transfer the balance in Cost of Goods Sold to the Income Summary account. Since the Cost of Goods Sold account is an expense, it is closed in the same manner as each of the other expense accounts. To illustrate, assuming a debit balance of $150,000 in the Cost of Goods Sold account at the end of the period, the closing entry would be:

```
Income Summary........................... 150,000
    Cost of Goods Sold...................           150,000
```

Under the perpetual inventory system there are no adjusting entries and only one closing entry (for Cost of Goods Sold), because the Inventory account is maintained up-to-date after each purchase and sale so that the ending balance in the Inventory account reflects the ending inventory that will be reflected on the balance sheet as a current asset. Similarly, the Cost of Goods Sold account balance reflects the accumulated cost of all goods sold for the period.

ADJUSTING AND CLOSING PHASES FOR THE PERIODIC INVENTORY SYSTEM

When the periodic inventory system is used, **two additional adjusting entries** are required: (a) the beginning inventory amount, which has been reflected in the Inventory account throughout the period, must be transferred to Income Summary; and (b) the ending inventory amount, which has just been determined by physical count, must be recorded as an asset. To illustrate, assume that the Inventory account (periodic inventory system) reflects a $40,000 debit on the trial balance taken from the ledger at the end of the period on December 31, 1974. Since no entries are made in the Inventory account during the year, under the periodic approach this balance reflects the **beginning** inventory. That is, it is the amount of inventory that was carried over from the last period. Assume further that the ending inventory on December 31, 1974, determined by physical count, amounted to $35,000. The two adjusting entries would be (these amounts agree with page 180):

```
a.  To transfer the beginning inventory balance:
Income Summary........................... 40,000
    Inventory (beginning)................           40,000
b.  To record the ending inventory:
Inventory (ending)....................... 35,000
    Income Summary.......................           35,000
```

In respect to closing entries under the periodic inventory system, the ending balance in the Purchases account is closed to Income Summary along with the other expense accounts. To illustrate, assuming an ending balance in the Purchases account of $515,000, the closing entry would be as follows:

```
c.  Income Summary.....................  515,000
        Purchases.....................              515,000
```

After these entries are posted, the Income Summary account would appear as follows:

Income Summary Account

Operating Expenses (not illustrated)		Revenues (not illustrated)	
(a) Beginning inventory	40,000	(b) Ending inventory	35,000
(c) Purchases	515,000		

Observe that the net of the three amounts shown above in the Income Summary account is a debit of $520,000, which is the amount of Cost of Goods Sold (see page 180).[10] If there are accounts for Transportation-in and Purchase Returns and Allowances, they would be closed to Income Summary along with the Purchases account.

Inventory shrinkage. Inventory shrinkage occurs as a result of theft, shoplifting, breakage, and spoilage. The measurement of inventory shrinkage is important for internal management uses. The amount of shrinkage is reported on internal financial statements, but seldom if ever are such amounts reported separately on external financial statements. The measurement of this loss often is directly related to the inventory system used.

When the periodic inventory system is used, measurement of this loss is often difficult, if not impossible. The physical inventory, taken at the end of the period, does not, in itself, provide a basis for measurement of the shrinkage. Under this system, since cost of goods sold is a residual amount (i.e., beginning inventory + purchases − ending inventory = cost of goods sold), the shrinkage loss is buried in the cost of goods sold amount.

Alternatively, a perpetual inventory system will provide data on shrinkage. The inventory record provides both cost of goods sold and the ending inventory. These data make it possible to measure shrinkage loss. To illustrate, assume the inventory record shows cost of goods sold for the period to be 19 units, $5,700 (Exhibit 6–2) and the ending inventory to be 21 units, $6,300. Assume further that a physical inventory is taken at the end of the period that shows 20 units on hand. In the absence of clerical error, an inventory shrinkage would be reported as 1 unit, $300. An investigation may convince the management

---

[10] Some accountants prefer to set up a *temporary* Cost of Goods Sold account under the periodic inventory system to facilitate the three adjusting and closing entries illustrated above. Under this procedure the three amounts, beginning inventory, ending inventory, and purchases would be transferred to it. The resultant balance in the Cost of Goods Sold account ($520,000 in the above instance) would then be closed to the Income Summary account.

that the shrinkage is due to theft. The entry to record the shrinkage, assuming a perpetual inventory system, would be:

```
Inventory Shrinkage (or Loss Due to Theft)....... 300
    Inventory.....................................      300
```

Demonstration case for self-study

ROTE'S APPLIANCE STORE, INCORPORATED

(Try to resolve the case before studying the suggested solution that follows.)

Rote's Appliance Store has been operating for a number of years. It is a relatively small but profitable retail outlet for major appliances, such as refrigerators and air conditioners. Approximately 10% of the sales are on credit. This case has been selected and simplified to demonstrate information processing when there are significant selling activities; the service activities have been deleted. The case has been structured to illustrate the application of both perpetual and periodic inventory systems with the same data. The annual fiscal period ends December 31, 1974. Two situations will be assumed:

Situation A—Perpetual inventory system is assumed to be used.

Situation B—Periodic inventory system is assumed to be used.

The trial balance derived from the ledger at December 31, 1974, was:

Accounts	System A—Perpetual Inventory System Used Debit	System A—Perpetual Inventory System Used Credit	Situation B—Periodic Inventory System Used Debit	Situation B—Periodic Inventory System Used Credit
Cash.............................	$ 24,100		$ 24,100	
Accounts Receivable.................	15,000		15,000	
Allowance for Doubtful Accounts.....		$ 1,000		$ 1,000
Merchandise Inventory:*				
Jan. 1, 1974......................			20,000	
Dec. 31, 1974....................	16,000			
Store Equipment....................	30,000		30,000	
Accumulated Depreciation, Store				
Equipment.......................		9,000		9,000
Accounts Payable....................		8,000		8,000
Income Taxes Payable..............				
Capital Stock.......................		40,000		40,000
Retained Earnings, Jan. 1, 1974.......		9,000		9,000
Sales Revenue......................		102,000		102,000
Sales Returns and Allowances........	2,000		2,000	
Cost of Goods Sold*................	60,000			
Purchases*.........................			57,000	
Purchases Returns and Allowances*...				1,000
Expenses (not detailed)..............	21,900		21,900	
Depreciation Expense................				
Income Tax Expense................				
	$169,000	$169,000	$170,000	$170,000

* These account balances are different because of the effects of the inventory system used.

Data developed as a basis for the adjusting entries at December 31, 1974, were:

a. Credit sales in 1974 amounted to $10,000; the average bad-debt-loss rate is estimated to be 1% of credit sales.

b. The store equipment originally cost $30,000 and is being depreciated on the basis of an estimated ten-year useful life with no residual value.

c. On December 31, 1974, the periodic inventory count of goods on hand reflected $16,000.

d. The corporate income tax rate is 22%.

The beginning inventory, January 1, 1974, is shown on the trial balance.

Required:

(a) Based upon the above data, complete a worksheet at December 31, 1974, similar to that shown in Exhibit 5–2. You may omit the pair of columns for Adjusted Trial Balance. Prepare a separate worksheet for each situation. See discussion below.

(b) Based upon the worksheet, present, in parallel columns, the adjusting entries for each situation at December 31, 1974.

(c) Based upon the worksheet, present, in parallel columns, the closing entries for each situation at December 31, 1974.

In preparing the worksheet when the **perpetual inventory system** is used no new complications are presented. The inventory amount is extended across the worksheet as an asset since the balance under the perpetual system reflects the ending inventory. The expense item—cost of goods sold—is extended to the Income Summary, debit column along with all the other expenses. See Exhibit 6–4.

In preparing the worksheet when the **periodic inventory system** is used both the beginning and ending inventory amounts must be used. First, the beginning inventory must be transferred to Income Summary. This may be done by means of an adjusting entry that credits the Inventory account and debits Income Summary. A special line, Income Summary–Inventories, is added to the bottom of the worksheet to accommodate this debit. Next, the ending inventory (determined by physical count) must be entered on the worksheet. This may be done by means of another adjusting entry that debits the Inventory account and credits Income Summary. On the worksheet this credit is entered on the special line that was added—Income Summary–Inventories. The beginning inventory amount is carried across as a debit to the income statement column because it is an *addition* to cost of goods sold. In contrast, the ending inventory is carried across (a) as a credit to the income statement because it is a *deduction* from cost of goods sold and (b) as a debit on the balance sheet because it is an asset at the end of the period.[11] See Exhibit 6–4.

---

[11] There are several mechanical ways of handling the inventories on the worksheet when the periodic inventory system is used. Some accountants view the inventory entries as closing rather than adjusting entries. The various approaches arrive at the same net result and each has its particular mechanical advantages and disadvantages.

Suggested Solution:

Requirement (b)

Adjusting Entries
December 31, 1974

		Situation A		Situation B	
		Perpetual Inventory		*Periodic Inventory*	
(a)	Expenses (bad debt loss)............	100		100	
	Allowance for Doubtful Accounts		100		100
	Bad debt loss estimated, $10,000 \times 1\% = \$100$.				
(b)	Depreciation Expense..............	3,000		3,000	
	Accumulated Depreciation, Store Equipment.................		3,000		3,000
	Depreciation for one year, $30,000 \div 10$ years $= \$3,000$.				
(c-1)	Income Summary.................	(Not applicable)		20,000	
	Inventory (beginning)..........				20,000
	Transfer beginning inventory to Income Summary.				
(c-2)	Inventory (ending)...............	(Not applicable)		16,000	
	Income Summary.............				16,000
	Record ending inventory per physical count.				
(d)	Income Tax Expense..............	3,300		3,300	
	Income Taxes Payable.........		3,300		3,300
	Income taxes for year, $15,000 \times 22\% = \$3,300$.				

Requirement (c)

Closing Entries
December 31, 1974

(1)	Sales Revenue......................	102,000		102,000	
	Sales Returns and Allowances....		2,000		2,000
	Income Summary..............		100,000		100,000
	To transfer the revenue accounts to Income Summary.				
(2)	Income Summary..................	(Not applicable)		56,000	
	Purchase Return Allowances........			1,000	
	Purchases.....................				57,000
	To transfer purchase amounts to Income Summary.				
(3)	Income Summary.................	60,000		(Not applicable)	
	Cost of Goods Sold...........		60,000		
(4)	Income Summary..................	28,300		28,300	
	Expenses (not detailed)..........		22,000		22,000
	Depreciation Expense...........		3,000		3,000
	Income Tax Expense............		3,300		3,300
	To transfer expense accounts to Income Summary.				
(5)	Income Summary..................	11,700		11,700	
	Retained Earnings..............		11,700		11,700
	To transfer net income to Retained Earnings.				

Worksheets compared for periodic and perpetual inventory systems

ROTE'S APPLIANCE STORE, INCORPORATED
Worksheet, December 31, 1974
Assuming Perpetual Inventory System Is Used (Situation A)

	Trial Balance		Adjusting Entries		Income Statement		Balance Sheet	
	Debit	Credit	Debit	Credit	Debit	Credit	Debit	Credit
Cash	24,100						24,100	
Accounts Receivable	15,000						15,000	
Allowance for Doubtful Accounts		1,000		(a) 100				1,100
Merchandise Inventory	16,000						16,000	
Store Equipment	30,000						30,000	
Accumulated Depreciation, Equipment		9,000		(b) 3,000				12,000
Accounts Payable		8,000						8,000
Income Taxes Payable				(d) 3,300				3,300
Capital Stock		40,000						40,000
Retained Earnings, Jan. 1, 1974		9,000						9,000
Sales Revenue		102,000				102,000		
Sales Returns and Allowances	2,000				2,000			
Cost of Goods Sold	60,000				60,000			
Expenses (not detailed)	21,900		(a) 100		22,000			
Depreciation Expense			(b) 3,000		3,000			
Income Tax Expense			(d) 3,300		3,300			
Net Income					11,700			11,700
Totals	169,000	169,000	6,400	6,400	102,000	102,000	85,100	85,100

ROTES APPLIANCE STORE, INCORPORATED
Worksheet, December 31, 1974
Assuming Periodic Inventory System Is Used (Situation B)

	Trial Balance		Adjusting Entries		Income Statement		Balance Sheet	
	Debit	Credit	Debit	Credit	Debit	Credit	Debit	Credit
Cash	24,100						24,100	
Accounts Receivable	15,000						15,000	
Allowance for Doubtful Accounts		1,000		(a) 100				1,100
Merchandise Inventory	20,000		(c-2) 16,000	(c-1) 20,000			16,000	
Store Equipment	30,000						30,000	
Accumulated Depreciation, Equipment		9,000		(b) 3,000				12,000
Accounts Payable		8,000						8,000
Income Taxes Payable				(d) 3,300				3,300
Capital Stock		40,000						40,000
Retained Earnings, Jan. 1, 1974		9,000						9,000
Sales Revenue		102,000				102,000		
Sales Returns and Allowances	2,000				2,000			
Purchases	57,000				57,000			
Purchases Returns and Allowances		1,000				1,000		
Expenses (not detailed)	21,900		(a) 100		22,000			
Depreciation Expense			(b) 3,000		3,000			
Income Tax Expense			(d) 3,300		3,300			
Income Summary—Inventories			(c-1) 20,000	(c-2) 16,000	20,000	16,000		
Net Income					11,700			11,700
Totals	170,000	170,000	42,400	42,400	119,000	119,000	85,100	85,100

Summary   This chapter focused on the measurement of the effects on net income of the selling and purchasing activities in various types of businesses. A new expense on the income statement was introduced known as "Cost of Goods Sold." Cost of goods sold is the *cost* of the merchandise represented in the sales revenue amount. In conformity with the matching principle, the total cost of those items sold during the period must be matched with the total sales revenue earned during the period. When cost of goods sold is matched or deducted from sales revenue for the period, the difference is known as gross margin on sales. From this amount, the other expenses must be deducted to derive net income.

The chapter also discussed and illustrated the effect on cost of goods sold of beginning and ending inventories of goods held for resale. We observed that the ending inventory of one period is the beginning inventory of the next period. Two systems were discussed for measuring the quantity of merchandise on hand at the end of the period and the cost of goods sold: (1) the perpetual inventory system, which is based on the maintenance of detailed inventory records for each kind of goods stocked; and (2) the periodic inventory system, which is based upon a physical count of the goods on hand at the end of each period.

Important terms	Cost of goods sold	Allowance for doubtful accounts
	Gross margin on sales	Revenue deductions
	Gross margin ratio (or percent)	Beginning inventory
	Revenue principle	Ending inventory
	Matching principle	Perpetual inventory system
	Gross sales	Periodic inventory system
	Net sales	Goods available for sale
	Sales returns and allowances	Physical inventory
	Sales discounts	Purchases returns and allowances
	Trade discounts	Transportation-in
	Bad debt losses	Cash equivalent cost
	Allowance method	Purchase discounts
	Offset (or contra) account	Inventory shrinkage

Appendix A   DATA PROCESSING—CONTROLLING ACCOUNTS AND SUBSIDIARY LEDGERS

This appendix explains an accounting procedure designed to facilitate record keeping and internal control in situations where a large number of similar transactions recur continuously. It does not involve accounting theory, principles, or standards, but deals with the mechanics of data processing. The use of *control accounts* and *subsidiary ledgers* will be explained and illustrated for accounts receivable; however, the procedure is also applicable in any situation that involves numerous transactions that are similar and require detailed record keeping, such as accounts payable and fixed assets.

In the preceding discussions and illustrations, charge sales or services were credited to a revenue account and debited, in the *general,* or regular, *ledger* to an account designated *"Accounts Receivable."* Subsequently, upon payment, the Accounts Receivable account was decreased or credited. We did not illustrate the manner in which the account receivable for each *individual customer* was maintained. Some businesses carry thousands of individuals on a credit status. The business could maintain some kind of "filing system" that would show (a) the amount of sales and services provided each customer on credit, (b) how much was collected from each customer on credit previously extended, and (c) the balance owed by each customer at any point in time. Alternatively, it could maintain a separate receivable account for each customer in the *general ledger.* This would require, in the above example, several thousand such accounts in that ledger.

A more efficient procedure involves the use of a single *control account* in the general ledger for Accounts Receivable and a separate *subsidiary ledger* that carries an individual account for each credit customer. Thus, in the above example, the general ledger would include Accounts Receivable as a *single control account* and the *subsidiary ledger* would include the several thousand *individual receivable accounts.* At any given point, the *sum* of the *accounts* in the receivable subsidiary ledger, in the absence of error, would equal the *single balance* in the *Accounts Receivable control account* in the general ledger. The Accounts Receivable account in the general ledger is called a control account because it controls the subsidiary ledger. The individual customer accounts, as subdivisions of it, are subsidiary to the control or summary account; thus the designation, subsidiary ledger.

To illustrate the data processing with a control account and a subsidiary ledger for Accounts Receivable, we will assume several transactions for the Mayo Department Store. Although most businesses that have a large volume of transactions such as these will use a computerized system, we will illustrate a manual system for instructional purposes. First, assume that on January 5, 1974, sales were made on credit to six different customers. These sales could be recorded in the general journal as follows:

GENERAL JOURNAL   Page 1

Date		Folio	Debit	Credit
Jan. 5	Accounts Receivable	12	2,400	
	Sales	61		2,400
	To record the following			
	credit sales:			
	Adams, J. K. $ 740	√		
	Baker, B. B. 120	√		
	Ford, C. E. 340	√		
	Moore, W. E. 320	√		
	Price, V. T. 430	√		
	Ward, B. L. 450	√		
	Total $2,400			

Posting of the above journal entry to the control account in the general ledger is indicated by entering the account numbers in the folio column in the usual manner, and posting to the individual customer accounts in the subsidiary ledger is indicated by entering a check mark (✔) in the folio column of the journal. Thus, we posted the total amount to the control account, Accounts Receivable (a debit total of $2,400), and we posted the several single amounts to the subsidiary and the subsidiary ledger are illustrated below. Note that the debit-credit-balance form is used rather than the T-account form that is used for instructional purposes.

GENERAL LEDGER

Date 1974	Cash #11	Folio	Debit	Credit	Balance
Jan 12		3	1 000		
	Accounts Receivable Control #12				
Jan 5		1	2 400		2 400
7		2		140	2 260
12		3		1 000	1 260
	Sales #61				
Jan 5		1		2 400	2 400
	Sales Returns #62				
Jan 7		2	140		140

SUDSIDIARY LEDGER

	Adams, J.K.				
Jan 5		1	740		740
7	Return	2		140	600
12		3		400	200
	Baker, B. R.				
Jan 5		1	120		120
	Ford, C. E.				
Jan 5		1	340		340
12		3		340	– 0 –
	Moore, W. E.				
Jan 5		1	320		320
12		3		220	100
	Price, V. T.				
Jan 5		1	430		430
12		3		40	390
	Ward, B. L.				
Jan 5		1	450		450

Now, assume that on January 7 one customer, J. K. Adams, returned as unsatisfactory some of the goods purchased on January 5. Mayo accepted the goods and gave him a credit memorandum. The resultant journal entry was:

GENERAL JOURNAL   Page 2

Jan. 7	Sales Returns	62	140	
	Accounts Receivable	12		140
	To record the return			
	of goods:			
	Adams, J. K. $140	√		

The folio column reveals that the above entry has been posted in total to the control account in the general ledger and that the single amount has been posted to the individual customer account in the subsidiary ledger.

Now, let's complete the example by assuming subsequent collections on accounts from some of the customers. The collections assumed resulted in the journal entry given below. The folio column indicates that the entry has been posted in total to the control account and each single amount to the individual customer accounts in the subsidiary ledger.

GENERAL JOURNAL   Page 3

Jan. 12	Cash	11	1,000	
	Accounts Receivable	12		1,000
	To record collections on			
	accounts as follows:			
	Adams, J. K. $ 400	√		
	Ford, C. E. 340	√		
	Moore, W. E. 220	√		
	Price, V. T. 40	√		
	Total $1,000			

The subsidiary ledger should be frequently reconciled with the control account. This is accomplished by summing the balances in the subsidiary ledger to determine whether that total agrees with the total shown by the control account in the general ledger. This check can be done by simply running an adding machine tape from the subsidiary ledger or by preparing a schedule or listing of the individual customer account balances. When there are a large number of credit sales and collections, a frequent reconciliation is advisable. A reconciliation schedule for Mayo follows:

MAYO DEPARTMENT STORE
Schedule of Accounts Receivable, January 28, 1974

Account	Amount (*per subsidiary*)
Adams, J. K.	$ 200
Baker, B. B.	120
Moore, W. E.	100
Price, V. T.	390
Ward, B. L.	450
Total Accounts Receivable (per control account)	$1,260

In this instance the subsidiary ledger total agrees with the balance in the control account. If there is disagreement, of course, an error is indicated; however, the mere fact of agreement does not necessarily mean there are no errors. One could post a debit or credit to the wrong individual account and the two ledgers would still reconcile in total.

In the above situation, the *Sales* account also could have been established as a control account supported by a subsidiary ledger that would contain individual accounts for the sales of *each department* or for *each product*. A very common application also relates to *accounts payable* when there are numerous purchases on credit.

Another common application relates to *fixed assets*. For example, the Office Equipment account is included in the general ledger, usually as a control account. In such instances, the control account is supported by a subsidiary ledger of office equipment that incorporates an account for each different kind of office equipment, such as copiers, typewriters, calculators, and furniture. You can appreciate from these examples that the control account/subsidiary ledger procedure is an important aspect of the information-processing system of most enterprises.

In the journal entries given above, the amounts relating to each individual customer account were listed in the "Explanation" column of the journal and were then posted to the subsidiary ledger. There are two approaches to simplifying this particular phase of the record keeping. Obviously, one could transfer directly from the charge tickets and credit memoranda to the subsidiary ledger accounts and thus avoid the detailed listing in the journal entry. This approach is used frequently by small companies that use a manual system. Another approach involves the use of a related procedure known as *special journals*. This procedure is explained and illustrated in Appendix B to Chapter 8.

A particular advantage of the use of subsidiary ledgers in a manual system is that it facilitates the subdivision of work. A person can be trained in a short time to maintain a subsidiary ledger since a knowledge of the broad field of accounting is not required for such routine record-keeping tasks.

Although our illustration used a manual approach to subsidiary ledgers, such is not the usual case. Most companies of any size apply the procedure by means of accounting machines or electronic computers. The computer can be programmed to process credit sales, returns, collections on account, reconciliation of account balances, and a printout of monthly bills to be mailed to the customers.

Appendix B   AGING ACCOUNTS RECEIVABLE

It is generally recognized that the older an account receivable, the greater the probability of its uncollectibility. The analysis of accounts receivable, in terms of "age," provides management with valuable information in respect to probable cash inflows, losses due to uncollectible accounts, and the general effectiveness of the credit and collection activities of the company. The aging analysis also is used by some companies to provide information needed to make the *adjusting entry* at the end of each period for estimated bad debt expense.

Instead of relating bad debt losses to credit sales for the period, as illustrated in the chapter (page 173), the aging approach relates bad debt losses to the uncollected account balances (i.e., the balance in Accounts Receivable) at the end of each period. The approach is addressed to the problem of analyzing the individual uncollected balances to estimate the portion that will ultimately be worthless. The amount estimated to be ultimately uncollectible represents the balance at the end of the period that should be in the account "Allowance for Doubtful Accounts." The *difference* between the actual balance in that account and the amount estimated that should be reflected in it is the amount used for the adjusting entry at the end of the period.

To illustrate, assume the general ledger for Macon Appliance Store, whose fiscal year ended December 31, 1974, reflected the following account balances:

> Accounts Receivable.................... $ 40,000 (debit balance)
> Allowance for Doubtful Accounts........   900 (credit balance)
> Sales on credit for 1974................. 200,000

The adjusting entry for bad debt *expense* is being prepared at December 31, 1974. The company utilizes the aging method for determining the amount for the adjusting entry to record estimated bad debt expense. As a consequence, the following analysis of accounts receivable by age was completed:

Analysis of Accounts Receivable by Age, December 31, 1974						
Customer	*Total*	*Not Yet Due*	*1–30 Days Past Due*	*31–60 Days Past Due*	*61–90 Days Past Due*	*Over 90 Days Past Due*
Adams, A. K.	$ 600	$ 600				
Baker, B. B.	1,300	300	900	100		
Cox, R. E.	1,400			400	900	100
Day, W. T.	3,000	2,000	600	400		
Zoe, A. B.	900					900
Total	$40,000	$17,200	$12,000	$8,000	$1,200	$1,600
Percent	100%	43%	30%	20%	3%	4%

The management, on the basis of past experience and knowledge of specific situations, can use the above analysis as a basis for realistically estimating the probable *rates of uncollectibility for each age group.* Assume the management determined the following probable loss rates: not yet due, 1%; 1–30 days past due, 3%; 31–60 days, 6%; 61–90 days, 10%; over 90 days, 25%. Now the following estimating schedule can be prepared:

Estimate of Probable Uncollectible Accounts, December 31, 1974			
Age	*Amount of Receivable*	*Percent Estimated to be Uncollectible*	*Balance Needed in Allowance for Doubtful Accounts*
Not yet due	$17,200	1	$172
1–30 days past due	12,000	3	360
31–60 days past due	8,000	6	480
61–90 days past due	1,200	10	120
Over 90 days past due	1,600	25	400
Total	$40,000		$1,532

The resultant adjusting entry on December 31, 1974, would be:

Dec. 31   Bad Debt Expense.................................... 632
                     Allowance for Doubtful Accounts..............   632
              To adjust Allowance for Doubtful Accounts to
              estimated balance needed:
                     Balance needed (per schedule above)...... $1,532
                     Balance before adjustment...............   900
                     Difference—adjustment needed (increase) $ 632

Some would argue that this approach to estimating the amount of bad debt expense does not comply with the matching principle as well as the method discussed in the chapter. There the estimate was based on the amount of credit sales from which the uncollectible accounts came. In contrast, the aging method, since it is based on the balance in Accounts Receivable, may be influenced by several factors rather than the credit sales for the period; however, it may provide a more accurate basis for measuring accounts receivable since it takes into account the actual age distribution of the amounts in each account.

Questions for discussion

1. In an enterprise characterized by extensive selling and purchasing activities, cost of goods sold must be matched with sales revenue. Explain.
2. What is the difference between gross sales and net sales?
3. What is gross margin on sales? How is the gross margin ratio computed?
4. Explain what is meant by sales discount. Use 1/15, n/60, in your explanation.
5. What is the distinction between sales allowances and sales discount?
6. A sale is made for $500, terms are 2/10, n/30. At what amount should the sale be recorded?
7. Since the actual time of cash collection is not relevant in determining the date on which a sale should be given accounting recognition, what factor is relevant?
8. Why is it essential that bad debt losses be estimated?
9. Briefly contrast the charge-off method with the allowance method in accounting for bad debt losses.
10. Why does the charge-off method of accounting for bad debt losses violate the matching principle?
11. What is a contra account?
12. Define the book value of accounts receivable.
13. Why should estimated bad debt losses be based on credit sales rather than on total sales?
14. Briefly distinguish between a perpetual and a periodic inventory system. Basically, how does each measure (a) inventory and (b) cost of goods sold?
15. What is the purpose of a perpetual inventory record for each item stocked?
16. What account is debited for a purchase of goods for resale (a) when the perpetual inventory system is used, and (b) when the periodic inventory system is used?
17. Why is transportation-in considered to be a cost of purchasing merchandise?
18. Why is it necessary to take a physical inventory count at the end of the period when the periodic inventory system is used?

19. Under the cost principle, at what amount should a purchase be recorded?

20. Why is there no Purchases account when the perpetual inventory system is used?

Exercises   E6–1. Supply the missing amounts for the income statement of Johnson Retailers.

Case	Sales	Beginning Inventory	Pur-chases	Total Avail-able	Ending Inventory	Cost of Goods Sold	Gross Margin	Ex-penses	Net In-come or (Loss)
A	900	100	700	800	200	600	300	200	100
B	900	200	750	950	150	800	100	100	0
C	900	150	800	950	300	650	250	100	150
D	900	300	600	900	200	700	200	150	50
E	900	250	650	900	100	800	100	150	(50)

E6–2. The following summarized data were provided by the records of Melody's Music Store, Incorporated, for the year ended December 31, 1974:

Sales of merchandise for cash....................	$100,000
Sales of merchandise on credit...................	40,000
Purchases......................................	81,000
Operating expenses.............................	50,000
Merchandise inventory, Jan. 1, 1974..............	32,000
Sales returns and allowances....................	3,000
Purchase returns and allowances.................	1,000
Freight-in.....................................	4,000

Corporate income tax rate, 22%.
Number of shares of common stock outstanding, 10,000.
Physical inventory of goods on hand, December 31, 1974, $59,000.
(The company uses the periodic inventory system.)

Required:

Based upon the above data, prepare an income statement. Show income tax expense separately. There were no extraordinary items. Compute the gross margin ratio and the profit margin ratio.

E6–3. The following data were taken from the records of King Corporation on December 31, 1974:

Sales of merchandise for cash....................	$255,000
Sales of merchandise for credit..................	150,000
Sales returns and allowances.....................	5,000
Operating expenses.............................	153,500
From perpetual inventory records:	
Cost of goods sold..........................	220,000
Inventory....................................	50,000

Estimated bad debt loss, 1% of net credit sales
Corporation income tax rate, 22%
Number of shares of common stock outstanding, 15,000

Required:

(a)   Based on the above data, prepare an income statement. There were no extraordinary items.

(b)   Compute the gross margin ratio and the profit margin ratio.

E6–4.   During the month of January, the AB Corporation sold goods to two customers. The sequence of events was as follows:

Jan. 3   Sold goods for $500 to J. Smith and billed him for that amount subject to terms, 2/10, n/30.

Jan. 5   Sold goods to B. Brown for $900 and billed him for that amount subject to terms, 2/10, n/30.

Jan. 12   Collected cash due from J. Smith.

Feb. 4   Collected cash due from B. Brown.

Required:

Give the appropriate entry for each date. Assume the periodic inventory system is used.

E6–5.   The following list of transactions involving Parson's Men's Store were selected from the records for January 1974:

(1)   Sales: Cash, $110,000; on credit, $32,000.

(2)   Merchandise sold on credit in (1) and subsequently returned: $2,000.

(3)   Purchases: Cash, $60,000; on credit $18,000.

(4)   Merchandise purchased and subsequently returned for credit: $400.

(5)   Shipping costs paid in cash on merchandise purchased: $300.

(6)   Bad debt losses, on the basis of past experience, are estimated to be one-half of 1% of credit sales net of sales returns and allowances.

(7)   An account receivable amounting to $140 was written-off as uncollectible. The sale was made two years earlier.

Required:

(a)   Give the journal entry that would be made for each transaction, assuming the company uses a periodic inventory system.

(b)   Prepare an income statement for January, 1974, through the caption "Gross Margin on Sales." The December 31, 1973, inventory of merchandise was $80,000 and the physical inventory of merchandise taken on January 31, 1974, amounted to $90,000.

E6–6.   During 1974, Stanton's Ready-to-Wear Shop sold merchandise amounting to $94,000, of which $30,000 was on credit. At the start of 1974 the Allowance for Doubtful Accounts reflected a $450 credit balance.

Required:

(a)   On December 31, 1974, an account receivable of $500 from a prior year was determined to be uncollectible; therefore, it was written off immediately. Give the journal entry for the write-off.

(b)   On December 31, 1974, on the basis of past experience, it was decided to continue the accounting policy of basing estimated bad debt losses on credit sales for the year. The rate was estimated to be 1% of such sales. Give the adjusting journal entry required.

(c)   Determine the balances in the following ledger accounts on December 31, 1974, after the entries in (a) and (b) have been posted.

> Allowance for Doubtful Accounts...... $_____
> Bad Debt Expense.................... $_____

(d)   Show how Accounts Receivable and Allowance for Doubtful Accounts should be reported on the balance sheet at December 31, 1974. Assume a balance in Accounts Receivable of $16,500.

E6–7.   Don's Sport Shop sells on credit terms of 2/10, n/60. A sale of $500 was made to Jim Tolbert on February 1, 1974. In due time, Jim paid the account in full.

Required:

(a)   Give the entry to record the credit sale.

(b)   Give the entry assuming Jim paid the account in full on February 9, 1974.

(c)   Give the entry assuming, instead, that Jim paid the account in full on March 29, 1974.

On March 1, 1974, Don's purchased from a supplier, on credit, sporting goods costing $8,000; the terms were 1/20, n/30.

Required:

(d)   Give the entry to record the purchase on credit. Assume periodic inventory system.

(e)   Give the entry assuming Don's paid the account in full on March 18, 1974.

(f)   Give the entry assuming Don's paid the account in full on March 28, 1974.

E6–8.   The Adams Company uses a perpetual inventory system. Since it is a small business and sells only five different high-cost items, a perpetual inventory record is maintained for each item. The following selected data relate to Item A for the month of January:

(a)   Beginning inventory—quantity 4, cost $90 each.

(b)   Purchased—quantity 3, cost $85 each; paid $15 total freight.

(c)   Sold—quantity 5, sales price $175 each.

(d)   Returns—one sold in (c) was returned for full credit.

Required:

(1) Give the entries for the above transactions assuming a perpetual inventory system and cash transactions.
(2) Prepare the perpetual inventory record to Item A.
(3) What was the gross margin on sales for Item A in January?

E6–9. The Sutter Company uses a perpetual inventory system that provides amounts for the period for (a) cost of goods sold and (b) the ending inventory. Physical inventory counts are made from time to time to verify the perpetual inventory records. On December 31, 1974, the end of the fiscal year, the perpetual inventory record for stock item #18 showed the following (summarized):

	Units	Unit Cost	Total Cost
Beginning inventory...........	500	$2	$1,000
Purchases during the period....	900	2	1,800
Sales during the period (sales price $3.50)................	800	2	1,600

Required:

(a) Give the entry to record the purchases for cash during the period.
(b) Give the entry to record the sales for cash during the period.
(c) What is the ending inventory as reflected by the perpetual inventory record?
(d) Assume a physical inventory count is made and it reflects 590 units of Item #18 on hand. Give any entry required.

E6–10. The trial balance for Home Appliances, Incorporated, at December 31, 1974, end of the fiscal year, is given below. Only selected items have been used in order to shorten the case. The company uses a perpetual inventory system. All of the accounts you will need are listed in the trial balance.

Trial Balance
Dec. 31, 1974

Cash............................	$ 11,800	
Accounts Receivable.............	12,000	
Allowance for Doubtful Accounts..		$ 700
Merchandise Inventory............	60,000	
Fixed Assets.....................	40,000	
Accumulated Depreciation.........		12,000
Accounts Payable.................		7,000
Income Taxes Payable		
Capital Stock....................		60,000
Retained Earnings, Jan. 1, 1974....		19,300
Sales Revenue....................		101,000
Sales Returns and Allowances......	1,000	
Cost of Goods Sold..............	56,000	
Expenses (not detailed)...........	19,200	
Bad Debt Expense................		
Depreciation Expense		
Income Tax Expense..............		
	$200,000	$200,000

Additional data developed for the adjusting entries:
- (a) Estimated bad debt expense is 2% of net credit sales. Credit sales for 1974 amounted to $40,000.
- (b) The fixed assets are being depreciated $4,000 each year.
- (c) The corporate income tax rate is 22%.

Required:

Set up a worksheet similar to the one in the demonstration problem (omit columns for Adjusted Trial Balance). Enter the trial balance and the adjusting entries and complete the worksheet.

E6–11. The trial balance for The Variety Store, Incorporated, at December 31, 1974, the end of the annual fiscal year, is given below. Only selected and summary accounts are given in order to shorten the case. Also, the amounts have been simplified for this same purpose. The company uses a periodic inventory system. With the exception of the ending inventory, all of the accounts you will need are listed in the trial balance.

	Debit		Credit	
Cash..................	$ 7,600	Allowance for Doubtful		
Accounts Receivable....	3,000	Accounts.............	$	150
Merchandise Inventory,		Accumulated Deprecia-		
Jan. 1, 1974..........	4,000	tion.................		900
Store Supplies..........	250	Accounts Payable.......		5,000
Store Equipment........	3,000	Wages Payable..........		
Sales Returns..........	150	Capital Stock..........		6,000
Purchases.............	6,000	Retained Earnings.......		1,870
Bad Debt Expense......		Sales..................		13,000
Depreciation Expense....		Purchases Returns......		80
Other Operating				
Expenses.............	3,000			
	$27,000			$27,000

Data developed as a basis for the adjusting entries at December 31, 1974, were:
- (a) Estimated bad debt expense for 1974 (based on net credit sales), $100.
- (b) Inventory of store supplies at December 31, 1974, reflected $50.
- (c) Depreciation on store equipment, which originally cost $3,000, is based on an estimated useful life of ten years; no residual value.
- (d) Wages earned up to December 31, 1974, but not yet paid amounted to $400.
- (e) Inventories: The beginning inventory is shown in the above trial balance. A physical inventory of merchandise on hand and unsold, taken at December 31, 1974, reflected $2,070.

Required:

Set up a worksheet similar to the one in the demonstration case (omit columns for Adjusted Trial Balance). Enter the trial balance, adjusting entries, and ending inventory and complete the worksheet. (This is a Subchapter S corporation, hence, there will be no corporate income taxes.)

Problems P6–1. Brown Equipment Company, Incorporated, sells heavy construction equipment. There are 10,000 shares of capital stock outstanding. The company uses a perpetual inventory system for inventory control and accounting purposes. The annual fiscal period ends on December 31. The following condensed trial balance was taken from the general ledger on December 31, 1974:

	Debit	Credit
Cash....................................	$ 11,000	
Accounts Receivable.....................	20,000	
Allowance for Doubtful Accounts..........		$ 1,000
Inventory..............................	90,000	
Fixed Assets...........................	40,000	
Accumulated Depreciation................		8,000
Liabilities..............................		17,000
Capital Stock..........................		100,000
Retained Earnings, Jan. 1, 1974...........		20,000
Sales..................................		204,000
Sales Returns and Allowances.............	4,000	
Cost of Goods Sold......................	120,000	
Selling Expenses........................	37,000	
Administrative Expenses..................	10,000	
Interest Expense........................	3,000	
Loss Due to Storm Damage................	5,000	
Income Tax Expense (40% average rate).....	10,000	
	$350,000	$350,000

Required:

(a) Prepare an income statement.
(b) Compute the gross margin ratio and the profit margin ratio (before extraordinary items).

P6–2. Grady's is a local grocery store organized seven years ago as a corporation by three individuals. At that time, 10,000 shares of common stock were issued to the organizers. The store is in an excellent location and sales have increased each year. At the end of 1974 the bookkeeper prepared the following statement (assume all amounts are correct):

GRADY'S
Profit and Loss
December 31, 1974

	Debit	Credit
Sales...		$301,000
Purchase returns and allowances...		700
Merchandise inventory, per count, Dec. 31, 1974...		112,300
Sales returns and allowances...	$ 1,000	
Purchases...	181,700	
Freight-in...	800	
Selling expenses...	60,000	
Administrative and general expenses...	30,000	
Interest expense...	500	
Merchandise inventory, per count, Dec 31, 1973...	100,000	
Loss on fixed assets due to fire...	4,000	
Income tax expense (on operations $12,000 less $1,200 saved on the fire loss)...	10,800	
Net profit (difference)...	25,200	
	$414,000	$414,000

Required:

(a) Prepare an income statement. The company utilizes periodic inventory procedures. Assume a flat 30% income tax rate.

(b) Compute the gross margin ratio and the profit margin ratio (before extraordinary items).

P6–3. The transactions listed below have been selected from those occurring during the month of January 1974 for the Minton Department Store, Incorporated. A wide line of goods is offered for sale: however, clothing lines are limited. Credit sales are extended to a few select customers. The usual credit terms are n/EOM. Selected transactions (summarized for January) are:

(a) Sales to customers: Cash... $320,000
                  On credit... 10,000

(b) Unsatisfactory merchandise returned
     by customers: Cash... 4,000
                   Credit... 1,000

(c) Merchandise purchased from vendors on credit; terms 1/20, n/60:
     Rox Supply Company, amount billed, before discount 1,000
     From other vendors, amount billed, before discount 99,000

(d) Freight paid on merchandise purchased; paid cash (set up a separate account for this)... 1,800

(e) Collections on accounts receivable... 9,000

(f) The accounts payable were paid in full during the period as follows (cash paid):
     Rox Supply Company, paid after the discount period 1,000
     Other vendors, paid within the discount period... 98,010

(g) Purchased two new typewriters for the office; paid cash... 900

(h) An account receivable from a customer amounting to $200 was determined to be uncollectible and was written off. Before this write-off, the Allowance for Doubtful Accounts reflected a credit balance of $700.

(i) At the end of January the adjusting entry for Estimated Loss on Uncollectible Accounts is to be made. The loss rate, based on past experience, is one-half of 1% of net credit sales for the period (i.e., on credit sales less credit returns).

Required:

(1) Prepare journal entries for the above items assuming a periodic inventory system.

(2) Assume the debit balance in Accounts Receivable on January 1, 1974, was $1,000. Show how Accounts Receivable and the related allowance account would be reported on the balance sheet; provide amounts.

P6–4. College Shop, Incorporated, is known as a "student co-op." It has been operating successfully for a number of years. The corporate Board of Directors is composed of faculty and student members. On January 1, 1974, when this case starts, the beginning inventory was $200,000; the Accounts Receivable debit balance was $2,000 and the Allowance for Doubtful Accounts credit balance was $300. The following transactions (summarized) have been selected from the month of January for case purposes:

(a) Merchandise sales for cash...................... $185,000

(b) Merchandise returned by customers as unsatisfactory, for cash.................................... 1,100

(c) Merchandise purchased from vendors on credit; terms 2/20, n/30:
    May Supply Company, invoice price, before discount.................................... 3,000
    Other vendors, invoice price, before discount....... 97,000

(d) Purchased equipment for use in the store; paid cash... 1,000

(e) Purchased office supplies to be used immediately in the store; paid cash............................ 400

(f) Freight paid on merchandise purchased; paid cash (set up a separate account for this)................. 500

(g) The accounts payable were paid in full during the period as follows (cash paid):
    May Supply Company, paid after the discount period 3,000
    Other vendors, paid within the discount period...... 95,060

Required:

(1) Prepare journal entries for each of the above items. Assume periodic inventory procedures are used.

(2) Give the end-of-the-period adjusting entries for the beginning inventory and the ending inventory of $208,000 taken at the end of business on January 31, 1974.

P6–5. The Strong Machinery Company uses a perpetual inventory system for the ten different kinds of construction machinery it stocks and sells. The following selected data relate to the lowest cost item of equipment stocked during the month of January 1974. To simplify we will refer to this item as Machine #10.

(a) Beginning inventory—quantity 7, cost $400 each.

(b) Purchased—quantity 9, cost $380 each plus $180 total freight-in.

(c) Sales—quantity 12, sales price $750 each.

(d) Returns—Strong accepted a return of one of the machines sold in (c) because it was not needed by the customer and had not been used.

Required: (assume all transactions were cash)

(1) Prepare the perpetual inventory record for Machine #10.

(2) Give entries for each of the above transactions assuming perpetual inventory procedures.

(3) Prepare the income statement for January 1974 through gross margin on sales as it relates to Machine #10. What was the gross margin ratio?

P6–6. The Mabry Company uses a perpetual inventory system. During the month of January 1974, the perpetual inventory record for Item A, which is one of the 23 items stocked, showed the following (summarized):

PERPETUAL INVENTORY RECORD

Date	Explanation	Receipts Units	Receipts Total Cost	Issues Units	Issues Total Cost	Balance Units	Balance Total Cost
(a)	Beginning inventory					40	3,200
(b)	Purchase (at $80 ea.)	20					
(c)	Sale (sales price $150 ea.)			31			
(d)	Purchase return (one unit)						
(e)	Purchase (at $80 ea.)	30					
(f)	Sale return (one unit)						
(g)	Sale (sales price $150 ea.)			29			

Required:

(1) Complete the above perpetual inventory record.

(2) Give the journal entry for each transaction (assume all entries are cash).

(3) Complete the following
Income Statement:

Sales	$_____
Cost of goods sold	$_____
Gross margin on sales	$_____
Gross margin ratio	_____
Balance Sheet:	
Inventory	$_____

P6–7. The following transactions, relating to one product sold by Sanders Company, were completed in the order given during January:

(a) Purchased—quantity 100, cost $20 each.

(b) Sold—quantity 80 at $30 each.

(c) Purchase return—returned one of the units purchased in (a) because it was the wrong size.

(d) Sales return—accepted two units from a customer that were sold in (b). The units were unused and the customer did not need them.

(e) Inventories:

Beginning inventory, Jan. 1–30 units at total cost of $600.
Ending inventory, Jan. 31—per perpetual inventory, 51 units @ $20 = $1,020.

(f) Cost of goods sold for January—78 units @ $20 = $1,560.

Required:

You are to compare the journal entries that would be made for the above transactions assuming: Case A—the perpetual inventory system is used; Case B—the periodic inventory system is used. To do this, set up the following form (assume cash transactions):

		Amounts			
		Perpetual		*Periodic*	
Date	*Accounts and Explanation*	*Debit*	*Credit*	*Debit*	*Credit*
(a)	To record the purchase				
(b)	To record the sale				
(c)	To record the purchase return				
(d)	To record the sales return				
(e)	To record the adjusting entries for inventories				
(f)	To record the closing entry for cost of goods sold				

P6–8. (Note: This is an extended problem designed to review Chapters 4, 5, and 6.) Quality Furniture Store, Incorporated, has been in operation for a number of years and has been quite profitable. The losses on uncollectible accounts and merchandise returns are about the same as for other furniture stores. The company uses a perpetual inventory system. The annual fiscal period ended December 31, 1974, and the end-of-the-period information-processing cycle has been started. The following trial balance was derived from the general ledger at December 31, 1974:

Cash..	$ 16,880	
Accounts Receivable.............................	36,000	
Allowance for Doubtful Accounts...................		$ 4,600
Merchandise Inventory...........................	120,000	
Store Equipment................................	20,000	
Accumulated Depreciation........................		8,000
Accounts Payable...............................		10,000
Income Taxes Payable...........................		
Interest Payable................................		
Notes Payable, Long-term........................		48,000
Capital Stock, par $100...........................		70,000
Retained Earnings, Jan. 1, 1974....................		11,400
Dividends Paid.................................	10,000	
Sales Revenue..................................		441,000
Sales Returns and Allowances.....................	25,000	
Cost of Goods Sold.............................	213,350	
Selling Expenses................................	102,700	
Administrative Expenses..........................	49,070	
Bad Debt Expense...............................		
Depreciation Expense............................		
Interest Expense................................		
Income Tax Expense.............................		
	$593,000	$593,000

Data for adjusting entries:
(a) Bad debt losses due to uncollectible accounts estimated to be $6,000.
(b) Store equipment that cost $20,000 when originally acquired is being depreciated over an estimated useful life of ten years and no residual value.
(c) The long-term note of $48,000 was for a two-year loan from a local bank. The interest rate is 8%, payable at the end of each 12-month period. The note was dated April 1, 1974. (Hint: Accrue interest for nine months.)
(d) Assume a flat 40% corporate income tax rate.

Required:

(1) Based upon the above data, complete a worksheet similar to the one illustrated in the chapter for the demonstration case (omit columns for Adjusted Trial Balance). The company uses a perpetual inventory system.
    (Hint: Net income is $24,000.)
(2) Based upon the completed worksheet, prepare an income statement, statement of retained earnings, and balance sheet.
(3) Based upon the completed worksheet, prepare adjusting and closing entries for December 31, 1974.

P6–9. (Note: This is an extended problem designed to review the materials discussed in Chapters 4, 5, and 6.) Central Appliances, Incorporated, is owned by six local investors. It has been operating for four years and is at the end of the 1974 fiscal year. For case purposes, certain accounts have been selected to demonstrate the information-processing activities at the end of the year for a corporation that sells merchandise rather than services. The following trial balance, assumed to be correct, was taken from the general ledger on December 31, 1974. The company uses a periodic inventory system.

Debit		Credit	
Cash....................	$ 18,000	Allowance for Doubtful	
Accounts Receivable......	28,000	Accounts.............	$ 600
Merchandise Inventory,		Accumulated Depreciation.	12,000
Jan. 1, 1974...........	80,000	Accounts Payable........	15,000
Prepaid Insurance.......	300	Notes Payable, Long-term.	30,000
Store Equipment........	40,000	Capital Stock, par $10.....	40,000
Cash Dividends Paid		Retained Earnings, Jan. 1,	
(during 1974).........	12,000	1974.................	14,000
Sales Returns...........	3,000	Sales....................	400,000
Purchases..............	250,000	Purchase Returns.........	7,000
Freight-in..............	11,000		
Operating Expenses......	76,300		
	$518,600		$518,600

Additional data for adjusting entries:
(a) Credit sales during the year were $100,000; based on past experience, a 1% loss rate on credit sales has been established.
(b) Insurance amounting to $100 expired during the year.
(c) Store equipment, costing $40,000 when acquired, is being depreciated over a ten-year estimated useful life and no residual value.
(d) The long-term note payable for $30,000 was dated May 1, 1974, and carries an 8% interest rate per annum. The note is for three years and interest is payable at the end of each year.
(e) Corporate tax rates are: first $25,000 earnings, 22%; over $25,000, 48%.
(f) Inventories:
   Beginning inventory, January 1, 1974 (per above trial balance), $80,000.
   Ending inventory, December 31, 1974 (per physical inventory count), $75,000.

Required:
(1) Prepare a worksheet at December 31, 1974, similar to the one shown in the demonstration problem in the chapter. You may omit columns for Adjusted Trial Balance. In order to save time and space, all operating expenses have been summarized. However, you should set up additional expense accounts for depreciation, bad debts, interest, and income taxes. Also, you will need additional liability accounts for interest payable and income taxes payable.
   (Hint: Net income is $35,100.)
(2) Based upon the completed worksheet, prepare an income statement, statement of retained earnings, and balance sheet.

(3) Based upon the completed worksheet, prepare the adjusting and closing journal entries at December 31, 1974.

P6–10. (Related to Appendix A.) Town's Department Store, Incorporated, is a large department store located in a midwestern town of approximately 200,000 population. The store carries top brands and attempts to appeal to "quality customers." Approximately 80% of the sales are on credit. As a consequence, there is a significant amount of detailed record keeping related to charge sales, returns, collections, and billings. Some years ago the accounts receivable records were maintained manually. A change was made to a mechanized system and now the store is considering computerizing this phase of the information system. Included in the general ledger is a control account for customer receivables. Supporting the control account is an accounts receivable subsidiary ledger that carries individual accounts for over 20,000 customers. For case purposes only, a few accounts and transactions with simplified amounts have been selected. The case requirement is intended to indicate the nature of the data-processing work that is to be computerized; however, here it will be completed manually.

On January 1, 1974, the Accounts Receivable control account (#52), in the general ledger, reflected a debit balance of $4,000 and the subsidiary ledger reflected the following balances:

Akins, A. K.	$400	May, O. W.	$800
Blue, V. R.	700	Nash, G. A.	100
Daley, U. T.	900	Roth, I. W.	600
Evans, T. V.	300	Winn, W. W.	200

During the month of January the following transactions and events relating to sales activities occurred (use notation at left for date):
(a) Sales of merchandise on credit:

Akins, A. K.	$300	Daley, U. T.	$ 70
Blue, V. R.	250	Roth, I. W.	370
Winn, W. W.	730	Evans, T. V.	410
May, O. W.	140		

(b) Unsatisfactory merchandise returned:

Roth, I. W.	$ 30	Akins, A. K.	$ 20
Winn, W. W.	70		

(c) Collections on accounts receivable:

Winn, W. W.	$800	Blue, V. R.	$750
May, O. W.	940	Daley, U. T.	600
Akins, A. K.	200		
Roth, I. W.	700		

(d) The account with G. A. Nash has been inactive for several years. After an investigation, the management decided that it was uncollectible; therefore, it is to be written off immediately.
(e) The bad debt losses are based on credit sales; the estimated loss rate is 2% of net credit sales (i.e., on credit sales less returns for credit).

Required:

(1) Set up the general ledger control account for Accounts Receivable. Also set up the general ledger account for Allowance for Doubtful Accounts (#53) with a credit balance of $600. Indicate the beginning balance as "Bal." and for convenience use T-accounts.

(2) Set up an accounts receivable subsidiary ledger in good form; use three columns—Debit, Credit, and Balance. Enter the beginning balances with the notation "Bal."

(3) Prepare journal entries for each of the above transactions. Include a folio column for posting to both the control account and the subsidiary ledger. Assume periodic inventory.

(4) Post the entries prepared in (3) to the Accounts Receivable control account, Allowance for Doubtful Accounts, and the subsidiary ledger. Use folio numbers for control accounts and checks for subsidiary.

(5) Prepare a schedule of accounts receivable to show how much each customer owed at the end of January.

(6) Show how accounts receivable and the related allowance would be reported in the January balance sheet.

7 Costing methods for measuring cost of goods sold and inventory

In measuring the amount of inventory at a given date, whether the perpetual or the periodic inventory system is used, the following basic questions must be considered:

1. What items should be included in the inventory?
2. What cost should be assigned to those items included in the inventory?

In this chapter we will focus on the answers to these two questions and their implementation in the information-processing system.[1]

Inventory often is the largest single asset owned by a business. Its measurement directly affects the amount of net income reported for the period. The amount of inventory, measured at the end of the accounting period, affects not only the net income for that period but also the amount of net income for the following period. This two-period effect is due to the fact that the ending inventory for one period is the beginning inventory for the next period. To illustrate these effects, assume that the 1973 and 1974 income statements for Company A reflected net incomes of $5,000 and $6,500, respectively, measured as follows:

---

[1] *Fundamentals of Management Accounting* discusses inventory measurement in a manufacturing business.

214

	1973		1974	
Sales..................................		$100,000		$110,000
Cost of goods sold:				
Beginning inventory.................	$ –0–		$10,000	
Purchases........................	70,000		58,000	
Goods available for sale...........	70,000		68,000	
Ending inventory..................	10,000		–0–	
Cost of goods sold...............		60,000		68,000
Gross margin.......................		40,000		42,000
Expenses........................		35,000		35,500
Net Income (pretax).................		$ 5,000		$ 6,500

Observe that the ending inventory, as measured and reported at December 31, 1973, amounted to $10,000. This amount also is reported as the inventory at the **beginning** of 1974.

Now, let's assume that the ending inventory was remeasured, at December 31, 1973, and determined to be $11,000 (i.e., $1,000 more than shown above). The changed amount in the inventory could have been due to either one or both of the following factors:

(1) In physically counting the inventory items, some were incorrectly left out. They had a cost of $1,000.

(2) Although the physical count was correct, in applying the unit costs, a higher purchase cost was used in the remeasurement. This higher cost increased the amount of the inventory by $1,000.

We now will see how this error of $1,000 in the inventory will affect the net income amounts for each of the two years. The income statements may be restated to reflect the increased inventory amount as follows:

	1973		1974	
Sales..................................		$100,000		$110,000
Cost of goods sold:				
Beginning inventory.................	$ –0–		$11,000	
Purchases........................	70,000		58,000	
Goods available for sale...........	70,000		69,000	
Ending inventory..................	11,000		–0–	
Cost of goods sold...............		59,000		69,000
Gross margin.......................		41,000		41,000
Expenses........................		35,000		35,500
Net Income (pretax).................		$ 6,000		$ 5,500

Observe that, in comparison with the preceding income statements, the net income for 1973 is greater by $1,000, and less by the same amount for 1974. Thus, a comparison of the two sets of income statements demonstrates the following generalizations:

a. In the period of the change:
    An increase in the amount of the ending inventory for a period increases net income for that period by the same amount. To the contrary, a decrease in the amount of inventory decreases net income for that period by the same amount.

b. In the next period:
    An increase in the amount of the ending inventory for a period decreases the net income of the *next period* by the same amount. To the contrary, a decrease in the amount of the ending inventory for a period increases the net income of the *next period* by the same amount.

The above illustrations and the demonstrated effects on the measurement of net income indicate the importance of careful measurement of inventory. Care must be exercised in (a) determining what physical items should be included in the inventory, and (b) applying the dollar unit cost to the units counted as being on hand.

What items should be included in inventory

Inventory usually is represented by tangible personal property that is held for sale in the ordinary course of business or is to be consumed in the near future in producing goods or services for sale. Inventory is reported on the balance sheet as a current asset because it normally will be converted into cash within one year or within the operating cycle of the business. It usually is listed below Accounts Receivable because it is less liquid. The kind of inventory normally held depends upon the characteristics of the business:[2]

Retail or wholesale business
Merchandise inventory—Goods held for resale in the ordinary course of business. The goods usually are acquired through purchase as completely manufactured and ready for sale without further processing.

Manufacturing business
Finished-goods inventory—Goods manufactured by the business, completed and ready for sale.
Goods-in-process inventory—Goods in the process of being fabricated or manufactured but not yet completed as finished goods. Goods-in-process inventory, when completed, become finished-goods inventory.
Raw-materials inventory—Items acquired by purchase, exploitation of natural resources, or growth (such as food products) for the purpose of processing into finished goods. Raw-materials inventory, when used, flows into work in process; then, when processing is completed, to finished goods.

---

[2] Supplies on hand are reported as prepaid expenses. This topic is discussed on page 237.

The discussions to follow focus on merchandise and finished-goods inventories.

In measuring the physical quantity of the inventory, a company should include all items to which it has legal title; that is, all goods owned, irrespective of their location. In business transactions involving inventories, accounting focuses on when legal title passes. When title passes, one party has made a sale and the other party has made a purchase. In a purchase/sale transaction, the basic guideline is that title to the goods passes at the *time intended by the parties* to the transaction. Generally, title passes when the goods are delivered by the seller to the buyer; however, there are situations where this is not the case. There also are situations where the intentions of the parties as to the time of passage of title are not clear. In such situations, all of the circumstances must be assessed and judgment applied as to when the buyer and seller intended title to pass. For example, goods may be sold on credit and the buyer requests the vendor to hold the goods pending shipping instructions. In this instance, title appears to have passed, irrespective of the delivery date. A similar question arises when a third party, usually a transportation firm, has physical possession of the goods for a period of time. The question is: Who owns goods during the period in transit? If the terms of the sale provide that the buyer pays the transportation charges (known as FOB shipping point), then title generally is assumed to pass when the vendor delivers the goods to the transportation agent. In contrast, if the terms of the sale are FOB destination (i.e., the seller pays the freight), title generally is assumed to pass when the goods are delivered to the buyer at destination.[3] The passage-of-title test of who owns the goods is a part of the revenue principle previously discussed (Exhibit 2–1). The passage-of-title guideline has a legal basis and prevails in the accounting process in respect to both the sale and purchase of goods. In the absence of the passage-of-title test, the financial statements could be manipulated to overstate net income by entering all sales orders received up through the last day of the period, irrespective of the fact that title to the goods ordered may not have passed. Conversely, purchases may not be recorded intentionally even though title to the goods has passed.

A company may have possession of goods that it does not own; these should be excluded from the inventory. The usual situation of this kind is where goods are held on consignment for sale on a commission basis. When goods are on consignment, the supplier (known as the consignor) legally retains title to the goods although they are in the physical possession of the party that will sell them (known as the consignee). The consignor, although the goods are not in his physical possession, should include them in his inventory. The consignee, al-

---

[3] FOB stand for "free on board"; it is used in business to indicate who is responsible for paying the transportation charges: FOB destination, seller pays the freight; FOB shipping point, buyer pays the freight.

though he has possession of them, should exclude them from his inventory.

In summary, in identifying the goods to be included in the inventory at a specific date, ownership or legal title, rather than physical possession, is controlling. The inventory should include only, but all of, the goods to which the company has legal title.

Inventory cost

In Chapter 6 we discussed the application of the cost principle to the purchase of goods for resale. Goods in inventory are costed in accordance with the *cost principle*. Its application to inventories has been stated as follows:

> The primary basis of accounting for inventory is cost, which has been defined generally as the price paid or consideration given to acquire an asset. As applied to inventories, cost means, in principle, the sum of the applicable expenditures and charges directly or indirectly incurred in bringing an article to its existing condition and location.[4]

We also explained that, in accordance with the cost principle, incidental expenditures related to the purchase of goods, such as freight, insurance, and storage, conceptually should be included in measuring the purchase cost of the goods acquired. When any of those goods remain in inventory, these elements should be included in measuring the inventory cost. However, since these incidental amounts frequently are not *material in amount* when related to the total purchase cost, and since there is often no convenient method of apportioning such costs to each item of goods, they often are not assigned to the inventory cost. Thus, for practical reasons, some companies use the *net invoice price* when assigning a unit cost to goods purchased or to inventory.

ASSIGNING COST TO THE INVENTORY

The previous chapter discussed the perpetual and periodic inventory systems. These two systems are used for *measuring* the amounts for cost of goods sold and for final inventory. Even though the mechanics of applying the two systems differ, the fundamental accounting relationship on which they focus is the same. That relationship is:

$$\left(\begin{array}{c} \text{Cost of Beginning} \\ \text{Inventory} \end{array} + \begin{array}{c} \text{Cost of Additional} \\ \text{Inventory Acquired} \\ \text{(Purchases)} \end{array} - \begin{array}{c} \text{Cost of} \\ \text{Ending} \\ \text{Inventory} \end{array} = \begin{array}{c} \text{Cost of} \\ \text{Goods} \\ \text{Sold} \end{array} \right)$$

Algebraically, this relationship can be represented as follows for each of the two systems:

Perpetual Inventory System:

$$BI + P - CGS = EI$$

[4] American Institute of Certified Public Accountants, *Accounting Research Bulletins* (ARB No. 43), Chapter 4, Statement 3, New York, 1961.

(since this system focuses on measuring and recording the amount of cost of goods sold currently for each separate sale).

Periodic Inventory System:

$$BI + P - EI = CGS$$

(since this system focuses on measuring, i.e., physically counting, the ending inventory at the *end of the period* and then determining cost of goods sold by subtraction).

Thus, both systems focus on the central objective of the measurement of both cost of goods sold and ending inventory. The perpetual inventory system accomplishes the objective on a *current* basis by means of detailed inventory records. In contrast, the periodic inventory system accomplishes the objective on a *end-of-the-period* basis by means of a physical count of the goods remaining on hand.

In the discussions to follow we must constantly remember that the central objective is not solely to measure the amount of goods on hand in order to obtain the balance sheet amount, but it also is to measure cost of goods sold, which is an important determinant in the measurement of net income.

THE UNIT COST PROBLEM

In Chapter 6, to simplify the illustrations, we assumed that the beginning inventory and the additional purchases of goods during the period were at the same unit cost. The normal situation, however, is that goods will be purchased during the period at different unit costs. To illustrate, assume the data given in Exhibit 7–1 for one product stocked and sold regularly by Summer's Retail Store.

Exhibit 7–1

SUMMER'S RETAIL STORE
Unit cost data

Transaction	Symbol	Number of Units	Unit Cost	Total Cost	
Beginning inventory (carried over from last period)...............	BI	100	$6		$ 600
Purchases during the period:					
Jan. 3, First purchase............	P	50	7	$ 350	
June 12, Second purchase.........	P	200	8	1,600	
Dec. 20, Third purchase...........	P	120	9	1,080	3,030
Total goods available for sale...............	GA	470			$3,630
Sales during the period:					
Jan. 6, Unit sales price, $10.......	S	40	?		$?
June 18, Unit sales price, 12.......	S	220	?		$?
Dec. 25, Unit sales price, 14.......	S	60	?		$?
Total Goods Sold.........	CGS	320			$?
Ending inventory.........	EI	150	?		$?

In the above example there are four different unit cost prices that make up the $3,630 amount for goods available for sale (i.e., $6, $7, $8, and $9). The accounting objective is to recognize these different unit costs in apportioning the total amount of goods available for sale ($3,630) between cost of goods sold and final inventory on a rational basis. As explained above, the perpetual and periodic inventory systems represent two different approaches for accomplishing this measurement objective. However, when *unit costs* change over time, as they did for Summer's, *either* system obviously must cope with this vexing problem. This problem of measuring the cost of goods sold and the ending inventory can be portrayed graphically as in Exhibit 7–2.

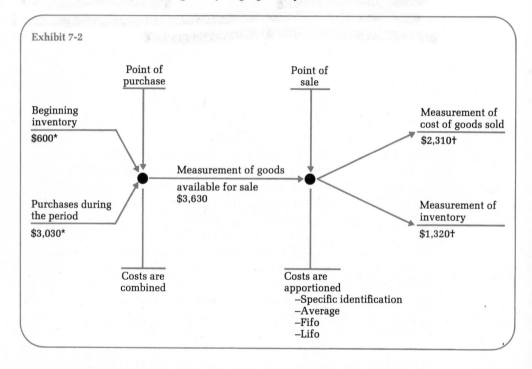

Exhibit 7-2

* Data from Exhibit 7–1.
† Fifo basis, Exhibit 7–5.

The apportionment of cost of goods available for sale between cost of goods sold and ending inventory requires the use of an inventory costing method. The four inventory costing methods commonly used are known as: (1) specific identification; (2) average; (3) first-in, first-out (Fifo); and (4) last-in, first-out (Lifo). First, we will discuss the characteristics of each of these inventory costing methods. Following that discussion, we will illustrate the application of each method separately for the perpetual and periodic inventory systems. Throughout these discussions we will use the data for Summer's Retail Store.

INVENTORY COSTING METHODS

A choice among the inventory costing methods is necessary only when there are different unit costs in the beginning inventory and/or purchases. These are cost-assignment methods and do not necessarily relate to the physical flow of goods on and off the shelves. Generally accepted accounting principles require that the inventory costing method used must be "rational and systematic."

Specific identification method. One way of assigning unit costs to cost of goods sold and the ending inventory is to keep track of the units of each separate purchase—that is, specific identification of the purchase cost of each item. This is done either by simply coding the cost price on each unit before placing it in stock or by keeping a separate record of the unit and identifying it with a serial number. When a sale is made, the cost of that unit is identified and recorded. For example, using the data in Exhibit 7–1, if the 40 units sold on January 6 were identified specifically as, say, units that were purchased for $6 (i.e., from the beginning inventory), the cost-of-goods-sold amount for that sale would be measured as 40 units × $6 = $240. Alternatively, if 20 of the units were identified as costing $6 (from the beginning inventory) and the other 20 as costing $7 (from the January 3 purchase), costs of goods sold would be measured as (20 units × $6) + (20 units × $7) = $260.

The specific identification method would be rather tedious and impractical where (a) a large number of different items are stocked; (b) unit costs change frequently; and (c) unit costs are low. On the other hand, where there are "big ticket" items such as automobiles and expensive jewelry, it is especially appropriate since each item tends to be different from the other items. In such situations, it is rational because the *selling price* is based on a markup over specific cost. The method is not systematic when the units are identical. One can manipulate the cost of goods sold and the ending inventory amounts simply by "picking and choosing" from among the several available unit costs, even though the goods are identical in every other respect. To illustrate, in the above example, cost of goods sold was either $240 or $260, depending on the choices made. In that example, net income would be different by $20, depending on the "identification."

Average-cost method. This method involves computation of the weighted average unit cost of the goods available for sale. The average unit cost is then applied to (a) the number of units sold to measure cost of goods sold and (b) the number of units in the ending inventory to measure the dollar inventory amount. To illustrate, at the end of the period, the method would be applied to the data given in Exhibit 7–1 as follows:[5]

To compute average cost:

$$\frac{\text{Goods available for sale—at cost}}{\text{Goods available for sale—units}} = \frac{\$3,630}{470} = \$7.72 \begin{cases} \text{average cost} \\ \text{per unit for} \\ \text{the period} \end{cases}$$

The cost assignment then would be:

	Units		Amount
Cost of goods sold:	320	@ $7.72 =	$2,472
Ending inventory:	150	" =	1,158
Goods available for sale:	470	" =	$3,630

The average-cost method is used often since it is rational, systematic, easy to apply, and not subject to manipulation. It weights the number of units purchased and unit costs during the period (including the unit cost of the beginning inventory). Thus, it is representative of the costs that occurred during the entire period rather than of the cost at the beginning, end, or at one point during the period.

First-in, first-out method. This method, frequently referred to as Fifo, assumes that the oldest unit costs (i.e., the first costs in) are the first units sold (i.e., the first costs out). In other words, the units in the beginning inventory are treated as if they were sold first, the units from the first purchase sold next, and so on until the units left in the ending inventory all come from the latest purchases. It follows that the oldest unit costs are apportioned to cost of goods sold and the latest unit costs apply to the ending inventory. Frequently, Fifo is justified on the basis that it is consistent with the actual physical flow of the goods. It is said that the first goods placed in stock tend to be the first goods sold. However, the method is applied irrespective of the actual physical inflow and outflow of goods because it is a cost-assignment procedure used to measure cost of goods sold and ending inventory. To illustrate, using the data given in Exhibit 7–1, the Fifo method would be applied as follows for the sale of January 6:

Goods available for sale on Jan. 6:

Jan. 1,	Beginning inventory 100 units @ $6 =	$600
Jan. 3,	First purchase	50 units @ $7 =	350
	Total		$950

Cost of goods sold for 40 units sold on Jan. 6:

At the oldest unit cost: 40 units × $6 = $240

Inventory remaining after sale of Jan. 6:

At latest unit costs: 60 units × $6 = $360
50 units × $7 = 350 $710

---

[5] This illustration shows the application when the periodic inventory system is used. For the perpetual inventory system a weighted moving average is used. Both applications are illustrated in more detail in subsequent paragraphs.

The Fifo method is widely used since it is rational, systematic, easy to apply, and not subject to manipulation. On the balance sheet, under Fifo, the ending inventory amount is at the most recent unit costs and, therefore, it is likely to be a realistic value prevailing at the balance sheet date. In direct contrast, on the income statement, cost of goods sold is at the oldest unit costs. The significance of the impact of Fifo on the income statement (i.e., cost of goods sold and net income) and the balance sheet (i.e., the inventory amount under current assets) depends on the extent to which unit costs increase or decrease during the period. This is illustrated later.

Last-in, first-out method. This method, frequently referred to as Lifo, assumes that the most recently acquired goods are sold first. Irrespective of the physical flow of goods, Lifo treats the costs of the most recent units acquired as the cost of goods sold. This leaves the unit costs of the beginning inventory and the earliest purchases in the ending inventory. Thus, the Lifo method attains results that are inverse to Fifo. That is, under Lifo, the total inventory cost is measured at the oldest unit costs and cost of goods sold is measured at the newest unit costs. To illustrate, using the data in Exhibit 7–1, the Lifo method would be applied as follows for the sale of January 6:

Goods available for sale on Jan. 6:

Jan. 1,	Beginning inventory 100 units @ $6 =		$600
Jan. 3,	First purchase	50 units @ $7 =	350
	Total		$950

Cost of goods for 40 units sold on Jan. 6:

At the newest unit cost:	40 units × $7 =	$280

Inventory remaining after sale of Jan. 6:

At oldest unit costs:	100 units × $6 = $600	
	10 units × $7 = 70	$670

The Lifo method is acceptable since it is deemed rational and systematic. However, it is amenable to manipulation by buying, or not buying, goods at the end of a period when unit costs have changed in order to affect cost of goods sold and, hence, net income. On the income statement under Lifo, cost of goods sold is based on the latest unit costs. In contrast, on the balance sheet the ending inventory amount is based on the earliest unit costs. The significance of the impact of Lifo will be discussed later.

INVENTORY COSTING WITH A PERPETUAL
INVENTORY SYSTEM

To measure cost of goods sold and inventory during the period, the perpetual inventory system is used. This system requires the maintenance of a detailed **perpetual inventory record** for each kind of goods or merchandise stocked and sold. This record is designed to show units and dollars, at all times, for (a) the goods received (purchased), (b) the goods sold (issued), and (c) the balance of goods on hand on a continuing basis. Each purchase and each sale transaction is entered on the record when it occurs. The perpetual inventory record may be maintained manually, mechanically, or by means of the electronic computer. The perpetual inventory record is designed so that cost of goods sold and the inventory are measured on a perpetual or continuous basis.

In the discussions to follow, a perpetual inventory record will be illustrated for each of the four inventory costing methods. To illustrate each application, we will use the data for Summer's Retail Store given in Exhibit 7–1. We also will use a manual system for instructional purposes. The beginning inventory of 100 units at a unit cost of $6 would have been carried over in the records from the prior period. Recall from Chapter 6 that each purchase would be recorded as follows and, at the same time, entered on the perpetual inventory record (see Exhibit 7–5):

```
Jan. 3:
    Inventory (50 units @ $7).....................  350
        Cash (or Accounts Payable).................         350
```

Also recall that a sale generates *two* companion entries when a perpetual inventory system is used:

```
Jan. 6:
    Cash.........................................  400
        Sales Revenue (40 units @ $10)............         400
    Cost of Goods Sold (Fifo basis)..............  240
        Inventory (40 units @ $6).................         240
```

Specific identification method applied. When this method is applied, as each unit is sold it is identified, usually by a code on the item, with a specific prior purchase unit cost. Exhibit 7–3 illustrates application of the specific identification method. The inventory reflects the beginning inventory in units and dollars in the column headed "Inventory Balance." The January 3 purchase of 50 units at $7 each is recorded under the "Received" column and the Balance column is changed to reflect the new balance. The Balance column is maintained so that the number of units on hand at each unit cost is reflected at all times. Now, assume that the sale of 40 units on January 6 was "identified" as consisting of 20 units that cost $6 each (from the beginning inventory) and 20 units that cost $7 each (from the January 3 purchase). The perpetual inventory would reflect this transaction as shown in Exhibit 7–3. The cost of goods sold for this transaction of $260 is reflected in the Issued column, and the inventory level, in units and amounts, is shown in the Balance column. The sales revenue and cost

Exhibit 7–3

Specific identification method—perpetual inventory system

PERPETUAL INVENTORY RECORD

Item   Item A   Code   13   Minimum Level Stocked _____
Location   320   Cost basis   Specific Identification
                                                 Maximum Level Stocked _____

	Received (purchases)			Issued (sales)			Inventory Balance		
Date	Units	Unit Cost	Total Cost	Units	Unit Cost	Total Cost	Units	Unit Cost	Total Cost
1/1 Balance							100	6	600
1/3	50	7	350				50	7	350
1/6				20	6	120	80	6	480
				20	7	140	30	7	210

of goods sold for this transaction would be entered in the accounts as shown above (for Fifo basis).

Average-cost method applied. When the average-cost method is applied with a perpetual inventory system, a **moving weighted average unit cost** usually is used. This is used because the cost-of-goods-sold amount must be measured and recorded at the time of each sale. Instead, if one were to apply the concept of an *annual* weighted average, the recording of costs of goods sold would be delayed until year end since it is not until that time that such an average can be computed.

In applying a moving average, a *new* average unit cost is computed during the period at the time of *each purchase.* Cost of goods sold and the remaining inventory are measured at the prevailing moving average unit cost. To illustrate, the perpetual inventory record for the data given in Exhibit 7–1 would be as shown in Exhibit 7–4. The moving average was recomputed three times during the period since there were three purchases. Units sold are removed from the inventory

Exhibit 7–4

Moving average method—perpetual inventory system

PERPETUAL INVENTORY RECORD
(Heading—Same as in Exhibit 7–3, except Cost Basis: Moving Average)

Date	Received (purchases)			Issued (sales)			Inventory Balance		
	Units	Unit Cost	Total Cost	Units	Unit Cost	Total Cost	Units	Unit Cost	Total Cost
1/1 Bal.							100	6.00	600
1/3	50	7.00	350				150	6.33*	950
1/6				40	6.33	253	110	6.33	697
6/12	200	8.00	1,600				310	7.41*	2,297
6/18				220	7.41	1,630	90	7.41	667
12/20	120	9.00	1,080				210	8.32*	1,747
12/25				60	8.32	499	150	8.32	1,248

* New average computed.

record at the then average unit cost. For example, the moving average was computed on the date of the first purchase as follows:

	Units	Cost
Beginning inventory	100	$600
Purchase, Jan. 3	50	350
Totals	150	$950

Moving average unit cost: $950 ÷ 150 = $6.33 per unit.

The companion entries for the sale on January 6 would reflect sales revenue of $400 and cost of goods sold of $253 (from the inventory record). The inventory at year end is 150 units @ $8.32 = $1,248. The moving average method is used widely with the perpetual inventory system.

Fifo method applied. When the Fifo method is applied with a perpetual inventory system, the remaining quantities on hand must be identified separately after each issue on the perpetual inventory record for *each unit cost.* These groups frequently are referred to as "inventory cost layers." The identification of inventory cost layers is necessary because goods sold are removed from the record in Fifo order; that is, the oldest unit cost is taken off first. To illustrate, the perpetual inventory record on a Fifo basis is shown in Exhibit 7–5. Each purchase and each sale of goods are entered on the record at the time of occurrence. At each time, the balance on the perpetual inventory record is restated to show the units and amount on hand for each different unit cost. At

Exhibit 7–5

Fifo method—perpetual inventory system

PERPETUAL INVENTORY RECORD
(Heading—Same as in Exhibit 7–3, except Cost Basis: Fifo)

Date	Received (purchases) Units	Unit Cost	Total Cost	Issued (sales) Units	Unit Cost	Total Cost	Inventory Balance Units	Unit Cost	Total Cost
1/1 Bal.							100	6	600
1/3	50	7	350				100	6	600
							50	7	350
1/6				40	6	240	60	6	360
							50	7	350
6/12	200	8	1,600				60	6	360
							50	7	350
							200	8	1,600
6/18				60	6	360			
				50	7	350			
				110	8	880	90	8	720
12/20	120	9	1,080				90	8	720
							120	9	1,080
12/25				60	8	480	30	8	240
							120	9	1,080

the same time, each transaction would be recorded in the accounts. The entry to record the sale of June 18 is:

```
June 18:
  Cash..................................... 2,640
      Sales Revenue (220 units @ $12)........      2,640

  Cost of Goods Sold....................... 1,590
      Inventory............................      1,590
      From Exhibit 7-5, $360 + $350 + $880 =
        $1,590.
```

The perpetual inventory record in Exhibit 7–5 reflects the following measurements at the end of the month:

(a) Cost of goods sold for the year (sum of the column
   Issued, Total Cost—$240 + $360 + $350 + $880 + $480). . $2,310
(b) Final inventory (last balance amounts—$240 + $1,080). 1,320
(c) Goods available for sale (beginning inventory plus purchase). $3,630

Lifo method applied. When the Lifo method is applied with a perpetual inventory system, the inventory cost layers must be identified
separately on the perpetual inventory record, as was the case with Fifo.
This identification is necessary so that the **unit costs** for the number of
units for each sale can be removed from the inventory record in the
reverse order that they came in; that is, the newest unit cost is removed
from the record. To illustrate, the perpetual inventory record on a Lifo
basis is shown in Exhibit 7–6.

Exhibit 7–6

Lifo method—perpetual inventory system

PERPETUAL INVENTORY RECORD
(Heading—Same as in Exhibit 7–3, except Cost Basis: Lifo

Date	Received (purchases)			Issued (sales)			Inventory Balance		
	Units	Unit Cost	Total Cost	Units	Unit Cost	Total Cost	Units	Unit Cost	Total Cost
1/1 Bal.							100	6	600
1/3	50	7	350				100	6	600
							50	7	350
1/6				40	7	280	100	6	600
							10	7	70
6/12	200	8	1,600				100	6	600
							10	7	70
							200	8	1,600
6/18				200	8	1,600			
				10	7	70			
				10	6	60	90	6	540
12/20	120	9	1,080				90	6	540
							120	9	1,080
12/25				60	9	540	90	6	540
							60	9	540

The Lifo method required that the sale of 40 units on January 6 be measured, recorded in the accounts, and removed from the perpetual inventory card at the latest unit purchase price, which was $7 per unit. The record measures cost of goods sold for the year as $2,550 (sum of the Issued column) and the ending inventory as $1,080 (Balance column).

To summarize, in respect to the four inventory pricing methods, let's recall that the central objective was to measure cost of goods sold for the income statement and ending inventory for the balance sheet. Each method applied with the perpetual inventory system met this objective continuously as each transaction happened. With the same data for beginning inventory, purchases, and sales, however, each method provided *different* amounts for costs of goods sold (and hence for net income) and for ending inventory (and hence current assets on the balance sheet).

INVENTORY COSTING WITH A PERIODIC INVENTORY SYSTEM

Recall that in a periodic inventory system the measurement and recording of cost of goods sold is deferred until the end of the period. At that time, the ending inventory is determined by a physical count and then **costed** by using one of the inventory costing methods. Goods available for sale (i.e., beginning inventory plus purchases during the period) less the amount of the ending inventory, thus determined, is the cost-of-goods-sold amount. Thus, the inventory costing methods with a periodic inventory system are applied to measure the dollar cost of the units remaining on hand as determined by the physical inventory count, and cost of goods sold is measured as the difference between goods available for sale and the ending inventory amount.

To illustrate, using the data for Summer's Retail Store given in Exhibit 7–1, application of the four inventory costing methods with the periodic inventory system may be focused on as follows:

Goods available for sale:

Beginning inventory (carried over from prior year)............................	100 units @ $6 =	$ 600
Purchases during the year (from the Purchases account)		
Jan. 3.............................	50 units @ $7 =	350
June 12............................	200 units @ $8 =	1,600
Dec. 20............................	120 units @ $9 =	1,080
Goods available for sale.................	470	$3,630

Ending inventory:

Units by physical count..................	150	
Dollar amount........................		$?
Difference—Cost of goods sold...........	320	$?

Thus, having completed the physical count and found 150 units on hand, the **dollar amount** of the ending inventory must be determined by applying one of the inventory pricing methods.

Application of specific identification method. When this method is used with a periodic inventory system, the unit cost of each item in the ending inventory must be identified with a specific unit purchase price. For example, assume that when the physical count was made at December 31 by Summer's, the unit costs for the 150 units on hand were identified from the "code" on each item as follows:

Units	Unit Cost	Total Cost
20	$ 6	$ 120
50	8	400
80	9	720
150		$1,240

With these data, cost of goods sold would be derived as follows:

Goods available for sale (per above).....	$3,630
Less ending inventory (specific identification).......................	1,240
Cost of goods sold..............	$2,390

Application of weighted average cost method. When this method is used with the periodic inventory system, the weighted average is computed at year end; thus, it is an *annual* average rather than the moving average as is used with the perpetual inventory system. In computing the weighted average, the beginning inventory and all of the purchases during the year are included in the average. To illustrate, using the data given in Exhibit 7–1, the annual weighted average would be computed as follows:

	Units	Total Cost
Beginning inventory...........................	100	$ 600
Purchases: Jan. 3.........................	50	350
June 12.........................	200	1,600
Dec. 20.........................	120	1,080
Totals.....................	470	$3,630

Weighted average: $3,630 ÷ 470 = $7.72 per unit.

With these data, cost of goods sold would be derived as follows:

Goods available for sale (per above)..........	$3,630
Less ending inventory (average):	
150 units @ $7.72 =.....................	1,158
Cost of goods sold..............	$2,472

Application of Fifo method. When this method is applied with a periodic inventory system, the number of units in the ending inventory are costed from the latest inventory layers, starting with the unit cost for the last purchase, then moving to the next to last one, and so on, until all units in the ending inventory are costed. To illustrate, for Summer's the 150 units physically counted as being on hand would be costed as follows:

	Units	Unit Cost	Total Cost
From Dec. 20 purchase.................	120	$9	1,080
From June 12 purchase.................	30	8	240
Ending inventory amount......	150		$1,320

With this data, cost of goods sold would be derived as follows:

Goods available for sale (per above)..........	$3,630
Less ending inventory (Fifo).................	1,320
Cost of goods sold..............	$2,310

Application of Lifo. When this method is used with periodic inventory procedures, the units in the ending inventory are costed at the oldest unit costs for the period starting with the beginning inventory, then to the first purchase, and so on. To illustrate, using the data from Exhibit 7–1, the 150 units in the ending inventory would be costed as follows:

	Units	Unit Cost	Total Cost
From beginning inventory.................	100	$6	$600
From Jan. 3 purchase.................	50	7	350
Ending inventory amount...........	150		$950

With this data, cost of goods sold would be derived as follows:

Goods available for sale (per above)...........	$3,630
Less ending inventory (Lifo).................	950
Cost of goods sold....................	$2,680

COMPARISON OF INVENTORY COST METHODS

Four alternative inventory costing methods were explained and illustrated in the preceding paragraphs. Each method is in accordance with generally accepted accounting principles, although they may produce significantly different net income and asset (i.e., ending inventory) amounts.

With the same data assumed, the moving average used with a perpetual inventory system will derive a different result than the weighted annual average used with a periodic system. Similarly, Lifo applied with a perpetual system usually will derive a somewhat different result than when applied with a periodic system. In contrast, Fifo will always derive the same result under both systems, as will specific identification.

To illustrate, following are the comparative results for Summer's Retail Store:

	Sales Revenue	Cost of Goods Sold	Gross Margin	Balance Sheet (Inventory)
Perpetual System:				
Specific identification....	$3,880	$2,390	$1,490	$1,240
Moving average........	3,880	2,382	1,498	1,248
Fifo.................	3,880	2,310	1,570	1,320
Lifo.................	3,880	2,550	1,330	1,080
Periodic System:				
Specific identification....	3,880	2,390	1,490	1,240
Weighted average.......	3,880	2,472	1,408	1,158
Fifo.................	3,880	2,310	1,570	1,320
Lifo.................	3,880	2,680	1,200	950

A comparison of the results shown above for the four **methods** will increase our understanding of their characteristics. First, we can readily perceive that, in the case of a constant or single inventory cost, all methods would provide the same net income and the same inventory amounts. Second, in the case of changing unit cost, each method tends to give a different net income and a different inventory amount. On this point, observe that the difference in *net income* among each of the methods is the same as the difference as in the inventory amounts. The method that provides the higher ending inventory amount also provides the higher net income amount. Third, the net income and inventory amounts may be affected by the inventory **system** used (i.e., compare the Lifo results under each system) and the costing method used. Fourth, the average-cost method tends to give net income and inventory amounts that fall between the Fifo and Lifo extremes.

We will now focus on a comparison of the Fifo and Lifo methods since they usually represent the extreme, and opposite, effects. Note in the comparison above that unit costs were *increasing* and that Lifo provided the lowest net income and inventory amounts, whereas Fifo provided the highest net income and inventory amounts. In comparing the effects of Fifo and Lifo, it is important to note that the comparative effects will depend upon the direction of change in unit cost. *When unit*

costs are rising, Lifo will result in lower net income and a lower in-
ventory valuation than will Fifo. Conversely, when unit costs are de-
clining, Lifo will result in higher net income and higher inventory
valuation than will Fifo.

Let's turn our attention to the income tax effects for the moment.
Since all four methods are acceptable for income tax purposes, in
recent years why have some businesses opted for Lifo? Clearly, the
reason is that it tended to minimize income tax payments. Prices have
been rising and, with rising prices, Lifo reports less net taxable income,
so the income tax bill is lower. Of course, the inventory effect suggests
that, should prices decline at some future date, those businesses may
want to change from Lifo to Fifo to minimize income taxes on the
downward trend of prices. It is difficult, however, to obtain permission
from the Internal Revenue Service to change the inventory costing
method.

No one method of inventory costing can be considered as the "best."
It would be impractical to assume that the tax consequences are not
important in the choice of method. Many observers believe that businesses, in setting selling prices, often do so within a "Lifo assumption"
since the goods sold must be replaced on the shelf at the latest cost
rather than at earlier cost.

Many accountants believe that the best inventory costing method is
the one that best matches the sales pricing policy of the company. Companies do price units for sale in each of the ways implied by these four
costing methods. These accountants believe that the only conceptually
sound basis for selecting the best costing method for a particular company depends upon the sales pricing policy followed. Other accountants
believe that the choice should be based upon whether the measurement
emphasis should be on the income statement or on the balance sheet.
Those who believe that the income statement should be accorded primary emphasis tend to defend Lifo since it matches the most recent
purchase cost with current sales revenue. To the contrary, those who
prefer to emphasize the balance sheet tend to prefer Fifo since it reports
the inventory (an asset) at the most current cost price. Because of
these considerations, it is not difficult to understand why the accounting
profession, and the income tax laws, have accepted several alternative
inventory costing methods.

INVENTORIES AT NET REALIZABLE VALUE

Merchandise on hand that is damaged, obsolete, or shopworn should
not be measured and reported at original cost but at present **net realizable value** when it is below cost. Net realizable value is the *estimated
amount* that is expected to be realized when the goods are sold in their
deteriorated condition, less disposal costs. For example, assume a

company selling television sets has on hand two sets that have been used as demonstrators; when purchased, the sets cost $200 each. In the light of their present condition, realistic estimates are:

	Per Set
Sales value in present condition.........	$140
Estimated disposal costs................	30
Estimated net realizable value...........	$110

On the basis of these estimates, the two television sets would be included in the inventory at $110 each, or a total of $220, rather than at the total original cost of $400. Net realizable value is used because it records the loss in the period in which it occurred rather than in the period of sale and does not overstate the asset.

INVENTORIES AT LOWER-OF-COST-OR-MARKET

We have emphasized that inventories should be measured at their unit purchase cost in accordance with the cost principle. However, when goods in the ending inventory can be replaced at a lower cost at inventory date, that lower unit cost should be used. This is known as measuring inventories on a **lower-of-cost-or-market basis.** It is a departure from the cost principle in favor of the exception principle—conservatism—in order to recognize a "holding" loss in the period when the replacement cost drops, rather than in the period when the goods are sold. To illustrate, assume that an office-equipment dealer has ten electronic calculators to be included in the ending inventory. The calculators were purchased for $150 each about a year earlier and marked to sell at $199.95. At the date of the ending inventory, however, the same calculators can be purchased for $100 and will sell for $129.95. Under the lower-of-cost-or-market basis the ten calculators should be costed in the ending inventory at $100 each. In this context, market is defined as the current market replacement cost of the item in the quantities usually purchased.

Let's look carefully at the effect of using a replacement cost of $100 against using the original purchase cost of $150 for the ten computers to be included in the ending inventory. By costing them at $50 per unit below their purchase cost, net income will be $500 (10 × $50), less than it would have been had they been costed in the inventory at $150 per unit. This $500 loss in **inventory utility** was due to a decline in the replacement cost. Because it is included in the cost of goods sold, net income will be reduced by $500 in the period in which the cost fell, rather than in the later period when the goods are sold. Thus, the loss is matched with the accounting period in which it occurred. These effects are demonstrated in Exhibit 7–7. The lower-of-cost-or-market usually is applied to all inventories.

Exhibit 7–7

Effect of inventory measurement at lower-of-cost-or-market

	Inventory Measured at	
	Cost (Fifo)	Lower-of-Cost-or-Market
Sales.....................................	$12,500	$12,500
Cost of goods sold:		
Beginning inventory.............	$6,750	$6,750
Add purchases..................	2,250	2,250
Goods available for sale..........	9,000	9,000
Less ending inventory		
(10 computers):		
At purchase cost of $150.....	1,500	
At lower-of-cost-or-market		
of $100........................		1,000
Cost of goods sold......................	7,500	8,000
Gross margin on sales.....................	5,000	4,500
Expenses...........................	4,000	4,000
Net Income...........................	$ 1,000	$ 500

Estimating inventory   When the periodic inventory system is used, a physical inventory count is essential for each date on which financial statements are to be prepared. Taking a physical inventory at the end of each period for which financial statements are derived is a time-consuming task in many businesses. As a consequence, physical inventories may be taken only once a year. Nevertheless, the management of many businesses desire financial statements on a monthly or, at least, a quarterly basis. When a periodic, rather than a perpetual, inventory system is used, some businesses *estimate* the ending inventory for the monthly or quarterly financial statements. The gross margin method has been developed for this purpose, using the gross margin ratio as the basis for the computation. Recall that the gross margin ratio is derived by dividing gross margin on sales by net sales (page 169). The gross margin method assumes that the *gross margin ratio* for the current period should be essentially the same as it was in the immediate past. Therefore, based on the *ratio* in the immediate past, a gross margin ratio is estimated for the current period. This estimated ratio can then be used to compute *estimated amounts* for (1) gross margin on sales, (2) cost of goods sold, and (3) ending inventory. To illustrate, assume Patz Company is preparing *monthly* financial statements at January 30, 1974. The accounting records would provide the sales, beginning inventory, purchases, and expense amounts as they are listed on the following page.

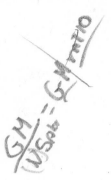

Income Statement
For the month ending January 30, 1974

Net sales..........................		$100,000*
Cost of goods sold:		
Beginning inventory.............	$15,000*	
Add purchases.................	65,000*	
Goods available for sale.........	80,000	
Less ending inventory...........	To be estimated	
Cost of goods sold...........		?
Gross margin on sales.............		?
Less expenses...................		30,000*
Net Income......................		$?

* Provided by the accounts.

The amount of the ending inventory each month is to be *estimated* rather than determined by physical count. Assume that the net sales for 1973 amounted to $1,000,000 and gross margin was $400,000; therefore, the actual gross margin ratio for 1973 was $400,000 ÷ $1,000,000 = .40. Using that ratio as our estimate for 1974, we can compute an *estimated* inventory valuation. The computational steps, in lettered sequence, are shown below.

Income Statement
For the month of January 1974 (estimated)

			Computations (sequence *a, b, c*)
Net sales..............		$100,000	Per accounts
Cost of goods sold:			
Beginning inventory...	$15,000		Per accounts
Add purchases........	65,000		Per accounts
Goods available for sale	80,000		
Less ending inventory..	20,000		(c) $80,000 − $60,000 = $20,000
Cost of goods sold...		60,000	(b) $100,000 − $40,000 = $60,000*
Gross margin on sales...		40,000	(a) $100,000 × .40 = $40,000
Less expenses.........		30,000	Per accounts
Net Income...........		$ 10,000	

* Or alternatively, $100,000 × (1.00 − .40) = $60,000.

The balance sheet is completed by entering the $20,000 estimated ending inventory amount under current assets.

The gross margin method has several other uses apart from preparation of the monthly or quarterly financial statements. Auditors and accountants may use it to test the reasonableness of the amount of the inventory determined by other means. If the current gross margin ratio has changed materially from past experience, it may suggest an error in the inventory determination. As another example, the method also is used in the case of a fire where an inventory of goods is burned and its valuation must be estimated for settlement purposes with the insurance company.[6]

---

[6] Another method, known as the retail method of estimating the ending inventory, is used widely by department stores. It is essentially the same as the

Supplies
inventories

The term **inventory,** as commonly used, means only merchandise inventory (either purchased or manufactured), raw materials to be used directly in the manufacture of goods for resale, and goods in process in varying stages of completion. Other types of inventories do exist; they include unused office supplies, janitorial supplies, store supplies, and maintenance supplies. When supplies are purchased for *immediate use,* an appropriately designated expense account is debited at the date of purchase of the supplies. On the other hand, supplies may be purchased for *future use* in the business. Supplies purchased for future use have been briefly discussed in the previous chapters as **prepaid expenses.** Recall that a prepaid expense is reported on the balance sheet as a current asset. When supplies are purchased for future use, an appropriately designated prepaid expense account is charged (i.e., debited). As the supplies are used, the prepaid expense account is credited and an expense account is debited. To illustrate, assume Company X purchased office supplies costing $200 on January 3, 1974 for future use. The purchase would be recorded as follows:

```
Prepaid Office Supplies (or Office
     Supplies Inventory)........................... 200
         Cash........................................         200
```

Now, assume it is December 31, 1974, end of the fiscal period. A count of the office supplies still unused and costed at their purchase price showed $40. Thus, the supplies actually used during the period amounted to: $200 − $40 = $160. Therefore, an adjusting entry must be made on December 31, 1974, as follows:

```
Office Supplies Expense......................... 160
     Prepaid Office Supplies (or Office
         Supplies Inventory)......................         160
```

The effect of these entries on the financial statements for 1974 will be:

```
Income statement:
     Office Supplies Expense........................... $160
Balance sheet:
     Current asset:
         Prepaid Expense (Office Supplies Inventory)...... $ 40
```

Office supplies on hand are not included with the "inventories" because they are not being held for resale.

---

gross margin method, but differs in detail. Discussion of it is deferred to more advanced books.

Consistency
in
accounting

In this and the preceding chapter, several alternative approaches in measuring cost of goods sold and inventory were discussed and illustrated. Some of these alternatives produce different income statement and balance sheet results under identical situations (see page 232). In addition to these situations, there are alternatives in many other areas of accounting. Recall that in Chapter 3 we illustrated 11 different accounting policies that were reported by J. C. Penney Company, Inc. Some of these policies reflected the company's choice of one of several alternatives available. In view of the **consistency principle** (Exhibit 2–1), a company cannot capriciously shift from one alternative to another. The consistency principle holds that in the accounting process all concepts, principles, and measurement approaches should be applied in a similar or consistent way from one period to the next in order to assure that the data reported in the financial statements are comparable over time. This principle prevents "willy-nilly" changes from one accounting or measurement approach to another. The consistency principle is not inflexible. It permits changes in accounting when the change is to an approach that tends to improve the measurement of financial results.

Demonstra-
tion case for
self-study

METAL PRODUCTS, INCORPORATED

(Try to resolve the requirements before proceeding to the suggested solution.)

This case focuses on the effects of a misstatement of the ending inventory. It does not introduce any new accounting concepts or procedures.

Metal Products, Incorporated, has been operating for eight years as a distributor of a line of metal products. It is now the end of 1974 and for the first time the company will undergo an audit by an independent CPA. The company uses the periodic inventory system. The annual income statements, prepared by the company, were:

	For the Year Ended, December 31	
	1974	1973
Sales	$800,000	$750,000
Cost of goods sold:		
Beginning inventory	40,000	45,000
Add purchases	484,000	460,000
Goods available for sale	524,000	505,000
Less ending inventory	60,000	40,000
Cost of goods sold	464,000	465,000
Gross margin on sales	336,000	285,000
Operating expenses*	306,000	275,000
Net Income	$ 30,000	$ 10,000

* As a Subchapter S Corporation there are no income taxes.

During the early stages of the audit, the independent CPA discovered that the ending inventory for 1973 had been understated by $15,000.

Required:

(a) Based on the above income statements, compute the gross margin ratio for each year. Do the results suggest the inventory error? Explain.
(b) Reconstruct the two income statements on a corrected basis.
(c) Answer the following questions.
    (1) What are the corrected gross margin ratios? Explain.
    (2) What effect did the $15,000 understatement of the ending inventory have on 1973 net income? Explain.
    (3) What effect did it have on 1974 net income? Explain.

Suggested Solution:

Requirement (a), Gross margin ratios as reported:
1973: $285,000 ÷ $750,000 = .38
1974: $336,000 ÷ $800,000 = .42

The change in the gross margin ratio from .38 to .42 suggests the possibility of an inventory error in the absence of any other explanation for this significant change.

Requirement (b), Income statements corrected:

	For the Year Ended, December 31	
	1974	*1973*
Sales..........................	$800,000	$750,000
Cost of goods sold:		
Beginning inventory.............	55,000	45,000
Add purchases..................	484,000	460,000
Goods available for sale........	539,000	505,000
Less ending inventory............	60,000	55,000
Cost of goods sold..............	479,000	450,000
Gross margin on sales.............	321,000	300,000
Operating expenses...............	306,000	275,000
Net Income......................	$ 15,000	$ 25,000

Requirement (c)

(1) Corrected gross margin ratios:
    1973: $300,000 ÷ $750,000 = .40
    1974: $321,000 ÷ $800,000 = .401

The inventory error of $15,000 was responsible for the variation in the gross margin ratios reflected in Requirement (a). The inventory error in 1973 affected gross margin for both 1973 and 1974, in the opposite direction but by the same amount ($15,000).

(2) Effect on net income in 1973:   *Ending inventory understatement* ($15,000) caused an *understatement of net income* by the *same amount*.

(3) Effect on net income in 1974:   Beginning inventory *understatement* (by the same $15,000) since the inventory amount is carried over from the prior period caused an *overstatement* of net income by the same amount.

An inventory misstatement in one year affects pretax net income by the amount of the error and in the next year affects net income again by the same amount but in the opposite direction.

Summary   This chapter focused on the problem of measuring the cost of goods sold and the ending inventory. The inventory should include all the items on hand for resale to which the entity has title. Costs flow into inventory when goods are purchased (or manufactured) and flow out when the goods are sold or otherwise disposed of. When there are several unit cost figures representing the inflow of goods for the period, one is confronted with the necessity of using a rational and systematic method to assign unit cost figures to the units in the inventory and to the units sold (cost of goods sold). The chapter discussed and illustrated four different methods with a perpetual inventory system and a periodic inventory system. Each of the methods is in accordance with the cost principle. The methods discussed were: specific identification, average cost, Fifo, and Lifo. The method of inventory costing used is particularly important since it will affect reported net income and the inventory valuation reported on the balance sheet. In a period of rising prices, Fifo gives a higher net income than does Lifo; in a period of falling prices the opposite results occur.

Damaged, obsolete, and deteriorated items in inventory should be assigned a unit cost that represents their estimated net realizable value. Also, when market value (i.e., replacement cost) has declined below the actual cost of the goods on hand, the inventory should be measured on a lower-of-cost-or-market basis.

This chapter presented another fundamental accounting principle (Exhibit 2–1) known as the consistency principle. This principle holds that in the accounting process all concepts, principles, and measurement approaches should be applied in a similar or consistent way from period to period so that the financial statements will be comparable over time.

Important
terms

Merchandise inventory
Goods-in-process inventory
Finished-goods inventory
Specific identification
Average cost
Moving average cost
First-in, first-out (Fifo)
Last-in, first-out (Lifo)

Inventory costing methods
Perpetual inventory record
Net realizable value
Lower-of-cost-or-market
Gross margin method
Consistency principle
Passage of title

Questions
for
discussion

1. Match the type of inventory with the type of business in the following matrix.

Type of Inventory	Type of business	
	Trading	Manufacturing
Merchandise		
Finished goods		
Goods in process		
Raw materials		

2. Why is inventory an important item to both management and external users of financial statements?

3. Fundamentally, what items should be included in inventory?

4. In measuring cost of goods sold and inventory, why is passage of title an important issue? When does title to goods usually pass? Explain.

5. Explain the application of the cost principle to the cost of an item in the ending inventory.

6. When a perpetual inventory system is used, unit costs must be known at the date of each sale. In contrast, when a periodic inventory system is used, unit costs must be known at the end of the accounting period. Explain.

7. The chapter discussed four inventory costing methods: (a) specific identification, (b) average cost, (c) Fifo, and (d) Lifo. Explain each.

8. Some accountants believe the specific identification method is subject to manipulation. Explain.

9. When a perpetual inventory system is used a *moving average* may be used. In contrast, when a periodic inventory system is used, an *annual weighted average* may be used. Explain why the different averages are used.

10. Contrast the balance-sheet effects of Lifo versus Fifo on reported assets

(i.e., the ending inventory) when (a) prices are rising and (b) when prices are falling.

11.   Contrast the income statement effects of Lifo versus Fifo (i.e., on net income) when (a) prices are rising and (b) where prices are falling.

12.   When should net realizable value be used in costing an item in the ending inventory?

13.   The chapter discussed the gross margin method to estimate inventories. Briefly explain it and indicate why it is used.

14.   Briefly explain the consistency principle. How might it relate to the inventory costing methods?

Exercises   **E7–1.**   The records at the end of January 1975 for Bill's Place showed the following for a particular kind of merchandise:

	Units	Total Cost
Inventory, Dec. 31, 1974	20	$200
Purchase, Jan. 9, 1975	50	550
Sale, Jan. 11, 1975 (at $20 per unit)	33	
Purchase, Jan. 20, 1975	30	360
Sale, Jan. 27, 1975 (at $21 per unit)	35	

Required:

Assuming a periodic inventory system, compute the amount of (1) the ending inventory and (2) cost of goods sold at January 31, 1975, under each of the following inventory costing methods (show computations):

a.   Specific identification (assume the sale on January 11 was "identified" with the purchase of January 9, the sale of January 27 was "identified" with the purchase of January 20, and any excess identified with the beginning inventory).

b.   Weighted average cost.

c.   First-in, first-out.

d.   Last-in, first-out.

E7–2.   The Masters Company uses a perpetual inventory system and the Fifo inventory costing method. The records reflected the following for January 1975.

	Units	Unit Cost
Beginning inventory, Jan. 1	100	$1.00
Purchase, Jan. 6	200	1.20
Sale, Jan. 10 (at $2.40 per unit)	110	
Purchase, Jan. 14	100	1.30
Sale, Jan. 29 (at $2.60 per unit)	160	

Required (show detailed computations):

a. Compute goods available for sale for January.
b. Compute cost of goods sold for January.
c. Compute the ending inventory for January.
d. Give journal entries indicated by the above data through January 10 (assume cash transactions).

E7–3. Use the data given in Exercise 7–1 for this exercise (assume cash transactions and perpetual inventory system).

Required:

a. Prepare a perpetual inventory record on a moving average basis. Round to even cents on unit costs and even dollars on total cost.
b. Give journal entry to record the purchase of Jan. 9, 1975.
c. Give the journal entries to record the sale on Jan. 11, 1975.
d. On Jan. 27, 1975, what would be the balance in (1) the Cost of Goods Sold account and (2) the Inventory account?

E7–4. Use the data given in Exercise 7–1 for this exercise (assume cash transactions and perpetual inventory system).

Required:

a. Prepare a perpetual inventory record (1) on a Fifo basis and (2) on a Lifo basis.
b. Give the journal entry to record the purchase of Jan. 9, 1975.
c. Give the journal entries to record the sale on Jan. 11, 1975 (1) on a Fifo basis and (2) on a Lifo basis.
d. On Jan. 27, 1975, what would be the balance, under each method, in (1) the Cost of Goods Sold account and (2) the Inventory account?

E7–5. Complete the following cost-of-goods-sold section of the income statement under three different inventory costing methods assuming a periodic inventory system. Show your computations of the ending inventory.

	Fifo	Lifo	Average
Cost of goods sold:			
Beginning inventory (480 units).............	$ 9,600	$ 9,600	$ 9,600
Purchases (520 units).....................	13,000	13,000	13,000
Goods available for sale..................			
Ending inventory (530 units)..............			
Cost of goods sold.......................			

11,250

In this situation, which method gives the highest net income? Which gives the lowest net income? Explain.

E7–6. During January 1974, Brush Company sold 6,100 units at $20 each of the only kind of merchandise stocked. The inventory for December 31, 1973, showed 5,600 units on hand, valued at $44,800. During January 1974, two purchases of the item were made: the first one was for 1,000 units at $9 per unit; the second one was for 6,000 units at $10 each. The periodic inventory reflected 6,500 units on hand on January 31, 1974. Operating expenses for the month summed to $62,100.

Required:

a. On the basis of the above information, complete summary income statements under Fifo and Lifo. Use a single list of side captions and set up three separate columns as follows: Units; Fifo; and Lifo. Show your computations of the ending inventory.
b. Which method gives the highest net income? Why?

E7–7.   In November 1974, a fire destroyed the inventory of the Kaplan Retail Store. The accounting records were not destroyed; hence, they provided the following information:

	1972	1973	1974 to Date of Fire
Sales.	$120,000	$142,000	$115,000
Cost of goods sold.	73,200	85,200	?
Gross margin on sales.	46,800	56,800	?
Expenses.	34,800	42,800	37,000
Net income.	$ 12,000	$ 14,000	?
Ending inventory.	$ 20,000	$ 22,000	?
Purchases during year.	70,000	87,200	68,000

Required:

Compute the inventory fire loss and prepare an income statement for 1974 up to the date of the fire. Show detail for the cost of goods sold.

E7–8.   The income statement for four consecutive years for Cable Company reflected the following summarized amounts:

	1971	1972	1973	1974
Sales.	$60,000	$70,000	$80,000	$65,000
Cost of goods sold.	36,000	38,300	50,100	39,000
Gross margin.	24,000	31,700	29,900	26,000
Expenses.	15,000	16,700	19,100	15,800
Net income (pretax).	$ 9,000	$15,000	$10,800	$10,200

Subsequent to development of the above amounts, it has been determined that the physical inventory taken on December 31, 1972, was overstated by $3,000.

Required:

a. Recast the above income statement summary to reflect the correct amounts, taking into consideration the inventory error.
b. Compute the gross margin ratio for each year (1) before the

correction and (2) after the correction. Do the results lend confidence to your corrected amounts? Explain.

E7–9. The Stacy Company is completing the annual information-processing cycle on December 31, 1974. The company uses large quantities of store supplies in regular operations. To obtain lower prices, store supplies are bought in large quantities far in advance of actual use. When purchased, the cost is debited to a store supplies inventory account. At December 31, 1974, the account reflected the following debits:

Balance, Jan. 1, 1974.................... $ 600
Purchases during 1974..................   1,400

A physical count at December 31, 1974, costed at purchase price, reflected supplies on hand amounting to $850.

Required:

What entry should be made on December 31, 1974, to reflect the effect of the inventory count?

Problems   P7–1. The Reynolds Company has just completed a physical inventory at year end, December 31, 1974. Only the items on the shelves, in storage, and in the receiving area were counted and extended at cost on a Fifo basis. The inventory summed to $73,500. During the audit the independent CPA developed the following additional information:

a. Reynolds Company, on the date of the inventory, received notice from a supplier that goods ordered earlier, at a cost of $900, had been delivered to the transportation company on December 27; the terms were FOB shipping point. Since the shipment had not arrived, it was excluded from the physical inventory.

b. On December 31, 1974, Reynolds shipped $600 worth of goods to a customer FOB destination. The goods are expected to arrive at destination no earlier than January 8, 1975. Since the goods were not on hand, they were not included in the physical inventory.

c. One of the items sold by Reynolds is high-priced and moves slowly. In order to induce Reynolds to carry the item, the manufacturer–supplier provides the item on a consignment basis. At the end of each month, Reynolds (the consignee) renders a report to the manufacturer on the number sold and remits cash for the cost. At the end of December 1974, Reynolds had five of these items on hand; hence, they were included in the physical inventory at $1,400 each.

d. Goods costing $100 were out on trial by a customer; hence, they were excluded from the inventory.

e. Goods in transit from a supplier with terms FOB destination on December 31, 1974, amounted to $350. Since these goods had not arrived, they were excluded from the physical inventory.

f. On December 31, 1974, goods in transit to customers with terms FOB shipping point amounted to $600 (expected delivery date January 10, 1975). Since the goods had been shipped, they were excluded from the physical inventory.

g. On December 28, 1974, a customer purchased goods for cash amounting to $800 and left them "for pickup on January 3, 1975." Reynolds had paid $500 for the goods and, since they were on hand, included the latter amount in the physical inventory.

Required:

Determine the correct amount for the ending inventory. Explain the basis for any changes that you make to the initial $73,500 amount. (Hint: The correct amount is $67,600; set up 3 columns: Items, Amount, and Explanation.)

P7–2. The Ryan Company has just completed taking the periodic inventory of merchandise on hand at the end of the fiscal year, December 31, 1974. There is some question concerning inventory costing for five different items on which we will focus attention. The inventory reflected the following:

		Units	Original Unit Cost
a.	Item A—The two units on hand have been damaged because they were used as demonstrators. It is estimated that they may be sold at 10% below cost and that disposal costs will amount to $50 each.	2	$180
b.	Item B—Because of a drop in the market, this item can be replaced from the original supplier at 8% below the original cost price. The sales price also was reduced.	20	50
c.	Item C—Because of style change, it is highly doubtful that this item can be sold; it has no scrap value.	5	14
d.	Item D—This item will no longer be stocked; as a consequence it will be marked down from the regular selling price of $80 to $40. Cost of selling is estimated to be 15% of the original cost price.	4	60
e.	Item E—Because of high demand and quality, the cost of this item has been raised from $120 to $144; hence, all replacement for inventory in the foreseeable future will be at the latter price.	10	120
f.	The remaining items in inventory pose no valuation problems; their costs sum to $32,000.		

Required:

1. Compute the total amount of the ending inventory. List each of the above items separately.

2. For each of the five items, separately identified, explain the basis for the unit amount you used in completing Requirement 1.

P7-3. At the end of January 1974, the records of the Lewis Company showed the following for a particular item that sold at $9.95 per unit:

	Units	Amount
Inventory, Jan. 1, 1974.	500	$3,000
Sale, Jan. 10.	(400)	
Purchase, Jan. 12.	600	3,720
Sale, Jan. 17.	(550)	
Purchase, Jan. 26.	310	1,953
Purchase return, Jan. 28.	(10)	Out of Jan. 26 purchase

Required:

a. Prepare the cost-of-goods-sold section of the income statement under each method of inventory: (1) specific identification, (2) average cost, (3) Fifo, and (4) Lifo. For specific identification, assume the first sale was out of the beginning inventory and the second sale out of the Jan. 12 purchase. Show the inventory computations in detail. Assume periodic inventory system.

b. Prove the cost-of-goods-sold amount for each of the four methods.

c. Between Fifo and Lifo, which one produces the higher net income? Why?

P7-4. The Clark Company executives are considering their inventory policies. They have been using the moving average method with the perpetual inventory system. They have requested an "analysis of the effects of Fifo and Lifo." The income statement, just completed for the month of January 1974, based upon the moving average method, follows:

	Units	Amounts
Sales.	180	$9,400
Cost of goods sold.	180	5,710
Gross margin on sales.		3,690
Expenses.		1,700
Net income.		$1,990

Transactions during the month were:

Beginning inventory 50 units @ $30
Jan. 6   Sold 40 units @ $50
Jan. 9   Purchased 100 units @ $32
Jan. 16 Sold 80 units @ $52
Jan. 20 Purchased 110 units @ $33
Jan. 28 Sold 60 units @ $54

Required:

a. Copy the above income statement and extend it to the right by adding columns for Fifo and Lifo using the perpetual inventory system. This will provide one basis for analyzing the different results among the three inventory costing methods. Show the ending inventory separately for Fifo and Lifo. Show your computations.

b. Between Fifo and Lifo, which one produces the higher net incomes? Why?

P7–5. Haven's Appliance Store uses a perpetual inventory system. In this problem we will focus on one item stocked, which is designated as Item A. The beginning inventory was 200 units @ $4. During January the following transactions occurred that affected Item A:

Jan. 5   Sold 50 units at $10 per unit.
Jan. 10   Purchased 100 units at $5 per unit.
Jan. 16   Sold 180 units at $10 per unit.
Jan. 18   Purchased 230 units for $1,380.
Jan. 24   Sold 60 units at $11 per unit.

Required (assume cash transactions):

a. Prepare a perpetual inventory record for January (1) on a Fifo basis and (2) on a Lifo basis.
b. Give the entry for the purchase on Jan. 10.
c. Give the entries under both methods for the sale on Jan. 16.
d. At the end of January what would be the inventory balance under (1) Fifo and (2) Lifo? Also complete the following income statement under each method.

Sales............................	$	?
Cost of goods sold.................	$	?
Gross margin......................	$	?
Expenses.........................	$	1,200
Net income.......................	$	?

Current assets:
Merchandise inventory............. $?

P7–6. This is a hypothetical case to demonstrate the effect on net income of (a) rising prices and (b) falling prices in comparing Fifo with Lifo. Net income is to be evaluated under four different situations as follows:

Situation A—Prices rising, *Fifo* is utilized.
Situation B—Prices rising, *Lifo* is utilized.
Situation C—Prices falling, *Fifo* is utilized.
Situation D—Prices falling, *Lifo* is utilized.

The basic data common to all four situations are: sales, 600 units for $5,300; beginning inventory, 500 units; purchases, 500 units, ending inventory, 400 units; and expenses, $3,000. The following tabulated income statements for each situation have been set up for analytical purposes:

	Prices Rising		Prices Falling	
	Situation A Fifo	Situation B Lifo	Situation C Fifo	Situation D Lifo
Sales.................	$5,300	$5,300	$5,300	$5,300
Cost of goods sold:				
Beginning inventory...	1,000	?	?	?
Purchases............	1,500	?	?	?
Goods available for sale	2,500	?	?	?
Ending inventory......	1,200	?	?	?
Cost of goods sold.....	1,300	?	?	?
Gross margin..........	4,000	?	?	?
Expenses..............	3,000	3,000	3,000	3,000
Net income............	$1,000	?	?	?

Required:

1. Complete the above tabulation for each situation. In Situations A and B (prices rising), assume the following: beginning inventory, 500 units @ $2.00 = $1,000; purchases, 500 units @ $3.00 = $1,500. In Situations C and D (prices falling), assume the opposite; that is: beginning inventory, 500 units @ $3.00 = $1,500; purchases, 500 units @ $2.00 = $1,000. Use periodic inventory procedures.

2. What effect on net income is demonstrated by Requirement 1 when prices are rising and when prices are falling?

P7-7. The president of Amis Company has just been presented with the March 1974 financial statement. It reflects data for three months as summarized below:

	Quarterly Income Statements			
	January	February	March	Quarter
Sales...................	$100,000	$106,000	$90,000	$296,000
Cost of goods sold.......	58,000	61,500	?	?
Gross margin on sales.....	42,000	44,500	?	?
Expenses................	32,000	33,500	32,000	97,500
Net income.............	$ 10,000	$ 11,000	$?	$?
Gross margin ratio.....	.42	.4198	.42 (estimated)	
Ending inventory.......	$ 14,000	$ 16,000		

The company uses the periodic inventory system. Although monthly statements are prepared, a monthly inventory count is not made. Instead, the company uses the gross margin method for monthly purposes.

Required:

a. Complete the computations in the following form to estimate the results for March.

	Amounts	*Computations*
Cost of goods sold:		
Beginning inventory.........	$16,000	From records
Purchases...................	51,000	From records
Goods available for sale....	?	?
Ending inventory............	?	?
Cost of goods sold..........	?	

b. Complete the quarterly income statements given above.

P7–8. The income statement for Mason Company summarized for a four-year period showed the following:

	1971	*1972*	*1973*	*1974*
Sales...............	$100,000	$120,000	$130,000	$110,000
Cost of goods sold..	60,000	61,000	87,000	65,000
Gross margin........	40,000	59,000	43,000	45,000
Expenses............	30,000	32,800	36,200	31,700
Net income..........	$ 10,000	$ 26,200	$ 6,800	$ 13,300

An audit revealed that in determining the above amounts the ending inventory for 1972 was overstated by $10,000. Reconstruct the statements on a corrected basis. What effects did this inventory error have on the statements? The company uses a periodic inventory system.

8 Cash, temporary investments in securities, and receivables

Purpose of the chapter In this chapter we will focus our attention on the measurement and reporting of a group of assets known as liquid assets: cash, temporary investments in securities, and receivables. They are designated as liquid assets because of their primary characteristic: they are either money or relatively close to conversion to money. Thus, they possess the characteristics of a current asset. The chapter will deal with the three parts in order.

PART ONE: SAFEGUARDING AND REPORTING CASH

Cash is the most liquid asset that a business owns. Cash includes money and any instrument, such as a check, money order, or a bank draft, that banks normally will accept for deposit and immediate credit to the depositor's account. Cash excludes such items as notes receivable, IOU's, and postage stamps (a prepaid expense) and is generally divided into three categories: cash on hand, cash deposited in banks, and other instruments that meet the above definition. It is not unusual for a business to have several bank accounts. Even though a separate cash account may be maintained for each bank account, they are combined as one amount for financial reporting purposes.

Because cash is the most liquid asset and is continuously being generated and used, it imposes heavy responsibilities on the management of an entity. These may be summarized as follows:

1. Safeguarding to prevent theft, fraud, loss through miscounting, etc.
2. Accurate accounting so that relevant reports of cash inflows, outflows, and balances may be prepared periodically.

3. Control to assure a sufficient amount of cash on hand (a) to meet current operating needs, (b) to meet maturing liabilities, and (c) to meet unexpected emergencies.
4. Planning to prevent excess amounts of idle cash from accumulating—idle cash produces no revenue. In many cases, idle cash is invested in securities and in other ways to derive a return, pending need for the cash.

Internal control of cash

Internal control refers to those policies and procedures of the business designed primarily to safeguard the assets of the enterprise. Internal control should extend to all assets: cash, receivables, investments, fixed assets, etc. An important phase of internal control focuses on cash. Effective internal control of cash normally should include:

1. Definite and precise assignment to designated individuals of the responsibilities for all activities related to cash handling and accounting for cash.
2. Establishment of definite and separate routines for (a) handling the inflow of cash, (b) handling the outflow of cash, and (c) the accounting process for both cash receipts and disbursements.
3. Separation of the physical handling of cash (in all forms) from the accounting function. Individuals that handle cash receipts or make cash disbursements (whether cash or by check) should not have access to the cash records. Similarly, those that are involved in maintaining the records should not have access to cash.
4. Complete separation of the function of receiving cash from the function of disbursing cash.
5. Require that all cash receipts be deposited in a bank daily. Keep cash on hand under strict controls.
6. Require that all significant cash payments be made by check with a separate approval requirement. For example, the person authorized to approve payments should be different from the person authorized to sign checks.

The separation of responsibilities and the use of prescribed routines are particularly important phases in the control of cash. A clear-cut separation of duties and responsibilities between people necessitates collusion between two or more persons if cash is to be embezzled and the theft concealed in the accounting records. Prescribed routines are designed so that the work done by one individual is checked by the results reported by other individuals. For example, the routine for handling cash received through the mail may be designed so that one designated person opens the mail and makes a list of the cash. Then the cash received must follow a prescribed channel to the bank deposit, and another channel is prescribed for the flow of the related cash forms and documents. Finally, the accounting process for cash is another prescribed routine. Thus, the individuals that handle the cash should be separated at all times from those that maintain the related records in the cash-processing cycle. All cash disbursements should be made with prenumbered checks, except as explained in the next paragraph. For cash payments there should be separate routines and responsibilities for (a) approvals, (b) check preparation, and (c) check signing. If procedures similar to these are followed, it is very difficult to conceal a fraudulent cash disbursement without the collusion of two or more persons. The level of internal control, which is subject to review by the internal auditor, tends to increase the reliability that users can accord to the financial statements of the business.

Bank accounts

When a depositor first opens a bank account, he must complete a signature card that lists the names and signatures of persons authorized to sign checks against the account. When a deposit is to be made, the depositor must fill out a deposit slip or ticket that includes the name of the account, the account number, and a listing of the coins, currency, and checks. In recent years most banks have gone almost exclusively to personalized checks; that is, the name, address, and account number of the depositor is preprinted on each check. Obviously, this is an important safety feature for all parties concerned.

THE BANK STATEMENT

Each month the bank provides the depositor with a bank statement that lists (a) each deposit made during the period; (b) each check cleared during the period; (c) a running balance of the depositor's account; (d) copies of the deposit slips; and (e) all canceled checks that cleared through the bank during the period covered by the statement. The bank statement also will reflect any bank charges or deductions (such as service charges) made directly to the depositor's account by the bank. A typical bank statement (excluding the deposit slips and cashed checks) is shown in Exhibit 8–1.

On Exhibit 8–1 there are three items that require comment. First, observe that on June 20 there is listed under Checks and Debits a deduction for $18.00 coded with "NC."[1] This code indicates an "NSF check charge" (in slang, a "hot" or "rubber" check); NSF stands for Not Sufficient Funds. A check for $18.00 was received and deposited by

---

[1] These codes vary between banks.

Exhibit 8–1

Bank statement

BANK CAPITAL
THE CAPITAL NATIONAL BANK

ACCOUNT NUMBER	STATEMENT DATE	PAGE NO.
877–95861	6–30–74	1

John Doe Company
1000 Blank Road
Austin, Texas 78703

STATEMENT OF ACCOUNT

Please examine statement and checks promptly. If no error is reported within ten days, the account will be considered correct. Please report change of address.

ON THIS DATE	YOUR BALANCE WAS	DEPOSITS ADDED NO.	DEPOSITS ADDED AMOUNT	CHECKS AND DEBITS SUBTRACTED NO.	CHECKS AND DEBITS SUBTRACTED AMOUNT	SERVICE COST	RESULTING BALANCE
6–1–74	7,562.40	5	4,050.00	23	3,490.20	6.00	8,122.20

CHECKS AND DEBITS						DEPOSITS	DATE	DAILY BALANCE
							6–1–74	7,562.40
						3,000.00	6–2–74	10,562.40
500.00							6–4–74	10,062.40
55.00		5.00		40.00			6–5–74	9,962.40
100.00						500.00	6–8–74	10,362.40
8.20		16.50		160.00			6–10–74	10,177.70
2,150.00		10.00				*100.00 CM	6–12–74	8,177.70
7.50		15.30					6–16–74	8,094.90
35.00		1.50				150.00	6–17–74	8,208.40
40.20		15.00		6.00			6–18–74	8,147.20
*18.00 NC							6–20–74	8,129.20
125.50		80.00		2.00			6–21–74	7,921.70
18.90						300.00	6–24–74	8,202.80
7.52		19.60					6–27–74	8,175.68
15.00		32.48					6–28–74	8,128.20
*6.00 SC							6–30–74	8,122.20

Code:
CM – Credit Memo––Customer note collected
NC – Insufficient funds
SC – Service charge

* Note to student: John Doe Company did not know about these items until the bank statement was received. Therefore, John Doe Company must record them in the accounts. See page 259.

John Doe Company from a customer, say J. Roe. Capital National Bank processed it through banking channels to Roe's bank. Roe's account did not have sufficient funds to cover it; therefore, his bank returned it to the Capital National Bank, which then charged it back to John Doe Company. The NSF check is now a receivable, and the John Doe Company must make an entry debiting Receivables and crediting Cash for the $18.00.

The second item on Exhibit 8–1 that requires comment is the $6.00 listed under checks and coded "SC." This is the code for bank service charges. Included with the bank statement would be a memo prepared by the bank explaining this charge. John Doe Company must make an entry to reflect this $6.00 decrease in the bank balance by debiting an appropriate expense account, such as Bank Service Expenses, and crediting Cash.

The third item to be noted is the $100.00 listed on June 12 under deposits and coded "CM" for "credit memo." In this instance, the John Doe Company had asked the bank to collect a note receivable that had been received from a customer. The bank collected the note and increased the depositor account in favor of the John Doe Company. The bank service charge mentioned above was in part for this service. The John Doe Company now must make an entry debiting Cash and crediting Notes Receivable for the $100.

Reconciling the bank balance. Normally, when the bank statement arrives, the ending cash balance shown by the bank will not agree with the ending balance shown by the Cash account on the books of the depositor. For example, assume the Cash account in the ledger at the end of June of the John Doe Company reflected the following:

Cash

June 1	Balance	7,010.00*	June	Checks written	3,800.00
June	Deposits	5,750.00			

(Ending balance $8,960.00)

* Including $200 undeposited cash held for change.

The $8,122.20 shown on the bank statement as the ending bank balance is different from the $8,960.00 ending book balance shown on the books of the John Doe Company because some transactions affecting cash may have been recorded in the books of the depositor but have not been recognized on the bank statement. Also, there may be some transactions that have been recognized on the bank statement but have not been recorded in the books of the depositor. The most common causes of the difference between the ending bank balance and the ending book balance of cash are:

1. Outstanding checks—checks drawn by the depositor and recorded in his Cash account as credits but have not yet cleared the bank. The outstanding checks are determined by comparing the checks returned with the bank statement with the record of checks drawn (such as the check stubs) and maintained by the depositor.

2. Deposits in transit—deposits made up by the depositor, taken to the bank, and recorded in his Cash account as debits but not yet recorded by the bank and not reflected on the bank state-

ment. This usually happens when deposits are made one or two days before the bank statement is received by the depositor. These are known as **deposits in transit** and are determined by comparing the deposits listed on the bank statement with the copies of the deposit slips retained by the depositor.

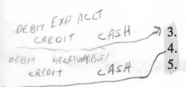

3. Bank service charges—explained above.
4. Charges for NSF checks—explained above.
5. Errors—both the bank and the depositor are susceptible to errors, especially when the volume of cash transactions is large.

In view of these several factors, a **bank reconciliation** should be made by the depositor (whether for a business or a personal account) immediately after each bank statement is received. A bank reconciliation is an important element of internal control and is needed for accounting purposes. To encourage bank reconciliation by depositors, many banks provide a format on the back of the bank statement for such purposes. Instructions for completing the reconciliation also may be given. A typical form is shown in Exhibit 8–2.

Exhibit 8–2

Suggested form and instructions for bank reconciliation

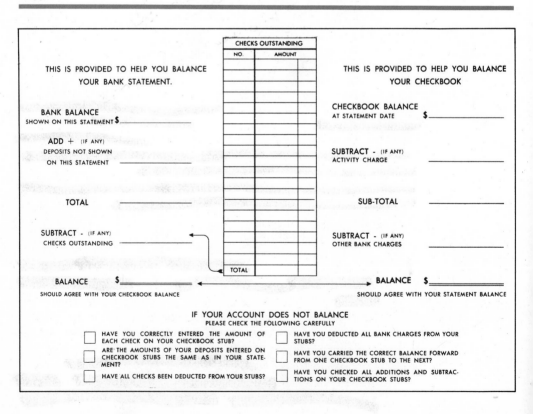

Bank reconciliation illustrated. A bank reconciliation prepared by the John Doe Company to reconcile the ending bank balance (Exhibit 8–1, $8,122.20) with the ending book balance (page 255, $8,960.00) is shown in Exhibit 8–3. A bank reconciliation has two accounting purposes: (1) to reconcile the ending bank and book cash balances, and (2) to develop the *correct balance* for the Cash account for reporting on the balance sheet. Observe on the completed reconciliation that the *correct* cash balance in Exhibit 8–3 is $9,045.00, which is different from both the reported bank and book balances before the reconciliation.

Although the layout of a bank reconciliation can vary, the most simple and flexible one follows a balancing format with the "Depositor's Books" and the "Bank Statement" identified separately. This format starts with the reported ending balance per books and the reported ending balance per bank statement. Provision then is made for additions and subtractions from each balance so that the last line reflects the same correct cash balance. This correct balance represents the amount that finally *should be* reflected in the Cash account after the reconciliation. It is also the amount of cash that should be reported on the balance sheet. Exhibit 8–3 for the John Doe Company reflects these features.

Exhibit 8–3

JOHN DOE COMPANY
Bank Reconciliation
At June 30, 1974

Depositor's Books			*Bank Statement*	
Ending Cash Balance per Books .	$8,960.00		Ending Cash Balance per Bank Statement	$ 8,122.20
Additions:			*Additions:*	
Proceeds of note collected by bank		100.00	Deposit in transit	1,800.00
Error in recording check No. 137		9.00	Cash on hand	200.00
		9,069.00		10,122.20
Deductions:			*Deductions:*	
NSF check of J. Roe $18.00 .			Outstanding checks	1,077.20
Bank service charges 6.00 .	24.00			
Correct Cash Balance	$9,045.00		*Correct Cash Balance*	$ 9,045.00

The John Doe Company followed these steps in completing the bank reconciliation:

1.   Identification of the outstanding checks—A comparison of the canceled checks returned by the bank with the records of the company of all checks drawn revealed the following checks to be outstanding at the end of June:

Check No.	Amount
101................	$ 145.00
123................	815.00
131................	117.20
Total........	$1,077.20

The total was entered on the reconciliation as a deduction from the bank account (the checks will be deducted by the bank when they clear).

2. Identification of the deposits in transit—A comparison of the deposit slips on hand with those listed on the bank statement revealed that a deposit made on June 30 for $1,800 was not listed on the bank statement. This amount was entered on the reconciliation as an addition to the bank account (it will be added by the bank when it is recorded).

3. Cash on hand—On the date of the bank statement, cash on hand (i.e., undeposited cash) amounted to $200. Since this amount is included in the Cash account balance but is not in the bank balance, it was entered on the reconciliaton as an addition to the bank balance (as it would be, if deposited).

4. Items on bank statement not yet recorded in the books of the John Doe Company:

(a) Proceeds of note collected, $100.00 (explained above)—entered on the bank reconciliation as an addition to the book balance; it is already included in the bank balance. A journal entry is required to increase the Cash account balance for this item.

(b) NSF check of J. Roe, $18.00 (explained above)—Entered on the bank reconciliation as a deduction from the book balance; it has already been deducted from the bank balance. A journal entry is required to reduce the Cash account balance for this item.

(c) Bank service charges, $6.00 (explained above)—Entered on the reconciliation as a deduction from the book balance; it has already been deducted from the bank balance. A journal entry is required to reduce the Cash account balance for this item.

5. Error—At this point the John Doe Company found that the reconciliation did not balance by $9.00. Since this amount is divisible by 9 they suspected a transposition. (A transposition will always cause an error that is divisible by 9). Upon checking the journal entries, they found that a check written by John Doe Company to pay an account payable for $56 had been recorded as $65 by the company; the incorrect entry was a debit to Accounts Payable and a credit to Cash for $56 instead of $65. Therefore, $9.00 (i.e., $65 − $56) must be added to the book cash balance on the reconciliation; the bank cleared the check

for the correct amount. A correcting entry must be made in the accounts: Cash debit $9.00 and Accounts Payable credit $9.00. In summary, observe that the "Depositor's Books" and the "Bank Statement" now reconcile at $9,045.00. This amount will be reported on the balance sheet. After the following journal entries have been made and posted to the ledger, the Cash account will reflect this balance:[2]

	Journal Entries from Bank Reconciliation		Balance in Cash Account
	Debit	Credit	
Balance before reconciliation..................			$8,960.00
Entries from the reconciliation:			
Cash.....................................	100.00		+100.00
Notes Receivable.....................		100.00	
To record note collected by bank.			
Accounts Receivable (J. Roe)...............	18.00		
Cash................................		18.00	− 18.00
To record NSF check.			
Bank Service Expenses.....................	6.00		
Cash................................		6.00	− 6.00
To record bank service charges.			
Cash.....................................	9.00		+ 9.00
Accounts Payable (name)..............		9.00	
To correct transposition made in prior journal entry.			
Correct cash balance......................			$9,045.00

(margin handwritten note: Just add or subtract entries for cash)

The importance of the bank reconciliation procedure in generating entries to *update* the Cash account should not be overlooked. This feature is important in measuring the correct cash balance for reporting on the balance sheet.

Cash over and short
Irrespective of the care exercised, when a large number of cash transactions are involved, errors in handling cash inevitably occur. These errors cause cash shortages or cash overages at the end of the day when the cash is counted and compared with the cash records for the day. Cash overages and shortages must be recognized in the accounts. To illustrate, assume that at the end of a particular day the cash from sales, as counted, amounted to $1,347.19 and the cash register tapes for sales totaled $1,357.19—a cash *shortage* of $10.00 is indicated. The sales for the day should be recorded as follows:

---

[2] It may be useful to observe that all of (and only) the additions and deductions on the "Depositor's Books" side of the reconciliation require journal entries to correct the Cash account balance. Otherwise, the correct cash balance will not accord with what should be reported on the balance sheet and reflected in the Cash account. All other reconciling differences are adjustments to the "Bank Statement" side.

```
Cash................................... 1,347.19
Cash Over and Short...................    10.00
  Sales...............................           1,357.19
  To record cash sales and
  cash shortage.
```

Alternatively, in the case of a cash *overage,* the Cash Over and Short account would be credited. At the end of the period, the Cash Over and Short account, in the case of a cumulative debit balance, is reported as a miscellaneous expense. If a credit balance exists, it would be reported as a miscellaneous revenue.

Petty cash

In the discussion of internal control we stated that all major disbursements of cash should be made by prenumbered check. Many businesses find it quite inconvenient and costly in terms of paperwork and employee time to write checks for small payments for items such as collect telegrams, taxi fares, newspapers, and small amounts of supplies. To avoid this inconvenience and cost, businesses frequently establish a **petty cash fund,** and small, miscellaneous payments are made from this fund. To establish a petty cash fund a check should be drawn (in favor of Petty Cash) and cashed for the amount desired; whenever cash runs low and at the end of each period, the expenditures from the fund are summarized and an accounting entry is made to reflect the activities of the fund and to record the check written to reimburse the fund for the amount spent. The details of accounting for a petty cash fund are included in Appendix A to this chapter.

Compensating balances

A recent accounting issue that has created some concern is referred to as **compensating balances.** In the past, information concerning compensating balances has not been included in the financial statements. A compensating balance is the minimum amount of cash a bank requires the business to maintain in its bank account. A minimum, or compensating balance, may be required by the bank explicitly (by a loan agreement), or implicitly (by informal understanding), as part of a credit-granting arrangement. Often, it is difficult for the independent auditor to know whether or not an informal understanding exists. Information on compensating balances is important to statement users since there are two major effects on the business: (1) a compensating-balance requirement imposes a restriction on the amount of cash readily available in the checking account; and (2) it increases the real rate of interest on the loan since not all of the cash borrowed can be readily used.

Many accountants believe that information concerning compensating balances should be reported in the financial statements because of its importance to statement users. The accounting profession currently is faced with the two problems of how a compensating balance (the restriction) should be reported and how the impact on interest cost should be reported. It seems clear that such information should be reported, as a minimum, in the notes to the financial statements. This would serve to fulfill the principle of full disclosure in serving the interest of the statement users.

Data processing for cash   In most small businesses the processing of accounting information on cash inflows and cash outflows is done manually. In medium-sized companies much of the cash information processing may be mechanized through the use of various accounting machines. In the still larger businesses much of the cash information processing is accomplished by means of electronic computers. The nature of these data-processing activities broadly are the same whether manual, mechanical, or electronic approaches are used. For instructional purposes their characteristics are best viewed in terms of a manual system. Appendix B to this chapter presents a data-processing procedure known as "special journals." Two of these special journals relate to data processing for cash inflows and outflows. As you read the appendix, although a manual system is illustrated, mechanical or electronic-computer applications should be apparent in the broad sense.

PART TWO: MEASURING AND REPORTING TEMPORARY INVESTMENTS

To employ idle cash and for other business reasons, a company may invest in commercial paper (such as certificates of deposit), or in the capital stock or bonds of another company. Such investments are facilitated because commercial paper is sold by local banks, and the stocks and bonds of most of the large corporations are "listed" on the New York and American stock exchanges. Capital stock of smaller unlisted companies frequently can be bought and sold over the counter or between individuals and companies directly.

When bonds of another company are acquired, the purchaser has become a creditor of the issuing company, since they represent debt owed by the other company similar to a long-term note payable. As the holder of a bond, the investor is entitled to receive interest on the principal of the bond and the principal if held to maturity. In contrast, when shares of capital stock are purchased as an investment, the purchaser becomes one of the owners (frequently called stockholders, shareholders, or equity holders) of the company that issued the stock.

As an owner, the stockholder receives dividends when they are declared and paid by the Board of Directors of the other company. Since most capital stock confers voting rights, the stockholder is provided an opportunity to exercise some control over the issuing company. The amount of control, obviously, is dependent upon the number of shares owned by the shareholder in relationship to the total number of shares of stock outstanding.

Investments made by one company in the stocks or bonds of another company may be either (1) temporary investments or (2) long-term investments (sometimes called permanent investments). This chapter discusses the measurement and reporting of temporary investments; long-term investments are discussed in Chapter 14.

Temporary
investments
defined

Temporary investments frequently are called short-term investments. To be classified as a temporary investment a security must meet the twofold test of (1) marketability and (2) a short-term holding period. Marketability means that the security must be regularly traded on the market so that there is a continuous market available and a determinable market price. Therefore, temporary investments generally are listed stocks and bonds, or short-term government securities. A short-term holding period means that it must be the intention of the management to convert the securities into cash in the near future for normal operating purposes.[3] Short-term refers to the longer of the normal operating cycle or one year as specified in the definition of current assets (Chapter 3). The distinction between temporary and long-term investments is important because the former should be classified as a current asset, whereas the latter is reported under a noncurrent caption, Funds and Investments.

Measurement of temporary investments. In accordance with the cost principle, temporary investments, when acquired, are measured and recorded at their cost. Cost includes the market price paid plus all additional costs incurred to purchase the security. To illustrate, assume the Brown Corporation had $50,000 in cash that would not be needed for operations for the next eight to ten months. Brown purchased 1,000 shares of American Telephone and Telegraph (AT&T) stock for $51,000, including all broker's fees and transfer taxes related to the purchase.

The transaction would be recorded in the accounts as follows:

---

[3] We shall see later that long-term investments frequently are comprised of marketable securities. Thus, the primary distinction between temporary and long-term investments turns on the intention of management in respect to their expected disposal date. The same security may be a temporary investment in one company and a long-term in another company depending upon the intentions of the respective managements.

```
Temporary Investments......................  51,000
    Cash..................................               51,000
    Purchase of 1,000 shares of AT&T stock as
    a temporary investment.
```

Assume that two months after the purchase a quarterly cash dividend of $.70 per share is received. The revenue on the temporary investment would be recorded as follows:

```
Cash.........................................  700
    Investment Revenue........................               700
    Cash dividend of $.70 per share on temporary
    investment (AT&T stock); $.70 × 1,000
    shares = $700.
```

Temporary investments held at the end of the accounting period are reported, at cost, on the balance sheet as a current asset (one exception is discussed later). The current market value at that date should be shown parenthetically. For example, the Brown Corporation would report the temporary investment of AT&T stock as follows:

```
Current assets:
    Cash....................................  $62,000
    Temporary Investments, at Cost (current
        market value $51,800)...................   51,000
```

Investment revenue earned would be reported on the income statement.

When a temporary investment is sold, normally a loss or gain on sale must be recognized. To illustrate, assume Brown sold one-half of the temporary investment in AT&T stock for $26,000 cash, after deducting broker's fees and the sale taxes. It would be recorded as follows:

```
Cash.........................................  26,000
    Temporary Investment......................               25,500
    Gain on Sale of Investments...............                  500
    Sale of 500 shares of AT&T stock at $52
    per share.
```

When a company owns securities in several other companies, the securities held generally are referred to collectively as the portfolio. A portfolio of temporary investments is managed (i.e., acquired, held, and sold) with the objective of maximizing the return while minimizing the risk. Thus, a portfolio of securities tends to be managed and accounted for as a whole rather than as a number of separate investments.

Temporary investments valued at lower-of-cost-or-market. Although temporary investments are measured and recorded at cost when acquired and *generally* are measured at cost thereafter in conformity with the cost principle, there is an exception. The exception occurs when their *current* market value drops below their purchase cost.

In Chapter 7, relating to inventories of merchandise, we explained that items of merchandise in the inventory for which the replacement cost had dropped below original cost should be measured under the lower-of-cost-or-market basis. The same principle applies to all current assets, including temporary investments. It is reasoned that, because of the drop in market value, the temporary investment potentially has lost a part of its usefulness as a source of cash. This is viewed as a holding loss that should be recognized in the period in which the drop occurred. However, a corresponding line of reasoning is not applied when the current market value is *above* the purchase cost. Although this reasoning violates both the cost principle and the consistency principle, the lower-of-cost-or-market basis in this situation is applied because of the principle of conservatism (see page 270). Thus, investments are restated on a lower-of-cost-or-market basis. To illustrate, let's return to the above example. Recall that the Brown Corporation still owns 500 shares of AT&T stock at a cost of $25,500 (i.e., $51.00 per share). Assume that it is at the end of the accounting period and the financial statements are to be prepared. Assume further that the current market value of the stock is $49.50 per share; the total market value, therefore, is 500 shares × $49.50 = $24,750. Although the stock is not sold at this date, under the lower-of-cost-or-market (LCM) basis a holding loss would be recognized at the end of the accounting period in an adjusting entry as follows:

```
Loss on Investments—Reduction to LCM............ 750
    Temporary Investments.......................        750
    To reduce temporary investments to lower-of-
    cost-or-market basis ($25,500 - $24,750 = $750)
```

Once a temporary investment is written down to an amount lower than cost, it is not considered acceptable to restore the amount previously written off even though the market subsequently rises to as much or more than the original cost. To do so would violate the principle of conservatism because an *unrealized* holding gain would be recognized. After the write-down illustrated above, the balance sheet would report the temporary investment as follows:

Current assets:
    Temporary Investment, at lower-of-cost-or-
        market (cost $25,500).................... $24,750

When the lower-of-cost-or-market rule is applied to temporary investments, the measurement is based upon the *total cost* versus *total market* amounts rather than on an item-by-item basis. To illustrate, a company having three stocks in its portfolio of temporary investments *could* derive the measurement at the end of the accounting period in either of two ways:

| Security | Cost | Market on Basis of: | |
		Total Market	Item-by-Item
A Company common stock.............	$ 5,000	$ 5,000	$ 5,000
B Company preferred stock.............	8,500	8,000	8,000
C Company common stock.............	9,000	9,200	9,000
Totals....................	$22,500	$22,200	$22,000

Under the lower-of-cost-or-market basis, as applied to the portfolio as a whole, the Temporary Investment account would be written down to $22,200 rather than to $22,000.[4]

Certificates of deposit. In recent years a common short-term investment strategy to employ idle cash has been to purchase certificates of deposit (CD's). A "CD" is an investment contract (a certificate is received) that an investor may purchase from a bank for cash. The contract specifies (a) a limited period of time for the investment, such as 90 days, 6 months, 1 year, etc.; and (b) a guaranteed interest rate. Generally, the larger the amount of the certificate (the amount invested), the higher the interest rate. The interest rate also tends to be different for various time periods. Certificates of deposit and similar commercial paper are widely used for the short-term employment of idle cash because of the relatively high interest return and the liquidity factor.

Certificates of deposit are measured and accounted for in a manner similar to that discussed above for other temporary investments. They are accounted for separately from the regular cash and the interest earned is reported as investment revenue. For external reporting purposes, certificates of deposit are reported as a current asset, either separately or in combination with the regular cash as follows:

```
Current assets:
      Cash...................................$200,000
      Certificates of Deposit....................  300,000
```

or

```
Current assets:
      Cash and Certificates of Deposit............$500,000
```

PART THREE: MEASURING AND REPORTING
RECEIVABLES

Broadly speaking, receivables encompass all claims of the entity for money, goods, or services from other entities or persons. In most businesses there are two types of receivables: trade receivables and

---

[4] In contrast, when the lower-of-cost-or-market rule is applied to merchandise inventories, the item-by-item basis is used since merchandise is not viewed "as a whole" but as separate items. Thus, the lower-of-cost-or-market basis would use $22,000 as the market amount for merchandise.

special receivables. Trade receivables include **Trade Accounts Receivable** and **Trade Notes Receivable.** These arise from the regular operating activities of the business; that is, the sale of merchandise and/or services. Special receivables arise from other transactions, such as the sale of fixed assets and loans to employees. Receivables often are large in amount and, for that reason, careful measurement and adequate reporting are important to statement users.

Trade accounts receivable almost always are designated as accounts receivable and special receivables are given other designations. Accounting and reporting for accounts receivable, including the allowance for doubtful accounts, were discussed in Chapter 6. *Special receivables* should be given descriptive titles as "Receivables from Employees." They should not be included in the caption "Accounts Receivable." Other than for appropriate reporting classification, special receivables generally do not involve any unusual measurement and reporting problems. Special receivables may or may not be properly classified as current assets, depending upon their maturity.

Many businesses *factor* their accounts receivable instead of holding them to due date for collection. **"Factoring"** is a term used for the sale of accounts receivable, usually at the date of the sale transaction, to a financial institution. It is widely used because the business receives the cash immediately for sales; however, the rate of interest for factoring arrangements tends to be high. A discussion of the detailed accounting involved is beyond the objectives of this book.

Interest calculations

Interest represents the **time cost of money.** To the maker of a promissory note, interest is an expense, whereas, to the payee, it is a revenue. The formula for computing interest is:

Principal $\times$ Annual Rate of Interest $\times$ Fraction of Year $=$ Interest Amount

It is important to remember that **interest rates** are quoted on an **annual basis** and, therefore, must be restated for time periods of less than one year. Thus, the interest on a $1,500, 8%, 90-day promissory note would be calculated as follows:

$$\$1,500 \times .08 \times 90/360 = \$30$$

When a note specifies a number of days, the exact days must be counted on the calendar to determine the due date and then related to 365 days. However, for computing interest, it is often assumed that the year encompasses 360 days, so that each day's interest is $\frac{1}{360}$ of a year rather than $\frac{1}{365}$. This has the effect of making the actual interest cost for a short-term loan slightly higher than the stated amount of interest.[5]

_____

[5] For convenience in the learning process, throughout this book, interest dates are given so as to avoid the needless counting of exact days on a calendar.

Notes
receivable   Notes receivable may be either trade notes receivable or special notes receivable, depending upon the source of the note. A promissory note is an unconditional promise in writing to pay a definite sum of money (i.e., the face amount or principal) on demand or at a definite future date known as the maturity or due date. The person who signs a promissory note is known as the maker, and the person to whom payment is to be made is known as the payee. The maker views a note as a "note payable," whereas the payee views the note as a "note receivable." Notes are said to be either interest-bearing or noninterest-bearing. An interest-bearing note specifies a rate of interest to be paid on the principal of the note at one or more specific future dates, usually at the maturity of the note. In the case of long-term notes, interest frequently is required to be paid annually or semiannually.

In the case of a so-called noninterest-bearing note, no interest rate is specified by the note and only the face or principal amount of the note is paid at maturity. Strictly speaking, all notes require the payment of interest since money has a time value that cannot be avoided. In the case of a so-called noninterest-bearing note, the interest is included in the principal of the note. For example, if one were to borrow cash and give the lender a noninterest-bearing note for $1,000, due in one year, and if the going rate of interest was 8%, one would receive cash in the amount of $925.93 (i.e., $1,000 ÷ 1.08).[6]

An overdue *noninterest*-bearing note immediately draws interest at a legal rate (usually specified by law) from due date.

Accounting for notes receivable. Notes receivable usually arise in a business as a result of selling merchandise or services. Although most businesses use open accounts (i.e., accounts receivable), those selling high-priced items on credit frequently require notes from their customers. Assuming a $1,500, 8% promissory note was received from a customer as a result of the sale of goods, the payee would record it on the date of the sale as follows:

```
Notes Receivable (Trade).....................  1,500
    Sales Revenue.........................            1,500
    To record 90-day, 8% note received from
    customer.
```

(Note: Assuming the note was in settlement of an open account receivable, which frequently happens, the credit would have been to Accounts Receivable instead of to Sales.)

The entry, at maturity date 90 days later, when collection is made, would be:

---

[6] This may be verified as follows:

Amount of cash received.....................	$ 925.93
Interest expense ($925.93 × 8%)..............	74.07
Amount of cash disbursed..................	$1,000.00

(Note: In some cases the interest is computed on the $1,000 face amount; this would result in cash of $920 and would serve to increase the interest cost.)

```
Cash.......................................... 1,530
     Notes Receivable (Trade)................          1,500
     Interest Revenue.......................             30
     To record collection of a 90-day, 8% note
     plus interest ($1,500 × .08 × 90/360 =
     $30) received from a customer.
```

Default of a note receivable. A note receivable that is not collected at maturity is said to be **dishonored** or **defaulted** by the maker. Immediately after default, an entry should be made by the payee transferring the amount due from the Notes Receivable account to a special account such as, Receivable—Defaulted Notes. Since the maker is responsible for both the unpaid principal and the unpaid interest, the receivable account should reflect the full amount to be collected by the payee. To illustrate, assuming the above note was defaulted by the maker, the entry in the accounts of the holder or payee would be:[7]

```
Special Receivable-Defaulted Notes........... 1,530
     Notes Receivable (Trade)................          1,500
     Interest Revenue.......................             30
     To record the principal and interest earned
     on defaulted note.
```

Special Receivable—Defaulted Notes is reported as a current or noncurrent asset depending upon the probable collection date.

Discounting a note receivable. Many businesses prefer a negotiable note receivable rather than an open account receivable from customers involved in large amounts of credit. One primary reason is that when promissory notes are *negotiable,* they often can be sold to a financial institution, such as a bank, or to individuals in order to obtain needed cash *before* the maturity date. Selling a note receivable to a financial institution frequently is referred to as **discounting** a note receivable. A negotiable instrument is one that can be transferred by endorsement (there are other technical legal requisites for negotiability). The most common negotiable instrument is a check. Notes and a number of other instruments generally can be transferred by endorsement. An endorsement may be simply by signature of the holder, in which case it is said to be "with recourse." This means that, in case of default, as in the case of a "hot" check (i.e., one that the depositor's bank has turned down because of insufficient funds in the depositor's account), the endorser is liable contractually for repayment. In contrast, an endorsement may be made "without recourse" by writing this phrase on the instrument next to the endorsement signature. This means

---

[7] When a note is the result of a sale of goods or a service, some accountants prefer to debit "Accounts Receivable" rather than "Receivable—Defaulted Notes." Also, some question the propriety of recognizing the interest revenue until collection is made (if it is).

that the endorser cannot be held liable contractually in the case of default by the maker.[8] Businesses seldom will accept endorsements without recourse; that is, a discounted note receivable usually is endorsed with recourse and, as a result, the financial institution can rely on both the maker and the endorser. An endorsement with recourse makes the endorser **contingently liable;** that is, if the maker does not pay the note at maturity the endorser must do so. The full disclosure principle (Exhibit 2–1) requires that such **contingent liabilities** be reported on the financial statements. This is usually done by means of a note to the financial statements (see page 270).

To illustrate the discounting of notes receivable, assume that the $1,500, 8%, 90-day note receivable (page 267) was sold to the Capital National Bank after 30 days at a **discount rate** of 9% per annum. The discount rate is the annual rate of interest required by the bank and may be more or less than the interest rate specified on the note. The discount rate is applied to the **maturity value**—that is, the principal amount of the note *plus* the amount of interest due at maturity. The discount rate of interest applies to the number of days the bank will hold the note (in this case, 60 days). Computation of the amount the bank will pay for the note is:

Discounting a Note Receivable

Note: Principal, $1,500; 8% per year, 90-days
Discounted: Thirty days after date; discount rate, 9% per year.

Principal amount.	$1,500.00
Interest due at maturity ($1,500 × .08 × 90/360).	30.00
Maturity value—amount subject to discount rate.	1,530.00
Discount—interest charged by bank:	
($1,530 × .09 × 60/360).	22.95
Proceeds—amount the bank pays for the note.	$1,507.05

The discounting or sale of the note receivable would be recorded by the payee as follows:[9]

```
Cash...................................  1,507.05
     Notes Receivable (Trade)...........           1,500.00
     Interest Revenue...................               7.05
To record the sale of an 8%, 90-day,
note receivable to the bank, 30 days
after date, at a 9% discount rate.
```

---

[8] The endorser or transferor may not be held liable contractually. However, the transferor may be held liable under *warranty* liability since the endorsement "without recourse" does not disclaim warranties such as title to the instrument. These legal distinctions are beyond the scope of this course.

[9] The credit of $7.05 to Interest Revenue may be explained. Had the payee held the note to maturity, he would have earned $30 interest revenue; however, the bank charged interest amounting to $22.95. The difference is $7.05, which is the net interest earned by the payee for holding it 30 of the 90 days. The discount rate is applied to the maturity value of the note since that is the amount the bank will advance, less the interest due them.

Although the note was sold by the payee, as an endorser, the *contingent liability* on the note must be disclosed by means of a note to the balance sheet similar to the following:

Note: At December 31, 1974, the company was contingently liable for notes receivable discounted in the amount of $1,530.00.

Exception principle

In the preceding chapters, the term "materiality" (or material amount) was used. Similarly, the term "conservatism" has been used. The principle of conservatism was referred to on page 234 and 264 as the basis for using the lower-of-cost-or-market basis in measuring inventory and marketable securities. These terms, materiality and conservatism, refer to one of the fundamental accounting principles listed in Chapter 2 (Exhibit 2–1). It was designated there as the "exception principle."

The exception principle is comprised of the following three subprinciples: (1) materiality; (2) conservatism; and (3) industry peculiarities.

Although accounting must recognize that measurement and compliance with accounting principles are essential, from a practical point of view, the benefits of high accuracy in measurement and strict compliance with concepts often are offset by other considerations. The exception principle holds that in certain limited situations the exception principle may override one or more other principles. These conditions are specified in the three sub-principles as follows:

1. Materiality—The fundamental accounting principles must be applied when the amount involved is material (i.e., significant) in relationship to the overall financial effect; however, small or insignificant amounts, although they must be accounted for, need not be accorded theoretically correct treatment. For example, in accounting for bad debts, the "charge-off" method (although it violates the matching principle) rather than the estimated allowance method may be used when bad debt losses are quite small in relationship to net income (see page 172). In this instance, materiality is permitted to override the matching principle.

2. Conservatism—Where more than one accounting or measurement alternative is permissible, the one having the least favorable immediate effect on net income or owners' equity usually should be selected. For example, in measuring the amount of a temporary investment or a merchandise inventory, the lower-of-cost-or-market basis is used. In this case, conservatism is permitted to override the cost principle. There are numerous situations, however, where conservatism does not prevail, as in the case of selecting Fifo over Lifo when prices are rising.

3. Industry peculiarities—The unique characteristics of an industry

may require use of special accounting approaches and measurement procedures in order to produce realistic financial reporting. For example, in the insurance and oil industries, accounting does not conform, in all respects, to generally accepted principles.

Demonstration case for self-study

DOTTER'S EQUIPMENT COMPANY, INCORPORATED

(Try to resolve the case before studying the suggested solution that follows.)

Dotter's Equipment Company, Incorporated, has been selling farm machinery for over 30 years. The company has been quite successful in both sales and repair services. A wide range of farm equipment, including trucks, is sold. The company strives for "high volume and quality service, at the right price." Credit terms with varying conditions are typical. Although most of the credit granted is carried by several financial institutions, Dotter's will carry the credit in special circumstances. As a result, the company accepts a promissory note and keeps it to maturity from time to time. However, if a cash need arises, some of these notes may be sold (i.e., discounted) to the local bank with which Dotter's carries its checking account. This case focuses on two farm-equipment notes that were received during 1974. By following these notes from date of sale of the farm equipment to final collection, we can see the various measurement problems posed and their resolution. The fiscal year for accounting purposes ends December 31, 1974.

The series of transactions in respect to the two notes follows:

Equipment Note No. 1

Jan. 15, 1974 Sold a farm tractor to Sam Scott for $8,000 and received a 25% cash down payment plus a $6,000 equipment note for the balance. The note was due in nine months and was interest-bearing at 8% per annum. A mortgage on the tractor was taken as a part of the agreement.

April 15, 1974 The Scott equipment note was sold to the local bank at an 8½% per annum discount rate. Dotter endorsed the note, with recourse, and the proceeds were deposited in Dotter's checking account.

Oct. 15, 1974 Scott paid the bank the principal amount of the note plus the interest ($6,000 + $360 = $6,360).

Required:

a. Give appropriate journal entries on each of the three dates. Show the interest computations.

b. Assume, instead of payment, that on October 15, 1974, Sam Scott defaulted on the note. The bank contacted Dotter's, which paid the note in full. Give the appropriate entry for this assumption and one for the further assumption—that Scott later paid in full on December 1, 1974.

Equipment Note No. 2

Oct. 1, 1974	Sold a farm truck to Bill Day for $4,000; received a down payment of $400 and set up an account receivable for the balance; terms, n/30.
Nov. 1, 1974	Day came in and wanted an extension on the account receivable "until he sold some products." After some discussion it was agreed to settle the account with a six-month, 8% interest-bearing note. Day signed the note and a mortgage on this date.
Dec. 31, 1974	End of the fiscal period. An adjusting entry is required.
Jan. 1, 1975	Start of the new fiscal period.
May 1, 1975	Since this was the due date, Day came in and paid the note plus interest in full. The note was marked paid and the mortgage was canceled.

Required:

c. Give appropriate journal entries on each date, including any adjusting entries at year end. Omit closing entries at year end. Provide explanations for each journal entry.

Suggested Solution:

Requirement (a) Note No. 1:

Jan. 15, 1974	Cash...............................	2,000.00	
	Equipment Notes Receivable............	6,000.00	
	Sales Revenue......................		8,000.00
	Sale of tractor to Sam Scott for cash and equipment note; terms of note, nine months, 8%, interest-bearing, including a mortgage.		
April 15, 1974	Cash...............................	6,089.70	
	Equipment Notes Receivable.........		6,000.00
	Interest Revenue...................		89.70
	Discounted Scott equipment note receivable at bank discount rate of 8½%. Proceeds computed:		
	Principal amount......................		$6,000.00
	Interest to maturity ($6,000 × .08 × $\frac{9}{12}$)..		360.00
	Maturity value.......................		6,360.00
	Discount ($6,360 × .085 × $\frac{6}{12}$).........		270.30
	Proceeds............................		$6,089.70
Oct. 15, 1974	No entry required; Scott paid the bank that owned the note. During the period April 15, 1974, until the note was paid, Dotter's was contingently liable for the note should Scott default.		

Requirement (b) Note No. 1:

Under the assumption that Scott defaulted on the note on due date, Dotter's would have to pay it in full and make the following entry:

Oct. 15, 1974　Accounts Receivable (Defaulted Note)........... 6,360
　　　　　　　　　　Cash.................................... 　　　　　6,360
　　　　　　　　Scott note defaulted; payment to bank of the
　　　　　　　　$6,000 principle plus interest ($6,000 × .08 × 9/12
　　　　　　　　= $360).

Dec. 1, 1974　Cash... 6,360
　　　　　　　　　　Accounts Receivable (Defaulted Note)....... 　　　6,360
　　　　　　　　Payment received in full on Scott note in default.
　　　　　　　　(Note: In most states, Dotter's could have also
　　　　　　　　assessed Scott interest at the *legal* rate on the
　　　　　　　　$6,360 amount overdue; in this case, there would
　　　　　　　　be a credit to Interest Revenue.)

Requirement (c) Note No. 2:

Oct. 1, 1974　Cash.. 400
　　　　　　　Accounts Receivable.......................... 3,600
　　　　　　　　　Sales Revenue............................ 　　　4,000
　　　　　　　Sold truck to Bill Day; terms of the receivable,
　　　　　　　n/30.

Nov. 1, 1974　Equipment Notes Receivable.................... 3,600
　　　　　　　　　Accounts Receivable...................... 　　　3,600
　　　　　　　Settled account receivable with a six-month,
　　　　　　　8%, interest-bearing note.

Dec. 31, 1974　Interest Receivable........................... 48
　　　　　　　　　Interest Revenue......................... 　　　48
　　　　　　　Adjusting entry for two months' interest accrued
　　　　　　　at 8% on Day equipment note
　　　　　　　($3,600 × .08 × 2/12)

Jan. 1, 1975　No entry is required on this date; however, a reversal of the adjust-
　　　　　　　ing entry could be made to facilitate the subsequent entry when the
　　　　　　　interest is collected. The *optional reversing entry* would be (see Ap-
　　　　　　　pendix A, Chapter 5):
　　　　　　　Interest Revenue............................. 48
　　　　　　　　　Interest Receivable....................... 　　　48

May 1, 1975　This entry to record collection of the principal plus interest will vary
　　　　　　　depending on whether the above reversing entry was made:
　　　　　　　(a)　Assuming reversing entry was made:
　　　　　　　Cash... 3,744
　　　　　　　　　Equipment Notes Receivable............... 　　　3,600
　　　　　　　　　Interest revenue
　　　　　　　　　　($3,600 × .08 × 6/12).................. 　　　144
　　　　　　　(b)　Assuming reversing entry was not made:
　　　　　　　Cash... 3,744
　　　　　　　　　Equipment Notes Receivable............... 　　　3,600
　　　　　　　　　Interest Receivable
　　　　　　　　　　($3,600 × .08 × 2/12).................. 　　　48
　　　　　　　　　Interest Revenue
　　　　　　　　　　($3,600 × .08 × 4/12).................. 　　　96
　　　　　　　Collection of Day equipment note plus interest.

Summary　　　　This chapter focused on the measurement and reporting of cash, temporary investments, and receivables. Since cash is the most liquid of all assets and is continually flowing in and out of a business, it can be one of the most critical problems facing the management. It is also of critical importance to the decision maker relying on the financial statements for relevant information. The measurement and reporting of cash includes such problems as control of cash, safeguarding cash, reconciliation of bank balances, petty cash, and the recording of all cash inflows and outflows.

The use of temporary investments to employ idle cash was considered. Temporary investments are short-term investments in marketable securities. The intention of management in respect to the holding period is fundamental in the classification of an investment as temporary, as opposed to long-term. Temporary investments are accounted for in accordance with the cost principle; however, in accordance with the principle of conservatism, the lower-of-cost-or-market basis is applied at the end of each accounting period. Long-term investments are deferred for discussion in a later chapter.

Receivables include trade receivables (usually called accounts receivable), special receivables, and notes receivable. Each of these should be accounted for separately. Interest calculations and discounting of notes receivable were discussed and illustrated.

The chapter emphasized the importance of careful measurement of these liquid assets and the importance of examining their characteristics before classifying them as current assets for reporting purposes. Financial statement users often are faced with decisions in which these liquid assets are critical; therefore, they should be properly measured and adequately reported.

Important terms		
Internal control	**Holding loss**	
Bank reconciliation	**Lower-of-cost-or-market**	
Cash over and short	**Principle of conservatism**	
Petty cash	**Certificates of deposit (CD's)**	
Compensating balances	**Contingent liability**	
Temporary investments	**Materiality**	

Appendix A   PETTY CASH

A petty cash fund is established to avoid the inconvenience and cost of writing checks for the many small payments that occur daily in some businesses. This appendix discusses and illustrates the detailed accounting and record keeping for a petty cash fund.

Establishing the petty cash fund. To establish a petty cash fund (sometimes called an imprest fund), a check should be written for the estimated amount needed to meet the expected payments, say for an average month. The check is made payable to "Petty Cash," is cashed, and the money kept in a safe place under the direct control of a *designated individual* as the *custodian.* The entry for the check would be:

Petty Cash 100
    Cash   100
        To record establishment of a petty cash fund.

Disbursements from the petty cash fund. The petty cash system should require that the custodian responsible for disbursements from the fund maintain a running, or perpetual, record of all disbursements and the amount of cash on hand. No entry is made in the regular accounts at the time each payment is made from the petty cash fund by the custodian. Rather, the custodian maintains a *Petty Cash Record* in which each disbursement is recorded when made. This record is supported by signed bills, vouchers, and receipts for each payment made. As an internal control feature, the custodian should expect occasional surprise counts of the fund and examinations of the records of disbursements. "Borrowing" from the fund by the custodian or others should not be allowed. Careless handling of petty cash has often led to defalcations and theft.

Replenishment of the petty cash fund. When the amount of petty cash on hand gets low, and at the end of each accounting period, the fund should be reimbursed, or replenished, with an amount of cash sufficient to restore it to the original amount (to $100 in the example). This is accomplished by having the custodian turn in the Petty Cash Record and the supporting documents. On the basis of these records, a check to "Petty Cash" is written for the amount of cash needed for replenishment. The check is cashed and the money is given to the custodian. An entry in the regular accounts for the amount of the check is made to record the expenditures. The petty cash documents turned in by the custodian provide the underlying support for this entry.

To illustrate, assume that, by the end of the month, there remained $8.50 petty cash on hand of the $100. This means that cash expenditures by the custodian amounted to $91.50 for the month. Assuming no shortage or overage, the bills, vouchers, and receipts accumulated by the custodian should sum to this amount. They provide the supporting documents for the additional check to petty cash for $91.50. These supporting documents provided the detailed data for recording the replenishment check in the following journal entry:

Telegrams 12.40
Office Supplies 6.32
Postage Expense 21.45
Freight-In 6.33
Taxi Fare Expense 14.87
Repair of Office Equipment 5.00
Supplies for Coffee Bar 10.04
Miscellaneous Expenses 15.09
    Cash 91.50

It should be emphasized that Petty Cash is debited only when the petty cash fund is first established. The Petty Cash account carries a stable balance at all times ($100.00 in the above example). Expense accounts, not Petty Cash, are debited when the fund is replenished. Hence, there will be no further entries in the petty cash fund once it is established unless it is decided to discontinue the fund or to increase or decrease the original amount on a permanent basis. The fund must be replenished when the balance of cash in the fund is low, and always at the end of the accounting period, whether low or not. This is necessary in order to record the expenses incurred by the fund up to the date of the financial statements. The petty cash fund should be subject to rigid internal control procedures to remove all temptations to misuse it.

Appendix B   SPECIAL JOURNALS

Up to this point in your study of accounting, we have utilized the *general journal* to record all transactions in chronological order (i.e., by order of date). The general journal is flexible in that any transaction can be recorded in it. However, it is inefficient if used for recording transactions that have a very high rate of occurrence, such as credit sales, credit purchases, cash receipts, and cash payments. It is inefficient at two points in the process: in recording the journal entry and in posting to the ledger. Special journals are designed to reduce these inefficiencies.

In discussing and illustrating special journals, we emphasize that no accounting principles or concepts are involved—we are simply dealing with the mechanics of data processing. Although special journals can, and should, be designed to meet a special need when a particular type of data-processing problem arises, we will limit this discussion to the four special journals that are often used: credit sales, credit purchases, cash receipts, and cash payments.

Sales journal. This journal is designed to accommodate *only credit sales.* Cash sales are entered in the cash receipts journal as explained below. You will recall that the journal entry to record a credit sale is:[10]

```
Jan. 3  Accounts Receivable................................. 100
           Sales.........................................       100
        To record credit sale to K. L. Adams; Invoice No. 324,
        terms n/30.
```

The sales journal is designed specifically to simplify the recording of only this kind of entry and the subsequent posting to the ledger. The design of a sales journal is shown in Exhibit 8–4.

Posting the sales journal. Posting the special sales journal involves two distinct phases. First, the individual charges (i.e., debits) must be posted daily to the customers individual accounts in the accounts receivable *subsidiary ledger.* Second, periodically (usually weekly or

---

[10] For instructional purposes, we will utilize simplified amounts, a limited number of transactions and customers, and T-accounts. We remind you again that a manual system and T-accounts are illustrated for instructional purposes. In many companies these procedures are completely computerized.

Exhibit 8–4

		SALES JOURNAL				Page 9
Date	Customer Name		Terms	Invoice Number	Folio	Amount
Jan. 3	Adams, K. L.		n/30	324	✓	100
4	Small, C. C.		n/30	325	✓	60
6	Baker, C. B.		n/30	326	✓	110
10	Roe, R. R.		n/30	327	✓	20
11	Mays, O. L.		n/30	328	✓	200
16	Roe, R. R.		n/30	329	✓	90
18	Null, O. E.		n/30	330	✓	30
20	Baker, C. B.		n/30	331	✓	180
21	Small, C. C		n/30	332	✓	150
31	Null, O. E.		n/30	333	✓	260
	Total					1,200
	Posting					(34) (81)
Feb. 1	Etc.					

monthly), the totals are posted to the *general ledger* accounts: Accounts Receivable (debit) and Sales (credit).

Posting on a daily basis to the subsidiary ledger is indicated in the folio column either by a check mark (as illustrated above) or by the account number for each individual customer. Daily posting to the subsidiary ledger is necessary because the customer may, on any day, want to pay the current balance then owed.

The daily posting during January to the accounts receivable subsidiary ledger is shown below.

ACCOUNTS RECEIVABLE SUBSIDIARY LEDGER

Adams, K. L.

Jan. 3		9	100		

Baker, C. B.

Jan. 6		9	110		
20		9	180		

Mays, O. L.

Jan. 11		9	200		

Null, O. E.

Jan. 18		9	30		
31		9	260		

Roe, R. R.

Jan. 10		9	20		
16		9	90		

Small, C. C.

Jan. 4		9	60		
27		9	150		

The second phase in posting the sales journal is to transfer to the general ledger the total credit sales for the month. Thus, the $1,200 total will be posted to the general ledger as (1) a debit to the Accounts Receivable *control account,* and (2) as a credit to the Sales account. This posting is shown below; note in the sales journal that two ledger account numbers were entered for the $1,200 total to indicate the posting procedure.

Accounts Receivable (control) #34		Sales #81	
Jan. 31 9 1,200			Jan. 31 9 1,200

The sales journal can be readily adapted to record sales taxes by adding a column headed "Sales Taxes Payable," and separate sales columns can be added to accumulate sales by department or product. You should observe the efficiencies attained in that: (1) recording in the sales journal is much less time-consuming than separately entering each credit sale in the general journal; (2) posting is significantly reduced by transferring the *total* to the ledger as opposed to posting separate debits and credits for each sales transaction.

Purchases journal. Following exactly the same pattern as described above, the purchases journal may be designed as shown below to accommodate the entry common to all purchases on credit, viz:

Jan. 8 Purchases... 392
           Accounts Payable...................................   392
        To record purchase on credit from C. B. Smith, Purchase
        Order #139, invoice dated January 5, 1974, terms 2/10,
        n/30. Recorded at net of discount, $400 × .98 = $392.

Only credit purchases would be recorded in the purchases journal. Cash purchases would be entered in the cash payments journal as illustrated later. The design of a purchases journal generally is as shown in Exhibit 8–5.

Observe that purchases are recorded net of the purchase discount as explained in Chapter 6, page 170. The cash payments journal will provide for recording the subsequent payment of cash for the purchase involving situations where the purchase discount is lost.

The above form was not completed in detail for illustrative purposes since it follows essentially the same pattern already illustrated for the sales journal, both in respect to entries therein and the two phases in posting. Daily posting would involve transfer to the creditors' individual accounts in the *accounts payable subsidiary ledger.* Periodically, the total would be posted to the *general ledger* as: (1) a debit to the Purchases account and (2) a credit to the Accounts Payable control account.

Exhibit 8–5

PURCHASES JOURNAL						Page 4	
Date	Creditors Account	Purchase Order No.	Date of Invoice	Terms	Folio	Amount	
Jan 8	Smith C. B.	139	Jan. 5	2/10, n/30	✓	392	
	Etc.						
	Total					784	
	Posting					(91)	(41)

Cash receipts journal. The design of a special journal to accommodate *all* cash receipts is more complex since there are a number of different accounts that are variously *credited* when the Cash account is debited. In order to resolve this problem, more than one credit column is necessary to accommodate the various credits. The number and desig-

Exhibit 8–6

		DEBITS	CREDITS					
Date	Explanation	Cash	Account Title	Folio	Accounts Receivable	Sundry Accounts	Cash Sales	
Jan. 2	Cash sales	1,237		—			1,237	
3	Cash sales	1,482		—			1,482	
4	Sale of land	2,500	Land	43		2,000		
			Gain on sale of land	91		500		
4	Cash sales	992		—			992	
6	Invoice #324	100	Adams, K. L.	✓	100			
6	Cash sales	1,570		—			1,570	
10	Bank loan	1,000	Notes payable	54		1,000		
15	Invoice #328	200	Mays, O. L.	✓	200			
26	Cash sales	1,360		—			1,360	
31	Invoice #326	110	Baker, C. B.	✓	110			
31	Cash sales	1,810		—			1,810	
	Totals	12,361			410	3,500	8,451	
	Posting	(12)			(34)	(NP)	(81)	

CASH RECEIPTS JOURNAL   Page 14

nation of the debit and credit columns will depend upon the character of the cash receipts transactions in the particular business.

A typical cash receipts journal with some usual transactions recorded is shown in Exhibit 8–6. Notice in particular that there are separate debit and credit sections. Each column illustrated is used as follows:

1. Cash Debit—This column is used for *every* debit to cash. The column is totaled at the end of the period and posted as one debit amount to the Cash account in the general ledger. The posting number at the bottom indicates the total was posted to account number "12," the Cash account.[11]

2. Accounts Receivable Credit—This column is used to enter the individual amounts collected and to be posted to the individual customer accounts in the accounts receivable *subsidiary* ledger (as indicated by the check marks in the folio columns). The total of this column is posted at the end of the period as a credit to the Accounts Receivable control account in the general ledger as indicated by the posting number "34."

3. Sundry Accounts Credit—This column is used for recording credits to all accounts other than Accounts Receivable and Sales. The titles of the accounts to be credited as listed in this column are entered under the column "Accounts Credited." Since this column represents a number of accounts, the *total* is not posted; rather, each individual amount is posted as a credit directly to the indicated account in the ledger. Account numbers entered in the related folio column indicate the posting has been made.

4. Cash Sales Credit—This column is used to record *all* cash sales. The total at the end of the month is posted as a credit to the Sales account in the general ledger.

Posting the cash receipts journal involves the same two phases explained previously for the sales and purchases journals. The daily posting phase encompasses posting the individual credits to the accounts receivable subsidiary ledger. The second phase involves posting the totals at the end of the period to the accounts in the general ledger, with the exception of the column total for "Sundry Accounts," as explained above.

The individual accounts shown in the "Sundry Accounts" column can be posted daily or at the end of the period. Posting through January is indicated by account code numbers and "checks" in the illustrated cash receipts journal.

---

[11] This design assumes that the company correctly records credit sales at net of discounts. If credit sales are recorded at "gross," then a Sales Discount Debit column would also be needed in this special journal.

The representative entries shown in the illustrative cash receipts journal are summarized below in general journal form, for convenience in assessing the increased efficiencies of the cash receipts journal approach in journalizing and posting a large number of cash receipts transactions.

Jan. 2 Cash...	1,237	
Sales..		1,237
To record total cash sales for the day.		
Jan. 3 Cash...	1,482	
Sales..		1,482
To record total cash sales for the day.		
Jan. 4 Cash...	2,500	
Land.......................................		2,000
Gain on Sale of Land..........................		500
To record sale of land for $2,500 that originally cost $2,000.		
Jan. 4 Cash...	992	
Sales..		992
To record total cash sales for the day.		
Jan. 6 Cash...	100	
Accounts Receivable..........................		100
To record collection of K. L. Adams account for Invoice #324 within the discount period.		
Jan. 6 Cash...	1,570	
Sales..		1,570
To record total cash sales for the day.		
Jan. 10 Cash...	1,000	
Notes Payable...............................		1,000
To record bank loan, 90-day, 6%.		
Jan. 15 Cash...	200	
Accounts Receivable..........................		200
To record collection of O. L. Mays account for Invoice #328 within the discount period.		
Jan. 26 Cash...	1,360	
Sales..		1,360
To record total cash sales for the day.		
Jan. 31 Cash...	110	
Accounts Receivable..........................		110
To record collection of C. B. Baker account, Invoice #326.		
Jan. 31 Cash...	1,810	
Sales..		1,810
To record total cash sales for the day.		

Other debit and credit columns can be added to the cash receipts journal to accommodate repetitive transactions that also involve cash receipts.

Cash payments journal. The special cash payments journal (often called the check register) is designed to accommodate efficiently the recording of all cash payments. The basic credit column, of course, is "Cash Credits"; other columns are incorporated into the format to accommodate repetitive transactions that involve cash payments. The cash payments journal, of necessity, must also include a column for "Sundry Accounts Debited" to accommodate the non-recurring transactions involving cash payments.

A typical cash payments journal with some usual transactions recorded is shown in Exhibit 8–7. Observe that, in common with the

Exhibit 8–7

			CREDITS	DEBITS					
Date	Check No.	Explanation	Cash	Account Name	Folio	Accounts Payable	Sundry Accounts	Cash Purchases	
Jan. 2	101	Purchased mdse.	1,880		–			1,880	
4	102	Invoice #37	2,970	Ray Mfg. Co.	✓	2,970			
5	103	Jan. Rent	1,200	Rent Expense	71		1,200		
8	104	Purchased mdse.	250		–			250	
10	105	Freight on mdse.	15	Freight in	63		15		
14	106	Invoice #42	980	Bows Supply Co	✓	980			
15	107	Bank loan plus	2,464	Notes Payable	54		2,400		
		interest paid		Interest Expense	79		64		
20	108	Insurance premium	600	Prepaid Insurance	19		600		
26	109	Purchased mdse.	2,160		–			2,160	
29	110	Invoice #91 – after	500	Myar Corp.	✓	490			
		discount period		Discount lost	80		10		
31	111	Wages	1,000	Wage Expense	76		1,000		
		Totals	14,019			4,440	5,289	4,290	
		Posting	(12)			(51)	(NP)	(61)	
Feb. 1		Etc.							

CASH PAYMENTS JOURNAL   Page 16

cash receipts journal, there are separate debit and credit sections. Each column illustrated is used as follows:

1. Cash Credit—This column is for every *credit* to the Cash account. The column is totaled at the end of the month and posted as a credit to the Cash account in the general ledger.
2. Accounts Payable Debit—This column is used to enter the individual amounts paid on accounts payable. The individual amounts are posted as debits to the accounts payable subsidiary ledger (as indicated by the check marks under folio) and the total at the end of the period is posted as a debit to the Accounts Payable control account in the general ledger.
3. Sundry Accounts Debit—This column is used to record all accounts

debited other than Accounts Payable and Purchases. The titles of the accounts to be debited are entered under the column "Account Name." Since this column represents a number of accounts, the total cannot be posted; rather, each individual amount is posted as a debit directly to the indicated account in the general ledger.

4. Cash Purchase Debit—All cash purchases are entered in this column. The total at the end of the month is posted as a debit to the Purchases account in the ledger.

Posting the cash payments journal involves two phases: (1) daily posting of the individual credit amounts to the accounts payable subsidiary ledger; and (2) posting of the totals to the general ledger, with the exception of the total of "Sundry Accounts." The posting of the individual amounts in the "Sundry Accounts" column can be done during the period, say daily, or at the end of the period.

The illustrative transactions entered in the cash payments journal were:

Jan. 2 Issued check #101 for cash purchase of merchandise costing $1,880.

Jan. 4 Issued check #102 to pay account payable owed to Ray Manufacturing Company within the discount period. Discount allowed: 1%; Invoice #37, $3,000.

Jan. 5 Issued check #103 to pay January rent, $1,200.

Jan. 8 Issued check #104 for cash purchase of merchandise costing $250.

Jan. 10 Issued check #105 for freight-in on merchandise purchased, $15.

Jan. 14 Issued check #106 to pay account payable owed to Bows Supply Company within the discount period. Discount allowed: 2%; Invoice #42, $1,000.

Jan. 15 Issued check #107 to pay $2,000 note payable plus 8% interest for 120 days.

Jan. 20 Issued check #108 to pay three-year insurance premium, $600.

Jan. 26 Issued check #109 for cash purchase of merchandise costing $2,160.

Jan. 29 Issued check #110 to pay account payable to Myar Corporation, terms 2/10, n/30, Invoice #91, $500; therefore, accounts payable to Myar was credited for $490 at the purchase date (see Chapter 6, page 182). The payment was made after the discount period; therefore, the full invoice price of $500 was paid and purchase discount lost of $10 was recorded.

Jan. 31 Issued check #111 to pay wages amounting to $1,000.

Additional debit and credit columns can be added to the cash payments journal to accommodate other repetitive transactions involving cash disbursements.

The larger companies generally use a *voucher system* for controlling expenditures rather than the purchases and the cash payments journals. A voucher system is particularly adaptable to computerized accounting and provides tight control mechanisms on the sequence of events for each transaction from incurrence until final cash payment. The voucher system is explained and illustrated in Chapter 10, Appendix B.

In summary, special journals do not involve new accounting principles or concepts. Rather, they represent a mechanical technique designed to increase the efficiency in the data-processing cycle. Special journals are not standardized; they should be especially designed to fit each particular situation. Although a manual approach has been illustrated for instructional purposes, many companies have fully computerized the procedures represented by special journals. In computerized systems, essentially the same mechanics illustrated for the manual system are accomplished by the computer.

<table>
<tr><td>Questions
for
discussion</td><td>1.</td><td>Define cash in the accounting context and indicate the types of items that should be included.</td></tr>
<tr><td></td><td>2.</td><td>Explain the purpose and nature of internal control.</td></tr>
<tr><td></td><td>3.</td><td>What are the primary characteristics of an effective internal control system for cash?</td></tr>
<tr><td></td><td>4.</td><td>Why should cash-handling and cash-recording activities be separated? Generally, how is it accomplished?</td></tr>
<tr><td></td><td>5.</td><td>What is the purpose and nature of a bank reconciliation? Specifically, what balances are reconciled?</td></tr>
<tr><td></td><td>6.</td><td>Define a temporary investment. What is the twofold test for a temporary investment?</td></tr>
<tr><td></td><td>7.</td><td>Is a marketable security always a temporary investment? Explain.</td></tr>
<tr><td></td><td>8.</td><td>How does the cost principle apply in accounting for temporary investments?</td></tr>
<tr><td></td><td>9.</td><td>What is the rationale for application of the lower-of-cost-or-market basis to temporary investments?</td></tr>
<tr><td></td><td>10.</td><td>Distinguish between accounts receivable and special receivables.</td></tr>
<tr><td></td><td>11.</td><td>Define a promissory note indicating the names of the parties and explain what is meant by principal, maturity date, and interest rate.</td></tr>
<tr><td></td><td>12.</td><td>Distinguish between an interest-bearing and noninterest-bearing note.</td></tr>
<tr><td></td><td>13.</td><td>What is a negotiable promissory note?</td></tr>
<tr><td></td><td>14.</td><td>What is a defaulted note? Who is responsible for its payment? Explain.</td></tr>
<tr><td></td><td>15.</td><td>What is meant by discounting a note receivable?</td></tr>
<tr><td></td><td>16.</td><td>What is a contingent liability? How does one arise in respect to a note receivable?</td></tr>
<tr><td></td><td>17.</td><td>What is the purpose of petty cash? What safeguards should be prescribed?</td></tr>
<tr><td></td><td>18.</td><td>Why are special cash journals frequently needed?</td></tr>
</table>

Exercises   E8–1. The bookkeeper for the Davis Service Company prepared a balance sheet on which cash was reported as $5,847.11. The following items were found to have been included in the reported cash balance:

IN	1.	Balance, City Bank............................	$3,832.51
EX	2.	A deposit made to the local electric utility...........	1,200.00
EX	3.	Postage stamps on hand........................	32.60
ACJR	4.	Check signed by Harry Mills, returned for NSF......	25.00
INC	5.	Petty cash on hand............................	25.00
R	6.	IOU's signed by employees......................	52.00
R	7.	Check from company president for an advance; to be held until he "gives the word to cash it.".........	500.00
INC	8.	Money orders on hand (received from customers)....	30.00
R	9.	Receipt from freight company that involved a $10 overpayment to them. They have indicated "a check will be mailed shortly."........................	10.00
INC	10.	A money order obtained from the post office to be used to pay for a special purchase upon delivery; expected within the next five days.................	140.00
		Total............................	$5,847.11

Required:

The reported cash balance has been questioned. You are to compute the correct cash balance and indicate appropriate reporting for any items that you exclude.

E8–2. The Samson Company operates several branches and, as a consequence, has cash in several locations. The general ledger at the end of 1974 showed the following accounts: Petty Cash—Home Office, $200; City Bank—Home Office, $27,300; Petty Cash—Branch A, $50; National Bank—Branch A, $1,458; Petty Cash—Branch B, $75; Southwest Bank—Branch B, $864; Petty Cash—Branch C, $100; State Bank—Branch C, $965; and Metropolitan Bank—General, $1,000.

Required:

A single Cash control account is to be used in the general ledger in the future. Explain how you would use the subsidiary ledger procedure to accomplish this end. Use the above amounts in your illustration.

E8–3. The Maxey Company has just received the June 30, 1974, bank statement, which is summarized below:

	Checks	Deposits	Balance
Balance, June 1................			$ 4,500
Deposits during June...........		$17,000	21,500
Checks cleared through June.....	$17,700		3,800
Bank service charges...........	7		3,793
Balance, June 30...............			3,793

The Cash account showed the following for June:

Cash

June 1 Balance	4,100	June checks	18,000
June deposits	19,000		

Required:

(a) Reconcile the bank account, assuming that a comparison of the checks written with the checks that have cleared the bank show outstanding checks to be $800 and that cash on hand on June 30 is $100. (Note: Some of the checks that cleared in June were written prior to June; there were no deposits in transit carried over from May.)

(b) Give any entries that would be made as a result of the bank reconciliation.

(c) What is the balance in the Cash account after the reconciliation entries?

(d) What amount of cash would be reported on the balance sheet at June 30?

E8–4. The Wilson Company has just received the September 30, 1974, bank statement, which is summarized below:

	Checks	Deposits	Balance
Balance, Sept. 1.....................			$ 5,100
Deposits recorded during September.....		$27,000	32,100
Checks cleared during September........	$27,300		4,800
NSF check—J. J. Jones...............	50		4,750
Bank service charges.................	10		4,760
Balance, Sept. 30....................			4,760

Cash on hand on Sept. 1 and Sept. 30 amounted to $200.
The Cash account for September reflected the following:

Cash

Sept. 1 balance	5,300	September checks	28,000
September deposits	29,500		

Required:

(a) Reconcile the bank account.
(Hint: You may find an error made by either the bank or the company.)

(b) Give any entries that would be made based upon the bank reconciliation.

(c) What should be the balance in the Cash account after the reconciliation entries?

(d) What amount of cash should be reported on the September 30 balance sheet?

E8–5. The Bailey Company has just received the March 31, 1974, bank statement, which is summarized below:

	Checks	Deposits	Balance
Balance, March 1....................			$ 8,600
Deposits during March...............		$28,000	36,600
Note collected for depositor (including $24 interest)..............		924	37,524
Checks cleared during March..........	$32,200		5,324
Bank service charges.................	8		5,316
Balance, March 31...................			5,316

The Cash account in the ledger showed the following for March:

Cash

Balance, March 1	8,200	Checks written during March	32,500
Deposits during March	31,000		

A comparison of deposits recorded with deposits on the bank statement showed deposits in transit to be $3,000. Similarly, outstanding checks at the end of March were determined to be $900. Cash on hand was $190 at March 31.

Required:

(a) Prepare a bank reconciliation for March.
(Hint: There is a cash overage or shortage involved; however, the bank figures have been verified to be correct.)
(b) Give any entries that should be made based on the reconciliation.
(c) What amount should be reflected as the ending balance of cash after the reconciliation entries? What amount of cash should be reflected on the balance sheet at the end of March?

E8–6. The Fanin Company, in July 1974, had accumulated approximately $10,000 in cash that would not be needed for "10 to 15 months." In order to employ the idle cash profitably, the management decided to purchase some shares of stock as a temporary investment. This series of transactions occurred:

July 30, 1974 Purchased 2,000 shares of the common stock of XY Corporation on the exchange. The price was $4.50 per share; paid cash. Also paid fees and costs related to the acquisition in the amount of $400.

Dec. 15, 1974 Received a cash dividend of $.20 per share on the XY shares.

Dec. 30, 1974 Sold 1,000 of the XY shares at $5.00 per share for cash less brokerage fees of $50.

Required:

(a) Give appropriate journal entries on each date for the temporary investment.
(b) How would the temporary investment be reported on the balance sheet at December 31, 1974? Assume the same market value as on December 30.

E8–7. The Dowd Company, in view of some idle cash, decided to purchase some common stock in RS Corporation as a temporary investment. The following transactions reflect what happened following this decision:

Feb. 1, 1974 Purchased for cash 5,000 shares of RS Corporation common stock at a cost of $19,600. Brokerage and related fees also were paid amounting to $400.

Aug. 15, 1974   Received a cash dividend on the RS stock of $.15 per share.

Dec. 30, 1974   Sold 1,500 shares of the RS stock at $3.60 per share (including brokerage fees).

Dec. 31, 1974   End of the fiscal year for accounting purposes.

Required:

(a)   Give appropriate journal entries for each date for the temporary investment in RS stock.

(Hint: An entry should be made on December 31.)

(b)   How would the temporary investment be reported on the balance sheet at December 31, 1974? The market value did not change on December 31.

E8–8.   The Wilson Company, in order to use some idle cash, in March 1974 acquired 100 shares of common stock in each of three corporations: Corporation A, cost $5,000; Corporation B, cost $4,000; and Corporation C, cost $7,000. At the end of the fiscal period, December 31, 1974, the quoted market prices per share were: Corporation A, $52; Corporation B, $40, and Corporation C, $63.

Required:

(a)   Give entry to record the acquisition of the temporary investments.

(b)   Give entry to reflect the temporary investments at lower-of-cost-or-market. Show computations.

(c)   Show how the temporary investments would be reported on the balance sheet at December 31, 1974.

E8–9.   Approximately 40% of the merchandise sold by the Royal Company is on credit. Accounts that are overdue, if material in amount, are "converted" to notes receivable when possible. This exercise traces one sale through accounts receivable, to notes receivable and to final collection. The related transactions during 1974 were:

January 10   Sold merchandise on account to J. K. Mier for $1,200; terms, n/30.

March 1   The account was unpaid; therefore, Royal Company asked Mier to sign a 120-day, 8% interest-bearing note for the account. Mr. Mier executed the note on this date.

July 1   Mier paid the note including interest.

Required:

Give the entry required on each of the three dates.

E8–10.   The Sloan Company sells a line of products that have a high unit sales price. Credit terms are traditional in the industry; accordingly, Sloan frequently takes a promissory note for the sales price. This exercise follows one promissory note, taken at date of sale, through final collection. The fiscal year for accounting purposes ends December 31. The series of transactions and events were:

Dec. 1, 1974   Sold merchandise to R. E. Gee on a 90-day, 8% interest-bearing note for $6,000.

Dec. 31, 1974   End of fiscal period; adjusting entry.

Jan. 1, 1975   Start of new fiscal period.

March 1, 1975 Collected the note, plus interest, in full.

Required:

Give appropriate entries at each of the four dates; if none, so state. To simplify the computations, assume 30-day months and 360 days in the year.

E8–11. The Logan Company frequently sells merchandise on a promissory note, which is later sold (i.e., discounted) to the local bank to obtain cash needed before maturity date. The following series of transactions relates to one note that followed this pattern:

April 1, 1974   Sold merchandise for $7,500 to D. E. Day; took a six-month, 8% interest-bearing note.

June 1, 1974   Discounted the note at the local bank at an 8½% discount rate; received the proceeds upon endorsement of the note to the bank.

Oct. 1, 1974   Due date of the note plus interest.

Required:

(a)   Give appropriate journal entries at each date assuming D. E. Day paid the bank for the note on due date.

(b)   Give appropriate entry on October 1, 1974, assuming Day defaulted on the note and Logan Company had to make it good, including a $10 protest fee.

E8–12. (Based on Appendix A.) On January 1, 1974, Exalto Company established a petty cash fund amounting to $100 by writing a check to "Petty Cash." The fund was assigned to Jane Wright, an employee, to administer as custodian. At the end of January there was $10 cash remaining in the fund. Signed receipts for expenditures during January were summarized as follows: postage $23; office supplies $18; transportation $31; newspapers $14; and miscellaneous $4.

Required:

(a)   Give entry to establish the fund.

(b)   Give entry to replenish the fund.

(c)   What balance would be reflected in the Petty Cash account in the ledger at January 31? Explain.

Problems   P8–1. The bookkeeper at the Ford Company has not reconciled the bank statement with the Cash account, saying, "I don't have time." You have been asked to prepare a reconciliation and review the procedures with the bookkeeper, since it is believed that "more than time is involved!" The April 30, 1974, bank statement has just been received and shows the following (summarized):

	Checks	Deposits	Balance
Balance, April 1			$19,000
Deposits during April		$38,000	57,000
Note collected for depositor (including $80 interest)		1,080	58,080
Checks cleared during April	$44,700		13,380
NSF check—A. B. Cage	70		13,310
Bank service charges	10		13,300
Balance, April 30			13,300

The Cash account in the ledger for the month of April showed the following:

Cash

Balance, April 1	18,200	Checks issued during April	
Deposits during April	42,000		44,500

The balance in the Petty Cash account at the beginning and end of April was $300. A comparison of checks written before and during April with the checks cleared reflected outstanding checks at the end of April to be $600. No deposits in transit were carried over from February.

Required:

(a) Prepare a detailed bank reconciliation.
(Hint: Don't overlook petty cash.)

(b) Give any entries that are indicated to be needed by the reconciliation.

(c) What are the balances in the cash accounts at the end of April?

(d) What amount of cash should be reported on the balance sheet at the end of April?

P8–2. The Massey Company has just received the following bank statement for the month of August 1974:

	Checks	Deposits	Balance
August 1			$14,500
2	$ 100		14,400
3		$7,000	21,400
4	400		21,000
5	200		20,800
9	900		19,900
10	300		19,600
15		9,000	28,600
21	700		27,900
24	21,000		6,900
25		8,000	14,900
30	800		14,100
31		1,080*	15,180
31	10†		15,170

* $1,000 note collected plus interest.
† $10 bank service charge.

The Cash account (detailed) reflected the following for August:

Cash

Balance, August 1	14,000	Checks written:	
Deposits:		August 2	300
August 2	7,000	4	900
12	9,000	15	600
24	8,000	17	500
31	6,000	18	800
		18	700
		23	21,000

Cash on hand at the end of August amounted to $200. There were three outstanding checks at the end of July: $200, $400, $100; there were no deposits in transit at that time.

Required:

(a) Determine the deposits in transit at the end of August.
(b) Determine the outstanding checks at the end of August.
(c) Prepare a bank reconciliation for August.
(d) Give any entries that are indicated on the reconciliation that should be made.
(e) After the reconciliation entries, what balance would be reflected in the Cash account in the ledger?
(f) What amount of cash should be reported on the August balance sheet?

P8–3. The Dyke Company, in order to use idle cash, usually acquires common stocks as a temporary investment. This case focuses on the purchase of three different common stocks during 1974. The annual fiscal period for accounting purposes ends December 31. The sequence of transactions was:

April 2, 1974   Purchased for cash, as a temporary investment, the following common stocks:

Corporation	Number of Shares	Total Price per Share
X	200	$40
Y	400	50
Z	100	70

Sept. 8, 1974   Received a cash dividend of $3.00 per share on Corporation Z stock.

Dec. 30, 1974   Sold the stock in Corporation Y for $56 per share.

Dec. 31, 1974   Quoted market prices on this date were: Corporation X stock, $38; Corporation Y stock, $56, and Corporation Z stock, $75.

Required:

(a) Give appropriate entry on each date.
(b) Illustrate how the temporary investment should be reflected on the balance sheet at December 31, 1974.

P8–4. The Jones Manufacturing Company produces and sells one main product. There is seasonality in demand and the unit price is relatively high. The fiscal year for accounting purposes ends December 31. Typically, in the high months of the cycle the company generates cash, which is idle during the low months. As a consequence, they consistently acquire temporary investments in order to earn a return on the otherwise idle cash. Recently, the company purchased 1,000 shares of common stock in each of two other corporations, designated for case purposes as Corporations A and B. The prices per share, including fees and related costs, were: A, $28; and B, $64. The sequence of transactions was:

March 15, 1974	Purchased the common stock of Corporations A and B.
Oct. 3, 1974	Received a cash dividend of $.40 per share on the stock of Corporation B.
Dec. 30, 1974	Sold 600 shares of the stock of Corporation A at $24 per share and 500 shares of the stock of Corporation B at $66 per share.
Dec. 31, 1974	End of fiscal period.

Required:

(a) Give appropriate entries at each of the dates. Omit any closing entries.

(b) ˙ Illustrate how the temporary investment would be reported on the balance sheet at December 31, 1974.

P8–5. The Dale Company sells approximately 60% of the merchandise marketed on credit; terms, n/30. Occasionally, as a part of the collection process of a delinquent account, a promissory note will be received. This case focuses on two different sales that ultimately generated promissory notes. The annual fiscal period for accounting purposes ends December 31. The sequence of transactions was:

Note No. 1:

Feb. 15, 1974	Sold merchandise for $1,600 to R. E. May; received $600 cash and the balance was charged to Accounts Receivable.
March 15, 1974	Received a promissory note in settlement of the overdue account of R. E. May. Terms of the note were 120 days, 9%, interest-bearing.
July 15, 1974	Due date for note; May defaulted.
Sept. 15, 1974	May paid the defaulted note plus interest, plus 6% interest on the defaulted amount for the period July 15–Sept. 15. The 6% is the legal rate of interest on overdue obligations.

Required:

(a) Give appropriate entries on each date. Show interest calculations.

Note No. 2:

Oct. 1, 1974	Sold merchandise for $1,000 to D. E. Wall; received $200 cash and the balance was charged to Accounts Receivable.
Nov. 1, 1974	Received a promissory note in settlement of the overdue account from Wall. The terms of the note were 90 days, 9% interest-bearing.
Dec. 31, 1974	End of fiscal period.
Jan. 1, 1974	Start of new fiscal period.
Feb. 1, 1974	Maturity date of the Wall note; Wall paid the principal and interest in full.

Required:

(b) Give appropriate entries on each date (omit any closing entries). Show interest calculations. Specify any accounting assumptions you make. Assume full 30-day-month interest periods to avoid counting on the calendar.

P8–6. The Franklin Machinery Company sells heavy machinery. Credit terms are customary and generally involve promissory notes plus a mortgage on the machinery sold. Down payments of 20% to 33⅓% are required. The annual fiscal period for accounting purposes ends December 31. This problem focuses on two different promissory notes that were received in 1974. The transactions were:

Note No. 1:

Feb. 1, 1974	Sold equipment to A. B. Poe for $12,000; received a 25% cash down payment and a 120-day, 8% interest-bearing note for the balance.
March 1, 1974	Sold the note to the local bank at an 8½% discount rate; endorsed the note to the bank and received the proceeds.
June 1, 1974	Due date of the note plus interest.

Required:

(a) Give appropriate entry on each date. Show interest computations. Assume that Poe paid the bank for the note plus interest on due date.

(b) Give entry on due date, June 1, 1974, assuming Poe defaulted on the note and Franklin paid the note plus interest, plus a $10 protest fee.

Note No. 2:

Dec. 1, 1974	Sold equipment to C. O. Abel for $20,000; received $5,000 cash down payment and a 90-day, 8% interest-bearing note for the balance.
Dec. 31, 1974	End of fiscal period for accounting purposes.
Jan. 1, 1975	Start of new fiscal period.
March 1, 1975	Due date of the note plus interest; Abel paid the note plus interest in full.

Required:

(c)   Give appropriate entries on each of the four dates (omit any
closing entries). State any assumptions you make. Assume full
30-day months for interest purposes to avoid counting on the
calendar.

P8–7.   The Hall Manufacturing Company is a relatively small local business
that specializes in the repair and renovation of antique jewelry, brass
objects, and silverware. The owner is an expert craftsman. Although
a number of skilled workers are employed, there is always a large
backlog of work to be done. A long-time employee, who serves as
clerk-bookkeeper, handles cash receipts, keeps the records, and
writes checks for disbursements. The checks are signed by the
owner. Small claims are paid in cash by the clerk-bookkeeper, subject
to approval of the owner. Approvals generally are made in advance;
however, routine payments are approved later. Approximately 100
regular customers are regularly extended credit. Although credit losses
are small, in recent years the bookkeeper has established an allowance
for doubtful accounts.

Recently, Mr. Hall, the owner, decided to construct a building for
the business that would provide many advantages over the presently
rented space and would make possible needed expansion of facilities.
As a part of the considerations in financing, the financing institution
asked for "audited financial statements." There had never been an
audit of the company. Early in the audit, the independent CPA
found numerous errors and one combination of amounts, in particular, that worried him. There appeared to be evidence that a job
billed at $500 had been charged to a new account receivable. The
account was credited with a $500 collection a few days later. The
new account was never active again. He also observed that at about
the same time there had been three write-offs of Accounts Receivable
balances to the Allowance account as follows: Jones $125.32; Adams
$269.88, and Coster $104.80. These write-offs triggered his attention
because he knew the customers involved and believed they would
not default on their accounts.

Required:

(a)   Can you determine what caused the CPA to be "worried"?
Explain.
(b)   What recommendations would you make in respect to internal
control procedures for this small company?

P8–8.   (Based on Appendix B.) The Alexander Company has a wide variety of transactions each year. A number of them are repetitive in
nature; therefore, the company utilizes five journals: general; sales,
purchases, cash receipts; and cash payments. Selected transactions are
listed below that are to be entered in the appropriate journal. To
shorten the case, amounts have been simplified and the number of
transactions limited in each journal.

Selected transactions (use letter at left in lieu of a date):

a. Sold merchandise to K. K. May at invoice cost of $250; terms 2/10, n/20; Invoice No. 38.

b. Received merchandise from Sable Company, invoice cost $300; credit terms 1/10, n/20; Purchase Order No. 17.

c. Sold merchandise to B. B. Wise for $200 on credit; terms 2/10, n/20; Invoice No. 39.

d. Received merchandise from Rex Supply Company at an invoice cost of $200, on credit, terms 1/10, n/20; Purchase Order No. 18.

e. Sold merchandise to A. B. Cox for $150 cash.

f. Received merchandise from Baker Manufacturing Company at a cost of $360, paid cash (number the checks consecutively starting with No. 81).

g. Purchased a fixed asset (machinery) at a cost of $800; gave a 90-day, 8% interest-bearing promissory note for the purchase price.

h. Sold a tract of land for $9,000 that originally cost $3,000; collected cash.

i. Collected account receivable from B. B. Wise within the discount period; Invoice No. 39.

j. Paid $600 for a three-year insurance premium.

k. Obtained a $5,000 bank loan; signed a one-year, 8% interest-bearing note.

l. Paid account payable to Rex Supply Company within the discount period.

m. Paid monthly rent, $650.

n. Sold merchandise for cash, $1,400.

o. Purchased merchandise for cash, $980.

p. Sold merchandise on credit to C. C. Coe for $700; terms 2/10, n/20; Invoice No. 40.

q. Received merchandise on credit from Stubbs Company at an invoice cost of $400; terms 2/10, n/30; Purchase Order No. 19.

r. Collected account receivable from K. K. May after the discount period.

s. Paid account payable to Sable Company after the discount period.

t. Paid monthly salaries, $2,400.

u. By year end, six months of the prepaid insurance had expired.

Use the following account code numbers for posting: Cash 11; Accounts Receivable 14; Prepaid Insurance 16; Machinery 17; Land 19; Accounts Payable 21; Notes Payable 22; Purchases 31; Purchases Discount Lost 33; Sales 41; Sales Discount 43; Expenses 51; and Gain on Sale of Fixed Assets 53. For journals, use the following page numbers: General 15, Sales 18, Purchases 14, Cash Receipts 21, and Cash Payments 34.

Required:

(1) Draft a format for each of the journals, including the general journal, following the illustrations in Appendix B. Include folio columns.

(2) Enter each transaction in the appropriate journal. Sales and purchases are recorded net of discount.

(3) Indicate all postings to the *subsidiary ledgers* by entering check marks ($\sqrt{}$) in the folio columns.

(4) Sum the special journals and indicate all postings to the *general ledger* accounts by entering the account code numbers in the folio columns and below totals posted. Utilize the account code numbers given above.

(5) To save time, unless directed otherwise by your instructor, you need not set up the subsidiary ledgers and the accounts in the general ledger.

9 Operational assets — plant and equipment, natural resources, and intangibles

Purpose
of the
chapter Operational assets are those noncurrent assets that a business retains more or less permanently, not for sale but for utilization (physically or in terms of rights) in the course of normal operations. Thus, operational assets include land in use, plant and equipment, natural resources, and certain intangibles (such as a patent) used in operating the business. The degree of efficiency in the utilization of the operational assets will influence the earnings of the business over time. The nature and cost of the operational assets, their age and state of repair, and the future demands for funds needed to replace them loom large in many important decisions. The expense of maintaining and operating these assets often has a major effect on net income.

An operational asset is acquired by a business because of the future services potentially available from it through use by the entity. Thus, such assets can be viewed as a bundle of services that is purchased *in advance of usage*. As those services are used, as in the use of a machine, the prepaid cost of the asset is allocated to the periods of utilization as an expense. To illustrate, assume a truck is purchased at a cost of $5,000 for use in the business. The cost is debited to an asset account and, assuming a five-year useful life, each year a part of the prepaid cost is apportioned to expense. This apportionment of the prepaid cost of operational assets to expense is variously known as depreciation, depletion, and amortization, depending on the characteristics of the asset.

The financial statements provide financial information in respect to operational assets. The financial impact of operational assets on the balance sheet, income statement, and statement of changes in financial position is useful information to decision makers. This chapter focuses on the measurement and reporting problems related to operational assets and discusses the measurement of cost at acquisition date and the apportionment of that cost to expense as the assets are used.

Categories of operational assets

The effective management of a business requires a combination of assets with different characteristics and purposes. Each type of asset—be it current, investments, or operational—serves a particular purpose not served by the other types of assets. The optimum combination of resources varies with each business, and its determination is a central responsibility of the management. An objective of the financial statements is the reporting of the different assets classified by types and the measurement of the resources committed to each type. For measurement and reporting purposes, operational assets may be classified as follows:

1. Fixed assets—The assets that include the long-lived, tangible assets acquired for use in the operation of the business and not intended for resale. Examples are land, buildings, equipment, furniture, tools, vehicles, and mineral deposits. There are three kinds of fixed assets: land—not subject to depreciation; plant, equipment, and fixtures—subject to depreciation; natural resources—the wasting assets used in the operation of the business, such as mines, gravel pits, oil wells, and timber tracts. Natural resources are subject to depletion.

2. Intangible assets—the assets held by the business because of the special rights they confer. They have no physical substance. Examples are patents, copyrights, franchises, licenses, and trademarks. Intangible assets are subject to amortization.

Principles underlying accounting for operational assets

The primary aspects of accounting for operational assets are:

1. Measuring and recording the cost of the asset at acquisition date.
2. After acquisition, measurement of the cost of the asset and the expense of using it during its useful life.
3. Recording disposals of operational assets.

At the date of acquisition, an operational asset is measured and recorded in conformity with the cost principle. After acquisition, the cost of an operational asset (except land) is matched periodically with the revenues generated during its useful life in accordance with the matching principle.

Measuring
and
recording
acquisition
cost

All reasonable and necessary costs incurred in acquiring an operational asset and in placing it in its operational setting, less any cash discounts, should be recorded in an appropriate asset account. Cost represents the net cash paid or to be paid. Cost is easily determined when an operational asset is purchased for cash. For example, the acquisition cost of a machine may be measured as follows:

Invoice price of the machine..........................	$10,000
Less: Cash discount ($10,000 × .02)...................	200
Net cash price.......................................	9,800
Add: Transportation charges paid by purchaser........	150
Installation costs paid by purchaser..............	200
Sales tax paid ($10,000 × .02)...................	200
Cost—amount debited to the Machinery account........	$10,350

The acquisition of this fixed asset would be recorded as follows:

```
Machinery.................................... 10,350
    Cash....................................          10,350
```

When an operational asset is purchased and *noncash* consideration is given for it, cost is the cash equivalent measured as the fair market value of the noncash consideration. To illustrate, assume a tract of timber (a natural resource) was acquired by Fuqua Corporation. Payment in full was made as follows: $28,000 cash plus 2,000 shares of Fuqua no-par stock. At the date of the purchase, Fuqua stock was selling at $12 per share. The cost of the tract would be measured as follows:

Cash paid...	$28,000
Noncash consideration given	
(2,000 shares no-par stock @ $12)...................	24,000
	52,000
Title fees, legal fees, and other costs paid	
(incidental to the acquisition)......................	1,000
Cost—Amount debited to the asset account............	$53,000

The journal entry to record the acquisition of this natural resource would be:[1]

```
Timber Tract.............................. 53,000
    Cash....................................          29,000
    Capital Stock, No-par
        (2,000 shares @ $12)..............          24,000
```

---

[1] See Chapter 12 for discussion of capital stock.

When land is purchased, all of the incidental costs, such as title fees, sales commissions, legal fees, title insurance, delinquent taxes, and surveying fees, should be included in the cost of the land.

Not infrequently, an old building or used machinery is purchased for operational use in the business. Renovation and repair costs incurred prior to use should be debited to the asset account as a part of the cost of the asset. Repair costs incurred *after* the asset is placed in use are considered to be expenses.

Basket purchases. When two or more kinds of operational assets are acquired at the same time, the cost of each kind must be separately measured and recorded. For example, when a building and the land on which it is located are purchased, at least two separate accounts must be established: one for the building (which is subject to depreciation) and one for the land (which is not subject to depreciation).

When several different operational assets are purchased for a single lump sum the purchase cost must be allocated on some rational basis to the several different kinds of assets purchased. Relative fair-market value of the several assets is the most logical basis on which to make the allocation. Appraisals or tax assessments often have to be used as indications of the fair-market values. To illustrate, assume Fox Company purchased a building suitable for an additional plant and the land on which the building is located for a total of $150,000 cash. Since the true fair-market values of the building and land were not known separately, a professional appraisal was obtained that showed the following *estimated* fair-market values: building, $99,000; land, $81,000 (apparently the buyer got a good deal). The apportionment of the $150,000 purchase price was made as follows:

	Appraised Value		Apportionment of Lump Sum Purchase Cost	
Asset	Amount	Ratio	Computation	Apportioned Cost
Building...........	$ 99,000	.55*	$150,000 × .55 =	$ 82,500
Land..............	81,000	.45†	150,000 × .45 =	67,500
	$180,000	1.00		$150,000

* $99,000 ÷ $180,000 = .55
† $81,000 ÷ $180,000 = .45

The journal entry to record the acquisition costs would appear as follows:

```
Plant Building.......................  82,500
Land—Plant Site......................  67,500
     Cash............................          150,000
```

Matching
the cost of an
operational
asset with
future
revenues

The acquisition cost of an operational asset having a limited useful life represents the prepaid cost of a bundle of **future services** or benefits (i.e., future usefulness). The matching principle requires that the acquisition cost of such assets be apportioned as expense to the periods in which revenue is generated as a result of using those assets. Thus, the acquisition cost of this kind of operational asset is matched with the revenues to which it contributed by way of services and benefits.

We should make clear the distinction between three different terms that generally are used to describe the cost apportionment required by the matching principle for the different types of operational assets:

1. Depreciation—The systematic and rational apportionment of the acquisition cost of **fixed assets** to future periods in which the services or benefits contribute to revenue. Example—depreciation of the cost of a machine over its useful life:

```
Dec. 31, 1974:
    Depreciation Expense..................... 1,035
        Accumulated Depreciation,
            Machinery...........................        1,035
```

2. Depletion—The systematic and rational apportionment of the acquisition cost of **natural resources** to future periods in which the use of those natural resources contribute to revenue. Example—depletion of the cost of a timber tract over the period of cutting:

```
Dec. 31, 1974:
    Depletion Expense..................... 10,600
        Timber Tract (#20)................        10,600
```

3. Amortization—The systematic and rational apportionment of the acquisition cost of **intangible assets** to future periods in which the benefits contribute to revenue. Example—amortization of the cost of a patent over its economic life:

```
Dec. 31, 1974:
    Patent Expense............................... 500
        Patents...................................        500
```

Each of these terms relates to the same basic objective; namely, the apportionment of the purchase cost of an operational asset to the future periods in which the benefits of its use contributed to the earning of periodic revenue. The amounts of depreciation, depletion, and amortization measured and recorded during each period are reported as expense on the income statement for the period. In contrast, on the balance sheet, the amounts of depreciation, depletion, and amortization *accumu-*

lated since acquisition date are reported as a deduction from the assets to which they pertain. To illustrate, a fixed asset, such as a machine, would be reported on the balance sheet as follows:

Balance Sheet at December 31, 1974

Fixed Assets:
    Machinery............................. $10,350
    Less: Accumulated Depreciation......... 2,070 $8,280

We must realize that the amounts for operational assets reported on the balance sheet do not represent their "fair-market values" but, rather, are "book, or carrying, values"; that is, their acquisition cost less the accumulated apportionments to expense of that cost to the date of the balance sheet. This is in accordance with the cost principle. Under it, the cost of an operational asset is measured and recorded at acquisition date. It is not remeasured at subsequent balance sheet dates, aside from the expense allocation for depreciation, depletion, and amortization.

Fixed assets subject to depreciation

Three kinds of fixed assets were identified on page 298. In this section we will limit our discussion to land and those fixed assets subject to depreciation. The term "fixed asset" refers to all kinds of buildings, machinery, furniture, and other equipment used in the operation of the business. Although the term fixed asset is used widely, a more descriptive term, "property, plant, and equipment," often is used in published financial statements.

Buildings, machinery, furniture, and other fixed assets (except land) decrease in economic "use–utility" to the user because of a number of causative factors, such as wear-and-tear, the passage of time, effects of the elements (such as the weather), obsolescence (i.e., becoming out-of-date), technological changes, and inadequacy. These causative factors are always bearing down on a fixed asset during the period it is being used to generate revenues. Thus, under the matching principle, at the end of each accounting period an **adjusting entry** is needed to record these expense-causing effects. In developing the adjusting entry, a *rational and systematic* measurement approach must be used to match the acquisition cost of a fixed asset with periodic revenues as they are generated.

Because of the wide diversity of fixed assets subject to depreciation and the varying effects of the causative factors listed above, a number of **depreciation methods** have been developed that are acceptable for both accounting and income tax purposes. In the paragraphs to follow, we will discuss and illustrate methods of measuring and recording depreciation that are commonly used.

To measure depreciation expense each period, the methods require three amounts for each fixed asset: (1) the **actual acquisition cost**, (2) the **estimated net residual amount**, and (3) the **estimated useful life.**

It is important to observe that, of these three amounts, two are *estimates* (residual value and useful life); thus, the depreciation expense that is recorded and reported is an estimate. To illustrate, depreciation expense may be measured as follows:

Actual acquisition cost	$625
Less: estimated residual value	25
Amount to be depreciated over useful life	$600
Estimated useful life	3 years
Annual depreciation expense: $600 ÷ 3 =	$200

Estimated residual value[2] must be deducted from acquisition cost because it represents that part of the acquisition cost that is expected to be recovered by the user when he disposes of the asset. *Residual value* is the total estimated amount to be recovered less the costs of dismantling, disposal, and selling. Because these costs may approximately equal the gross amount recovered, many fixed assets are assumed to have no residual value. It is important to realize that the estimated net residual value is not the value of the fixed asset as scrap, but, rather, it is the expected net recovery to be realized at the date that the *current user* intends to dispose of it. For example, a company whose policy is to replace all trucks at the end of three years normally would use a higher estimated residual value than would a user of the same kind of truck whose policy is to replace the trucks at the end of five years.

Estimated useful life should be viewed as the *economic* useful life to the *present owner* rather than as the total useful life to all potential users. In the truck example above, for accounting purposes, one user would utilize a three-year useful life, whereas the other user would utilize a five-year useful life.

The several **methods of depreciation** will be discussed and illustrated. For this purpose we will use a common set of facts and notations:

	Symbols	Illustrative Amounts
Acquisition cost of a particular machine	C	$625
Estimated net residual value at end of useful life	R	$ 25
Estimated service life:		
In years	n	3
In units of output	n	10,000
Depreciation rate	r	
Dollar amount of depreciation expense per period	D	

[2] Residual value is also called "scrap value" or "salvage value," however, "residual value" is a more descriptive term because the asset may not be scrapped upon disposition; a subsequent buyer may renovate it and reuse it for many years.

Straight-line depreciation. This method has been widely used because of its simplicity and reasonableness in respect to many kinds of fixed assets. Under this method, an *equal portion* of the acquisition cost to be depreciated is allocated to each period during the useful life. Thus, the annual depreciation expense is measured as follows:

$$D = \frac{C - R}{n} \text{ or, } D = \frac{\$625 - \$25}{3} = \$200 \text{ depreciation per year}$$

The annual adjusting entry for depreciation expense on this machine would be the same for each of the three years of the useful life; viz:

```
Depreciation Expense............................ 200
    Accumulated Depreciation, Machinery..........        200
```

A **depreciation schedule** covering the entire useful life of the machine could be developed as follows:

Depreciation Schedule—Straight-Line Method

Year	Depreciation Expense	End of Year Balance in Accumulated Depreciation	Book Value
At acquisition.........			$625
1.....................	$200	$200	425
2.....................	200	400	225
3.....................	200	600	25
	$600		

The straight-line method is simple, rational, and systematic. It is especially appropriate where the use of the asset is essentially the same each period and is coupled with an approximately equal decline in the economic usefulness of the asset each period.

Productive-output method. This method, sometimes called the units-of-production method, is based upon the assumption that the benefits derived each period from the fixed asset are related to the periodic output of that asset. For example, many persons believe that certain equipment, such as a delivery truck, should be depreciated on the basis of miles driven each period (i.e., based on a measure of output) rather than on the mere passage of time as is assumed by the straight-line method. They feel that many productive assets do not generate revenues merely because time is passing but, rather, only when they are used.

Since the productive-output method relates acquisition cost less residual value to the estimated productive life of the asset in terms of units of output, a **depreciation rate per unit of output** is computed as follows:

$$r = \frac{C - R}{n} \text{ or, } r = \frac{\$625 - \$25}{10,000 \text{ units}} = \$.06 \text{ per unit of output}$$

Assuming 3,000 units of output in year 1, depreciation expense for year 1 would be:

$$D = r \times n, \text{ or, } D = \$.06 \times 3,000 = \underline{\$180}$$

The *adjusting entry* for depreciation at the end of year 1 would be:

```
Depreciation Expense...........................  180
    Accumulated Depreciation, Machinery..........        180
```

Assuming output to be 5,000 units in year 2 and 2,000 units in year 3, the depreciation schedule would be as follows:

Depreciation Schedule—Productive-Output Method

Year	Depreciation Expense		End of Year Balance in Accumulated Depreciation	Book Value
At acquisition...				$625
1...............	(3,000 × $.06)	$180	$180	445
2...............	(5,000 × .06)	300	480	145
3...............	(2,000 × .06)	120	600	25
		$600		

The productive-output method is simple, rational, and systematic. It is appropriate where output of the asset can be measured realistically and where the economic use–utility of the fixed asset tends to decrease with use rather than with time. Also, where use is quite variable from period to period, a more realistic measurement of expense to be matched with revenue is attained.

Accelerated depreciation. Accelerated depreciation is based upon the notion that there should be relatively large amounts of depreciation expense reported in the early years of the useful life and correspondingly reduced amounts of depreciation expense in the later years. The basis for this conclusion is that a fixed asset is more efficient in generating revenue in the early years than in the later years of its life. Also, repair expense tends to be low in the early years and higher in the later years. Accelerated depreciation has considerable appeal from the income tax viewpoint. Higher depreciation expense means lower reported profits in the early years, hence, lower income taxes. Of course, the effect reverses in the later years; however, an early tax deduction is to be preferred to later tax deduction because of the time value of money.[3]

There are several variations of accelerated depreciation; however, the two methods generally used are the sum-of-the-years'-digits method and the double-declining balance method.

Sum-of-the-years'-digits method. This method, frequently referred

---

[3] The time value of money refers to interest that can be earned on money when invested or used in the business. Also, there may be a distinct tax advantage of accelerated depreciation and early disposition because of the effects of the long-term capital gains tax provision.

to as the SYD method, is used primarily because it produces a significantly accelerated effect. Depreciation expense each year is computed by multiplying the acquisition cost, less residual value, by a fraction that is successively *smaller* each year. The decreasing fractions are determined by using the sum of the digits comprising the useful life as the denominator, and the specific year of life in *inverse order* as the numerator. The computations may be demonstrated by using the illustrative data previously given, as follows:[4]

Denominator:	Sum of digits (comprising the useful life): $1 + 2 + 3 = 6$
Numerators:	Digits (specific year of life) in inverse order: 3, 2, 1

Year of Life	Fraction
1	$\frac{3}{6}$
2	$\frac{2}{6}$
3	$\frac{1}{6}$
Total	$\frac{6}{6}$

Therefore, the depreciation expense each year for the useful life of the illustrative machine would be: year 1, $600 \times \frac{3}{6} = \$300$; year 2, $600 \times \frac{2}{6} = \$200$; and year 3, $600 \times \frac{1}{6} = \$100$.

The effects of SYD depreciation can be readily observed in the following depreciation schedule:

Depreciation Schedule—Sum-of-the-Years'-Digits Method

Year	Computations	Depreciation Expense	Balance in Accumulated Depreciation (End of Year)	Book Value (End of Year)
At acquisition				$625
1	$600 × ⅜ =	$300	$300	325
2	600 × ⅖ =	200	500	125
3	600 × ⅙ =	100	600	25
Total....		$600		

The adjusting entry for depreciation expense by year would be:

	Year 1	Year 2	Year 3
Depreciation Expense	300	200	100
Accumulated Depreciation, Machinery	300	200	100

----

[4] The sum of the digits can be computed by using the formula: $\text{SYD} = n\left(\dfrac{n+1}{2}\right)$. For example, a five-year life would be: $\text{SYD} = 5\left(\dfrac{5+1}{2}\right) = 15$.

Double-declining balance method.   This accelerated method came directly from the provision for income taxes. For income tax purposes, accelerated depreciation is permitted; however, depreciation expense for each period may not be more than double the amount that would result under the straight-line method, ignoring residual value. Since this approach is permitted for income tax purposes, and since it gives a significant accelerating effect, it has been widely used on the tax return. Although considered by many accountants as not theoretically sound, it nevertheless has become widely used for accounting purposes. This is the only method that ignores residual value in computing the rate. Depreciation expense is measured each year by multiplying a constant rate by the decreasing undepreciated cost of the asset (i.e., the book value), ignoring residual value. The rate used is *double* the straight-line rate, ignoring residual value. Depreciation stops when the book value equals the estimated residual value. Thus, depreciation expense would be computed as follows, utilizing the illustrative data:[5]

Straight-line rate: 3 years = .333 rate
Double straight-line rate: .667
Annual depreciation: .667 × book value of the asset

Depreciation Schedule—Double-Declining Balance Method

Year	Computations	Depreciation Expense	Balance in Accumulated Depreciation	Book Value
At acquisition.....				$625
1.................	.667 × $625	$417	$417	208
2.................	.667 × 208	139	556	69
3.................	.667 × 69	44*	600	25*

End of Year (spans Balance in Accumulated Depreciation and Book Value)

  * Although .667 × $69 = $46, depreciation expense in the last year is limited to the amount necessary to leave the book value equal to the residual value of $25.

The four methods of computing depreciation are different ways of measuring depreciation expense for the period. They will have different impacts on the measurement of net income, even though the asset cost, estimated life, and residual value are the same. This demonstrates how the selection of a particular accounting approach will cause a difference in the measurement of net income. The comparative effects of each method on the income statement (depreciation expense) and the balance sheet (book value) for the illustrative data are shown in the table below.

---

  [5] Accelerated depreciation is limited for tax purposes to assets having a useful life of over three years; the short period was used to simplify the illustrations. There are other special tax provisions that are too detailed to be considered in this book.

Depreciation Methods—Comparative Results

Year	Straight Line Depreciation Expense	Straight Line Book Value	Productive Output Depreciation Expense	Productive Output Book Value	Sum of Years' Digits Depreciation Expense	Sum of Years' Digits Book Value	Double Declining Depreciation Expense	Double Declining Book Value
At Acquisition...........		$625		$625		$625		$625
1.....................	$200	425	$180	445	$300	325	$417	208
2.....................	200	225	300	145	200	125	139	69
3.....................	200	25	120	25	100	25	44	25
At End................	$600	$ 25	$600	$ 25	$600	$ 25	$600	$ 25

Depreciation for short periods. The preceding illustrations assumed that a full years' depreciation is recorded at the end of each year by means of an adjusting entry. Some businesses record depreciation monthly. Also, a fixed asset may be acquired or disposed of during the year. These situations may require that depreciation expense be recorded for periods of less than one year. In such cases, it is customary to compute depreciation on a proportional basis to either the nearest month or six-month period. For example, depreciation for a full month may be assumed to start or end at the nearest first of the month. For all of the methods illustrated, except productive output, monthly depreciation normally is determined by computing the annual amount of depreciation as illustrated, then dividing by 12 to obtain the monthly amount. For example, in the above illustration for double declining-balance depreciation, the depreciation for the first year was determined to be $417. Assume the asset was acquired on August 12, 1974, with a December 31 fiscal year ending. The depreciation expense for 1974 would be:

$$\frac{\$417}{12} \times 5 = \$174$$

Since depreciation expense is an estimate, one should never record depreciation, say to even cents, since to do so would suggest a higher degree of accuracy than prevails. For this reason, depreciation amounts should always be rounded to even amounts—one, ten, or hundred dollars—depending upon the relative cost of the fixed asset.

Repairs and maintenance

After the acquisition of a fixed asset, related cost outlays often must be made for such items as ordinary repairs and maintenance, major repairs, replacements, and additions. The central measurement problem is the determination of which of these items should be recorded as an expense of the current period when incurred, and which should be recorded as an asset (i.e., as a prepayment) to be matched with future revenues. In measuring the cost of using operational assets, two basic types of expenditures must be considered. The term expenditure means the payment of cash or the incurring of a debt for an asset or service received. The purchase of a machine or the use of a service, such as repairs on the truck, may be for cash or on credit. In either case there is an expenditure. The *two* types of expenditure are:

1. Capital expenditures—These are expenditures for the acquisition of an asset and for the expansion or improvement of an asset already owned. A capital expenditure is an expenditure that will benefit one or more accounting periods beyond the current period; therefore, capital expenditures are recorded in asset accounts. For example, a plant addition costing $20,000 would be recorded as follows:

```
Plant...................................... 20,000
    Cash...................................          20,000
```

2. Revenue expenditures—These are expenditures for such normal operating items as ordinary repairs, maintenance, and salaries that benefit *only* the current period; therefore, revenue expenditures are debited directly to appropriate expense accounts.[6] For example, the payment of $150 for ordinary repairs to the plant would be recorded in the current period as follows:

```
Repair Expense................................. 150
    Cash.......................................          150
```

Each expenditure made subsequent to the acquisition of an operational asset must be carefully evaluated in order to classify it properly as either capital or revenue. The distinction between capital and revenue expenditures is essential in order to conform with the matching principle. The expenditures must be matched with the periodic revenue to which they relate. The purpose and nature of the expenditure is the controlling factor in its classification. In the next few paragraphs we will discuss the common types of outlays subsequent to acquisition of a fixed asset.

Ordinary repairs and maintenance. Ordinary repairs and maintenance are always classified as revenue expenditures and debited to an appropriate *expense* account in the period in which incurred. *Ordinary repairs and maintenance* are those relatively small recurring outlays essential to keep a fixed asset in normal operating condition. Ordinary *repairs* do not materially add to the economic value of the asset or to its originally contemplated useful life. Rather, they tend to restore and

[6] The term "revenue expenditure" is widely used. It suggests that the expenditure is to be deducted in the current period from revenue in deriving net income. However, a term such as "expense expenditure" would be more descriptive.

repair the effects of normal wear-and-tear that occurred in the past. As a consequence, normal repair and maintenance tend to assure the expected useful life and operating efficiencies. These reasons justify the matching of current repair and maintenance expenditures with revenues of the current period.

Extraordinary repairs. Extraordinary repairs are classified as capital expenditures and are debited to the related *asset* account and depreciated over the *remaining* life of that asset. *Extraordinary repairs* occur infrequently, involve relatively large amounts of money, and tend to increase the economic usefulness of the asset in the future because of either greater efficiency or longer life, or both. They are represented by major overhauls, complete reconditioning, and major replacements and betterments. For example, the complete replacement of a roof on the factory building would constitute an extraordinary repair, whereas, patching the old roof would constitute an ordinary repair.

To illustrate the accounting for extraordinary repairs, assume a machine is being used that originally cost $20,000 and is being depreciated on a straight-line basis over ten years with no residual value. At the beginning of the seventh year, a major reconditioning was completed at a cost of $3,200. The estimated useful life was unchanged; however, efficiency was improved. The sequence of entries would be:[7]

At acquisition:

```
Machinery...................................  20,000
    Cash...................................             20,000
    Purchase of machinery.
```

Annually at end of years 1 through 6:

```
Depreciation Expense........................   2,000
    Accumulated Depreciation................              2,000
    Adjusting entry, to record annual
    depreciation ($20,000 ÷ 10).
```

At start of 7th year:

```
Machinery...................................   3,200
    Cash...................................              3,200
    Expenditure for major repair.
```

---

[7] Some accountants prefer to debit the related asset account, as illustrated above, only when the major repair increases the efficiency above normal. In contrast, when it is estimated that the useful life is extended, the related accumulated depreciation account is debited. This distinction often is not made for practical reasons and because subsequent book value and depreciation expense would be the same, irrespective of which account is debited.

Annually at end of years 7 through 10:

```
Depreciation Expense........................ 2,800
    Accumulated Depreciation................          2,800
    Adjusting entry, to record annual
    depreciation.
```

Computations

Original cost...............................	$20,000	
Depreciation, years 1–6.....................	12,000	
Book value remaining.......................		$ 8,000
Extraordinary repair.......................		3,200
Balance to be depreciated over remaining life....		$11,200

Annual depreciation: $11,200 ÷ 4 years = $2,800.

Additions. Additions are extensions or enlargements of existing assets, such as the addition of a wing to a present building. Since these are capital expenditures, the cost of such additions should be debited to the existing account for the asset and depreciated over the remaining life of the asset.

Disposals of fixed assets

Fixed assets may be disposed of voluntarily by sale, trade-in, or retirement; or involuntarily as a result of a casualty, such as a storm, fire, or accident. Whatever the nature of the disposal, the cost of the asset and any accumulated depreciation must be removed from the accounts at the date of disposal. The difference between any resources received, such as cash, for a fixed asset and the **book value** of the asset at the date of disposal represents a "gain or loss on disposal of fixed assets." To illustrate, assume a machine is sold for $3,500 cash when the account balances showed: Machine, $10,000; Accumulated Depreciation, Machine, $7,000 (i.e., a book value of $3,000). The entry to record the disposal would be:

```
Cash....................................... 3,500
Accumulated Depreciation, Machine........... 7,000
    Machine................................          10,000
    Gain on Disposal of Fixed Asset........             500
```

Gain Computed

Sale price.....................................	$3,500
Book value at date of sale ($10,000 − $7,000).....	3,000
Difference—gain....................	$ 500

When a fixed asset is disposed of at any date other than the end of the accounting period, it may be necessary to record depreciation for the fraction of the year to the date of disposal. After this entry is made, the entry to record the disposal can be made. To illustrate, assume a machine that cost $6,000 when acquired on January 1, 1967, was disposed of through sale for $1,000 cash on June 30, 1974. The machine has been depreciated on a straight-line basis assuming an estimated useful life of ten years and no residual value. The sequence of entries from date of purchase through date of disposal would be as follows:

```
Jan. 1, 1967      Machinery...................  6,000
                       Cash....................          6,000
                  Purchase of machinery.

Annually
Dec. 31, 1967,    Depreciation Expense.........   600
through 1973           Accumulated Depreciation.         600
                  Adjusting entry, to record
                  annual depreciation
                  (repeated each year for
                  7 years).

June 30, 1974     Depreciation Expense.........   300
                       Accumulated Depreciation.         300
                  Depreciation from end of
                  last accounting period to
                  date of disposal, $600 ×
                  6/12 = $300. This assumes
                  depreciation is computed
                  on even months.

June 30, 1974     Cash........................  1,000
                  Accumulated Depreciation:
                  ($600 × 7 yrs.) + $300...... 4,500
                  Loss on Disposal of Fixed
                      Asset....................   500
                       Machinery...............          6,000
                  Sale of fixed asset, in-
                  cluding removal from the
                  accounts of original cost
                  and accumulated de-
                  preciation.
```

In the above illustration, the fixed asset when sold had a book value of $6,000 − $4,500 = $1,500. The difference between this book value and the sales price of $1,000 was the amount of the loss on disposal.

The gain or loss on disposal of fixed assets would be reported on the income statement, and the machinery would no longer be reported on the balance sheet.

Trading in used assets   It is not unusual, when acquiring a new fixed asset, to trade in an old asset and pay some cash difference (often called "boot"). In such instances, the new asset must be recorded in the accounts and the old asset removed from the accounts.

Accounting for the exchange of assets, and the boot paid, depends upon whether the two assets are *similar* or *dissimilar*.[8] The trading in of an old truck on a new truck would involve similar assets. In contrast, the trading in of a lot (i.e., real estate) on a new truck would involve dissimilar assets.

If the assets are similar, the cost of the new asset acquired is the sum of the cash paid plus the book value of the old asset exchanged if there is a gain. In this situation no gain will be reported on the disposal of the old asset. To illustrate, assume that the AB Company has an old machine that originally cost $4,000 and that the accumulated depreciation to date of trade-in is $3,000; (i.e., a book value of $1,000). It is traded in on a similar new machine that has a cash price of $7,000. It was agreed that the AB Company would trade in the old machine and pay $5,500 cash as boot. Since there was a gain [$7,000 − ($5,500 + $1,000) = $500] the transaction would be recorded as follows:

```
Machinery (new): $5,500 + $1,000............  6,500
Accumulated Depreciation (old machine)......  3,000
      Machinery (old)..........................       4,000
      Cash....................................       5,500
```

In the case of a loss, the new asset must be recorded at its cash equivalent price ($7,000). Assuming a book value of $2,000, a $500 loss would be recorded.[9]

On the other hand, if the assets exchanged are dissimilar, the cost of the new asset is its cash equivalent price under the cost principle. Because the trade allowance almost always is different from the book value of the old asset, a gain or loss on disposal of the old asset (by trade-in) will be reported. To illustrate, we will adapt the above example. Assume the old asset is an item of office equipment (say, an electronic computer) and the new asset is a dump truck. Clearly, they are dissimilar. The computer originally cost $4,000 and the accumulated depreciation is $3,000 (i.e., a book value of $1,000). The new dump truck has a cash equivalent cost of $7,000. The acquisition of the new truck and disposal of the computer by trade-in would be recorded:

```
Dump Truck (new).............................  7,000
Accumulated Depreciation (old computer)......  3,000
      Computer (old)...........................       4,000
      Cash....................................       5,500
      Gain on Disposal of Fixed Asset..........         500
   Purchase of new truck and removal from
   the accounts the original cost and the
   accumulated depreciation on the old asset
   traded in.
```

[8] APB *Opinion No. 29*, May 1973, par. 22.

[9] Under this opinion the asset acquired in an exchange should never be recorded at an amount greater than its cash equivalent price.

Computation of gain

Price received for the old machine:		
New machine..............................	$7,000	
Less cash paid...........................	5,500	$1,500
Book value of the old machine:		
Original cost.............................	4,000	
Less accumulated depreciation..............	3,000	1,000
Difference—gain on disposal..................		$ 500

Natural resources

A natural resource, such as a mineral deposit, oil well, or timber tract, often is referred to as a "wasting asset" since it is physically consumed, or **depleted,** as it is used. When acquired or developed, a natural resource is measured and recorded in the accounts in accordance with the cost principle. As the resource is consumed or used up, the acquisition cost, in accordance with the matching principle, must be apportioned to the periods in which the resulting revenues are recognized. The term **"depletion"** is used to describe this process of cost–assignment over the period of use of a natural resource. A **depletion rate** is computed by dividing the total acquisition and development cost by the *estimated* units that can be economically withdrawn from the resource. The depletion rate, thus computed, is then multiplied each period by the number of units actually withdrawn. To illustrate, assume that a gravel deposit was developed at a cost of $80,000 and that a reliable estimate was made that 100,000 tons of gravel could be economically withdrawn from it. The depletion rate would be computed as follows:

$$\$80,000 \div 100,000 \text{ tons} = \$.80 \text{ per ton (depletion rate)}$$

Depletion expense for the first year, assuming 5,000 tons of gravel were withdrawn during the year, would be recorded by means of the following adjusting entry:

```
Depletion Expense........................... 4,000
    Gravel Pit..............................        4,000
    Depletion for the year, 5,000 tons × $.80.
```

At the end of the first year, this natural resource should be reported as follows:

Fixed Assets:
    Gravel Pit (Cost $80,000 − $4,000 accumulated
        depletion).................................... $76,000

Because changes in the estimate of recoverable units from a natural resource are made frequently, the depletion rate must be revised often. This is a "change in estimate" rather than an error; hence, the undepleted acquisition cost is spread over the estimated remaining recoverable units. For example, assume in year 2 that the estimate of recoverable units remaining was changed from 95,000 to 150,000 tons. The depletion rate for year 2 would be:

$$(\$80,000 - \$4,000) \div 150,000 \text{ units} = \$.51 \text{ per ton}$$

When buildings and similar improvements are constructed in connection with the development and exploitation of a natural resource, they should be recorded in separate asset accounts and *depreciated*— not depleted—over the shorter of their estimated useful lives or the time required to exploit the natural resource.

Intangible assets

An intangible asset, like any other asset, has value because of certain rights and privileges conferred by law upon the owner of the asset. However, an intangible asset has no corporeal existence (i.e., no material or physical substance) as do tangible assets such as land and buildings. Thus, it is often said that intangible assets are characterized by their intangible nature and the special rights that ownership confers. Examples of intangible assets are patents, copyrights, franchises, licenses, trademarks, and goodwill.

An intangible asset may be acquired through purchase or by development within the company. For example, an entity may purchase a patent from someone else or it may develop a patent internally through its own efforts. In either case, the intangible asset has a cost that should be measured and recorded in the accounts and reported on the financial statements of the entity.

At acquisition, an intangible fixed asset is recorded at its cost in accordance with the cost principle. Cost is defined as the sum of all expenditures made to acquire or develop the rights or privileges. It sometimes is difficult to determine accurately the cost of an intangible asset that was developed internally. For example, the internal development of a patent by the research department of the company may have been intentional or accidental. There are numerous indirect costs incurred in a research department that would be difficult to realistically identify with a particular result such as a single patent. However, to the extent that such costs can be realistically identified with the patent, they should be measured and recorded as a part of the cost of the intangible asset.

Each intangible asset should be recorded in a separate asset account, at cost, when acquired. To illustrate, assume that on January 1, 1974, the Mason Company purchased a patent from its developer, John Doe, at a cash price of $1,700. The acquisition of this intangible asset would be recorded as follows:

```
Jan. 1, 1974  Patents...................... 1,700
                  Cash......................         1,700
              Purchase of patent rights
              from John Doe.
```

Under the cost principle, an intangible right or privilege, although it may have value, is not recorded unless there has been an identifiable expenditure of resources to acquire or develop it. For example, the demise of a competitor's patent may cause the company's patent to be more valuable. This increase in value would not be recorded since there was no expenditure of resources incident to it.

Amortization of intangibles

Intangible fixed assets normally have a limited life similar to tangible fixed assets; however, intangible assets seldom, if ever, have a residual value at the end of their useful life. Intangible assets have a limited life because the rights or privileges that give them value terminate or simply disappear. For example, a patent has a *legal* life of 17 years from the date it is granted; however, the right may cease to have utility, although still legally alive, before the end of the legal life. Therefore, the cost of a patent must be apportioned over its *economic life,* which cannot be longer than 17 years. The systematic write-off of the cost of an intangible asset over its economically useful life is referred to as amortization. To illustrate, assume the patent acquired by the Mason Company, recorded above, had an estimated ten-year remaining economic life. At the end of 1974 the adjusting entry to record amortization for one year would be:[10]

```
Dec. 31, 1974  Patent Expense.................... 170
               Patents......................         170
               Adjusting entry, to record
               amortization of patent over
               the estimated economic life
               of ten years.
```

The amount of patent amortization expense recorded for 1974 would be reported on the income statement as an expense. The patent would be reported on the balance sheet as follows on December 31, 1974:

Intangible assets:
    Patents (cost $1,700, less amortization)... $1,530

Formerly, certain kinds of intangibles, such as trademarks, were not amortized. In 1970, however, the APB recognized that all intangible assets, for all practical purposes, have a limited economic life and, to stop certain abuses, the APB issued *Opinion No. 17,* which requires that each intangible be amortized over the period of its benefit, which cannot exceed 40 years. The *Opinion* also precludes the arbitrary and immediate write-off of an intangible asset down to, say, a nominal amount

---

[10] Consistent with the procedure for recording depreciation, an Accumulated Amortization account may be used. However, as a matter of precedent, the Intangible Asset account itself generally is credited directly for the periodic amortization. Either procedure is acceptable.

of $1.00. Prior to *Opinion No. 17,* this sometimes was done under the guise of conservatism.

Although an intangible asset may be amortized by using any "systematic and rational" method that reflects the actual expiration of its economic usefulness, the straight-line method is used almost exclusively.

Copyrights. A copyright is similar to a patent. A copyright gives the owner the exclusive right to publish, use, and sell a literary, musical, or artistic piece of work for a period of 28 years (which can be renewed once). The same principles and procedures used in accounting for and reporting the cost of patents also are appropriate for copyrights.

Franchises and licenses. Franchises and licenses frequently are granted by governmental and other units for a specified period and purpose. For example, a city may grant one company a franchise to distribute gas to homes for heating purposes, or a company may sell franchises, such as Kentucky Fried Chicken, to local outlets. Franchises and licenses generally require the expenditure of resources by the franchisee to acquire them; therefore, they represent an intangible asset that should be accounted for as illustrated earlier for patents.

Leaseholds. Leasing is a common type of business contract whereby one party, the owner or lessor, for a consideration known as rent, extends to another party, the lessee, certain rights to use specified property. Leases may vary from simple arrangements, such as the month-to-month lease of an office or apartment or the daily rental of an automobile, to long-term leases having complex contractural arrangements. The rights granted to a lessee frequently are referred to as a leasehold.

In the case of long-term leases, a lump-sum advance rental payment sometimes is required. The advance payment is debited to an intangible asset account (frequently called Leaseholds) and is then amortized over the life of the lease. The true amount of annual rent expense includes the amortization of the leasehold; therefore, the annual amortization is debited to Rent Expense. To illustrate, assume that the Favor Company leased a building for its own use on January 1, 1974, under a five-year contract that required a payment in advance of $20,000. The advance payment would be recorded as follows:

```
Jan. 1, 1974  Leasehold (or Rent Paid
                 in Advance)................ 20,000
              Cash.....................          20,000
              Rent paid in advance.
```

At the end of 1974, and at the end of each of the remaining four years, the following adjusting entry would be made to reflect amortization of this intangible asset:[11]

---

[11] This discussion presumes the normal or operating type of lease. In some instances, a lease is in effect a sale/purchase agreement. Such leases, known as financing leases, involve complex accounting problems that are deferred to more advanced accounting books.

```
Dec. 31, 1974  Rent Expense................. 4,000
                   Leasehold (or Rent Paid
                     in Advance).............          4,000
                   Adjusting entry, to record
                   amortization of leasehold
                   over five years.
```

Leasehold improvements. In most instances, when buildings, improvements, or alterations are constructed by the lessee on leased property, they legally revert to the owner of the property at the end of the lease. The lessee has full use of such improvements during the term of the lease and they should be recorded in an intangible asset account entitled "Leasehold Improvements." These expenditures should be amortized over the estimated useful life of the improvement or the remaining life of the lease, whichever is shorter.

Goodwill. Generally, a successful business, if sold as a unit, will command a price somewhat in excess of the sum of the fair-market values of the recorded assets less the liabilities. The reason a business may command the excess price is that an intangible called goodwill attaches to a successful business. Goodwill represents the potential of a business to earn above a normal rate of profit on the recorded assets. It arises from such factors as customer confidence, reputation for dependability, efficiency or internal competencies, quality of goods and services, and financial standing. From the date of organization, a successful business is continually building goodwill. In this context, the goodwill is said to be "internally generated at no identifiable cost." On the other hand, when a business is purchased "lock, stock, and barrel," the purchase price presumably will include a payment for any goodwill that exists at that time. *In conformance with the cost principle, goodwill is recorded as an intangible asset only when it is actually purchased.* To illustrate, assume Richard Roe purchased the College Men's Store on January 1, 1975, for $200,000 cash. At date of purchase, it was determined that the recorded assets, which included no goodwill, had a total fair-market value of $160,000, comprised of inventory, $110,000; fixtures, $35,000; prepaid rent expense, $1,000; and other assets, $14,000. The purchase would be recorded by Roe as follows:

```
Jan. 1, 1975  Inventory.................. 110,000
                 Furniture and Fixtures.....  35,000
                 Prepaid Rent Expense.......   1,000
                 Other Assets..............  14,000
                 Goodwill..................  40,000
                     Cash.. ................           200,000
                 Purchase of College
                 Men's Store.
```

The intangible asset—goodwill—must be amortized over its estimated economic life but not to exceed 40 years (APB *Opinion No. 17*).

For convenience, assume a 40-year economic life. The amortization for 1975 would be recorded in an adjusting entry as follows:

```
Dec. 31, 1975  Goodwill Amortized (expense).. 1,000
                   Goodwill..................         1,000
               Adjusting entry, to record
               goodwill amortization for
               one year based on 40-year
               economic life.
```

Many other types of intangible assets may be observed in financial statements. Examples are formulas, processes, and film rights. These are not discussed in detail in this book since they are accounted for, and reported, as illustrated above.

Deferred charges

An asset category called deferred charges is reported occasionally on balance sheets. A deferred charge, like a prepaid expense, is an *expense paid in advance;* that is, goods or services are acquired that will be used to generate future revenues. A deferred charge is a long-term prepaid expense and, therefore, cannot be classified as a current asset. A prepaid expense is a short-term prepayment and, for this reason, is classified as a current asset.

Common examples of deferred charges are bond issuance costs (Chapter 11), start-up costs, organization costs, plant rearrangement costs, and research and development costs. In conformance with the matching principle, deferred charges are amortized to expense each period over the number of future periods benefited.

Demonstration case for self-study

DIVERSIFIED INDUSTRIES, INCORPORATED

(Try to resolve the requirements before turning to the suggested solution that follows.)

Diversified Industries, Incorporated, has been in operation for a number of years. It started as a construction firm and in recent years has expanded into a number of related activities. For example, in addition to heavy construction, its operations include ready-mix concrete, sand and gravel, construction supplies, and earth-moving services.

The transactions given below were selected from those completed during 1974. They focus on the primary issues discussed in this chapter. Amounts have been simplified for case purposes.

Jan. 1, 1974: The management decided to purchase a building that was approximately ten years old. The location was excellent and there was adequate parking space. The company bought the building and the land on which it was situated for $300,000 cash, plus $5,000 for title costs, legal fees, and other costs incidental to the purchase. A reliable appraiser appraised the property at the following fair-market values: land, $136,500; building, $188,500.

Jan. 12, 1974: Paid renovation costs on the building amounting to $38,100.

June 19, 1974: Purchased a third location (designated No. 3) for a gravel pit at a cost of $50,000 cash. The location had been carefully surveyed and it was estimated that 100,000 square yards of gravel could be removed from the deposit.

June 30, 1974: Paid $20,000 to a professor from the local university for the completion of a research contract. The research was to develop an improved concrete mix to be used primarily for high-rise construction. The results look good; therefore, the company will offer a new line of ready-mix. It is estimated that this line will bring in additional revenue over the next five years.

July 10, 1974: Paid $1,200 ordinary repairs on the building.

Aug. 1, 1974: Paid $10,000 for costs of preparing the gravel pit, acquired in June 1974, for exploitation.

Dec. 31, 1974 (end of the annual accounting period). The following data were developed as a basis for the adjusting entries:

   a.   The building will be depreciated on a straight-line basis over an estimated useful life of 30 years. The estimated residual value is $35,000.

   b.   During 1974, 12,000 square yards of gravel were removed from gravel pit No. 3. Use an Accumulated Depletion account.

   c.   The research and development costs will be amortized over the next five years. Assume one-half year for 1974.

   d.   The company owns a patent right that is utilized in operations. The Patent account on Jan. 1, 1974, reflected a balance of $3,300. The patent has an estimated remaining life of six years (including 1974).

Required:

   (a)   Give the journal entries for the transactions completed during 1974.

   (b)   Give the adjusting entries on December 31, 1974.

   (c)   Show the classification and amount for each of the following items as they should be reflected on the balance sheet, December 31, 1974: land, building, gravel pit, patent, and deferred research and development costs.

Suggested Solution:

Requirement (a)   Entries during 1974:

Jan. 1, 1974	Land (building site)............................	128,100	
	Building....................................	176,900	
	Cash....................................		305,000

Allocation of purchase price based on appraisal:

Item	Appraisal Value	Percent	Computation	Allocation
Land...........	$136,500	42%	× $305,000 =	$128,100
Building........	188,500	58%	× 305,000 =	176,900
Totals........	$325,000	100		$305,000

Jan. 12, 1974	Building...................................	38,100	
	Cash....................................		38,100
	Renovation costs on building.		
June 19, 1974	Gravel Pit (#3).............................	50,000	
	Cash....................................		50,000
	Purchased gravel pit; estimated production, 100,000 square yards.		
June 30, 1974	Deferred Research and Development Costs......	20,000	
	Cash....................................		20,000
	Payment on research contract; deferred to match with future revenues.		
July 10, 1974	Repair Expense.............................	1,200	
	Cash....................................		1,200
Aug. 1, 1974	Gravel Pit (#3).............................	10,000	
	Cash....................................		10,000
	Development costs.		

Requirement (b)   Adjusting entries, December 31, 1974:

(a)	Depreciation Expense, Building........................	6,000	
	Accumulated Depreciation........................		6,000

Computation:

Cost ($176,900 + $38,100).................	$215,000	
Less: Residual value.....................	35,000	
Cost to be depreciated..................	$180,000	

Annual depreciation: $180,000 ÷ 30 years = $6,000

(b)	Depletion Expense.......................................	7,200	
	Accumulated Depletion Gravel Pit (#3)...............		7,200

Computation:

Cost ($50,000 + $10,000)...............	$60,000	
Depletion rate:		
$60,000 ÷ 100,000 yards =	$.60	
Depletion expense:		
$.60 × 12,000 yards =	$ 7,200	

(c)	Research and Development Expense.......................	2,000	
	Deferred Research and Development Costs............		2,000

Computation:

$$\$20,000 \div 5 \text{ years} = \$4,000 \text{ per year}$$
$$\text{For 1974: } \$4,000 \times \tfrac{1}{2} = \$2,000.$$

(d) Patent Expense................................... 550
       Patent...   550

Computation:

$$\$3,300 \div 6 \text{ years} = \$550$$

Requirement (c)   Balance Sheet, December 31, 1974:

Assets

Fixed assets:
  Land......................... $128,100
  Building..................... $215,000
  Less: Accumulated deprecia-
    tion.......................   6,000   209,000
  Gravel pit...................   60,000
  Less: Accumulated depletion..   7,200   52,800
    Total Fixed Assets....... $389,900
Intangibles:
  Patent ($3,300 − $550)........   2,750
Deferred charges:
  Deferred research and develop-
    ment costs ($20,000 − $2,000).   18,000

Summary

This chapter focused on accounting for operational assets. These are the noncurrent assets that a business retains more-or-less permanently, not for sale, but for use in the course of normal operations. They include fixed assets and intangible assets. At acquisition, operational assets are measured and recorded in the accounts at cost, in conformity with the cost principle. Cost includes the purchase price plus all reasonable and necessary incidental expenditures made in acquiring the asset.

An operational asset is, in nature, a bundle of future services and benefits that has been paid for in advance. As an operational asset is used, this bundle of benefits gradually is used up in the generation of revenue. Therefore, in accordance with the matching principle the prepayment of cost is apportioned to periodic expense over the periods benefited. In this way the expense associated with operational assets is matched with the revenues generated. This apportionment process is known as depreciation in the case of plant, equipment, and furniture; as depletion in the case of natural resources; and as amortization in the case of intangibles.

Four methods of depreciation are used: straight-line, productive output, sum-of-the-years'-digits, and double-declining balance depreciation.

Expenditures after acquisition of a fixed asset are classified either as:

(1)   Capital expenditures—those that provide benefits for one or more periods beyond the current period; consequently, they

are debited to an asset account and depreciated, depleted, or amortized over their useful life; or as

(2) Revenue expenditures—those that provide benefits during the current period only; consequently, they are debited to appropriate current expense accounts when incurred.

Ordinary repairs and maintenance costs are revenue expenditures, whereas extraordinary repairs and additions are capital expenditures.

Operational assets may be disposed of voluntarily by sale or retirement, or involuntarily through casualty, such as storm, fire, or accident. Upon disposal, such assets must be depreciated, depleted, or amortized up to the date of disposal. The disposal transaction is recorded by removing the cost of the old asset and the related accumulated depreciation, depletion, or amortization amount from the accounts. Normally, a loss or gain on disposal of an operational asset will result since the disposal price generally is different from the book value of the old asset.

Important terms		
Operational assets		**Ordinary repairs**
Fixed assets		**Extraordinary repairs**
Natural resources		**Straight-line depreciation**
Intangible assets		**Productive-output depreciation**
Depreciation		**Sum-of-years'-digits depreciation**
Depletion		**Double-declining balance**
Amortization		**depreciation**
Basket purchase		**Leaseholds**
Residual value		**Deferred charges**

Questions for discussion

1. Define operational assets. Explain how they may be considered to be a "bundle of future services."

2. What are the classifications of operational assets? Briefly explain each.

3. Relate accounting for operational assets to the cost principle.

4. Relate accounting for operational assets to the matching principle.

5. Define and illustrate the book value of a fixed asset.

6. Under the cost principle, what amounts should be included in the acquisition cost of a fixed asset?

7. What is a "basket purchase"? What measurement problem does it pose?

8. Briefly distinguish between: depreciation, depletion, and amortization.

9. In computing depreciation, three values must be known; identify and explain the nature of each.

10. Estimated useful life and residual value of a fixed asset relate to the current owner or user rather than to all users. Explain.

11. What kind of a depreciation-expense pattern is provided under the straight-line method? When would its use be particularly appropriate?

12. What kind of depreciation-expense pattern emerges under the productive-output method? When would its use be particularly appropriate?

13. What are the arguments in favor of accelerated depreciation?

14. What kind of depreciation-expense pattern emerges under the accelerated methods? When would their use be particularly appropriate?

15. Explain how monthly depreciation should be computed using the sum-of-the-years'-digits method for an asset having a ten-year life.

16. Over what period should an addition or enlargement to an existing fixed asset be depreciated? Explain.

17. Distinguish between a capital expenditure and a revenue expenditure and give an example of each.

18. Distinguish between ordinary and extraordinary repairs. How is each accounted for?

19. Define an intangible asset.

20. An intangible asset may be acquired through purchase or developed internally. Explain.

21. Prepare a matrix like the one below and enter checks to indicate the appropriate classification.

	Subject to Normal:		
Fixed Asset	*Amortization*	*Depreciation*	*Depletion*
a. Plant site (in use)			
b. Patent			
c. Plant building			
d. Trademark			
e. Machinery			
f. Franchise			
g. Goodwill			
h. Research and development costs			
i. Leasehold			
j. Mineral deposits			

22. Define goodwill. When is it appropriate to record goodwill as an intangible asset?

23. Distinguish between a leasehold and a leasehold improvement.
24. Over what period should a leasehold improvement be amortized? Explain.

Exercises   E9–1. Prepare a matrix like the one below and enter check marks to indicate the appropriate responses.

Asset	Usually Subject to			None of these
	Amortization	Depreciation	Depletion	
a. Land				
b. Patent				
c. Building				
d. Cash				
e. Oil well				
f. Trademark				
g. Goodwill				
h. Leasehold				
i. Franchise				
j. Plant site in use				
k. Copyright				
l. Investment in common stock				
m. Mineral deposit				
n. Machinery				
o. License right				
p. Research and development costs				
q. Leasehold improvements				
r. Timber tract				
s. Tools				
t. Gravel pit				
u. Organization costs				

E9–2. A machine was purchased by X Company on March 1, 1974, at an invoice price of $15,000; terms 2/20, n/60. On date of delivery, March 3, 1974, X Company paid $9,800 on the machine. On March 5, 1974, $500 was paid for freight and installation costs relating to the machine. On March 18, 1974, X Company paid the $4,900 balance due on the machine.

Required:

a. Give journal entries on each of the above dates through March 18.
b. Give the adjusting entry for straight-line depreciation at the end of 1974, assuming an estimated useful life of ten years and a net residual value of $3,200. Depreciate to the nearest month. The fiscal period ends December 31, 1974.

E9–3. The RT Company purchased two machines for a total cash price of $8,600. In addition, they paid transportation costs on the machines of $200. Installation and renovation costs amounted to: machine A, $300; machine B, $600. An independent appraiser provided fair-market values of: machine A, $4,000; machine B, $6,000. A separate fixed asset account is to be set up for each machine.

Required:

a. Apportion the price, plus the transportation, to the two machines on the basis of the appraised values. Show computations.
b. Give the entry to record the purchase of the two machines, including all expenditures. Assume all expenditures were cash.

E9–4. The K Corporation purchased a machine at a cost of $310. The estimated useful life was four years and the residual value $10. Assume that the estimated productive life of the machine is 30,000 units and each year's production was: Year 1, 10,000 units; year 2, 7,000 units; year 3, 5,000 units; and year 4, 8,000 units.

Determine the amount for each cell in the following table. Show your computations.

| | Depreciation Expense | | | |
Year	Straight-Line	Productive-Output	Sum-of-the-Years'-Digits	Double-Declining Balance
1				
2				
3				
4				
Total				

E9–5.   The AV Company purchased a machine that cost $10,000. The estimated useful life was five years and the residual value $1,000. Assume the estimated useful life in productive units to be 45,000. Units actually produced were: Year 1, 8,000; year 2, 11,000. Determine the appropriate amounts for the table below. Show your computations.

	Depreciation Expense		Book Value at End of:	
Method of Depreciation	*Year 1*	*Year 2*	*Year 1*	*Year 2*
Straight-line..................	————	————	————	————
Productive-output.............	————	————	————	————
Sum-of-the-years'-digits........	————	————	————	————
Double-declining balance......	————	————	————	————

E9–6.   The AVCO Company acquired a machine that cost $480 on January 1, 1974. The estimated useful life is four years with no residual value. The machine is to be depreciated on a monthly basis. Compute depreciation expense for January 1974 and January 1975, assuming (a) the straight-line method and (b) the SYD method.

E9–7.   The Blue Company owns an existing building that was constructed at an original cost of $68,000. It is being depreciated on a straight-line basis over a 20-year estimated useful life and an $8,000 estimated residual value. At the end of 1973, the building was one-half depreciated. In January 1974, an addition to the existing building was completed at a cash cost of $11,000. It is estimated that this addition will last for the remaining life of the existing structure and will add $1,000 to the residual value.

Required:

a.   Give the entry to record completion of the addition in January 1974.
b.   Compute the amount of depreciation that should be recorded in 1974, assuming the annual accounting period ends December 31. Show computations.
c.   Give the adjusting entry for depreciation at December 31, 1974.

E9–8.   The Daley Company operates a small manufacturing facility as a supplement to its regular service activities. At the beginning of 1974, a fixed asset account for the company showed the following balances:

Manufacturing equipment....................	$62,000
Accumulated depreciation through 1973	
(10 years)................................	(40,000)

During 1974 the following expenditures were incurred for repairs and maintenance:

(1)	Routine maintenance and repairs on the equipment.........................	$ 800
(2)	Complete overhaul of the equipment..........	$4,000

The equipment is being depreciated on a straight-line basis over 15 years with a $2,000 estimated residual value. The annual accounting period ends on December 31.

Required:

a. Give the adjusting entry for depreciation for the manufacturing equipment that was made at the end of 1973.

b. Give the entries to appropriately record the two expenditures for repairs and maintenance during 1974.

c. Give the adjusting entry to be made at the end of 1974 for depreciation of the manufacturing equipment, assuming no change in the estimated life or residual value. Show computations.

E9–9. Prepare a matrix like the one below and enter check marks to indicate the appropriate classification.

		Type of Expenditure		
	Item	Capital	Revenue	Neither
a.	Paid $500 for ordinary repairs			
b.	Paid $6,000 for extraordinary repairs			
c.	Addition to old building; paid cash, $10,000			
d.	Routine maintenance; cost, $300; on credit			
e.	Purchased a machine, $6,000; gave long-term note			
f.	Paid $2,000 for organization costs			
g.	Paid three-year insurance premium, $600			
h.	Purchased a patent, $3,400 cash			
i.	Paid $10,000 for monthly salaries			

E9–10. The ST Company sold a large truck for cash and the records of the company reflected the following:

Delivery truck........................	$4,000
Accumulated depreciation..............	(3,000)

Required:

a. Give the entry for disposal of the truck, assuming the sales price was $1,000.

    b.   Give the same entry but assume that the sales price was $600.

    c.   Give the same entry but assume that the sales price was $1,400.

E9–11.   The records of the Mason Company on January 1, 1974, reflected the following data in respect to a particular machine:

> Machine, original cost $17,000
> Accumulated depreciation 9,000*
>   * Based on a five-year estimated useful life and a $2,000
> residual value.

On May 1, 1974, the machine was sold for $7,100 cash. The accounting period ends on December 31.

Required:

    a.   How old was the machine on January 1, 1974? Show computations.

    b.   Give entry, or entries, incident to the sale of the machine. (Hint: Record depreciation to May 1.)

    c.   Give entry, or entries, incident to the sale of the machine assuming the price was $6,900.

E9–12.   The records of the Carter Company reflected the following data in respect to a fixed asset:

> Delivery truck (at cost) $3,600
> Accumulated depreciation . . . . (2,800)

The company decided to purchase a new truck; the dealer demonstrated a truck that was suitable to the needs. The new truck had a list price of $4,500. However, the cash price without a trade-in was $4,200. The dealer required a cash payment of $3,200 in addition to the old asset.

Required:

    a.   Give the entry to record the exchange assuming similar assets.

    b.   Give the adjusting entry for depreciation on the new truck for the first year after acquisition assuming a six-year useful life and a 10% residual value.

    c.   Give the entry to record the exchange, assuming the two assets were dissimilar.

E9–13.   In February, 1974, Kleen Extractive Industries paid $200,000 for a mineral deposit. During the next March, $40,000 was spent in preparing the deposit for exploitation. It was estimated that 400,000 tons could be extracted economically. During 1974, 12,000 tons were extracted. During January 1975, another $17,200 was spent for additional developmental work. After conclusion of the latest work, the estimated recovery was increased to 500,000 tons over the remaining life. By the end of 1975, 30,000 tons had been exploited during the year.

Required:

Give the appropriate journal entry at the following dates:
a. February 1974 for acquisition of the deposit.
b. March 1974 for developmental costs.
c. Year 1974 for annual depletion (show computations).
d. January 1975 for developmental costs.
e. Year 1975 for annual depletion (show computations).

E9–14. The Pride Manufacturing Company owns two patents, which are utilized in the manufacturing activities. The patents were acquired as follows:

Patent No. 1—Purchased from James Smith on January 1, 1974, for a cash cost of $4,080. Smith had registered the patent with the U.S. Patent Office on January 1, 1969. Amortize over remaining legal life.

Patent No. 2—During 1973, two employees of the company developed this patent for the company, which was registered on January 1, 1974. The company identified the following costs incurred in development and registration: salaries, $30,000; facilities used and overhead, $5,000; and registration costs, $1,000. These costs were accumulated during 1973 in an account entitled "Deferred R&D Costs." It is estimated that this patent will have a useful economic life of 15 years; the legal life is 17 years.

Required:

a. Give entry to record each patent as an intangible fixed asset. Provide a brief explanation with the entries.
b. Give adjusting entry at December 31, 1974, for amortization of each patent. Show computations.

E9–15. The Royal Company is in the process of preparing the balance sheet at December 31, 1974. The following are to be included:

Prepaid insurance	$ 300
Investment in common stock of X Corporation, at cost	1,000 (market $1,200)
Patent (at cost)	3,400
Accumulated amortization of patents	800
Accounts receivable	20,000
Allowance for doubtful accounts	600
Franchise (at cost)	1,000
Accumulated amortization of franchises	300
Deferred research and development costs (unamortized)	4,000
Organization costs deferred	2,000

Required:

Show how each of the above assets would be reflected on the balance sheet under Assets. Use the following subcaptions: Current Assets,

Funds and Investments, Fixed Assets, Intangible Assets, Deferred Charges, and Other Assets. The company prefers to use the "accumulated" accounts as listed above.

(Hint: Intangible assets sum to $33,000 on the balance sheet.)

E9–16. The Z Company has three intangibles that are to be accounted for during 1975. The relevant facts are:

1. On January 1, 1975, the company purchased a patent from R. Baker for $2,550 cash. Baker had developed the patent and registered it with the Patent Office on January 1, 1973. Amortize over the remaining legal life.

2. On January 1, 1975, the company completed development of an item that was copyrighted immediately. The developmental costs were $2,800 and the legal life was 28 years. The company executives estimated that the copyright would be of no value by the end of 20 years. To simplify, credit Cash at this date for the cost.

3. The Z Company purchased another small company in January 1975 at a cash cost of $50,000. Included in the purchase price was $8,000 for goodwill, the balance being for plant, equipment, and fixtures. Amortize the goodwill over the maximum period permitted.

Required:

a. Give the entry to record the acquisition of each of the intangibles.

b. Give the adjusting entry that would be required at the end of the annual accounting period, December 31, 1975, in respect to each intangible. Include a brief explanation and computations.

E9–17. The T Company conducts operations in several different localities. In order to expand into still another city, the company obtained a ten-year lease, starting January 1, 1974, on a very good downtown location. Although there was a serviceable building on the property, the company had to construct an additional structure to be used for storage purposes. The ten-year lease required a $10,000 cash advance payment, plus cash payments of $2,000 per month during occupancy. During January 1974, the T Company spent $30,000 cash constructing the additional structure. The new structure has an estimated life of 12 years with no residual value.

Required:

a. Give the entry for the T Company to record the payment of the $10,000 advance on January 1, 1974.

b. Give the entry to record the construction of the new structure.

c. Give any adjusting entries required at the end of the annual accounting period for the T Company on December 31, 1974, in respect to: (1) the advance payment and (2) the new structure. Show computations.

Problems P9–1.   The Baker Company purchased three used machines for a cash price of $24,500. Transportation costs on the machines amounted to $500. The machines were immediately overhauled, installed, and started operating. Since the machines were essentially different, each had to be recorded separately in the accounts. An appraiser was employed to "estimate their fair-market value at date of purchase." The appraisal results, installation costs, and renovation expenditures were:

	Machine A	Machine B	Machine C
Appraised value...................	$6,000	$15,000	$9,000
Installation costs..................	200	300	100
Renovation costs..................	800	500	600

Required:

a.   Compute the cost of each machine by making an allocation based upon the appraised values.

b.   Give the journal entry to record the purchase of the three machines assuming all payments were cash. Set up a separate fixed asset account for each machine.

P9–2.   The AT Company purchased a machine that cost $40,000. The estimated useful life is ten years and the estimated residual value is 10% of cost. The machine has an estimated useful life in productive output of 120,000 units. Actual output was: year 1, 10,000; year 2, 15,000.

Determine the appropriate amounts for the table below. Show your computations.

	Depreciation Expense		Book Value at end of:	
Depreciation Method	*Year 1*	*Year 2*	*Year 1*	*Year 2*
Straight-line................	$_____	$_____	$_____	$_____
Productive-output............	_____	_____	_____	_____
Sum-of-the-years'-digits.......	_____	_____	_____	_____
Double declining-balance.....	_____	_____	_____	_____

P9–3.   The Scott Company purchased a machine that cost $920. The estimated useful life was three years and the residual value $20. The management is considering several depreciation methods and is concerned about the choice of a method. You have been asked to prepare a table that will reflect the relevant income statement and balance sheet amounts over the life of the machine. Accordingly, you have designed the following table:

Comparison of Depreciation Methods

	Relevant Amounts		
Depreciation Methods and Effects	*Year 1*	*Year 2*	*Year 3*
Straight-line:			
Depreciation expense on income statement.....			
Net amount reported on balance sheet........			
Productive-output: (a)			
Depreciation expense on income statement.....			
Net amount reported on balance sheet........			
Sum-of-the-years'-digits:			
Depreciation expense on income statement.....			
Net amount reported on balance sheet........			
Double-declining balance depreciation:			
Depreciation expense on income statement.....			
Net amount reported on balance sheet........			

(a) Additional data:

      Estimated useful life in productive output: 30,000 units.
      Actual productive output assumed: Year 1, 8,000; year 2,
      13,000; year 3, 9,000.

Required:

    Determine the appropriate amounts for each line for the three years in the table above. Show computations.

P9–4. The Richards Company, on January 1, 1974, acquired a machine that cost $1,850. The machine had an estimated useful life of five years and a net residual value of $350. The machine is to be depreciated on a monthly basis starting January 1974. Monthly depreciation is computed as a proportional part of the annual amount. Round to even dollars.

Required:

a. Give the adjusting journal entry for monthly depreciation at the end of January 1974 and January 1975 under (1) straight-line, (2) SYD, and (3) double-declining balance.

b. Below the entries show your computations of the monthly amount for each entry.

    (Hint: Depreciation expenses for January, straight-line method, is $25.)

P9–5. The Janes Manufacturing Company was organized a number of years ago by Mr. R. C. Janes. It is a local manufacturer of seat covers, floor mats, and similar items for automobiles and boats. There are two manufacturing operations: one does custom work, the other manufactures standard items that are distributed through retail channels in a number of states. In January 1971, the company purchased land, including a building that was approximately 15 years old, at a cost of $200,000. Transfer costs, surveys, appraisals, titles, and legal fees amounted to another $18,000.

    The property was appraised, at acquisition date, for loan purposes, with the following results: land, $81,600; building, $158,400; estimated remaining life, 20 years; estimated residual value, $20,000.

In January 1973, major renovations on the building were completed at a cost of $86,120. The estimated remaining life of the building after renovation was 22 years, and the estimated residual value was the same as before, $20,000.

Straight-line depreciation is to be used and a full years' depreciation for 1971, 1972, and 1973 seemed reasonable since the property was put to use immediately.

Required:

a. Give the entry to record the fixed asset in January 1971. Show computations.
b. Give the adjusting entry for depreciation on December 31, 1971. Show computations.
c. Give entry to record the renovation in January 1973.
d. Give the adjusting entry for depreciation on December 31, 1973. Show computations.
   (Hint: Depreciation expense is $8,982.)

P9–6. The North Company found it necessary to do some extensive repairs on its existing building and to add a new wing suitable for use during the next 10 years. The existing building originally cost $100,-000, and, by the end of 1973, it was one-half depreciated on the basis of a 20-year useful life and no residual value. During 1974 the following expenditures were made that were related to the building:

1. Ordinary repairs and maintenance expenditures for the year, $8,500 cash.
2. Extensive and major repairs to the roof of the building, $10,000 cash. These repairs were completed on June 30, 1974.
3. The new wing was completed on June 30, 1974, at a cash cost of $37,500.

Required:

a. Record each of the above transactions during 1974.
b. Give the adjusting entry that would be required at the end of the annual accounting period, December 31, 1974, for the building after taking into account your entries in a above. Assume straight-line depreciation. The company computes depreciation to the nearest month.
c. Show how the assets would be reported on the December 31, 1974, balance sheet.
   (Hint: The book value of the building is $90,000.)

P9–7. The Kyle Manufacturing Company operates a number of machines. One particular bank of machines consists of five identical machines acquired at the same date. At the beginning of 1975 the fixed asset account for the five machines showed the following:

Machinery (Type A, 5 machines)...................... $160,000
Accumulated depreciation (Type A machine)........... 105,000*

*Based on ten-year estimated useful life and $2,000 residual value per machine.

One of the Type A machines was disposed of on September 1, 1975.

Required:

a. How old were the Type A machines at the end of 1974? Show computations.
b. What was the book value of the machine at the date of disposal? Show computations. The company computes depreciation to even months.
c. Give entry, or entries, incidental to disposal of the machine, assuming:
   1. It was sold for $7,000 cash.
   2. It was exchanged for a new machine having a list price of $44,000 and a cash-equivalent price of $40,000. A trade-in allowance of $11,000 was agreed upon and the balance of $33,000 was paid in cash. Assume the machines were similar.

P9–8. During 1974, the Dowd Company disposed of three different assets. On January 1, 1974, prior to their disposal, the accounts reflected the following:

Assets	Original Cost	Residual Value	Estimated Life	Accumulated Depreciation (straight-line)
Machine A.........	$20,000	$2,000	10 years	$12,600 (7 years)
Machine B.........	35,400	3,000	9 years	21,600 (6 years)
Machine C.........	65,200	6,000	14 years	59,200 (14 years)

The machines were disposed of in the following ways:

Machine A: Sold on January 1, 1974, for $6,500 cash.
Machine B: Exchanged for a new machine of similar type on May 1, 1974. The new machine had a list price of $48,000 and a cash equivalent price of $45,000. A trade-in allowance of $18,000 was agreed upon and the balance was paid in cash, $30,000.
Machine C: On January 2, 1974, this machine suffered irreparable damage from an accident. On January 10, 1974, it was given to a salvage company at no cost. The salvage company agreed to remove the machine immediately at no cost to Dowd.

Required:

1. List each machine and its book value on the date of disposal. Show computations. The company computes depreciation to even months.
2. Give all entries incident to the disposal of each machine. Provide a short explanation of each entry.

P9–9.   The Cleary Company has six different intangible assets to be accounted for and reported on the financial statements. At issue is a decision by the management in respect to the amortization of the cost of each of the six intangibles. Certain facts concerning each intangible are:

(1)   Patent—The company purchased a patent for a cash cost of $23,800 on January 1, 1974. The patent had a legal life of 17 years from date of registration with the U.S. Patent Office, which was January 1, 1971. Amortize over the remaining legal life.

(2)   Copyright—The company developed an item at a cost of $5,600 and it was copyrighted on January 1, 1974. The legal life from that date is 28 years. It is estimated that the copyrighted item will have little or no value by the end of 20 years. To simplify, credit Cash for the cost.

(3)   Franchise—The company obtained a franchise from the X Company to make and distribute a special item. The franchise was obtained on January 1, 1974, at a cash cost of $2,000 and was for a ten-year period.

(4)   License—The company secured a license on January 1, 1974, from the city to operate a special service for a period of five years. Total cash expended in obtaining the license was $5,000.

(5)   Goodwill—The Cleary Company started business in January 1972 by purchasing the assets of another business for a cash lump sum of $300,000. Included in the purchase price was the item "Goodwill, $80,000." Cleary executives believe that "the goodwill is an important long-term asset to us." Amortize over maximum period permitted.

(6)   Organization costs—The Cleary Company is a corporation and was organized in January 1972 to purchase the company mentioned in (5) above. During organization, $3,000 was expended for legal, accounting, charter, and other organizational activities. Debit a deferred charge and amortize over five years.

Required:

a.   Give the entry for each of the acquisitions.

b.   Give the adjusting entry for each intangible asset that would be necessary at the end of the annual accounting period, December 31, 1974. Provide a brief explanation and show computations. If no entry is required for a particular item, explain the basis for your conclusion.

c.   Determine the book value of each intangible on January 1, 1975.

(Hint: The total book value for the six intangibles is $108,420.)

P9–10.   On January 1, 1974 the Perdue Corporation was organized by five individuals for the purpose of purchasing and operating a very successful business known as The Quality Store. The name was retained and all of the assets, except cash, were purchased for $200,-

000 cash. The liabilities were not assumed by Perdue Corporation. The transaction was closed on January 5, 1974, at which time the balance sheet of The Quality Store reflected the book values shown below:

THE QUALITY STORE
January 5, 1974

	Book Value	Fair-Market Value*
Accounts Receivable (net)............	$ 30,000	$ 30,000
Inventory........................	100,000	100,000
Fixed Assets (net).................	9,000	25,000
Other Assets......................	1,000	5,000
Total Assets................	$140,000	
Liabilities........................	$ 35,000	
Owners' Equity....................	105,000	
	$140,000	

* These values for the assets purchased were provided to the Perdue Corporation by an independent appraiser.

As a part of the negotiations, the former owners of The Quality Store agreed not to engage in the same or similar line of business in the same general region.

Required:

a. Give the entry by the Perdue Corporation to record the purchase of the assets of The Quality Store by the Perdue Corporation. Include the goodwill.

b. Give the adjusting entries that would be made by the Perdue Corporation at the end of the annual accounting period, December 31, 1974, for:

   (a) Depreciation of the fixed assets (straight-line), assuming an estimated remaining useful life of 20 years and no residual value.

   (b) Amortization of goodwill assuming a 40-year amortization period.

10 Measurement and reporting of liabilities

Purpose
of the
chapter A business generates or receives resources from three distinct sources: contributions by owners, extension of credit by creditors, and through the sale of goods and services. Creditors provide resources to the business through cash loans and by providing property, goods, and services to the entity on credit. These borrowing activities create for the entity liabilities to various creditors. *Liabilities can be defined as legal obligations that result from transactions requiring the future payment of assets or the future performance of services, which are definite as to amount or are subject to reasonable estimation. Liabilities generally have a definite and known payment date known as the maturity or due date.*

From the point of view of the user of the financial statements, the liabilities, reported on the balance sheet, and the expense incurred from borrowing funds (i.e., interest expense), reported on the income statement, often are important factors in evaluating the financial performance of the entity. Usually there are a number of different kinds of liabilities and a wide range of creditors; therefore, those interested in the business necessarily must rely on the financial statements for relevant information on this important facet of the financial activities of an entity. The accounting model, coupled with the audit made by an independent accountant, provides the user with a good level of confidence that all liabilities are identified, properly measured, and fully reported.

This chapter focuses on the measurement and reporting problems associated with the various classifications of liabilities. Throughout this chapter the discussions will emphasize (1) identification of liabilities,

338

(2) measurement of the amount of each liability, (3) accounting for the various types of liabilities, and (4) appropriate reporting. The chapter is divided into two parts: Part One discusses the accounting for liabilities; and Part Two focuses on an important concept in the measurement of liabilities, present and future value.

PART ONE: ACCOUNTING FOR LIABILITIES

Although there are various ways to classify liabilities, for accounting and reporting purposes the following classifications are widely recognized:

1. Current liabilities
   a. Accounts payable
   b. Short-term notes payable
   c. Other short-term obligations
2. Long-term liabilities
   a. Long-term notes payable and mortgages
   b. Bonds payable
   c. Other long-term obligations

Bonds payable will be discussed in Chapter 11. Each of the other classifications will be separately discussed and illustrated in this chapter.

Measurement of liabilities

Identification of the liabilities of an entity at the balance-sheet date generally is not difficult for the accountant; however, aside from identification, the problem of **measurement** of the amount of each liability may be more complex. Conceptually, the amount of a liability, at any point in time, is the present value of the future outlays of assets required to pay the liability in full; that is, the present value of the principal plus all future interest payments. This present value amount may be called the current cash equivalent amount.[1] A liability that requires the "going rate of interest" will always have a present value equal to its maturity amount. However, when the required rate of interest is different from the going rate, or interest is unspecified, the present value will be different from the maturity amount. As such liabilities approach maturity or due date the present value, or current cash equivalent amount, approaches the maturity amount. These concepts are discussed and illustrated in Part Two.

---

[1] Some persons find it useful to think of the current cash-equivalent amount of a liability as the figure that the two parties (the debtor and the creditor) that are involved would settle the obligation for at a given date (between the beginning and due date) on a fair and equitable basis. This figure may be constant over the life of the debt, as in the case of an interest-bearing note. In the case of a bond payable, issued at a discount or premium, the cash equivalent amount would be different each date (see Chapter 11).

Fundamentally, liabilities are measured in accordance with the *cost principle*. That is, the amount of a liability, when initially incurred, is equivalent to the cost value of the resources received when the transaction occurred. Although the amount of most liabilities is definitely specified in the initial transaction (such as in a note payable), there are situations where a liability is known to exist but the exact amount is not determinable until a later date. For example, television sets may be sold with a one-year guarantee against defects. For the vendor, the guarantee creates a liability, the actual amount of which depends on the performance of the sets during the year. Thus, liabilities can be said to be comprised of known obligations of a definite amount and known obligations of an estimated amount.

Current liabilities

Current liabilities are short-term obligations that will be paid within the current operating cycle of the business or within one year of the balance-sheet date, whichever is the longer. Thus, the definition presumes that current liabilities will be paid with current assets.[2]

An important financial relationship on the balance sheet is known as working capital. Working capital is the dollar difference between total current assets and total current liabilities. The relationship between current assets and current liabilities also is measured as the *working capital* ratio or, as it is sometimes called, the current ratio. The current ratio is computed by dividing total current assets by total current liabilities. To illustrate, assume the balance sheet for the XY Company on December 31, 1974, reported total current assets of $900,000 and total current liabilities of $300,000. The amount of working capital would be $900,000 − $300,000 = $600,000. The current ratio would be: $900,000 ÷ $300,000 = 3.00, or 3 to 1. That is, at balance-sheet date, for each $1 of current liabilities there were $3 of current assets. These relationships often assist creditors in assessing the ability of a company to meet its short-term maturing obligations.[3]

Current liabilities commonly encountered are trade accounts payable, short-term notes payable, accrued liabilities (such as wages payable, taxes payable, and interest payable), cash dividends payable, and revenues collected in advance (i.e., deferred revenues).

---

[2] Current assets and current liabilities were defined and discussed in Chapter 4. Current assets are defined as cash and other resources reasonably expected to be realized in cash or sold or consumed within one year from the date of the balance sheet or during the *normal operating cycle,* whichever is the longer. Current liabilities are defined as those liabilities normally to be paid out of the current assets as reported on the balance sheet. The AICPA Committee on Accounting Procedure defines current liabilities as follows: The term "current liabilities" is used principally to designate obligations whose liquidation is reasonably expected to require the use of existing resources properly classifiable as current assets, or the creation of other current liabilities.

[3] Interpretation of financial ratios is discussed in Chapter 16.

ACCOUNTS PAYABLE

Trade accounts payable were discussed in Chapter 6 since they are created by the purchases of goods and services. The term "accounts payable" is used in accounting to mean *trade* accounts payable. Typical entries are:

```
March 6, 1974:
    Purchases (or Inventory)...................... 980
        Accounts Payable..........................        980
        Purchase of merchandise on credit; terms 2/10,
        n/30. (Invoice price, $1,000 × .98 = $980)

March 31, 1974:
    Accounts Payable.............................. 980
        Cash......................................        980
        Payment of account payable within the discount
        period.
```

[margin handwritten notes: "AT OWED FOR PURCHASE", "PAID ACCT IN CASH"]

ACCRUED LIABILITIES

Accrued liabilities arise from expenses that have been incurred but are not yet paid at the end of the accounting period. They appeared in Chapter 5 in the discussion of adjusting entries. To illustrate a typical accrued liability, assume that on December 31, 1974, the amount of property taxes for 1974 was determined to be $1,600. At the end of the accounting period, December 31, 1974, the current liability must be recorded and reported since the amount will not be paid until January 15, 1975. Therefore, the following adjusting entry must be made:

[margin handwritten notes: "KNOW", "INCURRED BUT NOT PAID"]

```
December 31, 1974:
    Property Tax Expense...................... 1,600
        Property Taxes Payable................        1,600
        Adjusting entry to record property taxes
        incurred in 1974 but not yet recorded
        or paid.
```

The entry in the next year for payment of the liability would be:

```
January 15, 1975:
    Property Taxes Payable.................... 1,600
        Cash..................................        1,600
        Payment of liability for property taxes
        accrued in 1974.
```

PAYROLL LIABILITIES

Accrued liabilities are always incurred when salaries and wages are incurred. When employees perform services, the employer incurs an obligation to them that normally is paid on a weekly or monthly payroll basis. In the preceding discussions and illustrations, accounting for wage and salary expense has been simplified by disregarding payroll taxes and payroll deductions.

In addition to the obligation to the employee, payrolls create other liabilities that are directly related to the payment of salaries and wages. These additional liabilities generally arise as a result of federal and state laws, as well as contractual obligations, such as pension plans and union dues. Some of these liabilities are paid by the employee through the employer (as payroll deductions); others must be paid by the employer and are additional expenses to him.

The take-home pay of most employees is considerably less than the gross salary or wages because of payroll deductions for such items as employee income taxes withheld, social-security taxes that must be paid by the employee, and such other employee deductions as insurance and union dues. The employer is required to pay the amounts deducted from the wages to the designated governmental agencies and other organizations such as the union. From the date of the payroll deduction until the date of payment to the agencies or organizations, the employer must record and report the current liabilities that are owed to the designated units. Thus, a typical journal entry for a payroll would be as follows:

```
January 31, 1974:
  Salaries Expense........................ 50,000
  Wages Expense........................... 30,000
    Liability for Income Taxes Withheld--
      Employees..........................         16,000
    Liability for Union Dues Withheld--
      Employees..........................            300
    FICA Taxes Payable--Employees........          4,800
    Cash.................................         58,900
  To record the payroll including employee
  deductions.
```

In addition to the payroll taxes that the *employees* must pay through the employer, the *employer* himself is required by law to pay *additional* specified payroll taxes. These constitute an operating expense for the business. Therefore, a second entry related to the payroll is needed to record the taxes to be paid by the employer. A typical entry would be as follows:

```
January 31, 1974:
  Payroll Tax Expense..................... 7,600
    FICA Taxes Payable--Employer..........          4,800
    FUTA Taxes Payable--Employer..........            400
    State Unemployment Taxes Payable--
      Employer...........................          2,400
  Employer payroll taxes for January
  payroll.
```

The six current liabilities created in the two entries above are settled in the near future when the company pays the requisite amount of cash to the appropriate agencies. Details involved in payroll accounting are discussed and illustrated in Appendix A to this chapter. Payroll accounting does not entail any new concepts or accounting principles; however, there is a significant amount of procedural detail involved.

DEFERRED REVENUES

Deferred revenues arise from revenues that have been collected in advance during the current period but will not be earned until a later accounting period. Deferred revenues constitute a liability since the cash has been collected but there is a *present obligation* to render, in the future, the services or to provide the goods. To illustrate, assume that during December 1974 rent revenue collected amounted to $6,000, which was debited to Cash and credited to Rent Revenue. Assume further that at the end of 1974 it was determined that $1,000 of this amount was for January 1975 rent. Thus, there is a current liability for deferred rent revenue that must be recognized. The sequence of entries for this situation would be as follows:

```
December 1974:
   Cash.......................................  6,000
      Rent Revenue..........................            6,000
      Collection of rent revenue.

December 31, 1974 (adjusting entry):
   Rent Revenue..............................  1,000
      Prepaid Rent Revenue (or Rent Collected
         in Advance)........................            1,000
      Adjusting entry to record prepaid rent
      revenue at the end of the accounting
      period.
```

Long-term liabilities | Long-term liabilities encompass all legal obligations not classified as current liabilities. Long-term liabilities sometimes are referred to as fixed liabilities. They generally arise from the purchase of fixed assets or the borrowing of large amounts of cash to be used for the acquisition of operational assets and major expansions of the business. Long-term liabilities usually involve long-term notes payable or bonds payable. Frequently, a long-term liability is supported by a mortgage on specified assets of the borrower *pledged* as security for the liability. The mortgage involves a separate document that is appended to the note payable. A liability supported by a mortgage is said to be a "secured debt." An unsecured debt is one for which the creditor relies primarily on the integrity and general earning power of the borrower.

Long-term liabilities are reported on the balance sheet under a separate caption below "Current liabilities." As a long-term debt approaches the maturity date, the portion of it that is to be paid in the next current period is reclassified as a current liability. To illustrate, assume a five-year note payable of $50,000 was signed on January 1, 1972. Repayment is to be in two installments as follows: December 31, 1975, $25,000 and December 31, 1976, $25,000. The December 31, 1973 and 1974 balance sheets would report the following:

> December 31, 1973:
> Long-term liabilities:
> Note payable............................. $50,000
>
> December 31, 1974:
> Current liabilities:
> Maturing portion of long-term note......... $25,000
> Long-term liabilities:
> Long-term note.......................... $25,000

Notes payable may be either short-term or long-term. A short-term note payable usually has a maturity date within one year from the balance-sheet date and generally arises as a result of borrowing cash or from purchasing merchandise or services on credit. Bonds payable (see Chapter 11) are always long-term liabilities, except for any maturing portion as illustrated above for the long-term note payable.

Notes   A note payable is a written promise to pay a stated sum at one or
payable   more specified dates in the future. A note payable may require a single-sum repayment at the due or maturity date or it may call for installment payments. To illustrate, assume the purchase of a sailboat for $3,000, with a $1,000 cash down payment and a note payable for the balance. The note may be drawn to call for a single payment at the end of 12 months or, alternatively, for 12 monthly payments.

Notes payable require the payment of interest and, hence, the recording of interest expense. Interest expense is incurred on liabilities because of the **time value of money.** The word "time" is significant because the longer money is borrowed (used), the larger the total dollar amount of interest expense. Thus, one must pay more interest for a two-year loan of a given amount, at a given **interest rate,** than for a one-year loan. To the borrower, interest is an expense, whereas, to the lender (creditor), interest is a revenue. In calculating interest we must consider (1) the principal, (2) the interest rate, and (3) the time. Therefore the formula is

$$\text{Interest} = \text{Principal} \times \text{Rate} \times \text{Time}$$

To illustrate, assume $6,000 cash is borrowed by the Baker Company on November 1, 1974, and a six-month, 8% note payable is given. The interest is payable at the due date of the note. The computation of interest expense would be: $6,000 \times .08 \times 6/12 = \$240$. This note would be recorded in the accounts as follows:

```
November 1, 1974:
    Cash...................................... 6,000
        Note Payable, Short—term (8%, interest—
        bearing)...............................        6,000
        Borrowed on short—term note; terms six
        months at 8% per annum; the interest is
        payable at maturity.
```

Since interest accrues with the *passage of time,* it is measured, recorded, and reported on a time basis rather than when it is actually paid in cash. This is based on legal as well as on economic considerations. For example, were the $6,000 loan cited above to be paid off in two months instead of in six months, interest amounting to $6,000 \times .08 \times 2/12 = \$80$ would have to be paid. It is on this basis that the *adjusting entry* for Accrued Interest Payable would be made at the end of the accounting period. To illustrate, assume the accounting period ends December 31, 1974. Although the $240 interest for the six months will not be paid until April 30, 1975, two months' unpaid interest must be accrued by means of the following adjusting entry:

```
December 31, 1974:
    Interest Expense............................... 80
        Interest Payable...........................        80
        Adjusting entry to accrue two months' interest,
        $6,000 × .08 × 2/12 = $80.
```

At maturity date the payment of principal plus interest would be recorded as follows:[4]

```
April 30, 1975:
    Notes Payable, Short—term.................. 6,000
    Interest Payable (per above)..............     80
    Interest Expense ($6,000 × .08 × 4/12).....    160
        Cash ($6,000 + $240)...................        6,240
        To record payment of note payable including
        interest.
```

The accounting for a note payable is the same whether it is classified as a current or as a long-term liability. Accounting for a note payable also is the same, irrespective of the purpose for which the note was executed.

---

[4] This assumes no reversing entry was made on January 1, 1975. See Chapter 5, Appendix.

Interest on notes. A note may be either interest-bearing or non-interest-bearing. All notes involve interest, either explicitly or implicitly. An interest-bearing note is one that explicitly specifies (a) a stated rate of interest (such as 8%) on the note itself, and (b) that the interest is to be paid at maturity, or in future installments, in *addition to the face or principal amount* of the note. For example, a $30,000, 8%, six-month, interest-bearing note would (a) provide the borrower with $30,000 cash, (b) have a face or principal amount of $30,000, and (c) require the payment of the principal ($30,000) plus interest for six months ($1,200)—a total of $31,200.

In contrast, a noninterest-bearing note is one that does not specify a rate of interest on the note itself and where the interest is included in the face or principal amount. For example, a $30,000, six-month, non-interest-bearing note (assuming a going rate of interest of 8%) (a) may provide the borrower with $28,800 cash (i.e., $30,000 − $1,200 interest) and (b) would require the payment of only the face of the note at maturity date ($30,000).[5]

The accounting entries for these two different notes are tabulated below for comparison:

Transactions	Interest-bearing	Noninterest-bearing
November 1, 1974, date of note:		
Cash	30,000	28,800
Discount on Note Payable		1,200
Note Payable, Short-term	30,000	30,000
(8% interest; term, 6 months)		
December 31, 1974, end of accounting period:		
Interest Expense (2 months)	400	400
Accrued Interest Payable	400	
Discount on Note Payable		400
Adjusting entry for 2 months' accrued interest; $30,000 × 8% × 2/12 = $400.		
April 30, 1975, maturity date of note:*		
Notes Payable	30,000	30,000
Interest Expense (4 months)	800	800
Accrued Interest Payable	400	
Discount on Note Payable		800
Cash	31,200	30,000
Payment of note at maturity.		

KNOW

OWED BUT NOT YET PAID

* It would have simplified this entry if a *reversing entry* of the accrual of December 31, 1974, had been made on January 1, 1975. (See Chapter 5, Appendix.)

The above illustration suggests two important concepts in the measurement of liabilities and interest expense. The concept of *present value* is important in the measurement of liability. The present value of

[5] In some instances interest is computed on the cash received. Cash received would be computed as: $30,000 ÷ 1.04 = $28,846. Also see Chapter 8, Part Three.

a note is the value today of its future cash flows. In the case of the interest-bearing note, the present value and the face amount of principal are the same; i.e., $30,000. However, in the case of the noninterest-bearing note, the present value of the $30,000 face amount or principal is $28,800, the amount of cash received. Further discussion and illustration of the concept of present value are in Part Two.

In the measurement of interest cost, the concepts of the *stated* (or nominal) *interest rate* and the *effective* (or real) *interest rate* are important. The stated interest rate is the rate specified on the note (in the above illustration it was 8% per year). The effective interest rate is the real or true rate of interest. In the above example the stated and effective rates were the same for the interest-bearing note, viz:

Stated interest rate: Specified on the note	8%
Effective interest rate:	
$\dfrac{\text{Annual interest payable}}{\text{Cash proceeds received}} = \dfrac{\$2,400}{\$30,000} =$	8%

In contrast, the stated and effective interest rates on the noninterest-bearing note are different, viz:

Stated interest rate: Given as the going rate	8%
Effective interest rate:	
$\dfrac{\text{Annual interest payable}}{\text{Cash proceeds received}} = \dfrac{\$2,400}{\$28,800} =$	$8\frac{1}{3}\%$

From the borrower's point of view, he should strive to borrow on an interest-bearing note because the interest cost is thereby lower.

Deferred income taxes

Throughout the preceding chapters, income taxes paid by corporations have been discussed and illustrated. In those discussions, income tax expense was reflected on the income statement and income taxes payable was reflected on the balance sheet. In addition to income taxes payable, most balance sheets of corporations report another tax liability called deferred income taxes. This additional liability for income taxes arises because of a difference in the *timing* in which certain expense and revenue items are reflected on the income statement versus the income tax return. For example, the income statement for 1974 may show a particular revenue of $5,000, while that same revenue, because of a provision in the Internal Revenue Code, must be reported on the 1975 income tax return rather than on the 1974 return. Thus, there is said to be a timing difference on this item. Assuming a 40% tax rate, there would be a deferred tax liability to be reported on the 1974 balance sheet amounting to $5,000 × 40% = $2,000. The revenue was earned in 1974 but the tax on it will be paid in 1975. Thus, the $2,000 should be included in the amount of income tax expense for 1974. In 1975 this deferred tax liability would have been paid; hence, it is said to have "reversed" or "turned around" in 1975.

To illustrate the computation and accounting for deferred taxes, assume the following additional data:

	1974	1975
Net income, per income statement....................	$20,000	$22,000
Revenue item reported on the 1974 income statement but includable on the *1975* tax return...............	−5,000	+5,000
Taxable income (per tax return).....................	$15,000	$27,000

Using the above data, income tax *expense* and income taxes *payable* for each year would be computed as follows:

a. Income tax expense (based on net income, per the income statement):
    1974: $20,000 × 40%..................... $ 8,000
    1975: $22,000 × 40%..................... $ 8,800

b. Income taxes payable (based on taxable income):
    1974: $15,000 × 40%..................... 6,000
    1975: $27,000 × 40%.....................   10,800

Difference—Deferred taxes:
    1974: A credit........................... $ 2,000
    1975: A debit............................ $ 2,000

The entry to record the income tax effect each year would be as follows:

```
1974:  Income Tax Expense.................  8,000
         Deferred Income Taxes...........           2,000
         Income Taxes Payable (or Cash)..           6,000

1975:  Income Tax Expense.................  8,800
       Deferred Income Taxes..............  2,000
         Income Taxes Payable (or Cash)..          10,800
```

From this illustration, it can be seen that the income tax expense for 1974 included taxes on the $5,000 revenue amount that was reported on the 1974 income statement. The effect was to match the expense with the revenue. In 1975, the amount of income tax expense reported on the income statement did not include the taxes on the $5,000 revenue amount although the tax was actually paid in the latter year. This pinpoints the two arguments that are advanced for the allocation of income taxes between accounting periods, viz: it is necessary in order to match expenses with revenues, and, since the revenue was earned in the earlier year and a tax ultimately will have to be paid, the deferred tax liability should be recorded. Common situations that cause a tax deferral are use of different methods of depreciation on the income statement from those used on the tax return, and installment sales where revenue is recognized in a different period on the income statement from that on the tax return. The balance sheet for J. C.

Penney Company, Inc., shown in Chapter 3, reported deferred taxes under both current liabilities and long-term liabilities. This is because the deferred tax liability must be classified in this manner depending upon when it is expected that the deferred tax liability will materialize. In this company, as in many companies, deferred income taxes is a large amount among the liabilities. At one point a well-known company reported deferred income taxes greater in amount than the total of owners' equity. Practically all financial statements for large companies that you will encounter will report deferred income taxes.

The above discussions indicate that deferred taxes are credits (a liability). Although this is the usual case, deferred taxes may start out as a debit (a deferred charge). In either instance, the concept of deferred income taxes is the same.

Recognition of deferred income taxes is a controversial issue. The APB, in *Opinion No. 11* (December 1967), made it mandatory; however, there continues to be strong opposition to it on several conceptual and practical grounds. The arguments tend to center on the position that (1) there is no tax expense or tax liability until the legal requirements of the tax code establish them; (2) there is great uncertainty in the assumption that long-term items will eventually reverse in their effect; (3) it confuses statement users; and (4) on an aggregate basis, rather than on an item basis, there is no deferred tax liability in an expanding or stable company.

Lease liabilities

In recent years the practice of leasing equipment, rather than purchasing it, has increased by leaps and bounds. There are a number of economic reasons why businesses have increasingly obtained operational assets by leasing. A primary reason has been that leasing does not require an immediate outflow of cash or, in the opinion of many people, the incurrence of a large debt. The trend in leasing has posed some difficult problems in measuring and reporting liabilities. As a result, leasing has been called "off balance sheet financing."

To illustrate the issues, assume the Daly Construction Company urgently needs a heavy machine that is priced at $40,000 new. It has an estimated useful life of five years and no residual value. The management of the company is considering three alternative ways of acquiring the machine:

a. Purchase the machine outright—This would entail borrowing approximately all of the purchase price at 8% interest. If this alternative is selected, the machine would be recorded in the accounts as follows:

```
Machinery............................. 40,000
    Note Payable, Long-term...........          40,000
```

Each period, maintenance, operating expenses, depreciation, interest expense ($3,200 per year), etc., would be recorded.

b. Lease the machine on a month-to-month or year-to-year basis—It has been determined that the rental payments would be as follows:

Monthly basis...................... $ 2,500 (per month)
Yearly basis........................   20,000 (per year)

Each period, operating expenses would be paid and reported as expense, in addition to the rental payment.

c. Lease the machine on a five-year, noncancelable lease contract— This contract would provide that Daly be fully responsible for all expenses for maintenance, operating, insurance, taxes, etc., for the full five years and, in addition, would pay an annual rental of $10,000. At the end of the five years, the machine would be returned to the lessor.

In this situation, the Daly Construction Company selected the third alternative. Let's review some of the considerations that influenced the decision, giving particular attention to the impact on the financial statements of each alternative.

Alternative (*a*) was considered undesirable because (1) they might not need the machine for the full five years; (2) the interest rate was high; (3) there was difficulty in obtaining the $40,000, 8% loan; and (4) it was undesirable to increase the long-term liabilities on the balance sheet by $40,000, which would affect their current credit standing with the banks.

Alternative (*b*) was given very little consideration because of the extremely high rental payments required. Although the machine could be returned at any time with no further obligation under this alternative, the high rental payments would cause a significant decrease in net income. The income statement effect would be more than the company could stand, even though there would be no liability reflected on the balance sheet.

Alternative (*c*) was chosen because (1) no cash or loan would be required to obtain the machine; (2) the rental payment would be deductible on the income tax return each period; (3) no liability would be recorded on the balance sheet; and (4) the amount of the annual rental payment appeared to be reasonable. In short, this option made possible "off balance sheet financing" since the leasing company would purchase the machine, make it available to Daly, charge a flat rental payment each period, and no liability for it would appear on the balance sheet.

The third alternative is typical of current leasing contracts that involve high-cost machinery and equipment. It is a situation that has caused some difficult accounting and reporting problems. Some people view the situation outlined in alternative (*c*) as an ordinary or operating type of lease just as is alternative (*b*). This is the way Daly viewed it in its analysis. If viewed in this way, no entry would be made in the accounts at the inception of the lease. Each period, when the rental payment is made, the entry would be:

```
Rental Expense............................ 10,000
    Cash..................................          10,000
```

Many accountants are of the opinion that this constitutes inappropriate measurement and reporting of the liability that is implicit in the situation outlined in alternative (*c*). They believe that the essence of the long-term, noncancelable lease, for the life of the equipment, is in fact a purchase transaction. They believe that the leasing company is providing financing for Daly; therefore, they believe it is a *financing type of lease* rather than an *operating type of lease*. When viewed as a financing type of lease, the following entries would be necessary:

At date of inception of the lease:

```
Asset—Machinery.......................... 40,000
Discount on Financing Lease Obligations.... 10,000
    Liability—Obligations on Financing
        Lease................................          50,000
```

At date of first rental payment:

```
Liability—Obligations on Financing Lease.. 10,000
    Cash..................................          10,000

Interest expense ($50,000 × 8%)............  4,000
    Discount on Financing Lease Obliga-
        tions................................           4,000
```

You should not be concerned with the computation of the above amounts nor the details of the entries. Rather, observe that the effect of the accounting is to report the asset and the long-term liability on the balance sheet. This result essentially follows the accounting effect of alternative *a;* it places the financing on the balance sheet. There has been widespread opposition by companies, such as Daly, to accounting for these transactions as a *financing lease* because of the effect on their financial statements. It is interesting to note that the leasing company would record the long-term lease, outlined in alternative (*c*), as a sale at the date of the lease transaction. There are many related complexities; however, the above illustration should be sufficient to comprehend the basic measurement and reporting issues.

Contingent
liabilities

A contingent liability is not a legal or effective liability; rather it is a *potential* future liability. The amount of a contingent liability may be known or estimated. A contingent liability is defined as a potential future liability that has arisen as a result of an event or transaction that has *already occurred*. Its conversion to a legal liability, however, is dependent upon the occurrence of one or more *future* events or transactions (i.e., a future contingency). To illustrate, assume that in 1974 the Baker Company was sued for $100,000 damages arising from an accident involving one of the trucks owned by the company. The suit is scheduled for trial during March 1975. Whether or not there is a legal liability will depend upon the decision of the court at the termination of the trial. When financial statements are prepared at December 31, 1974, a contingent liability must be disclosed. Because of the past event, the company is contingently liable for the payment of damages.

A contingent liability is *not* recorded in the accounts. Rather, it is reported by means of a footnote to the financial statements. For example, the contingent future liability arising from the lawsuit may be disclosed by a footnote to the balance sheet similar to the following:

> The company is contingently liable for $100,000 because of a lawsuit based on an accident involving a company vehicle. Legal counsel believes that the suit is lacking in merit. Trial is scheduled for March 1975.

Controlling
expenditures

The purchase of merchandise, services, and fixed assets often requires the recording of either a short-term or long-term liability. As a consequence, in addition to the cash transactions for these purposes, a large number of other cash payments are made in a business. In a company of any size, control over these cash expenditures is essential to prevent the misapplication of cash in the cash-disbursement process. In a very small business it is often possible for the owner to personally give attention to each transaction when it is incurred and to make each cash payment himself. This personal attention may assure that the business is getting what it pays for, that cash is not being disbursed carelessly, and that there is no theft or fraud.

As a business grows and becomes more complex, the owner or chief executive cannot give personal attention to each transaction involving the acquisition of goods and services and the handling of cash disbursements. In such situations these activities must be assigned to various employees. The assignment of these responsibilities to others creates a need for systematic and effective procedures for the control of cash expenditures. This is an important function of a well-designed accounting system.

In Chapter 8 the essential features of effective internal control were discussed briefly. That chapter emphasized the control of cash receipts. Similar procedures were discussed in respect to cash disbursements: the separation of duties, disbursement of cash by check, petty cash, and the two special journals—the purchases journal and the cash disbursements journal. In larger companies and in computerized accounting systems, the method usually used for maintaining control over cash expenditures is known as the **voucher system.** This system replaces the cash disbursements journal procedures.

THE VOUCHER SYSTEM

The voucher system is designed to establish strict control over the incurrence of every legal obligation to make an expenditure and all disbursements of cash. The system requires that a **written authorization,** called a **voucher,** be approved by one or more designated managers at the time each transaction occurs. An approved voucher is required regardless of whether the transaction involves the purchase of merchandise or services, the acquisition of fixed assets, investments, or the payment of a liability. The system permits checks to be issued only in payment of properly prepared and approved vouchers. The check-writing and voucher-approval procedures are kept completely separate from the check-approval and issuing procedures.

The voucher system requires that every obligation be supported by a voucher and that each transaction be recorded when incurred. The incurrence of an obligation is treated as an independent transaction and each payment of cash is treated as another independent transaction. This sequence of voucher approval, followed by payment by check, is required even in strictly cash-disbursement transactions. To illustrate, the *cash* purchase of merchandise for resale would be recorded under the voucher system as follows:

1. To record the incurrence of an obligation:

```
Purchases (or Inventory).................... 1,000
    Vouchers Payable........................     1,000
```

2. To record payment of the obligation by check (immediately thereafter):

```
Vouchers Payable............................ 1,000
    Cash....................................     1,000
```

In the voucher system, the account designated **Vouchers Payable** replaces the account entitled Accounts Payable. Entries of the first type are entered in a **voucher register** and entries of the second type are entered in a **check register.**

The primary objective of the voucher system is to attain continuous control over each step in an expenditure from the incurrence of an obligation to the final disbursement of cash to satisfy the obligation. Thus, every single transaction leading to a cash payment, and the cash payment itself, is systematically reviewed, then subjected to an approval system based on separately designated responsibilities. Appendix B to this chapter discusses and illustrates the *mechanics* of the voucher system.

STOP

PART TWO: CONCEPTS OF FUTURE VALUE AND PRESENT VALUE

The measurement and reporting of liabilities, when they are first recorded in the accounts and during the period the debt is outstanding, often involve application of the concepts of future value and present value. These concepts also are used in measuring the effects of long-term investments in bonds, leases, pension plans, and sinking funds. However, most of the applications in accounting involve either the establishment of a fund or the measurement of a liability or a receivable.

a. Establishment of a fund—A company may decide to set aside a certain amount of cash to be used in the future for a specific purpose, such as to pay off a large debt that will mature ten years hence. Funds of this type were reported on the balance sheet shown in Exhibit 3–2 and were discussed on page 56. They are also discussed further in Chapter 11 (page 399).

b. Measurement of a liability or a receivable—Long-term liabilities and receivables usually involve significant amounts of principal and interest. The measurement of these two related amounts often requires the use of future and present value concepts.

The concepts of future and present value focus on the **time value of money,** which is another name for **interest.** The time value of money refers to the fact that a dollar received today is worth more than a dollar to be received one year from today (or at some other later date). A dollar received today can be invested, say at 8%, so that it grows to $1.08 during the year. In contrast, a dollar to be received one year from today denies one the opportunity to earn the $.08 interest for the year. The difference is due to interest, which is the cost of the use of money for a specific period of time, just as rent represents the cost for use of a tangible asset for a period of time. Interest may be specified (i.e., it is explicitly stated), as in the case of an interest-bearing note, or it may be unspecified (but it is there nonetheless; i.e., it is present implicitly).

For many years the time value of money was largely overlooked in accounting for some of the transactions cited above. In recent years, several *Opinions* issued by the APB have required the application of present-value determinations. Of particular significance was *Opinion No.*

21, issued in August 1971, entitled "Interest on Receivables and Payables." This *Opinion* requires the application of present value determinations to a number of transactions. For example, the *Opinion* states: "In the absence of established exchange prices for the related property, goods, or service or evidence of the market value of the note, the present value of a note that stipulates either no interest or a rate of interest that is clearly unreasonable should be determined by *discounting* all future payments on the notes using an imputed rate of interest as described in paragraphs 13 and 14." To illustrate, assume a machine is purchased for $12,000 and the purchaser is given two years in which to make payment. What amount should be debited to the Machine account in order to conform to the cost principle? Answer: The current cash equivalent cost, which is $10,288 (see page 361).

Basic concepts

Time value of money relates to four different concepts that involve interest calculations:

1. Future amount of $1.
2. Present value of $1.
3. Future amount of an annuity of $1.
4. Present value of an annuity of $1.

Tables, using $1 as the base, provide values for each of these situations for different periods of time (n) and at different rates of interest (*i*). Extracts from the four tables are shown on pages 357–58. Let's examine each of these concepts.

FUTURE AMOUNT OF $1

This concept is generally referred to as compound interest. The future amount is the amount to which $1 will increase at *"i"* interest rate for *"n"* periods. The future amount will be the principal plus interest. To illustrate, assume that on January 1, 1974, you deposited $1,000 in a savings account at 6% annual interest, compounded each year. How much would you have at the end of the third year; that is, on December 31, 1976? We can calculate the compound amount to be $1,191 as follows:

	Amount at Start of Year	+	Interest During the Year	=	Amount at End of Year
Year 1.......	$1,000	+	$1,000 × .06 = $60	=	$1,060
Year 2.......	1,060	+	1,060 × .06 = 64	=	1,124
Year 3........	1,124	+	1,124 × .06 = 67	=	1,191

However, we can avoid the detailed arithmetic by referring to Table 10–1, *Future Amount of $1,* as shown on page 357. For $i = 6\%$; $n = 3$, we find the value 1.191; therefore, we can compute the balance at the end of year 3 as $1,000 × 1.191 = $1,191. The increase of $191 was due to the time value of money; it would be interest revenue to you and interest expense to the savings institution. Assuming a positive interest rate, an amount of 1 will always be greater than 1. The symbol used for an amount of 1 usually is *"a."* Exhibit 10–1 presents a summary of the concept.

PRESENT VALUE OF $1

Present value of $1 is the value now (i.e., the present) of a dollar to be received at some date in the future. It can be said to be the inverse of the amount-of-$1 concept. To compute the present value of a sum to be received in the future, the sum is subjected to **compound discounting** at *"i"* interest rate for *"n"* periods. In compound discounting, the interest is subtracted rather than added, as in compounding. To illustrate, assume that today is January 1, 1974, and that you will receive $1,000 cash on December 31, 1976—that is, three years from now. Assuming an interest rate of 6% per year, how much would the $1,000 be worth today; that is, what is its present value (today, on January 1, 1974)? We could set up a discounting computation, year by year, as was done on page 355. However, to facilitate the computation, we can refer to a present-value-of-$1 table, like the one shown on page 358, Table 10–2. For *i* = 6%; *n* = 3, we find the present value of $1 to be .8396. The $1,000, to be received three years hence, has a present value of $1,000 × .8396 = $839.60. The difference (i.e., the discount) of $160.40 is due to the time value of money; it is the interest. The symbol commonly used for present value of $1 is *"p."* The concept of the present value of $1 is summarized in Exhibit 10–1.

FUTURE AMOUNT OF AN ANNUITY OF $1

Basically, the future amount of an annuity of $1 is the same as the future amount of $1, except for the addition of the concept of an **annuity.** The word "annuity" means an *equal amount* is contributed *each period* for two or more future periods. In contrast to an amount of $1, which involves a single contribution at the start, an annuity involves an equal contribution each period. A future amount of an annuity of $1 involves *compound interest* on *each* contribution. To illustrate, assume that you decide to put $1,000 cash in a savings account each year for three years at 6% interest per year (i.e., a total of $3,000). The first $1,000 contribution is to be made on January 1, 1974; the second one on January 1, 1975; and the third and last one on January 1, 1976. How much would you have in the savings account immediately after the third (and last) deposit on January 1, 1976? In this situation, the first $1,000 contribution would draw compound interest for two years (1974 and 1975); the second deposit would draw interest for one year (1975); and the third deposit would draw no interest (since we desire to know the amount in the savings account *immediately* after the third deposit). We could laboriously compute the interest for each contribution to derive the future value of this annuity. However, we can refer to Table 10–3, *Future Amount of Annuity of $1*. For $i = 6\%$; $n = 3$, where we find the value 3.1836.[6] This is the future value of an annuity of $1 at $i = 6\%$; $n = 3$. Therefore, your three contributions of $1,000 each would have increased to $1,000 × 3.1836 = $3,183.60 on January 1, 1976. The increase of $183.60 was due to the time value of money; it is interest revenue to you. The concept is summarized in Exhibit 10–1.

PRESENT VALUE OF ANNUITY OF $1

The present value of an annuity of $1 is the value now of a series of *equal amounts* (i.e., rents) to be received each period for some specified number of periods in the future. It can be said to be the inverse of the future amount of an annuity of $1 explained immediately above. It involves **compound discounting** of each of the equal periodic amounts. To illustrate, assume now is January 1, 1974, and that you are to receive $1,000 in cash on each January 1, 1975, 1976, and 1977. How much would these three $1,000 future amounts be worth now, on January 1, 1974 (i.e., the present value), assuming an interest rate of 6% per year? We could laboriously calculate the discounting on each rent; however, we can compute the present value readily by referring to Table 10–4, *Present Value of Annuity of $1*. For $i = 6\%$; $n = 3$ rents, we find the value 2.670 (rounded). This is the present value of an **annuity** of $1 at $i = 6\%$, and 3 equals periodic rents. Therefore, your three $1,000 amounts to be received in the future have a present value of $1,000 × 2.670 = $2,670. The difference (i.e., the discount) of $330 was due to the interest factor. This concept is summarized in Exhibit 10–1 (page 359).

Table 10–1

Future amount of $1, $a = (1 + i)^n$

Periods	2%	3%	4%	5%	6%	7%	8%
0	1.	1.	1.	1.	1.	1.	1.
1	1.02	1.03	1.04	1.05	1.06	1.07	1.08
2	1.0404	1.0609	1.0816	1.1025	1.1236	1.1449	1.1664
3	1.0612	1.0927	1.1249	1.1576	1.1910	1.2250	1.2597
4	1.0824	1.1255	1.1699	1.2155	1.2625	1.3108	1.3605
5	1.1041	1.1593	1.2167	1.2763	1.3382	1.4026	1.4693
6	1.1262	1.1941	1.2653	1.3401	1.4185	1.5007	1.5869
7	1.1487	1.2299	1.3159	1.4071	1.5036	1.6058	1.7138
8	1.1717	1.2668	1.3686	1.4775	1.5938	1.7182	1.8509
9	1.1951	1.3048	1.4233	1.5513	1.6895	1.8385	1.9990
10	1.2190	1.3439	1.4802	1.6289	1.7908	1.9672	2.1589

---

[6] The equal periodic amounts implicit in all annuities often are referred to in the literature as "rents."

Table 10–2

Present value of $1, $p = \dfrac{1}{(1+i)^n}$

Periods	2%	3%	4%	5%	6%	7%	8%
1	0.9804	0.9709	0.9615	0.9524	0.9434	0.9346	0.9259
2	0.9612	0.9426	0.9246	0.9070	0.8900	0.8734	0.8573
3	0.9423	0.9151	0.8890	0.8638	0.8396	0.8163	0.7938
4	0.9238	0.8885	0.8548	0.8227	0.7921	0.7629	0.7350
5	0.9057	0.8626	0.8219	0.7835	0.7473	0.7130	0.6806
6	0.8880	0.8375	0.7903	0.7462	0.7050	0.6663	0.6302
7	0.8706	0.8131	0.7599	0.7107	0.6651	0.6227	0.5835
8	0.8535	0.7894	0.7307	0.6768	0.6274	0.5820	0.5403
9	0.8368	0.7664	0.7026	0.6446	0.5919	0.5439	0.5002
10	0.8203	0.7441	0.6756	0.6139	0.5584	0.5083	0.4632

Table 10–3

Future amount of annuity of $1 (ordinary), $A = \dfrac{(1+i)^n - 1}{i}$

Period Rents	2%	3%	4%	5%	6%	7%	8%
1	1.	1.	1.	1.	1.	1.	1.
2	2.02	2.03	2.04	2.05	2.06	2.07	2.08
3	3.06	3.0909	3.1216	3.1525	3.1836	3.2149	3.2464
4	4.1217	4.1836	4.2465	4.3101	4.3746	4.4399	4.5061
5	5.2040	5.3091	5.4163	5.5256	5.6371	5.7507	5.8666
6	6.3081	6.4684	6.6330	6.8019	6.9753	7.1533	7.3359
7	7.4343	7.6625	7.8983	8.1420	8.3938	8.6540	8.9228
8	8.5830	8.8923	9.2142	9.5491	9.8975	10.2598	10.6366
9	9.7546	10.1591	10.5828	11.0266	11.4913	11.9780	12.4876
10	10.9497	11.4639	12.0061	12.5779	13.1808	13.8164	14.4866

Table 10–4

Present value of annuity of $1 (ordinary), $P = \dfrac{1 - \dfrac{1}{(1+i)^n}}{i}$

Period Rents	2%	3%	4%	5%	6%	7%	8%
1	0.9804	0.9709	0.9615	0.9524	0.9434	0.9346	0.9259
2	1.9416	1.9135	1.8861	1.8594	1.8334	1.8080	1.7833
3	2.8839	2.8286	2.7751	2.7232	2.6730	2.6243	2.5771
4	3.8077	3.7171	3.6299	3.5460	3.4651	3.3872	3.3121
5	4.7135	4.5797	4.4518	4.3295	4.2124	4.1002	3.9927
6	5.6014	5.4172	5.2421	5.0757	4.9173	4.7665	4.6229
7	6.4720	6.2303	6.0021	5.7864	5.5824	5.3893	5.2064
8	7.3255	7.0197	6.7327	6.4632	6.2098	5.9713	5.7466
9	8.1622	7.7861	7.4353	7.1078	6.8017	6.5152	6.2469
10	8.9826	8.5302	8.1109	7.7217	7.3601	7.0236	6.7101

Exhibit 10–1

Time value of money determinations

Table No.	Designation	Definition and Graphic Representation	Usual Symbol	Table Formula
10–1	Future amount of $1	The future amount (worth or value) of $1 at the end of n periods at i compound interest rate. This is simply the principal plus compound interest. Graphic representation:	a	$(1 + i)^n$

Present
Time

$1 $n = 3; i = 6\%$ $1.19

| 10–2 | Present value of $1 | The present value (worth now) of $1 due n periods hence, discounted at i compound interest rate. This is simply a future amount with compound discount applied to it. | p | $\dfrac{1}{(1 + i)^n}$ |

Present
Value
of $1   Future
                                         Principal

$.84 $n = 3; i = 6\%$ $1

| 10–3 | Future amount of annuity of $1 | The future amount (worth or value) of n periodic contributions (i.e., rents) of $1 each plus accumulated compound interest at i rate. The first rent is immediately and the future value is on the date of the last rent. | A | $\dfrac{(1 + i)^n - 1}{i}$ |

                                         Future Amount
Present   of n Rents
Time   of $1 each

$1 $1 $1
$n = 3$ rents; $i = 6\%$ $3.18

| 10–4 | Present value of annuity of $1 | The present value (worth now) of n periodic rents of $1 each to be received (or paid) each period, discounted at i compound discount rate per period. The first rent is at the end of the first period. | P | $\dfrac{1 - \dfrac{1}{(1 + i)^n}}{i}$ |

Present
Value of   Future
n Rents of $1   Time

$1 $1 $1
$n = 3$ rents; $i = 6\%$

$2.67

We have said that there are numerous transactions where the concepts of future and present value are used for accounting measurements.
Below are cited four different situations where they must be used.

CASE A—Company A, on January 1, 1974, set aside $150,000 cash
in a special building fund (an asset) to be used at the end
of five years to construct a new building. The fund will
earn 6% interest per year, which will be added to the fund
balance. On the date of deposit the company made the
following entry:

```
Jan. 1, 1974:
    Special Building Fund.................. 150,000
        Cash................................          150,000
```

Required:
(1)   What will be the balance of the fund at the end of the fifth year?

   Answer: This situation involves the future-amount-of-$1 con-
   cept.

   Principal $\times$ Table 10–1 value $(i = 6\%; n = 5)$ = Future Amount
   $150,000 $\times$ 1.3382   = $200,730

(2)   How much interest revenue was earned on the fund during the
   five years?
   Answer:

$$\$200,730 - \$150,000 = \underline{\$50,730}$$

(3)   What entry would be made on December 31, 1974, to record
   the interest revenue for the first year?
   Answer: Interest for one year on the fund balance is added
   to the fund and recorded as follows:

```
Dec. 31, 1974:
    Special Building Fund..................... 9,000
        Interest Revenue ($150,000 × .06)......          9,000
```

(4)   How much interest would be added to the fund at the end of
   the second year?
   Answer: Interest on the fund balance for 1 year.

$$(\$150,000 + \$9,000) \times .06 = \underline{\$9,540}$$

CASE B—On January 1, 1974, Company B purchased a new machine
to be used in the plant at a list price of $12,000, which
was payable at the end of two years. The going rate of
interest was 8%.

Required:
(1)   The company accountant is preparing the following entry:

```
Machinery...................................... $  ?
    Accounts Payable (special)..............      $  ?
```

What amount should be used in this entry?

Answer: This situation requires application of the present-value-of-$1 concept. Under the cost principle, the cost of the machine is the current cash-equivalent price, which is the present value of the future payment. The present value of the $12,000 is computed as follows:

$$\text{Future Amount} \times \text{Table 10-2}\,(i = 8\%; n = 2) = \text{Present Value}$$
$$\$12,000 \times .8573 \qquad\qquad\qquad = \underline{\$10,288}$$

Therefore, the entry would be as follows:[7]

```
Machinery...................................... 10,288
    Accounts Payable (special)..............          10,288
```

(2) What entry would be made at the end of the first and second years for interest expense on the account payable?

Answer: Interest expense for each year on the amount in the Accounts Payable account would be recorded by means of an adjusting entry, as follows:

```
End of Year 1:
    Interest Expense............................. 823
        Accounts Payable (special)................      823
    $10,288 × .08 = $823

End of Year 2:
    Interest Expense............................. 889
        Accounts Payable(special).................      889
    ($10,288 + $823) × .08 = $889
```

The effect of these two entries is to increase the balance in Accounts Payable to the new current cash equivalent amount. By maturity date the balance will have been increased to the maturity amount, $12,000, which is the current cash-equivalent amount at due date.

(3) What entry would be made to record the payment on due date?

Answer: At this date the balance in Accounts Payable is the current cash-equivalent amount, which is the same

---

[7] This entry could also be made as follows with the same ultimate result:

```
Machinery................................................. 10,288
Discount on Accounts Payable............................. 1,712
    Accounts Payable (special)...........................          12,000
```

as the maturity amount on due date. The amount to be paid would be $10,288 + $823 + $889 = $12,000. The entry would be:

```
Accounts Payable (special)................ 12,000
    Cash.................................           12,000
```

CASE C—Company C decided to make five annual deposits of $20,000 each with a financial institution to create a debt retirement fund. The deposits will be made on each January 1, starting on January 1, 1974. The fifth and last deposit will be made on January 1, 1978. The financial institution will pay 5% annual compound interest, which will be added to the fund at the end of each year.

Required:

(1) What entry should be made to record the first deposit?

Answer:

```
Jan. 1, 1974:
    Debt Retirement Fund.................... 20,000
        Cash................................          20,000
```

(2) What will be the balance in the fund immediately after the fifth and last deposit (i.e., on January 1, 1978)?

Answer: This situation requires application of future amount of an annuity of $1.

$$\text{Rent} \times \text{Table } 10\text{–}3\,(i = 5\%; n = 5) = \text{Future Amount}$$
$$\$20,000 \times 5.5256 \qquad\qquad = \underline{\$110,512}$$

(3) What entry would be made at the end of the first year for interest?

Answer: Interest for one year on the fund balance would be added to the fund and recorded as follows:

```
Debt Retirement Fund...................... 1,000
    Interest Revenue ($20,000 × .05)........        1,000
```

(4) What would be the amount of interest revenue to be recorded at the end of the second year?

Answer: Interest would be computed on the increased fund balance as follows:

$$(\$20,000 + \$1,000 + \$20,000) \times .05 = \underline{\$2,050}$$

CASE D—On January 1, 1974, Company D purchased a new machine at a cash price of $30,000. Since the company was short of cash, arrangements were made to execute a $30,000 note payable to be paid off in three equal yearly installments. Each installment would include principal plus interest on the unpaid balance at 7% per year. The equal annual installments are due on January 1, 1975, 1976, and 1977. The acquisition was recorded as follows:

```
Machinery.................................. 30,000
    Note Payable..........................         30,000
```

Required:

(1) What would be the amount of each annual installment?

  Answer: The $30,000 is the amount of the debt today; hence, it is the present value of the three future installment payments required (i.e., the rents). Therefore, $n = 3$; $i = 7\%$, and the present value is $30,000. To compute the equal rents required, the present value of an annuity of $1 must be used as follows:

  Rent $\times$ Table 10–4 Value ($i = 7\%$; $n = 3$) = Present Value
  Substituting:
  Rent $\times$ 2.6243   = $30,000
  Rent = $30,000 $\div$ 2.6243
       = $11,432 (amount of each annual payment)

(2) What was the amount of interest expense in dollars?

  Answer:

  $$(\$11,432 \times 3) - \$30,000 = \underline{\$4,296}$$

(3) What entry would be made at the end of each year to record the payment of this $30,000 note payable?

  Answer:

  (a) To record the first installment payment on the note at the end of year 1:

```
Note Payable..............................  9,332
Interest Expense ($30,000 × .07)..........  2,100
    Cash (computed above)..................         11,432
```

  (b) To record the second installment on the note at the end of year 2:

```
Note Payable..............................  9,985
Interest Expense ($30,000 – $9,332) × .07...  1,447
    Cash (computed above)..................         11,432
```

  (c) To record final installment on the note at the end of year 3:

```
Note Payable..............................  10,683
Interest Expense..........................     749
    Cash (computed above)..................          11,432
Interest: ($30,000 – $9,332 – $9,985) ×
.07 = $749 (rounded).
```

(4) Prepare a debt payment schedule that shows the effect on interest expense and the unpaid amount of principal each period.

Debt Payment Schedule

Date	Payment Cash (Cr.)	Interest Expense (Dr.)	Reduction of Principal (Dr.)	Unpaid Principal
1/1/74				30,000
1/1/75	11,432[a]	2,100[b]	9,332[c]	20,668[d]
1/1/76	11,432	1,447	9,985	10,683
1/1/77	11,432	749	10,683	–0–
Totals	34,296	4,296	30,000	

Sequential computations:
  (a) Annual payment: Computed above.
  (b) Interest expense: Unpaid principal $30,000 × .07 = $2,100.
  (c) Reduction of principal: Annual payment $11,432 − Interest $2,100 = $9,332.
  (d) New unpaid balance: Prior balance $30,000 − reduction $9,332 = $20,668.

Although there are many other applications of the concept of the time value of money in the recording and reporting processes, the above examples are typical. The application of these concepts to capital budgeting is deferred to *Fundamentals of Management Accounting*.

Summary   This chapter focused on accounting for three types of obligations: current, long-term, and contingent liabilities. The treatment of bonds payable has been deferred to Chapter 11. Liabilities are legal obligations of either a known or estimated amount. Detailed information concerning the liabilities of an entity is especially important to decision makers, whether internal or external to the enterprise. Identification by the decision maker of the kinds and amounts of liabilities would be practically impossible without reliable financial statements. The existence and amount of liabilities sometimes are easy to conceal from outsiders. The accounting model and the verification by the independent CPA constitute the best assurances that liabilities are fully disclosed.

Current liabilities are those obligations that will be paid from the resources reported on the balance sheet as current assets. Thus, they are short-term obligations that will be paid within the coming year or within the normal operating cycle of the business, whichever is the longer. All other liabilities (except contingent liabilities) are reported as long-term liabilities. A contingent liability is a potential claim due to some event or transaction that has already happened, but whether it will materialize as a legal liability is not certain and depends upon some future event or transaction. Contingent liabilities must be fully disclosed on the financial statements. Disclosure usually is by note to the financial statement.

Important terms	Current cash-equivalent amount	Contingent liabilities
	Current liabilities	Voucher system
	Working capital	Future amount of $1
	Long-term liabilities	Present value of $1
	Deferred taxes	Annuity
	Lease liabilities	Future amount of an annuity of $1
	Operating lease	Present value of an annuity of $1
	Financing lease	

Appendix A   PAYROLL ACCOUNTING

Accurate and detailed payroll accounting, although it does not involve any new accounting concepts or principles, is particularly important in most enterprises because of the necessity to pay the employees for their services promptly and correctly. In addition, detailed payroll accounting is necessary in order to fulfill legal requirements under state and federal laws with respect to taxes withheld, social-security taxes, and unemployment taxes. Further, the management of an enterprise, for planning and control purposes, must have detailed and accurate cost figures for wages and salaries. Frequently, this is the largest category of expense in an enterprise. As a consequence of these requirements, payroll accounting is characterized by a large amount of detailed record keeping. Payroll accounting is computerized in many businesses, including the production of individual checks for the employees.

The accounting requires a payroll record for each employee. The payroll record varies with the circumstances in each company; however, it must provide for each individual such data as social-security number, number of dependents (for income tax withholding), rate of pay, a time record (for hourly paid employees), deductions from gross pay, etc.

To understand payroll accounting, a distinction must be made between (a) payroll deductions and taxes that must be paid by the *employee* (i.e., deducted from his gross earnings); and (b) payroll taxes that must be paid by the *employer*. Both types of payroll items must be transmitted to the governmental unit or other party to whom the amount is owed. Payroll taxes and deductions apply only in situations where there is an employer–employee relationship. Independent contractors that are not under the direct supervision of the client, such as outside lawyers, independent accountants, and building contractors, are not employees; hence, amounts paid to them are not subject to payroll taxes and related deductions.

An employee generally receives take-home pay that is much less than his gross earnings for the period. This is due to two types of payroll deductions:

1. Deductions for taxes required by state and federal laws.
2. Deductions authorized by the employee for special purposes.

EMPLOYEE DEDUCTIONS FOR TAXES

There are two categories of taxes that the employee must pay and that are deducted from his gross earnings; they are income taxes and social-security taxes. The employer must pay the amount deducted to the appropriate government agency.

Employee income taxes. Practically every employee must submit a federal income tax return annually. Wages and salaries earned during the year must be included thereon as income. For many years, federal laws have required the employer to deduct an appropriate amount of income taxes each period from the gross earnings of each employee. The amount of the deduction is determined from a tax table (provided by the Internal Revenue Service) based upon the earnings and number of exemptions of the employee. The amount of income taxes withheld from the employee is recorded by the employer as a current liability between the date of deduction and the date of payment to the government. The total amount withheld must be paid to the Internal Revenue Service within a specified short period of time. An especially designed form to accompany the payment is provided by the Internal Revenue Service to identify the employees and the amounts withheld. Some states also require withholding for state income taxes.

Employee FICA taxes. These social-security taxes generally are called FICA taxes since they are a result of the Federal Insurance Contributions Act. That act provides that persons who are *qualified* under the provisions of the act, upon reaching age 62, may retire and receive monthly benefits for life, plus certain medical benefits after age 65.[8] It also provides benefits for the family of a deceased person who was qualified.

The funds required by the government to provide the benefits under the Social Security Act are obtained by payroll taxes, which are imposed in equal amounts on both the employee and the employer. Until January 1, 1974, the FICA rate had been 5.85% on the first $10,800 paid to each employee during the year. Effective January 1, 1974, the rate was kept at 5.85% but the wage maximum was changed from $10,800 to $12,600. Since FICA rates change frequently, for convenience in calculations we will use a flat rate of 6% for illustrative and problem purposes.

At the end of each year, the employer is required to provide each

---

[8] In order to qualify under the act for retirement and medical benefits, the employee must be in "covered" employment for a specified period of time. Covered employment requires payroll deductions for these taxes. The amount of benefits and the FICA tax deductions are frequently changed by the U.S. Congress.

employee with a **Withholding Statement, Form W-2,** which reports to the employee (a) his gross earnings for the year; (b) earnings subject to FICA taxes; (c) income taxes withheld; and (d) FICA taxes withheld. A copy of this form also is sent to the Internal Revenue Service.

EMPLOYEE DEDUCTIONS FOR SPECIAL PURPOSES

Many companies encourage programs of voluntary deductions from earnings by employees. Typical of these voluntary deductions are savings funds, insurance premiums, charitable contributions, supplementary retirement programs, repayments of loans, stock purchase plans, and the purchase of U.S. savings bonds. The employer agrees to make these deductions, subject to authorization by the employee, as a matter of convenience to the employees. The amounts deducted are remitted in a short time to the organization or agency in whose honor the deduction was authorized. Another type of deduction, not always voluntary, is for union dues as specified in the union contract. The employer usually is required to remit the deductions, along with the employee list, to the union each month.

ACCOUNTING FOR EMPLOYEE DEDUCTIONS

The employer must maintain detailed and accurate records of all deductions for each employee. From the employer's viewpoint, the employee deductions are *current liabilities* from the date of the payroll deduction to the date of payment.

To illustrate the basic accounting entry to be made for the payment of a payroll and the accrual of liabilities for the *employee* deductions, assume that X Company accumulated the following data in the detailed payroll records for the month of January 1974:

```
Gross earnings:
    Salaries.................................. $50,000
    Wages (hourly paid employees)..............  30,000
    Income taxes withheld......................  16,000
    Union dues withheld........................     300
    FICA taxes (rate 6%; assume no maximums
        were exceeded in January)..............   4,800
```

The entry to record the payroll and employee deductions would be:

```
January 31, 1974:
    Salaries Expense.......................................  50,000
    Wages Expense..........................................  30,000
        Liability for Income Taxes Withheld—Employees.......          16,000
        Liability for Union Dues Withheld—Employees.........             300
        FICA Taxes Payable—Employees ($80,000 × 6%).......            4,800
        Cash................................................          58,900
    Payroll for January, including employee payroll deductions.
```

EMPLOYER PAYROLL TAXES

Remember that the payroll taxes illustrated above are those levied on the *employees*. The employer simply serves as a tax collector with respect to them. In addition, specific payroll taxes are also levied on the employer. These taxes represent operating expenses for the business. The liability is extinguished when the taxes are remitted to the designated agencies of the state and federal governments. Generally, three different payroll taxes must be paid by the employer—FICA taxes, FUTA taxes, and state unemployment compensation taxes.

Employer FICA taxes. The employer must pay an additional FICA tax equal to the amount withheld from the employee. Thus, the FICA tax paid by the employer is at the same rate as the FICA employee tax and on the same amount of wages (i.e., 5.85% on the first $12,600 of gross earnings of each employee).

Employer FUTA taxes. The Social Security Act provides for another program known as unemployment compensation. This program derives its monetary support under the provisions of the Federal Unemployment Tax Act. The FUTA, or unemployment tax, is paid *only by the employer*. Currently, the federal tax amounts to 0.5% of the first $4,200 in wages paid to each employee during the year.

State unemployment compensation taxes. The unemployment program specified in the Federal Unemployment Tax Act is a joint federal–state program; consequently, each state participates in the program both in providing benefits and in funding the program through payroll taxes. Although state laws vary as to both benefits and tax rates, many states have a 2.5% to 3.0% rate on the first $4,200 wages paid during the year. Most states have a merit-rating plan that provides for a reduction in the tax rate for employers that establish a record of stable employment over a period of time.

ACCOUNTING FOR EMPLOYER PAYROLL TAXES

Payroll taxes paid by the employer are debited to Expense and credited to a current liability when the payroll is paid each period. To illustrate, the January entry for the employer's payroll taxes for X Company (data shown on page 367), assuming a 3% state unemployment tax rate, would be as follows:[9]

Payroll Tax Expense..	7,600	
FICA Taxes Payable—Employer ($80,000 × 6%).............		4,800
FUTA Taxes Payable—Employer ($80,000 × 0.5%)........		400
State Unemployment Taxes Payable—Employer		
($80,000 × 3%)......................................		2,400
To record employer payroll taxes.		

---

[9] In this and the preceding entries, it was assumed that none of the employees received remuneration above the $12,600 and $4,200 maximums for the year.

When the taxes are paid to the government, the liability accounts are debited and Cash is credited.

Appendix B THE VOUCHER SYSTEM

The voucher system is designed to attain strict control over cash expenditures from the point of incurrence of an obligation (by means of purchase of merchandise for resale, services, fixed assets, investments, etc.) through the payment of cash to satisfy it. The incurrence of an obligation and the payment of cash to satisfy it are viewed as separate and independent transactions. When a voucher system is used, an account called *Vouchers Payable* replaces the account *Accounts Payable* in the ledger. Similarly, a *voucher register* and a *check register* replace the purchases journal and the cash disbursements journal, respectively.

The basic document in the voucher system is the *voucher*. A voucher is a business form, prepared and used within the business, on which a transaction is (a) summarized and adequately supported; (b) approved; (c) analyzed for recording; and (d) approved for payment. Thus, it is a comprehensive document that follows a transaction from its date to the final cash payment. A voucher is prepared for *each* transaction involving the payment of cash, such as the purchase of assets, the use of services, the incurrence of expenses, and the payment of debt. The form of a voucher varies between companies since it should be designed to meet the internal requirements of the individual company. For control purposes, voucher forms are numbered consecutively when printed. Similarly, all checks are numbered consecutively when printed.

Each voucher, after approval, is entered in the voucher register in order of number. The voucher register is designed to record the basic information from the voucher, including the accounts to be debited and credited.

To illustrate the mechanics of the voucher system, we will follow a purchase of merchandise for resale through the system from the order date to the final cash payment date. Each step in the sequence may be illustrated and explained as follows:

Jan. 10, 1974:
  Merchandise ordered from Box Supply Company, cost $1,000, terms n/15. A purchase order is prepared and approved.
Jan. 12, 1974:
  Merchandise ordered from Box Supply Company on Jan. 10 is received; invoice is received.
  Voucher No. 47 is drawn and the purchase order is attached (see Exhibit 10–2).
  Goods are checked for quantity and condition; a receiving report is prepared.

Exhibit 10–2

Voucher

MAY DEPARTMENT STORE Boston, Mass.			Voucher No. __47__	

Date of Voucher __Jan. 12, 1974__   Date Paid __Jan. 27, 1974__

Pay to: __Box Supply Company__   Check No. __90__

__1119 Brown Street__

__Philadelphia, Pa.__

For the following goods or services: (attach all supporting documents)

Date Incurred	Terms	Explanation of Details	Amount
Jan. 12	n/15	Merchandise, Dept. 8	1,000.00
		Invoice No. 17-8132	
		Receiving Report No. 123	
		Net payable	1,000.00

Approvals:

    Voucher Approval: Date __1/12/74__   Signature __R. C. Roe__

    Payment Approval: Date __1/26/74__   Signature __A. B. Doe__

Accounting Analysis:

Account Debited:	Acct. No.	Amount
Purchases	91	1,000.00
Office Supplies		
Sales Salaries		
Fixed Assets		
Etc.		
Total, Voucher Payable Credit	41	1,000.00

Exhibit 10–3

Voucher register

Date	Vou. No.	Payee	Payment Date	Check No.	Vouchers Payable (Credit)	Purchases (Debit)	Selling Expense Control Account Code	Folio	Amount (Debit)	Adm. Expense Control Account Code	Folio	Amount (Debit)	Other Accounts to be Debited Account Name	Folio No. P	Amount (Debited)
Jan 12	47	Bro Supply Co.	1/27	90	1,000	1,000									
Jan 14	48	John Doy-Delay	1/15	89	600		64	✓	600						
Jan 31	98	Capital Nat'l Bank-Note			2,160								Notes payable	44 ✓	2,000.00
													Interest expense	82 ✓	160.00
		Totals			27,605.00	14,835.00			7,410.00			3,160.00			2,160.00
		Posting notations			(41)	(91)			(60)			(70)			(✓)

Receiving report and invoice sent to accounting department; they are attached to the voucher.

Voucher is approved and then recorded in the voucher register (see Exhibit 10–3).

Jan. 26, 1974:

Voucher is approved by designated manager for payment on Jan. 27 and sent to disbursements department; Check No. 90 is prepared.

Jan. 27, 1974:

Check No. 90 is signed by treasurer and mailed.

Jan. 28, 1974: The accounting department:

Enters Check No. 90 in the check register (see Exhibit 10–4).

Exhibit 10–4

Check register

Date		Payee	Voucher No. Paid	Check No.	Vouchers Payable (Debit)*	Cash (Credit)*
Jan	15	John Day	48	89	600	600
	27	Box Supply Co.	47	90	1,000	1,000
	31	Totals			18,751.00	18,751.00
		Posting notation			(41)	(11)

* These two columns could be combined.

Enters payment notation in the voucher register (see Exhibit 10–3).

Files the voucher in the *Vouchers Paid File.*

For illustrative purposes, two more transactions are recorded in the voucher register, one of which remains unpaid.

At the end of the month the voucher register and the check register are totaled and the equality of the debits and credits are checked. Posting to the ledger from these two special journals follows the same pattern explained in Chapter 8, Appendix A, for the special journals illustrated there. Posting involves two separate phases:

1. Current posting—During the period, and perhaps daily, the details in the Voucher Register columns are posted (a) to the selling expense subsidiary ledger (under the selling expense control); (b) to the administrative expense subsidiary ledger (under the administrative expense control); and (c) other accounts to be debited. There

is no current posting required from the check register as illustrated.

2. Monthly posting—The totals from the voucher register, except for the "Other Accounts to be Debited, total $2,160.00," are posted at the end of each month. The account number to which each total is posted is entered below the amount. The column for "Other Accounts" was posted individually, hence, the total should not be posted. The totals from the check register are posted to the accounts at the end of each month as indicated by the account numbers entered below the total.

The balance in the ledger account Vouchers Payable is reported on the balance sheet as a liability and on the financial statement is designated as Accounts Payable. The Vouchers Payable account is a control account, the balance of which represents all of the *unpaid* vouchers at any given time. The total of all vouchers in the *Unpaid Vouchers File* must agree with the balance of the Vouchers Payable account; therefore, the Vouchers Payable account replaces the Accounts Payable control account in the ledger.

In studying the mechanics of the voucher system, as illustrated above, you should not overlook its most important aspect—the high degree of control attained through formalization of the sequence of acquiring fixed assets, services, and merchandise, and in making the cash payments. The control feature rests upon (a) clear-cut separation and designation of specific approval responsibilities; (b) a prescribed routine for carrying out these responsibilities; and (c) accounting for the results.

Although a manual approach was illustrated, we emphasize again that these routines are easily adapted to the computer. The computer program is designed to accomplish the same steps and procedures illustrated above. Most companies of any size have computerized the voucher system in order to attain a high degree of control over expenditures and to accelerate the processing of a large volume of transactions, including cash disbursements.

Questions for discussion

1. Define a liability and distinguish between a current liability and a long-term liability.
2. How can external parties be informed in respect to liabilities of an enterprise? Explain.
3. Liabilities are measured and reported at their current cash-equivalent amount. Explain.
4. A liability is a known obligation of either a definite or estimated amount. Explain.
5. What is working capital?

6. What is the current ratio? How is it related to the classification of liabilities?

7. What is accrued liability? What kind of an entry generally reflects an accrued liability?

8. What is a deferred revenue? Why is it a liability?

9. Define a note payable and distinguish between a secured and unsecured note payable.

10. Distinguish between an interest-bearing note and a noninterest-bearing note.

11. Define deferred income taxes. Explain why deferred income taxes are said to reverse, or turn around, in subsequent periods.

12. What is a lease liability?

13. What is meant by a financing lease?

14. What is meant by "off balance sheet financing" in respect to long-term leases?

15. What is a contingent liability? How is a contingent liability reported?

16. Briefly explain the primary purpose of a voucher system.

17. When a voucher system is used, the account Vouchers Payable replaces Accounts Payable. Explain.

18. Briefly explain what is meant by the time value of money.

19. Explain the basic difference between present value and future value.

20. What is an annuity?

Exercises E10–1. The Mycote Company sells a wide range of goods through two retail stores that are operated in two adjoining cities. Most purchases of goods for resale are on invoices with credit terms of of 2/10, n/30. Occasionally, a short-term note payable is executed to obtain cash for current use. The following transactions were selected from those occurring during 1974:

  (1) On January 15, 1974, purchased merchandise on credit, $20,000, terms 2/10, n/30. Record at net; the company uses the periodic inventory system.

  (2) On March 1, 1974, borrowed $30,000 cash from City Bank and gave a note payable; face value, $30,000; due at the end of six months, with an annual interest rate of 8% payable at maturity.

Required:

  a. Give the entry for each of the above transactions. Record purchases and accounts payable at net.
     (Hint: See Chapter 6.)

  b. Give the entry assuming the purchase of January 15, 1974, was paid within the discount period.

  c. Give the entry assuming the purchase of January 15, 1974, was paid after the discount period.

    d.   Give the entry for the payment of the note payable plus interest on the maturity date.

E10–2. During 1974, the two transactions given below were completed by Prince Company. The annual accounting period ends December 31.

    (1)   Wages paid and recorded during 1974 amounted to $47,000; however, at the end of December 1974, there were two days' wages unpaid because the weekly payroll will not be paid until January 6, 1975. Wages for the two days amounted to $1,200.

    (2)   On December 15, 1974, the Prince Company collected rent revenue amounting to $800 on some office space that it rented to another party. The rent collected was for the month December 15, 1974, to January 15, 1975, and was credited to Rent Revenue.

Required:

    (a)   For each transaction give (1) the adjusting entry required on December 31, 1974; (2) the January 6, 1975, entry for payment of any unpaid wages from December 1974; and (3) the January 15, 1975, entry for collection of the rent.

    (b)   Show how any liabilities related to the above transactions should be reported on the balance sheet at December 31, 1974.

E10–3. On November 1, 1974, Long's Auto Parts Company borrowed $12,000 cash from the City Bank for working capital purposes and gave an interest-bearing note and the face amount was $12,000. The note was due in six months and the interest rate was 8% per annum payable at maturity.

Required:

    a.   Give the entry to record the note on November 1.

    b.   Give the adjusting entry that would be required at the end of the annual accounting period, December 31, 1974.

    c.   Give a reversing entry, if you deem one desirable, on January 1, 1975.

    d.   Give the entry to record payment of the note and interest on the maturity date, April 30, 1975.

E10–4. On November 1, 1974, Long's Auto Parts Company borrowed cash from the City Bank for working capital purposes and gave a noninterest-bearing note payable. The note was due in six months and the amount was $6,000. The going rate of interest was 8% per year. Cash received was $5,760.

Required:

    a.   Give the entry to record the note on November 1.

    b.   Give the adjusting entry that would be required at the end of the annual accounting period, December 31, 1974.

c.   Give a reversing entry, if you deem one desirable, on January 1, 1975.

d.   Give the entry to record payment of the note at maturity on April 30, 1975.

E10–5.   Assume you needed to borrow exactly $1,000 cash on a one-year note payable. The City Bank charges 8% interest per annum on such loans. You are to respond to the following questions (show computations):

a.   What would be the face amount of the note, assuming the bank agreed to accept an interest-bearing note?

b.   What would be the face amount of the note, assuming the bank insisted on a noninterest-bearing note? Assume interest is based on the face amount of the note.

c.   What would be the journal entry to record the note in a? In b?

d.   What would be the journal entry at date of maturity in a? In b?

e.   What would be the real or effective rate of interest paid in a? In b?

E10–6.   The comparative income statement for the Oakland Company at December 31, 19B reflected the following data (summarized and excluding income taxes):

	Annual Income Statement for	
	19A	19B
Sales..........................	$50,000	$60,000
Expenses......................	40,000	48,000
Pretax net income.............	$10,000	$12,000

Included on the 19B income statement was an expense amounting to $3,000 that had to be included as a deduction on the income tax return in 19A. Assume a tax rate of 22%.

Required:

(a)   For each year compute (1) income tax expense; (2) income taxes payable; and (3) any deferred taxes.

(b)   Give the entry for each year to record income taxes, including any deferred taxes.

E10–7.   The comparative income statement for the Modern Company at December 31, 19B reflected the following data (summarized and excluding income taxes):

	Annual Income Statement for	
	19A	19B
Revenues......................	$90,000	$94,000
Expenses......................	75,000	78,000
Pretax income.................	$15,000	$16,000

Included on the 19B income statement was a revenue item amounting to $5,000 that had to be included on the 19A income tax return. Assume a flat tax rate of 22%.

Required:

(a) For each year compute (1) income tax expense; (2) income taxes payable; and (3) any deferred taxes.
(Hint: Deferred taxes will have a debit balance for 19A.)
(b) Give the entry for each year to record income taxes, including any deferred taxes.

E10–8. The Travis Manufacturing Company has completed the payroll for January 1974, reflecting the following data:

Salaries and wages earned......................	$50,000
Employee income taxes withheld...............	10,000
Union dues withheld.........................	1,000
FICA payroll taxes*.........................	3,000
FUTA payroll taxes..........................	250
State unemployment taxes.....................	1,500

* Assessed on both employer and employee at a 6% rate for each.

Required:

a. Give the entry to record payment of the payroll and employee deductions.
b. Give the entry to record employer payroll taxes.

E10–9. On January 1, 1974, you deposited $5,500 in a savings account. The account will earn 5% annual interest, which will be added to the fund balance at the end of each year. You recorded the deposit as follows:

Savings Account.....	5,500	
Cash........		5,500

Required:

(1) What will be the balance in the savings account at the end of ten years?
(2) What is the time value of money in dollars for the ten years?
(3) How much interest revenue did the fund earn in (a) year 1; (b) year 2?
(4) Give the entry to record interest revenue at the end of year 1 and year 2.

E10–10. On each January 1, you plan to deposit $500 in a savings account. The account will earn 5% annual interest, which will be added to the fund balance at the end of each year. You recorded the first deposit as follows:

Jan. 1, 1974:		
Savings Account.............................	500	
Cash..		500

Required:

(1) What will be the balance in the savings account on the date of the tenth deposit?

(2) What is the time value of money in dollars for the ten deposits?

(3) How much interest revenue did the fund earn in (a) year 1; (b) year 2?

(4) Give the entry for interest revenue at the end of year 1 and year 2.

E10–11. You have decided to take a trip around the world upon graduation, four years from now. Your grandfather desires to deposit sufficient funds for the purpose in a savings account for you now. A carefully drawn budget on your part indicates that you will need $5,000 at that time. The savings account will draw 5% annual interest, which will be added to the savings account at the end of each year. *Required* (round to even dollars for convenience):

(1) How much should your grandfather deposit in the savings account now so that there will be a $5,000 balance at the end of four years? (Indicated entry: Debit, Savings Account, $?; Credit, Cash, $?).

(2) What is the time value of money in dollars for the four years?

(3) How much interest revenue would the fund earn in year 1; year 2?

(4) Give the accounting entry for the interest revenue at the end of year 1 and year 2.

E10–12. You have decided to attend college for four years and have budgeted the cost at $1,500 per year. This amount will be needed each September 1, starting in 1974. Your father has decided to deposit a single sum of money now, which will pay you the $1,500 each September 1. The savings account will earn 5% annual interest, which will be added to the savings account at the end of each year. Your father will make the single deposit on September 1, 1973. (Indicated entry: Debit, Savings Account, $?; Credit, Cash, $?)

Required:

(1) How much should your father deposit in the savings account?

(2) What is the time value of money in dollars?

(3) How much interest revenue would the fund have earned at the end of year 1 and year 2?

(4) Give the accounting entry for interest revenue at the end of year 1 and year 2.

Problems   P10–1.   The Baker Company completed the transactions listed below during 1974. The annual accounting period ends on December 31, 1974.

Jan. 8   Purchased merchandise for resale at an invoice cost of

$40,000; terms 2/10, n/60. Record at net (see Chapter 8); assume a periodic inventory system.

Jan. 17 Paid invoice of Jan. 8.

April 1 Borrowed $18,000 from the National Bank for general use; executed a 12-month, 8%, interest-bearing note payable.

June 3 Purchased merchandise for resale at an invoice cost of $23,000; terms 1/20, n/30; record at net.

July 5 Paid invoice of June 3.

Aug. 1 Rented two rooms in the building owned by Baker and collected six-months' rent in advance amounting to $1,800.

Dec. 31 Wages earned but not paid on December 31 amounted to $3,400 (disregard payroll taxes).

Required:

a. Prepare journal entries for the above transactions.

b. Prepare any adjusting entries required on December 31, 1974.

c. Show how all of the liabilities arising from the above transactions would be reported on the balance sheet at December 31, 1974.

P10–2. The Litton Company completed the transactions listed below during 1974. The annual accounting period ends on December 31.

Jan. 20 Purchased merchandise for resale at an invoice cost of $30,000; terms 2/10, n/30; record at net and assume a perpetual inventory system (see Chapter 6).

Jan. 28 Paid invoice of Jan. 20.

May 1 Purchased a fixed asset for $68,000; paid $20,000 cash and gave a 12-month, 8%, interest-bearing note payable for the balance.

June 5 Purchased a machine (a fixed asset) at an invoice cost of $10,000; terms 3/10, n/60. (Hint: Interest expense is not a part of the cost of a fixed asset.)

June 14 Paid invoice of June 5.

Sept. 1 Collected rent revenue on some office space rented to another company; the rent of $3,000 was for the next six months.

Dec. 31 Received a tax bill for property taxes for 1974 in the amount of $900; the taxes are payable no later than March 1, 1975.

Required:

a. Give the journal entries for the above transactions.

b. Prepare any adjustment entries required on December 31, 1974.

c. Show how all liabilities arising from the above transactions would be reported on the balance sheet at December 31, 1974.

P10–3. On April 1, 1974, the Jones-Lane Company purchased equipment (a fixed asset) at a cost of $100,000. A cash down payment was made of $40,000. An interest-bearing note (including a mortgage on the equipment) for $60,000 was given for the balance. The note specified 8% interest, payable each April 1, and two payments of $30,000 each on the principle plus interest on the unpaid balance on April 1, 1975, and April 1, 1976. (Note: These will be unequal payments.)

Required:

a. Give the indicated entries at the following dates: April 1, 1974; December 31, 1974 (end of the annual accounting period); and April 1, 1975.
b. Show how the liabilities related to the purchase should be shown on the balance sheet at December 31, 1974.

P10–4. This is a hypothetical situation designed to illustrate accounting for (a) an interest-bearing note payable and (b) a noninterest-bearing note payable. The annual accounting period ends December 31 in both cases.

Assume Company X executed a note payable in favor of the City Bank for a loan of cash on April 1, 1974. The loan was for 12 months with a maturity date of March 31, 1975. The bank charges an 8% annual rate on loans of this type. The amount of cash borrowed was $3,000. We will assume:

Case A—The note was interest-bearing—that is, the principal plus the interest is payable at maturity. (Face amount of note, $3,000.)

Case B—The note was noninterest bearing—that is, the interest was included in the face amount of the note. (Face amount of note, $3,240.)

Required:

a. Record the issuance of the note on April 1, 1974, under each of the two case assumptions. Your solution can be simplified by setting up five columns: Account titles; Case A (debit and credit) and Case B (debit and credit). Thus, the two cases can be presented in your solution in parallel columns.
b. Give the journal entry to record the adjusting entry that would be required for each case on December 31, 1974.
c. Give the appropriate reversing entry for each case on January 1, 1975.
d. Give the entry to record payment of the note under each case at maturity, March 31, 1975.
e. In respect to each case show the following:
   (1) Liabilities that would be reported on the balance sheet at December 31, 1974.
   (2) Interest expense that would be reported on the income statements for 1974 and 1975 (separately).

P10–5. The Stony Company is in the process of preparing comparative statements at December 31, 19B. The records reflect the following summarized income statement date, exclusive of income tax expense:

	19A	19B
Revenues.....................	$150,000	$160,000
Expenses.....................	(110,000)	(129,000)
Extraordinary item..............	(10,000)	4,000
Net before income tax expense.....	$ 30,000	$ 35,000

Included in 19B revenues of $160,000 is an item of revenue amounting to $10,000 that was required to be included on the 19A income tax return. Also included in 19B expenses of $129,000 was an item of expense amounting to $6,000 that had to be deducted on the 19A income tax return. Assume a flat 30% income tax rate.

Required:

(a) For each year, compute (1) income tax expense; (2) income tax liability; and (3) any deferred taxes.
(b) Give the entry for each year to record income tax expense, including any deferred taxes.
(c) Restate the comparative income statement, including the appropriate presentation of income taxes for each year.
(Hint: Allocate income tax expense between operations and extraordinary items. Net income restated for 19B is $24,-500.)

P10–6. On January 1, 1974, the Nash Company signed a contract with the Z Company. The Nash Company was required to deposit with an independent trustee $20,000 cash as a performance guarantee. The trustee agreed to pay 4% annual interest on the fund and to add it to the fund balance at the end of each year. At the end of the third year, the contract was satisfactorily completed and the trustee returned the balance of the fund to the Nash Company. The entry to record the deposit was as follows:

| Performance Fund............................ | 20,000 | |
| Cash....................................... | | 20,000 |

Required:

(1) What was the balance of the fund at the end of the three years?
(2) What was the time value of money in dollars for the three years?
(3) How much interest revenue did the fund earn in each year?
(4) Give the following accounting entries for the Nash Company:
(a) To record interest revenue for each of the three years.
(b) To record receipt of the fund balance in 1976.

P10–7. On January 1, 1974, the management of the Nash Company agreed to set aside a special fund in order to provide sufficient cash to pay off a $50,000 long-term debt due at the end of five years. The single deposit will be made with an independent party (a bank), which will pay 5% annual interest on the fund balance. The interest will be added to the fund balance at the end of each year. The indicated entry for the single deposit on January 1, 1974, is as follows:

Debt Retirement Fund............................ $?
    Cash.. $?

Required:

(1) How much must be deposited as a single sum on January 1, 1974, to satisfy the agreement?
(2) What was the time value of money in dollars for the five years?
(3) How much interest revenue would the fund earn in year 1? In year 2?
(4) Give accounting entries for the following for the Nash Company:
    (a) To record the deposit.
    (b) To record the interest revenue for years 1 and 2.
    (c) To record payment of the maturing liability in 1978.

P10–8. On January 1, 1974, the management of the Lewis Company agreed to set aside, in a special fund, sufficient cash to have a $50,000 balance on hand to pay a maturing debt that was incurred on January 1, 1973. The Lewis Company will make five equal deposits on each January 1, 1974, 1975, 1976, 1977, and 1978. The fund will earn 5% annual interest, which will be added to the balance of the fund at the end of each year. The fund needed must be available immediately after the last deposit. Deposits will be recorded as follows:

Date:
    Debt Retirement Fund............................ $?
        Cash.. $?

Required:

(1) How much must be deposited each January 1?
    (Hint: Use Table 10–3 and divide instead of multiplying; round table value to three places.)
(2) What will be the time value of money in dollars for the fund?
(3) How much interest revenue will the fund earn in year 1? In year 2?
(4) Give accounting entries for the following for the Lewis Company:
    (a) To record the first deposit on January 1, 1974.
    (b) To record interest revenue at the end of year 1; at the end of year 2.
    (c) To record payment of the debt on January 1, 1978.

P10–9.　On January 1, 1974, the Lewis Company sold to the K Company a new machine for $40,000. A cash down payment of $10,000 was made by the K Company. A $30,000, 8% note was signed by the K Company for the balance due. The note is to be paid off in three equal installments due on January 1, 1975, 1976, and 1977. Each payment is to include principal plus interest on the unpaid balance. The sale was recorded as follows:

Jan. 1, 1974:　Cash............................　10,000
　　　　　　　Notes Receivable..................　30,000
　　　　　　　Sales Revenue.................　　　　40,000

Required:

(1)　What is the amount of the equal annual payment that must be made by the K Company?
(Hint: Use Table 10–4 and divide instead of multiplying.)
(2)　What was the time value of money, in dollars, on the note?
(3)　Give the entry for the Lewis Company to record the collection of (a) the first installment (on January 1, 1975) and (b) the second installment (on January 1, 1976).

P10–10.　On January 1, 1973, you purchased a new Super-Whiz automobile for $4,000. You paid a $1,000 cash down payment and signed a $3,000 note to pay the balance in four equal installments on each January 1, the first payment to be made on January 1, 1974. The interest rate is 7% per year on the unpaid balance. Each payment will include payment on principal plus the interest.

Required:

(a)　Compute the amount of the equal payments that you must make.
(b)　What is the time value of money in dollars for the installment debt?
(c)　Complete a debt amortization and interest expense schedule using the following format.

Date	Cash Payment	Interest Expense	Reduction of Principal	Unpaid Principal
1/1/73				$3,000
1/1/74.	$886	$3,000 × .07 = $210	$886 − $210 = $676	2,324
1/1/75				
1/1/76				
1/1/77		$544		–0–

Note: After completing the table, explain the fact that interest expense decreases each year, whereas, reduction of principle increases each year.

P10–11. (Based on Appendix A.)   The Tappen Company has just completed the salary and wage payroll for March 1974. Details provided by the payroll were as follows:

> Salaries and wages earned $100,000*
> Employee income taxes withheld   24,000
> Union dues withheld   1,000
> Insurance premiums withheld   500
>
> FICA tax rate, 6%
> FUTA tax rate, 0.5%
> State unemployment tax rate, 2.5% (based on
>   same amount of wages as FUTA taxes)
>
>   * Subject in full to payroll taxes.

Required:

a. Give the entry to record the payroll for March, including employee deductions. Show computations.
b. Give the entry to record the employer's payroll taxes.
c. Give a combined entry to reflect remission of amounts owed to governmental agencies and other organizations.

P10–12. (Based on Appendix B.)   The Holt Company uses a voucher system to attain control of expenditures. The following transactions have been selected from December 1974 for problem purposes. The accounting year ends December 31.

You are to design a voucher register and a check register similar to those shown in Appendix B. The transactions to follow will be entered in these two special journals.

Dec. 2   Purchased merchandise from AB Wholesalers for resale $2,000; terms 2/10, n/30; record purchases at net and assume a periodic inventory system (see Chapter 8); Invoice No. 14; start with Voucher No. 11.

Dec. 7   Approved contract with Ace Plumbing Co. for repair of plumbing, $450; account: Building Repairs, #77.

Dec. 11 Paid Voucher No. 11; start with Check No. 51.

Dec. 22 Purchased store supplies for future use from Crown Company; Invoice No. 21 for $90; account: Store Supplies Inventory, #16.

Dec. 23 Advertising for pre-Christmas sale $630; bill received from Daily Press and payment processed immediately; account: Advertising Expense, #54.

Dec. 31 Monthly payroll voucher, total $2,500; $1,500 was selling expense (Sales Salaries, #52) and $1,000 was administrative expense (Administrative Salaries, #62); voucher was supported by the payroll record, therefore, one voucher is prepared for the entire payroll; voucher was approved for immediate payment; six checks with consecutive numbers were issued.

Required:

a. Enter the above transactions in the voucher register and the check register.

b. Total the special journals and check the equality of the debits and credits. Set up T-Accounts and post both registers. Complete all posting notations. The following accounts may be needed:

Title	No.
Cash	01
Store Supplies Inventory	16
Vouchers Payable	30
Purchases	40
Selling Expense Control	50
Subsidiary ledger:	
Sales Salaries	52
Advertising Expense	54
Administrative Expense Control	60
Subsidiary ledger:	
Administrative Salaries	62
Building Repairs	77

c. Reconcile the Vouchers Payable account balance with the Unpaid Vouchers File at the end of December.

11 Measurement and reporting of bonds payable

Purpose of the chapter

The sale and issuance of bonds is a primary way of obtaining resources for growth and expansion by businesses, nonprofit organizations (such as colleges), and public subdivisions (such as municipalities and water districts). Bonds are evidences of long-term debt. When bonds are sold, they become an investment to the buyer and an obligation to the issuer. Accounting for bonds as debt is complex because of the wide range of characteristics they may possess. To be efficient in their decision making, both the issuing entity and the investor need to understand the characteristics of bonds and their varying economic effects. Accounting seeks to measure and report these economic effects.

Because of the special characteristics of bonds and the complexities in accounting for them, they were deferred for separate consideration. The purposes of this chapter are (1) to impart a knowledge of the characteristics of bonds payable and (2) to explain the accounting approaches used to measure, record, and report their economic impact. To provide flexibility the chapter is divided into two parts: Part One presents the fundamentals of measuring and reporting bonds payable; Part Two presents some accounting complexities often encountered in measuring and reporting bonds payable.

PART ONE: FUNDAMENTALS OF BONDS PAYABLE

Nature of bonds payable

Funds required for long-term purposes, such as the acquisition of high-cost machinery or the construction of a new plant, may be obtained by issuing long-term notes payable (discussed in Chapter 10) or

386

bonds payable. Bonds payable represent a long-term liability and may be secured by a mortgage on specified assets. Bonds are almost always in denominations of $1,000 and, in rare instances, in denominations of $100,000. They usually are negotiable (i.e., transferable by endorsement) and are bought and sold daily by investors. The bonds of most leading companies are quoted on the security exchanges.[1]

The principal of a bond is the amount payable at the maturity or due date as specified on the bond certificate. This amount frequently is called its par value or its face amount. Throughout the life of a bond, the issuing company makes periodic interest payments, usually semi-annually, to the bondholders.

A company desiring to sell a bond issue must draw up a bond indenture, which specifies the legal provisions of the bonds, such as due date, rate of interest to be paid, dates of interest payments, and conversion privileges (explained later). When a bond is sold, the investor receives a bond certificate (i.e., a bond). All of the bond certificates for a single bond issue are identical in that there is specified on the face of each certificate the same maturity date, interest rate, interest dates, and the other provisions. When a company issues bonds, it normally sells them to an underwriter, who, in turn, markets them to the public. A third party, called the trustee, usually is appointed to represent the bondholders; his duties are to ascertain that the issuing company fulfills all of the provisions of the bond indenture.

Classification of bonds

Bonds may be classified in a number of different ways, depending upon their characteristics. The following classifications should be understood:

1. On the basis of the underlying security:
   a. Unsecured bonds—bonds that do not include a mortgage or pledge of specific assets as a guarantee of repayment at maturity date. These usually are called debentures.
   b. Secured bonds—bonds that include a mortgage or a pledge of specific assets as a guarantee of repayment. Secured bonds tend to be designated on the basis of the type of assets pledged, such as real estate mortgage bonds and equipment trust bonds.
2. On the basis of repayment of principal:
   a. Ordinary or single-payment bonds—the principal is payable in full at a single specified due date in the future.
   b. Serial bonds—the principal is payable in installments on a series of specific dates in the future.

---

[1] In addition to bonds that are issued by most large corporations, many bonds are issued by governmental units, such as state governments, cities, counties, school districts, water districts, and nonprofit institutions. The discussions in this chapter apply to both types, although we will focus mainly on those issued by corporations.

3. On the basis of early retirement:
   a. Callable bonds—bonds that may be called for early retirement at the option of the *issuer*.
   b. Redeemable bonds—bonds that may be turned in for early retirement at the option of the *bondholder*.
   c. Convertible bonds—bonds that may be converted to other securities of the issuer (such as common stock) after a specified date in the future at the option of the *bondholder*.
4. On the basis of payment of interest:
   a. Registered bonds—the name and address of the owner must be currently on file (registered) with the issuing company. Payment of interest is made by check, which is mailed only to the person shown in the bond register.
   b. Coupon bonds—bonds to which a printed coupon is attached for each interest payment throughout the life of the bond. When an interest date approaches, the bondholder "clips" the coupon, signs it, and mails it to the issuing company. In turn, an interest check is sent to the person and address shown on the completed coupon.

Advantages of issuing bonds

Bonds payable often represent an attractive avenue for obtaining large amounts of funds needed by a corporation. The advantages of issuing bonds stem from the fact that the bondholders are creditors and not owners, as are stockholders. A bondholder does not share in the management, the accumulated earnings, or the growth in assets, as does the shareholder. Payments of resources to bondholders are limited to (a) the amount of interest specified on the bond and (b) to the principal or face amount of the bond at maturity. The rate of interest paid to bondholders may be more or less than the dividend rate being paid to shareholders. Using borrowed assets to enhance the return to the owners is spoken of as leverage, which is an important advantage for the stockholders. To illustrate, assume X Corporation earns approximately 15% return on total assets, while at the same time it is paying 7% interest to the bondholders. The interest differential on the portion of resources provided by the creditors clearly will be to the benefit of the shareholders. The leverage factor in favor of the shareholders frequently is significant. The favorable leverage factor increases when the proportion of assets provided by creditors is high in relation to the resources provided by the owners.

Of course, dividends normally are paid to stockholders only if profits have been earned. In contrast, interest payments to bondholders legally must be paid each period, irrespective of whether the corporation earns a profit or incurs a loss. This "fixed charge" to expense each period is a distinct disadvantage of bonds; however, there is an important compensating factor for the issuing company. Interest expense is *deductible* on the income tax return, whereas, dividends paid to stockholders are not deductible. This fact serves to reduce significantly the net cost of funds acquired by issuing bonds. For example, a corporation in the 48% tax bracket, paying 9% interest per annum on bonds payable, would incur a net interest cost on the bonds of $9\% \times 52\% = 4.68\%$. Despite the advantages of leverage, sound financing of a large business requires a realistic *balance* between the amounts of debt (i.e., notes and bonds payable) and owners' equity (i.e., common and preferred stock and retained earnings).

Measuring bonds payable and bond interest expense

The accounting approach used in measuring, recording, and reporting bonds payable is determined primarily by the cost and matching principles. When a bond is sold (i.e., issued), the issue price (or proceeds) is the net cash received, or the fair-market value of any noncash resources received. Under the cost principle, bonds payable are recorded at their issue price; that is, at their current cash equivalent amount. Subsequent to issuance, the bonds continue to be measured and reported at their current cash equivalent amount. This amount will change from period to period if the bonds were issued at a discount or at a premium.

Bonds may be sold at par; that is, at the face or maturity amount. If sold above par, they are said to have been issued at a premium. If sold below par, they are said to have been issued at a discount. To illustrate, if the issuing corporation received $1,000 cash for a bond having a $1,000 par value, there would be no premium or discount. Alternatively, if the corporation received $960 for the bond, there would be a discount of $40; or if $1,050 cash were received, there would be a premium of $50. Typically, bond prices are quoted on the security exchanges as a percent of par or face amount. A bond quoted at 100 sells at par; if quoted at 96 it sells at a discount of 4% below its face amount; if quoted at 105 it sells at 5% above its face amount.

Each period the bond interest is measured, recorded, and reported in conformance with the matching principle. Since interest is incurred on the basis of time, at the end of each period the amount of interest unpaid must be accrued and reported as expense so that it will be matched with the period in which it was incurred. The measurement and reporting of interest has already been discussed in respect to both notes receivable and notes payable. When bonds are issued at a premium or discount, however, an additional measurement problem arises, because these affect both the price of the bond and the amount of interest expense. This measurement problem is discussed subsequently.

In the paragraphs to follow, we will utilize a common set of illustrative data for the Mason Corporation. Assume the Board of Directors and the shareholders of the corporation approved a bond issue with the following provisions:

500 SHARES

Bonds payable authorized ($1,000 per bond)............... $500,000
Date on each bond.................................... January 1, 1974
Maturity in ten years, on December 31, 1983.
Interest, 6% per annum, payable 3% each six months on
    June 30 and December 31.

Mason Corporation, end of the annual accounting period:
    December 31.

Using the above data, we will discuss and illustrate three different assumed situations: (1) the bonds are sold at par; (2) the bonds are sold at a discount; (3) the bonds are sold at a premium.

BONDS SOLD AT PAR

Bonds sell at their par value when the buyers (investors) are willing to invest in them at the stated interest rate on the bond. To illustrate, assume that on January 1, 1974, the Mason Corporation issued $400,000 in bonds payable and received $400,000 in cash for them. The bonds were dated to start interest on January 1, 1974. The entry by the Mason Corporation to record the issuance of the bonds would be:

c A
LT LIAB

```
January 1, 1974:
  Cash................................. 400,000
    Bonds Payable.....................          400,000
  Sold $400,000, 6%, ten-year bonds
  payable at par.
```

Subsequent to the sale of the bonds, interest at 3% on the face amount of the bonds must be paid on each June 30 and December 31 until maturity. The entries to record the interest payments during 1974 would be as follows:

```
June 30, 1974:
  Bond Interest Expense.................. 12,000
    Cash...............................          12,000
  Paid semiannual interest on bonds
  payable ($400,000 x .03 = $12,000).

December 31, 1974:
  Bond Interest Expense.................. 12,000
    Cash...............................          12,000
  Paid semiannual interest on bonds
  payable ($400,000 x .03 = $12,000).
```

At the end of the accounting period, December 31, 1974, the financial statements would report the following:

Income statement:
    Bond interest expense...................... $ 24,000

Balance sheet:
    Long-term liabilities:
        Bonds payable, 6% (due Dec. 31, 1983)...... $400,000

In this situation, the Mason Corporation received $1,000 cash for each $1,000 bond sold and will pay back $1,000 + ($30 × 20) = $1,600. The $600 difference is the amount of interest expense for the ten years; therefore, the interest cost was $60 per year and the *effective rate of interest* was $60 ÷ $1,000 = 6% per year. The *stated* or *nominal rate* called for on the bond also was 6%.

BONDS SOLD AT A DISCOUNT

ISSUED FOR LESS THAN WHAT PRINCIPAL IS AT MATURITY

Bonds sell at a discount when the buyers (investors) are willing to invest in them only at a rate of interest that is *higher* than the stated interest rate on the bond. In this situation the *effective rate of interest* is more than the *stated interest rate* on the bonds. To comprehend this situation you must understand that the *dollar amount* of interest paid on a bond remains the same each period. The dollar amount of interest paid each period is the face or par amount multiplied by the interest rate *stated* on the bond. To illustrate, for each $1,000 bond payable, the Mason Corporation will pay interest amounting to $1,000 × .03 = $30. This is true whether the bond was sold at par, at a discount, or at a premium. With this fact in mind, let's see what the *effective rate of interest* would be, assuming the Mason Corporation issued a $1,000 bond for $980 (i.e., at 98). An analysis of the issuance of this $1,000 bond could be made as follows:

Cash received when bond was sold......................		$ 980
Cash paid back: Principal at maturity..................	$1,000	
Interest ($30 × 20)...................	600	1,600
Difference: Amount of interest paid...................		$ 620

Effective rate of interest: $620 ÷ 10 years = $62
$62 ÷ $980 = 6.33% per year.

INT/YR ÷ CASH PRICE

This computation suggests that the Mason Corporation, because the bond sold at a discount, incurred an *effective rate of interest* of 6.33%, although the stated rate on the bond was 6% per year.[2] The discount served to increase the effective rate above the nominal rate of interest. From this illustration you can see that the investor who desires a *higher* effective rate of interest than the *stated interest rate* on the bond will invest in these bonds only if he can purchase them at a discount.

To illustrate the effect on the accounting and reporting of bonds payable sold at a discount, assume $400,000 of the Mason bonds were issued for $392,000 (i.e., at 98) on January 1, 1974. The entry to record the issuance would be:

---

[2] A more precise and conceptually preferable computation can be made based on present-value concepts explained in Chapter 10. The effective rate of interest is sometimes called the real rate.

```
January 1, 1974:
  Cash...................................  392,000
  Discount on Bonds Payable.............    8,000
    Bonds Payable.......................            400,000
    Sold $400,000, 6%, 10-year bonds
    payable at 98; $400,000 × .98 =
    $392,000, cash received.
```

In the above entry the amount of the discount was recorded in a separate account as a *debit* because it must be accorded special treatment and because the accounts should reflect the maturity amount of $400,000 and the current cash equivalent of $400,000 − $8,000 = $392,000.

The analysis presented on page 391 demonstrated that the discount had the effect of increasing the effective rate of interest; therefore, bond discount, in the economic sense, represents an *increase in bond interest expense*. To give accounting effect to this, the $8,000 debit to Bond Discount must be apportioned to each interest period as an increase in bond interest expense from the date of issuance to maturity date. There are two different methods for doing this: (1) *straight-line* amortization and (2) *effective-interest* amortization. Straight-line amortization is easy to understand and compute; however, it is conceptually deficient. Effective-interest amortization requires use of the future- and present-value concepts discussed in Part Two of Chapter 10. First, we will present straight-line amortization because it is easy to follow. The more complex effective-interest method will be presented in Part Two of this chapter.

Straight-line amortization. To amortize the $8,000 discount over the period from date of issuance to maturity date on a straight-line basis, we allocate an equal dollar amount of it to each interest period. Since there are 20 six-month interest periods, the computation would be: $8,000 ÷ 20 periods = $400, amortization on each semiannual interest date. Therefore, the payments of interest on the bonds during 1974 would be recorded as follows:[3]

---

[3] The amount of interest expense each semiannual period may be confirmed as follows:

Cash to be paid out by the borrower:	
Face amount of the bonds—payable at maturity.........	$400,000
Interest payments ($12,000 × 20 semiannual	
payments)..	240,000
Total cash payments............................	640,000
Cash received by the borrower........................	392,000
Total interest expense over 10 years.............	$248,000
Interest expense per semiannual period	
($248,000 ÷ 20 periods).........................	$ 12,400

DEC OF (margin)
ACCUR LIAB (margin)
DEL (margin)
CUR ASST (margin)

```
June 30, 1974:
    Bond Interest Expense................... 12,400
        Discount on Bonds Payable
            ($8,000 ÷ 20 periods).............          400
        Cash ($400,000 × .03)..............        12,000
    Payment of semiannual interest on
    bonds payable and amortization of
    bond discount for six months.
```

AMT PAYP (margin)
DEC OF (margin)
CUR -IB (margin)
DEL ASST (margin)

```
December 31, 1974:
    Bond Interest Expense................... 12,400
        Discount on Bonds Payable...........          400
        Cash................................        12,000
    Payment of semiannual interest on
    bonds payable and amortization of
    bond discount for six months.
```

In accordance with the thrust of APB *Opinion No. 21,* bonds payable should be measured and reported on the balance sheet at their *current cash-equivalent amount;* that is, the maturity amount less any unamortized bond discount. Therefore, at the end of the accounting period, December 31, 1974, the financial statements would report the following:

Income Statement:
    Bond interest expense........................ $ 24,800

Balance Sheet:
    Long-term liabilities:
        Bonds payable, 6%, due Dec. 31, 1983......... $400,000
        Less unamortized discount.................   7,200 $392,800

8000 - 800 (margin)

Or, alternatively:

400,000 - 7,200 (margin)

    Bonds payable, 6%, due Dec. 31, 1983 (maturity amount $400,000, less unamortized discount)................................ $392,800*

    * This is called the current cash-equivalent amount; some prefer to call it the net liability.

Each succeeding year the unamortized discount will *decrease* by $800 and, as a consequence, the current cash-equivalent amount (net liability) will *increase* each year by $800. At the maturity date of the bonds, the unamortized discount (i.e., the balance in the Discount account) will be zero. At that time the maturity or face amount of the bonds and the current-cash equivalent amount will be the same—$400,000.

BONDS SOLD AT A PREMIUM

When lenders are willing to accept an effective rate of interest that is *lower* than the stated interest rate on the bonds, the bonds will sell at a premium. When the issue price is greater than par, the cash received is greater than the base amount (par) on which the dollars of interest to be paid is calculated. Therefore, when the cash received is related to the dollars of interest paid, based on the lesser par amount, the effective rate of interest is lower than the stated rate of interest.

To illustrate the issuance of bonds at a premium, assume the Mason Corporation issued the $400,000 bonds on January 1, 1974, and received $408,000 in cash (i.e., at 102). An analysis of this issuance could be made as follows:

Cash received when bonds were sold.....................		$408,000
Cash paid back: Principal at maturity.....................	$400,000	
Interest ($400,000 × .03 × 20 periods).....	240,000	640,000
Difference: Amount of interest paid.....................		$232,000

Effective rate of interest: $232,000 ÷ 10 years = $23,200
$23,200 ÷ $408,000 = 5.69% per year.

Although the bonds carried a stated rate of interest of 6% per year, the effective rate of interest was 5.69%. The lesser amount reflects the effect of the issuance premium (computations based on straight-line amortization).

The measurement and recording of the issuance of these bonds at a premium, for 1974, would be:

```
January 1, 1974:
  Cash.................................... 408,000
    Premium on Bonds Payable...........            8,000
    Bonds Payable......................          400,000
  Sold $400,000, 6%, bonds payable
  at 102; $400,000 × 1.02 =
  $408,000.

June 30, 1974:
  Bond Interest Expense..................  11,600
  Premium on Bonds Payable...............     400
    Cash...............................           12,000
  To record payment of interest for
  6 months ($400,000 × .03 =
  $12,000) and to amortize bond
  premium for 6 months ($8,000 ÷
  20 periods = $400).

December 31, 1974:
  Bond Interest Expense..................  11,600
  Premium on Bonds Payable...............     400
    Cash...............................           12,000
  To record payment of interest for
  6 months and to amortize bond
  premium for 6 months as computed
  above.
```

In the entry to record the sale of the bonds, the premium was recorded in a separate account as a *credit*. The premium has the effect of *decreasing* interest expense; therefore, in each period a portion of it is amortized to interest expense. Observe that in the above illustration bond interest expense is reduced by $400 each semiannual period since straight-line amortization is assumed.[4] At the end of 1974, the financial statements will reflect the following:

Income statement:
Bond interest expense........................ $ 23,200

Balance sheet:
Long-term liabilities:
Bonds payable, 6% (due Dec. 31, 1983)...... $400,000
Add unamortized premium................. 7,200 $407,200

Or, alternatively:

Bonds payable, 6%, due Dec. 31, 1983 (maturity
amount $400,000 plus unamortized premium)............. $407,200*

* This is called the current cash-equivalent amount; some prefer to call it the net liability.

[handwritten: 8000 − 600 = 7200]
[handwritten: ADD BECAUSE IT IS AN ASSET]
[handwritten: CURRENT CASH EQUIVALENT AMT.]

At maturity date, after the last interest payment, the bond premium of $8,000 will be fully amortized and the maturity or face amount and the current cash-equivalent amount for the bonds will be the same— $400,000. At maturity, December 31, 1983, the bonds will be paid off, resulting in the following entry:

```
December 31, 1983:
    Bonds Payable......................... 400,000
        Cash...............................          400,000
    To retire 6% bonds payable
    at maturity date.
```

The discussions and illustrations in this part of the chapter have focused on the fundamental issues in measuring and reporting bonds payable. The background essential to understanding the economic impact on the issuing company and to comprehending financial statements that report bonds payable is provided. The next part focuses on some complexities often encountered in accounting for bonds payable.

---

[4] The amount of interest expense each semiannual period may be confirmed as follows:

Cash paid out by the borrower:
Face amount of bonds at maturity............... $400,000
Interest payments ($12,000 × 20 periods)......... 240,000
Total cash payments....................... 640,000
Cash received by the borrower.................. 408,000
Total interest expense over 10 years.......... $232,000
Interest expense per semiannual period
($232,000 ÷ 20 periods)....................... $ 11,600

PART TWO: SOME COMPLEXITIES IN ACCOUNTING
FOR BONDS PAYABLE

This part of the chapter focuses primarily on three complexities usually encountered in accounting for bonds payable because important dates related to the bond issue are not the same as the ending of the accounting period. Bonds payable sold between interest dates, adjusting entries for accrued bond interest, and effective-interest amortization will be discussed and illustrated. Also treated will be a related issue—bond sinking funds.

As a basis for the discussions to follow, we will utilize a common set of data for the Mendez Corporation. Assume that the following bond issue was approved:

/ ○○

Bonds payable authorized ($1,000 per bond)..................... $100,000
Date on each bond....................................... June 1, 1974
Maturity in 10 years on June 1, 1984.
Interest, 6% per annum, payable 3% each June 1 and December 1.
Additional data:
   Mendez Corporation: End of the annual accounting period, December 31.
   Bonds issued: Entire issue sold on August 1, 1974, for $96,460.

In order to focus on the effect of different dates on the accounting for a bond issue, the time scale shown in Exhibit 11–1 may be helpful.

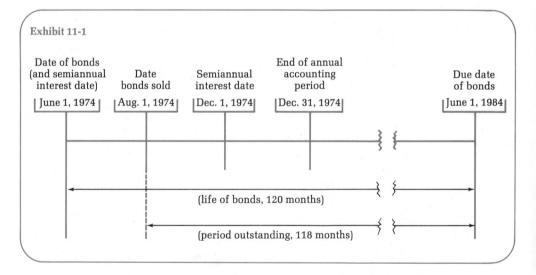

Exhibit 11-1

| Date of bonds (and semiannual interest date) | Date bonds sold | Semiannual interest date | End of annual accounting period | | Due date of bonds |
| June 1, 1974 | Aug. 1, 1974 | Dec. 1, 1974 | Dec. 31, 1974 | | June 1, 1984 |

(life of bonds, 120 months)

(period outstanding, 118 months)

Accounting for bonds sold between interest dates

The bond certificates specify the date and amount of each interest payment. Although bonds may be sold on an interest date, more frequently than not market factors cause them to be sold *between* interest dates. Nevertheless, the exact amount of interest specified on the bond certificate for each interest date will be paid, irrespective of whether a bond is sold on or between an interest date. Therefore, when bonds are sold between two interest dates, the lender (i.e., the buyer) must *pay the accrued interest* since the last interest date in addition to the market price of the bond. Because the next interest payment will be for a full interest period, the accrued interest is then effectively returned to him. In view of this standard practice, the investor will realize interest revenue only for the number of months the bonds were held by him from the date of sale. Similarly, the issuing corporation will incur interest expense for the same period. This presents two complexities in accounting for bonds: (1) the amount of accrued interest charged to the buyer must be included in the entry to record the sale of bonds; and (2) any premium or discount is amortized over the remaining **period outstanding** —that is, the period from date of sale to date of maturity of the bonds.

To illustrate, the above data for the Mendez Corporation states that the bonds were sold on August 1, which was *two* months after the last semiannual interest date of June 1, for $96,460 (i.e., at a discount of $3,540). On August 1, date of sale of the bonds, the Mendez Corporation would receive cash for the sales price of the bonds, *plus* two months accrued interest, computed as follows (refer to the time scale above):

Market price...	$96,460
Add accrued interest for 2 months:	
$100,000 × .03 × 2/6..............................	1,000
Total cash received.............................	$97,460

The entry to record the issuance of the bonds payable would be as follows:

```
August 1, 1974:
  Cash (per above)....................... 97,460
  Discount on Bonds Payable
    ($100,000 - $96,460)................. 3,540
      Bonds Payable.....................            100,000
      Bond Interest Expense (per above)...            1,000
    Sale of bonds 2 months
    after interest date.
```

In this entry, Bond Interest Expense is credited because the $1,000 accrued interest collected from the purchaser will be refunded to him when the first interest payment is made. That payment will be recorded as a credit to Cash and a debit to Bond Interest Expense. This is illustrated below.

The bond discount debit of $3,540 must be amortized over the *period outstanding* of 118 months; therefore, straight-line amortization would be: $3,540 ÷ 118 months = $30 per month. The entry to record the first interest payment would include amortization of discount only for the four months that the bonds have been outstanding. Therefore, the first interest payment would be recorded as follows:

```
December 1, 1974:
  Bond Interest Expense.................... 3,120
    Discount on Bonds Payable
      ($30 × 4 mos.)......................           120
    Cash ($100,000 × .03).................         3,000
  Payment of bond interest for 6 months
  and amortization of discount
  for 4 months.
```

After the two entries are posted, the Bond Interest Expense account would reflect a balance of $2,120, which is equivalent to four months' interest ($100,000 × .03 × ⁴⁄₆ = $2,000) plus four months' discount amortization ($30 × 4 = $120), viz:

Bond Interest Expense

12/1/74	3,120	8/1/74	1,000

(Balance $2,120)

Adjusting
entry for
accrued bond
interest

In accounting for notes payable, you will recall that, at the end of each accounting period, an adjusting entry was made for any interest expense accrued since the last interest payment date. The same adjusting procedure must be applied to bonds payable. However, in the case of bonds, the adjusting entry must include both the accrued interest and amortization of the bond discount or premium. To illustrate for 1974 for the Mendez Corporation, recall that the last interest payment date was December 1, 1974; therefore, on December 31 there is accrued interest for one month. Bond discount also must be amortized for one more month. The adjusting entry would be:

```
December 31, 1974:
  Bond Interest Expense......................... 530
    Discount on Bonds Payable.................          30
    Bond Interest Payable.....................          500
  Adjusting entry to record bond interest
  payable for 1 month, $100,000 × .03 × ⅙ =
  $500; and to amortize bond discount
  for 1 month, $30.
```

After this entry is posted, the Bond Interest Expense account will reflect a debit balance of $2,650, which represents interest expense for the five months that the bonds have been outstanding during 1974 (August 1 to December 31). This amount may be verified as follows:

$$
\begin{array}{lr}
\text{Interest: } \$100{,}000 \times .03 \times 5/6\ldots\ldots\ldots & \$2{,}500 \\
\text{Add discount amortized: } \$30 \times 5\ldots\ldots & 150 \\
\text{Total interest expense for 1974}\ldots\ldots & \$2{,}650 \\
\end{array}
$$

This amount will be closed to Income Summary and will be reported on the income statement for 1974 as Bond Interest Expense.

Bond sinking fund

On the maturity date of bonds payable, the issuing company must have available a large amount of cash to pay off the bondholders. Such a large cash demand might place the issuing company in a severe financial strain. In order to avoid this situation, some companies build up a **cash fund** in advance by making equal contributions each year over a period of time in advance of maturity date. Such a cash fund generally is known as a **bond sinking fund.** A sinking fund is an asset and is reported on the balance sheet under the caption Funds and Investments.

A bond sinking fund also adds a measure of security for the bondholders since it assures them that funds will be available for retirement of the bonds at maturity. Each cash contribution usually is deposited with a trustee, a designated third party such as a bank. The trustee invests the funds received and pays interest each year on the balance of the fund. Interest earned on a sinking fund is recorded as an increase in the fund balance (the debit) and as interest revenue (the credit). Thus, a bond sinking fund has the characteristics of a regular savings account. At maturity of the bonds, the balance of the fund is used to pay off the bondholders. Any excess is returned to the issuing corporation, or, in the case of a deficit, it must be made up by the issuer.

To illustrate a bond sinking fund, assume the Mendez Corporation, in order to pay off the $100,000 bonds payable due June 1, 1984, decided to set up a bond sinking fund. The fund is to be built up over the last five years that the bonds are outstanding by making five equal annual deposits each December 31, starting in 1979. The sinking fund is to be deposited with the City Bank, as trustee, which will pay 5% annual interest on the fund balance. The amount of each deposit required was calculated to be $18,098. This was based on the time-value-of-money concepts discussed and illustrated in Chapter 10, Part Two. If the fund earned no interest, obviously each deposit would have to be $100,000 ÷ 5 contributions = $20,000. Instead of $20,000, the annual deposit required is $18,098 because the interest earned each year will be added to the fund balance. (Note: This will provide a $100,000 fund balance six months before maturity date.) The required annual deposit was computed as follows:

Situation:
 Future amount needed.............................. $100,000
 Period of accumulation; (n), equal annual contributions..   5 rents
 Assumed interest earnings rate on the fund balance......   5% per year

Computation (application of future amount of annuity):
 Future Amount = Periodic Rent × Future Amount of Annuity of $1
         (n = 5; i = 5%)

 Substituting:
  $100,000 = ? × 5.5256 (from Table 10–3)
  Periodic Rent = $100,000 ÷ 5.5256
      = $18,098

The entries for 1979 and 1980 to be made by the Mendez Corporation for this sinking fund would be:

```
Dec. 31, 1979 (1st deposit):
  Bond Sinking Fund........................ 18,098
     Cash.................................           18,098
     To establish a bond sinking fund;
     1st deposit.

Dec. 31, 1980 (interest added to the fund):
  Bond Sinking Fund........................    905
     Interest Revenue......................              905
     To record sinking fund earnings during
     1st year ($18,098 × .05 = $905).

December 31, 1980 (2nd deposit):
  Bond Sinking Fund........................ 18,098
     Cash.................................           18,098
     To record 2nd deposit in bond sinking
     fund.
```

Identical entries with different interest amounts, because of the increasing balance in the fund, would be made for each of the five years of the accumulation period. At maturity date of the bonds, the following entry would be made upon payment to the bondholders:

```
At maturity date:
  Bonds Payable........................... 100,000
  Cash....................................   2,500
     Bond Sinking Fund.................            102,500
     To record payment of bonds payable
     at maturity from the bond sinking
     fund and the return of the $2,500
     excess in the bond sinking fund
     (i.e., 5% interest on $100,000 for
     six months).
```

At December 31, 1980, the financial statement would reflect:

   Income statement:
    Interest Revenue................... $ 905

   Balance sheet:
    Funds and Investments:
     Bond Sinking Fund............. $37,101*

    * Computation: $18,098 + $905 + $18,098 = $37,101.

The bond sinking fund is only one of several funds that a company may establish from time to time to meet future needs. For example, it is not uncommon for a company to accumulate, in a similar manner, a "building fund" in anticipation of the future cash needs for the construction of a large building. All such funds, appropriately labeled, are accounted for and reported as discussed and illustrated above.[5]

Effective-interest amortization on bonds payable

Effective-interest amortization of bond discount or bond premium is a conceptually sound approach for measuring both (1) the true or effective interest expense on bonds and (2) the carrying amount of the bonds (at the current cash-equivalent amount). It uses the concept of present value discussed in Chapter 10, Part Two. Conceptually, it is somewhat complex; however, APB *Opinion No. 21* requires this approach when the discount or premium amount is material. At this stage in your study of accounting, we are not concerned with all of the computational complexities but, rather, stress understanding of the concept. It is similar to the situation when one purchases an automobile on an installment payment basis where equal monthly payments are made on the debt. Each equal payment made on the debt consists of two parts: (1) a payment on the principal and (2) payment of interest.

Let's see how this same concept applies to bonds payable (similarly, a debt). We will use a simplified situation to illustrate the concept. Assume that Company X issued a $1,000 bond payable on January 1, 1974, and received $948 cash. Assume also that the bond carried a stated interest rate of 6%, payable at the end of each year, and that the life of the bond is three years. A $1,000, 6% bond issued at $948 results in an effective-interest rate of 8% (the $948 was taken from a bond table). The issuance of the bond was recorded as follows:

```
January 1, 1974:
  Cash.........................................  948
      Bonds Payable (maturity amount, $1,000)....        948
      Issued $1,000, 6% bond at $52 discount.
```

Note: The discount could have been set up separately as a debit to a bond discount account as illustrated in a prior paragraph. In either case, the effect will be the same.

The three annual interest payments would be recorded as follows, assuming effective-interest amortization:

	Year 1	Year 2	Year 3
Bond Interest Expense.......	76	77	79
Cash ($1,000 × .06)......	60	60	60
Bonds Payable*..........	16	17	19

  * Computed below.

---

[5] In connection with such funds, a company may also restrict, or appropriate, an equivalent amount of retained earnings as a dividend restriction. The restriction of retained earnings by a corporation is discussed in Chapter 13.

The financial statements at the end of each year would reflect the following:

	Year 1	Year 2	Year 3
Income Statement:			
Bond Interest Expense...................	$ 76	$ 77	$79
Balance Sheet:			
Bonds Payable (maturity amount, $1,000),			
less unamortized discount...............	$964	$981	$1,000*

* Just prior to retirement of the bonds.

The underlying concept of the measurement of interest expense is indicated on the income statement; interest expense changes in amount each year. Had straight-line amortization been used, interest expense would have been constant in amount each year. The underlying concept of the measurement of the **current cash-equivalent amount** of the debt is reflected in an increasing amount on the balance sheet from the issue price to the maturity or face amount of the bond (at maturity date).

We should not be overly concerned with the details of the computation of the periodic interest expense and the current cash-equivalent amount. Nevertheless, the computations are tabulated below because they also reveal the conceptual basis for effective-interest amortization. Observe that the effective rate of interest (8% in this example), rather than the stated rate of interest, is basic to the computations.

Date	Cash Paid for Interest each Period	Effective Interest each Period; Based on Unpaid Balance and Effective Rate	Amount Applied to Restate the Principal	Amount of Unpaid Principal
1/1/74 (issuance)............				$ 948
End Year 1...........	$ 60*	$948 × .08 = $ 76	$16†	964‡
End Year 2..........	60	964 × .08 = 77	17	981
End Year 3..........	60	981 × .08 = 79	19	1,000
Totals...........	$180	$232	$52	

* $1,000 × .06 = $60.
† Col. 2, $76 minus Col. 1, $60 = $16.
‡ $948 plus Col. 3, $16 = $964.

Effective-interest amortization is conceptually superior to straight-line amortization because, for each period, consistent with the issue price of the bonds, it measures (1) the true amount of interest expense on the income statement and (2) the true current cash-equivalent amount of the bonds outstanding (net liability) on the balance sheet. Straight-line amortization provides only approximations of these amounts.

Demonstra-
tion case for
self-study

REED COMPANY, INC.

(Try to resolve the requirements before studying the suggested solution that follows.)

In order to raise funds to construct a new plant, the management of Reed Company, Inc., decided to issue bonds. Accordingly, a proposed bond indenture was submitted to the Board of Directors and approved. The provisions in the bond indenture and specified on the bond certificates were:

> Face value of bonds to be issued ($1,000 bonds)..... $600,000
> Date of bond issue—Feb. 1, 1974, due in 10 years
>   on Feb. 1, 1984.
> Interest—6% per annum, payable 3% on each
>   Feb. 1 and Aug. 1.

The bonds were sold on June 1, 1974, at 102½ plus accrued interest. The annual accounting period for Reed Company, Inc., ends on December 31.

Required:

(a) How much cash was received by Reed Company, Inc., from the sale of the bonds payable on June 1, 1974? Show computations.

(b) What was the amount of premium on the bonds payable? Over how many months will it be amortized?

(c) Compute the amount of amortization of premium per month and for each six-month interest period; use straight-line amortization. Round to even dollars.

(d) Give entry on June 1, 1974, to record the sale of the bonds payable.

(e) Give entry for payment of interest and amortization of premium for the first interest payment on August 1, 1974.

(f) Give adjusting entry required on December 31, 1974, at the end of the accounting period.

(g) Give the optional reversing entry that could be made on January 1, 1975.

(h) Give entry to record second interest payment and amortization of premium on February 1, 1975.

(i) Show how bond interest expense and bonds payable would be reported on the financial statements at December 31, 1974.

Suggested Solution:

Requirement (a):

> Sales price of the bonds: ($600,000 × 1.025)............. $615,000
> Add accrued interest for 4 months (Feb. 1 to June 1)
>   ($600,000 × .06 × 4/12).........................   12,000
>   Total cash received from the bonds payable........ $627,000

Requirement (b):

Premium on the bonds payable ($600,000 × .025) ..... $ 15,000

Months amortized: From date of sale, June 1, 1974,
to maturity date, Feb. 1, 1984
120 months − 4 months = ... 116 months

Requirement (c):

Premium amortization: $15,000 ÷ 116 months = $129 per month, or $774 each six
month interest period.

Requirement (d):

```
June 1, 1974:
   Cash (per Req. (a) above)............. 627,000
      Premium on Bonds Payable (per
         Req. (b) above)................                 15,000
      Interest Expense ($600,000 ×
         .06 × 4/12)....................                 12,000
      Bonds Payable.....................                600,000
   To record sale of bonds payable
   at 102½ plus accrued interest for
   4 months, Feb. 1, 1974, to
   June 1, 1974.
```

Requirement (e):

```
Aug. 1, 1974:
   Bond Interest Expense................. 17,742
   Premium on Bonds Payable ($129 ×
      2 months)..........................    258
      Cash ($600,000 × .03).............                 18,000
   To record payment of semiannual
   interest and to amortize premium for
   2 months, June 1 to Aug. 1, 1974.
```

Requirement (f):

```
Dec. 31, 1974:
   Bond Interest Expense................. 14,355
   Premium on Bonds Payable ($129 ×
      5 months)..........................    645
      Accrued Bond Interest Payable
         ($600,000 × .06 × 5/12).........                 15,000
   Adjusting entry for 5 months' in-
   terest accrued plus amortization of
   premium, Aug. 1 to Dec. 31.
```

Requirement (g):

```
Jan. 1, 1975:
   Accrued Bond Interest Payable..........  15,000
      Premium on Bonds Payable...........             645
      Bond Interest Expense..............          14,355
   Reversing entry; optional.
```

Requirement (h):

```
Feb. 1, 1975:
   Bond Interest Expense................  17,226
   Premium on Bonds Payable
      (per Req. (c))....................     774
      Cash ($600,000 × .06 × 6/12)......          18,000
   To record payment of semiannual in-
   terest and to amortize premium for
   6 months.
```

Requirement (i):

Interest expense to be reported on the 1974 income statement should be for the period outstanding during the year; that is, for seven months, June 1 through December 31. Interest expense, per the above entries, is $17,742 + $14,355 − $12,000 = $20,097; or, alternatively, ($600,000 × .06 × 7/12 = $21,000) minus ($129 × 7 months = $903) = $20,097.

Income Statement for 1974:
  Interest expense.................................... $20,097

Balance Sheet, Dec. 31, 1974:
  Long-term Liabilities:
    Bonds payable, 6% (due Feb. 1, 1984)... $600,000
    Add unamortized premium*............   14,097 $614,097

* ($15,000 − ($258 + $645) = $14,097.)

Summary   In this chapter we discussed bonds payable, the issuance of which is one of the primary ways to obtain funds needed for acquiring fixed assets and to expand the business. An important advantage of bonds payable is that the cost of the funds—interest expense—is deductible for income tax purposes. This serves to reduce the net interest cost to the business. Bonds are measured and reported at their current cash-equivalent amount.

Bonds may be sold at their face, or par, amount; at a premium; or at a discount, depending upon the stated interest rate on the bonds, compared with the effective or market rate of interest that the buyers demand. The price of a bond varies inversely with the effective or market rate of interest. If the market rate is higher than the stated rate on the bond, the bonds will sell at a discount. Conversely, if the market rate is lower than the stated rate on the bond, the bonds will sell at a premium.

Discount and premium on bonds payable, in effect, are adjustments to the interest expense incurred by the issuing company. As a consequence, discount or premium on bonds payable is amortized to interest expense over the *outstanding* life of the bonds.

To pay off bonds payable at maturity, a company may set aside cash in advance by means of equal periodic contributions to a bond sinking fund. Such a fund is similar to a savings account. The bond sinking fund normally is administered by an outside third party, such as a bank (called the trustee). Interest earned on the fund balance is added to the fund. At the maturity date of the bonds, the fund is used to pay off the bondholders. Such a fund is reported on the balance sheet under the caption Funds and Investments. Interest earned on the fund is reported on the income statement as "Interest revenue."

Important terms		
Bond indenture		**Straight-line amortization**
Leverage		**Effective-interest amortization**
Bond discount		**Bond premium**
Effective rate of interest		**Bond sinking fund**
Stated rate of interest		

Questions for discussion

1. What is a bond payable? For what purpose are bonds payable usually issued?
2. What is the difference between the bond indenture and the bond certificates?
3. Distinguish between secured and unsecured bonds.
4. Distinguish between callable, redeemable, and convertible bonds.
5. Distinguish between registered and coupon bonds.
6. What are some advantages to the issuer in raising funds by the issuance of bonds, as compared with issuing capital stock?
7. The higher the tax bracket, the lower the net cost of borrowing money. Explain.
8. At date of issuance, bonds are recorded at their current cash-equivalent amount. Explain.
9. What is the nature of discount and premium on bonds payable?
10. What is the relationship between the stated interest rate and the effective interest rate on a bond?
11. Distinguish between the stated and effective rates of interest on a bond payable (a) sold at a discount; (b) sold at a premium.

12. Why is bond discount or bond premium amortized over the outstanding life of the bonds payable?

13. In respect to bonds payable, what is meant by "net liability"?

14. Why is the lender (i.e., the purchaser of a bond payable) charged for the accrued interest from the last interest date to date of purchase of the bonds?

15. Explain the basic difference between straight-line amortization and effective-interest amortization of bond discount or premium.

Exercises E11-1. Holiday, Incorporated, is considering borrowing $40,000 on a three-year note payable. The interest rate will be 8% per annum, payable each year. The company computed its return on total investment (i.e., net income ÷ liabilities + owners' equity) to be 12%. The average tax rate for the company is 40%.

Required:

a. What amount of interest would be paid the first year?
b. Considering the effect of income taxes, what would be the net interest cost?
c. List two advantages to Holiday in favor of the note payable versus selling more of its capital stock.

E11-2. Sosa Company, Inc., has approved a $100,000, 5% bond issue. The bonds are dated January 1, 1974, and are for ten years. Interest is paid each January 1. They have not yet been placed on the market. You are to give the entry to record their issuance, on January 1, 1974, under three different assumptions:

Assumption A—They sell at 100.
Assumption B—They sell at 99.
Assumption C—They sell at 102.

E11-3. Renolds, Incorporated, sold a $100,000, 5% bond issue on July 1, 1974, at 98. The bonds were dated July 1, 1974, and pay interest each December 31 and June 30. The bonds mature ten years from July 1, 1974.

Required:

a. Give the entry to record the issuance of the bonds.
b. Give the entry to record the interest payment on December 31, 1974. Assume straight-line amortization.
c. Show how the bond interest expense and the bonds payable would be reported on the December 31, 1974, annual financial statements.

E11-4. Davis Company, Inc., sold a $60,000, 7% bond issue on July 1, 1974, at 103. The bonds were dated July 1, 1974, and pay interest each December 31 and June 30. The bonds mature in 15 years from July 1, 1974.

Required:

a. Give the entry to record the issuance of the bonds.
b. Give the entry for the interest payment on December 31, 1974. Assume straight-line amortization.
c. Show how the bond interest expense and the bonds payable would be reported on the December 31, 1974, annual financial statements.

E11–5. Vieux-Carre, Incorporated, issued $100,000 bonds payable on January 1, 1974, that were due in ten years. The bonds sold for $106,000 on that date. Interest at 3% per semiannual period is payable each January 1 and July 1.

Required:

a. Give the entry to record the issuance of the bonds on January 1, 1974.
b. Give the entry to record the first interest payment on July 1, 1974. Assume straight-line amortization.

E11–6. In order to obtain cash for a purchase of fixed assets, the Harris Corporation, whose annual accounting period ends on December 31, issued the following bonds:

> Date of bonds: January 1, 1974.
> Maturity amount and date: $100,000, due in 10 years (December 31, 1983).
> Interest: 3% each June 30 and December 31.
> Date sold: January 1, 1974.

Required:

a. Give the entry to record the issuance and the first two interest payments under each of three different assumptions. Assume straight-line amortization.
   (1) The bonds sold at par.
   (2) The bonds sold at 97.
   (3) The bonds sold at 103.
b. On a separate piece of paper provide the following amounts to be reported on the financial statements at the end of 1974:

	Assumption 1	Assumption 2	Assumption 3
Interest expense	$	$	$
Bonds payable			
Unamortized premium or discount			
Net liability			

E11–7. The Strong Corporation issued the following bonds payable:

> Bonds payable authorized......................... $50,000
> Date on each bond............................. Jan. 1, 1974
> Maturity date (10 years)........................ Dec. 31, 1983
> Interest, 6% per year, payable each December 31.

Strong sold all of the bonds on March 1, 1974, and received $51,180 cash plus any accrued interest.

Required:

(a) What was the amount of discount or premium?
(b) Over what period of time should the discount or premium be amortized?
(c) What would be the amortization amount per month assuming straight-line amortization?
(d) Give entry to record the issuance.
(e) Give entry on first interest payment date.

E11–8. The Bay Corporation has a $50,000 bond issue outstanding that is due four years hence. They desire to set up a bond sinking fund for this amount by making five equal annual contributions. The first contribution will be made immediately and the last one on the due date. They will deposit the contributions with a bank as trustee, which will increase the fund at the end of each year for 6% on the fund balance that existed at the beginning of the year.

Required:

(a) Compute the annual contribution or rent.
(b) Give entry for the first and second contributions, including interest.
(c) Show how the effects of the fund would be reported on the financial statements at the end of the second year.

E11–9. The Fluger Corporation issued a $1,000 bond payable on January 1, 1974. The bond specified an interest rate of 7% payable at the end of each year. The bond matures in three years. It was sold at an effective rate of 5% per year. In respect to the issuance of the bond, the following computation has been completed:

Date	Cash	Interest	Principal	Balance
Jan. 1, 1974 (issuance)...				$1,054
End of Year 1.........	$70	$53	$17	1,037
End of Year 2.........	70	52	18	1,019
End of Year 3.........	70	51	19	1,000

Required:

Respond to the following questions:
(a) What was the issue price of the bond?
(b) Did the bond sell at a discount or a premium? How much?
(c) What amount of cash was paid each year for bond interest?
(d) What amount of interest expense should be shown each year on the income statement?
(e) What amount(s) should be shown on the balance sheet for bonds payable at each year end (assume last year, just before retirement of the bond)?

(f) What method of amortization was used? Explain.
(g) Show how the following amounts were computed for year 2:
     (1) $70; (2) $52; (3) $18; (4) $1,019.
(h) Why is the method of amortization used preferable?

Problems P11–1. Haywood, Incorporated, issued bonds with the following provisions:

Maturity value:	$100,000
Interest:	6% per annum payable semiannually each Dec. 31 and June 30.
Terms:	Bonds dated Jan. 1, 1974, due in 10 years from that date.

The annual accounting period for Haywood ends December 31. The bonds were sold on January 1, 1974, for $103,600.

Required:

a. Give journal entry to record the issuance of the bonds.
b. Give journal entries at the following dates (assume straight-line amortization): June 30, 1974; Dec. 31, 1974; June 30, 1975.
c. How much interest expense would be reported on the income statement for 1974? Show how liabilities relating to the bonds would be reported on the December 31, 1974, balance sheet.

P11–2. Griffin, Incorporated, issued $100,000 bonds payable, due in ten years, at 3% interest per semiannual period. The bonds were dated March 1, 1974, and interest is payable each March 1 and September 1. The bonds were sold on April 1, 1974, for $94,050, plus any accrued interest. The annual accounting period ends December 31.

Required:

a. Give the entry to record the issuance of the bonds on April 1, 1974.
b. Give the entry to record the first interest payment and amortization of discount on September 1, 1974. Assume straight-line amortization.
c. Give the required adjusting entry on December 31, 1974.
d. Give the amounts that should be reported on the 1974 financial statements for:
    Interest expense.
    Bonds payable.
    Unamortized discount.
    Net liability.

P11–3. Assume a $200,000, 6% bond issue was sold on March 1, 1974. The bonds pay interest each June 30 and December 31 and will mature ten years from January 1, 1974. Using this data, on a separate sheet of paper complete the table below under three separate cases as follows (show computations and assume straight-line amortization):

Case A—The bonds sold for $200,000.
Case B—The bonds sold for $195,280.
Case C—The bonds sold for $204,720.

	Case A	Case B	Case C
Income Statement for 1974:			
Bond interest expense..............	═══	═══	═══
Balance Sheet at Dec. 31, 1974:			
Long-term Liabilities:			
Bonds payable, 6%...............	———	———	———
Unamortized discount............	———	———	———
Unamortized premium............	———	———	———
Net liability..................	═══	═══	═══

P11–4. In order to expand to a new region, the Elgin Manufacturing Company decided to construct a new plant and warehouse. It was decided that approximately 60% of the resources required would be obtained through a $600,000 bond issue. Accordingly, the company developed and approved a bond indenture with the following provisions:

Date of bonds:................. March 1, 1974, due in 10 years
Amount authorized:............ $600,000 (maturity amount)
Interest:...................... 6% per annum, payable 3% each
March 1 and September 1

The annual accounting period ends on December 31. The bonds were sold on March 1, 1974, at 102.

Required:

a. How much cash was received by Elgin on March 1, 1974?
b. What was the amount of the premium? Over how many months will it be amortized?
c. On a separate sheet of paper complete the following table (use straight-line amortization):

	Per Month
Interest payment..........................	$_____
Premium amortization.....................	$_____
Net interest expense.......................	$_____

d. Give entries, if any, at each of the following dates: March 1, 1974; September 1, 1974; December 31, 1974; January 1, 1975; and March 1, 1975.
e. In respect to the financial statements for December 31, 1974:
   (1) How much interest expense would be reported?
   (2) Show how the liabilities related to the bonds would be reported on the balance sheet.

P11–5. On January 1, 1963, the Donnee Corporation issued $500,000, 6% bonds payable due at the end of 15 years. The bonds specified semiannual interest payments on each June 30 and December 31. The bonds sold at 103. Additionally, the bond indenture called for the establishment of a bond sinking fund to be accumulated over the last five years by deposits of $90,000 on each January 1, starting in 1974. Interest on the fund is to be deposited in the fund at the end of each year.

Required:

a. Give entry for issuance of the bonds on January 1, 1963.
b. Give entry for the semiannual interest payment on the bonds. Assume straight-line amortization.
c. Give entry on January 1, 1974, for the first contribution of cash to the sinking fund.
d. Give the sinking fund entry at the end of 1974, assuming the interest earned on the first contribution amounted to $4,000.
e. Give the entry to retire the bonds at maturity assuming the total bond sinking fund accumulation to be $493,000.

P11–6. Johnson, Incorporated, in order to obtain funds to acquire additional long-term assets, approved the following bond indenture:

Maturity value authorized:	$600,000 (in $1,000 denominations)
Interest:	6% per annum, payable 3% each June 1 and Dec. 1
Maturity:	10 years from June 1, 1974
Bond sinking fund:	Starting at the beginning of the 8th bond year, deposit $150,000 annually in a bond sinking fund under the control of Trustee X. Interest earned by the fund shall be deposited in the fund. The bond sinking fund shall be used only to retire the bonds at maturity.

The annual accounting period for Johnson ends on December 31. The bonds were sold on August 1, 1974, for $623,700, which included two months' accrued interest (June 1 to August 1).

Required:

a. Give the entry to record issuance of the bonds.
b. Give the entries at the following dates (assume straight-line amortization):
   (1) First interest date.
   (2) End of first annual accounting period (1974).
   (3) Beginning of second accounting period (1975).
   (4) Second interest date.
c. In respect to the 1974 financial statements:
   (1) How much interest expense would be reported on the 1974 income statement?
   (2) Show how the liabilities related to the bonds would be reported on the December 31, 1974, balance sheet.
d. Give the entry to record:
   (1) The first contribution to the sinking fund.
   (2) Interest earned on the sinking fund on the first contribution; amount, $6,000.

e. Give the entry to retire the bond issue at the end of the tenth year assuming the bond sinking fund has a balance of $510,000. (Note: The fund earnings rate varied from year to year).

P11–7. The Royal Corporation issued bonds payable and received cash in full for the issue price. The bonds were dated and issued on January 1, 1974. The stated interest rate was payable at the end of each year. The bonds mature at the end of four years. In respect to the issuance of the bonds, the following computations have been completed:

Date	*Cash*	*Interest*	*Principal*	*Balance*
Jan. 1, 1974..........				$5,173
End of Year 1........	$350	$310	$40	5,133
End of Year 2........	350	308	42	5,091
End of Year 3........	350	305	45	5,046
End of Year 4........	350	304	46	5,000

Required:

Respond to the following questions:
(a) What was the maturity amount?
(b) How much cash was received upon issuance?
(c) Was there a premium or a discount? How much?
(d) How much cash will be disbursed for interest each period? In total?
(e) What method of amortization is being used? Explain.
(f) What is the stated rate of interest?
(g) What is the effective rate of interest?
(h) Show how the following amounts for year 3 were computed: (1) $350; (2) $305; (3) $45; (4) $5,046.
(i) What amount of interest expense should be reported on the income statement each year?
(j) Show how the bonds should be reported on the balance sheet at the end of each year (show the last year immediately before retirement of the bonds).
(k) Why is the method of amortization being used preferable to other methods?

12 Measurement and reporting of owners' equity

Owners' equity is defined as the excess of total assets over total liabilities. It is a residual amount that represents the book value of the owners' interest in the business enterprise. Owners' equity appears somewhat differently on the balance sheet (and in the accounts) for a sole proprietorship, partnership, and corporation. With the same set of transactions, however, the *total amount* of owners' equity on a given date would be the same (except for income tax effects), irrespective of the type of business organization. The accounting entries and financial reporting for the three types of business organizations essentially are the same in all situations, *except for those entries that directly affect owners' equity*. This commonality exists because the underlying fundamentals of accounting (Exhibit 2–1) apply equally to each of the three types of business organizations.

Because of certain legal requirements and the full-disclosure principle, owners' equity for each of the three types of business organizations must be accounted for and reported in slightly different ways. Accounting for the owners' equity of a corporation is more complex than for a sole proprietorship or for a partnership. The purpose of this chapter is to expand the prior discussions of owners' equity. Part One will focus on corporations and Part Two on sole proprietorships and partnerships.

PART ONE: SHAREHOLDERS' EQUITY

The corporation is the dominant type of business organization in the United States. This is because the corporate form has three important advantages over the sole proprietorship and the partnership. First, the

414

corporate form facilitates the bringing together of large amounts of funds through the sale of shares to the public. Second, it facilitates the transfer of separate ownership interests because the shares can be easily transferred to others. Third, it affords the investor or stockholder limited liability.[1]

In contrast to a sole proprietorship or partnership, a corporation is recognized in law as a separate legal entity. Legally, it is separate and distinct from the owners and enjoys a continuous existence separate and apart from them. It may own property, sue others, be sued, and execute contracts independently of the stockholder owners.

Ownership in a corporation is evidenced by shares of capital stock, which are freely transferable without affecting the corporation. The owners of a corporation are known as stockholders or shareholders.

Each state has laws that govern the organization and operation of corporations. The laws of each state establish the requirements that must be met to organize a corporation. To form a corporation, an application for a charter must be submitted to the appropriate state official. The application must specify the name of the corporation, the purpose (type of business), kinds and amounts of capital stock authorized, and the financial contributions (through the sale of capital stock) at date of organization. Most states require a minimum of three stockholders, initially. Upon approval of the application, the state issues a charter (sometimes called the articles of incorporation). The governing body of a corporation is the Board of Directors, which is elected by the shareholders.

When a person buys shares of capital stock, he receives a stock certificate as evidence of his ownership interest in the corporation. The certificate will indicate the name of the stockholder, date purchased, type of stock, number of shares represented, and a description of the characteristics of the stock. Exhibit 12–1 shows a stock certificate for 100 shares of common stock. On the back of the certificate are instructions and blanks to be completed when the shares are sold and transferred to another party.

The charter granted by the state specifies the maximum number of shares of stock the corporation can issue. To illustrate, assume the charter for the Rogers Corporation specified "authorized capital stock, 10,000 shares; par value, $10 per share." Assume further that the corporation immediately sold and issued 6,000 shares. The following terms are used to describe the status of the 10,000 shares permitted:

1. Authorized shares—the maximum number of shares of the stock

---

[1] In case of insolvency of a corporation, the creditors have recourse for their claims only to the assets of the corporation. Thus, the stockholders stand to lose, as a maximum, only their equity in the corporation. In contrast, in the case of a partnership or sole proprietorship, creditors have recourse to the personal assets of the owners in case the assets of the business are insufficient to meet the outstanding debts of the business.

Exhibit 12–1

Stock certificate

that can be sold and issued as specified in the charter of the corporation. For the Rogers Corporation, the authorized shares would be 10,000.

2. Issued shares—the number of shares of capital stock that have been issued by the corporation to date. For the Rogers Corporation, the issued shares would be 6,000 to date.

3. Unissued shares—the number of authorized shares of capital stock that have not been issued by the corporation to date. For the Rogers Corporation, the unissued shares would be 4,000.

4. Subscribed shares—A corporation may sell some stock on credit and not issue it until payment is received. These are called subscribed shares. To illustrate, assume the Rogers Corporation sold 500 shares to an individual and has not issued them because the sales price has not been collected. In this instance there would be 500 subscribed shares.

5. Treasury stock—A corporation may purchase some of its own shares previously sold. Shares of the corporation that have been sold and issued and subsequently repurchased by the issuing corporation are referred to as treasury stock. They are considered issued but not outstanding. To illustrate, assume the Rogers Corporation purchased 200 of its own shares from a stockholder. The corporation then would have 200 shares of treasury stock.

6. Outstanding shares—the number of shares currently owned by stockholders. It is the number of shares *issued* less the number of shares of treasury stock held by the corporation. For example, for the Rogers Corporation, it would be:

TOTAL # ISSUED — TREASURY STOCK AMT (SHARES)

Issued shares	6,000
Less treasury stock	200
Outstanding shares	5,800

Types of capital stock

The capital stock of a corporation may consist of only one kind of stock, which would be known as **common stock**; or it may consist of two kinds of stock—common stock and **preferred stock.** Common stock may be conveniently viewed as the "usual" or "normal" stock of the corporation. In contrast, preferred stock is distinguished because it grants certain **preferences.** These preferences generally specify that the preferred shareholders must receive their dividends *before* any dividends can be paid to the common shareholders. Because of the important differences between common and preferred stock, they are separately identified in the accounting and reporting processes.

COMMON STOCK

When only one class of stock is issued, it must be common. It has the voting rights and often is called the **residual equity** since it generally ranks after the preferred stock for dividends and assets distributed upon dissolution. However, since it has no dividend limits comparable with those associated with preferred, it has greater possibilities for dividends and increases in market value. The two primary classifications of common stock are par value and no-par value.

Par-value and no-par-value stock. Some years ago, all capital stock was par value. Par value is a **nominal** value per share established for the stock in the charter of the corporation and is printed on the face of each stock certificate. Stock that is sold by the corporation to investors above par value is said to sell at a premium, whereas, stock sold below par is said to sell at a discount. In recent years the laws of all states have been changed to forbid the initial sale of stock by the corporation to investors below par value.[2] Originally, the concept of par value was established as a protection to creditors and investors by means of a "cushion" of assets that could not be impaired. Par value does not establish market value or worth, and the idea that it represented a

---

[2] The discussions throughout this chapter in respect to the sale of stock refer to the initial sale of the stock by the corporation rather than to later sales between investors, as is the common situation in the day-to-day transactions of the stock markets. Since the sale of stock by a corporation at a discount is no longer legal, no further discussion of it is included. The sale of stock between individuals is not recorded in the accounts of the corporation.

financial cushion was ill-conceived. Today, par value, when specified, only serves to identify the stated or legal capital of the corporation.

The par-value concept proved to be ineffective in protecting either creditors or stockholders. For that reason, many states enacted legislation permitting no-par-value stock. No-par-value common stock does not have an amount per share specified in the charter; therefore, it may be issued at any price without involving a discount. It also avoids giving the impression of a value that may be present. When no-par stock is used by a corporation, the legal, or stated, capital is as defined by the state law. State laws generally define it as (1) a stated amount per share set by the corporation itself (i.e., if it is not specified in the charter), or (2) as the amount for which the stock was sold originally. The term legal capital, or stated capital, is a matter of specification by the state incorporation laws. It varies between states; however, it is generally viewed as the par value of the stock outstanding (in the case of par-value stock) or the stated value set by the company (in the case of no-par-value stock) or the amount for which the stock was sold. We shall see later that legal capital generally cannot be used as the basis for dividends. The stock certificate shown in Exhibit 12–1 is for no-par-value stock.

PREFERRED STOCK

When one or more classes of stock in addition to common are issued, the additional classes are called preferred stock. Preferred stock involves some modification that makes it different from the common stock. The usual modifications, or features, one or more that characterize preferred stock are:

(1)   Dividend preferences.
(2)   Conversion privileges.
(3)   Asset preferences.
(4)   Nonvoting specifications.

Thus, preferred stock generally has both favorable and unfavorable characteristics, in comparison with common stock.[3] Preferred stock almost always has a par value. For example, a corporation charter may specify "Authorized capital stock: nonvoting, 5% preferred stock, 5,000 shares, par value $20 per share; common stock, 100,000 shares, no-par value."

A corporation may choose to issue more than one class of stock (a) to obtain favorable arrangements from its own point of view; (b) to issue stock without voting privileges; and (c) as an appeal to a wide range of investors with special provisions on the preferred stock.

---

[3] A majority of corporations issue only common stock. Large corporations tend to have both common and preferred in their financial structure. Some large companies also issue more than one class of preferred stock.

The dividend preferences of preferred stock will be discussed and illustrated later in the chapter. The other features may be briefly explained as follows:

Convertible preferred stock extends to the preferred stockholders the option to turn in their preferred shares and receive in return shares of common stock held for issuance by the corporation. The terms for the conversion will specify dates and a conversion ratio. To illustrate, in the example above, the charter could have read: "Each share of preferred stock, at the option of the shareholder, can be converted to two shares of the no-par common stock anytime after January 1, 1976."

Asset preferences almost always are specified for preferred stock. It is a preference as to the distribution of assets (a) in the event that the corporation *dissolves* or (b) in the event the corporation "calls" the preferred stock. The asset preference often is somewhat higher than the par value; that is, upon redemption or dissolution, the preferred stockholders would receive cash equal to the asset preference of their stock before any distribution would be made to the common stockholders. To illustrate, in the above example, the asset preference could have been specified as $25 per share. If it were, then a holder of the preferred stock would be entitled to receive on dissolution, for example, $25 per share before a shareholder of common stock would receive anything.

Nonvoting preferred stock is quite common, despite the fact that the nonvoting feature is undesirable to the investor. This feature denies the preferred stockholder the right to vote at stockholder meetings. It is one avenue for obtaining capital without lessening the control of the common stockholders.

Accounting and reporting capital stock

In accounting and reporting for shareholders' equity, accountants follow the concept of sources. Under this concept, the capital or owners' equity from different sources is recorded in separate accounts and reported separately in the Stockholders' Equity section of the balance sheet. The two basic sources of stockholders' equity are:

1. Contributed capital—the amounts invested by stockholders through the purchase of shares of stock from the corporation. It is comprised of two separate elements: (1) amounts derived from the sale of common stock and (2) amounts derived from the sale of preferred stock. This is also sometimes referred to as paid-in capital.

2. Retained earnings—the cumulative amount of net income earned since organization of the corporation less the cumulative amount of dividends paid by the corporation since organization.

First, we will discuss and illustrate contributed capital. For illustrative purposes in this section, we will use the Siesta Corporation. Assume the charter specified two types of capital stock as follows:

Authorized capital stock:
  Preferred stock, 5%, 1,000 shares, $10 par value per share.
  Common stock, 200,000 shares, $1 par value per share.

SALE OF CAPITAL STOCK

When par-value stock is sold and issued, Cash is debited and an appropriately designated contributed capital account for each type of stock is credited. The difference between the selling price and the par value of the stock is credited to a separate contributed capital account entitled "Contributed Capital in Excess of Par." To illustrate, assume the Siesta Corporation sold 400 shares of preferred stock at $15 per share and 100,000 shares of common stock at $5 per share. The entry would be:

```
Cash ($6,000 + $500,000)..................  506,000
    Preferred Stock (400 shares × $10 par
        value)...............................              4,000
    Contributed Capital in Excess of Par,
        Preferred 400 shares × ($15 - $10).               2,000
    Common Stock (100,000 shares × $1 par
        value)...............................            100,000
    Contributed Capital in Excess of Par,
        Common 100,000 shares × ($5 - $1)..              400,000
```

Observe in the above entry that the two capital stock accounts were credited for the *par value* of the shares sold and the differences between selling price and the par value were credited to two other contributed capital accounts. There were *two* basic "sources" to be recognized—preferred and common stock—and each source was subdivided between the par value and the excess received over par.[4]

Now, assume a balance sheet is prepared after the above entry. The **stockholders' equity** would be reported as follows:

Stockholders' Equity

Contributed Capital:
  5% Preferred stock, par $10; authorized 1,000 shares,
    issued and outstanding, 400 shares.............. $ 4,000
  Common stock, par $1; authorized 200,000 shares,
    issued and outstanding, 100,000 shares..........   100,000
  Contributed capital in excess of par:
    Preferred stock..............................   2,000
    Common stock.................................   400,000
        Total Contributed Capital................ $506,000
Retained earnings illustrated later.

---

[4] Contributed capital in excess of par sometimes is called "premium on stock" or "paid-in capital above par." In recent years, corporations have tended to set the par value per share far below the intended selling price for flexibility and in order to avoid any implication of a "discount."

Capital stock sold for noncash assets. When noncash considerations, such as buildings, land, machinery, and services (e.g., attorney fees), are received in payment for capital stock issued, the assets received (or expenses, in the case of services) should be recorded by the issuing corporation at the fair-market value of the stock issued at the date of the transaction in accordance with the cost principle. Alternatively, if the fair-market value of the stock issued cannot be determined, then the fair-market value of the consideration received should be used. To illustrate, assume the Siesta Corporation issued 50 shares of common stock for legal services when the stock was selling at $5 per share. The entry would be:

```
Legal Expense (50 shares × $5)..................... 250
    Common Stock (50 shares × $1 par)...........           50
    Contributed Capital in Excess of Par, Common
        Stock (50 shares × $4).....................          200
```

Accounting for no-par stock. No-par stock does not have a particular "value" specified in the charter of the corporation. As a consequence, when no-par stock is sold and issued, it may be recorded in one of two ways, depending on the laws of the particular state that granted the charter. In some states the law requires the corporation, after the charter is granted for no-par stock, to set a *stated* value per share. This stated value becomes the *legal* capital and is credited to the no-par capital stock and any excess is credited to "Contributed Capital in Excess of Stated Value." To illustrate, assume that the Elgin Corporation sold and issued 1,000 shares of its no-par common stock at $25 per share. Assume further that the corporation established a *stated value* of $20 per share. The sale and issuance of the no-par stock would be recorded as follows:

```
Cash........................................ 25,000
    No-par Common Stock (1,000
        shares × $20).......................          20,000
    Contributed Capital in Excess of
        Stated Value; No-par Common Stock....          5,000
    Sale and issuance of 1,000 shares
    of no-par common stock at $25 per
    share; stated value, $20 per share.
```

In contrast, the corporation may be chartered in a state where the laws require that the corporation must credit *all* of the proceeds from the sale of its capital stock to the No-par Capital Stock account. In this situation there would be no "stated" value. To illustrate, under these circumstances, the Elgin Corporation would record the sale and issuance of the no-par common stock at $25 per share as follows:

```
Cash.......................................... 25,000
    No–par Common Stock....................                    25,000
    Sale and issuance of 1,000 shares
    of no–par common stock at $25 per
    share.
```

At this point it may be emphasized that there is no difference in accounting between preferred and common stock, except that each is recorded in separate accounts. Similarly, on the financial statements, they are reported in the same manner, although separately.

Treasury
stock

Treasury stock is a corporation's own capital stock that was sold, collected for, issued, and subsequently reacquired by the corporation. Corporations frequently purchase shares of their own capital stock for sound business reasons—to obtain shares needed for employee bonus plans; to influence the market price of the stock; to increase their earnings per share amount; or to have shares on hand for use in the acquisition of other companies. Treasury stock, while held by the issuing corporation, has no voting, dividend, or other stockholder rights.[5]

When a corporation purchases its own capital stock, the assets (usually cash) of the corporation and the stockholders' equity are reduced by equal amounts. When treasury stock is sold, the opposite effects occur. Purchases of treasury stock generally are recorded by debiting the cost to a *negative* stockholders' equity account called Treasury Stock (type of stock) and crediting Cash. Since the Treasury Stock account has a debit balance, it is often referred to as a negative stockholders' account. When treasury stock is sold, the Treasury Stock account is credited at cost and Cash is debited. Generally, the purchase and selling prices will be different, necessitating recognition of the difference in an appropriately designated contributed capital account in the entry to record the sale. To illustrate accounting for treasury stock, assume the balance sheet for the May Corporation reflected the following on January 1, 1974:[6]

---

[5] The laws of most states impose certain restrictions on the amount of treasury stock a corporation can hold at any one time since this is an avenue for taking resources out of the corporation by the owners (stockholders), which may jeopardize the rights of creditors. The law in some states limits the cost of treasury stock that can be purchased to the balance reflected in the Retained Earnings account.

[6] There are two alternative approaches to accounting for treasury stock—the cost method and the par-value method. We will limit our discussions to the cost method since it is less complex and more widely used. The par-value method is discussed in most accounting texts at the intermediate level.

MAY CORPORATION
Summarized Balance Sheet, January 1, 1974

Assets		*Stockholders' Equity*	
Cash...............	$ 30,000	Contributed capital:	
Remaining assets.....	70,000	Common stock, par $10, authorized	
		10,000 shares, issued 8,000 shares....	$ 80,000
		Retained earnings...................	20,000
Total Assets.....	$100,000	Total Stockholders' Equity.......	$100,000

Assume that on January 2, 1974, the May Corporation purchased 300 of the outstanding shares of its own common stock at $12 per share. The transaction would be recorded as follows:

```
January 2, 1974:
  Treasury Stock, Common (300 shares
    at cost)................................ 3,600
    Cash.......................................        3,600
  Purchased 300 shares of treasury stock
  at $12 per share.
```

The effect of this entry is to contract, or reduce, both the assets and stockholders' equity by $3,600. Now, assume that on February 14, 1974, one-third of the treasury shares were resold at $13 per share. This transaction will have the effect of expanding both assets and stockholders' equity by $1,300. These effects are reflected in the following entry to record the resale of 100 of the treasury shares:

```
February 14, 1974:
  Cash....................................... 1,300
    Treasury Stock, Common (100 shares
      at cost)............................          1,200
    Contributed Capital, Treasury Stock
      Transactions.......................           100
  Sold 100 shares of treasury stock at
  $13; cost, $12 per share.
```

The Treasury Stock account has a debit balance, although owners' equity accounts normally carry a credit balance. Since the balance in the Treasury Stock account reflects a contraction of stockholders' equity, it is a negative equity account and is subtracted from the total. To illustrate, a balance sheet at February 15, 1974, assuming no other transactions by the May Corporation, would be:[7]

[7] Some people argue that the debit balance in the Treasury Stock account should be reported on the balance sheet as an asset rather than as a reduction in stockholders' equity. This position is supported by the argument that the treasury stock could be sold for cash just as readily as the shares of other corporations. The argument is fallacious; all *unissued* stock of the corporation presumably also could be sold for cash.

MAY CORPORATION
Summarized Balance Sheet, February 15, 1974

Assets		*Stockholders' Equity*	
Cash................	$27,700	Contributed Capital:	
Remaining assets......	70,000	Common stock, par $10, authorized	
		10,000 shares, issued 8,000, of	
		which 200 shares are held as trea-	
		sury stock....................	$ 80,000
		Contributed capital, treasury stock	
		transactions...................	100
		Total contributed capital.......	80,100
		Retained earnings................	20,000
		Total......................	100,100
		Less cost of treasury stock held......	2,400
Total Assets..........	$97,700	Total Stockholders' Equity.	$ 97,700

Upon resale of the 100 shares of treasury stock, contributed capital was increased by $100, which was the difference between cost and sales price of the treasury shares sold. Observe that this difference was *not* recorded as a gain as would be done for the sale of an asset. The basic accounting concept is that "gains or losses" on transactions involving a corporation's own stock are balance sheet (*stockholder equity*) items and not income statement items.

You should also observe in the preceding balance sheet that the May Company, on February 15, 1974, has both treasury stock and unissued stock; there are 200 shares of treasury stock held and 2,000 shares of unissued stock. The purchase and/or resale of treasury stock does not affect the number of shares of unissued (or issued) stock; however, the number of shares of outstanding stock is affected. The only difference between treasury stock and unissued stock is that treasury stock has been sold at least once and recorded in the accounts.

To illustrate the resale of treasury stock at a price *less than cost,* assume that an additional 50 shares of the treasury stock were resold by the May Corporation on March 1, 1974, at $11 per share; that is, $1.00 per share below cost. The resulting entry would be:

```
March 1, 1974:
  Cash.......................................... 550
  Contributed Capital, Treasury Stock Transac-
    tions....................................... 50
      Treasury Stock, Common (50 shares) ........     600
    Sold 50 shares of treasury stock at $11
    per share; cost, $12 per share.
```

Note that the "loss" is debited to the same contributed capital account to which the "gain" in the preceding entry was credited. Retained Earnings would be debited for the amount of the deficiency if there is no credit balance or an insufficient credit balance in the account Contributed Capital, Treasury Stock Transactions.

Accounting
for
dividends

A dividend is a distribution to stockholders by a corporation. Dividends must be voted by the Board of Directors of the corporation before they can be paid. Dividends may involve the distribution of cash, other assets of the corporation, or the corporation's own stock (i.e., a stock dividend). The term *"dividend,"* without a qualifier, generally is understood to mean a cash dividend, which is the most common type. Dividends normally are stated in terms of so many dollars per share, or as a percent of par value.

For illustrative purposes in this section, we will use the Monarch Corporation and will assume capital stock outstanding and retained earnings as follows:

5% Preferred stock, par $20, shares outstanding 2,000 . . . . . . $40,000
Common stock, par $10, shares outstanding 5,000 50,000
Retained earnings 40,000

To illustrate the payment of a cash dividend, assume the Board of Directors voted the following:

"The Board of Directors of the Monarch Corporation declared an annual cash dividend of $2 per share on the common stock and 5% per share on the preferred stock to the stockholders on date of record, payable on December 15, 1974." The entry to record the payment of the cash dividend would be:

```
December 15, 1974:
   Dividends Paid, Common Stock............. 10,000
   Dividends Paid, Preferred Stock.......... 2,000
      Cash...................................         12,000
   To record payment of a cash dividend:
   Common stock, 5,000 shares × $2 = $10,000
   Preferred stock, $40,000 × .05 = $2,000
```

In the above entry the debits were to Dividends Paid. This account is closed to Retained Earnings at the end of the period. Some accountants prefer to make the debits directly to Retained Earnings rather than maintaining separate Dividends Paid accounts. The effect is precisely the same in either case. The important point to observe is that the payment of a cash dividend has two effects: (1) assets are decreased and (2) retained earnings (i.e., owners' equity) is decreased by the same amount.

Nature of
a cash
dividend

An investor expends cash to acquire shares of stock as an investment. The incentive for buying the shares is to earn an economic return on the investment. Specifically, the investor expects cash inflows in the future that will return both his initial investment and a gain. His cash inflows in the future from the stock investment are expected to come from two sources: (1) current cash inflows in the form of dividends on the shares; and (2) a cash inflow at the time he sells the stock. He anticipates that the sum of these two cash inflows will be greater than his investment in the shares. The cash inflow from dividends is considered by him to be revenue. The other cash inflow (from sale of the shares) usually will result in a market gain or loss, depending on whether he sells the shares above or below the acquisition price. The amounts and frequency of dividends paid by a corporation generally have a definite effect on the market price of the stock.

Now, let's look at a cash dividend from the viewpoint of the corporation. A corporation has the earning of income on the resources provided by the stockholders as a primary objective. Its ability to attract and retain investments by present and potential stockholders in the long run depends in good measure on their earnings record. The profits of a corporation may be retained in the business for corporate expansion or paid to the shareholders as dividends. One of the significant decisions faced by the Board of Directors of a corporation is how much of the earnings should be retained and how much should be distributed to the shareholders as dividends each year.

In the entry above to record the cash dividend, it is significant to note that both assets (i.e., cash) and owners' equity (i.e., retained earnings) are decreased by the amount of the dividend. This fact suggests that there are two fundamental requirements for the payment of a cash dividend:

(1) Sufficient retained earnings—The corporation must have accumulated a sufficient amount of retained earnings to cover the amount of the dividends. State laws place a restriction on cash dividends. The laws tend to limit dividends to the balance in Retained Earnings. As a matter of financial policy, and to meet growth objectives, corporations seldom disburse more than 50–70% of the earnings as dividends.

(2) Sufficient cash—The corporation must have access to cash sufficient to pay the dividend, and in addition, sufficient cash to meet the continuing operating needs of the business. The mere fact that there is a large *credit* in the Retained Earnings account does not indicate sufficient cash. The cash generated by earnings represented in the Retained Earnings account may have been expended in acquiring inventory, purchasing fixed assets, or paying liabilities. There is no necessary relationship between the balance of retained earnings and the balance of cash.

Dividends on preferred stock

Common stock represents the basic, residual issue of stock. You will recall that preferred stock grants to its holders certain rights that have precedence over the rights granted by common stock. The primary feature of preferred stock is the dividend preference. The dividend preferences may be classified as follows:[8]

1. Current dividend preference.
2. Cumulative dividend preference.
3. Participating dividend preference.

Preferred stock may have one or a combination of these three dividend features. The charter of the corporation must state specifically the distinctive features of the preferred stock.

CURRENT DIVIDEND PREFERENCE

Preferred stock always carries a current dividend preference. This preference assures the preferred shareholders that, if any current dividends are paid, their current dividend must be paid before any dividends can be paid on the common stock. When the current dividend preference is met and no other preference is operative, the balance of the dividends is paid to the common-stock shareholders. The current dividend preference almost always is a specified percent of the par value of the preferred stock. To illustrate, the preferred stock of the Monarch Corporation was: "5% preferred stock, par $20 per share, 2,000 shares outstanding, total par value outstanding $40,000." The current dividend preference is $20 × .05 = $1 per share of preferred. Therefore, current dividends paid by the Monarch Corporation, under four different assumptions in respect to the total dividends paid, would be divided between the preferred and common shareholders as follows:

MONARCH CORPORATION
Current Dividend Preference

		Amount of Dividend Paid to Shareholders	
		5% Preferred Stock	Common Stock
	Total	*(2,000 shares @ $20*	*(5,000 shares @ $10*
Assumption	*Dividends Paid*	*par = $40,000)* *	*par = $50,000)*
A	$1,000	$1,000	$ –0–
B	2,000	2,000	–0–
C	3,000	2,000	1,000
D	8,000	2,000	6,000

* Preferred dividend preference, $40,000 × .05 = $2,000.

CUMULATIVE DIVIDEND PREFERENCE

If preferred stock has this feature, it is said to be "cumulative preferred stock." This means that if all or a part of the specified dividend

---

[8] A dividend preference does not mean that dividends will be paid automatically. Dividends are paid only when *formally* declared by the corporation's Board of Directors. Thus, the declaration of a dividend is discretionary.

(5% in the above example) is not paid in a given year, the unpaid amount becomes dividends in arrears. If the preferred stock is cumulative, the dividends in arrears must be paid subsequently before any dividends can be paid to the common. To illustrate, assume in the above example for the Monarch Corporation that no dividends were paid in the two preceding years. Therefore, a current dividend payment, under four different assumptions, would be divided between the preferred and common stock as follows:

MONARCH CORPORATION
Cumulative Preferred Stock

		Amount of Dividend Paid to Shareholders	
Assumption	*Total Dividends Paid*	*5% Preferred Stock** *(2,000 shares @ $20 par = $40,000)*	*Common Stock (5,000 shares @ $10 par = $50,000)*
A	$ 4,000	$4,000	$ –0–
B	6,000	6,000	–0–
C	8,000	6,000	2,000
D	15,000	6,000	9,000

* Current dividend preference, $40,000 × .05 = $2,000; dividends in arrears preference, $2,000 × 2 years = $4,000.

Of course, if the preferred stock is noncumulative, dividends can never be in arrears and, in effect, are lost to the preferred stockholders. Because of this highly unfavorable feature, preferred stock usually is cumulative.

PARTICIPATING DIVIDEND PREFERENCE

Preferred stock may be (a) nonparticipating, (b) fully participating, or (c) partially participating. These features relate to dividends that might be paid to preferred shareholders *above* the current dividend preference (i.e., above the 5% of par value in the above example) and above any cumulative dividends in arrears.

Most preferred stock is nonparticipating; that is, the amount of dividends payable to preferred shareholders in any one year is limited, in the absence of dividends in arrears, to the specified rate or amount. If the stock is cumulative, the preferred dividends are limited to the amount in arrears plus the specified dividend preference for the current year. To illustrate, assume the Monarch 5% preferred stock is nonparticipating and *non*cumulative. Under this assumption, dividends on the preferred stock would be limited to the maximum of 5% of par (i.e., $1 per share) in any one year. However, if the Monarch preferred stock were nonparticipating and cumulative, the preferred shareholders would be limited to the $1 per share for the current dividend *plus* the dividends in arrears.

Alternatively, preferred stock may be **fully participating**. This means that the preferred stock participates pro rata with common stock above the specified preference rate (5% in the above example) and with no upper limit to the annual dividend rate. When the preferred stock is fully participating, after the specified preference on the preferred stock is satisfied each year, the common stockholders then would receive an equivalent percentage amount, after which each group of stockholders would participate on an equivalent pro rata basis. To illustrate, dividends for the Monarch Corporation under two different assumptions as to the preferred stock would be divided between the preferred and common shareholders as follows:

MONARCH CORPORATION
Participating Preferred Stock

	Amount of Dividend Paid to:		
Assumptions	*Preferred Share-holders (Total par $40,000)*	*Common Share-holders (Total par $50,000)*	*Total Dividends Paid*
Case A—Preferred stock is cumulative and nonparticipating (2 years in arrears). Total dividends paid $13,000.			
Arrears...	$4,000		$ 4,000
Current dividend................................	2,000	$7,000	9,000
Totals.......................................	$6,000	$7,000	$13,000
Case B—Preferred stock is cumulative and fully participating (2 years in arrears). Total dividends paid $13,000.			
Arrears.......................................	$4,000		$ 4,000
Current preference.............................	2,000		2,000
Equivalent amount to common.....................		$2,500	2,500
Balance divided in ratio of par value:			
($40,000/$90,000) × ($13,000 − $8,500)...........	2,000		2,000
($50,000/$90,000) × ($13,000 − $8,500)...........		2,500	2,500
Totals.......................................	$8,000	$5,000	$13,000

Partially participating preferred stock is the same as fully participating, except that the participating preference above the current dividend rate is limited to a stated percent of par. For example, the charter may read, ". . . and partially participating up to an additional two percent." Fully participating and partially participating preferred stock preferences are rather rare.[9]

Stock dividends   Instead of paying a cash dividend, the Board of Directors of a corporation may decide to distribute to the stockholders, on a *pro rata*

---

[9] Refer to more advanced books for additional discussion and illustrations of the participating features and the payment of a dividend in assets other than cash, such as property and stock of other corporations being held as an investment.

basis, additional shares of the corporation's own unissued stock. This is known as a stock dividend. Stock dividends almost always consist of common stock being distributed to holders of common stock. To illustrate, assume the Monarch Corporation distributed a 10% common-stock dividend to the shareholders. For each ten shares of common stock held, one additional common share would be issued.

In contrast to a cash dividend, a stock dividend does *not affect the assets* of a corporation or the *total* amount of stockholders' equity. A stock dividend causes only an internal change in stockholders' equity. In accounting for a stock dividend, *Retained Earnings* is decreased (i.e., debited) and *Contributed Capital* is increased (i.e., credited) by the amount of the stock dividend. The 10% stock dividend for the Monarch Corporation would require the company to issue 500 additional shares (i.e., 5,000 shares outstanding × 10%) of the unissued common stock. The entry to record the distribution of the stock dividend, assuming a current market value of $15 per share, would be:[10]

```
Retained Earnings (500 shares × $15)....... 7,500
    Common Stock (500 shares × $10 par)....        5,000
    Contributed Capital in Excess of
    Par, Common Stock (500
    shares × $5).......................        2,500
Common stock dividend of 10% distributed
when market value per share was $15.
```

The transfer of retained earnings to permanent or contributed capital by means of a stock dividend often is referred to as capitalizing earnings. To restate: The only effects on the corporation issuing a stock dividend is to reshuffle the internal content of stockholders' equity and to increase the number of shares outstanding. From the viewpoint of the stockholder, he receives additional shares of stock but owns the same *proportion* of the shares outstanding after the stock dividend as he did before.

Observe in the above illustration of the stock dividend that the amount for the stock dividend transferred from Retained Earnings to Contributed Capital was the *current fair-market value* of the shares issued (i.e., $15 × 500 shares = $7,500). This amount is considered appropriate when the stock dividend is "small"; that is, when it is less than 25% of the previously outstanding shares. In those rare cases where a stock dividend is "large" (i.e., over 25%), some accountants believe that the amount transferred should be the par value of the shares issued. Par value is considered to be the absolute minimum. Fair market value is preferred by many accountants primarily because (1) it is the amount that would be credited to Contributed Capital if

---

[10] Some accountants prefer to debit an account called "Stock Dividends Distributed," which is closed to Retained Earnings at the end of the period. The effect is precisely the same.

the stock were sold at the current price, and (2) it is the amount that would be debited to Retained Earnings for a cash dividend equal to the current cash equivalent of the stock issued.

Reasons for stock dividends. Stock dividends are quite common since they serve very useful purposes, both from the viewpoint of the corporation and the individual stockholder. The two primary purposes of a stock dividend are:

(1) To maintain dividend consistency—Many corporations prefer to declare dividends each year. In the case of a cash shortage, the dividend record may be maintained by issuing a stock dividend. Stock dividends tend to satisfy the demands of stockholders for continuing dividends and yet avoid the demand on cash. Also, a stock dividend is not considered to be revenue to the shareholder for income tax purposes. Shareholders view stock dividends as quite different than a cash dividend.

(2) To "capitalize" retained earnings—A stock dividend is used to transfer accumulated earnings to permanent capital and thus remove such earnings from dividend availability. When a corporation consistently retains a substantial percent of its earnings for growth, the related funds are, more or less, permanently invested in long-term assets such as plant and other property. Therefore, it is considered realistic to transfer those accumulated earnings to permanent capital. A stock dividend is the most convenient approach for doing this. In profitable corporations that are expanding rapidly, this is perhaps the most fundamental reason for stock dividends.

Stock split. A stock dividend should not be confused with a stock split. In a stock split, the number of shares is increased by a specified amount, such as a 2-for-1 split. In this instance, each share held is called in and two shares are issued in its place. A stock split is accomplished by reducing the par value per share, so that the total par value outstanding is unchanged. For example, assuming $20 par-value stock before a split, the 2-for-1 split would involve reducing the par value to $10 per share. In contrast to a stock dividend, a stock split, although it increases the number of shares outstanding, does not result in a transfer of Retained Earnings to Contributed Capital. No transfer is needed in view of the change in the par value per share to accomplish the increased number of shares. The primary reason for a stock split is to reduce the market price *per share,* which tends to increase the market activity of the stock.

Dividend dates The preceding discussions assumed that a dividend was paid immediately after its declaration by the Board of Directors. There often is a time lag involved. For example, a typical dividend declaration would be as follows: "On November 20, 1974, the Board of Directors of XY Corporation declared a $.25 per share cash dividend on the 200,000 shares of no-par common stock outstanding. The dividend will be paid on January 15, 1975, to stockholders of record at December 15, 1974." In this declaration there are three identified dates. Strict accounting in respect to each date would be:

(1)   Declaration date—November 20, 1974: This is the date on which the Board of Directors officially voted the dividend. As soon as public announcement of the declaration is made, legally it is nonrevocable, hence, a dividend *liability* immediately comes into existence. Accordingly, on this date the **declaration** by XY Corporation would be recorded as follows:

```
Nov. 20, 1974:
  Retained Earnings (or Dividends Paid).... 50,000
     Dividends Payable...................           50,000
  Cash dividend declared; 200,000
  shares × $.25 = $50,000.
```

DEC O/E
INC LIAB

The December 31, 1974, balance sheet would report Dividends Payable as a current liability.

(2)   Date of record—December 15, 1974: This date follows the declaration date, usually by about one month, as specified in the declaration. It is the date on which the corporation takes from its stockholders' records the list of individuals owning shares. The dividend is payable only to those names listed on the record date. Thus, share transfers between buyers and sellers reported to the corporation before this date result in the dividend being paid to the new owner. Changes reported after this date are ineffective insofar as this particular dividend is concerned. No accounting entry would be made on this date.

(3)   Date of payment—January 15, 1975: This is the date on which the cash will be disbursed to pay the dividend. It will follow the date of record as specified in the dividend announcement. The entry to record the cash disbursement by XY Corporation would be as follows:

```
Jan. 15, 1975:
  Dividends Payable...................... 50,000
     Cash...............................           50,000
  Paid dividend declared and recorded
  on Nov. 20, 1974.
```

For instructional purposes this time lag usually is disregarded since it does not pose any substantive issues.

Stockholder
records

A corporation must maintain a record of each stockholder. The record includes at least the name, address, number of shares purchased of each type of stock, certificate numbers, dates acquired, and shares sold. Such a record is known as the stockholders' subsidiary ledger. The Capital Stock account serves as the controlling account in the general ledger for this subsidiary ledger. Sales of shares by a stockholder to others must be reported to the corporation so that new stock certificates can be issued and the stockholders' subsidiary ledger can be changed accordingly. Dividends are sent only to the names and addresses shown in the stockholders' subsidiary ledger. Large corporations with thousands of stockholders generally pay an independent stock transfer agent to handle the transfer of shares and the issuance of stock certificates and to maintain the equivalent of a stockholders' subsidiary ledger.

A particularly important record that must be maintained by all corporations is called the minute book. This is an official record of the actions taken at all meetings of the Board of Directors and of the stockholders. The independent auditor is required to inspect the minute book as a part of the audit program. The minute book not infrequently finds its way into the courtroom since the courts have tended to accord it some legal recognition.

Reporting
retained
earnings

In the preceding chapters, it has been emphasized that the income statement reports two *income* amounts: (1) income before extraordinary items and (2) net income (i.e., after extraordinary items). Net income is closed to the Income Summary account and is also reported on the statement of retained earnings. APB *Opinion No. 30* (dated June 1973) defines extraordinary items as those transactions and events that meet two criteria: (1) unusual in nature for the business and (2) infrequency of occurrence. They are set out separately on the income statement to help the statement user to focus on recurring normal operations since this is the best measure of earnings potential. We have also explained and illustrated the requirement by APB *Opinion No. 15* that earnings per share amounts be reported on the income statements for a corporation.

Similarly, we have discussed and illustrated the statement of retained earnings. Although not a required statement, it is almost always presented to meet the full-disclosure principle. Since retained earnings is one of two basic components of stockholders' equity, we should extend our knowledge of it at this point. A typical statement of retained earnings is shown in Exhibit 12–2.

The statement of retained earnings shown in Exhibit 12–2 reports two kinds of items that have not been discussed: (1) prior period adjustments and (2) restrictions on retained earnings.

Exhibit 12–2

FERRARI CORPORATION
Statement of Retained Earnings
For the Year Ended December 31, 1974

Retained earnings balance, Jan. 1, 1974...............		$240,000
Prior period adjustment:		
Deduct adjustment of 1971 federal income taxes.....		24,000
Balance as restated............................		216,000
Net income for 1974.............................		34,000
Total.................................		250,000
Deduct dividends declared in 1974:		
On preferred stock...........................	$ 6,000	
On common stock............................	12,000	18,000
Retained earnings balance, Dec. 31, 1974		
(see Note 5)...................................		$232,000

Note 5. Restrictions on retained earnings; total, $137,400:
   (a) Treasury stock—The corporation has treasury stock that cost $37,400.
        The state law requires that retained earnings be restricted by the cost of
        all treasury stock held.
   (b) Bonds payable—The bond indenture requires that retained earnings be re-
        stricted in accordance with an agreed schedule. The schedule amount for
        1974 and 1975 is $100,000.

Prior period adjustments. This category of events is defined in APB *Opinion No. 9* essentially as follows:

> Prior period adjustments are those rare adjustments, material in amount, which (a) are directly related to prior periods, (b) are not the result of events in the current or future periods, (c) resulted from determinations of persons other than the management of the business, and (d) were not susceptible to reasonable estimation as to their economic effect when the prior event occurred. Since a prior period adjustment must meet *all* of these criteria, they very rarely occur.

Examples of prior period adjustments are: (1) tax adjustments from prior years; (2) settlement of lawsuits initiated in prior periods; and (3) correction of accounting errors. Prior period adjustments are recorded in special accounts and are closed directly to Retained Earnings at the end of the period rather than to Income Summary. Consistent with this, they *must* be reported on the statement of retained earnings as illustrated in Exhibit 12–2 rather than on the income statement. A prior period adjustment is not an extraordinary item. Observe in the definitions above that they are quite different in concept.

Restrictions on retained earnings. Corporations frequently have restrictions on retained earnings. Basically, such a restriction removes that amount of retained earnings from availability for dividends. When the restriction is removed, the amount that was restricted then resumes dividend–availability status. Restrictions on retained earnings may be voluntary or involuntary. For example, the two restrictions reported on Exhibit 12–2 would be considered involuntary; one was imposed by law (i.e., the treasury stock restriction) and the other was imposed by contract. On occasion, the management may voluntarily establish a restriction on retained earnings such as "retained earnings restricted (or appropriated) for profits invested in plant and equipment." Of course, the management can remove this restriction at will.

The full-disclosure principle requires that restrictions on retained earnings be reported on the financial statements. The approach most widely used follows the illustration in Exhibit 12–2.

A practice widely used in past years, but seldom used now, is to set up special retained earnings accounts for each appropriation. These accounts, somewhat illogically, are often called "reserves." To illustrate, if the Ferrari Corporation had followed this approach, it would have made the following entry:

```
Retained Earnings...................... 137,400
    Reserve for Cost of Treasury Stock...        37,400
    Reserve for Bonds Payable...........        100,000
```

In preparing the statement of retained earnings, these two accounts would be included and the footnotes then would be unnecessary. When the restrictions are removed, the above entry is reversed.

PART TWO: OWNERS' EQUITY FOR SOLE PROPRIETORSHIP AND PARTNERSHIP

Owner's
equity for
a sole
proprietor-
ship

A sole, or single, proprietorship is a business owned by one person. As a consequence, the accounting for owner's equity is simple. The only owner's equity accounts needed are: (1) a capital account for the proprietor (for example, John Doe, Capital; or John Doe, Owner's Equity), and (2) a drawing account for the proprietor (for example, John Doe, Drawings; or John Doe, Withdrawals). The capital account is used to record investments by the owner and it absorbs the net income (or loss) for each period. Thus, the Income Summary account is closed to the capital account at the end of each accounting period. The drawing account is used to record withdrawals from the business of cash or other assets by the owner or the payment of the owner's personal obligations with assets of the business. The drawing account is closed to the capital account at the end of each accounting period; thus, the capital account cumulatively reflects all investments by the owner, plus all earnings of the entity, less all withdrawals of resources from the entity by the owner. In all other respects the accounting for a sole proprietorship is the same as for a corporation.

The following sequence of selected entries for Doe's Retail Store is presented to illustrate the accounting and reporting of owner's equity for a single proprietorship:

Jan. 1, 1974:   John Doe started a retail store by investing $150,000 of his personal savings. The accounting entry would be as follows:

```
Cash.................................... 150,000
    John Doe, Capital..................         150,000
    Investment by owner.
```

Dec. 30, 1974:   Mr. Doe withdrew $1,000 cash from the business for personal living costs each month during the year. Accordingly, each month the following entry was made:

```
John Doe, Drawings.......................... 1,000
    Cash....................................         1,000
    Withdrawal of cash by owner for per-
    sonal use.
```

Note: Clearly, at Dec. 31, 1974, after the last withdrawal, the drawing account will reflect a debit balance of $12,000.

Dec. 31, 1974:   Normal accounting entries for the year, including adjusting and closing entries for the revenue and expense accounts, resulted in an $18,000 *credit balance* in the Income Summary account (i.e., $18,000 net income). The next closing entry will be:

```
Income Summary............................. 18,000
    John Doe, Capital.....................         18,000
    Closing entry to transfer net income
    for the year to the owner's equity
    account.
```

Dec. 31, 1974:   The entry required on this date to close the drawing account would be:

```
John Doe, Capital.......................... 12,000
    John Doe, Drawings....................         12,000
    Closing entry to transfer drawings for
    the year to the capital account.
```

The financial statements of a sole proprietorship basically follow the same format as for a corporation, except in respect to **owner's equity** on the balance sheet. In conformity with the full-disclosure principle, the balance sheet at December 31, 1974, for Doe's Retail Store would report the owner's equity as follows:[11]

Owner's Equity

John Doe, Capital, January 1, 1974................	$150,000
Add: Net income for 1974......................	18,000
Total....................................	$168,000
Less: Withdrawals for 1974....................	12,000
John Doe, Capital, December 31, 1974.............	$156,000

Since a sole proprietorship, as a business entity, does not pay income taxes, the financial statements will not reflect income tax expense or income taxes payable. The net income of a sole proprietorship must be included on the personal income tax return of the owner. Also, since an individual cannot enter into an employer/employee contractual relationship with himself, a "salary" to the owner usually is not recognized as an expense of a sole proprietorship.

Owners' equity for a partnership

The Uniform Partnership Act, which has been adopted by many states, defines a partnership as "an association of two or more persons to carry on as co-owners a business for profit." The partnership form of business is used by small businesses and professional people, such as doctors, lawyers, and accountants. A partnership is formed by two or more persons reaching mutual agreement as to the terms of the partnership. The laws do not require an application for a charter as in the case for a corporation; however, the agreements between the partners constitute a **partnership contract** and, preferably, it should be in writing. The partnership contract or agreement should specify such matters as division of profits, management responsibilities, transfer or sale of partnership interests, disposition of assets upon liquidation, and procedures to be followed in case of the death of a partner. The primary advantages of a partnership are (1) ease of formation, (2) complete control by the partners, and (3) no income taxes on the business of the type assessed on a corporation. The primary disadvantage is the unlimited liability feature discussed in Chapter 1.

As with a sole proprietorship, accounting for a partnership follows the same underlying fundamentals of accounting as any other form of business organization, **except for those entries that directly affect owners' equity.** Accounting for partners' equity follows the same pattern as illustrated earlier for a sole proprietorship, except that separate partner capital and drawing accounts must be established for *each* partner. Investments by each partner are credited to his capital account. Withdrawals of cash and other resources from the partnership by each partner are debited to the respective drawing accounts. The net income

---

[11] Alternatively, the balance sheet may reflect only "John Doe, Capital, December 31, 1974, $156,000," with a supplemental or supporting *statement of owner's equity* that would be the same as this illustration.

for the partnership is divided between the partners in the profit ratio specified in the partnership agreement. The Income Summary account is then closed to the respective partner capital accounts in accordance with the division of profits. The respective drawing accounts also are closed to the partner capital accounts. Therefore, after the closing process, the capital account of each partner cumulatively reflects all investments of the individual partner, plus the partner's share of all partnership earnings, less all withdrawals by the partner.

The following sequence of selected entries is presented to illustrate the accounting and reporting of partners' equity.

Jan. 1, 1974:   The AB Partnership was organized by Art Able and Bill Baker on this date. Able contributed $60,000 and Baker $40,000 cash in the partnership and agreed to divide profits 60% and 40%, respectively. The accounting entry to record the investment would be:

```
Cash.................................... 100,000
     A. Able, Capital.....................        60,000
     B. Baker, Capital.....................       40,000
Investment to initiate a partnership.
```

Dec. 30, 1974:   It was agreed that, in lieu of salaries, Able would withdraw $1,000 and Baker $650 per month in cash. Accordingly, *each month* the following entry for the withdrawals was made:

```
A. Able, Drawings........................  1,000
B. Baker, Drawings........................    650
     Cash.................................           1,650
Withdrawal of cash by partners for
personal use.
```

Dec. 31, 1974:   Assume the normal accounting entries for the revenue and expense accounts resulted in a $30,000 *credit balance* in the Income Summary account (i.e., $30,000 net income). The next closing entry would be:

```
Income Summary........................... 30,000
     A. Able, Capital.....................        18,000
     B. Baker, Capital.....................       12,000
Closing entry to transfer net income
to the respective capital accounts.
Net income divided as follows:
   A. Able:  $30,000 × .60 = $18,000
   B. Baker: $30,000 × .40 =  12,000
       Total................ $30,000
```

Dec. 31, 1974:   The entry required to close the drawings accounts would be:

```
A. Able, Capital.........................  12,000
B. Baker, Capital........................   7,800
    A. Able, Drawings.....................            12,000
    B. Baker, Drawings....................             7,800
Closing entry to transfer drawings for
the year to the respective capital
accounts.
```

After the closing entries the partners' accounts would reflect the following balances:

Income Summary.................... $ –0–
A. Able, Drawings.................   –0–
B. Baker, Drawings.................   –0–
A. Able, Capital.................. 66,000
B. Baker, Capital................. 44,200

The financial statements of a partnership follow the same format as for a sole proprietorship and a corporation, except (1) the income statement includes an additional section entitled "Distribution of Net Income," and (2) the partners' equity section of the balance sheet is detailed for each partner in conformity with the principle of full disclosure. To illustrate, the income statement and balance sheet for the AB Partnership for 1974 would reflect the following additional information:

Income Statement:
    Net income.......................... $30,000

    Distribution of net income:
        A. Able (60%).......... $18,000
        B. Baker (40%).........   12,000
                   $30,000

Balance Sheet:
                Partners' Equity
A. Able, Capital.......................... $66,000
B. Baker, Capital........................   44,200
      Total Partners' Equity........... $110,200

A separate statement of partners' capital usually is prepared to supplement the balance sheet similar to the following:

AB PARTNERSHIP
Statement of Partners' Capital
For the Year Ended December 31, 1974

	A. Able	B. Baker	Total
Investment, Jan. 1, 1974.....................	$60,000	$40,000	$100,000
Add: Additional investments during the year....	–0–	–0–	–0–
Net income for the year......................	18,000	12,000	30,000
Totals...........................	78,000	52,000	130,000
Less: Drawings during the year..............	12,000	7,800	19,800
Partners' Equity, Dec. 31, 1974................	$66,000	$44,200	$110,200

SHELLY CORPORATION

(Try to resolve the case before studying the suggested solution that follows.)

This case focuses on the organization and operations for the first year of the Shelly Corporation, which was organized officially on January 1, 1974, the date on which the charter was granted by the state. The laws of the state specify, for no-par stock, that the legal or stated capital is the full sales amount. The corporation was promoted and organized by ten local businessmen for the purpose of operating a hotel-supply business. The charter authorized the following capital stock:

> Common stock, no-par value, 20,000 shares authorized.
> Preferred stock, 5%, $100 par value, 5,000 shares authorized (cumulative, nonparticipating, and nonvoting; liquidation value, $110).

The following summarized transactions, selected from 1974, were completed on the dates indicated:

(1)	January 1974:	Sold 7,500 shares of no-par common stock to the ten promoters for cash at $52 per share. Credit the No-par Common Stock account for the total sales amount.
(2)	February 1974:	Sold 1,890 shares of preferred stock at $102 per share; cash collected in full.
(3)	March 1974:	Purchased land for a store site and made full payment by issuing 100 shares of preferred stock. Early construction is planned. Assume the preferred stock is selling at $102 per share.
(4)	April 1974:	Paid cash for organization costs amounting to $1,980. Set up an account entitled "Organization Costs."
(5)	May 1974:	Issued ten shares of preferred stock to A. B. Cain in full payment of legal services rendered in connection with organization of the corporation. Assume the preferred stock is still selling at $102 per share. Debit Organization Costs.
(6)	June 1974:	Sold 500 shares of no-par common stock for cash to C. B. Abel at $54 per share.
(7)	July 1974:	Purchased 100 shares of preferred stock that had been sold and issued earlier. The stockholder was moving to another state and "needed the money." The Shelly Corporation paid the stockholder $104 per share.

(8) August 1974: Sold 20 shares of preferred treasury stock at $105 per share.

(9) November 1974: Purchased fixed assets at a cost of $600,000; paid cash.

(10) Dec. 31, 1974: Borrowed $20,000 cash from the City Bank on a one-year, interest-bearing note. Interest is payable at 7% at maturity.

(11) Dec. 31, 1974: Gross revenues for the year amounted to $129,300; expenses, including corporation income taxes but excluding organization costs, amounted to $98,000. Assume, for simplicity, that these summarized revenue and expense transactions were cash.

(12) Dec. 31, 1974: The Shelly Corporation decided that a "reasonable" amortization period for organization costs, starting as of January 1, 1974, would be ten years. This is an intangible asset that must be amortized over a reasonable period.

(13) Dec. 31, 1974: Closing entries.

Required:

a. Give appropriate entries, with brief explanation, for each of the above transactions.

b. Give appropriate closing entries at December 31, 1974.

c. Prepare a balance sheet for the Shelly Corporation at December 31, 1974.

Suggested Solution:

Requirement (a)—Journal entries:

(1) January 1974:

```
Cash.................................... 390,000
     No-par Common Stock (7,500 shares)...          390,000
     Sale of no-par common stock ($52 ×
     7,500 shares = $390,000).
```

(2) February 1974:

```
Cash.................................... 192,780
     Preferred Stock, 5%, par $100 (1,890
        shares)............................          189,000
     Contributed Capital in Excess of Par,
        Preferred Stock...................            3,780
     Sale of preferred stock ($102 × 1,890
     shares = $192,780).
```

(3)   March 1974:

```
Land (store site)........................   10,200
    Preferred Stock, 5%, par $100 (100
        shares)...........................               10,000
    Contributed Capital in Excess of Par,
        Preferred Stock...................                  200
Purchased land for future store site;
paid in full by issuance of 100 shares
of preferred stock; implied fair-market
value, $102 × 100 shares = $10,200.
```

(4)   April 1974:

```
Organization Costs......................    1,980
    Cash................................                1,980
Paid organization costs.
```

(5)   May 1974:

```
Organization costs......................    1,020
    Preferred Stock, 5%, par $100 (10
        shares)...........................                1,000
    Contributed Capital in Excess of Par,
        Preferred Stock...................                   20
Organization costs (legal services)
paid by issuance of 10 shares of pre-
ferred stock; implied fair-market
value, $102 × 10 shares = $1,020.
```

(6)   June 1974:

```
Cash....................................    27,000
    No-par Common Stock (500 shares).....               27,000
Sold 500 shares of the no-par common
stock ($54 × 500 shares = $27,000).
```

(7)   July 1974:

```
Treasury Stock, Preferred (100 shares at
    $104)..................................   10,400
    Cash.................................               10,400
Purchased 100 shares of preferred
treasury stock ($104 × 100 shares =
$10,400).
```

(8)   August 1974:

```
Cash (20 shares at $105)................     2,100
    Treasury Stock, Preferred (20 shares
        at $104)............................                2,080
    Contributed Capital from Treasury
        Stock Transactions................                    20
    Sold 20 shares of the preferred
    treasury stock at $105.
```

(9) Nov. 1974:

```
Fixed Assets........................... 600,000
    Cash...............................            600,000
    Purchased fixed assets.
```

(10) Dec. 31, 1974:

```
Cash....................................  20,000
    Notes Payable.......................             20,000
    Borrowed on one-year, 7%, interest-
    bearing note.
```

(11) Dec. 31, 1974:

```
Cash.................................... 129,300
    Revenues...........................            129,300

Expenses...............................  98,000
    Cash...............................             98,000
    To record summarized revenues and
    expenses.
```

(12) Dec. 31, 1974:

```
Expenses...............................     300
    Organization Costs..................                300
    Adjusting entry to amortize organiza-
    tion expense for one year, $3,000 ÷ 10
    years = $300.
```

Requirement (b)—Closing entries:

(13) Dec. 31, 1974:

```
Revenues............................... 129,300
    Income Summary.....................            129,300

Income Summary.........................  98,300
    Expenses ($98,000 + $300)...........             98,300

Income Summary.........................  31,000
    Retained Earnings..................             31,000
```

Requirement (c):

SHELLY CORPORATION
Balance Sheet
For the Year Ended December 31, 1974

Assets

Current Assets:
Cash... $ 50,800

Fixed Assets:
Land.. $ 10,200
Fixed assets (undesignated)............................ 600,000   610,200

Intangible Assets:
Organization costs unamortized.....................   2,700
Total Assets................................ $663,700

Liabilities

Current Liabilities:
Note payable...................................... $ 20,000

Stockholders' Equity

Contributed Capital:
Common stock, no-par value, authorized 20,000 shares,
issued and outstanding 8,000 shares................ $417,000
Preferred stock, 5%, par value $100, authorized
5,000 shares, issued 2,000 shares of which 80 shares
are held as treasury stock......................... 200,000
Contributed capital in excess of par, preferred stock.....   4,000
Contributed capital from treasury stock transactions.....   20
Total Contributed Capital....................... 621,020

Retained earnings.......................................   31,000
Total..   652,020

Less cost of preferred treasury stock held (80 shares).......... 8,320
Total Stockholders' Equity............................   643,700
Total Liabilities and Stockholders' Equity......... $663,700

Summary   This chapter focused on the differences in accounting for and reporting of owners' equity for corporations, sole proprietorships, and partnerships. Other than owners' equity, the accounting and reporting basically is unaffected by the type of business organization. Accounting for owners' equity is based upon the concept of source. Each specific source of owners' equity should be accounted for separately. The two basic sources of owners' equity for a corporation are: contributed capital and retained earnings. Separate accounts are maintained for each type of capital stock.

The earnings of a corporation that are not retained in the business for growth and expansion are distributed to the stockholders by means of dividends. Dividends, to be paid, must be formally declared by the Board of Directors of the corporation. A cash dividend results in a decrease in assets (cash) and stockholders' equity (retained earnings). In contrast, a stock dividend does not change either total assets or total stockholders' equity. Significantly, a stock dividend results in a transfer of retained earnings to the permanent or contributed capital of the corporation by the amount of the stock dividend.

Not infrequently a corporation purchases its own stock in the marketplace. Such stock, having been sold and issued by the corporation and subsequently reacquired, is known as treasury stock. The purchase of treasury stock is viewed as a contraction of corporate capital, and the subsequent resale of the treasury stock is viewed as an expansion of corporate capital.

Important terms		
Corporation charter	**Treasury stock**
Common stock	**Cumulative dividends**
Preferred stock	**Participating preferred stock**
Par value	**Stock dividends**
No-par-value stock	**Stock split**
Convertible stock	**Prior period adjustments**

Questions for discussion

1. Define a corporation and give its primary characteristics.
2. What is the charter of a corporation?
3. Briefly explain each of the following terms: (a) authorized capital stock; (b) issued capital stock; (c) unissued capital stock; (d) outstanding capital stock.
4. Briefly distinguish between common and preferred stock.
5. Briefly explain the distinction between par-value and no-par-value capital stock.
6. What are the usual features or characteristics of preferred stock?
7. What are the two basic sources of stockholders' equity? Explain them briefly.
8. Owners' equity is accounted for by source. Explain what is meant by source.
9. Define treasury stock. Why do corporations acquire treasury stock?
10. How is treasury stock reported on the balance sheet? How is the "gain or loss" on treasury stock that has been sold reported on the financial statements?
11. What are the fundamental requirements essential to support a cash dividend? What is the effect of a cash dividend on assets and stockholders' equity?
12. Distinguish between cumulative and noncumulative preferred stock.
13. Distinguish between participating and nonparticipating preferred stock.
14. Define a stock dividend. In what major respects does it differ from a cash dividend?
15. What are the primary purposes in issuing a stock dividend?

16. Identify and briefly explain the three important dates in respect to dividends.

17. Define extraordinary items. Why is it desirable that they be reflected separately on the income statement?

18. Define retained earnings. What are the primary components of retained earnings?

19. Define prior period adjustments. How are they reported?

20. Explain what is meant by restrictions on retained earnings.

21. List and explain the basic purposes of each owner's equity account for a partnership.

Exercises   E12–1.   The Apache Corporation was organized in 1974 for the purpose of operating an engineering service business. The charter authorized the following capital stock: common stock, par value $20 per share, 10,000 shares. During the first year the following selected transactions were completed:

(1) Sold 5,000 shares of common stock for cash at $23 per share; the stock was immediately issued.

(2) Issued 200 shares of common stock for a piece of land that will be utilized as a facilities site; construction was started immediately. Assume the stock was still selling at $23 per share. Debit Land.

(3) Sold 1,000 shares of common stock for cash at $23 per share; issued the stock.

(4) At year end, the Income Summary account reflected a $6,000 loss. Since a loss was incurred, no income tax expense was recorded.

Required:

a. Give the indicated journal entry for each of the transactions listed above.

b. Assume it is the year end and the financial statements are being prepared. Show how stockholders' equity would be reported in the balance sheet.

E12–2.   The Brady Corporation was organized in January 1974 by 14 stockholders to operate an air-conditioning sales and service business. The charter issued by the state authorized the following capital stock:

Common stock, $10 par value, 25,000 shares.
Preferred stock, $20 par value, 5% nonparticipating, noncumulative, 5,000 shares.

During January and February 1974, the following stock transactions were completed:

(1) Collected $15,000 cash from each of the 14 organizers and issued each of them 1,000 shares of common stock.

       (2)   Sold 500 shares of preferred stock at $25 per share; collected the cash and immediately issued the stock.

Required:

a.   Give the journal entries to record the above stock transactions.

b.   Assume it is the end of the annual accounting period, December 31, 1974, and net income for the year was $23,000; also assume that cash dividends paid at year end amounted to $10,000. Prepare the stockholders' equity section of the balance sheet at December 31, 1974.

E12–3.   Video Systems, Incorporated, was issued a charter on January 15, 1974, that authorized the following capital stock:

Common stock, no-par, 25,000 shares.
Preferred stock, 5%, par value $10 per share, 10,000 shares.
The Board of Directors established a stated value on the no-par common stock of $20 per share.

    During 1974 the following selected transactions were completed in the order given:

   (1)   Sold 10,000 shares of the no-par common stock at $43 per share. Collected the cash and immediately issued the shares.

   (2)   Sold 2,000 shares of preferred stock at $13 per share. Collected the cash and immediately issued the shares.

   (3)   At the end of 1974 the Income Summary account reflected a credit balance of $11,000.

Required:

a.   Give the entry indicated for each of the above items.

b.   Prepare the stockholders' equity section of the balance sheet at December 31, 1974.

E12–4.   The Dobbins-Marsh Corporation obtained a charter at the start of 1974 that authorized 10,000 shares of common stock, par value $50 per share, and 5,000 shares of preferred stock, par value $10. The corporation was promoted and organized by six individuals who "reserved" 60% of the common-stock shares for themselves. The remaining shares are to be sold to the public at $70 per share on a cash basis. During 1974 the following selected transactions occurred:

   (1)   Collected $25,000 cash from each of the six organizers and issued 500 shares of common stock to each.

   (2)   Sold 3,000 shares of common stock to an "outsider" at $70 per share. Collected the cash and issued the stock.

   (3)   Sold 2,000 shares of preferred stock at $12 per share. Collected the cash and immediately issued the stock.

   (4)   At the end of 1974, the Income Summary account, after income taxes, reflected a credit balance of $16,000.

Required:

a.   Give journal entries indicated for each of the transactions listed above.

b. Prepare the stockholders' equity section of the balance sheet at December 21, 1974.

E12–5. The stockholders' equity section of the December 31, 1974, balance sheet for the Delwood Corporation is shown below.

Stockholders' Equity

Contributed Capital:

Preferred stock, par value $30, authorized 5,000 shares; ? issued, of which 100 shares are held as treasury stock.............................	$120,000
Common stock, no-par, authorized 10,000 shares; issued 7,000 shares..............................	630,000
Contributed capital in excess of par, preferred.........	6,000
Contributed capital, treasury stock transactions.......	500
Retained earnings.................................	40,000
Less: Treasury stock, preferred....................	(3,200)
	$793,300

Required:

Complete the following (show computations) on a separate sheet of paper:

a. The number of shares of preferred stock issued was _____.
b. The number of shares of preferred stock outstanding is_____.
c. The average sales price of the preferred stock when issued apparently was $_____ per share.
d. Have treasury stock transactions (1) increased corporate resources _____; or (2) decreased resources _____? By how much? $_____.
e. How much did the treasury stock held cost per share? $_____.
f. Total stockholders' equity is $_____.

E12–6. The balance sheet (summarized) for the Acme Corporation reflected the following:

ACME CORPORATION
Balance Sheet
December 31, 1973

Assets		*Liabilities*	
Cash..............	$189,000	Current liabilities..............	$ 60,000
All other assets.....	296,000	Long-term liabilities...........	80,000
			140,000

		Stockholders' Equity	
		Contributed Capital:	
		Common stock, par $50, authorized 10,000 shares; outstanding 6,000 shares....	300,000
		Contributed capital in excess of par...................	15,000
		Retained earnings...........	30,000
	$485,000		$485,000

During the next year the following selected transactions affecting stockholders' equity occurred:

Feb. 1, 1974: Purchased for cash, in the open market, 300 shares of Acme's own stock at $45 per share.

July 15, 1974: Sold 100 of the shares purchased on Feb. 1, 1974, at $47 per share.

Sept. 1, 1974: Sold 20 more of the shares purchased on Feb. 1, 1974, at $43.

Dec. 31, 1974: The credit balance in the Income Summary account was $17,000.

Required:

a. Give the indicated entries for each of the four dates listed above.

b. Prepare the stockholders' equity section of the balance sheet at December 31, 1974.

E12–7. Cullum, Incorporated, obtained a charter from the state in January 1974 that authorized 100,000 shares of common stock, $1 par value. The stockholders comprised 18 local citizens, each of whom purchased varying amounts of the stock at $3 per share. During the first year the following selected transactions occurred in the order given:

(1) Sold 60,000 shares of the common stock to the 18 shareholders at $3 per share. Collected cash and immediately issued the stock.

(2) During the year, one of the 18 stockholders moved to another state and wanted to get his money back. Accordingly, the corporation purchased his 5,000 shares at $3.50 per share.

(3) Two months later, 3,000 of the shares purchased from the departing stockholder were resold to another individual at $4.00 per share.

(4) On December 31, 1974, the end of the first year of business, the Income Summary account reflected a credit balance of $22,000.

Required:

a. Give the indicated journal entry, or entries, for each of the above items.

b. Prepare the stockholders' equity section of the balance sheet at December 31, 1974.

E12–8. The Farris Manufacturing Company has outstanding (a) 10,000 shares of $20 par-value common stock and (b) 2,000 shares of $10 preferred stock (6%). On December 1, 1974, the Board of Directors voted a 6% cash dividend on the preferred stock and a 10% common-stock dividend on the common stock (i.e., for each ten shares of common stock held an additional share of common stock is to be issued as a stock dividend). At the date of declaration, the common stock was selling at $27 and the preferred at $12 per share.

Required:

a. Give the entry to record the payment of the cash dividend. Assume immediate payment.
b. Give the entry to record the distribution of the stock dividend. Transfer retained earnings on the basis of market values.

E12–9. The Duncan Supply Company records reflected the following balances in the stockholders' equity accounts:

Common stock, par $10 per share, 10,000 shares outstanding.
Preferred stock, 5%, par $10 per share, 2,000 shares outstanding.
Retained earnings $80,000.

On September 1, the Board of Directors was considering the distribution of a cash dividend amounting to $25,000. No dividends have been paid during the past two years. You have been asked to determine the total and per-share amounts that would be paid to the common stockholders and to the preferred stockholders assuming (show computations):

a. The preferred stock is noncumulative and nonparticipating.
b. The preferred stock is cumulative and nonparticipating.
c. The preferred stock is cumulative and fully participating.

E12–10. The stockholders' equity section of the balance sheet of the Farr Corporation, on December 31, 1974, reflected the following:

Common stock, par $20, shares authorized
  50,000; shares outstanding 12,000............ $240,000
Contributed capital in excess of par............   12,000
Retained earnings........................ 100,000

Now, assume a one-for-five (i.e., a 20%) stock dividend is declared and issued (that is, one additional share will be issued for each five shares now held). The market value of the stock is $22.50 per share. Assume the market value is capitalized.

Required:

a. Give the entry to record the distribution of the stock dividend.
b. Reconstruct the stockholders' equity section of the balance sheet (1) immediately before the stock dividend and (2) immediately after the stock dividend.
(Hint: Use two columns.)

E12–11. The following account balances were selected from the records of the Barker Corporation at December 31, 1974, after all adjusting entries were completed:

30,000 × 2.

Common stock, par $20, authorized 40,000 shares; issued 30,000 shares, of which 100 shares are held as treasury stock......................	$600,000
Contributed capital in excess of par............	12,000
Bond sinking fund..........................	70,000
Dividends paid in 1974.......................	30,000
Retained earnings, Jan. 1, 1974................	60,000
Adjustment of prior years' income taxes (additional assessment).....................	8,000
Treasury stock at cost (100 shares).............	3,000
Income summary for 1974 (credit balance)........	40,000
Restriction on retained earnings for cost of treasury stock is required by law in this state.	

R E

6 2,000

Required:

Based upon the above data, prepare (a) the stockholders' equity section of the balance sheet and (b) the statement of retained earnings for 1974.

(Hint: Total stockholders' equity is $671,000.)

E12–12. Assume that at the beginning of 1974 the stockholders' equity accounts of the Sloan Corporation reflected the following:

Common stock, $10 par, 30,000 shares outstanding........	$300,000
Retained earnings (including a $50,000 restriction on retained earnings for bonds payable).................	170,000

Assume the following transactions were completed in the order given:

(1) Paid cash dividends during 1974 amounting to $2 per share.
(2) Received a $26,000 cash refund on prior income taxes that had been in litigation for three years.
(3) The Income Summary account on December 31, 1974, after closing all revenue and expense accounts, reflected a credit balance of $45,000.

Required:

a. Give the appropriate entries for each of the above three items.
b. Prepare a statement of retained earnings, after taking into account the entries made in requirement a.

E12–13. This exercise presents three separate cases. Assume in each case that the annual accounting period ended December 31, 1974, and that the Income Summary account at that date reflected a credit balance of $26,000.

Case A—Assume that the company is a sole proprietorship and that, prior to the closing entries, the owner's (Mr. X) equity accounts reflected the following: Capital, $60,-000; Drawings, $12,000.

Case B—Assume that the company is a partnership owned by Mr. X and Mr. Y, who divide profits equally. Prior to the closing entries, the owners' equity accounts reflected the following: X, Capital, $32,000; Y, Capital, $26,-000; X, Drawings, $12,000; Y, Drawings, $10,000.

Case C—Assume that the company is a corporation owned by ten stockholders. Prior to the closing entries, the stockholders' equity accounts reflected the following: Capital Stock, 10,000 shares, par value $10 per share; Retained Earnings, $18,000.

Required:

a. Give all of the closing entries indicated at December 31, 1974, for each of the three separate cases.
b. Show how the owners' equity section of the balance sheet would be reflected on December 31, 1974, for each case.

Problems   P12–1.   The Barker Corporation received its charter during January 1974. The charter authorized the following capital stock:

Preferred stock, 5%, par $20, authorized 10,000 shares.
Common stock, par $1, authorized 100,000 shares.

During 1974 the following transactions occurred in the order given:

(1) Issued 10,000 shares of the common stock to each of the six organizers at $5 per share. Cash was collected in full and the stock was issued immediately.
(2) Sold 2,000 shares of the preferred stock at $30 per share. Collected the cash and issued the stock immediately.
(3) Sold 1,000 shares of the common stock at $7 per share and 500 shares of the preferred stock at $30. Collected the cash and issued the stock immediately.
(4) Revenues for 1974 totaled $180,000 and expenses totaled $150,000 (including income taxes).

Required:

a. Give all entries, including any closing entries, for the above items.
b. Prepare the stockholders' equity section of the balance sheet at December 31, 1974.

P12–2.   The Wesley Corporation began operations in January 1974. The charter authorized the following capital stock:

Preferred stock, 5%, $10 par, authorized 10,000 shares.
Common stock, no-par, authorized 50,000 shares.
The corporation, in conformance with state laws, established a stated value per share of $2 for the no-par common stock.

During 1974, the following transactions occurred in the order given:

(1) Issued 10,000 shares of the no-par common stock to each of the three organizers. Collected $3 per share in full and issued the stock immediately.

(2) Sold 3,000 shares of the preferred stock at $12 per share. Collected the cash and issued the stock immediately.

(3) Sold 200 shares of the preferred stock at $13 and 500 shares of the no-par common stock at $5 per share. Collected the cash and issued the stock immediately.

(4) Operating results at the end of 1974 were reflected as follows:

> Revenue account............................ $120,000
> Expense account, including income taxes........... 100,000

Required:

a. Give the entries indicated, including closing entries, for the above items.

b. Prepare the stockholders' equity section of the balance sheet at December 31, 1974.

P12–3. The Walden Corporation was issued a charter in January 1974 that authorized 10,000 shares of common stock. During 1974, the following selected transactions occurred in the order given:

(1) Sold 5,000 shares of the stock for cash at $105 per share. Collected the cash and issued the stock immediately.

(2) Acquired land to be used as a future plant site; made payment in full by issuing 200 shares of stock. Assume a market value per share of $105.

(3) At the end of 1974, the Income Summary account reflected a credit balance of $21,000.

Required:

Complete the following requirements under three different case assumptions:

Case I: Assume the stock was $100 par value per share.

Case II: Assume the stock was no-par and that the total selling price is credited to the No-par Capital Stock account.

Case III: Assume the stock is no-par with a stated value, specified by the Board of Directors, of $80 per share.

For each case given:

a. Indicated entries for each of the above items.

b. The stockholders' equity section of the balance sheet at December 31, 1974.

(Hint: Total contributed capital and total stockholders' equity are the same in amount in all of the cases—$567,000.)

P12–4. The Morris Manufacturing Company was granted a charter by the state that authorized the following capital stock:

Common stock, no-par, 25,000 shares. Assume the no-par stock will not be assigned a stated value per share.

Preferred stock, 5%, par value $20, 10,000 shares.

During the first year, 1974, the following selected transactions occurred in the order given:

(1) Sold 10,000 shares of no-par common stock at $30 per share and 2,000 preferred stock at $21 per share. Collected cash and issued the stock immediately. On the no-par stock, credit the full selling price to the No-par Capital Stock account.

(2) Issued 400 shares of preferred stock as full payment for a plot of land to be used as a future plant site. Assume the stock is selling at $21.

(3) Purchased 300 shares of the no-par common stock sold earlier; paid cash, $22 per share.

(4) Sold all of the treasury stock (common) purchased in (3) above. The sales price was $23 per share.

(5) Purchased 200 shares of preferred stock as $21 per share at the request of a stockholder who was moving to another state.

(6) At December 31, 1974, the Income Summary account reflected a credit balance of $18,500.

Required:

a. Give the entries indicated for each of the above items.

b. Prepare the stockholders' equity section of the balance sheet at December 31, 1974, end of the annual accounting period.
(Hint: Total stockholders' equity is $365,000.)

P12–5. The Tolson Equipment Company had the following stock outstanding and retained earnings:

Common stock, $10 par, outstanding 20,000 shares........	$200,000
Preferred stock, 5%, $20 par, outstanding 5,000 shares.....	100,000
Retained earnings....................................	240,000

The Board of Directors is considering the distribution of a cash dividend to the two groups of stockholders. No dividends have been paid in the past two years. Four different case situations are assumed:

Case A—The preferred is noncumulative and nonparticipating; the total amount of dividends to be $30,000.

Case B—The preferred is cumulative and nonparticipating; the total amount of dividends to be $15,000.

Case C—Same as Case B, except the amount is $40,000.

Case D—The preferred is cumulative and fully participating; total amount, $40,000.

Required:

a. Compute the amount of dividends, in total and per share, that would be payable to each class of stockholders for each case. Show computations.

b. Give the entry to record the cash dividend paid in Case C. Reflect a separate dividend paid account for each class of stock.

c. Give the required entry assuming the declaration and issuance of a 10% stock dividend in common stock on the outstanding common stock. Assume the market value per share of common stock was $15.

P12–6. The accounts of the Pryor Corporation reflected the following balances on January 1, 1974:

Preferred stock, 5%, $50 par value, cumulative, authorized 10,000 shares, issued and outstanding 2,000 shares $100,000
Common stock, $10 par value, authorized 100,000 shares, outstanding 20,000 shares 200,000
Contributed capital in excess of par, preferred stock 5,000
Contributed capital in excess of par, common stock 10,000
Retained earnings 200,000
Total Stockholders' Equity $515,000

The transactions during 1974 relating to the stockholders' equity are listed below in order:

(1) Purchased 100 shares of preferred treasury stock at $110 per share.
(2) The Board of Directors declared and paid a cash dividend to the preferred shareholders. No dividends had been paid during the past two years. The dividend was sufficient to pay the arrears plus the dividend for the current year.
(3) The Board of Directors declared a 1-for-10 (i.e., 10%) common-stock dividend on the outstanding common stock. Fair-market value of $11 per share to be capitalized.
(4) Net income for the year, after taxes, was $25,000.

Required:

a. Give the entry for each of the above transactions, including the closing entries. Show computations.
b. Prepare the stockholders' equity section of the balance sheet and a statement of retained earnings at December 31, 1974.
(Hint: Total stockholders' equity is $514,750.)

P12–7. Walker, Incorporated, is in the process of completing the year-end accounting, including the preparation of the annual financial statements, at December 31, 1974. The stockholders' equity accounts reflected the following balances at the end of the year:

Common stock, par $10, shares outstanding 40,000 . . . . $400,000
Contributed capital in excess of par 50,000
Retained earnings, Jan. 1, 1974 (credit) 300,000
Dividends declared and paid during 1974 (debit) . . . . (24,000)
Income summary account for 1974 (credit balance; after tax) 50,000

The following selected transactions occurred near the end of 1974; they are not included in the above amounts:

(1) As a result of litigation in the tax court over the last three years the corporation was assessed additional taxes for 1971

amounting to $39,000. The amount was paid immediately on December 31, 1974.

(2) The Board of Directors voted a voluntary restriction on retained earnings amounting to $100,000. It is to be designated as "Earnings Reinvested in the Business," effective for 1974 financial statements.

Required:

a. Give the appropriate entries for the events listed immediately above. If no entry is given, explain why not.

b. Give the appropriate closing entries, based upon the above data and requirement a, at December 31, 1974.

c. Prepare the stockholders' equity section of the balance sheet and a statement of retained earnings at December 31, 1974.

P12–8. Crescent, Incorporated, has completed all of the annual information processing at December 31, 1974, except for preparation of the financial statements. The following account balances were reflected at that date:

Adjusted Trial Balance, December 31, 1974

Cash...	$ 62,000	
Accounts receivable (net)........................	58,000	
Merchandise inventory, Dec. 31, 1974.............	120,000	
Long-term investment in Company Y..............	20,000	
Bond sinking fund..............................	40,000	
Land...	15,000	
Buildings and equipment (net)....................	738,000	
Other assets...................................	29,200	
Accounts payable..............................		$ 86,000
Income taxes payable..........................		18,000
Bonds payable, 5%.............................		100,000
Preferred stock, par $100, authorized 5,000 shares, issued 1,000 shares.....................		100,000
Common stock, par $10, authorized 100,000 shares, issued 66,000 shares.....................		660,000
Contributed capital in excess of par, preferred......		6,100
Contributed capital in excess of par, common.......		19,900
Treasury stock, preferred, 10 shares at cost........	1,100	
Retained earnings, Jan. 1, 1974..................		163,300
1974 net income (after tax).................		40,000
1974 cash dividends on preferred............	26,000	
1974 stock dividends distributed............	70,000	
Adjustment of 1971 income taxes (additional assessment).................................	14,000	
	$1,193,300	$1,193,300

Note: Retained earnings is restricted to an amount equal to the bond sinking fund per the provisions of the bond indenture.

Required:

Prepare a clasified balance sheet and a statement of retained earnings.

(Hint: Total stockholders' equity is $878,200.)

P12–9.   The KL Partnership is owned and operated by Jim Kay and Hi Low. The annual accounting period ends December 31, 1974. At the end of December 1974, the accounts reflected the following:

Credit balance in capital accounts (Jan. 1, 1974):

J. Kay	$50,000
H. Low	30,000
Credit balance in Income Summary account	23,000

Debit balance in drawings accounts:

J. Kay	7,000
H. Low	6,000

The partners divide net income equally.

Required:

a.   Give the closing entries indicated.

b.   Prepare the December 31, 1974, statement of partners' capital.

P12–10.   Assume for each of the three separate cases below that the annual accounting period ends on December 31, 1974 and that the Income Summary account at that date reflected a debit balance of $20,000.

Case A—Assume that the company is a sole proprietorship owned by Mr. A. Prior to the closing entries, the capital account reflected a credit balance of $70,000 and the drawings account a balance of $6,000.

Case B—Assume that the company is a partnership owned by Mr. A and Mr. B. Prior to the closing entries, the owners' equity accounts reflected the following balances: A, Capital, $42,000; B, Capital, $40,000; A, Drawings, $7,000; B, Drawings, $6,000. Profits and losses are divided equally.

Case C—Assume that the company is a corporation. Prior to the closing entries, the stockholders' equity accounts showed the following: Capital Stock, par $20, authorized 20,000 shares, outstanding 4,000 shares; Premium on Capital Stock, $2,000; Retained Earning, $32,000.

Required:

(a)   Give all of the closing entries indicated at December 31, 1974, for each of the separate cases.

(b)   Show how the owners' equity section of the balance sheet would appear at December 31, 1974, for each case.

P12–11.   You are to refer to the financial statements of J. C. Penney Company, Inc., shown in Chapter 3, and respond to the following:

a.   What name was used for the statement of retained earnings?

b.   What items caused retained earnings to change during each year?

c.   In which year were dividends the higher?

d. Approximately what percent of net income was declared as dividends each year? Show computations.
e. What kinds and amounts of capital stock were authorized? Issued?
f. Was any stock issued in 1972 and 1973? Explain.

13 Measurement and reporting of long-term investments[1]

Purpose
of the
chapter

One corporation may invest in another corporation by acquiring either debt securities (e.g., bonds) or equity securities (e.g., capital stock) of the other corporation. These investments are classified for measurement and reporting purposes by the investing entity as either short-term investments or long-term investments, depending on the investment intentions of the management. In Chapter 8, short-term (or temporary) investments were defined as those that meet the two tests of ready *marketability* and *management intention* to convert them to cash in the short run. Those not meeting these two tests are classified as long-term investments. Short-term investments are classified on the balance sheet as a current asset. Long-term investments are classified on the balance sheet under the caption "Funds and Investments."

The purpose of this chapter is to discuss the measurement and reporting of long-term investments. In Part One we will focus on long-term investments in equity securities, except for those situations where consolidated financial statements must be prepared. This latter topic is deferred to Chapter 14. Part Two discusses long-term investments in bonds.

---

[1] We suggest that you review the discussion of short-term investments in Chapter 8 prior to studying this chapter.

Nature of
long-term
investments
in the capital
stock of
other
corporations

PART ONE: LONG-TERM INVESTMENTS IN EQUITY SECURITIES

A corporation may invest in the equity securities (either the common or preferred stock) of one or more other corporations for reasons such as the use of idle cash; the exercise of influence or control over the other company; the attainment of growth through sales of new products and new services; the obtaining of access to new markets and new sources of supply; and the achievement of other economic purposes. One corporation may acquire capital stock of another corporation by purchasing the shares for cash (or other assets), or by exchanging some of its own capital stock for capital stock of the other corporation.

The investing company (i.e., the investor) may acquire some or all of either the preferred or the common stock outstanding of the other corporation. If the purpose is to obtain influence or control, the typical situation involves investment in the *common stock* because it is the voting stock. The number of shares of stock acquired by one corporation of another corporation generally depends upon the investment objectives of the investing company (i.e., the acquiring company). For measurement and reporting purposes, three different levels of ownership are recognized. Each of these calls for different measurement and reporting approaches. The three levels generally are related to the number of shares of voting capital stock owned by the investing company in relationship to the total number of such shares that are outstanding.

For long-term investments in common stock, measurement of the investment amount to be reported on the balance sheet and the periodic investment revenue to be reported on the income statement depend upon the relationship between the investing company and the other company. To effectively interpret and use the periodic financial statements of companies reporting long-term investments, the measurement approaches and their economic impacts must be understood.

In accordance with the cost principle, long-term investments in the capital stock of another company are measured and recorded, at the date of acquisition of the shares, as the total consideration given to acquire them. This total includes the market price, plus all commissions and other buying costs. Subsequent to acquisition, measurement of the investment amount and the investment revenue depends upon the extent to which the investing company can exercise significant influence or control over the operating and financial policies of the other company. Significant influence and control are related to the number of shares owned of the other company in proportion to the total number of such shares outstanding.

For the measurement and reporting of long-term investments in the voting capital stock of another company, the APB, in *Opinion No. 18* (March 1971), defined the two terms "significant influence" and "control" essentially as follows:

(1) Significant influence—the ability of the investing company to affect, in an important degree, the operating and financing policies of another company in which they own shares of the voting stock. Significant influence may be indicated by (a) membership on the Board of Directors of the other company; (b) participation in the policy-making processes; (c) material transactions between the two companies; (d) interchange of management personnel; or (e) technological dependency. In the absence of a clear-cut distinction based upon these factors, significant influence is presumed if the investing company owns at least 20% but not more than 50% of the shares of the other company.

(2) Control—the ability of the investing company to determine the operating and financing policies of another company in which they own shares of the voting stock. For all practical purposes, control is assumed when the investing company owns over 50% of the outstanding voting stock of the other company.

The way these terms relate to the measurement and reporting of long-term investments in capital stock is as follows:

Level of Ownership	Measurement and Reporting Approach
1. Neither significant influence nor control	Cost method
2. Significant influence but not control	Equity method
3. Control	Consolidated statement method

Each of these approaches is outlined in Exhibit 13–1. The first two are discussed in the paragraphs to follow and the third is discussed in Chapter 14.

No significant influence or control (cost method)

When the investment by one corporation in the voting capital stock of another corporation does not give the former the ability to exercise significant influence or control, the cost method of accounting and reporting must be used. Under this method of accounting, the investment is measured in the accounts at cost. Subsequent to acquisition, the investment amount is considered to be cost and this amount is reported under Funds and Investments on the balance sheet for each period. Cash dividends declared by the other corporation are reported by the

Exhibit 13–1

Measurement and reporting of long-term investments in capital stock

Status of Ownership	Designation of Method	Measurement at Date of Acquisition	Measurement after Date of Acquisition	
			Investment	Revenue
1. Investor can exercise no significant influence or control. Presumed if investor owns less than 20% of the outstanding voting stock of the other company.	Cost Method	Investor records the investment at cost. Cost is the total outlay made to acquire the shares	Investor measures and reports the investment at cost on the balance sheet each period.	Investor recognizes revenue each period when dividends are declared from the other company.
2. Investor can exercise a significant influence, but not control, over the operating and financing policies of the other company. Presumed if investor owns 20% or more, but not more than 50%, of the outstanding voting stock of the other company.	Equity Method	Same as above.	Investor measures and reports the investment at cost *plus* the investor's share of the earnings (or less the losses) and *minus* the dividends received from the other company. (Dividends received are not considered revenue. To recognize them as revenue, rather than as a reduction in the investment, would involve double counting.)	Investor recognizes as revenue each period his proportionate share of the earnings (or losses) reported by the other company.
3. Investor can exercise control over the operating and financing policies of the other company. Control is presumed if the investor owns over 50% of the outstanding voting stock of the other company.	Consolidated Financial Statement Method	Same as above.	Consolidated financial statements required each period. Discussed in Chapter 14.	

investing entity as "Revenue from Investments" in the period declared. The cost method is essentially the same as the accounting and reporting previously discussed and illustrated for short-term investments in Chapter 8, except that the lower-of-cost-or-market rule is not applied to long-term investments.

To illustrate application of the cost method, assume that on February 1, 1974, the Able Corporation purchased in the market 1,000 shares of the outstanding common stock (par value $100 per share) of the Baker Corporation at a cash cost of $120 per share. At the date of the purchase, the Baker Corporation had 10,000 shares of the common stock outstanding. Since the Able Corporation acquired only 10% of the out-standing voting stock of the Baker Corporation, we presume that significant influence is not present; therefore, the cost method must be used. A normal sequence of entries on the books of the Able Corporation follows:

```
Feb. 1, 1974:
Investment in Common Stock, Baker Cor-
   poration (1,000 shares)............... 120,000
     Cash...............................          120,000
   Purchased 1,000 shares (10%) of the
   common stock of the Baker Corporation
   at $120 per share.

Dec. 15, 1974:
Cash.................................... 5,000
   Revenue from Investments (1,000
     shares × $5).....................          5,000
   Received a $5-per-share cash dividend
   on Baker Corporation common stock.
```

At the end of 1974, the financial statements for the Able Corporation, the investor, would report the following:

ABLE CORPORATION
Balance Sheet
At December 31, 1974

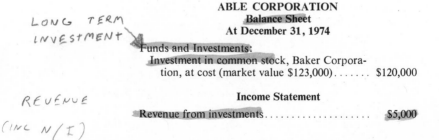

Funds and Investments:
   Investment in common stock, Baker Corpora-
      tion, at cost (market value $123,000)....... $120,000

Income Statement

Revenue from investments................... $5,000

The above entries clearly reflect application of the cost principle, hence, the designation "cost method." The Investment account is carried continuously at cost, and revenue is recognized from the in-vestment *only* in periods when dividends are declared. In the example above, the Baker Corporation declared and paid the dividends simul-taneously.

You should observe that the discussions above pertain only to the investing entity—the Able Corporation. The fact that the Able Corporation purchased 10% of the outstanding shares of the Baker Corporation had absolutely no affect on the accounting and reporting by the latter company.

Significant
influence
exists
(equity
method)

When the investment by one corporation in another corporation represents at least 20%, but not more than 50%, of the outstanding voting stock of the latter corporation, we can presume that significant influence is present; therefore, the equity method of measuring and reporting must be followed. When 20% or more, but not more than 50%, of the outstanding voting common stock of another corporation is owned, the degree of ownership is deemed to be sufficient to exercise significant influence over the financing and operating policies (including the dividend policies) of the other company.

When significant influence can be exercised over the dividend policies of another corporation, the net income of the other corporation can be obtained, almost at will (by means of dividends), by the investor company. As a consequence, under the equity method, each year the investor company recognizes its proportionate part of the *net income* (or net loss) of the other corporation as a part of its own net income rather than awaiting the receipt of dividends. At the time of recognition, since no cash is received, the offsetting debit is to the Investment account (an asset increase). Thus, under the equity method, both the Investment account and Investment Revenue reflect the investor's proportionate share of the profits of the other corporation. When dividends are received, they are credited to the Investment account. Thus, dividends received serve to reduce the Investment account balance and they are *not* credited to Investment Revenue. The revenue was recognized by the investor in the same period that the other company earned the income.

To illustrate the accounting and reporting under the equity method, assume that the Crown Corporation (the investor company), on January 15, 1974, purchased in the market 3,000 shares of the outstanding common stock of the Davis Corporation (often called the investee company) at a cash price of $120 per share. At the date of purchase, the Davis Corporation had outstanding 10,000 shares of common stock (par $100 per share). Since the Crown Corporation purchased 30% of the outstanding voting stock of the other corporation, the equity method must be used. At the date of acquisition, the investment would be recorded by the Crown Corporation at cost as follows:[2]

_____

[2] This example assumes that the investment was purchased at "book value." The accounting and reporting procedures for other situations are fairly complex

30

```
Jan. 15, 1974:
Investment in Common Stock, Davis Cor-
   poration (3,000 shares)............... 360,000
   Cash....................................              360,000
Purchased 3,000 shares (30%) of the
common stock of the Davis Corporation
at $120 per share.
```

After the acquisition date, each year when the other corporation reports net income (or net loss), the investor company records its percentage share of (i.e., equity in) the investment revenue. To illustrate, assume that, at the end of 1974, the Davis Corporation reported a net income of $50,000. The entry by the Crown Corporation (the investor company) to recognize its proportionate share of the net income would be:

INC ASST

INC O/E

```
Dec. 31, 1974:
Investment in Common Stock, Davis Corpora-
   tion..................................... 15,000
   Revenue from Investments...............              15,000
To record the proportionate share of 1974
net income reported by the Davis Cor-
poration ($50,000 × 30% = $15,000).
```

Proportionate

TOTAL × % owned by investor = share of net income

The proportionate share of the net income of the Davis Corporation was taken up by the Crown Corporation as revenue and as an *increase* in the Investment account. Therefore, when a dividend is received, to avoid counting the income twice, it is recorded as a debit to Cash and as a credit to the Investment account. This entry reflects the fact that a dividend represents the conversion of a part of the Investment account balance to cash. To illustrate, assume that on December 31, 1974, the Davis Company paid a cash dividend amounting to $10,000, of which 30%, or $3,000, was received by the Davis Corporation. The Davis Corporation would record the dividend as follows:

```
Dec. 31, 1974:
Cash..................................... 3,000
   Investment in Common Stock, Davis Cor-
      poration...............................              3,000
To record the receipt of a cash dividend
from the Davis Corporation ($10,000 ×
30% = $3,000).
```

To recapitulate, under the equity method, the balance in the Investment account initially starts at cost. Subsequently, it is increased on a

---

since they involve asset writeups and writedowns and, perhaps, the recognition of "goodwill." This chapter presents the fundamentals devoid of this complexity. More advanced books devote considerable attention to these complexities.

proportionate basis by the earnings of the investee company and decreased by the proportionate share of the dividends declared by that company. The investment and revenue accounts on the books of the investor company, the Crown Corporation, would be as follows:

Investment in Common Stock, Davis Corporation

1/15/74 Purchased 3,000 shares 360,000	12/31/74 Proportionate share of dividends of Davis Corp. 3,000
12/31/74 Proportionate share of 1974 net income of Davis Corp. 15,000	

(Debit balance $372,000)

Revenue from Investments

	12/31/74 Revenue from Davis Corp. 15,000

The financial statements for the Crown Corporation, the investor company, at the end of 1974 would reflect the following:

CROWN CORPORATION
Balance Sheet
At December 31, 1974

Funds and Investments:
Investment in common stock, Davis Corporation,
equity basis (cost $360,000; market $369,000)...... $372,000

Income Statement

Revenue from investments...................... $ 15,000

In interpreting and using financial statements that report long-term investments, information in respect to the method of measuring the investment and the related investment revenue is important. The financial statement must disclose the method used. In addition, regardless of whether the cost or the equity method is used, the original cost, current market value, and carrying value of the investment should be disclosed; this disclosure is illustrated in the preceding paragraphs.

The different methods used represent a compromise on the part of the accounting profession in respect to measuring the effects of long-term investments. Although not currently acceptable, many accountants believe that marketable securities should be measured and reported at their **fair-market value** at each balance-sheet date. Under this approach, both dividends received and changes in the market value of the stock since the last period would be reported as revenue (or loss) on the income statement. They take this position because they believe that it meets most closely the objective of reporting the economic consequences of holding an investment in marketable securities. The *cost method* measures the resources (dividends) received by the investor as revenue, but these may have absolutely no relationship to the earnings of the other company for the period. The cost method does not indicate to the investor or statement user the earnings pattern of the other company. The equity method tends to overcome this objection and is considered to be consistent with the concept of accrual accounting; however, it does not reflect the impact on the entity of market changes that are significant to the investor. After consideration of these and other factors, the accounting profession, for the present time, has accepted the three different measurement approaches for long-term investments in shares that are outlined in Exhibit 13–1.

PART TWO: LONG-TERM INVESTMENTS IN BONDS

Nature of
a bond
investment

In Chapter 11, the measurement and reporting of bonds as a long-term liability of the issuing corporation were discussed. In this part, we will focus on bonds of another company held as a long-term investment. Bonds are purchased as a long-term investment because they offer significantly different investment risks than does capital stock. Although bonds held as an investment do not confer voting privileges, as does capital stock, they do provide a stated rate of interest and a specified maturity value. As debt, they rank above shares, as a claim for both interest and principal. For example, assume that the Smith Company issued $100,000, 6%, 20-year bonds. At the specified maturity date, the investors in the bonds (i.e., the bondholders) receive exactly $100,000 cash in retirement of the bonds. The 6% stated interest on the face amount of the bond is received in cash each year, irrespective of the market price of the bonds or the earnings of the other company. The owner (i.e., the investor) of one or more of these bonds has no right to vote in the annual stockholders' meeting as he would have if he were the owner of some of the capital stock of the Smith Company.

Similar to capital stock, bonds are bought and sold in regular security markets. The market price of bonds fluctuates inversely with changes in the market rate of interest since the stated rate of interest, paid on the face amount of the bond, remains constant over the life of the bonds (see Chapter 11).

Measuring
and
reporting
bond
investments

Investors may buy bonds as an investment at their date of issuance or at subsequent dates during the life of the bonds. Irrespective of the timing of their acquisition, the investor must measure the (a) current cash equivalent amount of the investment at each balance-sheet date and (b) interest revenue earned each period, which is reported on the income statement. An understanding of the measurement approaches used is helpful in interpreting and using financial statements.

At date of acquisition, a bond investment is measured, recorded, and reported in accordance with the cost principle. The purchase cost, including all incidental acquisition costs (such as transfer fees and commissions), is debited to an investment account such as "Long-term Investment, Bonds of X Corporation." The cost recorded under the cost principle is the current cash-equivalent amount, and it may be the same as the maturity amount (if acquired at par); less than the maturity amount (if acquired at a discount); or more than the maturity amount (if acquired at a premium). The premium or discount on a bond investment usually is not recorded in a separate account; rather, the Investment account reflects the current cash-equivalent amount.

Subsequent to acquisition, a bond investment is measured as the *current cash-equivalent amount* at each subsequent date. If the bond investment was acquired at maturity value (at par), the current cash-equivalent amount remains constant over the life of the investment because there is no premium or discount to be amortized. In this situation, revenue earned from the investment each period is measured as the amount of cash interest collected (or accrued).

When a bond investment is acquired at a current cash-equivalent amount that is either more or less than the maturity amount (i.e., at a premium or discount), measurement of the investment after date of acquisition necessitates adjustment of the Investment account balance, from acquisition cost to maturity amount, over the life of the investment. This adjustment is the periodic amortization of the premium or discount. The periodic amortization is made as a debit or credit to the Investment account, depending on whether there was a premium or discount at acquisition, so that the Investment account at the end of each period reflects the *then current cash-equivalent amount*.

When a bond investment is acquired at a premium or discount, the revenue from interest each period is measured as the cash interest collected (or accrued), plus or minus the periodic amortization of premium or discount. As was illustrated in Chapter 11 for bonds payable, bond premium or discount may be amortized by using either the straight-line or effective-interest approach. The former is simpler, whereas, the latter is conceptually preferable. In the paragraphs to follow, we will assume straight-line amortization; effective-interest amortization is explained at the end of this part. In contrast to long-term investments, premium or discount is not amortized on bonds held as a short-term investment since the bonds will be converted to cash (i.e., sold) within the coming year instead of being held to maturity.

Accrual of interest revenue. After date of acquisition, interest revenue must be accrued (with an adjusting entry) for periods between the last date on which interest revenue was collected and the end of the accounting period. The procedure for accruing interest expense and interest revenue was discussed and illustrated in several prior chapters.

Bonds
purchased
at par

To illustrate a long-term investment in the bonds payable of another company, purchased at par, assume that on July 1, 1974, the Roth Company purchased $10,000, 20-year bonds of the Smith Company in the open market at a cost of $10,000 cash (i.e., purchased at par). The bonds were originally issued by the Smith Company on July 1, 1959, and mature on June 30, 1979; thus, the Roth Company purchased the bonds at 100, five years before the maturity date. The bonds call for 6% annual interest payable each July 1. The Roth Company adjusts and closes its book each December 31. The sequence of entries on the books of the Roth Company to account for this long-term investment in bonds payable is:

```
July 1, 1974:
Long-term Investment, Bonds of Smith
  Company.................................. 10,000
    Cash....................................          10,000
  Purchased at par, $10,000 maturity value,
  6% bonds of the Smith Company. (Note:
  Since the bonds were purchased on an
  interest date, there was no accrued
  interest.)


Dec. 31, 1974 (and each year until maturity):
Bond Interest Receivable..................   300
    Revenue from Investments*.............          300
  Adjusting entry to accrue 6 months' in-
  terest revenue on Smith Company bond
  investment ($10,000 × .06 × 6/12 = $300).

* Alternate titles are interest revenue and, sometimes, interest income.


July 1, 1975 (and each year until maturity):[3]
Cash ($10,000 × .06)......................   600
    Bond Interest Receivable (from Dec. 31
      entry)..............................          300
    Revenue from Investments..............          300
  Receipt of annual interest payment on the
  Smith Company bonds.


June 30, 1979:
Cash...................................... 10,000
    Long-term Investment, Bonds of Smith
      Company.............................          10,000
  Retirement of bonds at maturity date.
```

[3] This entry presumes that there was no reversal on January 1, 1975, of the prior adjusting entry. A reversing entry is optional since it serves only to facilitate the subsequent entry.

Since the bond investment was purchased at par or maturity value, there was no premium or discount to be amortized.

At the end of 1974, the financial statements of Roth Company would report the following:

Balance Sheet

Current Assets:
    Bond interest receivable.......................... $ 300
Funds and Investments:
    Investment in bonds, at cost (market $10,125)...... $10,000

Income Statement

Revenue from investments............................. $ 300

Bonds purchased at a discount

When investors demand a *higher* rate of interest than the stated rate on the bonds, they will sell in the market at a discount. When a bond investment is purchased at a discount, say at 98 (this means 98% of the bond's par value), the investor receives back in cash the periodic interest payments stated on the bond plus the maturity value (i.e., at 100). The discount serves to increase the interest revenue earned on the bond investment. To illustrate, assume that on July 1, 1974, the Roth Company purchased a $10,000, 6% bond issued by the Smith Company for $9,800 cash. The bond will mature in five years. Interest revenue of $10,000 × .06 = $600 will be collected annually. This investment can be analyzed to show that, although $600 cash is collected each year, the annual revenue *earned* from the investment is $640, due to amortization of the discount. The analysis, assuming straight-line amortization, is as follows:

Cash outflow for the investment:
    July 1, 1974—purchase of bond.................. $ 9,800
Cash inflows from the investment:
    Annual interest collected, July 1, 1974, through
        June 30, 1979 ($10,000 × .06 × 5 years)........ $ 3,000
        Collection of bond at maturity date, June 30, 1979.. 10,000   13,000
Difference: Net increase in cash (this is the total
    interest earned)..................................... $ 3,200

Revenue from investment per year: $3,200 ÷ 5 years = $640.

When a bond is purchased as an investment, the Long-term Investment account is debited for the current cash-equivalent amount in accordance with the cost principle. Therefore, when a bond investment is purchased at a discount, the Investment account balance at purchase date will be less than par or maturity value. Through amortization of the discount, the balance of the Investment account must be *increased* each period in order to be at the par amount at maturity date. Amortization of the discount each period over the remaining life of the bond also *in-*

creases the amount of interest revenue earned. To accomplish this, the amount of discount amortized each period is debited to the Investment account and credited to Interest Revenue. The effect of this periodic amortization, over the life of the investment, is (1) to carry the Investment account balance at the end of each period as the then current cash-equivalent amount, and (2) to increase interest revenue earned each year by the amount of the amortization.

To illustrate, in the preceding example, the Roth Company each year must amortize a part of the discount, $10,000 − $9,800 = $200, so that the total will be amortized over the remaining life of the bond investment. Assuming straight-line amortization, the amount of discount amortized each full year would be $200 ÷ 5 years = $40 per year.

The sequence of entries by the Roth Company, from the date of acquisition of the bond investment through maturity date, would be:

```
July 1, 1974:
Long-term Investment, Bonds of Smith
   Company....................................  9,800
      Cash....................................          9,800
   Purchased $10,000 maturity value, 6%
   bonds of the Smith Company at 98.


Dec. 31, 1974 (and each year until maturity):
Bond Interest Receivable ($10,000 × .06 ×
   6/12)....................................    300
Long-term Investment, Bonds of Smith
   Company (amortization: $40 × 6/12).......     20
      Revenue from Investments..............            320
   Adjusting entry to (1) accrue interest
   revenue for 6 months; (2) to amortize
   discount on the bond investment for 6
   months (July 1 to Dec.31).


July 1, 1975 (and each year until maturity):
Cash ($10,000 × .06).......................     600
Long-term Investment, Bonds of Smith Com-
   pany (amortization: $40 × 6/12)..........     20
      Bond Interest Receivable (From Dec. 31
      entry)................................            300
      Revenue from Investments..............            320
   Receipt of annual interest on Smith Com-
   pany bonds and amortization of discount
   for 6 months (Jan. 1 to July 1).


June 30, 1979:
Cash.......................................  10,000
      Long-term Investment, Bonds of Smith
      Company...............................         10,000
   Retirement of bonds at maturity.
```

The increase in the balance in the Long-term Investment account from cost at date of purchase to par value at maturity date that results from the amortization of the bond discount is reflected in the investment account as follows:[4]

Long-term Investment, Bonds of Smith Company

July 1, 1974, At Acquisition	9,800	June 30, 1979 Retirement	10,000
Amortizations:			
1974	20		
1975	40		
1976	40		
1977	40		
1978	40		
1979	20		
	10,000		10,000

At the end of 1974, the financial statements of the Roth Company would report the following:

Balance Sheet

Current Assets:
  Bond interest receivable........................ $ 300
Funds and Investments:
  Investment in bonds, at amortized cost
  (market $10,125)............................. $9,820

Income Statement

Financial Revenues:
  Revenue from investments........................ $ 320

Bonds purchased at a premium   When investors are willing to invest at a rate of interest *less* than the stated rate of interest on the bonds, the bonds will sell at a premium. When bonds are purchased at a premium, the Investment account is debited for an amount greater than the par or maturity value. Therefore, the premium must be amortized over the remaining life of the bonds as a *decrease* in the balance in the Investment account so that the balance of the Investment account is at par value on maturity date. The procedure parallels that illustrated above for a discount, except that each period the Investment account is credited and the premium amortization serves to *decrease* interest revenue.

To illustrate the accounting and reporting where there is a premium, assume that, in the preceding example, the Roth Company purchased

---

[4] Observe that the amortization of discount or premium on bond investments conceptually is the same as the amortization discussed and illustrated in Chapter 11 in the issuer's accounts. Here, we are simply looking at the other side of the transaction. A minor procedural difference may be noted. In Chapter 11, premium or discount was recorded in a separate account; in this chapter, the *net amount* (i.e., the cost) was recorded in the Investment account. Either procedure can be used in either situation with the same results. Common practice follows the procedures illustrated in the respective chapters.

the Smith Company bonds for $10,200 cash. The cash outflows and inflows for this investment may be analyzed to reflect the effect of the premium on interest revenue earned as follows:

10,000 + 200 Premium

Cash outflow for the investment:
July 1, 1974 purchase of bond................. $10,200

Cash inflows from the investment:
Annual interest collected, July 1, 1974, through
June 30, 1979 ($10,000 × .06 × 5 years)....... $ 3,000
July 30, 1979, collection of bond at maturity...... 10,000 13,000

Difference: Net increase in cash (this is the
total interest revenue earned)...................... $ 2,800

TOTAL INT

Revenue from investment, per year: $2,800 ÷ 5 years = $560.

The amount of premium amortization each full year, on a straight-line basis would be $200 ÷ 5 years = $40. The sequence of entries by the Roth Company for the bond investment, purchased at a premium, would be:

ORIGINAL COST

```
July 1, 1974:
Long-term Investment, Bonds of Smith Com-
   pany (at cost)........................... 10,200
      Cash....................................          10,200
   Purchased $10,000 maturity value, 6%
   bonds of the Smith Company at 102.


Dec. 31, 1974 (and each year until maturity):
Bond Interest Receivable ($10,000 × .06 ×
   6/12)...................................    300
      Long-term Investment, Bonds of Smith
      Company (amortization: $40 × 6/12)...              20
      Revenue from Investments..............             280
   Adjusting entry to (1) accrue interest
   revenue for 6 months; (2) to amortize
   premium on the investment for 6 months
   (July 1 to Dec. 31).


July 1, 1975 (and each year until maturity):
Cash ($10,000 × .06).......................    600
      Bond Interest Receivable (per Dec. 31
      entry)................................             300
      Long-term Investment, Bonds of Smith
      Company (amortization: $40 × 6/12)...              20
      Revenue from Investments..............             280
   Receipt of annual interest revenue on
   Smith Company bonds and amortization of
   premium for 6 months, Jan. 1 to July 1,
   1975.


June 30, 1979:
Cash.......................................  10,000
      Long-term Investment, Bonds of Smith
      Company...............................           10,000
   Retirement of bonds at maturity.
```

½ interest per ½ yr of 600 per yr less 300

REV = INT - AMOR
At PREMIUM

At the end of 1974, the financial statements of the Roth Company would report the following:

Balance Sheet

½ yrs intrest

Current Assets:
    Bond interest receivable......................... $ 300
Funds and Investments:
    Investment in bonds, at amortized cost   10,200 −20
    (market $10,125)............................. $10,180

Income Statement

300−20

Financial Revenues:
    Revenue from investments...................... $ 280

Bond investment purchased between interest dates

Investors generally purchase bond investments between the interest dates specified on the bonds. In these situations the investor must pay for the amount of interest accrued since the last interest date in addition to the purchase price of the bond. The bond market operates in this fashion because the holder of the bond at the interest date receives interest for the full period between interest dates, irrespective of the purchase date. The former owner of the bond is entitled to interest for the period of time that he held the bond (see Chapter 11). To illustrate, assume a $1,000 bond, 6% interest, payable each April 1 and October 1, is purchased on June 1, 1974, at 100 plus accrued interest. The purchase of the bond investment would be recorded as follows:

DEC o/E

```
June 1, 1974:
Long-term Investment, 6% Bond................ 1,000
Revenue from Investments ($1,000 × .06 ×
  2/12.......................................        10[5]
    Cash: $1,000 + ($1,000 × .06 × 2/12).....              1,010
  Purchase of a $1,000, 6% bond as a long-
  term investment at 100 plus accrued inter-
  est for 2 months, April 1 to June 1, 1974.
```

It is important to observe in this entry that the Long-term Investment account is debited for the *cost* of the investment, which excludes the accrued interest. The $10 accrued interest was paid for in cash by the purchaser; however, it will be refunded to the investor at the next interest date in October 1974. At that time, the investor will receive the full amount of interest for six months, although the bond has been owned by him for only four months (i.e., June 1 to October 1, 1974).

The entry to record the first interest collection after the purchase would be:

---

[5] Alternatively, an account, "Bond Interest Receivable," could have been debited on June 1 for $10 and then credited for that amount on October 1. The net effect would have been the same. When the end of the accounting period falls between the purchase date and the next interest date, this procedure may be less complex.

```
October 1, 1974:
Cash..................................................... 30
    Revenue from Investments......................          30
    Collected interest for 6 months on bond invest-
    ment ($1,000 × .03 = $30).
```

After these two entries are posted, the Revenue from Investments account will reflect interest earned for the four months since purchase as follows:

Revenue from Investments

6/1/74	10	10/1/74	30

(Balance, $1,000 × .03 × 4/6 = $20 credit)

Sale of a bond investment

When bonds are acquired as a long-term investment, they are accounted for with the expectation that they will be held to the maturity date. This is the basis for amortizing any premium or discount over the period from the date of purchase to the maturity date. Nevertheless, such long-term investments may be sold prior to the maturity date. When a bond investment is sold prior to maturity of the bonds, the difference between the sales price and the balance in the Investment account is recorded as a "gain (or loss) on the sale of investments."

To illustrate, assume the Carson Corporation has two $1,000, 6% bonds of the Drake Company that are being held as a Long-term Investment. Each bond was purchased at 104; therefore, the Long-term Investment account was debited for $2,080. Because of amortization to January 1, 1975, the Investment account balance is $2,040. On that date one of the bonds was sold for 100. The entry to record the sale would be as follows:

```
Cash........................................... 1,000
Loss on Sale of Investments.................     20
    Long-term Investment, Drake Co. Bonds....         1,020
    Sale of long-term investment.
```

Effective-interest amortization on bond investments

Effective-interest amortization of the discount or premium on a bond investment is conceptually identical with that discussed for bonds payable in Chapter 11 (page 401). This method of amortization is conceptually superior because (1) the true or effective interest revenue is measured each period for income statement purposes; and (2) the carrying amount of the investment is correctly measured for balance-sheet purposes at the end of each period. Each interest revenue collection (in cash) is assumed to consist of principal and interest. To illustrate the effective-interest approach, assume that on January 1, 1974, Company A purchased a three-year, $5,000 bond of Company B as a long-term investment. The purchase price was $4,869. The bond carried a stated rate of interest of 6% per year, payable each January 1. The purchase price, at a discount of $5,000 − $4,869 = $131, was recorded as follows:

```
Jan. 1, 1974:
Long-term Investment, Bond of Company B
   (maturity amount $5,000)................... 4,869
      Cash.....................................        4,869
   Purchase of long-term investment.
```

Computation of effective-interest amortization is shown in the following tabulation. Observe that the effective rate of interest, 7% in this example, is used to compute the revenue rather than the stated interest rate.

Period	Cash Received for Interest each Period	Effective Interest each Period: Based on Investment Balance and Effective Rate	Amount Added to Investment Balance	Investment Balance
1/1/74 (issuance)				$4,869
End of Year 1..........	$300*	$4,869 × .07 = $ 341	$ 41†	4,910‡
End of Year 2..........	300	4,910 × .07 = 344	44	4,954
End of Year 3..........	300	4,954 × .07 = 346	46	5,000
Totals..........	$900	$1,031	$131	

* $5,000 × .06 = $300.
† Col. 2, $341 minus Col. 1, $300 = $41.
‡ $4,869 plus Col. 3, $41 = $4,910.

The first amount column reflects the cash inflow each period for interest; the second column shows the interest revenue amount to be reported on the income statement each period; and the last column shows the amount of the investment to be reported on the balance sheet at the end of each period under "Funds and Investments." In addition, the entry for interest revenue each period can be taken directly from the table, viz:

	Year 1	Year 2	Year 3
Cash...........................	300	300	300
Long-term investment............	41	44	46
Revenue from investments.......	341	344	346

Conceptually, this method derives the true or effective-interest revenue earned during each period and the correct current cash-equivalent amount for the investment at the end of each period. The straight-line approach provides only approximations of these amounts. Straight-line amortization is often used because the amounts of premium or discount are not material. In such a case, the departure from the conceptually superior method is justified by the exception principle (i.e., materiality) of accounting.

| Demonstra-tion case for self-study | HOWELL EQUIPMENT, INCORPORATED |

HOWELL EQUIPMENT, INCORPORATED

(Try to resolve the case before turning to the suggested solution that follows.)

Howell Equipment, Incorporated, has been in operation for 18 years. The company sells a major line of farm equipment. In recent years its service department has expanded significantly. Both sales and services have been quite profitable. At the beginning of 1974, the company had considerable excess cash. At that time the management decided to invest in some securities of two of the manufacturers that supply most of the equipment purchased for resale. The annual accounting period ends on December 31.

This case focuses on the two long-term investments made in 1974. One investment was in equity securities and the other in debt securities. The transactions follow:

(a) Jan. 1, 1974: Purchased 2,000 shares of common stock of the Dear Company at $40 per share. This is 1% of the shares outstanding.

(b) Aug. 1, 1974: Purchased $100,000, 6% bonds payable of the Massey Company at 102, plus accrued interest.
The bonds pay semiannual interest on each June 1 and Dec. 1. The bonds mature on June 1, 1979. Brokerage fees amounted to $900.

(c) Dec. 1, 1974: Received semiannual interest on Massey Company bonds. Use straight-line amortization.

(d) Dec. 28, 1974: Received $4,000 cash dividend on the Dear Company stock.

(e) Dec. 31, 1974: Adjusting entry for accrued interest on the Massey Company bonds. The current market price of the stock is $42.

(f) Dec. 31, 1974: Closed the revenue from Investments account to Income Summary.

Required:

a. Give the journal entry for each of the above transactions.

b. Show how the two investments, the accrued interest receivable, and the related revenue would be reported on the balance sheet and income statement at December 31, 1974.

Suggested Solution:

Requirement (a):

```
(a) Jan. 1, 1974:
Long-term Investment, Stock of Dear Com-
  pany (2,000 shares)...................   80,000
  Cash...............................             80,000
  Purchased 2,000 shares Dear Company
  common stock at $40 per share.


(b) Aug. 1, 1974:
Long-term Investment, Bonds of Massey
  Company..............................  102,900
Revenue from Investments ($100,000 ×
  .03 × 2/6)...........................    1,000
  Cash...............................            103,900
  Purchased $100,000 bonds of the Massey
  Company:
    Cost ($100,000 × 1.02) +
    $900                    = $102,900
    Accrued interest for 2
    months ($100,000 × .03 ×
    2/6)                    =    1,000
             Total cash paid  $103,900


(c) Dec. 1, 1974:
Cash....................................    3,000
  Long-term Investment, Bonds of Massey
    Company...........................               200
  Revenue from Investments............             2,800
  Semiannual interest: $100,000
    × .03                   = $3,000
  Amortization of premium:
    $2,900 ÷ 58 months = $50 per
    month; $50 × 4 months*  =    200
  Revenue from investments   $2,800

    * Sept. 1, 1970, to June 30, 1975 = 58 months remaining life.


(d) Dec. 28, 1974:
Cash....................................    4,000
  Revenue from Investments............             4,000
  Received dividend on Dear Company
  stock.


(e) Dec. 31, 1974:
Accrued Interest Receivable...........      500
  Long-term Investment, Bonds of Massey
    Company...........................                50
  Revenue from Investments............              450
  Adjusting entry for accrued interest
  and premium amortization for one month
  on Massey Company bonds.
    Accrued interest receivable:
      $100,000 × .03 × 1/6       = $500
    Amortization of premium:
      $50 × 1 month              =    50
        Revenue from investments   $450
```

```
(f) Dec. 31, 1974:
Revenue from Investments................    6,250
    Income Summary.......................          6,250
    Closing entry: ($2,800 - $1,000 +
    $4,000 + $450 = $6,250).
```

Requirement (b):

HOWELL EQUIPMENT, INCORPORATED
Balance Sheet
At December 31, 1974

Current Assets:		
Accrued interest receivable.....................		$ 500
Funds and Investments:		
Stock of Dear Company, at cost, 2,000 shares		
(market $84,000).............................	$ 80,000	
Bonds of Massey Company, at amortized cost		
($100,000 maturity value).....................	102,650	182,650

Income Statement
For Year Ending December 31, 1974

Revenue from investments....................... $ 6,250

Summary

This chapter discussed the measuring and reporting of two types of long-term investments: the capital stock and the bonds of another company. A company may acquire a part or all of the outstanding capital stock of another corporation through purchase of the shares or by exchanging their own stock for shares in the other company. The measurement and reporting for a long-term investment in shares of capital stock of another company is determined by the percent of shares owned in relation to the total number outstanding.

If the ownership level is less than 20%, the **cost method** must be used. Under this method the investment amount reported by the investor company is the current cash-equivalent amount (i.e., cost), and dividends received from the other company are recognized as investment revenue.

If the ownership is at least 20% but not more than 50%, the **equity method** is used. Under this method the investment is recorded at cost by the investor company at date of acquisition. Each period thereafter, the investment amount is increased by the proportionate interest in the net income reported by the other company and decreased by the proportionate share of the dividends received from the other company. Each period, the investor company recognizes as revenue its proportionate share of the net income reported by the other company.

When there is a controlling interest—that is, over 50% ownership of the outstanding stock is held by the investor—the financial statements of the affiliated companies are **consolidated.** This subject is discussed in Chapter 14.

A corporation may purchase the bonds of another entity as a long-term investment. In contrast to capital stock, bonds are a liability of the issuing company, therefore (1) they have a specified maturity date and face amount; (2) they require the payment of a stated rate of interest at regular specified interest dates; and (3) they do not convey voting privileges. At the date of purchase, a long-term investment in bonds is recorded at cost, which may be at par, at a discount, or at a premium. When purchased at a premium or at a discount, amortization of such premium or discount over the remaining life of the bonds is required. The periodic amortization serves to adjust the investment amount (which is reported on the balance sheet) and interest revenue earned (which is reported on the income statement).

Important terms	**Significant influence** **Control** **Cost method** **Equity method**	**Current cash-equivalent amount** **Amortization of bond discount** **and premium**

Questions for discussion

1. Explain the difference between a short-term investment and a long-term investment.
2. Match the following:

    Measurement Method   *Level of Ownership of Capital Stock*
    _____Cost method.   a.   Over 50% ownership.
    _____Equity method.   b.   Under 20% ownership.
    _____Consolidation.   c.   At least 20% but not more than 50%.

3. Explain the application of the cost principle to the purchase of shares of capital stock in another company.
4. Under the cost method, why is revenue measured by the investor company only in periods when the other company pays a dividend?
5. Under the equity method, why is revenue measured on a proportionate basis by the investor company when earnings are reported by the other company, rather than when dividends are paid?
6. Under the equity method, dividends received from the investee company are not recorded as revenue. To record dividends as revenue would involve double counting. Explain.
7. Match the following relating to the balance of the long-term investment amount reported on the balance sheet of the investor company:

    Measurement Method   *Explanation of Balance in the Investment Account*
    _____Cost method.   (a)   Original cost of the investment.
    _____Equity method.   (b)   Original cost plus proportionate share of the net income of the subsidiary, less dividends received.

8. Explain why interest revenue must be accrued on a long-term investment in bonds but not on a long-term investment in capital stock.

9. Under what conditions will a bond sell at (a) par, (b) a discount, (c) a premium?

10. Distinguish between a long-term investment in bonds versus a long-term investment in capital stock of another company.

11. Why is it necessary to amortize premium or discount that arises from the purchase of a bond as a long-term investment above or below par? Over what period should the premium or discount be amortized?

12. When a bond investment is purchased between interest dates, the purchaser must pay accrued interest plus the purchase price of the bond. Explain why the accrued interest must be paid.

Exercises   **E13–1.** Company P purchased a certain number of the outstanding voting shares of Company S at $5.00 per share as a long-term investment. Company S had outstanding 10,000 shares of $10 par-value stock. On a separate sheet complete the following matrix relating to the measurement and reporting by Company P after acquisition of the shares of Company S stock.

Questions	Method of Measurement		
	Cost Method	Equity Method	Consolidated Statements
a. What is the applicable level of ownership by Co. P of Co. S to apply the method?	<20	20 30	>50
b. At acquisition, the Investment account on the books of Co. P should be debited at what amount?	Cost	cost	cost
c. When should Co. P recognize revenue owned on the stock of Co. S?	DECLARE DIVIDEND	WHEN S EARNS	✕
d. After acquisition date, when should Co. P change the balance of Investment account in respect to the stock of Co. S owned (other than for disposal of the investment)?	DON'T	' ' ' '	✕
For (e) and (f) that follow, assume the following: Number of shares acquired of Co. S stock Net income reported by Co. S in 1st year Dividends declared by Co. S in 1st year	1,000 $30,000 $10,000	3 3,000 $30,000 $10,000	✕
e. What would be the balance in the Investment account on the books of Co. P at the end of the 1st year?	5000	15,000 9,000 6,000 21,000	✕
f. What amount of revenue from the investment in Co. S will Co. P report at the end of the 1st year?	1000	900	✕

10%

15,000
9,000
-3000

30%
of the
income

E13–2. Mercury, Inc., acquired some of the 10,000 shares of the common stock of the Johnson Company as a long-term investment. The following transactions occurred during 1974. The accounting period for both companies ends on December 31.

July 2, 1974:   Purchased 1,500 shares at $20 per share.

Dec. 31, 1974: Received a copy of the 1974 annual financial statement for the Johnson Company. It reflected a net income of $11,000.

Dec. 31, 1974: The Johnson Company paid a cash dividend of $.50 per share.

Required:

a. Give the required entries by Mercury, Inc., for each transaction. If no entry is required, explain why.

b. Show how the long-term investment and the related revenue would be reported on the financial statements for Mercury, Inc., at December 31, 1974.

E13–3. The Reed Company acquired some of the 20,000 shares of outstanding common stock of Bledsoe, Inc., during 1974 as a long-term investment. The annual accounting period for both companies ends on December 31. The following transactions occurred during 1974:

Jan. 10, 1974: Purchased 5,000 shares of Bledsoe stock at $30 per share.

Dec. 31, 1974: Received the Dec. 31, 1974, financial statement of Bledsoe, Inc. The reported net income was $40,000.

Dec. 31, 1974: Bledsoe, Inc., paid a cash dividend of $1.50 per share.

Required:

a. Give the entries by the Reed Company for each of the above transactions. State if no entry is required and explain why.

b. Show how the long-term investment and the related revenue would be reported on the 1974 financial statements of Reed Company.

E13–4. During 1974, the Allen Company purchased some of the 100,000 shares of common stock of Mylar Marine, Inc., as a long-term investment. The annual accounting period for each company ends on December 31. The following transactions occurred during 1974:

Jan. 7, 1974:   Purchased 10,000 shares of Mylar stock at $6 per share.

Dec. 31, 1974: Received the 1974 financial statement of Mylar Marine, Inc. The reported net income was $55,-000.

Dec. 31, 1974: Mylar paid a cash dividend of $.50 per share.

Required:

a. Give the entries for the Allen Company for each of the above transactions. State if no entry is required and explain why.

b. Show how the long-term investment and the related revenue would be reported on the 1974 financial statements of the Allen Company.

E13–5. You are to use the same situation and data given in Exercise 13–4, *except* for the January 7, 1974, transaction. Assume it to be as follows:

Jan. 7, 1974:   Purchased 30,000 shares of Mylar stock at $6 per share.

(The data for December 31 are unchanged.)

Requirements a and b, as given in Exercise 13–4.

E13–6. On July 1, 1974, the Baker Company purchased at par a $10,000, 5%, 20-year bond of Case Corporation as a long-term investment. The bond interest is payable each year on July 1. The accounting period for the Baker Company ends on December 31. At the date of purchase, the bond had five years remaining before maturity.

Give the following entries on the books of the Baker Company in respect to the long-term investment:

(a) July 1, 1974, for acquisition.

(b) Dec. 31, 1974, adjusting entry at the end of the accounting period.

(c) July 1, 1975, collection of first interest.

(d) Maturity date of the bond.

E13–7. On July 1, 1974, the Mays Company purchased three different bonds as long-term investments. Data with respect to the three bonds and the purchase price were:

Bond Designation	Face of Bond	Annual Interest	Payable Semiannually	Remaining Years to Maturity	Purchase Price
A......	$1,000	6%	Dec. 31 and	5	$1,000
B......	1,000	5	June 30 each	5	980
C......	1,000	7	year	5	1,030

Required:

(a) Give the entries to record separately the purchase of each bond.

(b) Give the entries to record separately the receipt of interest on the first interest date after purchase. Use straight-line amortization.

(c) Give the entries to record separately the maturity of each bond.

E13–8.   On May 1, 1974, the Grove Company, as a long-term investment, purchased $8,000 maturity value bonds of the White Corporation at 97. The bond interest rate is 6% per annum payable each May 1 and November 1. The bonds mature in four years from May 1, 1974.

Required:

a. Give the entries by the Grove Company on May 1, 1974, Nov. 1, 1974, and Dec. 31, 1974 (adjusting entry for accrued interest). Use straight-line amortization.

b. Show how this long-term investment and the related revenue would be shown on the Dec. 31, 1974, annual financial statements of the Grove Company.

(Hint: Include the investment, interest receivable, and any revenue.)

E13–9.   On May 1, 1974, the Acme Company purchased $6,000, 6% bonds of Cook, Inc., at 104 as a long-term investment. The bonds pay interest each May 1 and November 1. The bonds mature in four years from May 1, 1974.

Required:

a. Give the entries by the Acme Company on May 1, 1974, Nov. 1, 1974, and Dec. 31, 1974 (adjusting entry for accrued interest). Use straight-line amortization.

b. Show how this long-term investment would be shown on the Dec. 31, 1974, annual financial statements of the Acme Company.

E13–10. On March 1, 1974, the Rogers Corporation purchased $5,000 bonds of the Barker Corporation as a long-term investment. The bonds pay 3% interest each January 1 and July 1. The bonds mature in ten years from January 1, 1974. The purchase price was $5,236, plus the accrued interest.

Required:

a. Give the entry by the Rogers Corporation to record the purchase on March 1, 1974.

b. Give the entry to record the interest received on July 1, 1974. Use straight-line amortization.

E13–11. On September 1, 1974, the Maple Company purchased, as a long-term investment, a $10,000 face value, 6% bond issued by Noonan Corporation, for $10,000 cash plus any accrued interest. The bond pays interest each year on June 30 and has five years' remaining life until maturity.

Required:

(a) Give the entry on the books of the Maple Company to record the purchase of the bond on Sept. 1, 1974.

(b) Give the adjusting and closing entries for bond interest at Dec. 31, 1974, assuming this is the end of the accounting period for Maple Company. Use straight-line amortization.

(c) Give the entry for the first collection of interest on the bond investment.

(d) Complete the following on a separate sheet (show computations):

	1974	1975
Income statement:		
Revenue from bond investment......... $_____	$_____
Balance sheet:		
Long-term investment, bonds,		
Noonan Corporation.................. $_____	$_____

E13–12. On January 1, 1974, the Bailey Company purchased, as a long-term investment, a $3,000 bond of the Caster Company for $2,923. The bond had a stated interest rate of 7%, payable each January 1. The bond matures in three years. The Bailey Company uses effective-interest amortization. As a consequence, the following table was developed:

Date	Cash Inflow	Interest Revenue	Investment Change	Investment Balance
Jan. 1, 1974.......				$2,923
End Year 1........	$210	234	$24	2,947
End Year 2........	210	236	26	2,973
End Year 3........	210	237	27	3,000

Required:

Respond to the following questions:

a. What was the total cash outflow and the total cash inflow over the life of this investment? What does the difference represent? Explain.

b. How much interest revenue will be recognized on the income statement each year and in total?

c. What amounts will be shown on the balance sheet each year? Give the last year just prior to collection of the maturity amount.

d. What was the effective rate of interest per year? Show computations.

e. How were the four different amounts computed that are listed on the line "End of Year 2"?

Problems P13–1. Company S had outstanding 5,000 shares of common stock, par value $10 per share. On January 1, 1974, Company P purchased some of these shares at $20 per share. At the end of 1974, Company S reported the following: net income, $20,000; cash dividends paid, $8,000.

Required:

(a) Give entries on the books of Company P at the dates indicated below for each of the two separate cases. If no entry is required, so indicate and explain.

	Accounts	*Case A—500 Shares Purchased*	*Case B—1,500 Shares Purchased*
1.	Entry to record the acquisition at Jan. 1, 1974:		
2.	Entry to recognize the net income reported by Company S for 1974:		
3.	Entry to recognize the dividends paid by Company S for 1974:		

(b) Give the amounts on a separate sheet that would be reported on the financial statements of Company P, for 1974, in respect to the investment in Company S as follows:

	Case A	*Case B*
Balance Sheet: Funds and Investments: Investment in Co. S............	$_____	$_____
Income Statement: Revenue from investment in Co. S.......................	$_____	$_____

P13–2. On January 1, 1974, the Lone Star Company purchased $50,000, 6% bonds of Acme, Inc., as a long-term investment, at 100. Interest is payable annually on December 31. The bonds mature in six years from December 31, 1973. The annual accounting period for Lone Star ends on December 31. In addition, on January 2, 1974, Lone Star purchased in the market 5% of the 10,000 shares of outstanding common stock of Acme, Inc., at $30 per share.

Required:

a. Give the entry by the Lone Star Company for the purchase of the bonds on Jan. 1, 1974.

b. Give the entry to record the purchase of the common stock on Jan. 2, 1974.

c. Give the entry assuming a cash dividend of $2.00 per share was received on the Acme stock on Dec. 28, 1974.

d. Give the entry for the receipt of the interest on the Acme bonds on Dec. 31, 1974.

e. Show how the long-term investments and the related revenues would be reported on the annual financial statements of the Lone Star Company at Dec. 31, 1974.

P13–3. The Century Company purchased, as a long-term investment, some of the 100,000 shares of the outstanding common stock of Smith Inc. The annual accounting period for each company ends on December 31. The following transactions occurred during 1974:

Jan. 10, 1974: Purchased shares of common stock of Smith, Inc., at $9 per share as follows:
Case A—10,000 shares purchased
Case B—30,000 shares purchased

Dec. 31, 1974: Received financial statement of Smith, Inc., for the year ended Dec. 31, 1974. The reported net income was $50,000.

Dec. 31, 1974: Received cash dividend of $.20 per share from Smith, Inc.

Required:

a. Give the entries by the Century Company for each case for the above transactions. State if no entry is required and explain why.
(Hint: You can save time by using parallel columns for Case A and Case B.)

b. Give the amounts for each case that would be reported on the financial statements of the Century Corporation at Dec. 31, 1974. Use the following format:

	Case A	*Case B*
Balance Sheet:		
Funds and Investments:		
Investment in Smith, Inc..........	_____	_____
Income Statement:		
Revenue from investments........	_____	_____

P13–4. On May 1, 1974, the Murray Company purchased $20,000 maturity value, 6% bonds of Patton, Inc., as a long-term investment. The interest is payable on each May 1 and November 1. The bonds mature in four years from May 1, 1974. The bonds were purchased at 96. In addition, brokerage fees of $224 were paid by the Murray Company.

Required:

a. Give the entries by the Murray Company on the following dates:
May 1, 1974—Purchase
Nov. 1, 1974—First interest date. Use straight-line amortization.
Dec. 31, 1974—Adjusting entry for accrued interest at the end of the annual accounting period

b. Show how the investment, interest receivable, and related revenue would be reported on the annual financial statements of the Murray Company on Dec. 31, 1974.

c. Give the entry at the maturity date of the bonds.

P13–5. On June 1, 1974, the Howard Company purchased $30,000, 6% bonds of Star, Inc., as a long-term investment. The interest is payable each May 1 and November 1. The bonds mature in five years from May 1, 1974. The bonds were purchased at 103. In addition, the Howard Company paid brokerage fees of $280. The annual accounting period for the Howard Company ends on December 31.

Required:

a. Give the entries by the Howard Company on the following dates:

June 1, 1974: Purchase plus accrued interest.

Nov. 1, 1974: First interest date. Use straight-line amortization.

Dec. 31, 1974: Adjusting entry for accrued interest.

b. Show how the investment, interest receivable, and related revenue would be reported on the annual financial statements of the Howard Company on Dec. 31, 1974.

c. Give the entry at the maturity date of the bonds.

P13–6. During 1974, the Royal Company purchased the following bonds of the Stone Corporation as a long-term investment:

	Series A	Series B	Series C	Series D
Maturity amount.............	$10,000	$10,000	$10,000	$10,000
Date purchased..............	7/1/74	7/1/74	7/1/74	9/1/74
Interest per annum..........	6%	5%	7%	6%
Interest dates, annual........	June 30	June 30	June 30	June 30
Maturity date...............	6/30/79	6/30/79	6/30/79	6/30/79
Purchase price*..............	100	95	106	100

* Excluding any accrued interest.

Required:

(a) Record the purchase on the books of the Royal Company for each series separately.

(b) Give the adjusting entry required on the books of the Royal Company for Dec. 31, 1974, assuming this is the end of the accounting period. Make a separate entry for each series. Use straight-line amortization.

(c) Give the entry on the books of the Royal Company for each series separately that should be made on June 30, 1975, for collection of the first interest payment.

(d) Compute on a separate sheet the following amounts that should be reflected on the Dec. 31, 1974, financial statements:

Income Statement:
    Revenue from bond investments..... $_____

Balance Sheet:
    Investment in bonds............... $_____

P13–7. On January 1, 1974, the Northern Corporation purchased, as a long-term investment, a bond of the Jacks Corporation. The following table was prepared based on the investment (table captions have been omitted intentionally):

		$I\text{-}2$	Am	$10,339
Jan. 1, 1974..........				$10,339
End of Year 1........	$800	$724	$76	10,263
End of Year 2........	800	718	82	10,181
End of Year 3........	800	713	87	10,094
End of Year 4........	800	706	94	10,000

$3200/9\ \eta\delta61$

Required:

Respond to the following questions:

a. What was the maturity amount of the bond?

b. What was the purchase price of the investment?

c. What entry was made at acquisition date?

d. Was the bond acquired at a premium or discount? How much?

e. What was the stated rate of interest per year? Show computations.

f. What method of amortization apparently will be used? Explain.

g. What was the effective rate of interest?

h. What was the total cash inflow and outflow on the investment? What does the difference represent? Explain.

i. How much interest revenue will be reported each period on the income statement? How does this relate to the difference in h?

j. What amount will be reported on the balance sheet at the end of each year? (Show Year 4 just before collection of the maturity amount.)

k. How were each of the four amounts computed that are in the table for Year 2? Show computations.

l. Why is the method of amortization being used conceptually superior to the straight-line method?

14 Consolidated statements — measurement and reporting

Chapter 13 discussed long-term investments in those situations where one company owns 50% or less of the outstanding voting stock of another corporation. This chapter focuses on those situations where there is a controlling interest evidenced by ownership of more than 50% of the outstanding voting stock of another corporation.

A general understanding of a controlling interest, consolidation concepts, and consolidated financial statements is important at this level of your study of accounting. Those who do not plan to study accounting beyond the first year need this general background in order to understand and evaluate business combinations by purchase and by pooling of interests, consolidated statements, and the underlying measurement issues. In subsequent business courses, financial statements often are encountered in various situations, and most of them will be consolidated statements. Outside the classroom, you will continually encounter consolidated statements, the issues of purchase and pooling, and the related measurement and reporting problems. For those who plan to study accounting further, this background will be quite useful. An understanding of the broad issues, measurement approaches, and underlying concepts of consolidated statements is important to the statement user. This chapter has as its primary objective the presentation of these basic issues.

When an investor company owns over 50% of the outstanding voting stock of another corporation, a **parent** and **subsidiary** relationship is said to exist. The **investing** company is known as the **parent** company and the **other** corporation is called a **subsidiary.** Both corporations continue as **separate legal entities** and separate financial statements for each are

490

prepared for certain purposes. However, because of their special relationship, they are viewed as a single economic entity for financial measurement and reporting purposes. They are generally called related or affiliated companies and the parent company is required to prepare consolidated financial statements. To accomplish this, the individual financial statements of each of the separate companies are combined into one overall or consolidated set of financial statements, as if there were only one entity. The three required statements—balance sheet, income statement, and statement of changes in financial position—are consolidated.

This chapter focuses on the interpretation and use of consolidated financial statements. Measurement approaches and reporting on a consolidated basis are accorded primary attention. The important differences that result between a pooling of interests and a combination by purchase are identified and discussed. For those who desire to gain a greater depth of understanding of the measurement procedures involved, Appendices A and B have been included.

The concept of consolidated statements

There are a number of operating, economic, legal, and technical advantages to the parent–subsidiary relationship. As a consequence, most large corporations, and many middle-sized corporations, own more than 50% of the outstanding voting stock of one or more other corporations.

Consolidated statements are prepared in situations where two basic elements are present that relate to two or more different corporations. The two basic elements are control and economic compatibility.

Control is presumed to exist when over 50% of the voting stock of another entity is owned by one investor. The nonvoting stock is not included in this determination because it does not extend any avenue for control to the owner. In special circumstances, effective control may not exist, even though over 50% of the voting stock is owned. This situation may exist when the subsidiary is located in a foreign country where governmental restrictions are such that the parent company is powerless to exert meaningful control. In such circumstances, since control is lacking, consolidated statements would be inappropriate.

Economic compatibility means that the operations of the companies are related so that one complements the other. For example, a company manufacturing a major item and a subsidiary manufacturing a component part of the major item would have economic compatibility. On the other hand, a manufacturing company and a bank would lack economic compatability and would not be consolidated.[1]

---

[1] When one company owns over 50% of the voting stock of another company, and for other reasons does not qualify for consolidation, the one is reported as a long-term investment on the balance sheet as "Investment in Unconsolidated Subsidiary." In this case it is accounted for under the equity method as discussed in Chapter 13 and is not consolidated.

The concept of consolidated statements relates *only to reporting* the financial results of the parent and subsidiary as one economic unit. Otherwise, the accounting for each business is unaffected. The fact that another company owns a controlling interest does not affect the accounting by the subsidiary. At the end of the accounting period, the subsidiary prepares its own financial statements. Similarly, the parent company carries out the accounting for its operations in the normal manner and prepares its own financial statements at the end of each period.

Under the concept of consolidated statements, the financial statements of the parent and the subsidiary, prepared in the normal manner, are combined, or aggregated, by the parent company on an **item-by-item basis** to develop the consolidated financial statements. Thus, the consolidated-statement concept does not affect the accounting for the parent and the subsidiaries but affects only the **reporting phase** of the combined entity represented by the parent company.

Acquiring a controlling interest

One corporation may acquire a controlling interest in another corporation either by (1) organizing a new entity and *retaining* over 50% of the capital stock of the new corporation; or (2) by *acquiring* over 50% of the outstanding stock of an existing corporation. Both approaches in acquiring a controlling interest (to establish a parent–subsidiary relationship) are widely used. In the latter approach the parent company may acquire over 50% of the voting capital stock of the other entity in one of two ways (or a combination of them) as follows:

(1)   Exchanging shares of its own capital stock for the acquired shares of capital stock of the subsidiary. This is known throughout industry as a combination by a **pooling of interests.**

(2)   Purchasing with cash, other assets, or debt, the acquired shares of capital stock of the subsidiary. This is known as a combination by **purchase.**

The different economic impacts and the related measurement problems were significant factors in the merger movement that characterized the 1960s. The merger trend is continuing, although somewhat diminished, in the 1970s. In the next few paragraphs, we will pinpoint some of these major impacts, the problems of measurement, and reporting on the consolidated financial statements.

Throughout the chapter we will use a continuing example to illustrate the measurement approaches involved and the consolidated financial statements. We will use data for Company P (the parent) and Company S (the acquired subsidiary). Assume that on January 1, 1974 (just prior to the acquisition), the balance sheets for Company P and Company S reported the data shown in Exhibit 14–1.

Exhibit 14–1

COMPANY P and COMPANY S
Separate Balance Sheets
January 1, 1974, Immediately before Acquisition

	Company P		*Company S*	
Cash...........................		$205,000		$ 35,000
Accounts receivable (net)*.........		15,000		30,000
Receivable from Co. S.............		10,000		
Inventories......................		170,000		70,000
Plant and equipment (net)*		100,000		45,000
Total.................		$500,000		$180,000
Accounts payable.................		$ 60,000		$ 20,000
Payable to Co. P.................				10,000
Stockholders' equity:				
Common stock (par $10).........	$300,000		$100,000	
Retained earnings..............	140,000	440,000	50,000	150,000
Total.................		$500,000		$180,000

* Accounts Receivable, less the Allowance for Doubtful Accounts and Plant and Equipment, less Accumulated Depreciation. The net amounts are used to simplify the example. The end results will be the same as they would have been had the separate accounts been used.

Pooling of interests

When one corporation acquires a controlling interest in the stock of another corporation without buying it but by *exchanging* its own shares, a purchase/sale transaction between the parties often is deemed not to have been consummated.[2] The acquiring company has simply issued its own stock certificates for the stock certificates of the other company. Because there was no purchase/sale transaction, the cost principle is not applied. Thus, under the consolidation concept, the exchange of stock, in many cases, is viewed as a pooling of interests rather than as a purchase. As a consequence, when the financial statements of the parent and subsidiary are combined, the book values of each, as shown on their respective financial statements, are added together with no consideration for the current market values of the assets of the subsidiary.

Now, assume that on January 2, 1974, Company P (the parent) acquired all of the stock of Company S (the subsidiary) by exchanging one share of its own stock for each share of Company S stock. Thus,

---

[2] APB *Opinion No. 16* (August 1970) states precise conditions under which a business combination *must* be measured and reported as a pooling of interests. The *Opinion* states: "The combination of existing voting common stock interests by the exchange of stock is the essence of a business combination accounted for by the pooling of interests." The *Opinion* specifies a number of additional conditions that, if present, *require* use of the pooling-of-interests method. Because of these conditions, not all stock exchanges qualify for the pooling-of-interests method. All combinations not meeting the specified conditions must be accounted for by the purchase method. The usual, although not exclusive, mode of combination in these latter situations is by disbursement of cash or by incurring debt for the stock.

the shareholders of Company S turned in all of their 10,000 shares and received in return 10,000 shares of Company P stock. After the exchange, Company P owns all of the outstanding shares of Company S; that is, it owns a 100% interest in Company S. Accordingly, Company P would make the following journal entry in its accounts:

```
Jan. 2, 1974:
Investment in Company S Stock (10,000
    shares; 100%)......................... 150,000
    Common Stock (10,000 shares).......           100,000
    Contributed Capital, from Pooling
        of Interests....................            50,000
Acquisition by pooling of interests.
```

Observe that the Long-term Investment account is debited for the *book value* of the Company S stock as shown on the books of Company S ($100,000 + $50,000). This amount is used because that is the book value of the owners' equity in Company S, which Company P now controls. The Common Stock account is credited for the number of shares issued times the par value per share, and Contributed Capital, from Pooling of Interests, is credited for the difference. The cost principle is not involved in the debit to the Investment account because there was no *purchase* of the stock, only a pooling of interests by exchanging "paper." The exchange of shares of stock would have no effect on the accounts of the subsidiary, Company S.

After the above journal entry is posted to the ledger accounts of Company P, the two separate balance sheets then would be changed as shown in Exhibit 14–2.

Exhibit 14–2

COMPANY P and COMPANY S
Separate Balance Sheets (Pooling-of-Interests Basis)
January 2, 1974, Immediately after Acquisition

	Company P	Company S
Cash.	$205,000	$ 35,000
Accounts receivable (net).	15,000	30,000
Receivable from Co. S.	10,000	
Inventories.	170,000	70,000
Investment in Co. S (100%).	150,000	
Plant and equipment (net).	100,000	45,000
Total.	$650,000	$180,000
Accounts payable.	$ 60,000	$ 20,000
Payable to Co. P.		10,000
Common stock, Co. P.	400,000	
Common stock, Co. S.		100,000
Contributed capital, from pooling of interests.	50,000	
Retained earnings, Co. P.	140,000	
Retained earnings, Co. S.		50,000
Total.	$650,000	$180,000

Now, let's combine the two separate balance sheets shown in Exhibit 14–2 into a single **consolidated balance sheet** as if there were a single entity represented by the parent company. To combine the two, we must be careful not to double count or to include any items that are strictly between the two companies. There are two such items in this situation:

(a)   The Investment account balance of $150,000, shown in the accounts of Company P, offsets the common stock of Company S of $100,000 (it is now 100% owned by Company P) and the contributed capital, from pooling of interests, of $50,000 (in the accounts of Company P). Thus, the following elimination or offsets must be made:

	Eliminations	
	Assets	*Shareholders' Equity*
Investment account—decrease............	− $150,000	
Common stock, Company S— decrease..............................		− $100,000
Contributed capital, from pooling of interests—decrease (for the difference)...........................		− 50,000

Another way of looking at the elimination of the Investment account is that, when the assets of the subsidiary are added to those of the parent, they replace the Investment account in the balance sheet of the parent. Therefore, to prevent double counting, the Investment account must be eliminated. Similarly, the owners' equity of the parent substitutes for the owners' equity of subsidiary, elimination is necessary to prevent double counting.

(b)   The accounts of Company P show a receivable of $10,000 from Company S, and the accounts of Company S show this as a debt to Company P. This is called an **intercompany debt.** When the two balance sheets are combined into a single consolidated balance sheet, this intercompany debt must be eliminated since there is no debt owed by the combined entity. Thus, the following elimination or offset must be made when combining the two balance sheets:

	Eliminations	
	Assets	*Liabilities*
Receivable from Company S—decrease.....	− $10,000	
Payable to Company P—decrease.........		− $10,000

The "two Separate Balance Sheets" are restated in Exhibit 14–3 and combined (aggregated) on a line-by-line basis, after deducting the

Exhibit 14–3

COMPANY P and Its Subsidiary, COMPANY S (100% Owned)
Consolidated Balance Sheet (Pooling-of-Interests Basis)
at January 2, 1974, Immediately after Acquisition

| | Separate Balance Sheets | | Eliminations* | Consolidated Balance Sheet |
	Company P*	Company S*	Eliminations*	Consolidated Balance Sheet
Assets:				
Cash...............................	$205,000	$ 35,000		$240,000
Accounts receivable (net)............	15,000	30,000		45,000
Receivable from Co. S...............	10,000		(b) − 10,000	–0–
Inventories........................	170,000	70,000		240,000
Investment in Co. S.................	150,000		(a) −150,000	–0–
Plant and equipment (net)...........	100,000	45,000		145,000
Total Assets..................	$650,000	$180,000		$670,000
Liabilities:				
Accounts payable...................	$ 60,000	$ 20,000		$ 80,000
Payable to Co. P...................		10,000	(b) − 10,000	–0–
Shareholders' Equity:				
Common stock, Co. P...............	400,000			400,000
Common stock, Co. S...............		100,000	(a) − 100,000	–0–
Contributed capital from pooling.....	50,000		(a) − 50,000	–0–
Retained earnings, Co. P............	140,000			} 190,000
Retained earnings, Co. S............		50,000		} 190,000
Total Liabilities and Shareholders' Equity.........................	$650,000	$180,000		$670,000

* Included for instructional purposes only. A worksheet is usually used to derive the consolidated amounts. See Appendixes A and B.

"Eliminations," to develop the "Consolidated Balance Sheet" shown in the last column. In an external consolidated financial statement, only the last column—the "Consolidated Balance Sheet" (and not the "Separate Balance Sheets")—would be reported.

In the "Consolidated Balance Sheet" on the pooling basis, as shown in Exhibit 14–3, the following measurement procedures are evident: (1) the amounts for the combined assets, liabilities, and shareholders' equity are the combined *book values* as reflected on the "Separate Balance Sheets"; (2) the intercompany amounts for investment, subsidiary common stock, contributed capital from pooling, and the intercompany debt are eliminated; and (3) the consolidated retained earnings is the sum of the two separate amounts ($140,000 + $50,000 = $190,000).[3] In the next section, we will compare these results with those that occur when the acquisition is by purchase instead of by pooling of interests.

Combination by purchase

When one corporation acquires a controlling interest in the voting stock of another corporation by *purchase* rather than by exchange of shares of stock, a purchase/sale transaction is deemed to have oc-

---

[3] The pooling of interest approach also requires that all statements presented for prior years must be restated.

curred.[4] This purchase/sale transaction requires that the **cost principle** be applied by the parent company in recording the long-term investment. That is, the investment account on the books of the parent company must be debited **at cost, which is the fair market value of the shares purchased.** The stock of the subsidiary, purchased by the parent, may be paid for in cash or a combination of cash, other assets, and debt.

Since the *fair-market value* of the subsidiary stock acquired must be recognized in a combination by purchase and *book values* must be used in a pooling of interests (as explained above), there are significantly different economic and reporting impacts as between pooling and purchasing.

To illustrate a combination by *purchase,* we will use the example of Companies P and S as given in Exhibit 14–1. Instead of the stock exchange, we will assume that, on January 2, 1974, Company P purchased 100% of the 10,000 shares of outstanding stock of Company S at $16.50 per share (i.e., for $165,000) and paid cash. On this date, Company P would make the following journal entry in its accounts:

```
Jan. 2, 1974:
Investment in Stock of Company S (10,000
    shares, 100%)........................ 165,000
    Cash..............................            165,000
Acquisition by purchase.
```

Note that Company P paid $165,000 cash for 100% of the owners' equity of Company S, although the total shareholders' equity of Company S that was purchased was only $150,000. Thus, Company P paid $15,000 more than "book value." In consolidating the two balance sheets, this $15,000 difference must be taken into account as explained below. We will assume also that the plant and equipment owned by Company S at this date had a fair-market value of $50,000. The purchase by Company P would have no effect on the accounting by the subsidiary, Company S.

After the above entry is posted to the accounts of Company P, the two separate balance sheets then would be changed as shown in Exhibit 14–4.

The consolidated balance sheet for Company P and its subsidiary, Company S, immediately after acquisition, is shown in Exhibit 14–5 on the **purchase basis.** The two separate balance sheets, given in Exhibit 14–4, were combined in a manner similar to that previously indicated for the pooling-of-interests basis. There are two intercompany items that

---

[4] Refer to footnote 2. In some instances, stock exchanges do not qualify for the pooling approach. In these instances, the purchase approach must be used, in which case the parent company must recognize the *fair-market values* for the subsidiary assets just as if cash and/or debt were exchanged for the stock of the subsidiary. These complexities are beyond the scope of this book.

Exhibit 14–4

COMPANY P and COMPANY S
Separate Balance Sheets, (Purchase Basis)
January 2, 1974, Immediately after Acquisition

	Company P	Company S
Cash....................................	$ 40,000	$ 35,000
Accounts receivable (net).......................	15,000	30,000
Receivable from Co. S.........................	10,000	
Inventories.................................	170,000	70,000
Investment in Co. S (100%)...................	165,000	
Plant and equipment (net).....................	100,000	45,000
Total.............................	$500,000	$180,000
Accounts payable............................	$ 60,000	$ 20,000
Payable to Co. S............................		10,000
Common stock, Co. P.........................	300,000	
Common stock, Co. S.........................		100,000
Retained earnings, Co. P......................	140,000	
Retained earnings, Co. S......................		50,000
Total.............................	$500,000	$180,000

Exhibit 14–5

COMPANY P and Its Subsidiary, COMPANY S (100% Owned)
Consolidated Balance Sheet (Purchase Basis)
At January 2, 1974 Immediately after Acquisition

	Separate Balance Sheets			Consolidated
	Company P*	Company S*	Eliminations*	Balance Sheet
Assets:				
Cash............................	$ 40,000	$ 35,000		$ 75,000
Accounts receivable (net)...........	15,000	30,000		45,000
Receivable from Co. S..............	10,000		(b) − 10,000	–0–
Inventories.......................	170,000	70,000		240,000
Investment in Co. S................	165,000		(a) −165,000	–0–
Plant and equipment (net)..........	100,000	45,000	(a) + 5,000	150,000
Goodwill†........................			(a) + 10,000	10,000
Total Assets................	$500,000	$180,000		$520,000
Liabilities:				
Accounts payable..................	$ 60,000	$ 20,000		$ 80,000
Payable to Co. P..................		10,000	(b) − 10,000	–0–
Shareholders' Equity:				
Common stock, Co. P..............	300,000			300,000
Common stock, Co. S..............		100,000	(a) −100,000	–0–
Retained earnings, Co. P...........	140,000			140,000
Retained earnings, Co. S...........		50,000	(a) − 50,000	–0–
Total Liabilities and Shareholders' Equity.......................	$500,000	$180,000		$520,000

* Included for instructional purposes only. A worksheet usually is used to derive the consolidated amounts. See Appendixes A and B.

† A title preferred by most accountants is "Excess of Cost over Book Value of the Assets of the Subsidiary." However, the length of this term causes the shorter term to be used extensively.

involve eliminations as illustrated for the pooling-of-interest approach; however, the first one is significantly different than before. The two eliminations or offsets are:

(a) The Investment account balance of $165,000, on the books of Company P, is at *fair-market value* (i.e., at cost). It is offset against the shareholders' equity of the subsidiary, which is at *book value*. In this case there is a difference and it must be recognized in the consolidated statement. The difference may be analyzed as follows:

Purchase price for 100% interest in Co. S..............	$165,000
Shareholders' equity purchased (common stock, $100,000, plus retained earnings, $50,000)........................	150,000
Difference—excess paid over book value of subsidiary.......	15,000
Analysis of the difference:	
Amount needed to write-up plant and equipment to fair-market value ($50,000 − $45,000)..................	5,000
Remainder—goodwill purchased......................	$ 10,000

Of the $15,000 paid over book value, $5,000 is attributed to the difference between the fair-market value of the plant and equipment of $50,000 over the book value of $45,000 reported by the subsidiary. The remainder is attributed to goodwill. Goodwill is the amount that Company P was willing to pay for the good reputation, customer appeal, and general acceptance of the business that Company S had developed over the years. All successful companies enjoy a measure of goodwill. Its "value" is never known except when the business is purchased, as it was in this instance.

To take care of the eliminations, or offsets, we must recognize the $5,000 and the $10,000 as follows:

	Eliminations	
	Assets	Shareholders' Equity
Plant and equipment—increase............	+$ 5,000	
Goodwill—increase......................	+ 10,000	
Investment—decrease....................	− 165,000	
Common stock Co. S—decrease............		−$100,000
Retained earnings, Co. S—decrease.........		− 50,000

(b) The intercompany debt must be eliminated as before, viz:

	Eliminations	
	Assets	Liabilities
Receivable from Co. S—decrease.............	−$10,000	
Payable to Co. P—decrease.................		−$10,000

The two "Separate Balance Sheets" are restated on Exhibit 14–5 and combined on a line-by-line basis, after the eliminations, to develop the "Consolidated Balance Sheet" shown in the last column. In an external consolidated financial statement, only the "Consolidated Balance Sheet" shown in the last column (and not the "Separate Balance Sheets") would be reported.

Comparing the effects on the balance sheet of pooling versus purchase

To gain some insight into the differences in measurement of balance sheet amounts that arise when the pooling-of-interests approach is used versus the purchase approach, we can compare the consolidated amounts shown in Exhibits 14–3 and 14–5 as follows:

	Acquisition Approach		
	Pooling Basis	Purchase Basis	Difference
Cash........................	$240,000	$ 75,000	$(165,000)
Plant and equipment (net)........	145,000	150,000	5,000
Goodwill.....................		10,000	10,000
Common stock, Co. P..........	400,000	300,000	(100,000)
Retained earnings, Co. P........	190,000	140,000	(50,000)

We can observe that, when a company elects the purchase approach, the cash position suffers; the $165,000 difference in cash was the purchase price. The $100,000 difference in the amount of common stock is due to the effect of issuing stock rather than paying cash when the pooling-of-interests approach is elected. The plant and equipment amount is higher when the purchase approach is used than when pooling of interests is used, because the former requires application of the cost principle so that *fair-market value* at date of acquisition rather than book value must be recognized for the assets of the subsidiary. Goodwill arises in purchase but does not in pooling of interests. These higher amounts for assets, of course, mean higher expenses will be reported on the income statements in the future periods when the combination is by purchase; i.e., for depreciation expense and amortization expense (for goodwill). Finally, under the pooling approach, the reported retained-earnings amount is higher because the amount of retained earnings of the subsidiary is added to that of the parent. In the case of purchase, the retained-earnings amount of the subsidiary is eliminated.

These constitute significant differences in the resultant consolidated financial statements of the pooling versus the purchase approach. If you consider them carefully, it should be apparent why most companies prefer the pooling to the purchase approach. The preference is not only because of the impact on the cash position but also because of the impacts on certain other reported amounts on the balance sheet and income statement in periods subsequent to the acquisition. These impacts generally are viewed as undesirable by the parent company.

Reporting
consolidated
operations
after
acquisition

The preceding discussions and illustrations focused on the impact of the pooling-of-interests approach versus the purchase approach on the balance sheet. The comparative impact on the income statement of the two approaches, for periods following the date of acquisition, are even more significant. Exhibit 14–6 presents the consolidated income statement and balance sheet for Company P and its subsidiary, Company S, after one year of operations (i.e., for 1974). The underlying data and consolidation procedures used to derive these two statements are shown in Appendix A, Exhibits 14–7 and 14–8.

The consolidation amounts, on a purchase basis, are based on the following assumptions:

Exhibit 14–6

COMPANY P and its Subsidiary, COMPANY S (100% Owned)
Consolidated Balance Sheet (Pooling and Purchase Approaches Compared)
At December 13, 1974, One Year after Acquisition

	Consolidated Statements	
	Pooling Basis	Purchase Basis
Income Statement (For Year 1974):		
Sales revenue	$510,000	$510,000
Expenses:		
Cost of goods sold	(279,000)	(279,000)
Expenses (not detailed)	(156,500)	(156,500)
Depreciation expense	(14,500)	(15,000)
Amortization expense (goodwill)		(500)
Income tax expense	(26,000)	(26,000)
Net Income (carried down to retained earnings)	$ 34,000	$ 33,000
Balance Sheet (At December 31, 1974):		
Assets:		
Cash	$271,500	$106,500
Accounts receivable (net)	46,000	46,000
Inventories	250,000	250,000
Plant and equipment (net)	130,500	135,000
Goodwill		9,500
Total Assets	$698,000	$547,000
Liabilities:		
Accounts payable	$ 74,000	$ 74,000
Shareholders' Equity:		
Common stock	400,000	300,000
Retained earnings	190,000	140,000
Add: Net income (from above)	34,000	33,000
Total Liabilities and Shareholders' Equity	$698,000	$547,000

(a)   The fixed assets of Company S, the subsidiary, at date of acquisition, had a market value of $5,000 in excess of their book value. These assets are being depreciated over a remaining life of 10 years by Company S.

(b)   The acquisition of Company S resulted in $10,000 goodwill to be recognized in consolidation under the purchase basis. This goodwill is to be amortized over the next 20 years.

The differences in impact between the pooling basis and the purchase basis on the consolidated statements of Company P and its subsidiary, Company S, after one year of operations are as follows:

		Acquisition Approach	
	Pooling Basis	Purchase Basis	Difference
Income Statement:			
Depreciation expense...........	$ 14,500	$ 15,000	$ 500
Amortization expense (goodwill)..		500	500
Net Income...................	34,000	33,000	$ 1,000
Balance Sheet:			
Cash........................	271,500	106,500	$165,000
Plant and equipment (net)........	130,500	135,000	(4,500)
Goodwill....................		9,500	(9,500)
Total................	698,000	547,000	$151,000
Common stock................	400,000	300,000	$100,000
Retained earnings.............	224,000	173,000	51,000
Total................	698,000	547,000	$151,000

The above comparison shows that net income was $1,000 less under the purchase basis than under pooling of interests. This difference was due to *additional* depreciation expense and amortization expense (goodwill) that must be recognized in consolidation when the assets of the subsidiary are recognized at their fair-market values, as is done in consolidation under the purchase basis (but not under pooling of interest). The causes of the $1,000 difference may be explained as follows:

(a)   Depreciation expense on pooling-of-interests basis
      (on subsidiary assets at book value)............. $14,500
      Add depreciation on the increased asset amount to
      fair-market value from book value
      ($5,000 ÷ 10 years).........................   500 $ 500
      Depreciation expense on purchase basis (on
      subsidiary assets at fair-market value)......... $15,000

(b)   Amortization expense on the goodwill recognized
      of $10,000, which is to be amortized over the next
      20 years ($10,000 ÷ 20 years)................   500
      (There is no goodwill recognized under pooling
      of interests.)
              Total..................................... $1,000

The additional expenses that must be recognized on the consolidated income statement in future periods cause less net income to be reported when the purchasing basis is used. Businesses do not like this unfavorable impact.

Likewise, the $151,000 difference in the balance-sheet totals is an important issue. In the example, this difference in results is caused by the different way in which the stock was acquired (shares exchanged versus cash payment) and the accounting measurements implicit in each of the two methods. These differences may be restated as follows:

Cash—The $165,000 difference reflects the price paid for the stock of the subsidiary purchased under the purchase basis as opposed to the exchange of shares under pooling-of-interests.

Plant and equipment (net)—This difference reflects the effects of including the fixed assets of the subsidiary at book value under the pooling-of-interests basis, compared with fair-market value under the purchase basis. The difference may be explained as follows:

Plant and equipment including subsidiary fixed assets at book value (pooling basis)	$130,500
Add difference between fair-market value and book value of subsidiary assets at date of acquisition	+5,000
Deduct depreciation on the difference for one year ($5,000 ÷ 10 years)	− 500
Plant and equipment, including subsidiary fixed assets at fair-market value (purchase basis)	$135,000

Common stock—The common stock of Company P is greater under a pooling of interests because of the issuance of shares in exchange for the shares of Company P.

Retained earnings—Retained earnings is $51,000 more under the pooling-of-interests basis than under the purchase basis. This $51,000 consists of the $50,000 elimination difference at date of combination plus the $1,000 difference in net income. Businesses normally consider this an unfavorable impact. This impact occurs because, under the pooling-of-interests approach, the retained-earnings amount for the subsidiary is added to derive the consolidated retained-earnings amount. In contrast, under the purchase basis, this amount must be eliminated as an offset to the Investment account.

Now, let's return to the merger movement, mentioned briefly on page 492, and assess some of the economic and motivational impacts of pooling of interests versus combination by purchase. Primarily, these impacts are related to the differences in measurement procedures used under each of these two accounting approaches. A comparison of these impacts may make clear why the merger movement depended, in good measure, on the option to use "pooling-of-interests accounting" rather than "purchase accounting" in many situations. Combination by pooling of interest was popular because it (1) requires no disbursement of cash or the creation of debt; (2) causes a higher net income to be reported than does purchase accounting; (3) reports higher retained earnings; and (4) lends itself to a high degree of flexibility. (This latter feature led to numerous abuses.)

In the merger movement, the pooling-of-interests approach generally was preferred because of the economic impacts; however, in the opinion of many, the opportunities for manipulation of net income were overriding. Four fairly common practices may be cited and illustrated:

(1) Instant Earnings—Company P acquired Company S through an exchange of stock; that is, by a pooling of interests. At the time, Company S owned three separate plants, each of which had a relatively low book value of, say, $100,000 and a high fair-market value of, say, $600,000. Following the pooling-of-interests approach, the $100,000 book value for each plant was reported on the consolidated balance sheet as an asset. Assume that during the next year one of the plants was sold for the $600,000 fair-market value. The result was a *gain* on the sale of fixed assets of $500,000 (disregarding income taxes), which then was reported on the income statement. This came to be referred to, in a derogatory way, as making "instant earnings." The reported gain would significantly increase *net income* and EPS and often caused the price of the shares of Company P to rise. At the higher stock prices, shares were sold to the public and/or used for another round of mergers following the same pattern and so on. Many people believe that there was no gain because the *cost* of the plant, to the acquiring company, was the fair-market value of the shares given in exchange; that is, $600,000. Under this view, no gain would be reported.

(2) Funny Money—This term, intended to be derogatory, refers to the use of peculiar and innovative securities that were designed to "qualify" an acquisition as a pooling of interests, when, in fact, its substance was an acquisition by purchase. These devious instruments were used because (1) the company wanted to use pooling-of-interests accounting, and (2) the shareholders of the acquired company (the subsidiary) wanted cash, not shares of stock of the acquiring company. Both objectives were accomplished by issuing a security (i.e., "funny money"). The security provided that, say, after one year, it could be turned in for either voting common stock or cash, at the option of the holder. This qualified superficially as a stock exchange (i.e., for pooling-of-interests accounting), while, at the same time, it made cash available in the short run to the shareholders of the subsidiary, as would be the case in a combination by purchase.

(3) Escalating EPS—This term refers to what was a common practice of seeking out smaller companies, usually near year end, to

acquire through a pooling-of-interests exchange, so that their earnings could be added to those of the parent (or to offset a loss). Thus, by the simple expedient of year-end pooling acquisitions, at no cash cost, the acquiring company could escalate net income reported on a consolidated basis by the parent company. Many of the year-end acquisitions for this purpose were consummated *after* the end of the year but before publication of the financial statements, in which case they were included in the consolidated statements of the past year. This became a favorite way to "doctor" net income at year end.

(4) Tricky Mixes—This situation represented the ultimate in misleading and illogical accounting. It was referred to as "part-purchase, part-pooling accounting." A corporation, in acquiring another company by pooling, often found a number of shareholders of the other company who would not accept shares in exchange; they wanted cash immediately. For example, it often worked out that, say, two-thirds of the shares of the subsidiary would be acquired by exchange of shares and the remaining third would be purchased for cash. In order to derive some of the "reporting benefits" of pooling-of-interests accounting, two-thirds of the acquisition would be accounted for on that basis and one-third on the purchase basis—thus part-purchase, part-pooling accounting. This mixture of accounting approaches not only was theoretically untenable but also was misleading and not subject to any rational explanation.

The merger movement came under considerable criticism because pooling-of-interests accounting often was used in situations that, in substance, did not meet the established criteria for its use. In response to extensive criticism the APB issued *Opinions Nos. 16* and *17* (August 1970). These tended to stop the abuses. *Opinion No. 16* states very specific conditions under which pooling-of-interests accounting is applicable. It is interesting to note that a number of the members of the APB strongly believed, both for conceptual and practical reasons, that pooling-of-interests accounting should be completely outlawed. The conceptual argument against pooling-of-interest reporting is that it ignores the market values on which the parties traded shares and substitutes, in violation of the cost principle, wholly irrelevant amounts—the book values carried in the accounts of the seller (i.e., the subsidiary). The practical argument against pooling-of-interest reporting is that it leads to abuses of the kinds cited above.

The primary arguments in favor of the pooling-of-interests method of reporting are (1) it avoids the problems of measuring the fair-market value of the different assets of the subsidiary at acquisition date; (2) it avoids the necessity to recognize goodwill, then having to amortize it as an expense in future periods; and (3) the exchange of shares is not a purchase/sale transaction but, rather, is a joining of common interests and risks.

Summary   This chapter discussed the use of consolidated statements that must be prepared in most situations when one corporation owns over 50% of the outstanding voting stock of another corporation. The concept of consolidated statements is based upon the view that a parent company and its subsidiaries constitute one economic entity. Therefore, the separate income statements, balance sheets, and statements of changes in financial position should be combined each period on an item-by-item basis as a single set of financial statements.

Ownership of a controlling interest (the outstanding stock) of another corporation may be obtained either by a pooling of interests or combination by purchase. The measurement of amounts to be reported on the income statement and the balance sheet is influenced to a significant degree by these two quite different accounting approaches.

A pooling of interests generally occurs when the acquiring company exchanges shares of its own voting stock for shares of the voting stock of the subsidiary. In this situation it is usually deemed that there was no purchase/sale (exchange) transaction. Rather, there is merely a joining of interests by exchanging stock certificates. As a consequence, the cost principle is not applied at acquisition date. In preparing consolidated statements, on a pooling-of-interests basis, the book values (i.e., those amounts reflected on the books) of each related company are added together and fair-market values are disregarded.

In a combination by purchase, the acquiring company usually pays cash and/or debt for the shares of the subsidiary. In these circumstances, a purchase/sale transaction has been effected and the acquisition is accounted for in conformance with the cost principle. Therefore, in preparing consolidated statements under the purchase basis, the assets of the subsidiary must be measured at their fair-market value before they are combined with the statements of the parent company.

Consolidation on a pooling-of-interests basis versus consolidation on a purchase basis causes significant differences on the consolidated financial statements. The pooling-of-interests basis has led to many abuses.

A large percentage of published financial statements of corporations are consolidated statements. It is important, therefore, that statement users understand the basic concept of consolidated statements and the measurement distinctions between the pooling basis and the purchase basis in reporting the results of business combinations.

The differences between pooling of interests and purchasing in measuring and reporting the results of business combinations may be generalized, for the usual case, as follows:

Item	Pooling of Interests	Purchasing
1. Measurement and recording at date of acquisition.	Acquisition is accomplished by exchanging shares of stock. A purchase/sale transaction is not assumed, hence, the cost principle is not applied. The Investment account is debited for the book value of the subsidiary stock acquired.	Acquisition usually is accomplished by purchasing the shares with cash and/or debt. A purchase/sale transaction is assumed, hence, the cost principle is applied. The Investment account is debited for the fair-market value of the resources acquired.
2. Goodwill	No goodwill is recognized.	Goodwill is recognized to the extent that the purchase price exceeds the fair-market value of the assets (less the liabilities) of the subsidiary.
3. Method of aggregating or combining to derive consolidated balance sheet.	Assets and liabilities of the acquired company are added, at book value, to those of the parent.	Assets and liabilities of the acquired company are added, at their fair-market value (as of the date of acquisition), to those of the parent.
4. Method of aggregating or combining to derive income statement.	Revenues and expenses, less any eliminations, as reported by each company are aggregated.	Revenues as reported, less any eliminations are aggregated. Expenses, plus additional depreciation and amortization of goodwill, less any eliminations, are aggregated.
5. Eliminations.	Eliminate all intercompany debts, revenues, and expenses. Eliminate Investment account on parent's books and owners' equity of subsidiary, excluding retained earnings.	Eliminate all intercompany debts, revenues, and expenses. Eliminate Investment account on parent's books and common stock of subsidiary, including retained earnings.
6. Usual effects on the consolidated financial statement.	Expenses—Lower Net income—Higher EPS—Higher Assets—Higher cash Noncash assets—Lower Liabilities—Same Capital stock—Higher Retained earnings—Higher	Expenses—Higher Net income—Lower EPS—Lower Assets—Lower cash Noncash assets—Higher Liabilities—Same Capital stock—Lower Retained earnings—Lower

Important terms

Parent company	**Combination by purchase**
Subsidiary company	**Consolidated balance sheet**
Single economic entity	**Consolidated income statement**
Consolidated statements	**Intercompany eliminations**
Control	**Goodwill**
Economic compatibility	**Amortization of goodwill**
Pooling of interests	

MEASUREMENT PROCEDURES FOR DERIVING
              CONSOLIDATED STATEMENTS—100% OWNERSHIP

The chapter has focused on the use of consolidated financial statements. This appendix discusses in depth the measurement procedures used in preparing consolidated financial statements. To accomplish this objective, we use the typical *consolidation worksheet* because, through it, the underlying concepts and measurement procedures come into sharp focus. The worksheets should be viewed as a learning device and not something to be mastered mechanically. At the outset we remind you that the worksheet and the entries made on it are *supplemental* to the accounts and the reports. *The worksheet entries are not recorded in the accounts under any circumstances; they are analytical devices only.* We will consider the various topics in the same order they were presented in the chapter. The example for Company P and its subsidiary, Company S, given on page 493, will be continued for all of the illustrations in this part.

CONSOLIDATED BALANCE SHEET IMMEDIATELY AFTER ACQUISITION

The consolidated balance sheets for Company P and its subsidiary, Company S, immediately after acquisition, were shown on the pooling-of-interests basis in Exhibit 14–3 and on the purchase basis in Exhibit 14–5. Those exhibits indicated in the first three columns the worksheet procedures essential to development of the statements. There is no need to repeat those discussions.

DEVELOPING CONSOLIDATED STATEMENTS FOR PERIODS SUBSEQUENT TO ACQUISITION

At the end of each accounting period after acquisition, a consolidated balance sheet, income statement, and statement of changes in financial position must be prepared. This section discusses the application of consolidation principles in the development of both a consolidated balance sheet and a consolidated income statement for periods subsequent to acquisition. We will illustrate a single worksheet that will meet this dual need.

To illustrate the development of a consolidation worksheet for both the balance sheet and the income statement, we will continue the situation involving the purchase of Company S stock by Company P given on page 496. You will recall that on January 2, 1974, Company P acquired 100% of the outstanding stock of Company S. To adapt the example, we will assume that it is now December 31, 1974, and, after operating for a year, each company has just prepared their separate income statements and balance sheets as follows:

Financial Statements for 1974

	At December 31, 1974	
	Company P	*Company S*
Income Statement (for 1974):		
Sales revenue	$400,000	$110,000
Revenue from investments		
(dividend from Co. S)	10,000	
Cost of goods sold	(220,000)	(59,000)
Expenses (not detailed)	(130,000)	(26,500)
Depreciation expense	(10,000)	(4,500)
Income tax expense	(20,000)	(6,000)
Net Income	$ 30,000	$ 14,000
Balance Sheet (at Dec. 31, 1974):		
Cash	$ 61,000*	$ 45,500
Accounts receivable (net)	18,000	28,000
Receivable from Co. S	6,000	
Inventories	185,000	65,000
Investment in Co. S		
(by purchase, at cost)	165,000*	
Plant and equipment (net)	90,000	40,500
	$525,000	$179,000
Accounts payable	$ 55,000	$ 19,000
Payable to Co. P		6,000
Common stock (par $10)	300,000*	100,000
Beginning retained earnings	140,000	50,000
Dividends paid during 1974		(10,000)
Net Income for 1974 (per above)	30,000	14,000
	$525,000	$179,000

* These amounts would be different under the pooling-of-interests basis.

At the end of 1974, the following data relating to intercompany eliminations were available:

(a) The Investment account balance was the same as at date of acquisition; the balance of retained earnings of Company S at acquisition was $50,000.

(b) At date of purchase, Jan. 1, 1974, the plant and equipment of Company S had a market value of $5,000 above book value and goodwill purchased amounted to $10,000.

(c) The intercompany debt owed by Company S to Company P was $6,000 at the end of 1974.

(d) The plant and equipment owned by Company S has a 10-year remaining life for depreciation purposes. The company uses straight-line depreciation.

(e) Any goodwill is to be amortized over 20 years on a straight-line basis.

(f) During December 1974, Company S declared and paid a $10,000 cash dividend. Accordingly, each company made the following entry in its accounts:

	Company P			*Company S*	
Cash.	10,000		Dividends Paid	10,000	
Revenue from					
Investments. . .		10,000	Cash		10,000

A consolidated income statement and a balance sheet for 1974 are to be developed for 1974. These statements were shown in Exhibit 14–6, assuming (1) pooling-of-interests basis and (2) consolidation by purchase. A separate consolidation worksheet is shown for each: Exhibit 14–7, pooling-of-interests and Exhibit 14–8, purchase. Each worksheet will be explained.

Pooling of interests—income statement and balance sheet. This worksheet (Exhibit 14–7) has side captions for each income-statement and balance-sheet item, and columns for the parent company, subsidiary, eliminations, and a final column for the *"consolidated balances."* The amounts entered in the first two amount columns are taken directly from the separate statements prepared by the parent and the subsidiary. The last column of this worksheet provided the data for the income statement and the balance sheet shown in Exhibit 14–6.

The worksheet is designed so that the eliminations are entered in debit and credit format. This provides an excellent check on the accuracy of the work. We remind you, however, that the elimination entries are *worksheet entries only;* they are never entered into the accounts of either the parent or the subsidiary. This is because reporting with consolidated statements is a *reporting concept* and does not affect the accounts of either the parent or the subsidiaries.

To complete the worksheet, the elimination entries must be developed, then each line is accumulated horizontally to derive the consolidated amount in the last column for each item listed on the income statement and the balance sheet. In this particular example, there are three elimination entries on the worksheet on the pooling-of-interests basis. They are briefly identified at the bottom of the worksheet; however, we will elaborate on them as follows:

(a)   The debit balance of $150,000 in the Investment account shown on the balance sheet of Company P is represented in its common stock ($100,000 issued in the exchange) and contributed capital accounts ($50,000). The $150,000 amount of stockholders' equity shown on the balance sheet of Company S is now "owned" by Company P. Thus, if we were to add the stockholders' equity shown on both balance sheets, there would be double counting of the $150,000. Also, under the consolidated-statement concept, the two companies are viewed as one entity. Thus, the Investment account balance of $150,000 cannot be included on the consolidated balance sheet. To remove these intercompany amounts, the Investment account balance of $150,000 is eliminated against the $100,000 stock balance of the subsidiary and $50,000 of the contributed capital recognized in the pooling entry. These eliminations are accomplished by means of the following intercompany elimination entry on the worksheet:

```
Common Stock, Co. S...................................  100,000
Contributed Capital, from Pooling-of-Interests..............   50,000
    Investment in Co. S................................          150,000
```

(b) The balance sheets show that Company S owes Company P $6,000 on account. This is known as an intercompany debt. When the two companies are combined, as if they were one entity, obviously this intercompany debt drops out as an economic reality. Therefore, the receivable shown by Company P and the payable shown by Company S must be eliminated. These eliminations are accomplished by means of the following intercompany elimination entry on the worksheet:

```
Payable to Company P....................................  6,000
    Receivable from Company S.............................       6,000
```

(c) During the year, Company S paid dividends amounting to $10,000. Since Company P owned 100% of the outstanding stock, all of this dividend was paid to Company P. This is an intercompany item that must be eliminated. The Investment Revenue account of Company P must be debited on the worksheet and the dividends paid account of the subsidiary credited for $10,000. Observe that a separate line is set up on the worksheet for dividends and net income for each company. This is simply a matter of convenience and clarity. The worksheet entry to accomplish these eliminations is:

```
Revenue from Investments................................  10,000
    Retained Earnings, Co. S (or Dividends Paid)............       10,000
```

Purchase–income statement and balance sheet. In this situation there will be a few more eliminations because of the fair-market values to be recognized when the consolidation is by purchase. The intercompany eliminations on Exhibit 14–8, purchase basis, may be explained as follows:

(a) This entry eliminates the Investment account, reported on the parent's balance sheet, against the owners' equity accounts, reflected on the balance sheet of the subsidiary. This eliminating entry will be the same as at date of acquisition for each succeeding period since it is based upon the values existing at the date of acquisition. The $15,000 difference between the purchase price and the book value is recorded, for convenience, in the temporary account "Differential" (Clearance). The worksheet entry is:

```
Common Stock, Co. S...................................  100,000
Retained Earnings, Co. S...............................   50,000
Differential (Clearance)................................   15,000
    Investment in Co. S (100%).........................          165,000
```

Exhibit 14–7

COMPANY P and Its Subsidiary, COMPANY S
Consolidation Worksheet (Pooling of Interests) for the Balance Sheet and Income Statement
December 31, 1974 (100% Ownership)

	Statements		Intercompany Eliminations		Consolidated Balances
	Company P	Company S	Debit	Credit	
Income Statement:					
Sales revenue	400,000	110,000			510,000
Revenue from investments	10,000		(c) 10,000		
Cost of goods sold	(220,000)	(59,000)			(279,000)
Expenses (not detailed)	(130,000)	(26,500)			(156,500)
Depreciation expense	(10,000)	(4,500)			(14,500)
Income tax expense	(20,000)	(6,000)			(26,000)
Net Income (carried down)	30,000	14,000			34,000
Balance Sheet:					
Cash	226,000	45,500			271,500
Accounts receivable (net)	18,000	28,000			46,000
Receivable from Co. S	6,000			(b) 6,000	
Inventories	185,000	65,000			250,000
Investment in Co. S*	150,000			(a) 150,000	
Plant and equipment (net)	90,000	40,500			130,500
	675,000	179,000			698,000
Accounts payable	55,000	19,000			74,000
Payable to Co. P		6,000	(b) 6,000		
Common stock, Co. P*	400,000				400,000
Common stock, Co. S		100,000	(a) 100,000		
Contributed capital from pooling*	50,000		(a) 50,000		
Beginning retained earnings, Co. P	140,000				140,000
Beginning retained earnings, Co. S		50,000			50,000
Dividends paid during 1974		(10,000)		(c) 10,000	
Net Income, 1974 (from above; not added across)	30,000	14,000			34,000
	675,000	179,000	166,000	166,000	698,000

Explanation of Eliminations:
   (a)   To eliminate investment account against common stock of subsidiary and contributed capital from pooling of interest.
   (b)   To eliminate the intercompany debt.
   (c)   To eliminate the intercompany revenue and dividends (paid by the subsidiary to the parent).
   * These amounts are based upon the pooling-of-interests approach. The parent would have made the following entry at acquisition date:

Investment in Co. S..	150,000	
Common Stock, Co. P...		100,000
Contributed Capital from Pooling of Interests..		50,000

(b) This entry allocates the differential to the fixed asset and goodwill accounts on the basis of an analysis of the purchase transaction. The analysis of the purchase was given on page 499. The worksheet entry is:

```
Plant and Equipment.....................................  5,000
Goodwill............................................... 10,000
    Differential.......................................         15,000
```

(c) At the end of 1974, the intercompany debt was $6,000. The following elimination entry is needed:

```
Payable to Co. P.......................................  6,000
    Receivable from Co. S...............................          6,000
```

(d) Since the plant and equipment amount for Company S has been increased by $5,000, for consolidation purposes we must record on the worksheet additional depreciation on that amount. The depreciation reflected on the statements of Company S does not include this item. Accordingly, the worksheet entry must be:

```
Depreciation Expense (Co. S)...............................  500
    Plant and Equipment (Co. S)............................           500
    $5,000 ÷ 10 years = $500.
```

(e) Goodwill is an intangible asset (see Chapter 9) that must be amortized over a period not longer than 40 years (APB *Opinion No. 17*). Company P has decided to use a 20-year life. Since $10,000 goodwill was recognized in entry (b) above, for consolidated statement purposes it must be amortized on the worksheet in the same manner as the depreciation in entry (d). Therefore, the worksheet entry to accomplish this effect is:

```
Amortization Expense (Goodwill)...........................  500
    Goodwill...........................................           500
    $10,000 ÷ 20 years = $500.
```

(f) During the year, Company S paid dividends amounting to $10,000. Since Company P owned 100% of the outstanding stock, all of this dividend was paid to Company P. This is an intercompany item that must be eliminated. The Investment Revenue account of Company P must be debited on the worksheet and the Dividends Paid account of the subsidiary credited for $10,000. Observe that a separate line is set up on the worksheet for dividends and net income for each company. This is simply for convenience and clarity. The worksheet entry to accomplish these eliminations is:

```
Revenue from Investments..................................  10,000
    Retained Earnings, Co. S (or Dividends Paid)...........           10,000
```

All of the intercompany eliminations have been effected. The worksheet is completed for the consolidated balances by cumulating the amounts horizontally for each item. The consolidated balances taken directly from the last column of the worksheet are classified in the

Exhibit 14–8

COMPANY P and Its Subsidiary, COMPANY S
Consolidation Worksheet (By Purchase) for the Balance Sheet and Income Statement
December 31, 1974 (100% Ownership)

	Statements		Intercompany Eliminations		Consolidated Balances
	Company P	Company S	Debit	Credit	
Income Statement:					
Sales revenue	400,000	110,000			510,000
Revenue from investments	10,000		(f) 10,000		
Cost of goods sold	(220,000)	(59,000)			(279,000)
Expenses (not detailed)	(130,000)	(26,500)			(156,500)
Depreciation expense	(10,000)	(4,500)	(d) 500		(15,000)
Amortization expense (goodwill)			(e) 500		500
Income tax expense	(20,000)	(6,000)			(26,000)
Net Income (carried down)	30,000	14,000			33,000
Balance Sheet:					
Cash	61,000	45,500			106,500
Accounts receivable (net)	18,000	28,000			46,000
Receivable from Co. S	6,000			(c) 6,000	
Inventories	185,000	65,000			250,000
Investment in Co. S (at cost)	165,000			(a) 165,000	
Plant and equipment (net)	90,000	40,500	(b) 5,000	(d) 500	135,000
Goodwill			(b) 10,000	(e) 500	9,500
	525,000	179,000			547,000
Differential			(a) 15,000	(b) 15,000	
Accounts payable	55,000	19,000			74,000
Payable to Co. P		6,000	(c) 6,000		
Common stock, Co. P	300,000				300,000
Common stock, Co. S		100,000	(a) 100,000		
Beginning retained earnings, Co. P	140,000				140,000
Beginning retained earnings, Co. S		50,000	(a) 50,000		
Dividends paid during 1974		(10,000)		(f) 10,000	
Net Income, 1974 (from above; not added across)	30,000	14,000			33,000*
	525,000	179,000	197,000	197,000	547,000

* Carried down from above.

Explanation of Eliminations:
   (a)   To eliminate the investment account against the subsidiary stockholders' equity.
   (b)   To allocate the difference between purchase price and book value purchased to the appropriate accounts.
   (c)   To eliminate the intercompany debt.
   (d)   To record additional depreciation for one year on the asset increase resulting from the acquisition.
   (e)   To record amortization for one year on the goodwill recognized.
   (f)   To eliminate intercompany revenue and dividends (paid by the subsidiary to the parent).

normal manner in preparing the consolidated income statement and balance sheet.

Appendix B   CONSOLIDATION MEASUREMENT PROCEDURES— CONTROLLING INTEREST LESS THAN 100% OWNERSHIP

When the parent company owns a controlling interest that is less than 100%, the consolidation procedures are identical, except that certain consolidation worksheet eliminations must be based upon the *proportionate* ownership level. When there is less than 100% owner-ship, there will be a group of stockholders of the subsidiary company known as the **minority stockholders.** Their interest in the subsidiary is unaffected by the parent's interest; therefore, the minority stockholders' interest must be accorded appropriate measurement and reporting rec-ognition. This gives rise to a new kind of owners' equity on the consoli-dated statements referred to as the **minority interest.** It includes their proportionate share of both the earnings and the stockholders' equity of the subsidiary.

Ownership interests of less than 100% generally are on the purchase basis since APB *Opinion No. 16* does not permit use of the pooling-of-interests basis when the ownership interest held by the parent company is less than 90%.

To illustrate the measurement of amounts for consolidated statements for a controlling interest of less than 100%, we will adapt the data for Company P and Company S given in Exhibit 14–1, page 493.

Assume that on January 2, 1974, Company P purchased 80% of the 10,000 shares of outstanding capital stock of Company S for $132,000 cash. At that date, Company P recorded the purchase of the 8,000 shares of capital stock as follows:

Jan. 2, 1974:
Investment, Stock of Company S (80% ownership)......... 132,000
   Cash....................................... 132,000
   Acquisition of 8,000 shares (80%) of the capital stock
   of Company S at $16.50 per share.

On the date of purchase, the owners' equity accounts of Company S reflected the following amounts: Capital Stock, $100,000, and Retained Earnings, $50,000. Company P paid $132,000 cash for 80% of the owners' equity of Company S, or $150,000 × .80 = $120,000. Thus, they paid $12,000 more than the book value of Company S. Of this amount, $4,000 was for the greater market value of the plant and equipment. The remaining amount, $8,000, was for *goodwill*. The analysis of the purchase transaction, at date of acquisition, follows:[5]

---

[5] Many accountants believe that the plant and equipment difference should be 100% (i.e., $5,000) rather than 80% (i.e., $4,000). This difference in opinion has not been resolved; however, it appears that most companies currently use the lower amount.

Purchase price for 80% interest in Co. S................	$132,000
Stockholders' equity (book value) of Co. S purchased	
($100,000 + $50,000) × .80	120,000
Difference—Excess paid over book value..............	12,000
Analysis of the difference:	
To plant and equipment ($50,000 − $45,000) × .80 ..	4,000
Remainder—Goodwill purchased....................	$ 8,000

Assume it is now December 31, 1974, and both companies have experienced one year's operations as affiliated companies. Each company has prepared the following separate 1974 financial statements:

Financial Statements for 1974

	At December 31, 1974	
	Company P	*Company S*
Income Statement (for 1974):		
Sales revenue	$400,000	$110,000
Revenue from investments (dividends from		
Co. S)................................	8,000	
Cost of goods sold........................	(220,000)	(59,000)
Expenses (not detailed)....................	(130,000)	(26,500)
Depreciation expense......................	(10,000)	(4,500)
Income tax expense.......................	(20,000)	(6,000)
Net Income.............................	$ 28,000	$ 14,000
Balance Sheet:		
Cash....................................	$ 92,000	$ 45,500
Account receivable (net)...................	18,000	28,000
Receivable from Co. S.....................	6,000	
Inventories..............................	185,000	65,000
Investment in Co. S (at cost)...............	132,000	
Plant and equipment......................	90,000	40,500
	$523,000	$179,000
Accounts payable.........................	$ 55,000	$ 19,000
Payable to Co. P.........................		6,000
Common stock (par $10)...................	300,000	100,000
Beginning retained earnings................	140,000	50,000
Dividends paid during 1974................		(10,000)
Net Income for 1974 (from above)...........	28,000	14,000
	$523,000	$179,000

Additional data developed for the consolidation worksheet:

(a) Investment account balance of $132,000 to be eliminated against 80% of stockholders' equity of subsidiary.

(b) Plant and equipment of Company S to be increased by $4,000 to fair-market value. Goodwill to be recognized, $8,000 (see analysis of purchase transaction above).

(c) Company S owed Company P $6,000 on Dec. 31, 1974.

(d) The plant and equipment is being depreciated over a remaining life of 10 years by Company S.

(e) Goodwill will be amortized over 20 years.

(f) Company S paid $10,000 cash dividends on Dec. 15, 1974.

Exhibit 14–9

COMPANY P and Its Subsidiary, COMPANY S
Consolidation Worksheet (Combination by Purchase) for the Balance Sheet and Income Statement
December 31, 1974 (80% Ownership)

	Statements		Intercompany Eliminations				Consolidated Balances
	Company P	Company S	Debit		Credit		
Income Statement:							
Sales revenue	400,000	110,000					510,000
Revenue from investments	8,000		(f)	8,000			
Cost of goods sold	(220,000)	(59,000)					(279,000)
Expenses (not detailed)	(130,000)	(26,500)					(156,500)
Depreciation expense	(10,000)	(4,500)	(d)	400			(14,900)
Amortization expense (goodwill)			(e)	400			(400)
Income tax expense	(20,000)	(6,000)					(26,000)
Net Income	28,000	14,000					33,200
Carried down:							
Minority interest ($14,000 × 20%)							2,800M*
Parent interest income							30,400
Balance Sheet:							
Cash	92,000	45,500					137,500
Accounts receivable (net)	18,000	28,000					46,000
Receivable from Co. S	6,000				(c)	6,000	
Inventories	185,000	65,000					250,000
Investment in Co. S (at cost)	132,000				(a)	132,000	
Plant and equipment (net)	90,000	40,500	(b)	4,000	(d)	400	134,100
Goodwill			(b)	8,000	(e)	400	7,600
	523,000	179,000					575,200
Differential			(a)	12,000	(b)	12,000	
Accounts payable	55,000	19,000					74,000
Payable to Co. P		6,000	(c)	6,000			
Common stock, Co. P	300,000						300,000
Common stock, Co. S		100,000	(a)	80,000			20,000M
Beginning retained earnings, Co. P	140,000						140,000
Beginning retained earnings, Co. S		50,000	(a)	40,000			10,000M
Dividends paid during 1974		(10,000)			(f)	8,000	(2,000)M
Net Income, 1974 (from above; not added across)	28,000	14,000					2,800M 30,400
	523,000	179,000	158,800		158,800		575,200

M—Minority interest.
* The minority interest in the earnings of the subsidiary is unaffected by the consolidation procedures of the parent company. Thus, the minority interest is $14,000 × 20% = $2,800. This amount is subtracted from consolidated income to derive the amount of consolidated income indentifiable with the controlling interest. The two separate amounts are then carried down to the balance-sheet section.
  Explanation of Eliminations:
  (a) To eliminate the investment account against 80% of the owners' equity of the subsidiary.
  (b) To allocate the difference between purchase price and book value to the appropriate accounts.
  (c) To eliminate the intercompany debt.
  (d) To record depreciation for one year on the asset increase resulting from the acquisition.
  (e) To amortize goodwill recognized (one year).
  (f) To eliminate intercompany revenue arising from dividends paid by the subsidiary.

The consolidation worksheet, on the purchase basis, is shown in Exhibit 14–9. It is the same as the worksheet shown in Exhibit 14–8 for 100% ownership, except for elimination entries (a), (b), (d), (e), and (f). These intercompany eliminations are the *same except for the amounts. They have been reduced to the 80% ownership level.*

Exhibit 14–10

COMPANY P and Its Subsidiary, COMPANY S
Consolidated Income Statement (Purchase Basis)
For the Year Ended December 31, 1974

Sales revenue..		$510,000
Cost of goods sold......................................		279,000
Gross margin..		231,000
Less:		
Expenses (not detailed).............................	$156,500	
Depreciation expense................................	14,900	
Amortization expense (goodwill)......................	400	
Income tax expense.................................	26,000	197,800
Consolidated net income................................		33,200
Less: Minority interest in net income....................		2,800
Controlling interest in net income.......................		$ 30,400

Earnings per share of common stock ($33,200 ÷ 30,000 shares) = $1.107 (some accountants prefer to use $30,400 as the numerator).

COMPANY P and Its Subsidiary, COMPANY S
Consolidated Balance Sheet (Purchase Basis)
At December 31, 1974

Assets

Current Assets:		
Cash...	$137,500	
Accounts receivable (net)...........................	46,000	
Inventories.......................................	250,000	$433,500
Fixed Assets:		
Plant and equipment (net)...........................		134,100
Intangible Assets:		
Goodwill (or Excess of cost over fair value of assets of		
subsidiary)......................................		7,600
		$575,200

Liabilities

Current Liabilities:		
Accounts Payable		$74,000

Stockholders' Equity

Contributed Capital:		
Common stock, par $10, 30,000 shares outstanding.......	$300,000	
Retained earnings.....................................	170,400	
Total..	470,400	
Minority interest.....................................	30,800*	
Total stockholders' interest....................		501,200
		$575,200

* $20,000 + $10,000 + $2,800 − $2,000 = $30,800.

On the worksheet the 20% representing the minority interest is designated with an "M." In the income statement part of the worksheet, 20% of the net income (i.e., $2,800) of the subsidiary is coded "M" and the remainder ($30,400) is identified with the parent. These consolidated balances, on the worksheet, are carried down to the balance-sheet section. The 20% of subsidiary stockholders' equity was not eliminated; therefore, it is carried across as the minority interest and coded "M." Aside from these adaptations, the "Consolidated Balances" column is completed as previously explained.

The consolidated income statement and balance sheet, based on the data in the "Consolidated Balances" column of the worksheet, are shown in Exhibit 14–10. The *minority* interest share of net income is separately identified on the income statement. Similarly, the minority interest share of stockholders' equity is separately identified on the balance sheet. The minority interest share of stockholders' equity often is shown as a special caption between liabilities and stockholders' equity rather than as illustrated in the exhibit.

Questions
for
discussion

1. Explain what is meant by a parent–subsidiary relationship.
2. Explain the basic concept underlying consolidated statements.
3. What two basic elements must be present before consolidated statements are used?
4. The concept of consolidated statements relates only to reporting as opposed to entries in the accounts. Explain.
5. Explain briefly what is meant by pooling of interests.
6. Explain briefly what is meant by combination by purchase.
7. When one corporation acquires a controlling interest in another corporation, the acquiring corporation debits a long-term investment account. In the case of a pooling of interests, basically, what amount is debited to the investment account?
8. Explain what is meant by intercompany eliminations, or offsets, in consolidation procedures.
9. Explain why the investment account must be eliminated against stockholders' equity.
10. Explain why the "book values" of the parent and subsidiary are aggregated on consolidated statements when there is a pooling of interests, but fair-market values of the subsidiary assets are used when the combination was by purchase.
11. Why is goodwill not recognized in a pooling of interests? Why is it recognized in a combination by purchase?
12. Explain why additional depreciation expense generally must be recognized on consolidation when the combination was by purchase.
13. Explain what is meant by goodwill when the combination was by purchase.

14. Explain why pooling of interests has been much more popular in the merger movement than combination by purchase.

15. Explain the basis for each of the following statements:
   a. Pooling of interests, given the same situation basically, reports a higher net income than does combination by purchase.
   b. The cash position, other things being equal, is better when there is a combination by pooling than when there is a combination by purchase.
   c. Pooling of interests, other things being equal, reports a higher amount of retained earnings than does combination by purchase.

Exercises E14–1. On January 2, 1974, Company P acquired all of the outstanding voting stock of Company S by exchanging, on a share-for-share basis, its own stock for the stock of Company S. Immediately after the stock exchange entry was posted by Company P, the separate balance sheets showed the following:

| | Balances, Jan. 2, 1974, Immediately after Acquisition | |
	Company P	Company S
Cash...	$ 38,000	$12,000
Receivable from Co. S.........................	7,000	
Inventory......................................	35,000	18,000
Investment in Co. S (100%)...................	60,000	
Fixed assets (net)............................	80,000	50,000
Total..................................	$220,000	$80,000
Liabilities....................................	$ 25,000	$13,000
Payable to Co. P..............................		7,000
Common stock (par $5)........................	140,000	40,000
Contributed capital from pooling of interests.....	20,000	
Retained earnings.............................	35,000	20,000
Total..................................	$220,000	$80,000

Required:

(a) Is this a pooling of interests or a combination by purchase? Explain.

(b) Give the entry that was made by Company P to record the acquisition. Assume pooling of interests.

(c) Prepare a consolidated balance sheet immediately after the acquisition. Follow the format of Exhibit 14–3.

(d) Were the assets of the subsidiary added to those of the parent, in the consolidated balance sheet, at book value or at market value? Explain.

E14–2. On January 1, 1974, Company P purchased a controlling interest of the shares of the outstanding common stock of Company S at $16 per share. At date of acquisition there were 10,000 shares of

Company S, $10 par value, common stock outstanding (issued at par) and the balance of retained earnings was $40,000. At date of acquisition it was determined that the fixed assets of Company S had a fair-market value of $6,000 in excess of book value as reflected on the books of Company S. Company P acquired 100% of the outstanding stock of Company S.

Required:

(a) Was this a combination by pooling-of-interest or by purchase? Explain.

(b) Give the entry on the books of Company P to record the acquisition.

(c) Analyze the purchase to determine the amount of goodwill purchased.

(d) In preparing a consolidated balance sheet, at what amounts would the subsidiary assets be included? Explain.

(e) Would there be any expenses to include on the consolidated income statement in future periods in addition to those reported by the parent and the subsidiary on their separate income statements? Explain.

E14–3. On January 1, 1974, Company P purchased 100% of the outstanding shares of Company S in the open market for $70,000 cash. On that date, *prior* to the acquisition, the separate balance sheets of the two companies were as follows (summarized):

| | Prior to Acquisition | |
	Company P	Company S
Cash	$ 80,000	$18,000
Receivable from Co. P		2,000
Fixed assets	80,000	60,000
	$160,000	$80,000
Liabilities	$ 28,000	$20,000
Payable to Co. S	2,000	
Common stock (par $10)	100,000	50,000
Retained earnings	30,000	10,000
	$160,000	$80,000

It was determined on date of acquisition that the fair-market value of the fixed assets of Company S were $4,000 in excess of their book value as reflected on the books of Company S.

Required:

(a) Was this a combination by pooling of interests or by purchase? Explain.

(b) Give the entry that should be made by Company P to record the acquisition.

(c) Analyze the acquisition to determine the amount of goodwill purchased.

(d) At what amount will the assets of Company S be included on the consolidated balance sheet? Explain.

(e) Prepare a consolidated balance sheet immediately after acquisition. Follow the format of Exhibit 14–5.

(f) Would there be any expenses to be included on the consolidated income statement in future periods in addition to those reported on the separate income statements of the parent and the subsidiary? Explain.

E14–4. On January 4, 1974, Company P acquired all of the outstanding stock of Company S for $10 per share cash. At the date of acquisition the balance sheet of Company S reflected the following:

Common stock, par $5..............	$ 50,000
Retained earnings...................	30,000

Immediately after the acquisition entry was posted, the balance sheets reflected the following:

	Balances, Jan. 4, 1974, Immediately after Acquisition	
	Company P	*Company S*
Cash.................................	$ 13,000	$17,000
Receivable from Co. P.................		3,000
Investment in Co. S (100%), at cost......	100,000	
Fixed assets.........................	122,000	70,000*
Total...................	$235,000	$90,000
Liabilities...........................	$ 22,000	$10,000
Payable to Co. S.....................	3,000	
Common stock (par $5)...............	150,000	50,000
Retained earnings....................	60,000	30,000
	$235,000	$90,000

* Determined by Company P to have a fair-market value of $78,000 at date of acquisition.

Required:

(a) Was this a combination by pooling of interests or by purchase? Explain.

(b) Give the entry that should be made by Company P to record the acquisition.

(c) Analyze the acquisition to determine the amount of goodwill purchased.

(d) At what amount will the assets of Company S be included on the consolidated balance sheet? Explain.

(e) Prepare a consolidated balance sheet immediately after acquisition. Follow the format of Exhibit 14–5.

(f) Would there be any expenses to be included on the consolidated income statement in future periods in addition to those reported on the separate income statements of the parent and the subsidiary? Explain.

E14–5. On January 1, 1974, Company P acquired all of the outstanding stock of Company S by exchanging one share of its own stock for each share of Company S stock. At the date of the exchange, the balance sheet of Company S showed the following:

Common stock, par $10...................... $40,000
Retained earnings........................... 10,000

One year after acquisition the two companies prepared their separate financial statements as shown on the following form:

COMPANY P and Its Subsidiary, COMPANY S (100% Owned)
Consolidated Balance Sheet and Income Statement (Pooling Basis)
For the Year Ended December 31, 1974

	Separate Balance Sheets			Consolidated Statements
	Company P	Company S	Eliminations	
Income Statement (for 1974):				
Sales revenue	96,000	42,000		
Revenue from investments	4,000			
Cost of goods sold	(60,000)	(25,000)		
Expenses (not detailed)	(17,000)	(10,000)		
Net income	23,000	7,000		
Balance Sheet (at Dec. 31, 1974):				
Cash	21,000	19,000		
Receivable from Co. P		2,000		
Investment in Co. S (100%)	50,000			
Fixed assets	59,000	47,000		
Total	130,000	68,000		
Liabilities	17,000	15,000		
Payable to Co. S	2,000			
Common stock, Co. P (par $10)	50,000			
Contributed capital from pooling of interests	10,000			
Common stock, Co. S (par $10)		40,000		
Beginning retained earnings, Co. P	28,000			
Beginning retained earnings, Co. S		10,000		
Dividend paid, 1974, Co. S		(4,000)		
Net income, 1974 (from above)	23,000	7,000		
Total	130,000	68,000		

Required:

a. Give the entry that was made by Company P to record the pooling of interests on January 1, 1974.

b. Complete the Eliminations column in the above form, then combine the two sets of statements in the last column for the income statement and the balance sheet.

(Hint: In completing the two columns, follow the pattern and approaches shown in Exhibit 14–3. Eliminate the revenue from invest-

524   *Fundamentals of financial accounting*

ments against the dividends paid since this represents intercompany revenue. The consolidated net income is $26,000.)

E14–6.   (Based on Appendix A.)   On January 1, 1974, Company P acquired 100% of the outstanding common stock of Company S for $106,000 cash. At that date, Company S reported the following for stockholders' equity: common stock (par $10), $60,000; retained earnings, $30,000. It also was determined that the fair-market value of the plant and equipment was $6,000 above the book value as reflected on the accounts of Company S. One year after acquisition date, December 31, 1974, the two companies prepared their separate financial statements as shown on the following consolidation worksheet. You are to complete the worksheet in every respect. Show the analysis of the purchase.

COMPANY P and Its Subsidiary, COMPANY S (100% Owned)
Consolidation Worksheet (Purchase Basis)
Income Statement and Balance Sheet, Dec. 31, 1974

	Statements		*Intercompany Eliminations*		*Consolidated Balances*
	Company P	*Company S*	*Debit*	*Credit*	
Income Statement (for 1974):					
Sales	80,000	47,000			
Revenue from investments (a)	4,000				
Cost of goods sold	(45,000)	(25,000)			
Expenses (not detailed)	(15,000)	(10,000)			
Depreciation expense (b)	(4,000)	(2,000)			
Amortization of goodwill (c)					
Net income	20,000	10,000			
Balance Sheet (at Dec. 31, 1974):					
Cash	15,000	10,000			
Accounts receivable (net)	19,000	9,000			
Receivable from Co. P		1,000			
Inventories	70,000	50,000			
Investment in Co. S (at cost)	106,000				
Plant and equipment (net)	80,000	40,000			
Goodwill					
	290,000	110,000			
Differential:					
Accounts payable	26,000	14,000			
Payable to Co. S	1,000				
Common stock, Co. P (par $10)	200,000				
Common stock, Co. S (par $10)		60,000			
Beginning retained earnings, Co. P	50,000				
Beginning retained earnings, Co. S		30,000			
Dividends paid during 1974, Co. P	(7,000)				
Dividends paid during 1974, Co. S		(4,000)			
Net income, 1974	20,000	10,000			
	290,000	110,000			

Additional data:
 (a) Dividends received from Co. S.
 (b) Plant and equipment has a remaining life of 20 years.
 (c) Assume goodwill is amortized over a period of 20 years.

E14–7.   (Based on Appendix A.)   On January 3, 1974, Company P purchased all of the outstanding stock of Company S at $2.50 per share.
At that date the balance sheet of Company S reflected the following:

Common stock, par $1 . . . . $20,000
Retained earnings   10,000

One year after acquisition, the two companies prepared their
separate financial statements as follows:

	Balances, Dec. 31, 1974	
Income Statement:	Company P	Company S
Sales	$ 99,000	$59,000
Revenue from investments	6,000	
Expenses (not detailed)	(71,000)	(40,400)
Depreciation expense	(9,000)	(3,600)
Net Income	$ 25,000	$15,000
Balance Sheet:		
Cash	$ 16,000	$ 6,000
Receivable from Co. P		4,000
Investment in Co. S	50,000	
Fixed assets (net)	90,000	40,000*
Total	$156,000	$50,000
Liabilities	$ 15,000	$11,000
Payable to Co. S	4,000	
Common stock, Co. P	80,000	
Common stock, Co. S		20,000
Beginning retained earnings, Co. P	32,000	
Beginning retained earnings, Co. S		10,000
Dividends paid, 1974		(6,000)
Net Income, 1974	25,000	15,000
Total	$156,000	$50,000

* Fair-market value of the fixed assets at date of acquisition was $12,000 more than
their book value. The fixed assets have a remaining life of 10 years from date of acquisition.

Required:

a.   Give the entry that would be made by Company P to record
the purchase on January 3, 1974.

b.   Analyze the stock purchase transaction to determine the amount
of goodwill purchased. Goodwill will be amortized over 20 years.

c.   Prepare a consolidation worksheet (purchase basis) for the
income statement and the balance sheet at December 31, 1974.

E14–8.   (Based on Appendix B.)   This exercise uses the data given in Exercise 14–3 for Company P and Company S, immediately prior to
acquisition, and all other data given, except with respect to the
number of shares purchased. Assume in this exercise that Company P purchased 70% of the outstanding shares of Company S
in the open market for $49,000 cash. Immediately after the pur-
chase, the balance sheets reflected the following:

Balance Sheet

	Company P	Company S
Cash..................................	$ 31,000	$18,000
Receivable from Co. P...................		2,000
Investment in Co. S (70%) at cost........	49,000	
Fixed assets...........................	80,000	60,000
Total........................	$160,000	$80,000
Liabilities............................	28,000	20,000
Payable to Co. S......................	2,000	
Common stock (par $10)...............	100,000	50,000
Retained earnings.....................	30,000	10,000
Total........................	$160,000	$80,000

Required:

(a) Give the entry on the books of Company P to record the purchase.

(b) Analyze the purchase to determine the amount of goodwill purchased.

(c) Prepare a consolidation worksheet for a balance sheet immediately after acquisition.

(d) What is the amount for minority interest that will be reported on the balance sheet?

Problems P14–1. On January 1, 1974, the separate balance sheets of two corporations showed the following:

Balances Jan. 1, 1974

	Company P	Company S
Cash...................................	$ 21,000	$ 9,000
Receivable from Co. P....................		4,000
Fixed assets............................	99,000	32,000
Total.............................	$120,000	$45,000
Liabilities.............................	$ 16,000	$10,000
Payable to Co. S........................	4,000	
Common stock (par $20).................	60,000	20,000
Retained earnings.......................	40,000	15,000
Total.............................	$120,000	$45,000

On January 3, 1974, Company P acquired all of the outstanding shares of Company S by exchanging one share of its own stock for two shares of Company S stock.

Required:

(a) Was this a combination by pooling of interests or by purchase? Explain.

(b) Company P made the following entry on its books, at date of acquisition, to record the investment:

Jan. 2, 1974:

Investment in Stock of Co. S............................	35,000	
Common Stock.......................................		10,000
Contributed Capital, from Pooling-of-Interests............		25,000

Explain the basis for each of the three amounts in this entry.

(c)   Will any goodwill be recognized on the consolidated balance sheet? Explain.

(d)   Prepare a consolidated balance sheet immediately after the acquisition. Follow the format shown in Exhibit 14–3.

(Hint: In the elimination, only $15,000 of the $25,000 contributed capital, from pooling-of-interests will be subtracted; the remainder is carried to the "Consolidated Balance Sheet" column.)

P14–2.   On January 2, 1974, Company P acquired all of the outstanding stock of Company S by exchanging its own stock for the stock of Company S. One share of Company P stock was exchanged for two shares of Company S stock. Immediately after the acquisition was recorded by Company P, the balance sheets reflected the following:

	Balances, Jan. 2, 1974 Immediately after Acquisition	
	Company P	Company S
Cash.................................	$ 38,000	$26,000
Receivable from Co. S..................	6,000	
Inventory............................	30,000	10,000
Investment in Co. S (100%).............	70,000	
Fixed assets (net)......................	90,000	50,000
Other assets..........................	6,000	4,000
Total.........................	$240,000	$90,000
Liabilities............................	$ 16,000	$14,000
Payable to Co. P......................		6,000
Common stock (par $5).................	125,000	50,000
Contributed capital, from pooling- of-interest.........................	45,000	
Retained earnings.....................	54,000	20,000
Total.........................	$240,000	$90,000

Required:

(a)   Was this a combination by pooling-of-interests or by purchase? Explain.

(b)   Give the journal entry that was made by Company P to record the acquisition on Jan. 2, 1974. Explain the basis for each amount included in the entry.

(c)   At what amounts will the assets of Company S be included on the consolidated balance sheet? Explain.

(d)   Will any goodwill be recognized on the consolidated balance sheet? Explain.

(e)   Prepare a consolidated balance sheet immediately after acquisition. Follow the format illustrated in Exhibit 14–3.

(Hint: In the eliminations, only $20,000 of the contributed capital, from pooling of interests, will be subtracted; the remainder will be carried over to the consolidated balance sheet.)

P14–3. On January 5, 1974, Company P purchased all of the outstanding stock of Company S for $100,000 cash. Immediately after the acquisition the separate balance sheets of the two companies reflected the following:

	Jan. 5, 1974, Immediately after Acquisition	
	Company P	Company S
Cash..............................	$ 22,000	$ 9,000
Accounts receivable (net)................	14,000	6,000
Receivable from Co. S..................	4,000	
Inventory...........................	50,000	25,000
Investment in Co. S (at cost).............	100,000	
Fixed assets (net)......................	153,000	67,000
Other assets..........................	7,000	3,000
Total.....................	$350,000	$110,000
Accounts payable.....................	$ 20,000	$ 16,000
Payable to Co. P......................		4,000
Bonds payable........................	90,000	
Common stock (par $5).................	180,000	60,000
Contributed capital, in excess of par.......	8,000	
Retained earnings.....................	52,000	30,000
Total.....................	$350,000	$110,000

The fixed assets of Company S were estimated to have a fair-market value at date of acquisition of $71,000.

Required:

(a) Was this a combination by pooling of interests or by purchase? Explain.

(b) Give the entry that would be made in the accounts of Company P at date of acquisition.

(c) Analyze the acquisition to determine the amount of goodwill purchased.

(d) At what amounts will the assets of Company S, the subsidiary, be included on the consolidated balance sheet immediately after acquisition? Explain.

(e) Prepare a consolidated balance sheet immediately after acquisition. Follow the format illustrated in Exhibit 14–5.

(f) Will there be any additional expenses to include on the income statements for future periods other than those reported on the separate income statements for the parent and the subsidiary? Explain.

P14–4. On January 4, 1974, Company P purchased 100% of the outstanding common stock of Company S for $240,000 cash. Immediately after the acquisition, the separate balance sheets for the two companies were prepared as shown in the form below.

It was determined at date of acquisition that, on the basis of fair-market value, compared with the book value of the assets as reflected on the books of Company S, the (a) Inventories should be reduced by $3,000; (b) Plant and Equipment should be increased by $11,000; and (c) Land should be increased by $2,000.

Required:

(a) Was this a combination by pooling of interests or by purchase? Explain.

(b) Give the entry that was made on the books of Company P to record the acquisition.

(c) Analyze the acquisition transaction to determine the amount of goodwill purchased. Use data from the form below if needed.

(d) At what amount will the assets of Company S be included on the consolidated balance sheet? Explain.

(e) Complete the "Eliminations" column in the form below and then extend the amounts for the consolidated balance sheet.

COMPANY P and Its Subsidiary, COMPANY S
Consolidated Balance Sheet
January 4, 1974 (Immediately after Acquisition)

	Separate Balance Sheets			
	Company P	Company S	Eliminations	Consolidated Balance Sheet
Assets:				
Cash	80,000	40,000		
Accounts receivable (net)	26,000	19,000		
Receivable from Co. P		8,000		
Inventories	170,000	80,000		
Long-term investment, bonds, Z Company	15,000			
Long-term investment, Co. S	240,000			
Land	12,000	3,000		
Plant and equipment (net)	157,000	130,000		
Goodwill				
	700,000	280,000		
Liabilities:				
Accounts payable	22,000	40,000		
Payable to Co. S	8,000			
Bonds payable, 5%	100,000	30,000		
Shareholders' Equity:				
Common stock, Co. P	500,000			
*Common stock, Co. S		150,000		
Retained earnings, Co. P	70,000			
Retained earnings, Co. S		60,000		
	700,000	280,000		

* Par $10.

P14–5. This problem presents the income statement and the balance sheet on a consolidated basis for Company P and its subsidiary, Company S, one year after acquisition, under two different assumptions: Case A—pooling-of-interests basis and Case B—purchase basis. The two different assumptions are used so that we can compare and analyze the differences.

On January 2, 1974, Company P acquired all of the outstanding common stock of Company S. At that date the shareholders' equity of Company S showed the following: common stock, par $10, $50,-000; retained earnings $20,000. The entry made by Company P to record the acquisition under each case was as follows:

Case A—Pooling-of-Interests Basis			*Case B—Purchase Basis*		
Investment in Co. S			Investment in Co. S		
(5,000 shares, 100%).	70,000		(5,000 shares, 100%).	80,000	
Common stock....		40,000	Cash............		80,000
Contributed capital,					
from pooling of					
interests........		30,000			

On January 2, 1974, date of acquisition, the acquisition by purchase was analyzed to determine the goodwill as follows:

Purchase price paid for 100% interest in Co. S.............	$80,000
Stockholders' equity of Co. S (at book value) purchased,	
$50,000 + $20,000....................................	70,000
Difference—Excess paid over book value..................	10,000
Analysis of the difference:	
To fixed assets (fair-market value, $42,000—book value,	
$40,000 = $2,000 increase).........................	2,000
Remainder—Goodwill purchased......................	$ 8,000

For consolidated statement purposes the fixed assets are being depreciated over 10 years' remaining life and the goodwill will be amortized over 20 years.

One year after acquisition, the two companies prepared separate income statements and balance sheets. These separate statements have been consolidated under each case as reflected on the next page.

Required:

(a) Prepare a schedule that shows what items are different on each statement for Case A, compared with Case B.

(b) Explain the reasons why net income is different under pooling versus purchase. Use the amounts from the two statements in your explanation and tell why they are different.

(c) Explain why the cash balance is different between the two cases.

(d) What was the balance in the account "Investment in Co. S" prior to its elimination? Explain.

(e) Explain why the fixed asset amount is different between the two cases.

(f) Why is there a difference in goodwill between the two cases?

(g) Why does goodwill reflect a balance of $7,600, compared with the $8,000 computed above for goodwill at date of acquisition?

(h) How much was eliminated for "Payable to Co. P"? Why was it eliminated?

(i) What was the amount of "Common stock, Co. S" that was eliminated? Why was it eliminated?

(j) Why was only $20,000 of the $30,000 of contributed capital, from pooling of interests, eliminated?

(k) Explain why the account "Contributed capital, in excess of par, $10,000," was not eliminated.

(l) Explain why "Beginning retained earnings, Co. S, $20,000," is shown under Case A (pooling) but not under Case B (purchase).

COMPANY P and Its Subsidiary, COMPANY S (100% Owned)
Consolidated Income Statement and Balance Sheet
For the Year Ended December 31, 1974

	Consolidated Statements Dec. 31, 1974	
	Pooling Basis (Case A)	*Purchase Basis (Case B)*
Income Statement (for Year Ended Dec. 31, 1974):		
Sales revenue	$236,000	$236,000
Revenue from investments ($4,000, eliminated)		
Cost of goods sold	(112,000)	(112,000)
Expenses (not detailed to simplify)	(75,500)	(75,500)
Depreciation expense	(12,500)	(12,700)
Amortization expense (goodwill)		(400)
Net Income	$ 36,000	$ 35,400
Balance Sheet (at Dec. 31, 1974):		
Assets:		
Cash	$128,000	$ 48,000
Accounts receivable (net)	53,000	53,000
Receivable from Co. S ($5,000, eliminated)		
Inventory	37,000	37,000
Investment in Co. S (eliminated)		
Fixed assets (net)	125,000	126,800
Goodwill		7,600
Total	$343,000	$272,400
Liabilities:		
Current liabilities	$ 30,000	$ 30,000
Payable to Co. P (eliminated)		
Bonds payable	50,000	50,000
Shareholders' Equity:		
Common stock, Co. P	140,000	100,000
Common stock, Co. S (eliminated)		
Contributed capital, in excess of par	10,000	10,000
Contributed capital, from pooling of interests ($20,000, eliminated)	10,000	
Beginning retained earnings, Co. P	47,000	47,000
Beginning retained earnings, Co. S	20,000	
Dividends paid in 1974 (eliminated)		
Net Income, 1974 (from income statement above)	36,000	35,400
Total	$343,000	$272,400

P14–6.   (Based on Appendix A.)   On January 1, 1974, Company P purchased 100% of the outstanding capital stock of Company S for
$98,000 cash. At that date the stockholders' section of the balance
sheet of Company S reflected the following:

Capital stock, $10 par, 5,000 shares outstanding..... $50,000
Retained earnings............................   30,000
                                              $80,000

At the date of acquisition, it was determined that the fair-market
value of certain assets of Company S, in comparison with the book
value of those assets as reflected on the balance sheet of Company S,
should be reflected by (a) decreasing Inventories by $2,000 and (b)
increasing Equipment by $8,000.

It is now one year after acquisition, December 31, 1974, and
each company has prepared the following separate financial statements (summarized):

	At Dec. 31, 1974	
	Company P	*Company S*
Balance Sheet:		
Cash.....................................	$ 52,000	$ 30,000
Accounts receivable (net).................	31,000	10,000
Receivable from Co. P.....................		3,000
Inventories..............................	60,000	70,000
Investment in Co. S (at cost)..............	98,000	
Equipment..............................	80,000	20,000
Other assets.............................	9,000	17,000
	$330,000	$150,000
Accounts payable.........................	$ 42,000	$ 30,000
Payable to Co. S.........................	3,000	
Bonds payable, 5%.......................	70,000	30,000
Capital stock ($10 par)....................	140,000	50,000
Beginning retained earnings................	50,000	30,000
Dividend paid during 1974................	(10,000)	(5,000)
Net Income for 1974 (from income		
statement)............................	35,000	15,000
	$330,000	$150,000
Income Statement (for 1974):		
Sales revenue............................	$360,000	$140,000
Revenue from investments.................	5,000	
Cost of goods sold.......................	(220,000)	(80,000)
Expenses (not detailed)...................	(106,000)	(44,000)
Depreciation expense.....................	(4,000)	(1,000)
Net Income.............................	$ 35,000	$ 15,000

Additional data during 1974:

(1)   Near the end of 1974, Company S declared and paid a cash
dividend amounting to $5,000.

(2)   The equipment is being depreciated on the basis of a 20-year
remaining life.

(3)   Goodwill is to be amortized over a 40-year period.

Required:

(a)   Give the entry on the books of Company P to record the acquisition of the capital stock of Company S on Jan. 1, 1974.

(b)   Analyze the acquisition of the stock to determine the purchased goodwill.

(c)   Prepare a consolidation worksheet (purchase basis) for the year 1974 as a basis for the 1974 income statement and balance sheet.
(Hint: Consolidated net income is $44,300.)

(d)   Prepare a classified income statement and balance sheet based on the data provided by the consolidation worksheet.

P14–7.   (Based on Appendix B.)   On January 1, 1974, Company P purchased 90% of the outstanding capital stock of Company S for $100,000 cash. At the date of acquisition, the stockholders' equity accounts of Company S reflected the following: Capital Stock (par $10), $60,000; Contributed Capital, in Excess of Par, $10,000; and Retained Earnings, $20,000. At that date it was determined that the book value of the fixed assets was $10,000 less than their fair-market value.

It is now December 31, 1974, and each company has independently prepared the following financial statements (summarized):

	At Dec. 31, 1974	
	Company P	*Company S*
Balance Sheet:		
Cash..................................	$ 23,000	$ 11,000
Accounts receivable (net).................	57,000	13,000
Receivable from Co. P		7,000
Inventories............................	110,000	24,000
Investment in Co. S (at cost; 90% owned).....	100,000	
Fixed assets (net).......................	120,000	50,000
Other assets...........................	6,000	5,000
	$416,000	$110,000
Accounts payable.......................	$ 30,000	$ 8,000
Payable to Co. S.......................	7,000	
Bonds payable, 5%.....................	80,000	10,000
Capital stock ($10 par)....................	200,000	60,000
Contributed capital, in excess of par.........	4,000	10,000
Beginning retained earnings...............	80,000	20,000
Dividends paid, 1974....................	(15,000)	(8,000)
Net Income (from income statement)........	30,000	10,000
	$416,000	$110,000
Income Statement (for 1974):		
Sales revenue..........................	$195,000	$ 75,000
Revenue from investments.................	7,200	
Cost of goods sold......................	(115,000)	(43,000)
Expenses (not detailed)...................	(52,200)	(19,500)
Depreciation expense....................	(5,000)	(2,500)
Net Income............................	$ 30,000	$ 10,000

Required:

(a) Give the entry on the books of Co. P to record and acquisition of the stock of Co. S.

(b) Analyze the stock purchase to determine the amount of purchased goodwill.

(c) Prepare a consolidation worksheet (purchase basis) for a balance sheet and income statement for 1974. Assume the fixed assets of Company S has a 10-year remaining life and that any goodwill will be amortized over 20 years.
(Hint: Consolidated net income is $31,400.)

(d) Prepare a classified income statement and balance sheet based upon the data provided by the consolidation worksheet.

15 The statement of changes in financial position

Throughout the previous chapters, we have emphasized that, for external reporting purposes, three basic statements must be presented: (1) an income statement, (2) a balance sheet, and (3) a statement of changes in financial position.[1] In the past, "funds-flow statements" were prepared by many companies, although they were not required. The statement of changes in financial position is similar in many respects to what formerly was called a funds-flow statement. Whereas the funds-flow statement usually was limited in scope (i.e., to working-capital analysis) the statement of changes in financial position now used is based on an all-resources concept. The latter statement has been required since the issuance of APB *Opinion No. 19,* dated March 1971.[2]

This chapter will focus on understanding and interpreting the statement of changes in financial position. Part One will discuss the statement prepared on a working-capital-flow basis. Part Two will discuss the statement prepared on a cash-flow basis. The Appendix discusses and illustrates the techniques used in the preparation of a statement of changes in financial position. The techniques are set out separately for

---

[1] Other supporting schedules, such as a statement of cost of goods sold, statement of retained earnings, statement of changes in capital, and a schedule of lease commitments, are essential in certain circumstances to meet the requirements of the full-disclosure principle.

[2] APB *Opinion No. 19* states:

> The Board concludes that information concerning the financing and investing activities of a business enterprise and the changes in its financial position for a period is essential for financial statement users. . . . A statement summarizing changes in financial position should be presented as a basic financial statement for each period for which an income statement is presented.

the convenience of those who do not desire to pursue the technical aspects of preparing the statement.

Concept of the statement of changes in financial position

Fundamentally, the statement of changes in financial position, as prescribed in APB *Opinion No. 19,* must be based on an all-resources concept. This means that it must report the following:

1. The inflow of *all* resources during the period.
2. The outflows of *all* resources during the period.
3. The net increase (or decrease) in resources during the period.

APB *Opinion No. 19* also provides that, for measurement purposes, *all resources* may be measured in terms of *either:* (*a*) working capital (i.e., the difference between current assets and current liabilities) or (*b*) cash.

The sources or inflows of resources (sometimes called funds) are said to represent the financing activities of the business during the period (i.e., where the resources came from). The uses or outflows of resources are said to represent the investing activities of the business during the period (i.e., where the resources went).

The words "changes in financial position" focus on the basic concept underlying the statement. It is a "change" statement because it reports the changes in the assets, liabilities, and owners' equity amounts during the period. As indicated in the above paragraph, these changes are due to the inflow of funds (i.e., the financing activities) and the outflow of funds (i.e., the investing activities). The diagram shown in Exhibit 5–1 (page 125) should be restudied at this point. It will aid in understanding the relationships of the statement of changes in financial position to the income statement and the balance sheet. The concept of reporting the *changes* in financial position for each accounting period may be diagramed as follows:

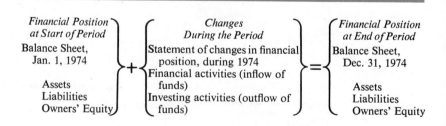

Financial Position at Start of Period	Changes During the Period	Financial Position at End of Period
Balance Sheet, Jan. 1, 1974	Statement of changes in financial position, during 1974	Balance Sheet, Dec. 31, 1974
	Financial activities (inflow of funds)	
Assets Liabilities Owners' Equity	Investing activities (outflow of funds)	Assets Liabilities Owners' Equity

The primary financing activities, or sources of funds, in most businesses are:

(1) Operations; revenues from the sale of goods and services, less the expenses incurred in generating those revenues.

(2) Issuance (usually through sale) of capital stock.

(3)   Sale of assets used in the business.

(4)   Borrowing (incurring debt).

The primary investing activities, or uses of funds, in most businesses are:

(1)   To purchase fixed assets and to expand the business.

(2)   To pay cash dividends to shareholders.

(3)   To pay debts.

The term "funds" was used a number of times in the above paragraphs. Since it is a *general* term, it must be clearly understood in the context used. When it is used in respect to the statement of changes in financial position, it means *either* cash or working capital. Both of these terms have been defined in prior chapters. In the context of the statement of changes in financial position, these two terms mean:[3]

(1)   Cash—cash plus the short-term investments (as defined in Chapter 8). Short-term investments generally are added to cash for this purpose because they are very near to cash and can be converted to cash at any time.

(2)   Working capital—current assets minus current liabilities. The usual current assets are cash, short-term investments, accounts receivable, and inventory. The current liabilities are short-term debts that presumably are to be paid out of the current assets. The difference between the current assets and the current liabilities is called working capital (or, sometimes, net working capital).[4]

The statement of changes in financial position may present the sources or inflows and the uses or outflows of funds on *either* a working-capital basis or a cash-flow basis. Each statement of changes in financial position should clearly indicate the basis on which it was prepared. We will consider each basis separately in the two parts that follow.

Illustrative case

Throughout this chapter, we will use the Fina Company, Inc. case as a basis for discussion and illustration. Assume it is December 31, 1974, the end of the annual accounting period. The Fina Company, Inc. has completed all of the year-end procedures, including the preparation of the income statement and the balance sheet. The remaining reporting

---

[3] Some accountants prefer to use the general term "resources" rather than "funds."

[4] The word "funds" also is used in other ways by accountants. It has been used to refer to assets, generally cash, set aside for specific future use, such as a building fund or a bond sinking fund; and in governmental accounting, it has an entirely different meaning. This wide range of inconsistent usage of the term suggests the desirability of using more descriptive terms, such as "cash" and "working capital," and the use of more descriptive titles, such as "statement of changes in financial position" rather than the older title, "funds-flow statement."

Exhibit 15–1

FINA COMPANY, INC.
Income Statement
For the Year Ending December 31, 1974

Sales...		$100,000
Cost of goods sold...........................		60,000
Gross margin.................................		40,000
Less expenses:		
Expenses (not detailed to simplify).........	$24,000	
Depreciation expense.....................	6,000	
Income taxes............................	2,000	32,000
Net Income.................................		$ 8,000

---

requirement is preparation of a **statement of changes in financial position** for 1974.

The income statement for 1974 is shown in Exhibit 15–1.

Comparative balance sheets for the current and past year are shown in Exhibit 15–2. The prior balance sheet, at December 31, 1973, is needed for analytical purposes, as discussed later.

Exhibit 15–2

FINA COMPANY, INC.
Balance Sheets
At December 31, 1974 and 1973

	December 31, 1974		*December 31, 1973**	
Current Assets:				
Cash.............................	$37,500		$30,000	
Accounts receivable (net)†...........	25,000		20,000	
Inventory.........................	20,000	$ 82,500	24,000	$ 74,000
Long-term Investments:				
Common stock of X Corp............		1,000		6,000
Fixed Assets:				
Equipment (net)†...................		59,000		60,000
Total Assets................		$142,500		$140,000
Current Liabilities:				
Accounts payable...................	$22,000		$20,000	
Income taxes payable................	500			
Short-term notes payable (nontrade)...	10,000	$ 32,500	14,000	$ 34,000
Long-term Liabilities:				
Bonds payable.....................		32,000		40,000
Stockholders' Equity:				
Capital stock (par $10)..............	60,000		50,000	
Contributed capital in excess of par....	6,000		5,000	
Retained earnings..................	12,000	78,000	11,000	66,000
Total Liabilities and Stock-				
holders' Equity...........		$142,500		$140,000

* An alternate dating would be Jan. 1, 1974, since the ending balance sheet for the past period is the beginning balance sheet for the current period.

† In analyzing and reporting changes in financial position, accounts receivable and assets generally are shown *net* of the allowance accounts as a matter of convenience.

PART ONE: CHANGES IN FINANCIAL POSITION— WORKING-CAPITAL BASIS

The concept of working capital

To understand and interpret the statement of changes in financial position prepared on a working-capital basis, one must clearly understand the concept of working capital as a "fund." In Exhibit 15–2, for the Fina Company, we can observe the following on the balance sheets:

	1974	1973	Working Capital Increase (Decrease) 1973 to 1974
Current assets.	$82,500	$74,000	$ 8,500
Less: Current liabilities.	32,500	34,000	1,500
Working capital.	$50,000	$40,000	$10,000

The $8,500 *increase* in current assets increased working capital by that amount, and the $1,500 *decrease* in current liabilities also increased working capital. The total increase during the year in working capital, therefore, was $10,000. You should clearly understand the effect on working capital of increases and decreases in current assets and current liabilities. The statement of changes in financial position, prepared on the working-capital basis, focuses on this point. That is, it measures the inflows and outflows of funds in terms of working capital (rather than in terms of cash, or current assets). To repeat, the statement reports where working capital came from (sources) and where working capital went (uses) and the resultant net increase or decrease in working capital during the period.

Working-capital basis illustrated

The Statement of Changes in Financial Position—Working-Capital Basis for the Fina Company for 1974 is shown in Exhibit 15–3. First, let's focus on the primary aspects of the statement. Basically, the statement includes two sections:

Section A—Sources and Uses of Working Capital.

Section B—Changes in the Internal Content of Working Capital.

Section A reports the financing activities (i.e., the sources or inflows of working capital) and the investing activities (i.e., the uses or outflows of working capital) during the period. Section A is the basic part of the report. For the Fina Company, it reports that, during the period, working capital flowed in from three sources: (1) Operations—net income (revenues minus expenses as adjusted); (2) Investors—from the sale of common stock for cash; and (3) Other sources—sale of a long-term investment. Similarly, it reports that working capital was used or applied during the period for three purposes: (1) to pay a cash dividend to stockholders; (2) to pay a long-term debt; and (3) to purchase a fixed asset (equipment). Section A concludes by reporting

Exhibit 15–3

FINA COMPANY, INC.
Statement of Changes in Financial Position—Working-Capital Basis
For the Year Ended December 31, 1974

Section A: Sources and Uses of Working Capital During the Period*

Sources of Working Capital (inflows)
From operations:
Net income... $ 8,000
    Add expenses not requiring working capital during the
    current period:
        Depreciation expense............................... 6,000
        Total working capital generated by operations........ $14,000
From other sources:
    Sale of unissued common stock......................... 11,000
    Disposal of long-term investment (Note A)................. 5,000
        Total working capital generated from other sources.... 16,000
        Total working capital generated during the period... 30,000

Uses of Working Capital (outflows)
Payment of cash dividend on common stock................. 7,000
Payment on bonds payable................................ 8,000
Acquisition of equipment (Note A)......................... 5,000
    Total working capital applied during the period.......... 20,000
Net increase in working capital during the period.............. $10,000

Section B: Changes in the Internal Content of Working Capital During the Period*

Changes in Working-Capital Accounts	Balances, December 31		Working-Capital Increase (Decrease)
	1974	*1973*	
Current assets:			
Cash.............................	$37,500	$30,000	$ 7,500
Accounts receivable (net)..............	25,000	20,000	5,000
Merchandise inventory.................	20,000	24,000	(4,000)
Total current assets...............	82,500	74,000	
Current liabilities:			
Accounts payable....................	22,000	20,000	(2,000)
Income taxes payable.................	500		(500)
Notes payable, short-term (nontrade).....	10,000	14,000	4,000
Total current liabilities.............	32,500	34,000	
Working Capital......................	$50,000	$40,000	$10,000

Note A: This equipment was acquired in exchange for common stock of the X Corporation, which was being held as a long-term investment.
* These two headings often do not appear on the statement; they are included here as an aid in the explanation of the concept. See Exhibit 15–6 for the source of the data.

---

the net effect of these several changes in financial position. The net effect was a $10,000 increase in working capital during the period.

Section B of the statement is a listing of each current asset, each current liability, and the resultant increases, and decreases in working capital. For example, it shows how much cash increased, how much inventory decreased, how much accounts payable increased, etc. Observe that it also reports a $10,000 increase in working capital during the period. Obviously, this amount must agree with the net effect (increase) reported in Section A. By comparing Section B with the comparative balance sheets given in Exhibit 15–2, you can see that it is copied directly from the balance sheet.[5]

It is important to understand that Sections A and B report two distinctly different aspects of working-capital flows:

(1) Section A—This section reports the basic sources and uses of working capital during the period. Thus, it focuses on the causes of the changes in working capital.

(2) Section B—In contrast to Section A, this section reports which working-capital accounts changed and by how much during the period. Thus, it focuses on changes in the internal content of working capital.

Sources of working capital

Transactions that increase working capital represent sources of working capital. Transactions of this type involve a debit to a current asset or current liability account and a credit to one or more nonworking-capital accounts. The four primary sources of funds listed on page 536 may be "explained" as follows:

(1) *Current operations*—Net income reflects the net results of operations. It is composed of total revenue less total expense. As goods and services are sold during the period, there is an inflow of cash and accounts receivable (both working-capital items). Also, during the period, as the expenses are incurred, there is a decrease in working capital occasioned by cash payments and the incurrence of current liabilities. Therefore, a reported net income would indicate an increase (source) of working capital.

The increase in working capital from operations, however, normally is somewhat more than the amount of net income for the period. This is due to the fact that the income statement usually includes expenses that do not involve the use of working capital during the period—depreciation, depletion, and amortization of intangible assets. For example, the income statement for the Fina Company, Exhibit 15–1, shows that there was an inflow of working capital of $100,000 from sales during the year. It also shows that there were outflows of working capital for cost of goods sold, $60,000; expenses, $24,000; and income taxes, $2,000 (i.e., a net inflow of $14,000). In making these computations we must recognize that there was no outflow of working capital for the depreciation expense of $6,000. This latter point is evident if we recall that the entry for Depreciation Expense was:

---

[5] For this reason, some accountants consider Section B to be redundant; however, it is required by APB *Opinion No. 19.*

```
Depreciation Expense.......................... 6,000
     Accumulated Depreciation................              6,000
```

This entry neither increased nor decreased working capital, although net income was decreased. The working-capital increase from operations, therefore, was:

Net income................................. $ 8,000
Add expenses that did not decrease working
    capital:
        Depreciation.......................... 6,000
Working capital inflow from operations......... $14,000

On the statement of changes in financial position, Exhibit 15–3, this source of working capital was reported as above.

(2) Sale of capital stock—The sale of capital stock causes an inflow of working capital since cash flows in for the sales price of the stock.

(3) Sale of noncurrent assets—When a long-term investment, a fixed asset, or "other" asset is sold, working capital is increased by the amount of the cash and/or receivable that results from its disposition.

(4) Long-term borrowing—When a loan is obtained on a long-term basis, working capital (cash) is increased by the amount of the proceeds of the loan. In contrast, when a short-term loan is obtained, working capital is not increased since a working-capital account (Cash) is increased and another working-capital account (a current liability) is increased by the same amount. Since the two increases offset each other, working capital (current assets minus current liabilities) does not change. To illustrate, assume the Fina Company borrowed $5,000 cash on a 90-day loan at the end of 1974. The working-capital effect would be (data from page 539):

	Before Short-Term Loan	Effect of Short-Term Loan	After Short-Term Loan
Current assets..........	$82,500	+5,000	$87,500
Current liabilities.....	32,500	+5,000	37,500
Working capital.........	$50,000	–0–	$50,000*

* Effect on working capital = (+$5,000) − (+$5,000) = 0.

Uses of working capital   Transactions that decrease working capital represent uses of working capital. Transactions of this type would involve a credit to a working-capital account and a debit to a nonworking-capital account. The three primary uses of funds that are listed on page 537 may be explained as follows:

(1) To purchase fixed assets and other noncurrent assets—Transactions of this type generally require a payment of cash and, some-

times, the creation of a debt. To the extent that cash is paid out or short-term debt is recorded, working capital is reduced.

(2) To pay cash dividends—In this transaction, there is an outflow of cash, hence, working capital is reduced (used) by that amount.[6]

(3) To pay a long-term liability—Payments on long-term notes, bonds, and other obligations involve an outflow of cash, hence, they represent a use of working capital. In contrast, the payment of a current liability does not change working capital for the same reason explained above in respect to borrowing (source) on a short-term debt basis.

The above explanations should make it clear that (1) working capital is not increased or decreased by transactions that involve debits and credits to working-capital accounts *only;* and (2) working capital usually is increased or decreased by transactions that involve debits and/or credits to working-capital accounts and debits and/or credits *also* to nonworking-capital accounts.

Reporting direct exchanges

A business may exchange two nonworking-capital items. For example, it is not unusual for a business to acquire an asset by means of a direct trade of another asset. In such cases there may be no cash paid or received. To illustrate, during 1974, the Fina Company acquired a machine worth $5,000. Instead of paying cash or incurring current debt for it, they used (traded) 100 shares of stock in another corporation (designated as Corporation X) that they owned as a long-term investment. The entry made by Fina to record the transaction was:

```
1974:
    Machinery...................................... 5,000
        Long-term Investment (100 shares of
            Corp. X stock)......................         5,000
```

Obviously, this transaction did not increase or decrease working capital. Yet, in effect, there were two economic activities:

(1) A financing activity—the long-term investment was disposed of to "generate" resources (financing) amounting to $5,000.

(2) An investing activity—resources amounting to $5,000 were expended (used) to acquire a fixed asset.

---

[6] When a dividend is declared, working capital is reduced by the amount of the dividend even though payment in cash is at a later date. The dividend payable is recorded as a current liability on declaration date. The cash payment later does not affect working capital since equal debits and credits to working-capital accounts will be made at that time. This distinction is important only when declaration and payment dates fall in different accounting periods.

Prior to APB *Opinion No. 19* (March 1971), transactions such as this were not reported on the old funds statements because working capital was unaffected by the swap. *Opinion No. 19* requires that such transactions be included as "financing and investing activities that did not affect working capital." They now are reported on the statement of changes in financial position as two activities (as if working capital actually increased and decreased by the same amount simultaneously). Such transactions, therefore, are reported under *both* sources and uses as an "in-and-out" item. For example, the swap by the Fina Company is reported in Exhibit 15–3 in two places as follows:

Working Capital From Other Sources:
    Disposal of long-term investment.......... $5,000

Uses of Working Capital:
    Acquisition of equipment................. $5,000

The new statement, in contrast to the old funds statement, is said to include "all financing and investing activities" rather than a very narrow report limited to direct working-capital effects. This is the significant aspect of the new concept of the statement and one of which users should be fully aware. Other examples of direct exchanges (swaps) are (a) settlement of debt with capital stock; (b) exchange of land for land; (c) exchange of machinery for other machinery; and (d) exchange of tangible assets for intangible assets. It is not uncommon now to see one or more direct exchanges reported on the statement of changes in financial position.

The preparation of a statement of changes in financial position is somewhat technical. A worksheet approach is almost essential. An efficient worksheet for this purpose is presented in the Appendix to this chapter.

PART TWO: CHANGES IN FINANCIAL POSITION—CASH BASIS

Cash-basis concept

A statement of changes in financial position prepared on a cash basis is identical in purpose and concept with one prepared on a working-capital basis *except* for the definition of "funds." As explained on page 537, cash, for this purpose, is defined as cash plus short-term investments. Since cash is one element of working capital, the statement on a cash basis will report *more* different types of transactions than would be reported on the working-capital basis. In fact, it will report the effect of *all* transactions that increased or decreased cash during the period. Hence, it is a more detailed statement than one on the working-capital basis.

The Statement of Changes in Financial Position—Cash Basis is shown in Exhibit 15–4 for the Fina Company for the year ended December 31, 1974. Fundamentally, the statement reports the **financing activities** for the period on a **cash-inflow** basis under the caption "Sources of Cash," and the **investing activities** for the period on a **cash-outflow** basis under the caption "Uses of Cash." In contrast to the working-capital basis, there is no "Section B" (comparable to that

Exhibit 15–4

FINA COMPANY, INC.
Statement of Changes in Financial Position—Cash Basis
For the Year Ended December 31, 1974*

Sources of Cash (inflows)†			
From operations:			
Revenues		$100,000	
Add (deduct) adjustments to convert to cash basis:			
Accounts receivable increase		(5,000)	
Cash generated from revenues			$95,000
Expenses		92,000	
Add (deduct) adjustments to convert to cash basis:			
Depreciation expense		(6,000)	
Merchandise inventory decrease		(4,000)	
Accounts payable increase		(2,000)	
Income taxes payable increase		(500)	
Cash disbursed for expenses			79,500
Total cash generated by operations			15,500
From other sources:			
Sale of unissued common stock		11,000	
Disposal of long-term investment (Note A)		5,000	
Total cash generated from other sources			16,000
Total cash generated during the period			31,500
Uses of Cash (outflows)†			
Payment of cash dividend on common stock		7,000	
Payment on bonds payable		8,000	
Payment on notes payable, short-term (nontrade)		4,000	
Acquisition of equipment (Note A)		5,000	
Total cash expended during the period			24,000
Net increase in cash during the period			$ 7,500

Note A: Equipment was acquired in exchange for common stock of the X Corporation, which was being held as a long-term investment.
* Source of data, Exhibit 15–7.
† Often referred to as "Cash Generated" and "Cash Applied," respectively.

shown in Exhibit 15–3) since there is no "internal content of cash" to be reported.

The statement for the Fina Company reports three typical sources of cash: (1) operations, (2) sale of unissued stock, and (3) disposal of an investment. Other common sources of cash are the sales of fixed assets and borrowing. The statement reports four typical uses of cash:

(1) cash dividends, (2) payment of long-term debt, (3) payment of short-term debt, and (4) purchase of fixed assets.

The total sources, $31,500, minus the total uses, $24,000, gives the increase in the cash balance of $7,500 during the period. This increase necessarily must agree with the increase in cash shown on the comparative balance sheets in Exhibit 15–2 (i.e., $37,500 − $30,000 = $7,500).[7]

Sources of cash

The typical sources of cash listed in the preceding paragraph do not need further elaboration, with one exception. Cash inflow (often called cash generated) from operations ($15,500) is a more complex issue because it reflects the **net cash effect** of all the revenue and expense transactions. Further, there are some important distinctions that must be understood between working-capital flows and cash flows from operations.

Operations generally is the primary source of cash for all businesses over the long term, and net income reflects the net effect of operations for the period on the **accrual basis.** As goods and services are sold during the period, there is an inflow of cash from these revenues; however, the cash inflow from the revenues is conditioned by the credit sales of the current and prior periods. To illustrate, assume a company sold goods amounting to $100,000, of which $20,000 remained uncollected at year end. In this case, the cash inflow would be: $100,000, minus the increase of $20,000 in accounts receivable, equals $80,000. Alternatively, if sales totaled $100,000 and, at the same time, accounts receivable decreased by $20,000, cash inflow would be $120,000 for the period. In comparison, the working-capital inflow in each instance was $100,000.

During the period, expenses are incurred that cause a cash outflow; however, the cash outflow for expenses is conditioned by the amount of expenses incurred on credit in the current and prior periods. To illustrate, assume a company incurred expenses during the year of $80,000, of which $10,000 was unpaid at year end. In this case, the cash outflow would be: $80,000, minus the $10,000 increase in accounts payable, equals $70,000. In addition, cash used during the current period to pay last year's expenses must be added to the $70,000. In contrast, the working-capital outflow was $80,000. The amount of the cash inflow from operations, therefore, generally will be different

---

[7] One of several alternate reporting forms starts with "Net Income" under "From operations." Adjustments for noncash items are then reported to derive the amount "Total cash generated by operations, $15,500." The form of presentation in Exhibit 15–2 is easier to understand and better reflects the underlying events. In other respects, the alternate forms tend to be the same.

from net income because of the effect of **noncash revenues and noncash expenses.**

To illustrate the adjustments to net income for the period in order to derive cash inflow (or cash generated) from operations, let's return to the Fina Company. The income statement shown in Exhibit 15–1 reported a net income of $8,000. On the basis of an **analysis** of the revenues on credit and the expenses on credit, including the noncash depreciation expense, the net income was converted to a **cash-inflow** basis as follows:

Revenues (as reported on the income statement; accrual basis)...		$100,000
Deduct increase in accounts receivable (as between the two balance sheets)*....		(5,000)
Cash inflow from revenues (revenues converted to cash basis)......		95,000
Expenses (as reported on the income statement; accrual basis) $60,000 + $32,000 =....	$92,000	
Deduct expense items not requiring cash during the current period (as between the two balance sheets)*:		
Depreciation expense	(6,000)	
Merchandise inventory decrease	(4,000)	
Accounts payable increase	(2,000)	
Income taxes payable increase....	(500)	
Cash outflow for expenses (expenses converted to cash basis)....		79,500
Total cash generated by operations (net income converted to cash basis)....		$ 15,500

* Some items may be added rather than deducted, as illustrated later.

The above computation is reported on the Statement of Changes in Financial Position—Cash Basis, Exhibit 15–4.

Observe in the above computation that the cash inflow generated by operations ($15,500) was *greater* than net income ($8,000). In some instances it will be less than net income. The adjustments to convert reported revenues and expenses (accrual basis) to a cash basis (cash generated from operations) often are quite varied. They may be grouped into 11 different items. The following tabulation is convenient for study and problem-solving purposes.[8]

---

[8] No useful purpose is served by memorizing this tabulation. The rationale for the "plus and minus" adjustments should be understood. It should be freely available for problem-solving purposes. The central purpose is to explain and illustrate the reasons for, and the nature of, the adjustments that are necessary to convert revenues and expenses (i.e., net income) from an accrual basis to a cash basis.

Nature of Item	Plus and Minus Adjustments	Illustration (Fina Company)
Revenue (as reported on income statement, accrual basis).....		$100,000
Adjustments to cash basis:		
1. Decrease in balance of trade receivables...... +		
2. Increase in balance of trade receivables ...... −	−5,000	
Revenue adjusted to cash basis............		$95,000
Expenses (as reported on income statement, accrual basis).....		92,000
Adjustments to cash basis:		
Cost of goods sold:		
3. Decrease in merchandise inventory........... −	−4,000	
4. Increase in merchandise inventory.......... +		
5. Increase in *trade* payables.................. −	−2,000	
6. Decrease in *trade* payables................ +		
Expenses (other than cost of goods sold):		
7. Increase in balance of accrued (unpaid) liabilities............................ −	− 500	
8. Decrease in balance of accrued (unpaid) liabilities............................ +		
9. Decrease in balance of prepayments.......... −		
10. Increase in balance of prepayments......... +		
11. Period's depreciation, amortization and depletion............................. −	−6,000	
Expenses adjusted to cash basis...........		79,500
Net cash generated from operations.................		$15,500

Direct (noncash) exchanges

Direct exchanges of noncash items for other noncash items are not uncommon. For example, a company may acquire an asset by swapping another asset for it and no cash difference is paid or received; or a company may retire its bonds payable by issuing common stock to the bondholders. If there is no cash difference involved (i.e., there was no "boot"), cash will not be increased or decreased. Nevertheless, such transactions must be included on the statement of changes in financial position "as if" there were simultaneous investing and financing activities (required by APB *Opinion No. 19*). The inclusion of these noncash exchanges is necessary in order for the statement to report on an all-resources basis (see page 536).

These types of transactions were discussed and illustrated on page 543 in respect to the statement on the working-capital basis. Trades and swaps are included on the cash-basis statements in the same manner as described there. For example, the exchange of stock of the X Corporation, held by the Fina Company as a long-term investment, for machinery having a fair-market value of $5,000 is reported in Exhibit 15–4 (cash basis) as a financing activity (source of cash) and also as an investing activity (use of cash). This item was similarly reported on Exhibit 15–3 (working-capital basis).

Summary   The preceding discussions should enable you to understand and interpret a statement of changes in financial position prepared on either a working-capital or cash basis. You should be able to understand the basic differences between a working-capital and a cash-basis statement. The concept of working capital, or cash, provided by **operations** is a particularly important aspect of the statement of changes in financial position. This concept focuses on the conversion of reported net income (i.e., revenues and expenses), an accrual-basis amount, to either working capital generated from operations or cash generated from operations. The statement of changes in financial position is relatively easy to understand and interpret if this basic concept is understood.

Although not essential to understanding and interpreting the statement, the technical aspects of preparing the statement, by means of a worksheet, are presented in the Appendix. Knowledge of the preparation procedures will serve to increase your level of understanding of this important statement. The statement of changes in financial position is prepared primarily by analyzing the balance sheet and the income statement, which are prepared from the accounts.

Appendix   PROCEDURES TO DEVELOP THE
STATEMENT OF CHANGES
IN FINANCIAL POSITION

The complexities involved in developing a statement of changes in financial position in situations where there are numerous transactions suggest the need for the worksheet approach. Worksheets are simply a matter of convenience. They are designed for orderly grouping of essential data, for an efficient and simplified approach to the analytical processes required, and for straightforward derivation of the basic data needed for the formal statement. In Chapter 5, Exhibit 5–2, a worksheet was illustrated and explained that was evolved for developing the income statement and the balance sheet. The development of the statement of changes in financial position similarly suggests the need for an appropriately designed convenience worksheet. A worksheet for this purpose may follow one of several mechanical approaches. Those presented in this chapter are widely used because (a) they are simple to understand; (b) they involve, in summary, repetition of certain basic accounting entries; and (c) they are capable of handling complex and voluminous data.[9] Separate worksheets will be presented for the working-capital basis and for the cash basis.

---

[9] Some worksheets are designed mechanically, so that the student is forced to *reverse* the debits and credits in the analysis, which frequently causes considerable confusion initially. In contrast, strictly from the pedagogical viewpoint, a T-account approach is quite useful. Although it is particularly useful for teaching purposes, it is not used in the real world of accounting because of its mechanical unsophistication and bulk. The worksheet presented in this chapter closely parallels

WORKSHEET FOR THE WORKING CAPITAL BASIS

In the preceding discussions, we emphasized that the *causes* of the changes in financial position are to be found in the *non*working-capital accounts. Therefore, we need a worksheet that will facilitate analysis of the **nonworking-capital accounts** in such a way that we can "pull out" the *sources* and *uses* of working capital that occurred during the period in an orderly and efficient manner. Since the changes to be explained are between the beginning and ending balance sheets (see page 536), the worksheet should incorporate (a) the beginning balance-sheet amounts; (b) the ending balance-sheet amounts; and (c) provision for an *analysis* of the transactions that occurred between the two balance-sheet dates. Observe in the skeleton worksheet shown below that a column has been provided for each of these items. The *analysis* has as its purpose identification of the *sources* of working capital and the *uses* of working capital during the period between the two balance-sheet dates. Thus, the skeleton worksheet below has three basic side captions: (1) a listing of the balance-sheet accounts since they will be "analyzed"; (2) sources of working capital; and (3) uses of working capital.

The skeleton worksheet form is as follows:

Skeleton Worksheet to Develop the Statement of Changes in Financial Position

	(a) Beginning Balance Sheet	(b) Analysis of Interim Entries	(c) Ending Balance Sheet
(1) Balance Sheet Accounts (listed)			
(2) Sources of Working Capital			
(3) Uses of Working Capital			

Utilizing the data from the beginning and ending balance sheets given in Exhibit 15–2 for the Fina Company, we can set up an efficient worksheet as shown in Exhibit 15–5. Note the three column headings explained above and the five side captions. The three side captions listed in the skeleton worksheet have been expanded to five because it is helpful to separately identify working capital (Item 1) and the increase or decrease in working capital (Item 5).

In completing the worksheet, the first step is to enter the amounts from the two balance sheets in the first and last columns. Since we are

the T-account approach since each account is analyzed in a straightforward debit and credit fashion. Also, the worksheet is so designed that the bottom portion can suffice for the formal statement in many problem situations.

analyzing the nonworking-capital accounts, each one is listed separately. The working-capital accounts are not listed individually; however, the amount of working capital for each date can be entered for balancing purposes (Item 1). The second step is to complete the *"Analysis of Interim Entries"* in the middle column, which has been split into debit and credit columns.

The "Analysis of Interim Entries" has as its purpose the analysis (in summary fashion) of all changes during the period in each *nonworking-capital* account entered on the worksheet. These changes are analyzed to determine those that either (a) generated working capital (increased working capital), (b) utilized or decreased working capital, and (c) those that did not affect working capital. The analytical entries are entered directly on the worksheet in the normal debit–credit fashion; however, instead of entering amounts in the working-capital accounts

Exhibit 15–5

FINA COMPANY, INC.
Worksheet to Develop Statement of Changes in Financial Position—Working-Capital Basis
For the Year Ended December 31, 1974

	Balances Dec. 31, 1973	Analysis of Interim Entries		Ending Balances Dec. 31, 1974
		Debit	Credit	
Debits				
(1) *Working Capital**	40,000	XXXXX	XXXXX	50,000
(2) *Nonworking-capital Accounts*				
Investments, long-term	6,000			1,000
Equipment (net)	60,000			59,000
	106,000			110,000
Credits				
Bonds payable	40,000			32,000
Capital stock (par $10)	50,000			60,000
Contributed capital, in excess of par	5,000			6,000
Retained earnings	11,000			12,000
	106,000			110,000
(3) *Sources of Working Capital*				
From operations:				
Net income				
Adjustments to net income:				
From other sources:				
(4) *Uses of Working Capital*				
(5) *Change—Increase (decrease) in Working Capital*				

* Current assets minus current liabilities. This line is inserted for balancing purposes only. Without it, the debits and credits in the first and last columns would not balance.

(they are not on the worksheet), the normal debits to working-capital accounts are entered in the lower section as "Sources of Working Capital" and the credits are entered as "Uses of Working Capital." It is important to understand that, when the worksheet analysis is completed, the interim entries for it will "account for" the change during the period for each nonworking-capital account listed on the worksheet.

The completed worksheet for the Fina Company is reflected in Exhibit 15–6. Data, in addition to the two balance sheets, needed for analytical purposes must be selected from the income statement and other accounting records. Detailed explanations of the source of the data and each *analytical entry* on the worksheet is given below. Worksheet entries are keyed for ready reference in study.

(a) Net income (from the income statement)—As explained earlier, net income generates working capital. The original entry for net income was: Debit—Income summary; Credit—Retained earnings. We record this is an *analytical entry* on the worksheet in essentially the same manner; that is;

```
Sources of Working Capital: From Operations.. 8,000
       Retained Earnings.......................      8,000
```

(b) Depreciation expense (from the income statement)—This expense was originally recorded as a debit to Depreciation expense and a credit to Allowance for Depreciation. It did not increase or decrease working capital; however, it did serve to reduce net income. Since it was a nonworking-capital deduction in deriving net income, it must be added back to net income to derive "Working Capital from Operations." This is accomplished on the worksheet by essentially following the original entry; the worksheet *analytical entry* to adjust net income for depreciation would be:

```
Sources of Working Capital: From Operations.. 6,000
       Allowance for Depreciation..............      6,000
```

Note: Amortization expense on intangible assets and depletion expense on natural resources would be treated the same way.

(c) Sales of capital stock (from the balance sheet and other records) —The worksheet reflects a $10,000 increase in capital stock and a $1,000 increase in contributed capital, in excess of par, during the period. Inspection of the records revealed that 1,000 shares of unissued capital stock were sold at $11 per share. The original entry was: Debit—Cash, $11,000; Credits—Capital Stock, $10,000, and Contributed Capital in Excess of Par: $1,000. Clearly, this transaction

Exhibit 15–6

FINA COMPANY, INC.
Worksheet to Develop Statement of Changes in Financial Position—Working-Capital Basis
For the Year Ended December 31, 1974

	Balances Dec. 31, 1973	Analysis of Interim Entries Debit	Credit	Ending Balances Dec. 31, 1974
Debits				
(1) *Working Capital*	40,000	XXXXX	XXXXX	50,000
(2) *Nonworking-capital Accounts*				
Investments, long-term	6,000		(f-1) 5,000	1,000
Equipment (net)	60,000	(f-2) 5,000	(b) 6,000	59,000
	106,000			110,000
Credits				
Bonds payable	40,000	(e) 8,000		32,000
Capital stock (par $10)	50,000		(c) 10,000	60,000
Contributed capital in excess of par	5,000		(c) 1,000	6,000
Retained earnings	11,000	(d) 7,000	(a) 8,000	12,000
	106,000			110,000
(3) *Sources of Working Capital*				
From operations:				
Net income		(a)† 8,000		
Adjustments to net income:				
Depreciation expense		(b) 6,000		
From other sources:				
Sale of unissued capital stock		(c) 11,000		
Disposal of long-term investment*		(f-1) 5,000		
(4) *Uses of Working Capital*				
Payment of dividend on capital stock			(d) 7,000	
Payment on bonds payable			(e) 8,000	
Acquisition of equipment*			(f-2) 5,000	
(5) Change—Increase in Working Capital				
(per line 1 above)			10,000	
		30,000	30,000	

* Equipment acquired in exchange for common stock of the X Corporation, which was being held as a long-term investment.
† These notations are keyed for ready reference to the textual discussions of the worksheet starting on page 552.

generated working capital in the amount of $11,000. The original entry essentially is repeated as a worksheet *analytical entry* as shown below:

```
Sources of Working Capital: From Other
    Sources.................................. 11,000
        Capital Stock........................          10,000
        Contributed Capital in Excess of Par...           1,000
```

(d) Dividends declared and paid (company records)—During the year, the Fina Company declared and paid a $7,000 cash dividend. The original entry to record this dividend was: Debit—Retained Earnings (dividends paid); Credit—Cash. Clearly, working capital was decreased by this transaction. The original entry essentially is repeated as a worksheet *analytical entry* as follows:

```
Retained Earnings............................ 7,000
      Uses of Working Capital..................          7,000
```

At this point you should observe on the worksheet that for the line "Retained earnings" the beginning balance (a credit) $11,000, minus the dividend (a debit) $7,000, plus net income (a credit) $8,000, equals the ending balance of $12,000. Similarly, as subsequent analytical entries are made, the remaining change in the balance of each nonworking-capital account will be exactly accounted for, at which time the worksheet is complete.

(e) Payment on bonds payable (balance sheet and other records)— The worksheet reflects a decrease of $8,000 in the balance in bonds payable. Other records reveal that, during the year, a payment of this amount was made on the bonds; the original entry was: Debit—Bonds Payable, $8,000; Credit—Cash, $8,000. Clearly, working capital was decreased by this transaction. Consistent with the original entry, the *analytical entry* on the worksheet is:

```
Bonds Payable................................ 8,000
      Uses of Working Capital..................          8,000
```

Note that this entry "clears" the bonds payable line.

(f) Exchange of long-term investment for equipment (company records)—Observe that the worksheet reflects a decrease in long-term investments of $5,000. Other records revealed that the company acquired some machinery and paid for it with some common stock of the X Corporation, which was being held as a long-term investment. It was a direct swap and no cash was disbursed or received. The original transaction was recorded as follows: Debit—Machinery, $5,000; Credit —Long-term Investments, $5,000. Clearly, this transaction completely bypasses working capital since it was an outright trade.

Since *all* financing and investing activities must be included in the statement of changes in financial position, analytical entries must be made on the worksheet as if there were two transactions: one for the sale of the investments and another for the purchase of the machinery. These *two analytical entries* on the worksheet are as follows:

(f-1)   To record the financing activity:

```
Sources of Working Capital: From Other
   Sources...................................... 5,000
         Investments, Long-term..................          5,000
```

(f-2)   To record the investing activity:

```
Machinery...................................... 5,000
      Uses of Working Capital.................          5,000
```

Upon completion of the above analytical entries on the worksheet, observe that the amount of change from the beginning to the ending balance for *each* nonworking-capital account on the worksheet has been accounted for exactly. This indicates that the analysis of the interim entries is complete. The worksheet is then completed by (a) drawing a double line under the two middle columns just above "Sources of Working Capital"; (b) determining the difference between the debits and credits in the lower portion of the worksheet ($10,000 for Fina); and (c) entering this difference to balance as the increase or decrease in working capital. Observe that, in the absence of error, this difference will correspond exactly with the difference on the first line of the worksheet ($50,000 − $40,000); that is, it will agree with the change in working capital for the period. This is a valuable check on the accuracy of your analysis of the changes.[10]

The bottom portion of the worksheet provides the detailed data for the statement of changes in financial position. The statement presented in Exhibit 15–3, with appropriate captions added, was taken directly from this portion of the worksheet.

WORKSHEET FOR CASH-FLOW BASIS

A facilitating worksheet to develop the statement of changes in financial position on a *cash basis* is fundamentally the same as that illustrated for working capital. The worksheet, however, is somewhat more tedious since *all of the balance-sheet accounts,* except the Cash account itself, must be analyzed to determine the *causes* of the inflows and outflows of cash. Simply reporting the debits and credits to the

---

[10] In studying the worksheet, you should have observed that (a) the *analytical entries* follow very closely the debits and credits of the original entry in the accounts; and (b) there is no provision thereon for debiting and crediting the individual accounts comprising working capital. The mechanical effect is that the original debits and credits to working-capital accounts are entered in the analytical entries as *debits to working capital* provided and as *credits to working capital* applied to the bottom portion of the worksheet. These mechanical features tend to "lead" the analyst to the correct *analytical entry* for each situation.

Cash account does not meet the purposes and specifications of the statement of changes in financial position. The statement must reflect the basic causes or reasons for the inflows and outflows of cash during the period, and, in addition, must include all noncash financing and investing transactions, such as the exchange of a long-term investment for machinery previously illustrated. A primary problem to be resolved on the worksheet is the conversion of revenues and expenses, as reported on the income statement on the accrual basis, to a strictly cash-flow basis (that is, to cash flow from operations). The nature of this conversion was explained on pages 547 and 548.

The worksheet presented in Exhibit 15–6 for working capital, adapted slightly, will conveniently accommodate the analysis necessary to develop a statement of changes in financial position on a cash basis. The adapted worksheet on a cash basis, completed for the Fina Company, is shown in Exhibit 15–7. It maintains all of the desirable mechanical features of the former worksheet. The analytical entries on the worksheet focus on the conversion from an accrual to a cash basis. The *analytical entries* are made in a straightforward manner as before. The worksheet is set up with precisely the same three column headings as before. Likewise, the five major side captions are essentially the same. The primary difference to be observed is that *all* of the accounts (and their balances) reported on the two balance sheets are captioned on the worksheet in the left column and the amounts are entered in first and last amount columns.[11] To illustrate, compare these columns with the asset, liability, and owners' equity account balances given for the Fina Company in Exhibit 15–2.

The final step in completing the worksheet is to record the *analytical entries* on the worksheet, similar to the approach illustrated and explained for the working-capital worksheet. The analytical entries are based upon data provided by the two balance sheets, the income statement, and other accounting records. Data, including the sources, to complete the analytical entries follow for the Fina Company for 1974. (Entries (a) through (f) are identical with those previously illustrated and explained for the working-capital analysis, pages 552 thru 555; therefore, the detailed *explanations* are not repeated.)

(a)   Revenues and expenses (from income statement)—The *analytical worksheet* entry, essentially the same as the original entry, is:

```
Sources of Cash: Revenues................. 100,000
      Expenses.............................          92,000
      Retained Earnings....................           8,000
```

---

[11] Observe that the Cash account is listed only for balancing purposes. It is blocked out for the analytical interim entries. Debits and credits to Cash in the original entries in the accounts are entered in the bottom position of the worksheet as *cash sources* (debits), or as *cash applied* (credits), as was done for working capital in the prior worksheet.

Exhibit 15–7

FINA COMPANY, INC.
Worksheet to Develop Statement of Changes in Financial Position—Cash Basis
For the Year Ended December 31, 1974

	Balances Dec. 31, 1973	Analysis of Interim Entries Debit		Analysis of Interim Entries Credit		Ending Balances Dec. 31, 1974
Debits						
(1) Cash Account	30,000	XXXXX		XXXXX		37,500
(2) Noncash Accounts						
Accounts receivable (net)	20,000	(h)	5,000			25,000
Merchandise inventory	24,000			(i)	4,000	20,000
Investments, long-term	6,000			(f-1)	5,000	1,000
Equipment (net)	60,000	(f-2)	5,000	(b)	6,000	59,000
	140,000					142,500
Credits						
Accounts payable	20,000			(j)	2,000	22,000
Income taxes payable				(k)	500	500
Notes payable, short-term (nontrade)	14,000	(g)	4,000			10,000
Bonds payable	40,000	(e)	8,000			32,000
Capital stock (par $10)	50,000			(c)	10,000	60,000
Contributed capital in excess of par	5,000			(c)	1,000	6,000
Retained earnings	11,000	(d)	7,000	(a)	8,000	12,000
	140,000					142,500
(3) **Sources of Cash**						
From operations:						
Revenues (accrual basis)		(a)†	100,000			
Adjustments to cash basis:						
Accounts receivable increase				(h)	5,000	
Expenses (accrual basis)				(a)	92,000	
Adjustments to cash basis:						
Depreciation expense		(b)	6,000			
Merchandise inventory decrease		(i)	4,000			
Accounts payable increase		(j)	2,000			
Income taxes payable increase		(k)	500			
From other sources:						
Sale of unissued capital stock		(c)	11,000			
Disposal of long-term investment*		(f-1)	5,000			
(4) **Uses of Cash**						
Payment of cash dividend				(d)	7,000	
Payment on bonds payable				(e)	8,000	
Acquisition of equipment*				(f-2)	5,000	
Payment on note payable, short-term (nontrade)				(g)	4,000	
(5) Change—Increase in cash (per line 1 above)					7,500	
			128,500		128,500	

* Equipment was acquired in exchange for common stock of the X Corporation, which was being held as a long-term investment.

† These notations are keyed for ready reference to the textual discussions of the worksheet starting on page 556.

This entry represents the transfer of net income of $8,000 from income summary to retained earnings. To facilitate analysis on the worksheet, total revenue and total expense amounts (that comprise net income) are entered separately.

(b)   Depreciation expense (from the income statement)—The *analytical entry* serves to record depreciation expense as an adjustment (added back) to expenses in deriving cash outflow paid for expenses. The analytical entry is:

```
Sources of Cash: Expenses (adjustment)....... 6,000
    Allowance for Depreciation..............          6,000
```

(c)   Sale of unissued capital stock (from balance sheet and other records)—The sale of unissued capital stock for $11,000 generated cash. The original entry is essentially recorded as the *analytical entry* on the worksheet as follows:

```
Sources of Cash: From Other Sources........ 11,000
    Capital Stock........................          10,000
    Contributed Capital in Excess of Par...           1,000
```

(d)   Cash dividends paid (company records)—The payment of a $7,000 dividend involved the expenditure of cash. The original entry is essentially recorded as the *analytical entry* as follows:

```
Retained Earnings........................... 7,000
    Uses of Cash............................          7,000
```

(e)   Payment on bonds payable (balance sheets and other records)—This transaction involved the expenditure of $8,000 cash payment on the bonds. The *analytical entry* is:

```
Bonds Payable............................... 8,000
    Uses of Cash............................          8,000
```

(f)   Exchange of long-term investment for equipment (company records)—The company acquired equipment, paying with some long-term investments being held rather than with cash. This transaction effectively bypassed cash; however, the statement of changes in financial position must report all financing and investing activities. Therefore, this transaction is analyzed as if there were two transactions: (1) the sale of long-term investments—a financing activity; and (2) the purchase of equipment —an investment activity. Accordingly, the *two analytical entries* are:

```
(f-1)  Sources of Cash: From Other Sources... 5,000
                Long-term Investments............         5,000
(f-2)  Equipment............................. 5,000
                Uses of Cash......................         5,000
```

(g)   Payment on current liability, short-term note payable (nontrade) (balance sheets)—During the period, the Fina Company paid $4,000 on nontrade, short-term notes payable, evidenced on the worksheet by the fact that the balance of this account decreased by this amount during the year. Thus, cash was used to reduce liabilities. The original entry was: Debit—Notes Payable, Short-term (nontrade); Credit—Cash. Therefore, the analytical entry would be:

```
Notes Payable, Short-term (nontrade)......... 4,000
       Uses of Cash...........................          4,000
```

We may note that the above analytical entry reflects the net change in nontrade notes payable during the year. It is a summary entry. There may have been several debit and/or credit entries to the note account during the year; however, for analytical purposes, only the net effect is reflected. This is true in respect to all of the analytical entries. Most of them are summary entries that reflect the net effect of numerous entries to the accounts being analyzed.

(h)   Accounts receivable, change in balance (balance sheets)—The worksheet reveals that the accounts receivable balance increased by $5,000. This amount reflects a difference between sales revenue on the accrual basis and cash inflow from operations. Consequently, this reflects an adjustment (reduction) to revenues to derive cash inflow from operations. The analytical entry to reflect this adjustment would be:

```
Accounts Receivable........................ 5,000
       Sources of Cash: Revenues (adjustment)...          5,000
```

Note that this involves a "credit" under Sources of Cash on the worksheet. The credit reflects the fact that this amount must be *subtracted* from revenues in deriving cash inflow from operations (also see page 548).

(i)   Inventory of merchandise, change in balance (balance sheets) —The two balance sheets revealed that inventory decreased by $4,000 during the year. This means that $4,000 of the cost-of-goods-sold amount of $60,000 (page 538) was represented by goods withdrawn from inventory rather than being purchased for cash this period. This amount reflects a difference in cost of goods sold between the accrual and cash basis. Therefore, since it represents a noncash expense this period, an adjustment (deduction) to expense must be made to derive cash outflow for expenses. The *analytical entry* to reflect this adjustment would be:

```
Sources of Cash: Expenses (adjustment)....... 4,000
        Inventory...............................       4,000
```

(j)   Accounts payable, change in balance (balance sheets)—The worksheets indicates that accounts payable (trade) increased by $2,000 during the year. This means that expenses (including cost of goods sold) amounting to $2,000 were deducted on the income statement but are not yet paid in cash. Therefore, an adjustment (addition) to expenses must be made to derive cash outflow for expenses during the period. The *analytical entry* to reflect this adjustment would be:

```
Sources of Cash: Expenses (adjustment)....... 2,000
        Accounts Payable.......................       2,000
```

(k)   Income taxes payable, change in balance (balance sheet)—The worksheet indicates an increase in income taxes payable (a current liability) of $500. Since income tax expense is reported on the income statement, this amount reflects a difference between the amount accrued and the amount paid in cash. Therefore, the $500 represents an *adjustment* (addition) to expenses to derive cash outflow to this expense. The *analytical entry* on the worksheet would be:

```
Sources of Cash: Expenses (adjustments).......... 500
        Income Taxes Payable.......................      500
```

After the above analytical entries are recorded on the worksheet, inspection of the worksheet will reveal that the change between the beginning and ending balances on each line (i.e., each balance-sheet account) will have been accounted for exactly. This indicates that the worksheet analysis is finished. At this point the double lines should be drawn across the two middle amount columns (Analysis of Interim Entries) just above the caption "Sources of Cash." The change in cash for the period, as indicated on Line 1, should be entered at the bottom of the worksheet and the bottom portion of the worksheet summed. The debit and credit columns should then be equal, which provides a partial check on the accuracy of the results.

The data provided at the bottom of the worksheet, with appropriate captions added, were used directly in preparing the formal Statement of Changes in Financial Position—Cash Basis as reflected in Exhibit 15–4.

Summary The annual financial statements must include, as a minimum, an income statement, a balance sheet, and a statement of changes in financial position. The latter statement has as its central purpose the explanation of the causes of the changes in assets, liabilities, and owners' equity that occurred during the period. It accomplishes this purpose by reporting the financing activities (sources of funds for the business) and the investing activities (uses of funds) during the period.

The primary source of funds during each period generally is operations. The sale of goods and services (revenues) cause an inflow of funds to the business during the period. The incurring of expenses during the period causes an outflow of funds; therefore, net income, adjusted for the nonfund items, represents a net source of funds. In the statement of changes in financial position, net income is converted to funds generated from operations. Other common sources of funds are the sale of fixed assets, borrowing, and the sale of capital stock.

The common uses of funds are the purchase of fixed assets, payment of debts, and payment of cash dividends.

Understanding and interpreting the statement of changes in financial position is not difficult; however, preparation of the statement is somewhat technical.

Important terms

Financing activities
Investing activities
Working captial

Direct exchanges
Working capital flow
Cash flow

Questions for discussion

1. What are the three basic statements that are now required to be included in the annual financial statements? Fundamentally, what does each report?
2. What "changes" are reported by the statement of changes in financial position?

3. What are the primary sources and uses of funds in a business?
4. Define working capital.
5. What are the two basic sections on the statement of changes in financial position—working-capital basis? Why is the second section considered by some to be redundant?
6. Explain the difference between (a) changes in the internal content of working capital and (b) causes of the changes in working capital.
7. Explain why net income (i.e., operations) is often the primary source of working capital in a business in the long term.
8. In developing "Working Capital Generated by Operations" on the statement of changes in financial position, why are depreciation, amortization of intangible assets, and depletion added back to net income?
9. Explain why a long-term loan affects working capital but a current or short-term loan does not.
10. Why are direct exchanges reported on the statement of changes in financial position although they do not change working capital?
11. What is the essential difference between a statement of changes in financial position (a) on a working-capital basis and (b) on a cash basis?
12. Company X acquired a tract of land in exchange for a $10,000 bond payable. Should this noncash, nonworking-capital exchange be included on the statement of changes in financial position (a) on the working-capital basis or (b) on the cash basis?
13. Assume you are completing a statement of changes in financial position—cash basis and have the data listed below. On a separate sheet, complete the blanks to the right.

Revenues (accrual basis).............................		$80,000	
Increase in accounts receivable................	$1,400	———	
Cash inflow from receivables...............			$———
Expenses (accrual basis).............................		70,000	
Depreciation expense.........................	1,500	———	
Amortization of patent.......................	200	———	
Decrease in merchandise inventory............	2,200	———	
Increase in accounts payable.................	1,000	———	
Cash outflow for expenses..................			———
Cash generated from operations for the period........			———

14. As a statement user interested in the statement of changes in financial position, would you prefer it on (a) the working-capital basis or (b) the cash basis? Explain.

Exercises E15–1. The following statement has just been prepared by the Wilson Company:

WILSON COMPANY
Statement of Changes in Financial Position—Working-Capital Basis
For the Year Ended December 31, 1974

Sources of Working Capital
From operations:
Net income.. $ 2,000
Add expenses not requiring working capital:
Depreciation expense............................ 4,000
Patent amortization expense..................... 1,000
Total working capital generated by operations .... $ 7,000

From other sources:
Sale of stock..................................... 10,000
Long-term loan.................................... 33,000
Sale of land (at cost)............................. 5,000
Total working capital from other sources. 48,000
Total working capital generated during the period 55,000

Uses of Working Capital
Acquisition of machinery.... 22,000
Payment of mortgage 20,000
Cash dividend.................................... 12,000
Total working capital applied during the period 54,000
Net increase in working capital during the period........... $ 1,000

Changes in Working-Capital Accounts

	Balances December 31		Working-Capital Increase (Decrease)
	1974	1973	
Current assets:			
Cash..............................	$ 1,000	$ 9,000	($ 8,000)
Accounts receivable.................	31,000	24,000	7,000
Inventory.........................	38,000	21,000	17,000
Total current assets	70,000	54,000	
Current liabilities:			
Accounts payable...................	18,000	15,000	(3,000)
Short-term notes payable	22,000	10,000	(12,000)
Total current liabilities	40,000	25,000	
Working Capital	$30,000	$29,000	$ 1,000

Required:

(a) Was there an increase in working capital?

(b) What was the primary source of working capital?

(c) What does your answer to (b) suggest as to the future potential of the company to generate working capital?

(d) Can you spot a potential problem in respect to the long-term and short-term liabilities?

(e) Explain how working capital of $55,000 was generated during the period when only $2,000 net income was earned.

(f) Assess the soundness of the cash dividend.

(g) Assess the cash-flow potentials of the company.

E15–2. The Darby Company has never prepared a statement of changes in financial position. At the end of 1974 the company bookkeeper, following instructions, assembled the following data (which has been determined to be correct) for such a statement:

		Balances at Dec. 31	
		1973	1974
(1)	From the Balance Sheet:		
	Current Assets:		
	Cash	$15,000	$20,000
	Accounts receivable (net)..................	24,000	17,000
	Merchandise inventory.....................	30,000	27,000
	Current Liabilities:		
	Accounts payable	(19,000)	(15,000)
	Notes payable, short-term	(10,000)	(12,000)
	Working capital....................	$40,000	$37,000
(2)	From the Worksheet:		
	Net income..............................		$21,000
	Depreciation expense		4,500
	Amortization of patent....................		500
	Purchase of fixed assets		(6,000)
	Sale of fixed assets (no gain or loss)		2,000
	Payment of long-term note payable		(40,000)
	Issuance of bonds payable.................		30,000
	Sale of common stock		10,000
	Payment of dividend on common stock		(25,000)
	Difference.......................		$ 3,000

Required:

Utilize the above data to prepare a statement of changes in financial position—working-capital basis for 1974. No worksheet is needed; the above data were taken directly from a worksheet.

E15–3. The White Company has completed preparation of the income statement and the balance sheet at year end, December 31, 1974. A worksheet to develop a statement of changes in financial position also has been developed. The balance sheet and the worksheet provided the following data:

		Balances at Dec. 31	
		1973	1974
(1)	From Balance Sheet:		
	Current Assets:		
	Cash	$ 8,000	$15,000
	Accounts receivable (net)..................	17,000	12,000
	Inventory	15,000	18,000
	Current Liabilities:		
	Accounts payable	10,000	12,000
	Notes payable, short-term.................	18,000	13,000
(2)	From Worksheet:		
	Net income..............................		$20,000
	Depreciation expense......................		6,000
	Purchase of long-term investment...........		15,000
	Payment of long-term note.................		5,000
	Sale of unissued capital stock...............		10,000
	Payment of cash dividend..................		8,000
	Purchased land for future plant site, issued		
	capital stock as payment..................		25,000

Required:

Prepare a statement of changes in financial position—working-capital basis.

E15–4. The accounting department of the Simons Company assembled the following data at December 31, 1974, end of the accounting period, as a basis for preparing a statement of changes in financial position —cash basis:

Transaction	Amount	
Net income (Revenue $200,000 − Expenses $168,000)......	$ 32,000	
Depreciation expense..................................	7,000	
Purchase of fixed assets for cash........................		$ 42,000
Accrued wages payable increase..........................	4,000	
Inventory decrease.....................................	3,000	
Accounts payable decrease..............................		8,000
Payment of cash dividend on common stock..............		20,000
Amortization of patent.................................	1,000	
Payment on short-term note payable (nontrade)...........		25,000
Sale of common stock for cash.........................	15,000	
Sale of fixed assets for cash (no gain or loss).............	9,000	
Accounts receivable increase............................		6,000
Long-term borrowing during the period..................	50,000	
Purchase long-term investment, stock X Co. (cash)........		30,000
Difference—decrease in cash.....................	10,000	
	$131,000	$131,000

Required:

Utilize the above data to prepare a statement of changes in financial position—cash basis. Assume all of the above amounts are correct. No worksheet is required; the above data were taken directly from a worksheet.

E15–5. The Watkins Company has completed the income statement and the balance sheet at December 31, 1974. The following data were taken from a worksheet completed as a basis for the statement of changes in financial position:

Net income (Revenues $150,000 − Expenses $128,000)....	$22,000
Depreciation expense...................................	4,000
Purchase of fixed assets for cash........................	15,000
Sale of long-term investment (at cost) for cash...........	6,000
Inventory increase during the period....................	3,000
Paid cash dividends....................................	8,000
Borrowed on short-term note...........................	20,000
Accounts payable decrease.............................	2,000
Payment of long-term note.............................	30,000
Acquired land for future use, issued capital stock in payment...	12,000

Required:

Prepare the statement of changes in financial position—cash basis. (Hint: Cash decreased by $6,000 during the year.)

E15–6.   Use the data given below to compute (a) total working capital generated by operations and (b) total cash generated by operations.

Transaction	(a) Working-Capital Basis	(b) Cash Basis
Net income reported (accrual basis)*	$18,000	$18,000
Depreciation expense, $2,000		
Increase in accrued wages payable, $1,500		
Decrease in trade accounts receivable, $800		
Increase in merchandise inventory, $2,300		
Amortization of patents, $300		
Increase in bonds payable, $10,000		
Decrease in trade accounts payable, $700		
Sale of common stock, $5,000		
Total working capital generated by operations	$	
Total cash generated by operations		$

* Revenues $78,000 − Expenses $60,000 = $18,000.

E15–7.   (Based on the Appendix.) The Humber Company is developing the annual financial statements at December 31, 1974. The income statement and the balance sheet have been completed and the statement of changes in financial position—working-capital basis is to be developed. The income statement and the balance sheet are summarized below:

	Balances, December 31	
	1973	1974
Balance Sheet:		
Cash	$12,800	$10,800
Accounts receivable (net)	9,000	10,500
Merchandise inventory	6,600	5,000
Fixed assets (net)	40,000	43,000
Patent	3,000	2,700
	$71,400	$72,000
Accounts payable	$11,000	$ 9,000
Income taxes payable	400	500
Notes payable, long-term	10,000	5,000
Capital stock (no-par)	42,000	45,000
Retained earnings	8,000	12,500
	$71,400	$72,000

Income Statement for 1974:	
Sales	$60,000
Cost of goods sold	35,000
Gross margin	25,000
Expenses (including depreciation, $4,000, and patent amortization, $300)	18,000
Net Income	$ 7,000

Additional data for 1974:
    Purchased fixed assets for cash, $7,000
    Paid $5,000 on long-term note payable
    Sold capital stock for $3,000 cash
    Declared and paid a $2,500 dividend on capital stock

Required:

(a) Based upon the above data, prepare a worksheet to develop the statement of changes in financial position—working-capital basis.

(Hint: Working capital decreased $200.)

(b) Prepare the formal statement of changes in financial position —working-capital basis.

E15–8. (Based on the Appendix.) The Whippet Company is developing the annual financial statements at December 31, 1974. The statements are complete except for the statement of changes in financial position—cash basis. The completed balance sheet and the income statement are summarized below:

	Balances at Dec. 31	
	1973	1974
Balance Sheet:		
Cash....................................	$ 20,000	$ 31,500
Accounts receivable (net)....................	26,000	25,000
Merchandise inventory......................	40,000	38,000
Fixed assets (net)..........................	64,000	67,000
	$150,000	$161,500
Accounts payable..........................	$ 24,000	$ 27,000
Accrued wages payable......................	500	400
Notes payable, long-term....................	35,000	30,000
Capital stock (no-par)......................	70,000	80,000
Retained earnings..........................	20,500	24,100
	$150,000	$161,500
Income Statement for 1974:		
Sales.....................................		$ 90,000
Cost of goods sold..........................		(52,000)
Expenses (including depreciation expense, $4,000).................................		(32,000)
		$ 6,000

Required:

(1) Set up a worksheet (cash basis) to develop the statement of changes in financial position—cash basis. Analytical entries should be made for the following:

a. Net income—from income statement.

b. Depreciation expense—from income statement.

c. Purchased fixed assets for cash, $7,000.

d. Paid $5,000 on the long-term note payable.

e. Sold unissued common stock for $10,000 cash.

f. Paid a $2,400 cash dividend on capital stock.

g. Accounts receivable decrease—from balance sheets.

h. Merchandise inventory decrease—from balance sheets.

i. Accounts payable increase—from balance sheets.

j. Accrued wages payable decrease—from balance sheets.

(2) Based upon the completed worksheet, prepare the formal statement of changes in financial position—cash basis.

Problems P15–1. The following statement has just been prepared by the Baker Corporation:

BAKER CORPORATION
Statement of Changes in Financial Position—Cash Basis
For the Year Ended December 31, 1974

Sources of Cash
From operations:

Revenues.....................................	$60,000	
Add (deduct) adjustments to convert to cash basis:		
Accounts receivable decrease..............	2,000	
Cash generated from revenues...........		$62,000
Expenses....................................	70,000	
Add (deduct) adjustments to convert to cash basis:		
Depreciation expense.....................	(3,000)	
Amortization expense....................	(300)	
Inventory increase......................	1,500	
Accounts payable decrease...............	1,000	
Prepaid insurance decrease...............	(200)	
Cash disbursed for expenses.............		69,000
Cash generated by operations..............		(7,000)
From other sources:		
Sale of capital stock.......................	10,000	
Long-term note payable.....................	30,000	
Land (exchanged for machinery).............	7,000	
Cash from other sources....................		47,000
Total cash generated during the period..........		40,000

Uses of Cash

Machinery (acquired in exchange for land)........	7,000	
Payment on mortgage.........................	6,000	
Cash dividends..............................	12,000	
Total cash expended during the period............		25,000
Net increase in cash during the period.............		$15,000

Required:

(1) What was the net income for 1974?

(2) How much did cash increase during 1974?

(3) Compute the difference in dollars between (1) and (2). What does it mean?

(4) Explain how management generated significantly more cash than profits.

(5) Did "operations" generate more or less cash than income? Explain.

(6) Explain the land transaction. Why is it reported on this statement?

(7) Explain why the decrease in accounts receivable increases the cash inflow from revenues.

(8) Explain why the inventory increase is added to expenses.

(9) Explain why the decrease in accounts payable is added to expenses.

(10) Do you have any reason to question the soundness of the cash dividend payment of $12,000?

P15–2. The following statement has just been prepared for the Amhurst Corporation:

AMHURST CORPORATION
Funds-Flow Statement
Year December 31, 1974

Funds Provided

Sales and other incomes.	$90,000
Accounts receivable change.	4,000
Expenses.	(70,000)
Depreciation.	2,000
Inventory change.	(3,000)
Accounts payable change.	1,000
Prepaid insurance change.	(100)
Cash from operations.	23,900
Other sources	
Capital stock.	5,000
Total sources.	28,900

Funds Applied

Equipment.	(7,000)
Bonds payable.	(10,000)
Dividends.	(2,000)
Total uses.	19,000
Increase in funds.	$ 9,900

Required:

(a) Is the above on a working-capital basis or cash basis? How did you determine the basis on which the statement was prepared?

(b) List the format and terminology deficiencies on the statement.

(c) Recast the above statement in good form.

P15–3. The Baker Company has completed all of the adjusting and closing procedures at the end of 1974. They also have prepared the 1974 income statement and balance sheet. A worksheet to develop the statement of changes in financial position has been completed. From these sources, the following data were taken:

(1) Balance sheet data:

	Balance at Dec. 31	
	1974	1973
Current Assets:		
Cash.	$20,000	$10,000
Accounts receivable (net).	15,000	16,600
Inventories.	29,000	17,000
Prepaid expenses.	1,500	1,400
Current Liabilities:		
Accounts payable.	6,000	8,000
Accrued wages payable.	500	1,000
Notes payable, short-term.	9,000	4,000

(2) Worksheet data:

Net income.	$22,000
Depreciation expense.	4,000
Purchase of fixed assets for cash—cost.	24,000
Sale for cash of long-term investment (at cost). . . .	6,000
Borrowed cash on long-term note	15,000
Sales of unissued capital stock (cash).	4,000
Payment of cash dividend.	5,000
Payment on long-term note.	4,000
Acquired land for future plant site and issued bonds payable (10-year) for full purchase price .	40,000

Required:

Prepare a statement of changes in financial position—working-capital basis for 1974.

P15–4. The Yancey Company has completed the balance sheet and the income statement at year end, December 31, 1974. A worksheet also has been completed as a basis for the statement of changes in financial position—cash basis. Data from the worksheet follow:

Net income (Revenue $140,000 − Expenses $100,000).	$40,000
Depreciation expense.	10,000
Paid long-term note.	25,000
Sale of fixed assets for cash (no gain or loss)	15,000
Amortization of patent.	2,000
Sale of unissued capital stock for cash.	20,000
Increase in accounts receivable.	3,000
Purchased fixed assets for cash.	34,000
Decrease in accounts payable.	4,000
Decrease in merchandise inventory.	6,000
Paid cash dividends.	8,000
Acquired future plant site, issued bonds payable in full settlement.	30,000

Required:

Prepare a statement of changes in financial position—cash basis. (Hint: Cash increased by $19,000 during the period.)

P15–5. The Koster Company is in the process of preparing the 1974 annual financial report. The company controller decided to prepare two statements of changes in financial position—one on the working-capital basis and the other on the cash basis. A worksheet on each basis has been completed and determined to be correct. The following data were taken from the cash-basis worksheet.

Items	Amounts	
Net income reported (accrual basis)................	$ 44,000*	
Depreciation expense.........................	8,000	
Purchase of long-term investment, stock Co. A.........		$ 40,000
Sale of fixed assets for cash (no gain or loss)...........	11,000	
Increase in income taxes payable....................	400	
Purchase of fixed assets for cash....................		11,000
Patent amortization expense.......................	600	
Payment of cash dividend on common stock...........		18,000
Increase in accounts payable......................	4,000	
Increase in merchandise inventory..................		9,000
Sale of common stock for cash.....................	20,000	
Payment on short-term note payable (nontrade)........		20,000
Decrease in accounts receivable....................	5,000	
Payment on long-term note payable.................		30,000
Issuance of bonds payable (received cash).............	50,000	
Difference—increase in cash......................		15,000
	$143,000	$143,000

* Revenues $144,000 — Expenses $100,000 = $44,000.

The beginning and ending balance sheets reflected the following:

	Balances, Dec. 31	
	1973	1974
Current assets:		
Cash.......................................	$55,000	$40,000
Inventory..................................	39,000	30,000
Accounts receivable (net).....................	15,000	20,000
Current liabilities:		
Accounts payable............................	(19,000)	(15,000)
Short-term notes payable (nontrade).............	-0-	(20,000)
Income taxes payable.........................	(1,400)	(1,000)
Difference—working capital....................	$88,600	$54,000

Required:

(a) Based upon the above data, prepare in good form a statement of changes in financial position—cash basis.

(b) Based upon data selected from the above, prepare in good form a statement of changes in financial position—working-capital basis.

P15–6. (Based on the Appendix.) The Davis Company is in the process of preparing the annual financial reports at December 31, 1974; included is a statement of changes in financial position—working-capital basis. In preparing the latter statement, the following worksheet has been set up:

DAVIS COMPANY
Worksheet to Develop Statement of Changes in Financial Position—Working-Capital Basis
For the Year Ended December 31, 1974

	Balances Dec. 31, 1973	Analysis of Interim Entries Debit	Analysis of Interim Entries Credit	Ending Balances Dec. 31, 1974
Debits				
Working Capital	21,000	XXXXX	XXXXX	27,400
Nonworking-Capital Accounts:				
Investments, long-term	5,000			6,000
Fixed assets (net)	50,000			51,000
Patent (net).	4,000			3,600
	80,000			88,000
Credits				
Bonds payable	15,000			10,000
Capital stock	40,000			50,000
Retained earnings	25,000			28,000
	80,000			88,000
Sources of Working Capital:				
From operations:				
From other sources:				
Uses of Working Capital:				
Change in Working Capital				

Additional Data:

(a) Net income was $7,000; (b) Depreciation expense, $2,000; (c) Amortization of patent, $400; (d) Purchase of long-term investment, $1,000; (e) Annual payment on bonds payable, $5,000; (f) Sale of unissued common stock, $10,000; (g) Paid cash dividend, $4,000; and (h) Purchased fixed assets, $3,000.

Required:

Complete the above worksheet on a working-capital basis.

P15–7.   (Based on the Appendix.) The Packard Company is in the process of developing the 1974 annual reports. A statement of changes in financial position—cash basis is being developed. The following worksheet has been set up to develop the statement:

PACKARD COMPANY
Worksheet to Develop Statement of Changes in Financial Position—Cash Basis
For the Year Ended December 31, 1974

	Balances Dec. 31, 1973	Analysis of Interim Entries Debit	Analysis of Interim Entries Credit	Ending Balances Dec. 31, 1974
Debits				
Cash Account	24,000	XXXXX	XXXXX	32,200
Noncash Accounts:				
Accounts receivable (net)	26,000			30,000
Inventory	30,000			28,000
Prepaid insurance	1,200			800
Investments, long-term	10,800			8,000
Fixed assets (net)	30,000			37,000
Patent (net)	3,000			2,700
	125,000			138,700
Credits				
Accounts payable	21,000			18,000
Accrued wages payable	3,000			2,000
Income taxes payable	1,000			1,200
Notes payable, long-term	25,000			20,000
Capital stock (par $10)	60,000			70,000
Retained earnings	15,000			27,500
	125,000			138,700
Sources of Cash:				
From operations:				
From other sources:				
Uses of Cash:				
Change in Cash Balance				

Additional Data:

(a) Revenues $120,000 − Expenses $100,000 = Net income $20,000; (b) Depreciation expense, $3,000; (c) Amortization of patent, $300; (d) Sale of long-term investment at cost, $2,800; (e) Purchase of fixed assets, $10,000; (f) Payment on long-term note payable, $5,000; (g) Sale of unissused capital stock for $10,000 cash; (h) Paid cash dividend, $7,500; (i) Increase in accounts receivable balance during the period, $4,000; (j) Decrease in inventory during the period, $2,000; (k) Decrease in prepaid insurance balance during the period, $400; (l) Decrease in accounts payable balance during the period, $3,000; (m) Decrease in accrued wages payable balance during the period, $1,000; and (n) Increase in income taxes payable balance during the period, $200.

Required:

Complete the above worksheet on a cash basis.

P15–8. (Based on the Worksheet.) The Reo Company is in the process of developing the annual financial statements, including a statement of changes in financial position—working-capital basis, at December 31, 1974. The balance sheet and the income statement are already prepared as summarized below:

	Balances at	
	Dec. 31, 1974	*Dec. 31, 1973*
Balance Sheet:		
Cash........................	$ 21,500	$ 15,000
Accounts receivable (net)....................	23,000	20,000
Merchandise inventory.......................	27,000	22,000
Prepaid insurance..........................	300	600
Investments, long-term......................	12,000	
Fixed assets (net)...........................	220,000	134,000
Patent (net)................................	16,000	
	$319,800	$191,600
Accounts payable............................	$ 18,000	$ 12,000
Notes payable, short-term (nontrade)..........	10,000	18,000
Accrued wages payable......................	800	1,000
Income taxes payable.......................	1,000	600
Notes payable, long-term....................	10,000	30,000
Bonds payable.............................	100,000	
Capital stock (par $10)......................	140,000	100,000
Contributed capital in excess of par...........	6,000	5,000
Retained earnings..........................	34,000	25,000
	$319,800	$191,600

Income Statement for 1974:		
Sales........................		$200,000
Cost of goods sold.............		126,000
Gross margin on sales...........		74,000
Expenses.....................	$39,000	
Depreciation expense............	14,000	
Amortization of patent..........	1,000	
Income tax expense.............	7,000	61,000
Net Income...................		$ 13,000

Additional Data for 1974:

(a) Net income for 1974 (per above); (b) Depreciation expense (per above); (c) Purchased patent on Jan. 1, 1974, for $17,000 cash; (d) Amortize patent over 17 years; (e) Purchased stock of S Corporation as a long-term investment for cash, $12,000; (f) Paid $20,000 on the long-term notes payable; (g) Sold 4,000 shares of unissued capital stock for $41,000 cash; (h) Declared and paid a $4,000 cash dividend; (i) Acquired a building (a fixed asset) and paid in full for it by issuing $100,000 bonds payable, at par, to the former owner; date of transaction was Dec. 30, 1974.

Required:

(a) Based upon the above data, prepare a worksheet to develop the statement of changes in financial position—working-capital basis.

(Hint: The increase in working capital was $16,000.)

(b) Based upon the completed worksheet, prepare the statement of changes in financial position—working-capital basis.

P15–9. (Based on the Appendix.) The Stutz Company is in the process of preparing the annual financial statements on December 31, 1974, including a statement of changes in financial position—cash basis. The balance sheet and the income statement have been completed and are summarized below:

	Balances at	
	Dec. 31, 1973	Dec. 31, 1974
Balance Sheet:		
Cash....................................	$ 10,000	$ 24,500
Accounts receivable (net)....................	19,000	23,000
Merchandise inventory......................	52,000	50,000
Prepaid insurance.........................		2,000
Investments, long-term......................	5,000	
Fixed assets (net).........................	111,000	151,000
Patent....................................	3,000	2,000
	$200,000	$252,500
Accounts payable..........................	$ 28,000	$ 25,000
Accrued wages payable.....................	2,000	1,500
Income taxes payable......................	3,000	4,000
Notes payable, short-term (nontrade)..........	5,000	
Notes payable, long-term....................	25,000	60,000
Capital stock (no-par)......................	107,000	130,000
Retained earnings..........................	30,000	32,000
	$200,000	$252,500

Income Statement for 1974:	
Sales......................................	$300,000
Cost of goods sold.........................	(170,000)
Expenses..................................	(85,000)
Depreciation expense.......................	(10,000)
Patent amortization........................	(1,000)
Income tax expense........................	(14,000)
Net Income................................	$ 20,000

Data summarized, needed for worksheet:

From income statement: (a) Net income, $20,000; (b) Depreciation, $10,000; (c) Patent amortization, $1,000.

From other records: (d) On Jan. 1, 1974, paid $3,000 for 3-year insurance premium; (e) Amortized ⅓ of the insurance premium; (f) Sold the long-term investment at cost, $5,000; (g) Paid the short-term note payable, $5,000; (h) Paid $15,-000 on the long-term note payable; (i) Sold unissued capital stock for $23,000 cash; (j) Declared and paid a cash dividend, $18,000.

From the balance sheets: (k) Accounts receivable increased $4,000; (l) Merchandise inventory decreased $2,000; (m) Accounts payable decreased $3,000; (n) Accrued wages payable decreased $500; (o) Income taxes payable increased $1,000.

From other records:

(p) On Dec. 31, 1974, acquired fixed assets and paid for them by issuing a $50,000 long-term note payable.

Required:

(1) Based on the above data, set up and complete a worksheet to develop the statement of changes in financial position—cash basis. There will be an analytical entry for each of the data summarized (a) through (p).

(2) Utilize the completed worksheet to develop the statement of changes in financial position—cash basis.
(Hint: Cash generated by operations is $27,500.)

16 Using and interpreting financial statements

Purpose
of the
chapter

Throughout the preceding chapters, your attention has been focused on developing an understanding of the financial reports prepared for use by external parties. The rationale, reasons, and conceptual basis for the major phases of the accounting process and the resulting financial statements were presented. Throughout those discussions, we also emphasized the use and interpretation of the various items and groups of items reported on the income statement, balance sheet, and statement of changes in financial position.

The broad fundamentals underlying accounting that were presented in the preceding chapters are summarized in Exhibit 16–1 for convenience in study. We have emphasized these fundamentals because an understanding of them and their impact on financial statements is essential to the statement user. The interpretation of financial reports and an appreciation of both their advantages and limitations rest basically on a knowledge of the broad fundamentals. They emphasize valuations, measurements, and the basic distinctions in the measurement and reporting processes. As a potential decision maker who must necessarily rely on financial statements, your understanding of these broad fundamentals should serve you to advantage.

The purpose of this chapter is to present some important uses and interpretations of external financial statements prepared in accordance with generally accepted accounting standards. Part Two of the chapter focuses on the impacts of price-level changes that are important in interpreting the financial statements correctly.

577

Exhibit 16–1

Summarization of the broad fundamentals underlying accounting

	Text Reference		
Fundamental	*Chapter*	*Page*	*Brief Explanation*
1. *Underlying Assumptions:*			
a. Separate-entity Assumption............	1	4	Accounting is concerned with a specifically defined entity. Thus, for accounting purposes, an enterprise is assumed to be an accounting unit separate and apart from the owners, creditors, and other entities.
b. Continuity Assumption............	2	35	In accounting, an enterprise is assumed to be a "going-concern." That is, for accounting purposes, it is assumed that the entity will not liquidate in the foreseeable future, but will continue to carry out its proprietary objectives in an orderly way.
c. Unit-of-measure Assumption............	1	3	With many diverse items and transactions to be accounted for, it is necessary that a single unit of measure be adopted. Accounting assumes the monetary unit—the dollar—as the common denominator in the measurement process.
d. Time-period Assumption............	5	126	Financial data must be reported for relatively short time periods: months, quarters, years. Society imposes this calendar constraint on accounting. Thus, accounting assumes that financial results must be reported for short time periods. This leads to the necessity for the accrual and deferral of revenues and expenses.
2. *Underlying Principles:*			
a. Cost Principle..........	2	35	This principle holds that cost (i.e., the resources given up in the acquisition of other goods and services) is the appropriate basis for initial recording and subsequent accounting for assets, liabilities, revenues, and expenses.
b. Revenue Principle.......	2	32	This principle defines revenue as the considerations received for the aggregate of products and services transferred by an entity to its customers. Under this principle, revenue is realized when title to the goods sold transfers and when services sold are rendered.
c. Matching Principle......	5	128	This principle holds that, for each period, the revenues of the period must be identified and recognized in the accounting process. Then, all of the costs incurred in generating that revenue, irrespective of the period in which the costs were incurred, must be identified with the period in which the revenues are recognized. Thus, under this principle, the costs of generating particular revenues are matched with those revenues, period by period. This principle requires the accrual and deferral of many costs.
d. Objectivity Principle...............	2	35	This principle holds that accounting should be based on objective data and objective determinations to the fullest extent possible. It should be free from bias. The accounting data recorded and reported should be verifiable.

Exhibit 16–1 (continued)

e. Consistency Principle............	7	238	This principle holds that the accounting process must apply all concepts, principles, standards, and measurement approaches on a consistent basis from one period to the next, in order to derive financial data that are comparable over time.
f. Full-disclosure Principle............	3	68	This principle holds that financial reporting should be complete and understandable to the typical user (i.e., the investor) and should include all significant information relating to the economic affairs of the entity.
g. Exception Principle.....	8	270	Accounting is applied to a very diverse range of situations and transactions across companies and industries; therefore, a reasonable degree of flexibility is essential. As a consequence, certain exceptions to the basic concepts, standards, and procedures are necessary. There are three types of exceptions that are permitted: (1) Materiality—Amounts of small significance (i.e., relatively small amounts) need not be accorded strict theoretical treatment. (2) Conservatism—Where more than one accounting alternative (or judgment) is permissible, the one having the least favorable immediate effect on owners' equity should be selected. (3) Industry peculiarities—Unique characteristics of an industry may require the development and application of special accounting approaches in order to produce realistic financial results.

3. *Accounting Practices and Procedures:*

                   Examples:

a. Those related to income and asset measurement. — Lifo versus Fifo; straight-line versus accelerated depreciation.

b. Those related to the reporting of accounting results. — Illustrated and discussed throughout the chapters. — Reporting extraordinary items; terminology in financial reports.

c. Those not related to asset or income measurement or to the reporting of results. — Control and subsidiary accounts; special journals, methods of processing and recording accounting data (manual, mechanical, and electronic).

PART ONE: INTERPRETING FINANCIAL STATEMENTS

Financial reports in the decision-making process

  The basic objective of financial statements is to help the decision maker make better decisions. Decision makers who use financial statements constitute two broad groups. The management of the business (i.e., internal decision makers) relies on financial data in making a preponderance of the important managerial decisions. This aspect of accounting is considered in *Fundamentals of Management Accounting.*

  The second broad group that uses financial reports is frequently referred to as "external" decision makers. This group consists primarily of investors (both present and potential owners), creditors (both short-term and long-term), and the public at large. Financial accounting and the "external" financial reports discussed in the preceding chapters are oriented toward serving this particular group of decision makers.

Irrespective of the particular decision maker, there are three fundamental purposes for using financial data:

1. Measurement of past performance—The decision maker needs to know how the business has performed in the past. Information concerning such items as net income, sales volume, extraordinary items, cash and working-capital flows, and return on the investment earned helps him assess the success of the business and the effectiveness of the management. It also helps the decision maker compare one entity with others.

2. Measurement of the present condition of a business—The decision maker must have data on how the entity stands today. Relevant questions include: How much debt does the business owe? What assets are owned? What is the cash position? How much of the earnings have been retained in the business? What is the debt/equity ratio? What is the inventory position? This helps the decision maker assess the successes and failures of the past; but, more importantly, it provides useful information in assessing the future potentials of the business.

3. Prediction of the future potentials of the business. Decision makers make decisions by selecting from several alternative courses of action. Each course of action will cause different effects *in the future* for the decision maker. Many of these future effects are financial in nature; thus, in decision making, one is faced with the problem of predicting the probable future impact. All decisions are future-oriented. They do not (and cannot) affect the past. However, in predicting the probable future impact of a decision, reliable measurements of what has happened in the recent past are valuable. This is particularly true when the decision relates to a business entity. The recent sales and profit trends of a business are very good indicators of what might be expected in the reasonable future.

Thus, decision makers must rely substantially on the past data presented in financial reports in making assessments and predictions of probable future potentials. Generally, this is the most important use of financial statements by decision makers.

Some decisions are made intuitively and without much supporting data. In these cases there is no systematic attempt to collect measurable data such as those provided in financial reports. The decision maker does not attempt to array, measure, and evaluate the advantages and disadvantages of each alternative. There are numerous reasons for intuitive decisions of this sort. Time and cost may prevent a careful analysis. Frequently, the decision maker is unsophisticated; he does not understand the systematic approach to decision making and is not aware of the basic factors bearing on the decision. Unsophisticated decision makers tend to oversimplify the decision-making process and quite frequently overlook the financial impacts.

In contrast, a sophisticated decision maker will pursue forcefully a systematic analysis of each alternative. Adequate information that bears on each alternative will be collected. In decisions relating to a business, the financial statements generally provide critical financial data bearing on the various alternatives. We must emphasize, however, that the financial impact is only one of several important factors that should be evaluated in most decisions.

To use financial data effectively, however, one must understand what they represent and how the measurements were accomplished. With a reasonable level of understanding of the fundamentals of the accounting process, one is able to evaluate effectively the **strength and weaknesses** (or limitations) of the financial data presented in the financial reports of a business. Your study of the preceding chapters should enable you to appreciate and evaluate these aspects. *Fundamentals of Management Accounting* will add to your level of sophistication in this respect.

Use and interpretation of financial statements
: The three basic financial statements—the income statement, balance sheet, and statement of changes in financial position—have evolved primarily to meet the special needs of "external" decision makers. These are the investors (present and potential owners), the creditors (short-term and long-term), financial analysts, and the public at large. Because of the varied needs of these users, special and supplementary financial data and analyses frequently are needed.

The creditors
: Financial institutions, and other parties to some extent, grant long-term and short-term credit to businesses. Those that grant credit to do so in order to earn a return, i.e., interest revenue. They expect to collect periodic interest during the credit period and the principal at maturity. As a consequence, in granting credit to a business, the creditor is basically concerned about (a) the profit potentials of the business; (b) its ability to generate cash; and (c) its financial position (assets owned and debts owed). Therefore, the credit grantors almost always look to the financial reports for information bearing on these issues. Not infrequently the financial institution requires that it be provided with "certified" financial statements prior to making a loan and throughout the credit period.

Short-term credit grantors are particularly concerned about the cash flow and working-capital position as reflected in the statement of changes in financial position and the balance sheet. Near-cash items, such as short-term investments, accounts receivable, and inventory balances, are especially relevant to their decision. Similarly, claims to cash, such as current liabilities and early maturities of long-term debt, are critical to them.

In contrast, long-term credit grantors are more concerned about such factors as profit-making potentials, assets as security for the loan, the ability to generate cash over long periods of time, and the overall performance of the enterprise. In addition, the notes to the financial statements and the "auditor's opinion" convey important information since they tend to disclose facts that are not quantified and certain future contingencies (such as major lawsuits pending).

This brief discussion should be sufficient to indicate the reliance that credit grantors necessarily place upon financial statements. The analytical techniques explained in the next section are widely used by credit grantors in interpreting financial statements.

The investors   Investors are the primary group to which external financial statements are addressed. As a group they include present owners (shareholders in the case of a corporation), potential owners (those that may become interested in purchasing shares), and investment analysts (those that advise investors). Investors include individuals, other businesses, and institutions, such as your university.

In Chapter 13, on long-term investments, we discussed the concept of a controlling interest. Aside from this issue, investors, when purchasing shares of stock, do so in the anticipation of receiving revenue in the form of dividends during the investment period and an increase, or growth, at disposition of the shares over the amount invested. Thus, when making an investment of this type or in selling an investment being held, the investor is faced with the problem of predicting the future **income** and **growth** potentials of the enterprise. In making these predictions, the investor should look at several different considerations, such as the nature of the industry, the characteristics of the company, and its financial record. The income statement provides him with significant data, such as revenue from products and services, extraordinary items, income tax impacts, net income, and earnings per share. Other relationships, such as gross margin, profit margin, and expense relationships, can be computed. Similarly, the balance sheet and the statement of changes in financial position, buttressed by the notes to the financial statements, provide a measurement of past performance and current position. These data constitute an important base from which to make predictions of future income and growth potentials. These data are particularly valuable when available for several past periods (see Exhibit 16–2).

In the next section, we will elaborate on the prior discussions and present some analytical techniques commonly used in the evaluation and interpretation of financial statements.

Analysis of
financial
statements

Financial statements necessarily include a large volume of quantitative data supplemented by descriptive notes. The notes are intended to be particularly helpful to users in interpreting the statements; therefore, they should be viewed as perhaps the most important aspect of the financial statement. They elaborate on accounting policies, major financial effects and events, and certain events not directly affecting the current quantitative measurements, but which may bear on the continued success of the firm. An example of the latter situation would be a major lawsuit or governmental action that is pending. The notes are intended to contribute to a full understanding of such factors.

In respect to the quantitative data presented in the financial statements, there are two techniques that are widely used to assist the user in interpreting the financial statements: (1) presentation of comparative statements and long-term summaries, and (2) use of ratio and percentage analyses.

Comparative
statements

For a number of years, the accounting profession has insisted on the presentation of comparative financial statements covering, as a minimum, the current year and the prior year. Examples are presented on page 63 for J. C. Penney Company, Inc., and in Exhibit 16–2.

Exhibit 16–2

_____

PACKARD COMPANY
Comparative Statements Illustrated
Comparative Income Statement (Simplified for Illustration)
For the Years Ended December 31, 1974 and December 31, 1973

| | Year Ended Dec. 31 | | Increase (Decrease) 1974 over 1973 | |
	1974	1973*	Amount	Percent
Sales.................................	$120,000	$100,000	$20,000	20.0
Cost of goods sold....................	72,600	60,000	12,600	21.0
Gross margin on sales.................	47,400	40,000	7,400	18.5
Operating expenses:				
Distribution expenses................	22,630	15,000	7,630	50.9
Administrative expenses..............	12,870	14,300	(1,430)	(10.0)
Interest expense......................	500	700	(200)	(28.6)
Total expenses.................	36,000	30,000	6,000	20.0
Pretax income........................	11,400	10,000	1,400	14.0
Income taxes.........................	2,600	2,000	600	30.0
Net Income..........................	$ 8,800	$ 8,000	$ 800	10.0

* Base amount.

Exhibit 16–2 (continued)

PACKARD COMPANY
Comparative Balance Sheet (Simplified for Illustration)
At December 31, 1974 and December 31, 1973

	At Year End, Dec. 31		Increase (Decrease) 1974 over 1973	
Assets	1974	1973*	Amount	Percent
Current Assets:				
Cash............................	$ 13,000	9,000	$ 4,000	44.4
Accounts receivable (net).............	8,400	7,000	1,400	20.0
Merchandise inventory..............	54,000	60,000	(6,000)	(10.0)
Prepaid expenses....................	2,000	4,000	(2,000)	(50.0)
Total Current Assets............	77,400	80,000	(2,600)	3.3
Investments:				
Real estate........................	8,000	8,000		
Operational Assets:				
Equipment and furniture.............	82,500	75,000	7,500	10.0
Less accumulated depreciation........	(23,250)	(15,000)	8,250	55.0
Total Operational Assets.........	59,250	60,000	(750)	(1.3)
Other assets.........................	1,900	2,000	(100)	(5.0)
Total Assets...............	$146,550	$150,000	($ 3,450)	(2.3)
Liabilities				
Current Liabilities:				
Accounts payable....................	$ 13,200	$ 12,000	$ 1,200	10.0
Notes payable, short-term............	15,000	20,000	(5,000)	(25.0)
Accrued wages payable..............	7,200	8,000	(800)	(10.0)
Total Current Liabilities.........	35,400	40,000	(4,600)	(11.5)
Long-term Liabilities:				
Notes payable, long-term............	7,150	10,000	(2,850)	(28.5)
Total Liabilities.................	42,550	50,000	(7,450)	(14.9)
Shareholders' Equity				
Common stock (par $10)..............	85,000	85,000		
Retained earnings....................	19,000	15,000	4,000	26.7
Total Shareholders' Equity..........	104,000	100,000	4,000	4.0
Total Liabilities and Shareholders' Equity.	$146,550	$150,000	($ 3,450)	(2.3)

* Base amount.
Note: The statement of changes in financial position would follow the same format.

As a consequence, practically all financial statements present, side by side, the results for the current and the preceding year (similar to the statements shown in Exhibit 16–2). As published, only two amount columns generally are shown, as on page 63, however, two additional columns may be added for (a) the amount of change for each item and (b) the percent of change. These additional **variance** columns are illustrated in Exhibit 16–2. The two variance columns facilitate **interpretation** by the statement user. Frequently the percent of change from the prior period is more helpful than the absolute dollar amount of change. Observe that the percents are determined independently on each line by dividing the amount of the change by the amount for the preceding year. For example, in Exhibit 16–2, the percentage on the Sales line was computed as $20,000 ÷ $100,000 = 20.0%.

In the interest of full disclosure, many companies also include in the annual report 5-, 10-, and even 20-year summaries of basic data, such as sales, net income, total assets, total liabilities, total owners' equity, and selected ratios. This kind of reporting is to be applauded from the standpoint of the statement user. Data for a series of years are particularly important in interpretation of the financial statements for the last period. There is considerable likelihood of misinterpretation and unwarranted conclusions when the user limits consideration to only the last one or two periods. The vagaries of transactions, economic events, and accounting are such that the financial reports for one relatively short period of time generally do not provide a sound basis for assessing the long-term potentials of an enterprise. Sophisticated financial analysts typically use data covering a number of periods so that significant trends may be identified and interpreted. An excellent 15-year Financial Summary, presented by the Clark Equipment Company, is shown in Exhibit 16–3.

In analyzing and interpreting comparative data, the items showing significant increases and decreases should receive special attention. Care should be exercised to identify evidence of significant turning points, either upward or downward, in trends for important items such as net income and cash flow. Fundamental to the interpretation is the need to determine the underlying causes for significant changes in either direction (favorable or unfavorable).

Ratio and percentage analysis

Some amounts on financial statements, such as net income, are highly significant in and of themselves; however, the significance of many amounts is highlighted by their relationship to other amounts. These significant relationships can be pinpointed and isolated effectively in many instances through the use of an analytical tool known as ratio or percentage analysis. A ratio or percent simply expresses the proportionate relationship between two different amounts. A ratio is computed by dividing one quantity by another quantity; the divisor is known as the *base* amount. For example, the fact that a company earned $500,000 net income assumes greater significance when that amount is compared with the stockholders' investment in the company. Assume stockholders' equity is $5,000,000 (i.e., the base amount); the relationship of earnings to shareholder investment would be: $500,000 ÷ $5,000,000 = .1, or 10%. Clearly, this ratio analysis has significant informational content for the user. It enables one to compare more easily and meaningfully across companies.

Fundamentally, there are two aspects of ratio analysis: (1) relation-

Exhibit 16–3

Clark Equipment Company

15-Year Financial Summary

Per-Share Amounts in Dollars
Other Dollar Amounts in Thousands

	1972	(a)1971	1970	1969	1968	1967
Operating Data						
Net Sales	$897,567	$742,172	$671,007	$645,446	$529,942	$507,676
Other Income	19,959	18,885	13,703	11,718	9,505	9,348
Total Sales & Other Revenues	917,526	761,057	684,710	657,164	539,447	517,024
Wages, Salaries & Employee Benefits	283,902	229,442	196,407	198,134	158,205	143,108
Cost of Materials, Supplies & Services	522,483	439,554	387,896	354,168	304,151	310,534
Depreciation	15,929	14,749	12,383	11,137	9,985	8,805
Interest & Service Charges	26,330	24,348	21,129	14,583	9,891	9,536
Total Costs & Expenses	848,644	708,093	617,815	578,022	482,232	471,983
Income Before Tax	68,882	52,964	66,895	79,142	57,215	45,041
Provision For Income Taxes	28,570	23,948	31,614	40,537	28,255	20,862
Net Income	40,312	29,016	35,281	38,605	28,960	24,179
(b) Income Per Share	3.01	2.36	2.92	3.21	2.43	2.05
Cash Dividends	19,431	17,112	16,935	16,446	13,623	12,939
(b) Dividends Per Share	1.45	1.40	1.40	1.40	1.20	1.15
Reinvested In The Business	20,881	11,904	18,346	22,159	15,337	11,240
Financial Data						
Current Assets	361,068	347,178	292,503	260,819	209,567	181,581
Current Liabilities	160,994	126,059	107,190	105,534	88,190	65,699
Working Capital	200,074	221,119	185,313	155,285	121,377	115,882
Current Ratio	2.2 to 1	2.8 to 1	2.7 to 1	2.4 to 1	2.4 to 1	2.8 to 1
Properties & Equipment—Net	142,701	133,679	116,390	97,898	88,971	80,440
Long-term Debt	75,698	97,548	102,955	76,894	58,221	58,732
Shareholders' Equity	318,535	293,676	233,550	214,429	188,788	171,343
(b) Book Value Per Share	23.69	22.03	19.29	17.76	15.81	14.49
Other Data						
Return on Net Sales	4.5%	3.9%	5.3%	6.0%	5.5%	4.8%
Return on Average Shareholders' Equity	13.2%	11.8%	15.7%	19.3%	16.0%	14.5%
Capital Expenditures	27,767	22,764	26,668	22,492	16,029	14,514
(b) Shares Outstanding at Dec. 31	13,446,986	13,329,716	12,107,650	12,074,230	11,940,722	11,826,521
Number of Shareholders	12,539	12,719	13,894	13,109	12,414	12,027
Number of Employees	28,259	26,825	22,100	21,640	19,300	17,300

(a) For comparative purposes, 1971 amounts have been restated to reflect the acquisition of Gysler Manufacturing Co.
(b) Adjusted for stock splits.

1966	1965	1964	1963	1962	1961	1960	1959	1958
$508,622	$423,662	$347,699	$263,505	$230,075	$173,320	$196,769	$208,184	$142,618
8,025	5,997	5,279	7,423	6,144	5,109	2,857	2,394	2,042
516,647	429,659	352,978	270,928	236,219	178,429	199,626	210,578	144,660
145,572	116,922	95,021	75,960	68,486	51,062	61,326	61,138	44,292
302,540	257,484	209,730	158,671	135,744	109,350	121,298	120,296	83,387
7,373	5,925	5,361	3,702	3,632	3,083	2,964	2,780	2,664
8,055	6,359	2,519	1,833	1,818	1,694	2,297	1,693	1,816
463,540	386,690	312,631	240,166	209,680	165,189	187,885	185,907	132,159
53,107	42,969	40,347	30,762	26,539	13,240	11,741	24,671	12,501
23,740	18,976	19,222	14,915	12,864	5,419	4,999	12,269	6,052
29,367	23,993	21,125	15,847	13,675	7,821	6,742	12,402	6,449
2.52	2.08	2.03	1.54	1.34	.81	.70	1.30	.67
10,871	9,226	8,064	6,921	6,140	5,793	5,728	5,363	4,786
1.00	.875	.775	.675	.60	.60	.60	.563	.50
18,496	14,767	13,061	8,926	7,535	2,028	1,014	7,039	1,663
205,222	170,328	132,483	113,397	95,454	66,524	80,336	93,085	71,365
97,964	74,024	58,738	47,227	34,230	17,901	31,391	44,075	20,628
107,258	96,304	73,745	66,170	61,224	48,623	48,945	49,010	50,737
2.1 to 1	2.3 to 1	2.3 to 1	2.4 to 1	2.8 to 1	3.7 to 1	2.6 to 1	2.1 to 1	3.5 to 1
70,893	52,273	46,060	42,207	34,163	32,080	31,656	31,263	30,594
58,377	47,840	35,743	36,418	36,500	29,750	30,500	28,650	30,700
157,689	135,373	114,396	100,070	90,539	73,040	70,353	68,641	62,173
13.49	11.72	10.98	9.69	8.85	7.56	7.34	7.22	6.54
5.8%	5.7%	6.1%	6.0%	5.9%	4.5%	3.4%	6.0%	4.5%
20.2%	18.8%	18.5%	15.8%	17.6%	10.9%	9.7%	19.0%	10.7%
27,248	10,272	7,719	5,509	3,527	3,542	3,384	3,501	3,964
11,692,885	11,552,717	10,422,044	10,324,994	10,229,156	9,661,732	9,588,252	9,507,852	9,511,652
12,423	10,787	9,544	9,198	9,285	7,989	7,825	7,150	7,245
18,300	16,900	13,750	11,400	9,750	8,170	8,169	9,520	8,014

ships within one period and (2) relationships between *periods*. In addition, ratios may be computed within one statement, such as the income statement or, between statements, such as the income statement and the balance sheet. In Exhibit 16–2, for the Packard Company, the percents of change represent a percentage analysis between periods within each statement.

There is no particular list of ratios or percentages that can be identified as appropriate to all situations. Each situation usually will evidence a need for particular ratios; however, there are a number of ratios or percentages that are widely used because they are appropriate to many situations. The next few paragraphs will discuss and illustrate the ratios and percentages that are commonly used.

Component percentages   A widely used technique known as component percentages expresses each item on a particular statement as a percentage of a single base amount.[1] Exhibit 16–4 presents a component analysis for the 1974 and 1973 income statements and balance sheets for the Packard Company. On the income statement, the single base amount used is net sales. Thus, each expense is expressed as a proportional part of net sales. On the balance sheet, the single base amount is total assets. The percents are derived by dividing the amount on each line by the base amount (total assets).

Exhibit 16–4

PACKARD COMPANY
Component Percentages Illustrated
Income Statement (Simplified for Illustration)
For the Years Ended December 31, 1974, and December 31, 1973

	Year Ended Dec. 31, 1974		Year Ended Dec. 31, 1973	
	Amount	*Percent*	*Amount*	*Percent*
Sales*............................	$120,000	100.0	$100,000	100.0
Cost of goods sold...................	72,600	60.5	60,000	60.0
Gross margin on sales...............	47,400	39.5	40,000	40.0
Operating expenses:				
Distribution expenses...........	22,630	18.9	15,000	15.0
Administrative expenses.........	12,870	10.7	14,300	14.3
Interest expense.....................	500	.4	700	.7
Total expense....................	36,000	30.0	30,000	30.0
Pretax income.......................	11,400	9.5	10,000	10.0
Income taxes........................	2,600	2.2	2,000	2.0
Net Income.........................	$ 8,800	7.3	$ 8,000	8.0

---

[1] Component percentage (or ratio) analysis often is referred to as vertical analysis.

Exhibit 16–4 (continued)

PACKARD COMPANY
Balance Sheet (Simplified for Illustration)
At December 31, 1974 and December 31, 1973

	At Year End, Dec. 31, 1974		At Year End, Dec. 31, 1973	
	Amount	Percent	Amount	Percent
Assets				
Current Assets:				
Cash..........................	$ 13,000	8.9	$ 9,000	6.0
Accounts receivable (net)............	8,400	5.7	7,000	4.6
Merchandise inventory..............	54,000	36.8	60,000	40.0
Prepaid expenses...................	2,000	1.4	4,000	2.7
Total Current Assets...........	77,400	52.8	80,000	53.3
Investments:				
Real estate......................	8,000	5.5	8,000	5.3
Operational Assets:				
Equipment and furniture............	82,500	56.3	75,000	50.0
Less accumulated depreciation.......	(23,250)	(15.9)	(15,000)	(10.0)
Total Operational Assets........	59,250	40.4	60,000	40.0
Other Assets......................	1,900	1.3	2,000	1.4
Total Assets*.............	$146,550	100.0	$150,000	100.0
Liabilities				
Current Liabilities:				
Accounts payable..................	$ 13,200	9.0	$ 12,000	8.0
Notes payable, short-term...........	15,000	10.2	20,000	13.3
Accrued wages payable.............	7,200	4.9	8,000	5.3
Total Current Liabilities.........	35,400	24.1	40,000	26.6
Long-term Liabilities:				
Notes payable, long-term............	7,150	4.9	10,000	6.7
Total Liabilities...............	42,550	29.0	50,000	33.3
Shareholders' Equity				
Common stock (par $10)............	85,000	58.0	85,000	56.7
Retained earnings...................	19,000	13.0	15,000	10.0
Total Shareholders' Equity.........	104,000	71.0	100,000	66.7
Total Liabilities and Shareholders' Equity*......................	$146,550	100.0	$150,000	100.0

* Base amount.

Component percentages often are quite useful in interpreting and evaluating the reported financial data. Percents have the distinct characteristic of revealing the proportional relationships existing between two or more amounts. For example, in Exhibit 16–4, on the income statement, we can observe that distribution expenses were 18.9% of sales in 1974, compared with 15% in 1973. On the balance sheet, for example, we may note that, at the end of 1974, merchandise inventory was 36.8% of total assets, compared with 40% for 1973. These changes in important relationships often suggest the need for further inquiry.

Numerous ratios can be computed from a single set of financial statements; however, only a selected few may be useful in a given situation. Thus, a common procedure is to compute certain widely used ratios and then decide what additional ratios are relevant to the particular type of decisions being contemplated. Since balance-sheet amounts relate to one instant in time, while the income statement figures refer to transactions and events over a period of time, care must be exercised in calculating ratios that use amounts from both statements. Thus, when an income-statement amount is compared with a balance-sheet amount, a balance-sheet *average* amount often is used. In the examples to follow, the selected balance-sheet average usually is computed as one-half of the sum of the amounts shown on the beginning and ending balance sheets. When additional information is available, such as monthly data, a more representative average often is preferable.

Commonly used financial ratios can be grouped loosely into four categories as follows:[2]

Tests of profitability
1.   Return on investment (on owners' equity).
2.   Return on investment (on total equities).
3.   Earnings per share (EPS).
4.   Profit margin.

Tests of liquidity
5.   Working-capital or current ratio.
6.   Quick or "acid-test" ratio.
7.   Receivable turnover ratio (or average collection period).
8.   Inventory turnover ratio (or average days' supply).

Tests of solvency and equity position
9.   Debt/equity ratio.
10.   Owners' equity to total equities.
11.   Creditors' equity to total equities.

Market tests
12.   Price/earnings ratio (P/E ratio).
13.   Dividend yield ratio.

TESTS OF PROFITABILITY

Continuing profitability is widely recognized as the primary measure of the overall success of a company; it is a necessary condition for survival. Investors and others would like to be able to rely on a *single measure* of profitability that would be meaningful in all situations. Unfortunately, no single amount has been devised to meet this compre-

---

[2] These numbers are maintained in the subsequent discussions for ease of reference.

hensive need. Tests of profitability focus on measuring the adequacy of net income by comparing it with one or more primary activities or factors that are measured in the financial statements. Four different tests of profitability commonly used are explained below.

Return on investment. This ratio is generally regarded as the most fundamental test of true profitability. It relates net income to the amount of investment that was committed to earning the net income. To measure the profitability of any investment, whether for a company, a project, or for an individual investment, the amount of profit must be gauged against the resources invested. Investors commit their funds to an enterprise because they expect to earn a return (i.e., a profit) on those funds. Fundamentally, the return on investment ratio is computed as follows:

$$(1) \quad \text{Return on Owners' Investment} = \frac{\text{Net Income}}{\text{Owners' Equity}}$$

$$\text{Packard Company, 1974} \quad = \frac{\$8,800^*}{\$104,000\dagger} = 8.5\%$$

(Exhibit 16–4)

* Income *before* extraordinary items should be used.
† Average owners' equity sometimes is used when it is available.

Thus, the Packard Company can be said to have earned 8.5%, after income taxes, on the investment provided by the owners. Return on investment is a particularly useful measure of profitability because it relates the two fundamental factors in any investment situation—the amount of the investment and the return earned on that investment.

Another view of the return-on-investment concept relates net income to total resources used (often called total investment or total equities) rather than to owners' investment only. Under this broader concept, return on investment would be computed as follows:

$$(2) \quad \text{Return on Total Investment} = \frac{\text{Net Income} + \text{Interest Expense}}{\text{Liabilities} + \text{Owners' Equity}}$$

$$\text{Packard Company, 1974} \quad = \frac{\$8,800 + \$500}{\$42,550 + \$104,000} = 6.3\%$$

Thus, it can be said that the management of Packard Company earned 6.3% on all of the resources employed during the year. This concept views *investment* as the amount of resources provided by both owners and creditors.

In computing return on *total* investment, interest expense must be added back to net income since it is the return on the creditors' investment and was deducted in deriving net income. The denominator represents *total* investment; therefore, interest expense clearly must be added back in order to also raise the numerator to a *total* return basis. Similarly, total investment sometimes is computed to omit *current* liabilities because they are viewed as not representing permanent capital. These differences in computing this ratio pose a very important issue. The computation of a particular ratio is not standardized. Neither the accounting profession nor the security analysts have prescribed the manner in which a ratio should be computed (except for earnings per share). Thus, each user of a financial statement should compute the various ratios in accordance with his own views and needs. There are no agreed-upon standards in this respect. As a consequence, before relying on a ratio or a series of ratios, the user should be informed as to the basic computational approach used. The discussions and illustrations in this section follow the approaches commonly used.

Return on total investment reflects the combined effect of both the operating and the financing and investing activities of a company (see Exhibit 16–5).

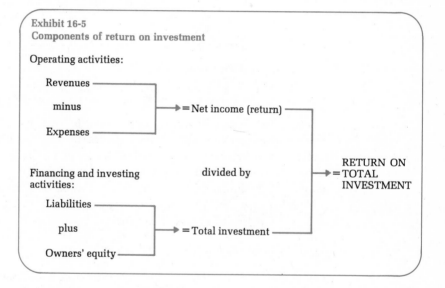

Exhibit 16–5
Components of return on investment

Operating activities:

Revenues

minus

Expenses

= Net income (return)

Financing and investing activities:

divided by

RETURN ON = TOTAL INVESTMENT

Liabilities

plus

Owners' equity

= Total investment

As a matter of actual practice, most analysts compute a return-on-investment ratio for both total investment and on owners' equity. Return on total investment is viewed as the preferable measure of **management performance;** that is, management performance in using all of the resources available to them. The return of owners' equity is viewed as particularly relevant to the owners since it tends to measure the return that has accrued to them.

Earnings per share (EPS). This ratio was illustrated in preceding chapters. This test of profitability is strictly from the common stockholders' point of view. It is intended to provide a measure of profitability that can be readily adjusted for the number of shares owned. Basically, earnings per share on common stock is computed as follows:

$$\text{(3) Earnings Per Share} = \frac{\text{Net Income}}{\text{Average Number of Shares of Common Stock Outstanding}}$$

$$\text{Packard Company, 1974} = \frac{\$8,800}{8,500} = \$1.04 \text{ per share}$$

As illustrated previously, EPS is computed on (a) income before extraordinary items, (b) extraordinary items, and (c) net income. Of the three EPS amounts, the first one generally is considered the more relevant.

Profit margin. This ratio relates only to the income statement. It is computed as follows:

$$\text{(4) Profit Margin} = \frac{\text{Net Income (Before Extraordinary Items)}}{\text{Net Sales}}$$

$$\text{Packard Company, 1974} = \frac{\$8,800}{\$120,000} = .073 \text{ (or 7.3\%)}$$

This profitability test simply expresses the percent of each sales dollar, on the average, that represents profit. It may be interpreted as follows:

(a) Net income was .073 of net sales.
(b) Net income was 7.3% of net sales.
(c) $.073 of each $1.00 of sales was profit.

This ratio also is reflected in the component percentages illustrated in Exhibit 16–4. Some appear to view this profitability test as the most important measure of overall profitability and, hence, as the fundamental indicator of managerial performance. This view is erroneous because the ratio does not take into account the amount of resources employed (i.e., total investment) to produce the net income. For example, the income statements of Company A and Company B may reflect the following:

		Company A	Company B
(a)	Sales......................................	$100,000	$150,000
(b)	Net income.............................	$ 5,000	$ 7,500
(c)	Profit margin (b) ÷ (a)...................	5%	5%
(d)	Total investment.........................	$ 50,000	$125,000
(e)	Return on total investment (b) ÷ (d)........	10%	6%

In this example, both companies reported the same profit margin (5%). Company A, however, appears to be doing much better because it is earning a 10% return on the total investment against the 6% earned by Company B. The profit margin percents do not reflect the effect of the $50,000 investment in Company A against a $125,000 investment in Company B. The effect of the different amounts of investment in each company is reflected in the return on investment percents. Thus, the profit margin percents omit one of the two important factors that must be used in evaluating return on the investment.

TESTS OF LIQUIDITY

Current liquidity refers to a company's ability to meet its currently maturing obligations; therefore, it has to do with the relationship between current assets and current liabilities. The ability of a company to meet its current liabilities is an important factor in short-term financial strength. There are two ratios that tend to reflect **current liquidity**; they are the working-capital ratio and the quick or acid-test ratio.

(5) Working Capital or Current Ratio $= \dfrac{\text{Current Assets}}{\text{Current Liabilities}}$

Packard Company $= 1973 \ \dfrac{\$80,000}{\$40,000} = $ **2.0 times or 2.0 to 1**

$1974 \ \dfrac{\$77,400}{\$35,400} = $ **2.2 times or 2.2 to 1**

The working capital or ratio (sometimes called the current ratio) tends to measure the adequacy of working capital as well as liquidity. It measures the cushion of working capital maintained in order to allow for the inevitable unevenness in the flow of "funds" through the working-capital accounts.[3]

(6) Quick or Acid-Test Ratio $= \dfrac{\text{Quick Assets (net)}}{\text{Current Liabilities}}$

Packard Company $= 1973 \ \dfrac{\$16,000}{\$40,000} = $ **.40 times or .40 to 1**

$1974 \ \dfrac{\$21,400}{\$35,400} = $ **.60 times or .60 to 1**

Quick assets include cash, temporary investments held in lieu of cash, and accounts receivable (net of the allowance for doubtful accounts). Quick assets are those assets that are presumed to be readily convertible into cash at approximately their stated amounts. Inventories are omitted because of the length of the period between their acquisition

---

[3] Occasionally, "working capital" is taken to mean total current assets. This is confusing and unnecessary since "total current assets" is a perfectly good term. Sometimes the term "net working capital" is used to describe the difference between current assets and current liabilities. Throughout this book, we have followed the more general usage of working capital to mean the difference between current assets and current liabilities.

and their ultimate conversion to cash. Prepaid expenses do not "convert" to cash; rather, they only "save" cash in the future, hence, they are also excluded. Thus, the quick or acid-test ratio is a much more *severe* test of current liquidity than is the working capital ratio.

The current liquidity position is related to the specific items of working capital. Their nearness to cash often is measured in terms of turnover. There are two ratios, in addition to the two illustrated above, that bear on this issue: the receivable turnover and the inventory turnover.

$$\text{(7) Receivable Turnover} = \frac{\text{Net Credit Sales}}{\text{Average Net Receivables}}$$

Packard Company
(Net credit sales
assumed to be
$77,000 for 1974)
$$= 1974 \ \frac{\$77,000}{(\$7,000 + \$8,400) \div 2} = 10 \text{ times}$$

This is a turnover ratio since it reflects how many times the receivables, on the average, were granted, collected, then granted again during the period. It expresses the relationship of the average balance in Trade Accounts Receivable and Trade Notes Receivable to the transactions that generated those receivables—credit sales. This turnover ratio tends to measure the effectiveness of the credit-granting and collection activities of the company. Obviously, granting credit to poor credit risks and ineffective collection efforts will cause this ratio to be low. The receivable turnover often is converted to a time basis known as the average age of the receivables. The computation is as follows:

$$\text{Average Age of Receivables} = \frac{\text{Days in Year}}{\text{Receivable Turnover}}$$

$$\text{Packard Company, 1974} = \frac{365}{10} = 36.5 \ \text{Average Days to Collect (or average age of accounts receivable)}$$

The effectiveness of credit and collection activities sometimes is judged by a "rule of thumb" that the *average days to collect* should not exceed 1½ times the credit terms. For example, if the credit terms are 2/10, n/30, the average days to collect should not exceed 45 days (i.e., not more than 15 days past due). Like all rules of thumb, this one is rough and has many exceptions. However, an increase or decrease in the receivable turnover or average days to collect, from one period to the next, would suggest that there were changes in the implementation of credit policies and/or changes in collection efficiency. An increase in the average collection period would indicate an increasing time lag between credit sales and cash realization.

Inventory turnover. Inventory turnover tends to measure the liquidity of the inventory. It is the relationship of the inventory to the volume of goods sold during the period. The computation is as follows:

$$(8) \quad \text{Inventory Turnover} \quad = \frac{\text{Cost of Goods Sold}}{\text{Average Inventory}}$$

$$\text{Packard Company, 1974} = \frac{\$72,600}{(\$60,000 + \$54,000) \div 2}$$

$$= 1.3 \text{ times}$$

The inventory may be said to have "turned over" 1.3 times on the average during the year since cost of goods sold was 1.3 times the average inventory level. Since a profit normally is realized each time the inventory is sold (i.e., turned over), an increase in the ratio is favorable, up to a point. The higher the ratio, the shorter the average "shelf life" for the items stocked. On the other hand, if the ratio is too high, sales may be lost because of items that are out of stock. The turnover ratio often is converted to a time-basis expression called the **average days' supply in inventory.** The computation would be:

$$\text{Average Days' Supply in Inventory} = \frac{\text{Days in Year}}{\text{Inventory Turnover}}$$

$$\text{Packard Company, 1974} = \frac{365}{1.3} = 281 \text{ Average Day's Supply in Inventory}$$

(Another example: A turnover ratio of 12.0 would convert as 365 ÷ 12.0 = 30 + average days' supply in inventory.) Turnover ratios are used widely because they are relevant, simple to compute, and easy to understand.

TESTS OF SOLVENCY AND EQUITY POSITION

We noted above that current liquidity refers to the current assets and current liabilities. In contrast, **solvency** refers to the ability of a company to meet its **long-term obligations** on a continuing basis. Equity position refers to the relative amount of resources provided by the two equities: creditors' equity (i.e., debt capital) and owners' equity (i.e., equity capital). Since the sum of these two equities equals total equities (i.e., total investment), certain critical relationships exist. There are three ratios that reflect these relationships.

$$(9) \quad \text{Debt/Equity Ratio} \quad = \frac{\text{Creditors' Equity}}{\text{Owners' Equity}}$$

$$\text{Packard Company, 1974} = \frac{\$42,550}{\$104,000} = .41$$

This ratio reflects the proportionate relationship between debt and owners' equity. Instead of this single ratio, some people prefer two ratios that measure the same relationship:

(10) Owners' Equity to
Total Equities

$$= \frac{\text{Owners' Equity}}{\text{Total Equities}}$$

(i.e., liabilities plus owners' equity)

$$\text{Packard Company, 1974} = \frac{\$104,000}{\$146,550} = .71 \text{ (or } 71\%)$$

(11) Creditors' Equity to
Total Equities

$$= \frac{\text{Creditors' Equity}}{\text{Total Equities}}$$

$$\text{Packard Company, 1974} = \frac{\$42,550}{\$146,550} = .29 \text{ (or } 29\%)$$

Obviously, the latter two ratios are complements of each other; they will always sum to 100%. They indicate the relative amount of total resources provided by each of the two groups of suppliers of capital to the business. Debt capital is risky for the debtor because there are (a) specific maturity dates for the principal amounts and (b) specific interest payments that must be made. Both claims are enforceable by law and do not depend upon the earning of income by the company. In contrast, capital supplied by owners does not give rise to similar obligations; that is, it is not fixed as to amounts and dates of repayment; thus, equity capital is much less risky for the company. However, there is a compensating factor—to obtain equity capital, which, conversely, is more risky for the *investor,* the company must incur an overall higher cost of obtaining capital. In the long-run, earnings rates on stockholders' equity normally must be higher than interest rates paid to creditors. Despite the element of debt risk to the company, it may be advantageous to the stockholders if the company derives significant amounts of capital through borrowing. For example, assume a company is earning 15% return on total equities (i.e., on total investment), while its borrowing rate on debt is 7% on the average. To the extent that there is capital provided by debt (at a 7% cost), the difference between the earnings rate on total resources of 15% and the 7% interest paid to the creditors accrues to the benefit of the stockholders.[4] In the long run, the stockholders benefit by the 15% earned on the resources provided by them, plus the difference between the 15% return and the 7% interest rate paid on the resources provided by the creditors. This effect is known as **trading on the equity.** A company with a high proportion of long-term debt (such as bonds payable) is said to be **highly**

---

[4] Interest expense on debt is a deductible expense on the income tax return; in contrast, payments to stockholders by means of dividends are not. Thus, funds obtained by means of debt tend to be less costly. The real cost of debt in the above example is only about 3.5%, depending upon the income tax rate.

levered. The debt/equity ratio or, alternatively, the two equity ratios indicate the balance that the management has brought about between these two sources of capital.

MARKET TESTS

A number of ratios have been developed to measure the "market worth" of a share of stock. Basically, these market tests attempt to relate the **current market price** of a share of stock to some indicator of the profit (or gain) that might accrue to an investor. There are two market test ratios that are widely quoted by analysts, stockbrokers, investors, and others. They are the price/earnings ratio and the dividend yield ratio.

(12) Price/Earnings Ratio $= \dfrac{\text{Current Market Price per Share}}{\text{Earnings per Share}}$

**Packard Company
(assuming a current market price of $15.60 per share),
1974** $= \dfrac{\$15.60}{\$1.04^*} = 15 \text{ to } 1$

* Page 593.

Thus, it is said that this stock was selling at 15 times the earnings per share. This ratio is frequently referred to as **the multiple.** Sometimes the components of this ratio are inverted, giving what is referred to as the **capitalization rate.** This is said to be the rate at which the stock market apparently is capitalizing the current earnings. For example, the computation would be $\$1.04 \div \$15.60 = 6.67\%$ (capitalization rate).

(13) Dividend Yield Ratio $= \dfrac{\text{Dividends per Share}}{\text{Market Price per Share}}$

For Packard Company (assuming dividends paid of $.75 per share), 1974 $= \dfrac{\$.75}{\$15.60} = .0481$ or 4.81%

The dividend yield ratio attempts to measure the potential return to the investor, based upon the dividends declared per share (which is income to him), against the cost of his investment as indicated by the market price per share. It is a volatile measure since the price of stock may change materially over short periods of time. This ratio is frequently referred to simply as the "yield."

Interpreting ratios

Ratio analyses, along the lines discussed in the preceding paragraphs, catch the attention of many people; however, ratios pose significant interpretative problems to the user. To evaluate a ratio, it must be compared, at least in the mind of the user, with some *standard* that represents an optimum or desirable level. For example, the return-on-investment ratio may be compared with a long-range objective expressed in this manner. Some ratios, by their characteristics, are unfavorable if they are *either* too high or too low. For example, in a certain company a working-capital ratio of approximately 2:1 may be considered optimum. In this situation, a ratio of 1:1 would tend to indicate a danger of being unable to meet maturing obligations; whereas, a ratio of 3:1 may indicate that excess funds are being left idle rather than being profitably employed. Another problem is posed in respect to differences in situations. An optimum ratio for one company frequently will not be the same as the optimum ratio for another company. Thus, comparisons of ratios between companies frequently are of questionable validity, particularly when there are important differences between companies, such as size, industry, and nature of operations. Another limitation is that most ratios represent *averages* and, therefore, may tend to obscure large variations in the underlying factors above and below the average.

Despite these difficulties there are four types of "standards" against which ratios and percents frequently are compared:

(1) Comparison of the present ratios with the historical ratios of the company, with particular attention to changes in the *trend* of each ratio over time.

(2) Experience of the analyst who has a "subjective feel for the right relationships" in a given situation. These subjective judgments of an experienced and competent observer tend to be more reliable than purely mechanical comparisons.

(3) Comparison of the present ratios with planned goals and objectives expressed as ratios. Many companies prepare, on a continuing basis, comprehensive profit plans (i.e., budgets) that incorporate realistic plans for the future. These plans generally incorporate planned goals for significant ratios, such as profit margin and return on investment. These internally developed standards clearly have less inherent difficulties than any of the other comparisons; however, they generally are not available to external parties.

(4) Comparison with external standards. These comparisons include the use of ratios and percents from other similar companies and from industry averages. Industry averages are published by many trade associations, governmental agencies, and certain profit-making enterprises. A variety of ratios will be found in the publications of Dun & Bradstreet, Inc. (ratios for 125 industry groups), Moody's *Manual of Investments,* and Standard and Poor's *Corporation Records.*

In summary, interpretation of amounts reported on financial statements may be enhanced by expressing certain relationships as ratios and

Exhibit 16–6

Clark Equipment Company

Statistical Data

Performance Review

Notwithstanding the cyclical nature of the capital goods industry, Clark has generated continuing growth in sales, net income, cash dividends and net worth. Such progress is shown in the following tabulation which averages these key indicators over three-year periods to even out the peaks and valleys characteristics of the heavy equipment business.

| | | AVERAGE ANNUAL | | |
Period	Sales	Net Income	Cash Dividends	Year-End Net Worth
1952-1954	$109,563,000	$ 5,464,000	$ 3,079,000	$ 39,832,000
1955-1957	139,900,000	9,055,000	4,791,000	53,434,000
1958-1960	182,524,000	8,531,000	5,292,000	67,056,000
1961-1963	222,300,000	12,448,000	6,285,000	87,883,000
1964-1966	426,661,000	24,828,000	9,387,000	135,819,000
1967-1969	561,021,000	30,581,000	14,336,000	191,520,000
1970-1972	770,249,000	34,870,000	17,826,000	281,920,000

Net Sales (in millions)

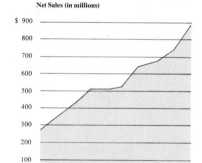

Cash Dividends (in millions)

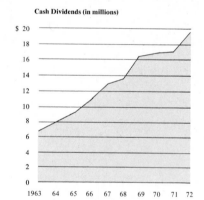

Net Income (in millions)

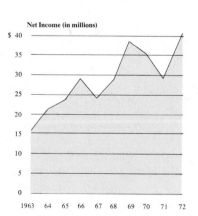

Shareholders' Equity (in millions)

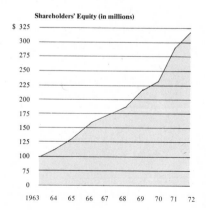

Clark Sales Growth

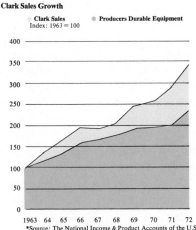

● Clark Sales
  Index: 1963 = 100   ● Producers Durable Equipment

*Source: The National Income & Product Accounts of the U.S.

Although subject to the capital goods cycle, Clark's sales performance has been consistently better than the general sales trend of durable goods producers.

Income and Dividends per Share

Adjusted for stock splits

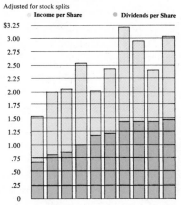

● Income per Share   ● Dividends per Share

Dividend payout to Clark Equipment Shareholders has averaged about 50 percent of net income since 1963.

Capital Expenditures and Depreciation*

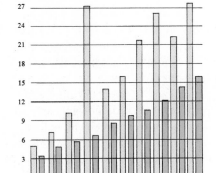

● Capital Expenditures   ● Depreciation

*In Millions of Dollars

Since 1966, Clark has invested approximately $130.3 million in new plant and equipment. Depreciation provisions during the period amounted to $73.0 million. Net plant at Dec. 31, 1972 amounted to $142.7 million.

Return on Sales and Equity

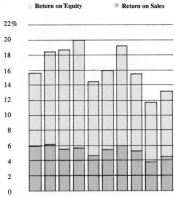

● Return on Equity   ● Return on Sales

In the last 10 years, Clark has shown an average return on shareholders' equity of 16.4 percent and an average return on sales at 5.4 percent.

Distribution of the Income Dollar

Wages, Salaries & Benefits 30.9¢   Materials, Supplies & Services 57.0¢

Depreciation 1.7¢
Interest 2.9¢
Income taxes 3.1¢
Dividends 2.1¢
Reinvested in business 2.3¢

percents. Although a great many ratios can be calculated, a few usually will suffice for a given decision that is under consideration. Having selected the relevant ratios, the analyst has the central problem of evaluating them. This evaluation involves the task of selecting one or more realistic standards with which to compare them. Four types of standards are frequently used: (1) historical standards; (2) experience; (3) planned standards; and (4) external standards. Experience and competence are particularly important. The interpretation of ratios often may suggest strengths and weaknesses in the operations and/or the financial position of the company that should be accorded in-depth investigation and evaluation if significant decisions are contemplated.

Selected ratios are commonly presented in the published financial statements. For example, the 15-year summary shown in Exhibit 16–3 reports the following ratios: (1) income per share; (2) dividends per share; (3) working-capital ratio; (4) book value per share; (5) return on net sales (i.e., profit margins); and (6) return on average share-holders' equity. Ratios frequently are presented in graphic format. For example, Exhibit 16–6 shows a presentation by the Clark Equipment Company in its 1972 annual report.

PART TWO: EFFECTS OF PRICE-LEVEL CHANGES IN FINANCIAL STATEMENTS

In using and interpreting financial statements, the impact of significant inflationary and deflationary trends should be appreciated. The impact of inflation on the economy in recent years has been a major concern of government, business, economists, accountants, and others. It is a very difficult issue from any point of view.

The impact of inflation on financial statements is difficult to assess by the user, particularly when price-level data do not appear on the statements. Accountants and business are not in agreement as to what should be done to assist the statement user in this respect. In this section we will briefly discuss the major issues and an approach that might prove helpful to the decision maker using financial statements.

The nature of price-level effects

Money is the common denominator for accounting measurements. It is a unit of measure of value. That is, a dollar will command a certain amount of **real goods and services** in the marketplace at a given time. Unfortunately, the dollar, or any other monetary unit, does not maintain a stable value in terms of the real goods and services that it will command. Over time, one unit of money (e.g., one dollar) will command less goods and services in the case of inflation, or, alternatively, more goods and services in the case of deflation; that is, its purchasing power changes. In applying the concept of historical cost (i.e., the cost principle), transactions are recorded in the accounts and subsequently reported in historical dollars. Many of those dollar amounts remain in the accounts and are reported in the financial statements over many years (such as the cost of a fixed asset). Thus, over a period of time, the accounting system accumulates and reports dollars having different purchasing power, given inflation or deflation. Under the concept of historical cost, dollars having different real values are aggregated on the balance sheet and matched on the income statement. Thus, during periods of significant inflation or deflation, the accounting figures are apt to reflect considerable distortion because of the effects of the changing value of the monetary unit. To illustrate, assume a company purchased a building for $200,000 when the general price-level index was 100. Assuming straight-line depreciation, no residual value, and a 40-year life, the annual depreciation would be $5,000 per year. Let's assume that the current year is year 30 (since acquisition) and that the current price-level index is 200.[5] At the end of year 30, the financial statements would show the following amounts, based on historical costs as recorded in the accounting system:

Balance Sheet:
    Fixed assets:
        Building (at cost)............................ $200,000
        Accumulated depreciation.................... 150,000
            Book value............................ $50,000

Income Statement:
    Depreciation expense......................... $ 5,000

Obviously, all the amounts shown above represent dollars "valued" at acquisition date. Those dollars had a purchasing-power equivalent of 100 (the index). On the balance sheet they are aggregated with other dollar amounts having a different purchasing-power equivalent. On the income statement the depreciation expense, expressed in the dollars at acquisition (index 100), are matched with revenue, which is in current dollars (index 200). The current general price-level index of 200 means that each current dollar will command (buy) only one-half (i.e., 100/200) as much real goods and services as when the index was 100. One could *adjust* the above amounts for the price-level change (inflation in this case). The adjustment can be accomplished by multiplying the historical cost amount by a price-level index ratio. Using the data

---

[5] A price-level index is a statistical value that expresses the average price level of each of a series of periods in relative terms. To construct a price-level index, the prices of primary items ordinarily bought are averaged, then expressed as an index number. A base year is selected and assigned the index number of 100. Changes in the average price level then are expressed in relationship to this base. Changes in the index number, from period to period, may be viewed as a measure of inflation (cheaper dollars) and deflation (dearer dollars). For example, a change in the price level from 100 to 200 would indicate significant inflation; on the average, when the index is 200, one dollar will buy only one-half as much real goods as when the index was 100.

given above, the ratio would be 200/100, or 2.0. Multiplication by this ratio raises the cost-based amounts to the current price level basis. The calculations and the resultant adjusted amounts for the data given above would be as follows:

	Historical Cost Basis	Computations	Adjusted to Current Price-Level Basis
Balance-Sheet Amounts:			
Fixed assets:			
Building....................	$200,000	× 200/100 =	$400,000
Accumulated depreciation.....	150,000	× 200/100 =	300,000
Book value............	$ 50,000		$100,000
Income Statement Amount:			
Depreciation expense...........	$ 5,000	× 200/100 =	$ 10,000

If all the other revenues and expenses were already expressed in current dollars, then the effect of this increase in depreciation expense would be to decrease reported net income by $5,000.

The adjustment to the current price-level basis is done each year. When reading a financial statement for 1973, one is most interested in (and thinks in terms of) 1973 dollars. In 1974, he thinks in terms of 1974 dollars. That is one rationale for restating the amounts each year in terms of the then current dollars (the then current price level).

In recent years, the accounting profession has become quite concerned about the distortion of accounting amounts on the financial statements as a consequence of continued inflationary trends. In periods of inflation, net income, unadjusted for the effects of inflation, tends to be overstated. In June 1969, the APB issued *Statement No. 3, Financial Statements Restated for General Price-Level Changes,* which recommended supplementary financial statements, in addition to the regular cost-basis statements, that present the amounts restated for general price-level changes. *Statement No. 3* recommends that a business present two sets of financial statements as follows: (1) on the traditional historical cost basis and (2) on an adjusted price-level basis. Some accountants, however, prefer that one set of financial statements be presented with separate columns for the historical cost basis and the adjusted price-level basis. Very few companies use either approach. They continue to limit their statements to the regular cost-basis statements.

As a basis for discussing and illustrating the basic concept of developing amounts for the financial statements adjusted for price-level changes, we will use a simplified situation. Assume the Cole Company has been operating for one year only, 1974. At the start of the year, the general price-level index was 100 and at the end of the year it was 120. (We are using a large price-level change to emphasize the effects.) At the end of 1974, the statements shown in Exhibit 16–7 were prepared following the usual accounting approaches (historical cost basis).

The company desires to add a column to each statement entitled "Adjusted for Price-Level Changes to the Current Price-Level Basis." The price-level data given in Exhibit 16–7 were developed to be used as a basis for the adjustment or restatement for the price-level changes.

To comprehend the restatement of amounts on the financial state-

Exhibit 16–7

COLE COMPANY
Balance Sheet
At December 31, 1974

	Historical Cost Basis
Assets	
Cash	$ 34,000
Land	10,000
Building (net)	60,000
Total	$104,000
Liabilities	
Note payable, long-term	$ 8,000
Stockholders' Equity	
Capital stock	80,000
Retained earnings	16,000
Total	$104,000

Income Statement
For Year Ending December 31, 1974

Revenues	$ 55,000
Expenses (for simplification, not detailed here)	(33,000)
Depreciation expense	(6,000)
Net Income	$ 16,000

Price-Level Data*

Item	General Price Level when Acquired or Incurred
Price level at beginning of the year—100	
Price level at end of the year—120	
Cash	106.25†
Land purchased	100
Building purchased	100
Note payable executed	100
Capital stock sold	100
Revenues	110†
Expenses	110†
Depreciation expense	100(same as the asset)

* The company desires to add a column to each statement entitled "Adjusted for Price-Level Changes to the Current Price-Level Basis." The price-level data given above were developed to be used as a basis for the adjustment or restatement for the price-level changes.

† Since a number of cash, revenue, and expense transactions occurred *uniformly* throughout the year, an average index is used for these items.

ments, a careful distinction must be made between two quite different types of items known as monetary items and nonmonetary items. They cause a quite different impact on the wealth of the holder of them, when the real value of the monetary unit changes (i.e., inflation or deflation). Monetary items have future amounts stated in dollars that are fixed by contract, such as a payable or receivable, or are otherwise fixed by their nature, such as cash. For example, the $8,000 note payable, reflected in Exhibit 16–7, requires this specific number of dollars to be paid at maturity, irrespective of inflation or deflation. Thus, the holders of monetary assets or liabilities gain or lose general purchasing power during periods of inflation or deflation simply as a result of changes in the general price level. For example, cash held during a period of inflation incurs a loss to the holder since each dollar held progressively buys fewer real goods and services. Similarly, if one owes a debt during a period of inflation, there will be a gain for the one owing the obligation because the debt at maturity will be paid off with the specified number of dollars each of which will command fewer real goods and services than when the debt was incurred; that is, the debt will be paid off with cheaper dollars. On the other side, the one to whom the debt is owed will have a loss. In settlement of the debt, he will receive dollars having less purchasing power. *Thus, the fundamental aspect of monetary items is that the holder of them incurs a "general price-level gain or loss" during periods of inflation or deflation.* The loss or gain reflects command over real goods and services. The loss or gain on monetary items must be recognized in accounting for price-level changes. Restatement to a price-level adjusted basis must recognize these losses or gains on the *income statement* but not on the balance sheet.

In contrast, nonmonetary items do not have a fixed future amount in dollars; they are free to move up and down in respect to the number of dollars they will command in the marketplace. For example, a tract of land purchased for $10,000 when the price index was 100 would tend to move up in terms of real goods to a current cash sales value of $12,-000 as the result of an increase to 120 of the general price index, other things being equal (i.e., $10,000 \times 120/100 = $12,000$). Thus, the holder would not incur a loss or gain on this nonmonetary asset due to the general price-level change. Under the assumption that other things are equal, in this situation he could sell the land that cost $10,000 for $12,000. The $12,000 then would buy the same quantity of real goods that the $10,000 would have bought at the purchase date of the land. Examples of nonmonetary items are inventories, investments in common stocks, property, fixed assets, and patents. *The fundamental aspect of nonmonetary items is that the holder does not gain or lose in real purchasing power as a result of changes in the general price level.* That is, there is no "general price-level gain or loss" to be recognized on nonmonetary items in accounting for price-level changes. Restatement to a price-level basis requires adjustment of nonmonetary items on the balance sheet. Since they do not create a gain or loss as a result of price-level changes, they do not affect the income statement in restatement.

Now, let's return to our example for the Cole Company and two financial statements given in Exhibit 16–7. We will restate them in terms of the current price level. The balance sheet reflects two monetary items —cash and notes payable. As explained above, the *monetary items* are not restated on the balance sheet since they have a fixed monetary amount in the future that cannot be changed. In contrast, the *non-monetary items* are restated on the balance sheet since their future command over dollars changes with the price level. The historical amount of each nonmonetary item is restated by multiplying each amount by an "index ratio." An index ratio is the index number at the end of the year divided by the index number when the transaction occurred. The restatement of the balance sheet is reflected in Exhibit 16–8. The computations are shown in detail.

The income-statement amounts are restated by multiplying the appropriate "index ratio" by each amount. The gain or loss on the *monetary* items is the difference between the historical cost amount and the restated amounts. The computation for the Cole Company is as follows:

Monetary Items	Historical Cost Basis	Restated to Price-Level Basis	Difference Gain (Loss)
Cash..................	$34,000	$34,000 × 120/106.25 = $38,400	($4,400)
Notes payable..........	8,000	$ 8,000 × 120/100 = $ 9,600	1,600
Net price-level loss on monetary items during the period............			($2,800)

A comparison of the balance-sheet items in Exhibit 16–8 shows that restatement increased total assets from $104,000 to $118,000, which is a 13.5% increase. In contrast, the income statement reflected a decrease in reported income from $16,000 to $14,000, which is a 12.5% decrease. When there is an inflationary trend, price-level adjusted net income usually will be lower than the cost-basis amount. Many observers have suggested that this is one of the primary reasons companies have shown little interest during the last few years in price-level adjusted statements. Another reason often cited is that users will not understand the implications of price-level adjustments; however, there are many who disagree with this presumption. Perhaps a more fundamental reason is that price-level adjusted statements do not deal adequately with the concept of fair-value statements.

The preceding discussions and illustrations focus on the impacts of significant inflationary trends on financial statements. Decision makers need to appreciate the fundamental nature of these impacts in using and interpreting financial statements. Restated amounts are particularly

Exhibit 16–8

COLE COMPANY
Balance Sheet
At December 31, 1974

	Historical Cost Basis	*Restatement Computations*	*Current Price-Level Basis*
Assets			
Cash...............	$ 34,000	Monetary item, no restatement....	$ 34,000
Land..............	10,000	Nonmonetary item, $10,000 × 120/100.....................	12,000
Building (net)........	60,000	Nonmonetary item, $60,000 × 120/100.....................	72,000
Total..........	$104,000		$118,000
Liabilities			
Note payable, long-term.........	$ 8,000	Monetary item, no restatement....	$ 8,000
Stockholders' Equity			
Capital stock........	80,000	Nonmonetary item, $80,000 × 120/100.....................	96,000
Retained earnings....	16,000	Restatement per income statement.....................	14,000
Total..........	$104,000		$118,000

Income Statement
For Year Ended December 31, 1974

Revenues..............	$ 55,000	$55,000 × 120/110...............	$ 60,000
Expenses..............	(33,000)	$33,000 × 120/110...............	(36,000)
Depreciation expense.............	(6,000)	$6,000 × 120/100...............	(7,200)
Net Income...........	$ 16,000		$ 16,800
Price-level gains (losses) on monetary items:			
Cash......................		$34,000 − ($34,000 × 120/106.25 = $38,400*) =	(4,400)
Notes payable..............		8,000 − ($8,000 × 120/100 = $9,600) =	1,600
Net income restated...			$ 14,000

* Rounded.

useful in many situations. Restatement of historical costs for price-level changes is somewhat complex and requires a significant amount of detail in respect to the exact dates when each item was acquired.

Despite the recommendations included in APB *Statement No. 3,* and significant inflationary trends, industry has exhibited considerable reluctance to publish supplementary statements restated for price-level changes. The opposition appears to be based upon the belief that two sets of statements for the same period would serve to confuse, rather than to enlighten, most of the users of financial statements. If inflationary trends continue, this attitude will have to change.

Concluding note

This volume focused on financial accounting and reporting to external parties, as represented by potential investors, creditors, and the public at large. We have emphasized the use and interpretation of financial statements by decision makers. The conceptual side of accounting also was emphasized in order to provide a higher level of sophistication in using and interpreting financial statements than is otherwise possible. This focus also provides the reasons underlying the various accounting concepts, measurements, and approaches. Procedures and mechanics were introduced only to the extent deemed essential to further one's study of the broad subject of accounting, particularly the important subject of management accounting.

In the next volume, attention is focused on the area of management accounting. Management accounting emphasizes the planning, controlling, and decision-making activities of management. It considers both the behavioral and quantitative implications of accounting in the management process. Throughout that volume you will find that most of the concepts and practices discussed and illustrated in this volume are applicable. However, managerial accounting is not constrained by "generally accepted accounting principles" since its primary focus is to serve internal management in effectively carrying out the broad functions of executive administration.

Important terms

Comparative statements	Turnover ratios
Ratio or percentage analysis	Trading on the equity
Component percentages	Price-level effects
Tests of profitability	Monetary items
Tests of liquidity	Nonmonetary items
Tests of solvency	Price-level restatement
Market tests	

Questions for discussion

1. What are the three fundamental uses of external financial statements by decision makers?
2. What are some of the primary items on financial statements about which creditors are concerned?
3. Explain why the notes to the financial statements are particularly important in use and interpretation.
4. What is the primary purpose of comparative financial statements?
5. Explain what is meant by ratio analysis.
6. What are component percentages?

7. Explain return on investment. Why is it considered to be the primary indicator of profitability?

8. Contrast the working-capital ratio with the quick ratio.

9. What does the debt/equity ratio reflect?

10. Why are statement users especially interested in financial summaries covering a number of years?

11. What is meant by a price-level change? Explain the meaning of a general price-level index.

12. What is meant by restatement of the financial statement for price-level effects?

13. Distinguish between monetary and nonmonetary items. Explain their impacts on the business when there is inflation.

14. Explain why monetary items are not restated on the balance sheet and why nonmonetary items are.

15. Explain why monetary items affect the income statement but nonmonetary items do not.

Exercises E16–1. The comparative financial statements prepared at December 31, 1974, for the Hudson Company reflected the following data (summarized):

	1973	1974
Income Statement:		
Sales.....................................	$140,000	$150,000*
Cost of goods sold.........................	85,000	90,000
Gross margin on sales.....................	55,000	60,000
Operating expenses and interest expense........	40,500	43,000
Pretax income............................	14,500	17,000
Income taxes.............................	4,500	5,000
Net Income	$ 10,000	$ 12,000
Balance Sheet:		
Cash....................................	$ 11,000	$ 8,000
Accounts receivable (net)...................	14,000	12,000
Inventory................................	28,000	30,000
Fixed assets (net).........................	43,000	50,000
	$ 96,000	$100,000
Current liabilities	$ 17,000	$ 15,000
Long-term liabilities (6% interest)...........	35,000	35,000
Common stock (par $10)....................	40,000	40,000
Retained earnings†........................	4,000	10,000
	$ 96,000	$100,000

* One-third were credit sales.
† During 1974, cash dividends amounting to $6,000 were declared and paid.

Required:

Complete the following columns for each item in the above comparative financial statements:

Increase (Decrease)
1974 over 1973

Amount   *Percent*

E16–2. Based on the comparative data given in Exercise 16–1 for Hudson Company, present component percentages for 1974 only.

E16–3. Based on the comparative data given in Exercise 16–1 for Hudson Company. Use a separate sheet and complete the following tabulation for 1974 only (assume a common stock price of $33 per share); add the ratios that should be included under each category:

Name and Computation of the Ratio (show computations)	*Brief Explanation and Meaning of the Ratio*

A.   Tests of profitability:
   (1)   Return on investment ratio
         (on total investment)
   (2) Etc.	

B.   Tests of liquidity
   (1)   Working-capital ratio
   (2) Etc.	

C.   Tests of solvency and equity position:
   (1)   Debt/equity ratio
   (2) Etc.	

D.   Market tests:
   (1)   Price/earnings ratio
   (2) Etc.	

E16–4. The Case Company has just prepared the comparative annual income statement for 1974.

CASE COMPANY
Income Statement
For the Years Ended December 31, 1974 and 1973

	For the Year Ended	
	1974	*1973*
Sales (one-half on credit).........	$100,000	$ 95,000
Cost of goods sold..............	48,000	46,000
Gross margin on sales............	52,000	49,000
Expenses (including $2,000 interest expense each year)............	34,000	33,000
Pretax income.................	18,000	16,000
Income taxes on operations (22%)	3,960	3,520
Income before extraordinary items.	14,040	12,480
Extraordinary loss.............. $3,000		
Less income taxes saved........ 660	2,340	
Extraordinary gain	$1,000	
Applicable income tax.........	220	780
Net Income..................	$ 11,700	$ 13,260

Balance Sheet at December 31, 1974 and 1973

	1974	1973
Assets:		
Cash	$ 47,200	$ 20,000
Accounts receivable (net)	35,000	30,000
Inventory	30,000	40,000
Fixed assets (net)	90,000	100,000
Total Assets	$202,200	$190,000
Liabilities:		
Accounts payable	$ 60,000	$ 50,000
Income taxes payable	1,500	1,000
Notes payable, long-term	25,000	25,000
Stockholders' Equity:		
Capital stock (par $10)	80,000	80,000
Retained earnings	35,700	34,000
Total	$202,200	$190,000

Required:

Compute for 1974 the tests of (a) profitability, (b) liquidity, (c) solvency, and (d) market. Assume the quoted price of the stock to be $26.50 for 1974. Dividends paid during 1974 amounted to $10,000.

E16–5.   The balance sheet for the Scott Company, prepared on the usual historical cost basis at December 31, 1974, has been completed. Supplemental statements are to be developed on a "restated price-level basis." The following four items were selected from the balance sheet:

Items	Historical Cost Basis (when acquired)	General Price-Level Index (when acquired)
Receivables	$69,000	115
Investment, stocks	42,000	105
Land, plant site	15,000	100
Payables	99,000	110

The price level at the end of 1974 was 120.

Required:

(a) Indicate which of the above items are monetary and non-monetary.

(b) Set up a table to derive the amount "Restated Price-level Basis" that should be shown on the supplementary balance sheet for each item. Show computations.

(c) Compute the loss or gain resulting from price-level changes that will be shown on the supplementary income statement. Show computations.

(d) Explain why certain of the items were omitted from your computation in (c).

E16–6.   In 1954, the Klassen Company purchased a plant site for $23,100. Immediately thereafter, construction of a plant building was started. The building was completed in June 1955 at a cost of $336,000. The building is being depreciated on a straight-line basis assuming an estimated useful life of 30 years and no residual value.

Assume the price-level index in 1954 was 110, in 1955 it was 112, and at the end of 1974 it was 180. Complete the following on a separate sheet of paper:

	Amount to be Reported Assuming:	
	Historical Cost Basis	*Price-Level Adjusted Basis*
Balance Sheet at December 31, 1974:		
Fixed assets:		
Land..........................		
Building......................		
Less accumulated depreciation (20 years).....................		
Income Statement for 1974:		
Depreciation expense.............		

Show your computations.

Problems   **P16–1.**   The Arrow Sales Corporation has just completed the comparative statements for the year ended December 31, 1974. At this point, certain analytical and interpretative procedures are to be undertaken. The completed statements (summarized) are as follows:

	1973	1974
Income Statement:		
Sales.....................................	$390,000	$400,000*
Cost of goods sold........................	218,000	220,000
Gross margin on sales.....................	172,000	180,000
Operating expenses and interest expense........	148,000	147,000
Pretax income............................	24,000	33,000
Income taxes.............................	7,000	9,000
Net income..............................	$ 17,000	$ 24,000
Balance Sheet:		
Cash	$ 2,700	$ 25,400
Accounts receivable (net)....................	30,000	24,000
Merchandise inventory......................	24,000	30,000
Prepaid expenses..........................	500	600
Fixed assets (net).........................	130,000	120,000
	$187,200	$200,000
Accounts payable	$ 20,000	$ 19,000
Income taxes payable......................	1,200	1,000
Bonds payable (5% interest rate).............	50,000	50,000
Common stock (par $10)....................	100,000	100,000†
Retained earnings‡........................	16,000	30,000
	$187,200	$200,000

* Twenty-five percent were credit sales.
† The market price of the stock at the end of 1974 was $24.00 per share.
‡ During 1974 the company declared and paid a cash dividend of $10,000.

Required:

(a) Prepare the "Increase (Decrease)" columns for "Amount" and "Percent" for 1974 over 1973.

(b) Compute the component percentages for 1974 only.

(c) Based upon the comparative data, complete the following tabulation for 1974 only (use separate sheet and show computations):

Name and Computation of the Ratio *(use those illustrated in the chapter)*	Brief Explanation of the Ratio
A. Tests of profitability:	
B. Tests of liquidity	
C. Tests of solvency and equity position:	
D. Market tests:	

P16–2. The Rundell Company has prepared the annual financial statements at December 31, 1974. The company is considering the development of supplemental statements on the "restated price-level basis." The following seven items were selected from the balance sheet:

	Items	Historical Cost Basis *(when acquired)*	General Price-Level Index *(when acquired)*
1.	Cash..............................	$ 14,800	148
2.	Merchandise inventory...............	58,000	145
3.	Accounts receivable (net)............	28,800	144
4.	Land...........................	12,000	100
5.	Building (net).....................	157,500	105
6.	Accounts payable..................	42,000	140
7.	Bonds payable....................	88,000	110

At the end of 1974 the price-level index was 150.

Required:

(a) Group the above items into two categories: monetary and nonmonetary.

(b) Set up a table and compute the amount "Restated Price-level Basis" that should be shown on the balance sheet for each of the seven items. Show calculations. Round to even $100 in the restatement.

(c) Compute the loss or gain resulting from the price-level changes that will be shown on the supplementary income statement. Show calculations.

(d) Explain why certain of the seven items were omitted from your computations in (c).

P16–3. At the end of the first year of operations, the Davis Company prepared the following balance sheet and income statement:

DAVIS COMPANY
Balance Sheet
At December 31, 1974

Assets:

Cash.....................................	$ 3,330
Accounts receivable (net)......................	5,650
Inventory...................................	46,000
Fixed assets (net)............................	55,000
Total.................................	$109,980

Liabilities:

Accounts payable............................	$ 3,480
Bonds payable..............................	23,000

Stockholders' Equity:

Capital stock...............................	66,000
Retained earnings...........................	17,500
Total.................................	$109,980

Income Statement
For the Year Ended December 31, 1974

Revenues......................................	$ 69,000
Expenses (not detailed)........................	(46,000)
Depreciation expense..........................	(5,500)
Net Income...................................	$ 17,500

	General Price Level When Acquired or Incurred
Price-level data:	
Price level at start of year—110	
Price level at end of year—120	
Cash	111*
Accounts receivable	113*
Inventory	115
Fixed assets	110
Accounts payable	116
Bonds payable	115
Revenues	115*
Expenses	115*
Depreciation expense	110
Capital stock	110

* Averages.

Required:

Recast the income statement and balance sheet with the following headings: (1) Historical Cost Basis; (2) Restatement Computations; (3) Current Price-Level Basis.

P16–4. After operating for one year, the Swenson Company completed the following income statement and balance sheet:

SWENSON COMPANY
Balance Sheet
At December 31, 1974

Assets:

Cash.	$ 42,300
Accounts receivable (net).	29,580
Long-term investment, stock of Co. X.	7,400
Land.	11,200
Plant (net).	140,000
Total.	$230,480

Liabilities:

Accounts payable.	$ 5,880
Bonds payable.	28,000

Stockholders' Equity:

Capital stock.	182,000
Retained earnings.	14,600
Total.	$230,480

Income Statement
For the Year Ending December 31, 1974

Revenues.	$ 87,000
Expenses (not detailed).	(58,400)
Depreciation expense.	(14,000)
Net Income	$ 14,600

Price-Level Data:	General Price Level When Acquired or Incurred
Price level at start of year	140
Price level at end of year	150
Cash	141*
Accounts receivable	141*
Long-term investment purchased	148
Land purchased	140
Plant acquired	140
Accounts payable	147*
Bonds payable sold	140
Capital stock	140
Revenues	145*
Expenses	146*
Depreciation expense	140*

* Averages of a number of transactions in each instance.

Required:

Recast the income statement and balance sheet with the following headings: (1) Historical Cost Basis; (2) Computations; (3) Current Price-Level Basis.

Index

FUNDAMENTALS OF FINANCIAL ACCOUNTING
Welsch and Anthony

List of Key Figures

Chapter 1

Exercises

1-1	None	None
1-2	None	None
1-3	Effective after-tax rate	4½%
1-4	Profit .... $	3,900
1-5	Net cash flow (negative)	8,900

Problems

1-1	Total expenses .... $	7,340
1-2	Profit before income taxes	2,470

Chapter 2

Exercises

2-1	None	None
2-2	None	None
2-3	Earnings per share .... $	2.106
2-4	Total depreciation expense for 1974	1,320
2-5	Balance sheet total	50,000
2-6	None	None
2-7	Decrease in cash	6,000
2-8	Cash distributed to owners	15,000

Problems

2-1	Earnings per share .... $	23.40
2-2	Correct balance sheet totals	210,640
2-3	None	None
2-4	Earnings per share	18.72
2-5	Building, book value, 1975	125,000
2-6	Total depreciation expense for 1974	4,500

Chapter 3

Exercises

3-1	Earnings per share .... $	2.96
3-2	Total assets	230,000
3-3	Increase in cash	19,000
3-4	None	None
3-5	Earnings per share	3.00
3-6	Net income	16,800
3-7	None	None
3-8	Total stockholders' equity	200,000
3-9	None	None
3-10	None	None
3-11	None	None
3-12	None	None

Problems

3-1	Net income, earnings per share.. $	2.31
3-2	Total shareholders' equity	239,000
3-3	Fixed assets, total	6,720
3-4	(Req. b) Effective interest rate ..	4.8%
3-5	None	None
3-6	None	None
3-7	None	None

Chapter 4

Exercises

4-1	Total owners' equity .... $	30,000
4-2	Depreciation expense (108)	200 debit
4-3	None	None
4-4	None	None
4-5	Balance in cash account	3,450
4-6	(Req. b) Net loss in January	1,000
4-7	Interest expense is a	800 debit

Problems

4-1	None	None
4-2	None	None
4-3	Net income .... $	15,300
4-4	(Req. 2) Operating expenses, total	32,980
4-5	(Req. 3) Trial balance total	79,000
4-6	Earnings per share	11.37
4-7	(Req. d) Net income $15,600; balance sheet total	57,100
4-8	(Req. 5) Net income $40,100; total assets	144,100
4-9	Net income corrected	21,640

Chapter 5

Exercises

5-1	None	None
5-2	None	None
5-3	None	None
5-4	None	None
5-5	None	None
5-6	None	None
5-7	Shipping supplies expense ...... $	7,000
5-8	None	None
5-9	Retained earnings balance	48,000
5-10	None	None

Problems

5-1	Interest expense, entry (7) ..... $	120
5-2	None	None
5-3	None	None
5-4	None	None
5-5	Service revenue earned in 1974, item (3)	6,500
5-6	Balance sheet totals, corrected ..	69,000
5-7	(Req. c) Net income, $20,000; balance sheet totals	46,500
5-8	(Req. 2) Net income, $30,000; balance sheet totals	72,100
5-9	(Req. 4) Net income $22,100; balance sheet totals	207,600
5-10	None	None

Chapter 6

Exercises

6-1	None	None
6-2	Earnings per share .... $	2.34
6-3	(Req. b) Profit margin ratio	.04875

10-10	(Req. 4) Interest revenue, year 2 $	51
10-11	(Req. 4) Interest revenue, year 2	216
10-12	(Req. 4) Interest revenue, year 2	204

Problems

10-1	(Req. c) Total current liabilities $	22,780
10-2	(Req. c) Total current liabilities	52,460
10-3	(Req. b) Long-term liabilities ...	30,000
10-4	(Req. e) Total current liabilities, Case A	3,180
10-5	(Req. c) Net income, 19B	24,500
10-6	(Req. 4) Interest revenue, 1976 .	866
10-7	(Req. 4) Interest revenue, 1975..	2,057
10-8	(Req. 4) Interest revenue, 1975..	927
10-9	(Req. 3) Interest revenue, Jan. 1, 1976	1,661
10-10	None	None
10-11	(Req. a) Cash credit	68,500
10-12	Voucher register, vouchers payable credit, total	5,630

Chapter 11

Exercises

11-1	None	None
11-2	None	None
11-3	(Req. c) Bond interest expense .. $	2,600
11-4	(Req. c) Bond interest expense ..	2,040
11-5	None	None
11-6	(Req. b) Interest expense (at 103)	5,700
11-7	None	None
11-8	(Req. c) Balance sheet, end of 2nd year, bond sinking fund balance	18,272
11-9	None	None

Problems

11-1	(Req. c) Bonds payable (net), Dec. 31, 1974 .... $	103,240
11-2	(Req. d) Interest expense	4,950
11-3	Net liability, Case C	204,320
11-4	(Req. e) Interest expense, 1974 ..	29,000
11-5	(Req. e) Cash credit	7,000
11-6	(Req. c) Unamortized premium	16,950
11-7	None	None

Chapter 12

Exercises

12-1	(Req. b) Total stockholders' equity .... $	136,600
12-2	(Req. b) Total stockholders' equity	235,500
12-3	(Req. b) Total stockholders' equity	467,000
12-4	(Req. b) Total stockholders' equity	400,000
12-5	None	None
12-6	(Req. b) Total stockholders' equity	354,060
12-7	(Req. b) Total stockholders' equity	196,500
12-8	None	None
12-9	(Req. c) Common stock, per share dividends	1.92
12-10	None	None
12-11	Total retained earnings	62,000
12-12	(Req. b) Retained balance, Dec. 31, 1974	181,000
12-13	None	None

Problems

12-1	(Req. b) Total stockholders' equity .... $	412,000
12-2	(Req. b) Total stockholders' equity	151,100
12-3	(Req. b) Total stockholders' equity, Case I	567,000
12-4	(Req. b) Total stockholders' equity	365,000
12-5	(Req. a) Case D, common stock, dividends, per share ...	1.00
12-6	(Req. b) Retained earnings balance, Dec. 31, 1974	188,750
12-7	(Req. c) Retained earnings balance, Dec. 31, 1974	287,000
12-8	Total stockholders' equity	878,200
12-9	None	None
12-10	(Req. b) Case B, equity Dec. 31, 1974, for partner B	24,000
12-11	None	None

Chapter 13

Exercises

13-1	None	None
13-2	(Req. b) Revenue from investments .... $	750
13-3	(Req. b) Revenue from investments	10,000
13-4	None	None
13-5	None	None
13-6	(Item b) Dec. 31, 1974, revenue from investments	250
13-7	(Req. b) Bond C, revenue from investments	32
13-8	(Req. b) Income statement, revenue from investments	360
13-9	(Req. b) Income statement, revenue from investments	200
13-10	None	None
13-11	None	None
13-12	None	None

Problems

13-1	(Req. b) (Case B) Balance sheet, investments .... $	33,600
13-2	None	None
13-3	(Req. b) (Case B) Income statement, revenue from investments	15,000
13-4	(Req. b) Revenue from investments	896
13-5	(Req. b) Revenue from investments	910
13-6	(Req. d) Income statement, total revenue from bond investments	1,090
13-7	None	None

Chapter 14

Exercises

14-1	(Req. c) Consolidated balance sheet column, total .... $	233,000
14-2	None	None
14-3	(Req. e) Consolidated balance sheet column, total	178,000
14-4	(Req. e) Consolidated balance sheet column, total	242,000
14-5	(Req. b) Consolidated statements column, total	146,000
14-6	Consolidated balances column, total	308,200

This book has been set in 10 and 9 point Times Roman, leaded 2 points. Part numbers are 24 point Melior Bold and chapter numbers are 48 point Melior Bold. Part and chapter titles are 24 point Melior. The size of the type page (maximum area) is 32 by 48 picas.